Praise for the Reformation Commentary on Scripture

"Protestant reformers were fundamentally exegetes as much as theologians, yet (except for figures like Luther and Calvin) their commentaries and sermons have been neglected because these writings are not available in modern editions or languages. That makes this new series of Reformation Commentary on Scripture most welcome as a way to provide access to some of the wealth of biblical exposition of the sixteenth and seventeenth centuries. The editor's introduction explains the nature of the sources and the selection process; the intended audience of modern pastors and students of the Bible has led to a focus on theological and practical comments. Although it will be of use to students of the Reformation, this series is far from being an esoteric study of largely forgotten voices; this collection of reforming comments, comprehending every verse and provided with topical headings, will serve contemporary pastors and preachers very well."

Elsie Anne McKee, *Archibald Alexander Professor of Reformation Studies and the History of Worship, Princeton Theological Seminary*

"This series provides an excellent introduction to the history of biblical exegesis in the Reformation period. The introductions are accurate, clear and informative, and the passages intelligently chosen to give the reader a good idea of methods deployed and issues at stake. It puts precritical exegesis in its context and so presents it in its correct light. Highly recommended as reference book, course book and general reading for students and all interested lay and clerical readers."

Irena Backus, *Professeur ordinaire, Institut d'histoire de la Réformation, Université de Genève*

"The Reformation Commentary on Scripture is a major publishing event—for those with historical interest in the founding convictions of Protestantism, but even more for those who care about understanding the Bible. As with IVP Academic's earlier Ancient Christian Commentary on Scripture, this effort brings flesh and blood to 'the communion of saints' by letting believers of our day look over the shoulders of giants from the past. By connecting the past with the present, and by doing so with the Bible at the center, the editors of this series perform a great service for the church. The series deserves the widest possible support."

Mark A. Noll, *Francis A. McAnaney Professor of History, University of Notre Dame*

"For those who preach and teach Scripture in the church, the Reformation Commentary on Scripture is a significant publishing event. Pastors and other church leaders will find delightful surprises, challenging enigmas and edifying insights in this series, as many Reformational voices are newly translated into English. The lively conversation in these pages can ignite today's pastoral imagination for fresh and faithful expositions of Scripture."

J. Todd Billings, *Associate Professor of Reformed Theology, Western Theological Seminary*

"The Reformers discerned rightly what the church desperately needed in the sixteenth century—the bold proclamation of the Word based on careful study of the sacred Scriptures. We need not only to hear that same call again for our own day but also to learn from the Reformation how to do it. This commentary series is a godsend!"

Richard J. Mouw, *President, Fuller Theological Seminary*

"Like the Ancient Christian Commentary on Scripture, the Reformation Commentary on Scripture does a masterful job of offering excellent selections from well-known and not-so-well-known exegetes. The editor's introductory survey is, by itself, worth the price of the book. It is easy to forget that there were more hands, hearts and minds involved in the Reformation than Luther and Calvin. Furthermore, encounters even with these figures are often limited to familiar quotes on familiar topics. However, the Reformation Commentary helps us to recognize the breadth and depth of exegetical interests and skill that fueled and continue to fuel faithful meditation on God's Word. I heartily recommend this series as a tremendous resource not only for ministry but for personal edification."

Michael S. Horton, *J. G. Machen Professor of Systematic Theology and Apologetics, Westminster Seminary, California*

"The Reformation was ignited by a fresh reading of Scripture. In this series of commentaries, we contemporary interpreters are allowed to feel some of the excitement, surprise and wonder of our spiritual forebears. Luther, Calvin and their fellow revolutionaries were masterful interpreters of the Word. Now, in this remarkable series, some of our very best Reformation scholars open up the riches of the Reformation's reading of the Scripture."

William H. Willimon, *Bishop of the North Alabama Conference of the United Methodist Church*

"The Reformation Scripture principle set the entirety of Christian life and thought under the governance of the divine Word, and pressed the church to renew its exegetical labors. This series promises to place before the contemporary church the fruit of those labors, and so to exemplify life under the Word."

John Webster, *Chair of Systematic Theology, University of Aberdeen*

"Since Gerhard Ebeling's pioneering work on Luther's exegesis seventy years ago, the history of biblical interpretation has occupied many Reformation scholars and become a vital part of study of the period. Reformation Commentary on Scripture provides fresh materials for students of Reformation-era biblical interpretation and for twenty-first-century preachers to mine the rich stores of insights from leading Reformers of the sixteenth century into both the text of Scripture itself and its application in sixteenth-century contexts. This series will strengthen our understanding of the period of the Reformation and enable us to apply its insights to our own days and its challenges to the church."

Robert Kolb, *Mission Professor of Systematic Theology and Director of the Institute for Mission Studies, Concordia Theological Seminary*

"The multivolume Ancient Christian Commentary on Scripture is a valuable resource for those who wish to know how the Fathers interpreted a passage of Scripture but who lack the time or the opportunity to search through the many individual works. This new Reformation Commentary on Scripture will do the same for the Reformers and is to be warmly welcomed. It will provide much easier access to the exegetical treasures of the Reformation and will hopefully encourage readers to go back to some of the original works themselves."

Anthony N. S. Lane, *Professor of Historical Theology and Director of Research, London School of Theology*

"This volume of the RCS project is an invaluable source for pastors and the historically/biblically interested that provides unparalleled access not only to commentaries of the leading Protestant reformers but also to a host of nowadays unknown commentaters on Galatians and Ephesians. The RCS is sure to enhance and enliven contemporary exegesis. With its wide scope, the collection will enrich our understanding of the variety of Reformation thought and biblical exegesis."

Sigrun Haude, *Associate Professor of Reformation and Early Modern European History, University of Cincinnati*

"The Reformation Commentary on Scripture series promises to be an 'open sesame' to the biblical exegesis, exposition and application of the Bible that was the hallmark of the Reformation. While comparisons can be odious, the difference between Reformation commentary and exposition and much that both preceded and followed it is laid bare in these pages: whereas others write about the Bible from the outside, Reformation exposition carries with it the atmosphere of men who spoke and wrote from inside the Bible, experiencing the power of biblical teaching even as they expounded it. . . . This grand project sets before scholars, pastors, teachers, students and growing Christians an experience that can only be likened to stumbling into a group Bible study only to discover that your fellow participants include some of the most significant Christians of the Reformation and post-Reformation (for that matter, of any) era. While here the Word of God is explained in a variety of accents: German, Swiss, French, Dutch, English, Scottish and more. Each one vibrates with a thrilling sense of the living nature of God's Word and its power to transform individuals, churches and even whole communities. Here is a series to anticipate, enjoy and treasure."

Sinclair Ferguson, *Senior Minister, First Presbyterian Church, Columbia, South Carolina*

"I strongly endorse the Reformation Commentary on Scripture. Introducing how the Bible was interpreted during the age of the Reformation, these volumes will not only renew contemporary preaching, but they will also help us understand more fully how reading and meditating on Scripture can, in fact, change our lives!"

Lois Malcolm, *Associate Professor of Systematic Theology, Luther Seminary*

"Discerning the true significance of movements in theology requires acquaintance with their biblical exegesis. This is supremely so with the Reformation, which was essentially a biblical revival. The Reformation Commentary on Scripture will fill a yawning gap, just as the Ancient Christian Commentary did before it, and the first volume gets the series off to a fine start, whetting the appetite for more. Most heartily do I welcome and commend this long overdue project."

J. I. Packer, *Board of Governors Professor of Theology, Regent College*

"There is no telling the benefits to emerge from the publication of this magnificent Reformation Commentary on Scripture series! Now exegetical and theological treasures from Reformation era commentators will be at our fingertips, providing new insights from old sources to give light for the present and future. This series is a gift to scholars and to the church; a wonderful resource to enhance our study of the written Word of God for generations to come!"

Donald K. McKim, *Executive Editor of Theology and Reference, Westminster John Knox Press*

"Why was this not done before? The publication of the Reformation Commentary on Scripture should be greeted with enthusiasm by every believing Christian—but especially by those who will preach and teach the Word of God. This commentary series brings the very best of the Reformation heritage to the task of exegesis and exposition, and each volume in this series represents a veritable feast that takes us back to the sixteenth century to enrich the preaching and teaching of God's Word in our own time."

R. Albert Mohler Jr., *President, The Southern Baptist Theological Seminary*

"Today more than ever, the Christian past is the church's future. InterVaristy Press has already brought the voice of the ancients to our ears. Now, in the Reformation Commentary on Scripture, we hear a timely word from the first Protestants as well."

Bryan Litfin, *Associate Professor of Theology, Moody Bible Institute*

"I am delighted to see the Reformation Commentary on Scripture. The editors of this series have done us all a service by gleaning from these rich fields of biblical reflection. May God use this new life for these old words to give him glory and to build his church."

Mark Dever, *Senior Pastor, Capitol Hill Baptist Church, and Director of 9Marks.org Ministries*

"Monumental and magisterial, the Reformation Commentary on Scripture, edited by Timothy George, is a remarkably bold and visionary undertaking. Bringing together a wealth of resources, these volumes will provide historians, theologians, biblical scholars, pastors and students with a fresh look at the exegetical insights of those who shaped and influenced the sixteenth-century Reformation. With this marvelous publication, InterVarsity Press has reached yet another plateau of excellence. We pray that this superb series will be used of God to strengthen both church and academy."

David S. Dockery, *President, Union University*

Reformation Commentary on Scripture

Old Testament XII

Ezekiel, Daniel

EDITED BY
Carl L. Beckwith

GENERAL EDITOR
Timothy George

ASSOCIATE GENERAL EDITOR
Scott M. Manetsch

IVP Academic
An imprint of InterVarsity Press
Downers Grove, Illinois

InterVarsity Press
P.O. Box 1400, Downers Grove, IL 60515-1426
World Wide Web: www.ivpress.com
E-mail: email@ivpress.com

InterVarsity Press® is the book-publishing division of InterVarsity Christian Fellowship/USA®, a movement of students and faculty active on campus at hundreds of universities, colleges and schools of nursing in the United States of America, and a member movement of the International Fellowship of Evangelical Students. For information about local and regional activities, write Public Relations Dept., InterVarsity Christian Fellowship/USA, 6400 Schroeder Rd., P.O. Box 7895, Madison, WI 53707-7895, or visit the IVCF website at <www.intervarsity.org>.

Design: Cindy Kiple
Images: Wooden cross: iStockphoto
The Protestant Church in Lyon: The Protestant Church in Lyon, called "The Paradise" at Bibliotheque Publique et Universitaire, Geneva, Switzerland, Erich Lessing/Art Resource, NY.

ISBN 978-0-8308-2962-0

Printed in the United States of America ∞

Library of Congress Cataloging-in-Publication Data

InterVarsity Press is committed to protecting the environment and to the responsible use of natural resources. As a member of Green Press Initiative we use recycled paper whenever possible. To learn more about the Green Press Initiative, visit <www.greenpressinitiative.org>.

Library of Congress Cataloging-in-Publication Data

Ezekiel, Daniel/edited by Carl L. Beckwith.
p. cm.—(Reformation commentary on Scripture. Old Testament ; 12)
Includes bibliographical references (p.) and indexes.
ISBN 978-0-8308-2962-0 (hardcover: alk. paper)
1. Bible. O.T. Ezekiel—Commentaries. 2. Bible. O.T. Daniel—Commentaries. I. Beckwith, Carl L.
BS1545.53.E99 2012
244'.40709031—dc23

2011047328

P 24 23 22 21 20 19 18 17 16 15 14 13 12 11 10 9 8 7 6 5 4 3 2 1
Y 33 32 31 30 29 28 27 26 25 24 23 22 21 20 19 18 17 16 15 14 13 12

Reformation Commentary on Scripture
Project Staff

Supervising Editor/Project Editor
Michael D. Gibson

Managing Editor
Allison Rieck

Copyeditor
Linda Triemstra

Editorial and Research Assistants
Benjamin M. McCoy
Rebecca Carhart
Kasey Durbin
Christina Jaske
Todd Hains

Assistants to the General Editors
David Anderson
David Barshinger
Gail Barton
Cheryl Cecil
Philip Cox
B. Coyne
Andre Gazal
Jihoon Jin
Le-Ann Little
Sam Noone
Elizabeth Wells

Administrative Support
Nathan Baker-Lutz

Design
Cindy Kiple

Design Assistant
Beth Hagenberg

Typesetters
Gail Munroe
Maureen Tobey

Proofreader
Keith Williams

Print Coordinator
Jim Erhart

InterVarsity Press

Publisher
Robert A. Fryling

Associate Publisher, Editorial
Andrew T. Le Peau

Associate Editorial Director
James Hoover

Production Manager
Anne Gerth

CONTENTS

ABBREVIATIONS

CE	*The Catholic Encyclopedia*. Edited by Charles G. Herbermann et al. 16 vols. New York: The Encyclopedia Press, 1907-1914.
CHB	*Cambridge History of the Bible*. 3 vols. Eds. P. R. Ackroyd, C. F. Evans,
G.W.H.	Lampe and S. L. Greenslade. Cambridge: Cambridge University Press, 1970-75.
CO	*Ioannis Calvini Opera Quae Supersunt Omnia*. 59 vols. Corpus Reformatorum 29-88. Eds. G. Baum, E. Cunitz and E. Reuss. Brunswich and Berlin, 1863-1900.
CSML	*The Complete Sermons of Martin Luther*. Ed. John Nicholas Lenker. Grand Rapids, MI: Baker Books, 2000.
CTS	Calvin's Commentaries. Calvin Translation Society. 46 vols. Edinburgh, 1843-55.
DMBI	*Dictionary of Major Biblical Interpreters*. Ed. Donald McKim. Downers Grove, IL: InterVarsity Press, 2007.
DNB	*Dictionary of National Biography*. Edited by Leslie Stephen and Sidney Lee. 63 vols. London: Smith, Elder, and Co., 1885-1900.
Inst.	*John Calvin. Institutes of the Christian Religion*. Edited by John T. McNeill. Translated by Ford Lewis Battles. 2 vols. Philadelphia: Westminster Press, 1960.
Lenker	*The Precious and Sacred Writings of Martin Luther*. Ed. John Nicholas Lenker. 31 vols. Minneapolis: Lutherans in All Lands, 1903-38.
LW	*Luther's Works* [American edition]. 55 vols. St. Louis, Mo.: Concordia Publishing House; Philadelphia: Fortress Press, 1955-86.
LXX	Septuagint
NICOT	New International Commentary on the Old Testament. Ed. Robert L. Hubbard. 23 vols. Grand Rapids: Eerdmans.
NPNF	P. Schaff, et al. A Select Library of the Nicene and Post-Nicene Fathers of the Christian Church. 2 series (14 vols. Each). New York: Christian Literature, 1887-1894. Reprint, Grand Rapids, MI: Eerdmans, 1952-56. Reprint, Peabody, MA: Hendrickson, 1994.
ODNB	*Oxford Dictionary of National Biography*. 60 vols. Oxford: Oxford University Press, 2004.
OER	*The Oxford Encyclopedia of the Reformation*. 4 vols. Oxford: Oxford University Press, 1996.

PL	J.P. Migne, ed. Patrologia cursus completus. Series Latina. 221 vols. Paris: Migne, 1844-64.
RC	*Racovian Catechism*. London: Longman, Hurst, Rees, Orme & Brown, 1818.
Tappert	*The Book of Concord: The Confessions of the Evangelical Lutheran Church*. Edited by Theodore G. Tappert. Philadelphia, PA: Fortress Press, 1959.
Vg	Vulgate
WA	*D. Martin Luthers Werke, Kritische Gesamtausgabe*. 72 vols. Weimar: Verlag Hermann Böhlaus Nachfolger, 1883-.
WADB	*D. Martin Luthers Wereke, Kritische Gesamtausgabe: Deutsche Bibel*. 12 vols. Weimar: Hermann Böhlaus Nachfolger, 1906-61.
WSA	J. E. Rotelle, ed. *Works of Saint Augustine: A Translation for the Twenty-First Century*. Hyde Park, NY: New City Press, 1995.

GENERAL INTRODUCTION

The Reformation Commentary on Scripture (RCS) is a twenty-eight-volume series of exegetical comment covering the entire Bible and gathered from the writings of sixteenth-century preachers, scholars and reformers. The RCS is intended as a sequel to the highly acclaimed Ancient Christian Commentary on Scripture (ACCS), and as such its overall concept, method, format and audience are similar to the earlier series. Both series are committed to the renewal of the church through careful study and meditative reflection on the Old and New Testaments, the charter documents of Christianity, read in the context of the worshiping, believing community of faith across the centuries. However, the patristic and Reformation eras are separated by nearly a millennium, and the challenges of reading Scripture with the reformers require special attention to their context, resources and assumptions. The purpose of this general introduction is to present an overview of the context and process of biblical interpretation in the age of the Reformation.

Goals

The Reformation Commentary on Scripture seeks to introduce its readers to the depth and richness of exegetical ferment that defined the Reformation era. The RCS has four goals: the enrichment of contemporary biblical interpretation through exposure to Reformation-era biblical exegesis; the renewal of contemporary preaching through exposure to the biblical insights of the Reformation writers; a deeper understanding of the Reformation itself and the breadth of perspectives represented within it; and the recovery of the robust spiritual theology and devotional treasures of the Reformation's engagement with the Bible. Each of these goals requires a brief comment.

Biblical interpretation. During the past half-century, biblical hermeneutics has become a major growth industry in the academic world. One of the consequences of the historical-critical hegemony of biblical studies has been the privileging of contemporary-philosophies and ideologies at the expense of a commitment to the Christian church as the primary reading community within which and for which biblical exegesis is done. Reading Scripture with the church fathers and the reformers is a corrective to all such imperialism of the present. One of the greatest skills required for a fruitful interpretation of the Bible is the ability to listen. We rightly emphasize the importance of listening to the voices of contextual theologies today, but in doing so we often marginalize or ignore another crucial context—the community of believing Christians through the centuries. The serious study of Scripture requires more than the latest Bible translation in one hand and the latest commentary (or niche study Bible) in the other. John L. Thompson has called on Christians today to practice the art of "reading the Bible with the dead."[1] The RCS presents carefully selected comments from the extant commentaries of the Reformation as an encouragement to more in-depth study of this important epoch in the history of biblical interpretation.

Preaching. The Protestant reformers identified the public preaching of the Word of God as an indispensible means of grace and a sure sign of the true church. Through the words of the preacher, the living voice of the gospel *(viva vox evangelii)* is heard. Luther famously said that the church is not a "pen house" but a "mouth house." The Reformation in Switzerland began when Huldrych Zwingli entered the pulpit of the Grossmünster in Zurich on January 1, 1519, and began to preach a series of expositional sermons chapter by chapter from the Gospel of Matthew. In the following years he extended this homiletical approach to other books of the Old and New Testaments. Calvin followed a similar pattern in Geneva. Many of the commentaries represented in this series were either originally presented as sermons or were written to support the regular preaching ministry of local church pastors. Luther said that the preacher should be a *bonus textualis*—a good one with a text—well-versed in the Scriptures. Preachers in the Reformation traditions preached not only about the Bible but also from it, and this required more than a passing acquaintance with its contents. Those who have been charged with the office of preaching in the church today can find wisdom and insight—and fresh perspectives—in the sermons of the Reformation and the biblical commentaries read and studied by preachers of the sixteenth century.

Reformation. Some scholars of the sixteenth century prefer to speak of the period they study in the plural, the European Reformations, to indicate that many diverse impulses for reform were at work in this turbulent age of transition from medieval to modern times. While this point is well taken, the RCS follows the time-honored tradition of using Reformation in the singular form to indicate not only a major moment in the history of Christianity in the West but also, as Hans J. Hillerbrand has put it, "an essential cohesiveness in the heterogeneous pursuits of religious reform in the sixteenth century."[2] At the same time, in developing guidelines to assist the volume editors in making judicious selections from the vast amount of commentary material available in this period,

[1]John L. Thompson, *Reading the Bible with the Dead* (Grand Rapids: Eerdmans, 2007).

[2]Hans J. Hillerbrand, *The Division of Christendom* (Louisville, Ky.: Westminster John Knox, 2007), p. x. Hillerbrand has also edited the standard reference work in Reformation studies, *OER*. See also Diarmaid MacCulloch, *The Reformation* (New York: Viking, 2003) and Patrick Collinson, *The Reformation: A History* (New York: Random House, 2004).

we have stressed the multifaceted character of the Reformation across many confessions, theological orientations and political settings.

Spiritual theology. The post-Enlightenment split between the study of the Bible as an academic discipline and the reading of the Bible as spiritual nurture was foreign to the reformers. For them the study of the Bible was transformative at the most basic level of the human person: *coram deo*. Luther's famous Reformation breakthrough triggered by his laborious study of the Psalms and Paul's letter to the Romans is well known, but the experience of Cambridge scholar Thomas Bilney was perhaps more typical. When Erasmus's critical edition of the Greek New Testament was published in 1516, it was accompanied by a new translation in elegant Latin. Attracted by the classical beauty of Erasmus's Latin, Bilney came across this statement in 1 Timothy 1:15: "Christ Jesus came into the world to save sinners." In the Greek this sentence is described as *pistos ho logos*, which the Vulgate had rendered *fidelis sermo*, "a faithful saying." Erasmus chose a different word for the Greek *pistos*—*certus*, "sure, certain." When Bilney grasped the meaning of this word applied to the announcement of salvation in Christ, he tells us that "immediately I felt a marvelous comfort and quietness, insomuch that my bruised bones leaped for joy."[3] The reformers all repudiated the idea that the Bible could be studied and understood with dispassionate objectivity, as a cold artifact from antiquity. Luther described the way the Bible was meant to function in the life of believers when he reproached himself and others for reacting to the nativity narrative with such cool unconcern. "I hate myself because when I see Christ laid in the manger or in the lap of his mother and hear the angels sing, my heart does not leap into flame. With what good reason should we all despise ourselves that we remain so cold when this word is spoken to us, over which everyone should dance and leap and burn for joy! We act as though it were a frigid historical fact that does not smite our hearts, as if someone were merely relating that the sultan has a crown of gold."[4] It was a core conviction of the Reformation that the careful study and meditative listening to the Scriptures, what the monks called *lectio divina*, could yield life-changing results. The RCS wishes to commend the exegetical work of the Reformation era as a program of retrieval for the sake of renewal—spiritual réssourcement for believers committed to the life of faith today.

Perspectives

In setting forth the perspectives and perimeters of the RCS, the following considerations have proved helpful.

Chronology. When did the Reformation begin, and how long did it last? In some traditional accounts, the answer was clear: the Reformation began with the posting of Luther's Ninety-five Theses at Wittenberg in 1517 and ended with the death of Calvin in

[3]See A. G. Dickens, *The English Reformation* (New York: Schocken, 1974), p. 79.
[4]WA 49:176-77, quoted in Roland Bainton, "The Bible in the Reformation," in *CHB*, p. 23.

Geneva in 1564. Apart from reducing the Reformation to a largely German event with a side trip to Switzerland, this perspective fails to do justice to the important events that led up to Luther's break with Rome and its many reverberations throughout Europe and beyond. In choosing commentary selections for the RCS, we have adopted the concept of the long sixteenth century, say, from the late 1400s to the mid-seventeenth century. Thus we have included commentary selections from early or pre-Reformation writers such as John Colet and Jacques Lefèvre d'Étaples to seventeenth-century figures such as Henry Ainsworth and Johann Gerhard.

Confession. The RCS concentrates primarily, though not exclusively, on the exegetical writings of the Protestant reformers. While the ACCS provided a compendium of key consensual exegetes of the early Christian centuries, the Catholic/Protestant confessional divide in the sixteenth century tested the very idea of consensus, especially with reference to ecclesiology and soteriology. While many able and worthy exegetes faithful to the Roman Catholic Church were active during this period, this project has chosen to include primarily those figures that represent perspectives within the Protestant Reformation. For this reason we have not included comments on the apocryphal or deuterocanonical writings.

We recognize that "Protestant" and "Catholic" as contradistinctive labels are anachronistic terms for the early decades of the sixteenth century before the hardening of confessional identities surrounding the Council of Trent. Protestant figures such as Philipp Melanchthon, Johannes Oecolampadius and John Calvin were all products of the revival of sacred letters known as biblical humanism. They shared an approach to biblical interpretation that owed much to Desiderius Erasmus and other scholars who remained loyal to the Church of Rome. Careful comparative studies of Protestant and Catholic exegesis in the sixteenth century have shown surprising areas of agreement when the focus was the study of a particular biblical text rather than the standard confessional debates.

At the same time, exegetical differences among the various Protestant groups could become strident and church-dividing. The most famous example of this is the interpretive impasse between Luther and Zwingli over the meaning of "This is my body" (Mt 26:26) in the words of institution. Their disagreement at the Colloquy of Marburg in 1529 had important christological and pastoral implications, as well as social and political consequences. Luther refused communion to Zwingli and his party at the end of the colloquy; in no small measure this bitter division led to the separate trajectories pursued by Lutheran and Reformed Protestantism to this day. In Elizabethan England, Puritans and Anglicans agreed that "Holy Scripture containth all things necessary to salvation: so that whatsoever is not read therein, nor may be proved thereby, is not to be required of any man" (article 6 of the Thirty-nine Articles of Religion), yet on the basis of their differing interpretations of the Bible they fought bitterly over the structures of the church, the clothing of the clergy and the ways of worship. On the matter of infant baptism, Catholics and Protestants alike agreed on its propriety, though there were various theories as to how a practice not mentioned in the Bible could be justified biblically. The Anabaptists were outliers on this subject. They rejected infant baptism altogether. They appealed to the example of the baptism of Jesus and to his final words as recorded in the Gospel of Matthew (Mt 28:19-20), "Go therefore, and make disciples of all nations, baptizing them in the name of the Father, and of the Son, and of the Holy Spirit, teaching them to observe all that I have commanded you." New Testament Christians, they argued, are to follow not only the commands of Jesus in the Great Commission, but also the exact order in which they were given: evangelize, baptize, catechize.

These and many other differences of interpretation among the various Protestant groups are reflected in their many sermons, commentaries and public disputations. In the RCS, the volume editor's introduction to each volume is intended to help the reader understand the nature and significance of doctrinal conversations and disputes that resulted in particular, and frequently clashing, interpretations. Footnotes throughout the text will be provided to explain obscure references, unusual expressions and other matters that require special comment. Volume editors have chosen comments on the Bible across a wide range of sixteenth-century confessions and schools of interpretation: biblical humanists, Lutheran, Reformed, Anglican, Puritan and Anabaptist. We have not pursued passages from post-Tridentine Catholic authors or from radical spiritualists and antitrinitarian writers, though sufficient material is available from these sources to justify another series.

The availability of digital resources has given access to a huge residual database of sixteenth-century exegetical comment hitherto available only in major research universities and rare book collections. The RCS has formed a partnership with the Alexander Street Press Digital Library of Classical Protestant Texts (DLCPT) to make available to our volume editors numerous imprints of sixteenth-century works in an online format. Through the help of RCS editorial advisor Herman Selderhuis, we have also had access to the special Reformation collections of the Johannes a Lasco Bibliothek in Emden, Germany. In addition, modern critical editions and translations of Reformation sources have been published over the past generation.

The design of the RCS is intended to offer reader-friendly access to these classic texts. Each volume in the RCS will include an introduction by the volume editor placing that portion of the canon within the historical context of the Protestant Reformation and presenting a summary of the theological themes, interpretive issues and reception of the particular book(s). The commentary itself consists of particular pericopes identified by a pericope heading; the biblical text in the English Standard Version (ESV), with significant textual variants registered in the footnotes; an overview of the pericope in which principal exegetical and theological concerns of the Reformation writers are succinctly noted; and excerpts from the Reformation writers identified by name according to the conventions of the *Oxford Encyclopedia of the Reformation*. Original translations of Reformation sources are given unless an acceptable translation already exists. Each volume will also include a bibliography of sources cited, as well as an appendix of authors and source works.

The Reformation era was a time of verbal as well as physical violence, and this fact has presented a challenge for this project. Without unduly sanitizing the texts, where they contain anti-Semitic, sexist or inordinately polemical rhetoric, we have not felt obliged to parade such comments either. We have noted the abridgement of texts with ellipses and an explanatory footnote. While this procedure would not be valid in the critical edition of such a text, we have deemed it appropriate in a series whose primary purpose is pastoral and devotional. When translating *homo* or similar terms that refer to the human race as a whole, we have used alternative English expressions to the word *man* (or derivative constructions used generically to signify humanity at large), whenever such substitutions can be made without producing an awkward or artificial construction.

As is true in the ACCS, we have made a special effort where possible to include the voices of women, though we acknowledge the difficulty of doing so for the early modern period when for a variety of social and cultural reasons few theological and biblical works were published by women. However, recent scholarship has focused on a number of female leaders whose literary remains show us how they understood and interpreted the Bible. Women who made significant contributions to the Reformation include Marguerite d'Angoulême, sister of King Francis I, who supported French reformist evangelicals including Calvin and who published a religious poem influenced by Luther's theology, *The Mirror of the Sinful Soul*; Argula von Grumbach, a Bavarian noblewoman who defended the teachings of Luther and Melanchthon before the theologians of the University of Ingolstadt; Katarina Schütz Zell, the wife of a former priest, Matthias Zell, and a remarkable reformer in her own right—she conducted funerals, compiled hymnbooks, defended the downtrodden and published a defense of clerical marriage as well as composing works of consolation on divine comfort and pleas for the toleration of Anabaptists and Catholics alike; and Anne Askew, a Protestant martyr put to death in 1546 after demonstrating remarkable biblical prowess in her examinations by church officials. Other echoes of faithful women in the age of the Reformation are found in their letters, translations, poems, hymns, court depositions and martyr records.

Lay culture, learned culture. In recent decades, much attention has been given to what is called "reforming from below," that is, the expressions of religious beliefs and churchly life that characterized the popular culture of the majority of the population in the era of the Reformation. Social historians have taught us to examine the diverse pieties of townspeople and city folk, of rural religion and village life, the emergence of lay theologies and the experiences of women in the religious tumults of Reformation Europe.[5] Formal commentaries by their nature are artifacts of learned culture. Almost all of them were writ-

[5]See Peter Matheson, ed., *Reformation Christianity* (Minneapolis: Fortress, 2007).

ten in Latin, the lingua franca of learned discourse well past the age of the Reformation. Biblical commentaries were certainly not the primary means by which the Protestant Reformation spread so rapidly across wide sectors of sixteenth-century society. Small pamphlets and broadsheets, later called *Flugschriften* ("flying writings"), with their graphic woodcuts and cartoon-like depictions of Reformation personalities and events, became the means of choice for mass communication in the early age of printing. Sermons and works of devotion were also printed with appealing visual aids. Luther's early writings were often accompanied by drawings and sketches from Lucas Cranach and other artists. This was done "above all for the sake of children and simple folk," as Luther put it, "who are more easily moved by pictures and images to recall divine history than through mere words or doctrines."[6]

We should be cautious, however, in drawing too sharp a distinction between learned and lay culture in this period. The phenomenon of preaching was a kind of verbal bridge between scholars at their desks and the thousands of illiterate or semi-literate listeners whose views were shaped by the results of Reformation exegesis. According to contemporary witness, more than one thousand persons were crowding into Geneva to hear Calvin expound the Scriptures every day.[7] An example of how learned theological works by Reformation scholars were received across divisions of class and social status comes from Lazare Drilhon, an apothecary of Toulon. He was accused of heresy in May 1545 when a cache of prohibited books was found hidden in his garden shed. In addition to devotional works, the French New Testament and a copy of Calvin's Genevan liturgy, there was found a series of biblical commentaries, translated from the Latin into French: Martin Bucer's on Matthew, François Lambert's on the Apocalypse and one by Oecolampadius on 1 John.[8] Biblical exegesis in the sixteenth century was not limited to the kind of full-length commentaries found in Drilhon's shed. Citations from the Bible and expositions of its meaning permeate the extant literature of sermons, letters, court depositions, doctrinal treatises, records of public disputations and even last wills and testaments. While most of the selections in the RCS will be drawn from formal commentary literature, other sources of biblical reflection will also be considered.

Historical Context

The medieval legacy. On October 18, 1512, the degree *doctor in biblia* was conferred on Martin Luther, and he began his career as a professor in the University of Wittenberg. As is well known, Luther was also a monk who had taken solemn vows in the Augustinian

[6]Martin Luther, *Passional* (1522). See R. W. Scribner, *For the Sake of Simple Folk: Popular Propaganda for the German Reformation* (Cambridge: Cambridge University Press, 1981), p. xi.

[7]Letter of De Beaulieu to Guillaume Farel (1561) in J. W. Baum, ed., *Theodor Beza handschriftlichen und anderen gleichzeitigen Quellen* (Leipzig: Weidmann, 1851) 2.92.

[8]Francis Higman, "A Heretic's Library: The Drilhon Inventory" (1545), in Francis Higman, *Lire et Découvire: la circulation des idées au temps de la Réforme* (Geneva: Droz, 1998), pp. 65-85.

Order of Hermits at Erfurt. These two settings—the university and the monastery—both deeply rooted in the Middle Ages, form the background not only for Luther's personal vocation as a reformer but also for the history of the biblical commentary in the age of the Reformation. Since the time of the Venerable Bede (d. 735), sometimes called "the last of the Fathers," serious study of the Bible had taken place primarily in the context of cloistered monasteries. The Rule of St. Benedict brought together *lectio* and *meditatio*, the knowledge of letters and the life of prayer. The liturgy was the medium through which the daily reading of the Bible, especially the Psalms, and the sayings of the church fathers came together in the spiritual formation of the monks.[9] Essential to this understanding was a belief in the unity of the people of God throughout time as well as space, and an awareness that life in this world was a preparation for the beatific vision in the next.

The source of theology was the study of the sacred page (*sacra pagina*); its object was the accumulation of knowledge not for its own sake but for the obtaining of eternal life. For these monks, the Bible had God for its author, salvation for its end and unadulterated truth for its matter, though they would not have expressed it in such an Aristotelian way. The medieval method of interpreting the Bible owed much to Augustine's *On Christian Doctrine*. In addition to setting forth a series of rules (drawn from an earlier work by Tyconius), Augustine stressed the importance of distinguishing the literal and spiritual or allegorical senses of Scripture. While the literal sense was not disparaged, the allegorical was valued because it enabled the believer to obtain spiritual benefit from the obscure places in the Bible, especially in the Old Testament. For Augustine, as for the monks who followed him, the goal of scriptural exegesis was freighted with eschatological meaning; its purpose was to induce faith, hope and love and so to advance in one's pilgrimage toward that city with foundations (see Heb 11:10).

Building on the work of Augustine and other church fathers going back to Origen, medieval exegetes came to understand Scripture as possessed of four possible meanings, the famous *quadriga*. The literal meaning was retained, of course, but the spiritual meaning was now subdivided into three senses: the allegorical, the moral and the anagogical. Medieval exegetes often referred to the four meanings of Scripture in a popular rhyme:

> The letter shows us what God and our fathers did;
> The allegory shows us where our faith is hid;
> The moral meaning gives us rules of daily life;
> The anagogy shows us where we end our strife.[10]

In this schema, the three spiritual meanings of the text correspond to the three theological virtues: faith (allegory), hope (anagogy) and love (the moral meaning). It should

[9]See the classic study by Jean Leclercq, *The Love of Learning and the Desire for God* (New York: Fordham University Press, 1961).

[10]A translation of the well-known Latin quatrain: *Littera gesta docet/Quid credas allegoria/Moralis quid agas/Quo tendas anagogia*. See Robert M. Grant, *A Short History of the Interpretation of the Bible* (New York: Macmillan, 1963), p. 119.

be noted that this way of approaching the Bible assumed a high doctrine of scriptural inspiration: the multiple meanings inherent in the text had been placed there by the Holy Spirit for the benefit of the people of God. The biblical justification for this method went back to the apostle Paul, who had used the words *allegory* and *type* when applying Old Testament events to believers in Christ (Gal 4:21-31; 1 Cor 10:1-11). The problem with this approach was knowing how to relate each of the four senses to one another and how to prevent Scripture from becoming a nose of wax turned this way and that by various interpreters. As G. R. Evans explains, "Any interpretation which could be put upon the text and was in keeping with the faith and edifying, had the warrant of God himself, for no human reader had the ingenuity to find more than God had put there."[11]

With the rise of the universities in the eleventh century, theology and the study of Scripture moved from the cloister into the classroom. Scripture and the Fathers were still important, but they came to function more as footnotes to the theological questions debated in the schools and brought together in an impressive systematic way in works such as Peter Lombard's *Books of Sentences* (the standard theology textbook of the Middle Ages) and the great scholastic *summae* of the thirteenth century. Indispensible to the study of the Bible in the later Middle Ages was the *Glossa ordinaria,* a collection of exegetical opinions by the church fathers and other commentators. Heiko Oberman summarized the transition from devotion to dialectic this way: "When, due to the scientific revolution of the twelfth century, Scripture became the *object* of study rather than the *subject* through which God speaks to the student, the difference between the two modes of speaking was investigated in terms of the texts themselves rather than in their relation to the recipients."[12] It was possible, of course, to be both a scholastic theologian and a master of the spiritual life. Meister Eckhart, for example, wrote commentaries on the Old Testament in Latin and works of mystical theology in German, reflecting what had come to be seen as a division of labor between the two.

An increasing focus on the text of Scripture led to a revival of interest in its literal sense. The two key figures in this development were Thomas Aquinas (d. 1274) and Nicholas of Lyra (d. 1340). Thomas is best remembered for his *Summa Theologiae,* but he was also a prolific commentator on the Bible. Thomas did not abandon the multiple senses of Scripture but declared that all the senses were founded on one—the literal—and this sense eclipsed allegory as the basis of sacred doctrine. Nicholas of Lyra was a Franciscan scholar who made use of the Hebrew text of the Old Testament and quoted liberally from works of Jewish scholars, especially the learned French rabbi Salomon Rashi (d. 1105). After Aquinas, Lyra was the strongest defender of the literal, historical meaning of Scripture as the primary basis of theological disputation. His *Postills,* as his notes were called,

[11]G. R. Evans, *The Language and Logic of the Bible: The Road to Reformation* (Cambridge: Cambridge University Press, 1985), p. 42.

[12]Heiko Oberman, *Forerunners of the Reformation* (Philadelphia: Fortress, 1966), p. 284.

were widely circulated in the late Middle Ages and became the first biblical commentary to be printed in the fifteenth century. More than any other commentator from the period of high scholasticism, Lyra and his work were greatly valued by the early reformers. According to an old Latin pun, *Nisi Lyra lyrasset, Lutherus non saltasset,* "If Lyra had not played its lyre, Luther would not have danced." While Luther was never an uncritical disciple of any teacher, he did praise Lyra as a good Hebraist and quoted him more than one hundred times in his lectures on Genesis, where he declared, "I prefer him to almost all other interpreters of Scripture."[13]

Sacred philology. The sixteenth century has been called a golden age of biblical interpretation, and it is a fact that the age of the Reformation witnessed an explosion of commentary writing unparalleled in the history of the Christian church. Kenneth Hagen has cataloged forty-five commentaries on Hebrews between 1516 (Erasmus) and 1598 (Beza).[14] During the sixteenth century, more than seventy new commentaries on Romans were published, five of them by Melanchthon alone, and nearly one hundred commentaries on the Bible's prayer book, the Psalms.[15] There were two developments in the fifteenth century that presaged this development and without which it could not have taken place: the invention of printing and the rediscovery of a vast store of ancient learning hitherto unknown or unavailable to scholars in the West.

It is now commonplace to say that what the computer has become in our generation, the printing press was to the world of Erasmus, Luther and other leaders of the Reformation. Johannes Gutenberg, a goldsmith by trade, developed a metal alloy suitable for type and a machine that would allow printed characters to be cast with relative ease, placed in even lines of composition and then manipulated again and again making possible the mass production of an unbelievable number of texts. In 1455, the Gutenberg Bible, the masterpiece of the typographical revolution, was published at Mainz in double columns in gothic type. Forty-seven copies of the beautiful Gutenberg Bible are still extant, each consisting of more than one thousand colorfully illuminated and impeccably printed pages. What began at Gutenberg's print shop in Mainz on the Rhine River soon spread, like McDonald's or Starbucks in our day, into every nook and cranny of the known world. Printing presses sprang up in Rome (1464), Venice (1469), Paris (1470), the Netherlands (1471), Switzerland (1472), Spain (1474), England (1476), Sweden (1483) and Constantinople (1490). By 1500, these and other presses across Europe had published some twenty-seven thousand titles, most of them in Latin. Erasmus once compared himself with an obscure preacher whose sermons were heard by only a few people in one or two churches while his books were read in every country

[13]LW 2:164.

[14]Kenneth Hagen, *Hebrews Commenting from Erasmus to Bèze, 1516-1598* (Tübingen: Mohr, 1981).

[15]See David C. Steinmetz, ed., *The Bible in the Sixteenth Century* (Durham: Duke University Press, 1990) and R. Gerald Hobbs, "Biblical Commentaries," *OER* 1:167-71.

in the world. Erasmus was not known for his humility, but in this case he was simply telling the truth.[16]

The Italian humanist Lorenzo Valla (d. 1457) died in the early dawn of the age of printing, but his critical and philological studies would be taken up by others who believed that genuine reform in church and society could come about only by returning to the wellsprings of ancient learning and wisdom—*ad fontes*, "back to the sources!" Valla is best remembered for undermining a major claim made by defenders of the papacy when he proved by philological research that the so-called Donation of Constantine, which had bolstered papal assertions of temporal sovereignty, was a forgery. But it was Valla's *Collatio Novi Testamenti* of 1444 that would have such a great effect on the renewal of biblical studies in the next century. Erasmus discovered the manuscript of this work while rummaging through an old library in Belgium and published it at Paris in 1505. In the preface to his edition of Valla, Erasmus gave the rationale that would guide his own labors in textual criticism. Just as Jerome had translated the Latin Vulgate from older versions and copies of the Scriptures in his day, so now Jerome's own text must be subjected to careful scrutiny and correction. Erasmus would be *Hieronymus redivivus*, a new Jerome come back to life to advance the cause of sacred philology. The restoration of the Scriptures and the writings of the church fathers would usher in what Erasmus believed would be a golden age of peace and learning. In 1516, the Basel publisher Froben brought out Erasmus's *Novum Instrumentum*, the first published edition of the Greek New Testament. Erasmus's Greek New Testament would go through five editions in his lifetime, each one with new emendations to the text and a growing section of annotations that expanded to include not only technical notes about the text but also theological comment. The influence of Erasmus's Greek New Testament was enormous. It formed the basis for Robert Estienne's *Novum Testamentum Graece* of 1550, which in turn was used to establish the Greek *Textus Receptus* for a number of late Reformation translations including the King James Version of 1611.

For all his expertise in Greek, Erasmus was a poor student of Hebrew and only published commentaries on several of the psalms. However, the renaissance of Hebrew letters was part of the wider program of biblical humanism as reflected in the establishment of trilingual colleges devoted to the study of Hebrew, Greek and Latin (the three languages written on the *titulus* of Jesus' cross [Jn 19:20]) at Alcalá in Spain, Wittenberg in Germany, Louvain in Belgium and Paris in France. While it is true that some medieval commentators, especially Nicholas of Lyra, had been informed by the study of Hebrew and rabbinics in their biblical work, it was the publication of Johannes Reuchlin's *De rudimentis hebraicis* (1506), a combined grammar and dictionary, that led to the recovery of *Veritas Hebraica*, as Jerome had referred to the true voice of the Hebrew Scriptures. The

[16]See E. Harris Harbison, *The Christian Scholar in the Age of the Reformation* (New York: Charles Scribner's Sons, 1956), p. 80.

pursuit of Hebrew studies was carried forward in the Reformation by two great scholars, Konrad Pellikan and Sebastian Münster. Pellikan was a former Franciscan friar who embraced the Protestant cause and played a major role in the Zurich reformation. He had published a Hebrew grammar even prior to Reuchlin and produced a commentary on the entire Bible that appeared in seven volumes between 1532 and 1539. Münster was Pellikan's student and taught Hebrew at the University of Heidelberg before taking up a similar position in Basel. Like his mentor, Münster was a great collector of Hebraica and published a series of excellent grammars, dictionaries and Jewish rabbinic texts. Münster did for the Hebrew Old Testament what Erasmus had done for the Greek New Testament. His *Hebraica Biblia* offered a fresh Latin translation of the Old Testament with annotations from medieval rabbinic exegesis.

Luther first learned Hebrew with Reuchlin's grammar in hand but took advantage of other published resources, such as the four-volume Hebrew Bible published at Venice by Daniel Bomberg in 1516 to 1517. He also gathered his own circle of Hebrew experts, his *sanhedrin* he called it, who helped him with his German translation of the Old Testament. We do not know where William Tyndale learned Hebrew, though perhaps it was in Worms, where there was a thriving rabbinical school during his stay there. In any event, he had sufficiently mastered the language to bring out a freshly translated Pentateuch that was published at Antwerp in 1530. By the time the English separatist scholar Henry Ainsworth published his prolix commentaries on the Pentateuch in 1616, the knowledge of Hebrew, as well as Greek, was taken for granted by every serious scholar of the Bible. In the preface to his commentary on Genesis, Ainsworth explained that "the literal sense of Moses's Hebrew (which is the tongue wherein he wrote the law), is the ground of all interpretation, and that language hath figures and properties of speech, different from ours: These therefore in the first place are to be opened that the natural meaning of the Scripture, being known, the mysteries of godliness therein implied, may be better discerned."[17]

The restoration of the biblical text in the original languages made possible the revival of scriptural exposition reflected in the floodtide of sermon literature and commentary work. Of even more far-reaching import was the steady stream of vernacular Bibles in the sixteenth century. In the introduction to his 1516 edition of the New Testament, Erasmus had expressed his desire that the Scriptures be translated into all languages so that "the lowliest women" could read the Gospels and the Pauline epistles and "the farmer sing some portion of them at the plow, the weaver hum some parts of them to the movement of his shuttle, the traveler lighten the weariness of the journey with stories of this kind."[18] Like Erasmus, Tyndale wanted the Bible to be available in the language of the common people. He once said to a learned divine that if God spared his life he would cause the boy who

[17]Henry Ainsworth, *Annotations Upon the First Book of Moses Called Genesis* (Amsterdam, 1616), preface.
[18]John C. Olin, *Christian Humanism and the Reformation* (New York: Fordham University Press, 1987), p. 101.

drives the plow to know more of the Scriptures than he did![19] The project of allowing the Bible to speak in the language of the mother in the house, the children in the street and the cheese monger in the marketplace was met with stiff opposition by certain Catholic polemists such as Johann Eck, Luther's protagonist at the Leipzig Debate of 1519. In his *Enchiridion* (1525), Eck derided the "inky theologians" whose translations paraded the Bible before "the untutored crowd" and subjected it to the judgment of "laymen and crazy old women."[20] In fact, some fourteen German Bibles had already been published prior to Luther's September Testament of 1522, which he translated from Erasmus's Greek New Testament in less than three months' time while sequestered in the Wartburg. Luther's German New Testament became the first bestseller in the world appearing in forty-three distinct editions between 1522 and 1525 with upwards of one hundred thousand copies issued in these three years. It is estimated that five percent of the German population may have been literate at this time, but this rate increased as the century wore on due in no small part to the unmitigated success of vernacular Bibles.[21]

Luther's German Bible (inclusive of the Old Testament from 1534) was the most successful venture of its kind, but it was not alone in the field. Hans Denck and Ludwig Hätzer, leaders in the early Anabaptist movement, translated the prophetic books of the Old Testament from Hebrew into German in 1527. This work influenced the Swiss-German Bible of 1531 published by Leo Jud and other pastors in Zurich. Tyndale's influence on the English language rivaled that of Luther on German. At a time when English was regarded as "that obscure and remote dialect of German spoken in an off-shore island," Tyndale, with his remarkable linguistic ability (he was fluent in eight languages), "made a language for England," as his modern editor David Daniell has put it.[22] Tyndale was imprisoned and executed near Brussels in 1536, but the influence of his biblical work among the common people of England was already being felt. There is no reason to doubt the authenticity of John Foxe's recollection of how Tyndale's New Testament was received in England during the 1520s and 1530s: "The fervent zeal of Christians in those days seemed much superior to these our days and times, as manifestly may appear by their sitting up all night and reading and hearing: also by their expenses and charges in buying of books in English, by whom some gave five marks, some more, some less, for a book; some gave a load of hay for a few chapters of St. James or of St. Paul in English."[23]

[19]This famous statement of Tyndale was quoted by John Foxe in his *Acts and Monuments of Matters Happening in the Church* (London, 1563). See Henry Wansbrough, "Tyndale," in Richard Griffith, ed., *The Bible in the Renaissance* (Aldershot, Vt.: Ashgate, 2001), p. 124.

[20]John Eck, *Enchiridion of Commonplaces*, trans. Ford Lewis Battles (Grand Rapids: Baker, 1979), pp. 47-49.

[21]The effect of printing on the spread of the Reformation has been much debated. See the classic study by Elizabeth L. Eisenstein, *The Printing Press as an Agent of Change* (Cambridge: Cambridge University Press, 1979). More recent studies include Mark U. Edwards Jr., *Printing, Propaganda and Martin Luther* (Minneapolis: Fortress, 1994) and Andrew Pettegree and Matthew Hall, "The Reformation and the Book: A Reconsideration," *Historical Journal* 47 (2004): 1-24.

[22]David Daniell, *William Tyndale: A Biography* (New Haven: Yale University Press, 1994), p. 3.

[23]John Foxe, *The Acts in Monuments*, 4:212.

Calvin helped to revise and contributed three prefaces to the French Bible translated by his cousin Pierre Robert Olivétan and originally published at Neuchâtel in 1535. Clément Marot and Beza provided a fresh translation of the Psalms with each psalm rendered in poetic form and accompanied by monophonic musical settings for congregational singing. The Bay Psalter, the first book printed in America, was an English adaptation of this work. Geneva also provided the provenance of the most influential Italian Bible published by Giovanni Diodati in 1607. The flowering of biblical humanism in vernacular Bibles resulted in new translations in all of the major language groups of Europe: Spanish (1569), Portuguese (1681), Dutch (New Testament, 1523; Old Testament, 1527), Danish (1550), Czech (1579-1593/94), Hungarian (New Testament 1541; complete Bible, 1590), Polish (1563), Swedish (1541) and even Arabic (1591).[24]

Patterns of Reformation

Once the text of the Bible had been placed in the hands of the people, in cheap and easily available editions, what further need was there of published expositions such as commentaries? Given the Protestant doctrine of the priesthood of all believers, was there any longer a need for learned clergy and their bookish religion? Some radical reformers thought not. Sebastian Franck searched for the true church of the Spirit "scattered among the heathen and the weeds" but could not find it in any of the institutional structures of his time. *Veritas non potest scribi, aut excrimi,* he said, "truth can neither be spoken nor written."[25] Kaspar von Schwenckfeld so emphasized religious inwardness that he suspended external observance of the Lord's Supper and downplayed the readable, audible Scriptures in favor of the word within. This trajectory would lead to the rise of the Quakers in the next century, but it was pursued neither by the mainline reformers nor by most of the Anabaptists. Article 7 of the Augsburg Confession (1530) declared the one holy Christian church to be "the assembly of all believers among whom the Gospel is preached in its purity and the holy sacraments are administered according to the Gospel."[26]

Historians of the nineteenth century referred to the material and formal principles of the Reformation. In this construal, the matter at stake was the meaning of the Christian gospel: the liberating insight that helpless sinners are graciously justified by the gift of faith alone, apart from any works or merits of their own, entirely on the basis of Christ's atoning work on the cross. For Luther especially, justification by faith alone became the criterion by which all other doctrines and practices of the church were to be judged. The cross proves everything, he said at the Heidelberg disputation in 1518. The distinction between law and gospel thus became the primary hermeneutical key

[24]On vernacular translations of the Bible, see *CHB* 3:94-140 and Jaroslav Pelikan, *The Reformation of the Bible/The Bible of the Reformation* (New Haven: Yale University Press, 1996), pp. 41-62.

[25]Sebastian Franck, *280 Paradoxes or Wondrous Sayings*, trans. E. J. Furcha (Lewiston, N.Y.: Edwin Mellen Press, 1986), pp. 10, 212.

[26]John H. Leith, ed., *Creeds of the Churches* (Atlanta: John Knox, 1963), p. 70.

that unlocked the true meaning of Scripture.

The formal principle of the Reformation, *sola scriptura,* was closely bound up with proper distinctions between Scripture and tradition. "Scripture alone," said Luther, "is the true lord and master of all writings and doctrine on earth. If that is not granted, what is Scripture good for? The more we reject it, the more we become satisfied with men's books and human teachers."[27] On the basis of this principle, the reformers challenged the structures and institutions of the medieval Catholic Church. Even a simple layperson, they asserted, armed with Scripture should be believed above a pope or a council without it. But, however boldly asserted, the doctrine of the primacy of Scripture did not absolve the reformers from dealing with a host of hermeneutical issues that became matters of contention both between Rome and the Reformation and within each of these two communities: the extent of the biblical canon, the validity of critical study of the Bible, the perspicuity of Scripture and its relation to preaching and the retention of devotional and liturgical practices such as holy days, incense, the burning of candles, the sprinkling of holy water, church art and musical instruments. Zwingli, the Puritans and the radicals dismissed such things as a rubbish heap of ceremonials that amounted to nothing but tomfoolery, while Lutherans and Anglicans retained most of them as consonant with Scripture and valuable aids to worship.

It is important to note that while the mainline reformers differed among themselves on many matters, overwhelmingly they saw themselves as part of the ongoing Catholic tradition, indeed as the legitimate bearers of it. This was seen in numerous ways including their sense of continuity with the church of the preceding centuries; their embrace of the ecumenical orthodoxy of the early church; and their desire to read the Bible in dialogue with the exegetical tradition of the church.

In their biblical commentaries, the reformers of the sixteenth century revealed a close familiarity with the preceding exegetical tradition, and they used it respectfully as well as critically in their own expositions of the sacred text. For them, *sola scriptura* was not *nuda scriptura*. Rather, the Scriptures were seen as the book given to the church, gathered and guided by the Holy Spirit. In his restatement of the Vincentian canon, Calvin defined the church as "a society of all the saints, a society which, spread over the whole world, and existing in all ages, and bound together by the one doctrine and the one spirit of Christ, cultivates and observes unity of faith and brotherly concord. With this church we deny that we have any disagreement. Nay, rather, as we revere her as our mother, so we desire to remain in her bosom." Defined thus, the church has a real, albeit relative and circumscribed, authority since, as Calvin admits, "We cannot fly without wings."[28] While the reformers could not agree with the Council of Trent (though some

[27]Martin Luther, "Defense and Explanation of All the Articles Which Were Rejected by the Roman Bull" (1521), WA 7:317.1-9; LW 32:11-12.

[28]John C. Olin, ed., *John Calvin and Jacopo Sadoleto: A Reformation Debate* (New York: Harper Torchbooks, 1966), pp. 61-62, 77.

recent Catholic theologians have challenged this interpretation) that Scripture and tradition were two separate and equable sources of divine revelation, they did believe in the coinherence of Scripture and tradition. This conviction shaped the way they read and interpreted the Bible.[29]

Schools of Exegesis

The reformers were passionate about biblical exegesis, but they showed little concern for hermeneutics as a separate field of inquiry. Niels Hemmingsen, a Lutheran theologian in Denmark, did write a treatise, *De Methodis* (1555), in which he offered a philosophical and theological framework for the interpretation of Scripture. This was followed by the *Clavis scripturae sacrae* (1567) of Matthias Flacius Illyricus, which contains some fifty rules for studying the Bible drawn from Scripture itself.[30] However, hermeneutics as we know it came of age only in the Enlightenment and should not be backloaded into the Reformation. It is also true that the word *commentary* did not mean in the sixteenth century what it means for us today. Erasmus provided both annotations and paraphrases on the New Testament, the former a series of critical notes on the text but also containing points of doctrinal substance, the latter a theological overview and brief exposition. Most of Calvin's commentaries began as sermons or lectures presented in the course of his pastoral ministry. In the dedication to his 1519 study of Galatians, Luther declared that his work was "not so much a commentary as a testimony *(ennaratio)* of my faith in Christ."[31] The exegetical work of the reformers was embodied in a wide variety of forms and genres, and the RCS has worked with this broader concept in setting the guidelines for this compendium.

The Protestant reformers shared in common a number of key interpretive principles such as the priority of the grammatical-historical sense of Scripture and the christological centeredness of the entire Bible, but they also developed a number of distinct approaches and schools of exegesis.[32] For the purposes of the RCS, we note the following key figures and families of interpretation in this period.

Biblical humanism. The key figure is Erasmus, whose importance is hard to exaggerate for Catholic and Protestant exegetes alike. His annotated Greek New Testament and fresh Latin translation challenged the hegemony of the Vulgate tradition and was doubtless a factor in the decision of the Council of Trent to establish the Vulgate edition as

[29]See Timothy George, "An Evangelical Reflection on Scripture and Tradition," *Pro Ecclesia* 9 (2000): 184-207.

[30]See Kenneth G. Hagen, "'*De Exegetica Methodo*': Niels Hemmingsen's *De Methodis* (1555)," in *The Bible in the Sixteenth Century*, ed. David C. Steinmetz (Durham: Duke University Press, 1990), pp. 181-96.

[31]See Kenneth Hagen, "What Did the Term *Commentarius* Mean to Sixteenth-Century Theologians?" in Irena Backus and Francis M. Higman, eds., *Théorie et pratique de l'exégèse* (Geneva: Droz, 1990), pp. 13-38.

[32]I follow here the sketch of Irena Backus, "Biblical Hermeneutics and Exegesis," *OER* 1:152-58. In this work, Backus confines herself to Continental developments, whereas we have noted the exegetical contribution of the English Reformation as well. For more comprehensive listings of sixteenth-century commentators, see Gerald Bray, *Biblical Interpretation* (Downers Grove, Ill.: InterVarsity Press, 1996), pp. 165-212 and Richard A. Muller, "Biblical Interpretation in the Sixteenth and Seventeenth Centuries," *DMBI*, pp. 22-44.

authentic and normative. Erasmus believed that the wide distribution of the Scriptures would contribute to personal spiritual renewal and the reform of society. In 1547, the English translation of Erasmus's *Paraphrases* was ordered to be placed in every parish church in England. John Colet first encouraged Erasmus to learn Greek, though he never took up the language himself. Colet's lectures on Paul's epistles at Oxford are reflected in his commentaries on Romans and 1 Corinthians.

Jacques Lefèvre d'Étaples has been called the "French Erasmus" because of his great learning and support for early reform movements in his native land. He published a major edition of the Psalter, as well as commentaries on Romans (1512), the Gospels (1522) and the Pastoral Epistles (1527). Guillaume Farel, the early reformer of Geneva, was a disciple of Lefèvre, and the young Calvin also came within his sphere of influence.

Among pre-Tridentine Catholic reformers, special attention should be given to Thomas de Vio, better known as Cajetan. He is best remembered for confronting Martin Luther on behalf of the pope in 1518, but his biblical commentaries (on every book in the Bible except the Song of Songs and Revelation) are virtually free of polemic. Like Erasmus, he dared to criticize the Vulgate on linguistic grounds. His commentary on Romans supported the doctrine of justification by grace applied by faith based on the "alien righteousness" of God in Christ. Jared Wicks sums up Cajetan's significance in this way: "Cajetan's combination of passion for pristine biblical meaning with his fully developed theological horizon of understanding indicates, in an intriguing manner, something of the breadth of possibilities open to Roman Catholics before a more restrictive settlement came to exercise its hold on many Catholic interpreters in the wake of the Council of Trent (1545-1563)."[33] Girolamo Seripando, like Cajetan, was a cardinal in the Catholic Church, though he belonged to the Augustinian rather than the Dominican order. He was an outstanding classical scholar and published commentaries on Romans and Galatians. Also important is Jacopo Sadoleto, another cardinal, best known for his 1539 letter to the people of Geneva beseeching them to return to the church of Rome, to which Calvin replied with a manifesto of his own. Sadoleto published a commentary on Romans in 1535. Bucer once commended Sadoleto's teaching on justification as approximating that of the reformers, while others saw him tilting away from the Augustinian tradition toward Pelagianism.[34]

Luther and the Wittenberg School. It was in the name of the Word of God, and specifically as a doctor of Scripture, that Luther challenged the church of his day and inaugurated the Reformation. Though Luther renounced his monastic vows, he never lost that sense of intimacy with *sacra pagina* he first acquired as a young monk. Luther provided three rules for reading the Bible: prayer, meditation and struggle *(tentatio)*. His exegetical

[33]Jared Wicks, "Tommaso de Vio Cajetan (1469-1534)," *DMBI*, pp. 283-87.

[34]See the discussion by Bernard Roussel, "Martin Bucer et Jacques Sadolet: la concorde possible," *Bulletin de la Société de l'histoire de protestantisme français* (1976): 525-50, and T. H. L. Parker, *Commentaries on the Epistle to the Romans, 1532-1542* (Edinburgh: T&T Clark, 1986), pp. 25-34.

output was enormous. In the American edition of Luther's works, thirty out of the fifty-five volumes are devoted to his biblical studies, and additional translations are planned. Many of his commentaries originated as sermons or lecture notes presented to his students at the university and to his parishioners at Wittenberg's parish church of St. Mary. Luther referred to Galatians as his bride, "my own epistle, to which I have plighted my troth; my Katie von Bora." He considered his 1535 commentary on Galatians his greatest exegetical work, although his massive commentary on Genesis (seven volumes in LW), which he worked on for ten years (1535-1545), must be considered his crowning work. Luther's principles of biblical interpretation are found in his *Open Letter on Translating* and in the prefaces he wrote to all the books of the Bible.

Philipp Melanchthon was brought to Wittenberg to teach Greek in 1518 and proved to be an able associate to Luther in the reform of the church. A set of his lecture notes on Romans was published without his knowledge in 1522. This was revised and expanded many times until his large commentary of 1556. Melanchthon also commented on other New Testament books including Matthew, John, Galatians and the Petrine Epistles, as well as Proverbs, Daniel and Ecclesiastes. Though he was well trained in the humanist disciplines, Melanchthon devoted little attention to critical and textual matters in his commentaries. Rather, he followed the primary argument of the biblical writer and gathered from this exposition a series of doctrinal topics for special consideration. This method lay behind Melanchthon's *Loci communes* (1521), the first Protestant theology textbook to be published. Another Wittenberger was Johannes Bugenhagen of Pomerania, a prolific commentator on both the Old and New Testaments. His commentary on the Psalms (1524), translated into German by Bucer, applied Luther's teaching on justification to the Psalter. He also wrote a commentary on Job and annotations on many of the books in the Bible. The Lutheran exegetical tradition was shaped by many other scholar-reformers including Andreas Osiander, Johannes Brenz, Caspar Cruciger, Erasmus Sarcerius, Georg Maior, Jacob Andreae, Nikolaus Selnecker and Johann Gerhard.

The Strasbourg-Basel tradition. Bucer, the son of a shoemaker in Alsace, became the leader of the Reformation in Strasbourg. A former Dominican, he was early on influenced by Erasmus and continued to share his passion for Christian unity. Bucer was the most ecumenical of the Protestant reformers seeking rapprochement with Catholics on justification and an armistice between Luther and Zwingli in their strife over the Lord's Supper. Bucer also had a decisive influence on Calvin, though the latter characterized his biblical commentaries as longwinded and repetitious. In his exegetical work, Bucer made ample use of patristic and medieval sources, though he criticized the abuse and overuse of allegory as a "blatant insult to the Holy Spirit." He declared that the purpose of his commentaries was "to help inexperienced brethren [perhaps like the apothecary Drilhon, who owned a French translation of Bucer's *Commentary on Matthew*] to understand each of the words and actions of Christ, and in their proper order as far as possible, and to retain an explanation of them in their natural meaning, so that they will not distort God's Word through age-old aberrations or by inept interpretation, but rather with a faithful comprehension of everything as written by the Spirit of God, they may expound to all the churches in their firm upbuilding in faith and love."[35] In addition to writing commentaries on all four Gospels, Bucer published commentaries on Judges, the Psalms, Zephaniah, Romans and Ephesians. In the early years of the Reformation, there was a great deal of back and forth between Strasbourg and Basel, and both were centers of a lively publishing trade. Wolfgang Capito, Bucer's associate at Strasbourg, was a notable Hebraist and composed commentaries on Hosea (1529) and Habakkuk (1527).

At Basel, the great Sebastian Münster defended the use of Jewish sources in the Christian study of the Old Testament and published, in addition to his famous Hebrew grammar, an annotated version of the Gospel of Matthew translated from Greek into Hebrew. Oecolampadius, Basel's chief reformer, had been a proofreader in Froben's publishing house and worked with Erasmus on his Greek New Testament and his critical edition of Jerome. From 1523 he was both a preacher and professor of Holy Scripture at Basel. He defended Zwingli's eucharistic theology at the Colloquy of Marburg and published commentaries on 1 John (1524), Romans (1525) and Haggai-Malachi (1525). Oecolampadius was succeeded by Simon Grynaeus, a classical scholar who taught Greek and supported Bucer's efforts to bring Lutherans and Zwinglians together. More in line with Erasmus was Sebastian Castellio, who came to Basel after his expulsion from Geneva in 1545. He is best remembered for questioning the canonicity of the Song of Songs and for his annotations and French translation of the Bible.

The Zurich group. Biblical exegesis in Zurich was centered on the distinctive institution of the *prophezei*, which began on June 19, 1525. On five days a week, at seven o'clock in the morning, all of the ministers and theological students in Zurich gathered into the choir of the Grossmünster to engage in a period of intense exegesis and interpretation of Scripture. After Zwingli had opened the meeting with prayer, the text of the day was read in Latin, Greek and Hebrew, followed by appropriate textual or exegetical comments. One of the ministers then delivered a sermon on the passage in German that was heard by many of Zurich's citizens who stopped by the cathedral on their way to work. This institute for advanced biblical studies had an enormous influence as a model for Reformed academies and seminaries throughout Europe. It was also the seedbed for sermon series in Zurich's churches and the extensive exegetical publications of Zwingli, Leo Jud, Konrad Pellikan, Heinrich Bullinger, Oswald Myconius and Rudolf Gwalther. Zwingli had memorized in Greek all of the Pauline epistles, and this bore fruit in his powerful expository preaching and biblical exegesis. He took seriously the role of grammar, rhetoric and historical research in explaining the biblical text. For example, he disagreed with Bucer

[35]Quoted in D. F. Wright, "Martin Bucer," *DMBI*, p. 290.

on the value of the Septuagint regarding it as a trustworthy witness to a proto-Hebrew version earlier than the Masoretic text.

Zwingli's work was carried forward by his successor Bullinger, one of the most formidable scholars and networkers among the reformers. He composed commentaries on Daniel (1565), the Gospels (1542-1546), the Epistles (1537), Acts (1533) and Revelation (1557). He collaborated with Calvin to produce the *Consensus Tigurinus* (1549), a Reformed accord on the nature of the Lord's Supper, and produced a series of fifty sermons on Christian doctrine, known as *Decades*, which became required reading in Elizabethan England. As the *Antistes* ("overseer") of the Zurich church for forty-four years, Bullinger faced opposition from nascent Anabaptism on the one hand and resurgent Catholicism on the other. The need for a well-trained clergy and scholarly resources, including Scripture commentaries, arose from the fact that the Bible was "difficult or obscure to the unlearned, unskillful, unexercised, and malicious or corrupted wills." While foreswearing papal claims to infallibility, Bullinger and other leaders of the magisterial Reformation saw the need for a kind of Protestant magisterium as a check against the tendency to read the Bible in "such sense as everyone shall be persuaded in himself to be most convenient."[36]

Two other commentators can be treated in connection with the Zurich group, though each of them had a wide-ranging ministry across the Reformation fronts. A former Benedictine monk, Wolfgang Musculus, embraced the Reformation in the 1520s and served briefly as the secretary to Bucer in Strasbourg. He shared Bucer's desire for Protestant unity and served for seventeen years (1531-1548) as a pastor and reformer in Augsburg. After a brief time in Zurich, where he came under the influence of Bullinger, Musculus was called to Bern, where he taught the Scriptures and published commentaries on the Psalms, the Decalogue, Genesis, Romans, Isaiah, 1 and 2 Corinthians, Galatians and Ephesians, Philippians, Colossians, 1 and 2 Thessalonians and 1 Timothy. Drawing on his exegetical writings, Musculus also produced a compendium of Protestant theology that was translated into English in 1563 as *Commonplaces of Christian Religion*.

Peter Martyr Vermigli was a Florentine-born scholar and Augustinian friar who embraced the Reformation and fled to Switzerland in 1542. Over the next twenty years, he would gain an international reputation as a prolific scholar and leading theologian within the Reformed community. He lectured on the Old Testament at Strasbourg, was made regius professor at Oxford, corresponded with the Italian refugee church in Geneva and spent the last years of his life as professor of Hebrew at Zurich. Vermigli published commentaries on 1 Corinthians, Romans and Judges during his lifetime. His biblical lectures on Genesis, Lamentations, 1 and 2 Samuel and 1 and 2 Kings were published posthumously. The most influential of his writings was the *Loci communes (Commonplaces)*, a

[36]Euan Cameron, *The European Reformation* (Oxford: Oxford University Press, 1991), p. 120.

theological compendium drawn from his exegetical writings.

The Genevan Reformers. What Zwingli and Bullinger were to Zurich, Calvin and Beza were to Geneva. Calvin has been called "the father of modern biblical scholarship," and his exegetical work is without parallel in the Reformation. Because of the success of his *Institutes of the Christian Religion* Calvin has sometimes been thought of as a man of one book, but he always intended the *Institutes,* which went through eight editions in Latin and five in French during his lifetime, to serve as guide to the study of the Bible, to show the reader "what he ought especially to seek in Scripture and to what end he ought to relate its contents." Jacob Arminius, who modified several principles of Calvin's theology, recommended his commentaries next to the Bible, for, as he said, Calvin "is incomparable in the interpretation of Scripture."[37] Drawing on his superb knowledge of Greek and Hebrew and his thorough training in humanist rhetoric, Calvin produced commentaries on all of the New Testament books except 2 and 3 John and Revelation. Calvin's Old Testament commentaries originated as sermon and lecture series and include Genesis, Psalms, Hosea, Isaiah, minor prophets, Daniel, Jeremiah and Lamentations, a harmony of the last four books of Moses, Ezekiel 1-20 and Joshua. Calvin sought for brevity and clarity in all of his exegetical work. He emphasized the illumination of the Holy Spirit as essential to a proper understanding of the text. Calvin underscored the continuity between the two Testaments (one covenant in two dispensations) and sought to apply the plain or natural sense of the text to the church of his day. In the preface to his own influential commentary on Romans, Karl Barth described how Calvin worked to recover the mind of Paul and make the apostle's message relevant to his day: "How energetically Calvin goes to work, first scientifically establishing the text ('what stands there?'), then following along the footsteps of its thought; that is to say, he conducts a discussion with it until the wall between the first and the sixteenth centuries becomes transparent, and until there in the first century Paul speaks and here the man of the sixteenth century hears, until indeed the conversation between document and reader becomes concentrated upon the substance (which must be the same now as then)."[38]

Beza was elected moderator of Geneva's Company of Pastors after Calvin's death in 1564 and guided the Genevan Reformation over the next four decades. His annotated Latin translation of the Greek New Testament (1556) and his further revisions of the Greek text established his reputation as the leading textual critic of the sixteenth century after Erasmus. Beza completed the translation of Marot's metrical Psalter, which became a centerpiece of Huguenot piety and Reformed church life. Though known for his polemical writings on grace, free will and predestination, Beza's work is marked by a strong pastoral orientation and concern for a Scripture-based spirituality.

Robert Estienne (Stephanus) was a printer-scholar who had served the royal household

[37]Quoted in A. M. Hunter, *The Teaching of Calvin* (London: James Clarke, 1950), p. 20.

[38]Karl Barth, *Die Römerbrief* (Zurich: TVZ, 1940), p. 11; ET: *The Epistle to the Romans* (London: Oxford University Press, 1933), p. 7.

in Paris. After his conversion to Protestantism, in 1550 he moved to Geneva, where he published a series of notable editions and translations of the Bible. He also produced sermons and commentaries on Job, Ecclesiastes, the Song of Songs, Romans and Hebrews, as well as dictionaries, concordances and a thesaurus of biblical terms. He also published the first editions of the Bible with chapters divided into verses, an innovation that quickly became universally accepted.

The British Reformation. Commentary writing in England and Scotland lagged behind the continental Reformation for several reasons. In 1500, there were only three publishing houses in England compared with more than two hundred on the Continent. A 1408 statute against publishing or reading the Bible in English, stemming from the days of Lollardy, stifled the free flow of ideas, as was seen in the fate of Tyndale. Moreover, the nature of the English Reformation from Henry through Elizabeth provided little stability for the flourishing of biblical scholarship. In the sixteenth century, many "hot-gospel" Protestants in England were edified by the English translations of commentaries and theological writings by the Continental reformers. The influence of Calvin and Beza was felt especially in the Geneva Bible with its "Protestant glosses" of theological notes and references.

During the later Elizabethan and Stuart church, however, the indigenous English commentary came into its own. Both Anglicans and Puritans contributed to this outpouring of biblical studies. The sermons of Lancelot Andrewes and John Donne are replete with exegetical insights based on a close study of the Greek and Hebrew texts. Among the Reformed authors in England, none was more influential than William Perkins, the greatest of the early Puritan theologians, who published commentaries on Galatians, Jude, Revelation and the Sermon on the Mount (Mt 5-7). John Cotton, one of his students, wrote commentaries on the Song of Songs, Ecclesiastes and Revelation before departing for New England in 1633. The separatist pastor Henry Ainsworth was an outstanding scholar of Hebrew and wrote major commentaries on the Pentateuch, the Psalms and the Song of Songs. In Scotland, Robert Rollock, the first principal of Edinburgh University (1585), wrote numerous commentaries including those on the Psalms, Ephesians, Daniel, Romans, 1 and 2 Thessalonians, John, Colossians and Hebrews. Joseph Mede and Thomas Brightman were leading authorities on Revelation and contributed to the apocalyptic thought of the seventeenth century. Mention should also be made of Archbishop James Ussher, whose *Annals of the Old Testament* was published in 1650. Ussher developed a keen interest in biblical chronology and calculated that the creation of the world had taken place on October 26, 4004 B.C. As late as 1945, the Scofield Reference Bible still retained this date next to Genesis 1:1, but later editions omitted it because of the lack of evidence on which to fix such dates.[39]

[39]*The New Scofield Reference Bible* (New York: Oxford University Press, 1967), p. vi.

Anabaptism. Irena Backus has noted that there was no school of "dissident" exegesis during the Reformation, and the reasons are not hard to find. The radical Reformation was an ill-defined movement that existed on the margins of official church life in the sixteenth century. The denial of infant baptism and the refusal to swear an oath marked radicals as a seditious element in society, and they were persecuted by Protestants and Catholics alike. However, in the RCS we have made an attempt to include some voices of the radical Reformation, especially among the Anabaptists. While the Anabaptists published few commentaries in the sixteenth century, they were avid readers and quoters of the Bible. Numerous exegetical gems can be found in their letters, treatises, martyr acts (especially *The Martyrs' Mirror*), hymns and histories. They placed a strong emphasis on the memorizing of Scripture and quoted liberally from vernacular translations of the Bible. George H. Williams has noted that "many an Anabaptist theological tract was really a beautiful mosaic of Scripture texts."[40] In general, most Anabaptists accepted the apocryphal books as canonical, contrasted outer word and inner spirit with relative degrees of strictness and saw the New Testament as normative for church life and social ethics (witness their pacifism, non-swearing, emphasis on believers' baptism and congregational discipline).

We have noted the Old Testament translation of Ludwig Hätzer, who became an anti-trinitarian, and Hans Denck that they published at Worms in 1527. Denck also wrote a notable commentary on Micah. Conrad Grebel belonged to a Greek reading circle in Zurich and came to his Anabaptist convictions while poring over the text of Erasmus's New Testament. The only Anabaptist leader with university credentials was Balthasar Hubmaier, who was made a doctor of theology (Ingolstadt, 1512) in the same year as Luther. His reflections on the Bible are found in his numerous writings, which include the first catechism of the Reformation (1526), a two-part treatise on the freedom of the will and a major work *(On the Sword)* setting forth positive attitudes toward the role of government and the Christian's place in society. Melchior Hoffman was an apocalyptic seer who wrote commentaries on Romans, Revelation and Daniel 12. He predicted that Christ would return in 1533. More temperate was Pilgram Marpeck, a mining engineer who embraced Anabaptism and traveled widely throughout Switzerland and south Germany, from Strasbourg to Augsburg. His "Admonition of 1542" is the longest published defense of Anabaptist views on baptism and the Lord's Supper. He also wrote many letters that functioned as theological tracts for the congregations he had founded dealing with topics such as the fruits of repentance, the lowliness of Christ and the unity of the church. Menno Simons, a former Catholic priest, became the most outstanding leader of the Dutch Anabaptist movement. His masterpiece was the *Foundation of Christian Doctrine* published in 1540. His other writings include *Meditation on the Twenty-fifth Psalm*

[40]George H. Williams, *The Radical Reformation* (Kirksville, Mo.: Sixteenth-Century Journal Publishers, 1992), p. 1247.

(1537); *A Personal Exegesis of Psalm Twenty-five* modeled on the style of Augustine's *Confessions; Confession of the Triune God* (1550), directed against Adam Pastor, a former disciple of Menno who came to doubt the divinity of Christ; *Meditations and Prayers for Mealtime* (1557); and the *Cross of the Saints* (1554), an exhortation to faithfulness in the face of persecution. Like many other Anabaptists, Menno emphasized the centrality of discipleship *(Nachfolge)* as a deliberate repudiation of the old life and a radical commitment to follow Jesus as Lord.

Reading Scripture with the Reformers

In 1947, Gerhard Ebeling set forth his thesis that the history of the Christian church is the history of the interpretation of Scripture. Since that time, the place of the Bible in the story of the church has been investigated from many angles. A better understanding of the history of exegesis has been aided by new critical editions and scholarly discussions of the primary sources. The *Cambridge History of the Bible,* published in three volumes (1963-1970), remains a standard reference work in the field. The ACCS built on, and itself contributed to, the recovery of patristic biblical wisdom of both East and West. Beryl Smalley's *The Study of the Bible in the Middle Ages* (1940) and Henri de Lubac's *Medieval Exegesis: The Four Senses of Scripture* (1959) are essential reading for understanding the monastic and scholastic settings of commentary work between Augustine and Luther. The Reformation took place during what has been called "le grand siècle de la Bible."[41] Aided by the tools of Renaissance humanism and the dynamic impetus of Reformation theology (including permutations and reactions against it), the sixteenth century produced an unprecedented number of commentaries on every book in the Bible. Drawing from this vast storehouse of exegetical treasures, the RCS allows us to read Scripture along with the reformers. In doing so, it serves as a practical homiletic and devotional guide to some of the greatest masters of biblical interpretation in the history of the church.

The RCS gladly acknowledges its affinity with and dependence on recent scholarly investigations of Reformation-era exegesis. Between 1976 and 1990, three international colloquia on the history of biblical exegesis in the sixteenth century took place in Geneva and in Durham, North Carolina.[42] Among those participating in these three gatherings were a number of scholars who have produced ground-breaking works in the study of biblical interpretation in the Reformation. These include Elsie McKee, Irena Backus, Kenneth Hagen, Scott H. Hendrix, Richard A. Muller, Guy Bedouelle, Gerald Hobbs, John

[41]J-R. Aarmogathe, ed., *Bible de tous les temps,* 8 vols.; vol. 6, *Le grand siècle de la Bible* (Paris: Beauchesne, 1989).

[42]Olivier Fatio and Pierre Franenkel, eds., *Histoire de l'exégèse an XVIe siècle: texts du colloqui international tenu Genève en 1976* (Geneva: Droz, 1978); David C. Steinmetz, ed., *The Bible in the Sixteenth Century* [Second International Colloquy on the History of Biblical Exegesis in the Sixteenth Century] (Durham: Duke University Press, 1990); Irena Backus and Francis M. Higman, eds., *Théorie et pratique de l'exégèse. Actes du troisieme Colloque international sur l'histoire de l'exégèse biblique au XVIe siècle, Genève, 31 août-2 septembre 1988* (Geneva: Droz, 1990); see also Guy Bedouelle and Bernard Roussel, eds., *Bible de tous les temps,* 8 vols.; vol. 5, *Le temps des Réformes et la Bible* (Paris: Beauchesne, 1989).

B. Payne, Bernard Roussel, Pierre Fraenkel and David C. Steinmetz. Among other scholars whose works are indispensible for the study of this field are Heinrich Bornkamm, Jaroslav Pelikan, Heiko A. Oberman, James S. Preus, T. H. L. Parker, David F. Wright, Tony Lane, John L. Thompson, Frank A. James and Timothy G. Wengert.[43] Among these scholars no one has had a greater influence on the study of Reformation exegesis than David C. Steinmetz. A student of Oberman, he has emphasized the importance of understanding the Reformation in medieval perspective. In addition to important studies on Luther and Staupitz, he has pioneered the method of comparative exegesis showing both continuity and discontinuity between major Reformation figures and the preceding exegetical traditions (see his *Luther in Context* and *Calvin in Context*). From his base at Duke University, he has spawned what might be called a Steinmetz school, a cadre of students and scholars whose work on the Bible in the Reformation era continues to shape the field. Steinmetz serves on the RCS Board of Editorial Advisors, and a number of our volume editors have pursued doctoral studies under his supervision.

In 1980, Steinmetz published "The Superiority of Pre-critical Exegesis," a seminal essay that not only placed Reformation exegesis in the context of the preceding fifteen centuries of the church's study of the Bible but also challenged certain assumptions underlying the hegemony of historical-critical exegesis of the post-Enlightenment academy.[44] Steinmetz helps us to approach the reformers and other pre-critical interpreters of the Bible on their own terms as faithful witnesses to the church's apostolic tradition. For them, a specific book or pericope had to be understood within the scope of the consensus of the canon. Thus the reformers, no less than the Fathers and the schoolmen, interpreted the hymn of the Johannine prologue about the preexistent Christ in consonance with the creation narrative of Genesis 1. In the same way, Psalm 22, Isaiah 53 and Daniel 7 are seen as part of an overarching storyline that finds ultimate fulfillment in Jesus Christ. Reading the Bible with the resources of the new learning, the reformers challenged the exegetical conclusions of their medieval predecessors at many points. However, unlike Alexander Campbell in the nineteenth century, their aim was not to "open the New Testament as if mortal man had never seen it before." Rather, they wanted to do their biblical work as part of an interpretive conversation within the family of the people of God. In the reformers' emphatic turn to the literal sense, which prompted their many blasts against the unrestrained use of allegory, their work was an extension of a similar impulse made by Thomas Aquinas and Nicholas of Lyra.

This is not to discount the radically new insights gained by the reformers in their dynamic engagement with the text of Scripture; nor should we dismiss in a reactionary way

[43]For bibliographical references and evaluation of these and other contributors to the scholarly study of Reformation-era exegesis, see Richard A. Muller, "Biblical Interpretation in the Era of the Reformation: The View From the Middle Ages," in *Biblical Interpretation in the Era of the Reformation: Essays Presented to David C. Steinmetz in Honor of His Sixtieth Birthday*, ed. Richard A. Muller and John L. Thompson (Grand Rapids: Eerdmans, 1996), pp. 3-22.

[44]David C. Steinmetz, "The Superiority of Pre-Critical Exegesis," *Theology Today* 37 (1980): 27-38.

the light shed on the meaning of the Bible by the scholarly accomplishments of the past two centuries. However, it is to acknowledge that the church's exegetical tradition is an indispensible aid for the proper interpretation of Scripture. And this means, as Richard Muller has said, that "while it is often appropriate to recognize that traditionary readings of the text are erroneous on the grounds offered by the historical-critical method, we ought also to recognize that the conclusions offered by historical-critical exegesis may themselves be quite erroneous on the grounds provided by the exegesis of the patristic, medieval, and reformation periods."[45]

George Herbert was an English pastor and poet who reaped the benefits of the renewal of biblical studies in the age of the Reformation. He referred to the Scriptures as a book of infinite sweetness, "a mass of strange delights," a book with secrets to make the life of anyone good. In describing the various means pastors require to be fully furnished in the work of their calling, Herbert provided a rationale for the history of exegesis and for the Reformation Commentary on Scripture:

> The fourth means are commenters and Fathers, who have handled the places controverted, which the parson by no means refuseth. As he doth not so study others as to neglect the grace of God in himself and what the Holy Spirit teacheth him, so doth he assure himself that God in all ages hath had his servants to whom he hath revealed his Truth, as well as to him; and that as one country doth not bear all things that there may be a commerce, so neither hath God opened or will open all to one, that there may be a traffic in knowledge between the servants of God for the planting both of love and humility. Wherefore he hath one comment[ary] at least upon every book of Scripture, and ploughing with this, and his own meditations, he enters into the secrets of God treasured in the holy Scripture.[46]

Timothy George
General Editor

[45]Richard A. Muller and John L. Thompson, "The Significance of Pre-critical Exegesis: Retrospect and Prospect," in *Biblical Interpretation in the Era of the Reformation: Essays Presented to David C. Steinmetz in Honor of His Sixtieth Birthday*, ed. Richard A. Muller and John L. Thompson (Grand Rapids: Eerdmans, 1996), p. 342.
[46]George Herbert, *The Complete English Poems* (London: Penguin, 1991), p. 205.

A GUIDE TO USING THIS COMMENTARY

Several features have been incorporated into the design of this commentary. The following comments are intended to assist readers in making full use of this volume.

Pericopes of Scripture

The scriptural text has been divided into pericopes, or passages, usually several verses in length. Each of these pericopes is given a heading, which appears at the beginning of the pericope. For example, the first pericope in the commentary on Ezekiel is "1:1-28 The Living Creatures and the Glory of the Lord." This heading is followed by the Scripture passage quoted in the English Standard Version (ESV) across the full width of the page. The Scripture passage is provided for the convenience of readers, but it is also in keeping with Reformation-era commentaries, which followed the patristic and medieval commentary tradition, in which the citations of the reformers were arranged around the text of Scripture.

Overviews

Following each pericope of text is an overview of the Reformation authors' comments on that pericope. The format of this overview varies among the volumes of this series, depending on the requirements of the specific book of Scripture. The function of the overview is to provide a brief summary of all the comments to follow. It tracks a reasonably cohesive thread of argument among reformers' comments, even though they are derived from diverse sources and generations. Thus, the summaries do not proceed chronologically or by verse sequence. Rather, they seek to rehearse the overall course of the reformers' comments on that pericope.

We do not assume that the commentators themselves anticipated or expressed a formally received cohesive argument but rather that the various arguments tend to flow in a plausible, recognizable pattern. Modern readers can thus glimpse aspects of continuity in the flow of diverse exegetical traditions representing various generations and geographical locations.

Topical Headings

An abundance of varied Reformation-era comment is available for each pericope. For this reason we have broken the pericopes into two levels. First is the verse with its topical heading. The reformers' comments are then focused on aspects of each verse, with topical headings summarizing the essence of the individual comment by evoking a key phrase, metaphor or idea. This feature provides a bridge by which modern readers can enter into the heart of the Reformation-era comment.

Identifying the Reformation Texts

Following the topical heading of each section of comment, the name of the Reformation commentator is given. An English translation (where needed) of the reformer's comment is then provided. This is immediately followed by the title of the original work rendered in English.

Readers who wish to pursue a deeper investigation of the reformers' works cited in this commentary will find full bibliographic detail for each reformation title provided in the bibliography at the back of the volume. Comments translated from original-language Reformation-era commentaries and sermon collections can be readily located in the source texts by Scripture reference. Information on English translations (where available) and standard original-language editions and critical editions of the works cited is found in the bibliography.

The Footnotes

To aid the reader in exploring the background and texts in further detail, this commentary utilizes footnotes. The use and content of footnotes may vary among the volumes in this series. Where footnotes appear, a footnote number directs the reader to a note at the bottom of the right-hand column, where one will find annotations (clarifications or biblical cross references), information on English translations (where available) or standard original-language editions of the work cited.

Where original-language texts have remained untranslated into English, we provide new translations. Where there is any serious ambiguity or textual problem in the selection, we have tried to reflect the best available textual tradition. Wherever current English translations are already well rendered, they are utilized, but where necessary they are stylistically updated. A single asterisk (*) indicates that a previous English translation has been updated to modern English or amended for easier reading. We have standardized spellings and made grammatical variables uniform so that our English references will not reflect the linguistic oddities of the older English translations. For ease of reading we have in some cases edited out superfluous conjunctions.

INTRODUCTION TO EZEKIEL & DANIEL

Although the books of Ezekiel and Daniel were widely used in sermons and theological writings by the reformers of the sixteenth and seventeenth centuries, they elicited unequal attention when it came to writing formal commentaries on them. Among the major sixteenth-century reformers, there are twice as many commentaries on Daniel as there are on Ezekiel. Reasons ranging from the length of the book of Ezekiel and the complexity of his visions to the provocativeness of his language and the difficulty of the Hebrew text may be given to account for this. And yet these same concerns arise for the other major prophets, Isaiah and Jeremiah, which both received significantly more commentaries by the reformers. Although any number of explanations for the lack of sixteenth-century commentaries on Ezekiel may be given, the ultimate reason could be innocent: lack of time. The canonical placement of Ezekiel after Isaiah and Jeremiah put it, in a sense, third in the queue.

The book of Daniel, by contrast, is not only unique among the prophets with its explicit prophecies about Christ and his eternal kingdom but also is of manageable size. The book divides naturally between history (Dan 1–6) and prophecy (Dan 7–12). Indeed, for a book of such modest length, it contains some of the most well-known events and prophecies of the Old Testament. Of great interest to the lay reader and commentator alike are the histories of the monarchs in the first and second part of Daniel. The great miracles that occurred in Daniel's day, such as the fiery furnace and the lions' den, captivate our attention and provide an enduring image of God's fatherly care for his faithful people. The striking punishment of Nebuchadnezzar and the unsettling handwriting on the wall before Belshazzar warn of God's strict justice and punishment of the idolatrous and proud. The second part of Daniel reveals the precise time of Christ's advent and gives a clear description of his saving benefits for us. Daniel's lengthy prayer (Dan 9) teaches with clarity the sinfulness of all humans and justification by faith alone—themes touching directly on the heart of the Reformation. Finally, the book ends with the promised deliverance of God's saints and the resurrection of all, some to eternal damnation and others to eternal life with Christ.

Whether it is concern over Ezekiel's length or fascination with Daniel's content, whatever the reason, the reformers produced more works on the book of Daniel. Although Ezekiel has four times more chapters than Daniel, the commentary section of this volume gives slightly more space to Daniel than Ezekiel because of the abundance of Reformation material. The remainder of this introduction will provide the historical context of our Reformation writers and their work on Ezekiel and Daniel, the theological themes discussed by them, the interpretive issues that arise in their works and, finally, the historical reception of their commentaries.

THE BOOK OF EZEKIEL

Historical Context

Despite the fact that the reformers produced few formal commentaries on the book of Ezekiel, there is no doubt that the prophet was widely read and used. Occasional comments on Ezekiel are found in dogmatic works, sermons and official confessions of faith throughout the sixteenth and seventeenth centuries. This is seen in such places as the index to John Calvin's *Institutes of the Christian Religion*, which shows an extensive use of Ezekiel in his theological reflection.[1] Likewise, the index to the *Book of Concord* (1580), the official confessions of sixteenth-century Lutheranism, reveals numerous citations and glosses on various verses from Ezekiel.[2] These uses of Ezekiel, however, are occasional and casual. That is to say, they are occasioned by specific theological issues, sometimes apologetically motivated, other times polemically, but rarely accompanied by exegetical comment. This type of engagement with Ezekiel is also casual. It lacks the formality of a sustained reading of the text that attends to, among other things, the context of a particular passage within the larger prophetic book, the historical and grammatical issues of the passage under consideration and the enduring relevance of the text for present-day believers. Given the nature of these sorts of comments, they are used only sparingly in this volume.

Martin Luther (1483–1546). Martin Luther wrote two prefaces for Ezekiel in 1532 and 1541, respectively. Luther's first preface is brief and deals mostly with the relationship between Jeremiah and Ezekiel. His only comment on the book of Ezekiel discusses the meaning of the final fifteen chapters, which address the kingdom of Christ and the heavenly Jerusalem. Luther's second preface is longer and more detailed. He offers lengthy comment on the opening and closing visions in Ezekiel, showing

[1]*Inst.* 2:1566.

[2]*The Book of Concord: The Confessions of the Evangelical Lutheran Church*, eds. Robert Kolb and Timothy Wengert (Minneapolis: Augsburg Fortress, 2000), p. 664.

especially their christological meaning. Luther's second preface is best understood as a summary of Ezekiel's principal visions.

John Calvin (1509–1564). John Calvin started lecturing on the book of Ezekiel at the end of his life. His lectures began on January 20, 1563, and came to an abrupt end on February 2, 1564. During that year, he endured numerous illnesses and, on occasion, needed to be physically carried to the lecture hall. His final lecture was on Ezekiel 20. After returning home that day, he was unable to continue and remained bedridden until his death on May 27, 1564. Although bedridden, Calvin remained alert and productive. From February to May, he continued to work on Ezekiel, completing Ezekiel 20 and revising his lectures for publication. The lectures on Ezekiel are Calvin's last work. Here we read the final thoughts of the Calvin who had endured ecclesiastical and theological battles, suffered disappointment and personal hardship and labored on behalf of the Reformation for thirty years.

John Mayer (1583–1664). John Mayer, an English separatist, was educated at Cambridge and served as a rector his whole life. He spent his time thoroughly digesting the exegetical works of the reformers and the early church fathers. His life's work was a commentary on the whole of Scripture, which was published in seven volumes from 1627 to 1653. The commentary on the prophets was published in 1652.[3] Mayer's lengthy and detailed exposition of Ezekiel offers comment on every chapter. These comments are not equal in length or interest. Mayer does not say much about the judgments against the nations (Ezek 25–32) or the oracles of Israel's restoration (Ezek 33–39). His main interests are the visions of Ezekiel, especially the final vision of the new Jerusalem.

William Greenhill (1591–1671). William Greenhill, an Independent minister, was educated at Cambridge and attained facility in Hebrew, Greek, Latin, history and theology.[4] He wrote an exhaustive and impressive commentary on Ezekiel. Greenhill delivered his *Exposition* as lectures in London and published them in five separate volumes (1645–1662). In the nineteenth century, these volumes were combined and circulated as a single volume. The *Exposition* remains in print to this day. Greenhill gives a detailed verse-by-verse exposition of the text. He begins by offering lexical and syntactical comments on the Hebrew, comparing, when appropriate, the Septuagint and Vulgate. Following these comments, Greenhill gives historical and theological observations on the verse. A good deal of engagement with earlier writers occurs in the "observations" section. Greenhill is aware, for example, of Calvin's partial commentary on Ezekiel. He also engages the works of the early church fathers.

Finally, the section on Ezekiel includes occasional comments by Johannes Oecolampadius, Hans Denck, Johann Gerhard, Giovanni Diodati, Jakob Raupius, Thomas Manton, John Owen, John Bunyan, Richard Baxter and Matthew Meade.

[3]*ODNB* 37:573.
[4]*ODNB* 23:601-3.

Johannes Oecolampadius, who is introduced at length in the section on Daniel below, lectured on Ezekiel at the University of Basel. His lecture notes were posthumously edited and published by Wolfgang Capito (1478–1541), his friend and first biographer.[5] These notes provide a general introduction to the theological themes of each chapter in Ezekiel and offer short comments on select verses.

Hans Denck (c. 1500–1527). The theology of Hans Denck is difficult to characterize. He was at home with the humanists, imbued with spiritualist notions and called the "pope of the Anabaptists" by Martin Bucer. Denck was critical of Luther's teaching on justification by faith alone and, in a sense, held beliefs more reminiscent of the relativism and individualism of postmodernity.[6] He was expelled from numerous cities because of his unorthodox views and was forced to wander for a time. Befriended by Oecolampadius and given refuge in Basel, he resisted all efforts to conform his theological positions to normative Protestant views. He died because of the plague in 1527. Denck coauthored a work on the book of Micah toward the end of his life. In this work, or reflection as it is styled, Denck appeals in places to Ezekiel.

Johann Gerhard (1582–1637). Johann Gerhard is the third most significant theologian in the Lutheran tradition after Martin Luther and Martin Chemnitz. He was appointed professor of theology at the University of Jena in 1616 and served there until his death in 1637. He is known for his dogmatic and apologetic writings, especially his impressive *Theological Commonplaces* (1610–1622), and his various devotional works, *Sacred Meditations* (1606), *Handbook of Consolations* (1611) and *Schola Pietatis* (1622–1623). The statements used in the commentary below come from his collected sermons or Postilla, as these collections were termed, and from his summary of the book of Ezekiel in his Theological Commonplaces.

Giovanni Diodati (1576–1649). Giovanni Diodati fled Italy because of religious persecution and settled in Geneva, where he taught Hebrew and theology at the Academy of Geneva. Diodati participated in the famous synod of Dort (1618), translated the Bible into Italian and published notes and annotations on the books of the Bible.[7] It is this last work that is used in the commentary below.

Jakob Raupius (1604–1677). Jakob Raupius was a Lutheran pastor for many years in Herleshausen, a small town in the north of Hesse. Although he never held an academic appointment, he wrote numerous commentaries on the Old Testament and one on the Gospels. His commentary on the major prophets was published in 1655. Raupius summarizes the main points of each chapter and provides an analysis of key verses in

[5]Cf. J. Brashler, "Oecolampadius, Johannes," *DMBI*, 781-84; Hughes Oliphant Old, "John Oecolampadius," in *The Reading and Preaching of the Scriptures in the Worship of the Christian Church*, 7 vols. (Grand Rapids: Eerdmans, 2002), 4:53-65.

[6]For a review of Denck's theology, see E. J. Furcha, ed., *Selected Writings of Hans Denck* (Lewiston, N.Y.: Edwin Mellen, 1989), viii-xviii. See also David C. Steinmetz, *Reformers in the Wings*, 2nd ed. (Oxford: Oxford University Press, 2001), pp. 146-52, 188-89.

[7]*OER* 1:485-86.

the chapter. His comments are brief and concerned mostly with questions pertaining to the Hebrew grammar. Raupius relied heavily on the works of others; he borrowed freely without attribution from the works of Johann Gerhard and Hugo Grotius (1583–1645), a Dutch theologian and jurist.

Thomas Manton (1620–1677). Thomas Manton, educated at Oxford, was a nonconformist minister and strong advocate of Presbyterianism.[8] He was known as a rigorous evangelical Calvinist who preached long expository sermons. At different times in his ecclesial career he worked side by side with Richard Baxter and John Owen. In his later life, Manton's nonconformist position led to his ejection as a clergyman from the Church of England (1662) and eventual imprisonment (1670). Although a voluminous writer, Manton was best known for his preaching. At his funeral in 1677, he was dubbed "the King of Preachers." The commentary below makes use of two sermons by Manton on Ezekiel 18.

John Owen (1616–1683). John Owen, theologian and Independent minister, was educated at Oxford.[9] Owen was a prolific writer, unrelenting opponent of Arminianism and renowned preacher. Owen published devotional works on sanctification and the Christian life, theological works on the Trinity and especially the Holy Spirit, numerous polemical and apologetic pieces, an extensive correspondence and collections of sermons. Owen's sermons are used below in the commentary.

John Bunyan (1628–1688). John Bunyan, a self-educated Independent preacher, is best known as the author of *The Pilgrim's Progress*.[10] His life was fraught with bouts of spiritual depression, controversy and imprisonment. In the commentary below, Bunyan's *Solomon's Temple Spiritualized* is used. In this work, Bunyan offers a spiritual interpretation of the temple and its various utensils. Bunyan's comments on the heavenly temple at the end of Ezekiel are used below.

Richard Baxter (1615–1691). Richard Baxter, largely self-educated, was a reluctant nonconformist who sought to bridge the theological and ecclesiological differences between the Presbyterian, Episcopalian and Independent groups in England.[11] Although disputatious, Baxter valued moderation and reasonableness. Theologically he sought a middle ground between Calvinism and Arminianism, rejecting double predestination and limited atonement. He was a prolific writer, composing devotional, pastoral, historical and exegetical works. In the commentary below, Baxter's *Call to the Unconverted* (1658), a lengthy reflection on Ezekiel 33, is used.

Matthew Meade (1628/29–1699). Matthew Meade, educated at Cambridge, was an uncompromising nonconformist.[12] Early in his ecclesial career he associated with

[8]*ODNB* 36:565-68.
[9]*ODNB* 42:216-31.
[10]*ODNB* 8:702-11.
[11]*ODNB* 4:418-33.
[12]*ODNB* 37:648-50.

William Greenhill, eventually joining his congregation at Stepney and becoming his assistant. Following Greenhill's death in 1671, Meade was called to serve as pastor in the church at Stepney. John Owen participated in Meade's ordination service. Meade was repeatedly fined as a nonconformist, along with Owen, and eventually imprisoned. Following Owen's death in 1683, Meade succeeded him as lecturer at Pinner's Hall in London. Meade's sermons on Ezekiel and lectures on Ezekiel's vision of the wheels are used below in the commentary.

Theological Themes

The book of Ezekiel may be divided into five sections: Ezekiel's call and opening visions (Ezek 1–3), prophecies of judgment against Israel (Ezek 4–24), judgments against the nations (Ezek 25–32), oracles of Israel's restoration (Ezek 33–39) and the vision of the new temple (Ezek 40–48). Certain themes recur throughout Ezekiel for our commentators. They emphasize God's covenantal promise to his people, who turn from him by embracing idolatry and the worship of the nations. God repeatedly warns his people of judgment and destruction. Despite these constant warnings through the prophet, the people persist in their idolatry and are punished. Although God speaks judgment against sin and idolatry, against his people, their city and temple, he always ends with comfort and words of promise. Restoration follows judgment. This restoration points to Christ and his eternal kingdom; he is the one who atones for our sins and clothes us with his righteousness. Here the visions of Ezekiel offer much. We glimpse through the prophet's words the advent of Christ, his saving work for us, his second coming, the new Jerusalem and the eternal city in which the saints will dwell forever with God. The larger point observed is that God continually cares for the faithful, who dwell amid an idolatrous and rebellious people.

The sections of Ezekiel that elicit the most comment are his visions (Ezek 1–3; 8–11; 37; 40–48). Our commentators emphasize the appearance of Christ to Ezekiel and the comfort of Christ's eternal kingdom as proclaimed in these visions. The final section in particular is a lengthy prophetic reflection on the new Jerusalem. This final section is regarded by our commentators as the most difficult as it is filled with numerous types and figures of the restoration of the church of God under the gospel.

There are other sections worthy of note. The allegory of unfaithful Jerusalem in Ezekiel 16 receives the greatest amount of comment outside of the vision narratives. A number of themes are emphasized in this chapter. God alone calls us to faith by his grace and adorns us with his benefits. Our great sin is to boast in these blessings from God as if we were the author of them. God judges such ingratitude and sinful boasting harshly. The chapter ends with comfort and the promise of God's everlasting faithfulness in keeping his covenant. This promise points to Christ's atonement for our sins.

Two of the best-known sections of Ezekiel for readers today receive only minimal attention from our commentators. The death of Ezekiel's wife is discussed almost in passing (Ezek 24:15-27) and commented on only in relation to the destruction of the temple and city. Her sudden death and Ezekiel's prohibition to mourn for her, who was his dearest comfort and the desire of his eyes, elicits no comment of sympathy for the double hardship now endured by the prophet, who not only loses his wife but also is prevented from mourning for her. Similarly, the valley of dry bones (Ezek 37:1-14) receives unequal attention from commentators. The preferred reading is that this section points to the restoration of Israel from captivity. The minority reading, which requires argument from those accepting it, is that this section concerns the general resurrection of the dead. For all of our commentators, however, the second part of the chapter, which promises the unification of Israel and Judah under the image of two sticks (Ezek 37:15-28), elicits more interest. The reason for this seems to be the number of exegetical and theological questions surrounding the image of two sticks. When does such reunification occur? Does this imply the salvation of the Jews? Who is this servant David who will be their one king and one shepherd forever? These questions occupy the attention of our commentators far more than the valley of dry bones.

Interpretive Issues

Attention to detail characterizes the observations of our commentators. From the peculiar beginning of the book to the description of heavenly Jerusalem at the end, our commentators are captivated by the inspired character of every detail recorded by Ezekiel. For example, why does the book begin with the word "and"? "And it came to pass" is a peculiar beginning to a book. There is no antecedent. There is no apparent need for the word *and*. Yet that is how this inspired book begins. To pass over something like this as trivial or to suggest that it is a mere Hebrew idiom, characteristic of many other books of the Bible, fails to appreciate the instruction for us in this word, which is also inspired. To think otherwise suggests that God's revelation to us is at times irrelevant and superfluous—a position not held by our commentators. Once this peculiar beginning is accounted for our commentators stumble on an equally perplexing phrase, "the thirtieth year." The thirtieth year of what or of whom? The text does not say. Again, a detail not to be overlooked. This attention to detail is especially observed throughout the final vision of the new temple. Nothing escapes notice or comment. Whether it is the wall, gates, chambers, steps and windows or the courts, porch and pillars of the temple, everything receives comment because all of Scripture is recorded for our learning.

The book of Ezekiel also raises a number of theological issues central to the Reformation that require a fair amount of exegetical comment. For example, in Ezekiel 14, God uses the example of Noah, Daniel and Job, who were all declared righteous. Ezekiel explains that even if these righteous men were amid God's sinful people, to whom the prophet Ezekiel is speaking, their righteousness would save only themselves. Likewise those to whom Ezekiel speaks will deliver their souls by their own righteousness (Ezek

14:20). If no person can stand before God by his own righteousness, then what does this verse mean? Our commentators argue that the righteousness here spoken about is not the righteousness of faith, which alone avails for our salvation, but the righteousness of the Christian life.

There are also issues that arise in Ezekiel that divide our commentators and reveal their confessional differences. In both Ezekiel 18 and Ezekiel 33, God declares through Ezekiel that he does not desire the death of the wicked but that all should repent and live. The question arises for our commentators whether God wishes all to be saved. Here differences emerge. At issue is election and whether God predestines to both salvation and damnation. Mayer and Gerhard reject double predestination. Gerhard explicitly argues against the Calvinists in his comment. Baxter and Manton both insist that sinners are to blame for their sins; they alone are the principal cause of their own destruction. Calvin and Greenhill argue that these two passages are not addressing election and God's sovereign decrees. Rather, these texts comfort those who repent with the knowledge that God indeed is ready to forgive.

A second issue, indeed what is perhaps a surprising exegetical issue for our commentators, occurs at the beginning of Ezekiel 44. Ezekiel is led back to the east gate and told that the gate is to remain shut forever. No man shall enter in by it because the Lord, the God of Israel, has entered in by it (Ezek 44:1-2). The early church fathers understood this text to be about the incarnation and the perpetual virginity of Mary. The gate that is closed and shall no more be opened indicates that Mary remained always a pure virgin. The reader will not be surprised, however, to see this theological position dismissed as "popish" by Greenhill. The reader may be surprised to see that both Gerhard and Mayer agree with the early church fathers. The blessed Virgin Mary is the closed gate. Joseph never knew her; brothers are cousins.

Finally, for Greenhill and Meade, an interpretive issue arises with God's promise of reuniting the houses of Israel and Judah (Ezek 37:21-22), his promise of an everlasting covenant (Ezek 37:26-27) and his promise to restore Israel (Ezek 39:25-29). These promises have not yet been fulfilled and point to the future conversion of the Jews when they will be gathered by one king, one shepherd, the Messiah, who is Christ.

Historical Reception of These Works

The historical reception of these works on Ezekiel is found within the works themselves. Although Luther wrote only prefaces on Ezekiel, these comments were known and used by Calvin. In turn, both Mayer and Greenhill engaged Calvin throughout their respective works. The enduring value of these works for modern readers follows a different trajectory. Luther and Calvin remain the two most significant Reformation voices for us today. Their works are widely available in English, and modern commentators, whether agreeing or disagreeing with them, must take their labors into account. The same cannot be said for our seventeenth-century writers. These figures are lesser known, and their works are less accessible. Mayer's impressive commentary on Ezekiel is not engaged by any major commentary series in our day. Greenhill's massive and detailed exposition of Ezekiel appears in only one series.[13] In the commentary below, however, Mayer and Greenhill are the featured writers. Therefore, their voices once again sound forth to instruct us on the book of Ezekiel.

THE BOOK OF DANIEL

Historical Context

The book of Daniel, like the book of Ezekiel, elicited broad interest from the reformers. Citations and glosses from Daniel appear throughout theological works, sermons, confessional documents, and other such writings during the sixteenth and seventeenth centuries. Unlike the book of Ezekiel, however, the reformers also produced a number of commentaries on the whole of Daniel or select portions.

Martin Luther (1483–1546). In 1530, Martin Luther published separately his German translation of the prophet Daniel (*Der Prophet Daniel Deudsch*) with a detailed and lengthy preface.[14] Luther intended the preface to provide a short introduction to this book by "St. Daniel" so that simple believers could know and understand the histories related by him. Luther summarizes the content of each chapter and offers detailed comment on such things as Nebuchadnezzar's dream (Dan 2), God's punishment of Nebuchadnezzar (Dan 4), Daniel's visions and prophecies of future kingdoms (Dan 7–8) and the seventy weeks (Dan 9). Luther also gives a lengthy explanation of the histories contained in Daniel 11. Although he spends a significant amount of time on the histories contained in Daniel, Luther ends by encouraging readers not to be so consumed with the history that they fail to refresh and comfort their hearts with the promises of Christ contained in Daniel. We read the history to better understand the advent of Christ. Put another way, biblical history has a purpose and an end: Jesus Christ.

Johannes Oecolampadius (1482–1531). Johannes Oecolampadius is not as well known as Luther or Zwingli but was just as active in the Reformation efforts of the 1520s. He studied law at Bologna and theology at Heidelberg, Tübingen and Basel. Around the year 1514, Oecolampadius came into contact with Philipp Melanchthon and began an association with Melanchthon's great-uncle, the distinguished Hebrew scholar Johannes Reuchlin (1455–1522). He was a close friend of Erasmus, whom he assisted with the publication of the Greek New Testament.[15] At this time, he also taught theology at the

[13]Daniel Block, *The Book of Ezekiel: Chapters 1–24*, NICOT (Grand Rapids: Eerdmans, 1997), pp. 65, 89, 216, 250, 305, 314; Daniel Block, *The Book of Ezekiel: Chapters 25–48*, NICOT (Grand Rapids: Eerdmans, 1998), p. 700.

[14]*LW* 35:294-316.

[15]P. G. Bietenholz and Thomas B. Deutsher, eds., *Contemporaries of Erasmus: A Biographical Register of the Renaissance and*

University of Basel and Heidelberg. Among his students were Hans Denck, with whom he would maintain a close friendship and eventually provide refuge in Basel at the end of his life, and Johannes Brenz (1499–1570), who unhesitatingly sided with Luther against Oecolampadius during the eucharistic controversy in the 1520s when Oecolampadius changed his position from Luther to Zwingli.[16]

Oecolampadius was appointed preacher and confessor at the cathedral of Augsburg in 1518, and, to the surprise of many, entered a monastery near Augsburg in 1520. He began a friendship with Zwingli in 1522 and theologically began to move in the direction of Zurich. At this point, he accepted an invitation to come to Basel to secure the budding Reformation in that city. It is here that Oecolampadius expended his efforts for the Reformation. He began lecturing at the University of Basel in 1523 and subsequently joined his reforming efforts with Zurich.[17] He died in 1531, a mere month after Zwingli's death at the battle of Kappel.

Oecolampadius published his commentary on Daniel in 1530.[18] The commentary covers the whole of Daniel and is divided into two books, corresponding to the division in Daniel between the historical (Dan 1–6) and prophetical books (Dan 7–12). Oecolampadius uses the Vulgate to introduce the text. He then offers detailed textual comments in light of the Hebrew, Aramaic or Greek, when appropriate. Finally, he provides lengthy historical and theological comments that are arranged according to verse or half-verse. Oecolampadius's love of the church fathers, as witnesses of the truth (*testes veritatis*), is evident throughout. The modern reader will be struck by how christological Oecolampadius's commentary is. Although Luther wrote only a preface, there is a good deal of agreement between the two reformers in their approach to Daniel.

Philipp Melanchthon (1497–1560). Philipp Melanchthon, humanist and reformer, is one of the most remarkable and interesting theologians of the sixteenth century.[19] His eloquence and calm demeanor made him an attractive figure to kings and princes, moderate cardinals and fellow evangelicals, who all requested his presence at imperial diets and theological colloquies in Germany, England and France. His literary efforts, erudition and persuasiveness garnered attention from gifted humanists like Erasmus, sympathetic reformers like Bucer and Calvin and undeniable foes like Eck and Cochlaeus. Melanchthon was an ecclesiastical statesman, gifted linguist, careful historian, insightful theologian and committed evangelical.

Reformation, 3 vols. (Toronto: University of Toronto Press, 1987), 3:26.

[16]On Brenz, see Steinmetz, *Reformers in the Wings*, pp. 76-82, 182.

[17]For a more detailed introduction to Oecolampadius, see Gordon Rupp, *Patterns of Reformation* (Philadelphia: Fortress, 1969), pp. 3-53; *OER* 3:169-71.

[18]Cf. Brashler, "Oecolampadius, Johannes," *DMBI*, 781-84; Old, "John Oecolampadius," in *The Reading and Preaching of the Scriptures*, 4:53-65.

[19]Cf. Heinz Scheible, "Philip Melanchthon," in *The Reformation Theologians*, ed. Carter Lindberg (Oxford: Blackwell, 2002), pp. 67-82; Steinmetz, *Reformers in the Wings*, pp. 49-57, 179-80; Heinz Scheible, *Melanchthon: Eine Biographie* (Munich: C. H. Beck, 1997).

Trained in Latin and Greek, Melanchthon accepted a call to teach Greek and New Testament at the University of Wittenberg in 1518. Luther and Melanchthon quickly became close associates and theological allies. Melanchthon brought theological order and systematic presentation to Luther's reforming efforts. Although they did not share the same theological demeanor and did not always agree on such things as the Lord's Supper, they remained colaborers on behalf of the Reformation in Germany and beyond throughout Luther's life.

Following Luther's death, Melanchthon struggled to maintain unity among the Lutherans during the difficult times of the Smalcald War (1546–1547) and the Augsburg and so-called Leipzig interims (1548). His continued modification of the Augsburg Confession and theological departure from Luther on such issues as free will and the relationship between good works and the article of justification by faith led to the rise of two opposing parties within Lutheranism: the so-called Philippists, supporters of Melanchthon's changing positions, and the Gnesio-Lutherans, the "genuine" Lutherans, who were faithful to the Unaltered Augsburg Confession and committed to the spirit of Luther's reforming efforts.

Melanchthon wrote some of the most influential works of the sixteenth century. He was the main author of the Augsburg Confession (1530) and its Apology (1531). He attempted to give order to Luther's theology by composing the first Protestant systematic theology, the *Loci Communes*.[20] This dogmatic work was a brief outline of the chief points of Scripture. Melanchthon also wrote on philosophical topics and church history; he published numerous letters, sermons and commentaries.

In 1543, Melanchthon wrote a commentary on Daniel. The reader of this commentary immediately discovers that he is reading the work of a dogmatic theologian. Melanchthon comments on a whole chapter at a time. In the first part of the commentary (Dan 1–6), he begins by giving the Vulgate text and then lists the dogmatic topics raised in the chapter. The commentary continues with subheadings that correspond to the list of dogmatic topics made by Melanchthon. He does not offer a separate comment for each dogmatic topic that he identifies. The second half of the commentary (Dan 7–12) offers a narrative exposition of the text with lengthy historical and theological excurses on such things as the antichrist, Alexander the Great, Antiochus Epiphanes, and the various kings mentioned in Daniel. An impressive amount of historical material is furnished by Melanchthon throughout the commentary.

John Calvin (1509–1564). John Calvin began his lectures on Daniel during the summer of 1559 and completed them in the spring of 1560. The lectures were lightly edited and

[20]In the *Tischreden*, Martin Luther famously said, "If anybody wishes to become a theologian, he has a great advantage, first of all, in having the Bible. This is now so clear that he can read it without any trouble. Afterward he should read Philipp's *Loci Communes*. This he should read diligently and well, until he has its contents fixed in his head. If he has these two he is a theologian, and neither the devil nor a heretic can shake him." Again, Luther is reported as saying, "There's no book under the sun in which the whole of theology is so compactly presented as in the *Loci Communes*. If you read all the fathers and sententiaries you have nothing. No better book has been written after the Holy Scriptures than Philipp's." See *LW* 54:439; WA, Tr 5, 204, no. 5511.

published in 1561. The published commentary, however, retains the feel and atmosphere of the lecture hall. Those elements often removed from polished prose, such as repetition, digressions and explicit verbal transitions, remain in the commentary. We are told that Calvin lectured without notes. He began by reading aloud the Hebrew or Aramaic, offering a translation of the text (glossing it as he went) and then giving his exposition.[21] Calvin shows an awareness of alternative translations and different theological interpretations. He is also familiar with the earlier commentaries by Oecolampadius and Melanchthon.

Heinrich Bullinger (1504–1575). Heinrich Bullinger, born out of wedlock, was the son of a Roman Catholic parish priest.[22] In 1519, he entered the University of Cologne to study the humanities. Here he began to kindle his lifelong interest in the early church fathers. His conversion to Protestantism came by reading the early works of Luther and Melanchthon's *Loci Communes* (1521). Their teaching, he determined, was in accord with Scripture and the church fathers in a way that Roman Catholic teaching was not. In 1523, he began teaching at the Cistercian monastery at Kappel and, at the same time, developed a close relationship with Huldrych Zwingli, which would continue until Zwingli's untimely death. In 1531, he was chosen as Zwingli's successor to be the chief minister (*antistes*) of the Grossmünster, a principal church in Zurich.

Bullinger actively participated in the eucharistic controversy between Wittenberg and Zurich. In 1549, he joined with John Calvin in producing the *Consensus Tigurinus*, which was a thorough rejection of the Lutheran position and the *Wittenberg Concord* of 1536. He authored the *Second Helvetic Confession* (1566), which was intended to be his personal testament of faith but instead became the most widely recognized Reformed confession of faith. Bullinger was also a tireless and profuse preacher. For the first ten years as chief minister of the Grossmünster, he preached six to eight sermons a week. By the end of his life, he had preached through all the books of the Bible (*lectio continua*). It is estimated that Bullinger delivered between seven thousand and seventy-five hundred sermons to the people of Zurich.

In 1565, Bullinger published sixty-six sermons on the book of Daniel. His homilies offer a running commentary on the entire text.[23] Bullinger's comments attend to textual, historical and theological issues. As with Oecolampadius, Bullinger's comments are often christological and, as would be expected of a homily, directed toward the current social and religious concerns of his hearers.

Johann Wigand (1523–1587). Johann Wigand was a staunch Lutheran who labored to secure Luther's reforming efforts amid the turmoil and divisions of sixteenth-century Lutheranism.[24] He was raised by devout Lutheran parents. He studied theology at the

[21]"Translator's Preface," *Daniel I: Calvin's Old Testament Commentaries* (Grand Rapids: Eerdmans, 1993), pp. ix-x.

[22]Bruce Gordon, "Heinrich Bullinger," in *The Reformation Theologians*, pp. 170-83; Steinmetz, *Reformers in the Wings*, pp. 93-99, 183-84. After his father's conversion to Protestantism in 1529, his parents married.

[23]On Bullinger's interpretation of Scripture, see R. L. Petersen, "Bullinger, Heinrich," *DMBI*, 256-60.

[24]For the following, see Ronald Diener, "Johann Wigand, 1523-1587," in *Shapers of Religious Tradition in Germany, Switzerland*

University of Wittenberg, where he heard lectures by Luther and Melanchthon. From the 1550s onward, Wigand became active in the theological controversies plaguing Lutheranism. He collaborated with Matthias Flacius (1520–1575) in vehemently opposing the Philippists. In 1573, he became acquainted with Martin Chemnitz and was appointed professor of theology at the University of Königsberg. In 1575, he became the bishop of Pomerania. Here he remained until his death in 1587 preaching, teaching, writing and visiting churches to ensure their faithfulness to the Scriptures and Lutheran theology.

Wigand wrote numerous theological and historical works, which were often motivated by controversy and written with polemical interest. He wrote catechetical works for the churches under his care. He proposed and implemented a theological program for the University of Königsberg. His sermons and sermon outlines were collected and disseminated for use among parish pastors.[25] In addition to these works, Wigand wrote a commentary on Daniel in 1571. The commentary is orderly and clear. He divides each chapter into historical and theological parts. He first offers a Latin translation of the text with comment. He then proceeds with annotations on nearly every verse. A section on the doctrinal points raised by the text is given next. Finally, at various places in the commentary, Wigand offers lengthy excurses on doctrinal issues related to the text, such as the ceremonial law, idolatry, pride, drunkenness, dreams, angels, and so on.

Andrew Willet (1562–1621). Andrew Willet was a prolific writer, controversialist and parish pastor.[26] He was born at Ely in 1562 and attended both Cambridge and Oxford. He took holy orders in 1585. Willet received his father's prebendal stall at Ely in 1587 and was appointed to the rectory of Barley in 1598. He retained both sources of revenue until his death in 1621, providing him a substantial income. Willet read extensively in the church fathers, canon law, the schoolmen and the chief writings of his own day, both Protestant and Roman Catholic. He composed works in Latin and English, publishing forty-two books in his lifetime. He wrote significant commentaries on Genesis, Exodus, Leviticus, 1 and 2 Samuel, Daniel and Romans—the latter being his most well-known. In 1610, he wrote a sixfold commentary on Daniel.

Willet's commentary is extraordinarily detailed and thorough. He discusses each chapter under six points. He begins by stating the argument of the chapter and then introduces the reader to the various renderings of the text from the original language to its various translations (Greek, Latin, English). Third, he turns to the questions and doubts raised throughout the history of interpretation. Fourth, he discusses the doctrinal topics raised in the chapter under consideration. Willet then addresses the places of controversy

and Poland, 1560-1600, ed. Jill Raitt (New Haven, Conn.: Yale University Press, 1981), pp. 19-38; *OER* 4:272-73.

[25]Wigand's interests ranged well beyond theology. His lifelong interest in science and natural history resulted in a book on the Prussian elk. He was also captivated by horticulture, providing an exhaustive botanical study of the herbs in Pomerania. See Diener, "John Wigand, 1523-1587," p. 26.

[26]*ODNB* 59:26-29.

in the fifth part. He ends each chapter, the sixth part, with moral observations from the text.

Throughout the commentary, Willet cites the authors he is engaging by placing their names in parentheses at the end of the sentence. These references add a significant amount of theological and ecclesial diversity to Willet's commentary. A figure who influenced most sixteenth-century Protestants and is used frequently by Willet is Nicholas of Lyra (c. 1270–1349). Nicholas was a Franciscan and noted biblical exegete. He was well-versed in Hebrew and had a rich knowledge of the early church. The reformers from Luther to Willet were especially attracted to Nicholas because of his attention to the plain sense of Scripture.[27]

Willet incorporates comments from two sixteenth-century Roman Catholic theologians. Benedict Pereira (1535–1610), whom Willet refers to as Pererius, was a Spanish Jesuit theologian and philosopher who wrote a commentary on Daniel in 1587.[28] Hector Pintus (1528–1584) was a Portuguese theologian and professor at Coimbra who published a commentary on Daniel in 1582. In addition to Calvin and Bullinger, Willet regularly cites two other Reformed theologians. Amandus Polanus (1561–1610), an important contributor to the development of Reformed orthodoxy, published a commentary on Daniel in 1599. Polanus published numerous commentaries on the Old Testament and later turned his attention to dogmatics.[29] Francis Junius (1545–1602), a Huguenot theologian, published an exposition on Daniel in 1593. Willet's esteem for Junius can be seen in the appendix attached to end of his commentary. In 1608, Conrad Graser (1557–1613), a historian and professor of Hebrew at the Reformed gymnasium in Thorn (modern-day Toruń, Poland), published an exposition of Daniel 9 that challenged the arguments of Francis Junius. Willet appends to his commentary on Daniel a refutation of Graser and defense of Junius.

Finally, in addition to Luther and Melanchthon, Willet appeals to Andreas Osiander (1498–1552), an accomplished Hebraist, controversialist and part-time Lutheran.[30] Osiander opposed nearly every friend he made: Philipp Melanchthon, Hans Denck, John Calvin and Martin Chemnitz, to name only a few. He participated in the Marburg Colloquy of 1529 with Luther and Zwingli but later opposed Luther's teaching on justification by faith. Osiander believed that Christ's righteousness was not merely imputed to the believer but substantially transferred to the individual. This position, referred to as Osiandrianism, was rejected by the Lutherans and others during the sixteenth century.

John Mayer (1583–1664). As mentioned above in the introduction to Ezekiel, Mayer wrote a commentary on the whole Bible. In his commentary on Daniel, Mayer comments

[27]Philip Krey and Lesley Smith, eds., *Nicholas of Lyra: The Senses of Scripture* (Leiden: Brill, 2000), pp. 1-18.
[28]*TCE* 11:664.
[29]Robert Letham, "Amandus Polanus: A Neglected Theologian?" *The Sixteenth-Century Journal* 21:3 (1990): 463-76.
[30]Steinmetz, *Reformers in the Wings*, pp. 64-69, 166.

with interest on every chapter. He demonstrates familiarity with most of the Protestant commentaries on Daniel noted above. He has a great interest in the historical details of the monarchies and the christological prophecies of Daniel.

Miscellaneous Commentators. The book of Daniel elicited comments from many writers during the sixteenth and seventeenth centuries. Although most of these comments, like those mentioned above with Ezekiel, are occasional and casual, some of them have been incorporated into the commentary below to further broaden the ecclesiastical diversity of the volume. Brief comments are again found from Hans Denck (c. 1500–1527), Johann Gerhard (1582–1637) and Giovanni Diodati (1576–1649), who were introduced above. In addition to Denck, two other Anabaptists, Menno Simons (c. 1496–1561) and Tieleman J. van Braght (1625–1664), are briefly cited in the commentary. Simons, a Roman Catholic priest, was rebaptized in 1536 and became the most significant Anabaptist theologian in the sixteenth century. Tieleman J. van Braght, a Dutch Mennonite, published sermons, hymns and a book on Christian martyrs. Comments from the book on martyrs are used below. A handful of other comments are added by Martin Chemnitz (1522–1586, Lutheran), William Pemble (1591/92–1623, Puritan) and Joseph Mede (1586–1638, Anglican). Chemnitz, a German Lutheran, labored to unite the divided voices of sixteenth-century Lutheranism around the *Book of Concord* (1580).[31] Pemble, a Puritan divine and committed Calvinist, was a well-known preacher who published exegetical and historical works. His historical work on the Persian monarchy is used below.[32] Mede, an Anglican biblical scholar known for his encyclopedic knowledge on various subjects and for his skill in Hebrew, produced a work on Daniel's seventy weeks.[33]

Theological Themes

The book of Daniel is divided into two parts by our commentators. The first part, Daniel 1–6, deals with well-known events like the fiery furnace, Nebuchadnezzar's punishment, the lions' den and the handwriting on the wall. These chapters, for the most part, describe events that occurred in Babylon during the exile. The second part, Daniel 7–12, presents numerous visions about the monarchies of the world, the kingdom of Christ and antichrist and the end of the world.

According to Heinrich Bullinger, some people in the sixteenth century refused to read Daniel, or indeed anything from the prophets, because they now possessed the Gospels and the apostolic teaching of the New Testament. Our commentators find such a view shameful and arrogant. They are not only committed to the continued study and preaching of the Old Testament but also are convinced that the teaching of

[31]Robert Kolb, "Martin Chemnitz," *The Reformation Theologians*, 140-53; Theodore R. Jungkuntz, *Formulators of the Formula of Concord* (St. Louis, Mo.: Concordia Publishing House, 1977), pp. 46-68.
[32]*ODNB* 43:508-10.
[33]*ODNB* 37:683-85.

the prophets provides great comfort and benefit to those who stand on the far side of the apostles. Christian experience commends the use of the prophets; the New Testament Scriptures direct us to their study (Mt 24:15; 1 Pet 1:10-12). As Peter puts it, the prophets served us and not themselves in searching out the sufferings of Christ and the subsequent glories.

Our commentators note many benefits in reading Daniel. The histories of the monarchs, the great miracles that occurred in Daniel's day and the comfort of God's fatherly care and watchful providence over his saints are all recorded for the encouragement of our faith. Moreover, we find explicit prophecies concerning Christ, the precise time of his coming and the promises of his benefits to us. Daniel's thorough description of the office of Christ (Dan 9) is a compendium of the chief articles of the Christian faith. Here Daniel gives clear testimony concerning the advent and death of Christ, the atonement for sins, justification by faith and the everlasting righteousness of Christ. All of these teachings are preceded by Daniel's great prayer of repentance. Here we learn that prayer is the chief exercise of faith; indeed, it is the prerogative of faith.

A constant theme for our commentators throughout their reading of Daniel, whether it is part one or two, is the continued appearance of or allusion to Christ in nearly every chapter of the book. For example, Christ is the stone cut out of the mountain (Dan 2); the one like the Son of God in the fiery furnace (Dan 3); the watcher and holy one (Dan 4); the Ancient of Days and Son of Man (Dan 7); the holy one or *Palmoni* (Dan 8); the atonement for sins and everlasting righteousness (Dan 9); the one in the likeness of man (Dan 10); and the one called Michael, who is the Son of God, Jesus Christ (Dan 12). To be sure, our commentators are not always in agreement on these appearances of Christ. Calvin is the most reluctant to find Christ in the places listed above; Wigand is the most willing.

Interpretive Issues

There are two types of interpretive issues for our commentators. First, there are issues where our commentators are in complete agreement with one another in their opposition to either Roman Catholic or Jewish interpretation. For example, our commentators devote significant space to questions concerning the canonicity and authority of Daniel and the apocryphal additions to the book.

Our commentators show some knowledge of the Jewish debate over the canonical placement of Daniel and the third-century attack on the authority of Daniel by the pagan philosopher Porphyry. Both of these issues touch on the character of Daniel's prophecy. Was the book of Daniel written by Daniel the prophet or was it composed years later, perhaps during the reign of Antiochus Epiphanes, as argued by Porphyry? To take the latter position rejects the inspiration of Daniel and introduces falsehood into the Scriptures. Our commentators reject this position. To accept the canonicity of Daniel in a provisional way, which is how they characterize the Jewish position, is motivated more by theological convictions than historical conclusions. Because Daniel presents the advent and death of the Messiah, his atoning work for all people and his eternal kingdom with more clarity and precision than any other Old Testament writer, this book is classed among the hagiographa (*kethubim*) and rarely read by the rabbis. Although modern scholars may take issue with how the reformers frame this question and characterize the rabbinic view, the significant point for us to observe is the theological motivation for their conclusion. All of our commentators see Daniel giving explicit and comforting prophecies about Christ and his eternal kingdom. This is why all good Christians read Daniel, as Luther puts it.

There are four additions to Daniel not found in the Masoretic text but only in the Greek versions of Daniel: Prayer of Azariah, Song of the Three Youths, Story of Susanna and Bel and the Dragon. The Roman Catholic Council of Trent (1546–1563) declared these to be canonical. Our commentators regard them as apocryphal and endorse the arguments of Jerome against their inclusion in the canon. For the most part, these additions do not occupy the attention of our commentators.

Second, there are a number of exegetical and interpretive issues within the book of Daniel that create difficulties for our commentators and yield diverse conclusions. These difficulties range from chronological questions concerning the reign of Nebuchadnezzar (Dan 2:1) to textual questions regarding the identity of *Palmoni* (Dan 8:13) and Michael (Dan 10:13; 12:1). As with Ezekiel, our commentators demonstrate throughout their commitment to a close reading of the text. When the reformers read that Nebuchadnezzar dreamed "in the second year of his reign," a number of issues arise. How does this agree with Daniel 1, which declares that he besieged Jerusalem in the first year of his reign? There would not be enough time for Daniel to be reckoned among the wise men and astrologers, as the text declares. A number of proposals are made by our commentators to account for the reckoning of years in Daniel 1 and Daniel 2.

We again see their concern for detail and their close reading of the text with two textual questions that arise in the second part of Daniel. First, should the Hebrew word *Palmoni*, which is used at Daniel 8:13, be translated or not? Willet, Mayer and Melanchthon all agree that this word should remain untranslated and understood as Christ. If translated, the word would be "excellent" or "wonderful" angel. When we consider that this "angel" or *Palmoni* is instructing and revealing mysteries known only to God and that it is another angel, perhaps Gabriel, who makes the inquiry on Daniel's behalf to this other "angel," the reformers conclude that this must be Christ himself. It is better, then, to keep the word *Palmoni* untranslated. If we were to translate it, Melanchthon suggests "somebody wonderful," which corresponds to "wonderful counselor," as Christ is elsewhere called (Is 9:6).

A similar issue arises with the identity of Michael (Dan 10:13; 12:1). Although some commentators are more reserved than others in their judgment on this question, nearly all acknowledge that Michael is the Son of God. Mayer and, to some extent, Calvin are the lone dissenters. Again, the reformers' conclusions arise from a close reading of the text and a theological consideration of the "work" assigned Michael. Since our commentators assume that "person" and "work" go together, when they read that Michael is the prince of the people, an office belonging only to Christ, they conclude that "Michael" is not to be understood as the angel but rather translated and understood as the one who is like God.

Two further examples show our commentators' concern for the details of the text and the hermeneutical challenges presented by an overly literal reading of it. When God punishes Nebuchadnezzar (Dan 4), Daniel relates that the king was driven from human society, forced to make his dwelling among the beasts of the field and made to eat grass as the oxen. The question arises to what extent this punishment is to be read according to the letter. Did God change Nebuchadnezzar's nature into that of a beast in order for him to be sustained by grass, something humans are incapable of doing, or was this change in mind only and not in body? Although none of the commentators suggest that Nebuchadnezzar underwent some sort of metamorphosis, nearly all of them are concerned to prevent their readers from drawing such a conclusion.

Another issue arises with Daniel's vision in Daniel 8. Was he physically in Susa, as the text says, or did he remain in Babylon? Calvin argues that he was in Babylon and in Susa by vision only. Any other argument is unreasonable. Mayer dismisses Calvin's position as contrary to what the text says. Mayer argues that Daniel was indeed taken to Susa by the Spirit as Ezekiel and Elijah had also been transported miraculously by the Spirit. Wigand finds the question too difficult to answer one way or the other.

Finally, as mentioned above, our commentators find an appearance or allusion to Christ in nearly every chapter in Daniel. They do not, however, all agree when and where these appearances occur. For example, who appeared in the fiery furnace with the three youths? Calvin says it was an angel; Bullinger argues it was an angel but type of Christ; Wigand and Mayer assert it was the very Son of God. All four offer exegetical support for their conclusion. The pattern of some seeing Christ and others not is repeated throughout the book of Daniel.

Historical Reception of These Works

The historical reception of the commentaries on Daniel begins with the reformers themselves. Luther's preface is used and known by Melanchthon and Wigand. Oecolampadius's commentary, which is the earliest one produced by the reformers on Daniel, is used by Melanchthon, Calvin, Bullinger, Willet and Mayer. Melanchthon is used by Calvin, Bullinger, Willet and Mayer. For modern commentators on Daniel, Luther and Calvin retain their place of significance. They are read and engaged, whether the reader agrees or disagrees with their interpretations. The other commentators, however, are less accessible to the modern reader. The works by Oecolampadius, Melanchthon, Bullinger and Wigand are available only in Latin. Although Willet and Mayer wrote in English, their works are not readily available and their English is cumbersome.

The commentary on Daniel that follows retains the importance of Luther and Calvin but gives the majority of space to these other reformers from the sixteenth and seventeenth centuries. What follows is only a sampling of the erudition and theological insight of their respective works; works that all deserve, in my estimation, to be translated into English and made available once again to a broad readership interested in the important and comforting words of the prophet Daniel.

EZEKIEL

PREFACE

Overview: Our commentators begin with the place of Ezekiel's prophesy in relationship to Jeremiah, highlighting specifically the role Ezekiel was to play for God. Ezekiel, like Jeremiah, tempers his harsh judgments against the people with promises of Christ's kingdom and the heavenly Jerusalem. Moreover, Ezekiel proved a real comfort to Jeremiah, who now had a companion in speaking the things of God. Finally, some comment is made about the reading restrictions historically placed on parts of Ezekiel among Jews and the various difficulties to be encountered in the book.

Jeremiah and Ezekiel. Johannes Oecolampadius: In the order of the books of the prophets, Ezekiel follows Jeremiah. They both have the same argument and both flourished at the same time. Jeremiah was older and preceded Ezekiel into the office of prophet. Jeremiah preached in Jerusalem and Ezekiel in Babylon. They both corroborated each other's prophecy. Ezekiel was taken to Babylon at the time of Jeconiah. Commentary on the Prophet Ezekiel.[1]

Jeremiah and Ezekiel. Martin Luther: Ezekiel, like Daniel and many more, along with King Jeconiah, went willingly into captivity in Babylon, following the counsel of Jeremiah. The prophet Jeremiah constantly advised that the people should surrender to the king of Babylon—and thus live; they should not resist—or they would be destroyed (Jeremiah 21). Now when the people arrived in Babylon, as Jeremiah shows in chapter 24, they became impatient and regretted beyond measure that they submitted. For they saw that those who stayed in Jerusalem and had not surrendered still possessed the city and everything else, and hoped to make Jeremiah a liar and to defend themselves against the king of Babylon and remain in their own land.

In Jerusalem the false prophets helped this notion along by constantly consoling the people that their city would not be captured, and that Jeremiah was a lying heretic. Along with this (as it usually does) went the fact that those at Jerusalem boasted that they were holding honestly and firmly to God and fatherland. They claimed that the others who had surrendered had deserted God and fatherland and were thus faithless traitors who were unable to trust or hope in God, but had gone over to the enemy because of the vile talking of Jeremiah, the liar. This hurt and embittered greatly those who had surrendered to Babylon, and their captivity became a double one. O how many a hefty curse they must have wished on Jeremiah, whom they had followed and who had led them astray so miserably!

For this reason God raised up in Babylon this prophet Ezekiel, to encourage the captives and to prophesy against the false prophets at Jerusalem, as well as to substantiate the word of Jeremiah. Ezekiel does this thoroughly; he prophesies much harder and far more than Jeremiah that Jerusalem shall be destroyed and the people perish, along with the king and princes. Yet he promises also that the captives

[1]*Commentarius in Ezechielem* (1553), 3.

shall return home to the land of Judah. This is the most important thing that Ezekiel did in his time; he deals with this matter down to chapter twenty-five.

After that, to chapter thirty-four, he extends his prophecy also to all the other lands round about, which the king of Babylon was to afflict. There follow in addition four chapters [34–37] on the spirit and kingdom of Christ, and after that on the last tyrant in Christ's kingdom, Gog and Magog [38–39]. At the end Jerusalem is rebuilt, and Ezekiel encourages the people to believe that they shall go home again [40–48]. Yet in the Spirit he means the eternal city, the heavenly Jerusalem, of which the Apocalypse also speaks [Rev 21]. PREFACE TO THE PROPHET EZEKIEL.[2]

JEREMIAH AND EZEKIEL. JOHN CALVIN: Before I proceed any farther, I will briefly consider the themes that Ezekiel discusses. He has almost everything in common with Jeremiah, as we have said, but especially this: that he announces final destruction to the people, because they were not holding back from piling evil deed upon evil deed, thereby inciting the vengeance of God more and more. Therefore, he threatens them, and not just once, because the hard-heartedness of the people was so great, that to utter the threats of God only three or four times would not be enough, unless he were to repeat them incessantly.

Yet Ezekiel also shows the reasons why God decided to deal with his people so severely, certainly because they were so polluted with many superstitions, because they were deceitful, greedy, merciless, filled with crime, given to extravagance, and depraved by lust. All these things are listed by our prophet, to show that the vengeance of God is not too severe, since the people continued to reach the greatest godlessness and to amass a great pile of evil deeds. . . .

The prophets demonstrate the guilt of the people with no other intention than to stir them to repentance, if only they would believe it is possible for those who are estranged from God to be reconciled to him. Accordingly this is the reason why whenever our prophet, as well as Jeremiah, rebukes the people, he tempers the severity of correction by weaving in promises. . . .

But after chapter 40 he deals more richly and extensively with the rebuilding of the temple and the city. According to this declaration he announces a new *position* of the people, royal authority would flourish and the priesthood would recover its former excellence. For the rest of the book he will explain the remarkable kindnesses of God, which were to be hoped for after the close of the seventy years. Here it is useful to remember what we observed in the case of Jeremiah. While the false prophets were promising the people a return after three or five years, the true prophets were proclaiming what would really happen, so the people might submit themselves patiently to God, enduring his just corrections, not discouraged by the duration of years. EZEKIEL 1.[3]

DIFFICULTY OF EZEKIEL. MATTHEW MEADE: It must be said of this prophecy, as was said of Paul's epistles, that there are some things in them hard to be understood, full of obscurity and difficulty, which made Jerome say, there is in this book a sea of Scripture so deep and a labyrinth of the mysteries of God so difficult, and therefore as the reading of the beginning of Genesis and the book of Canticles was forbidden to the Jews (as Jerome says) until they were thirty years of age, so was the beginning and ending of this prophecy.

There are in it dark visions hard to be unfolded, uncertain chronologies difficult to be found out, mystical parables hard to be opened and many enigmatic hieroglyphics not easily understood. Such as the portrait tile (Ezek 4),

[2]Lenker 6, 303-304* (WADB 11,1:392). [3]CTS 22:55-56 (CO 18:24-25).

the removing of the household baggage (Ezek 12), the useless vine branch (Ezek 15), the two eagles and a vine (Ezek 17), the boiling pot (Ezek 24), the dry bones (Ezek 37), and the like. But among all of them none has more darkness and difficulty attending it than of the wheel and cherubim mentioned in the first and tenth chapters. THE VISION OF THE WHEELS.[4]

WHO SHOULD READ EZEKIEL? MARTIN LUTHER: St. Jerome and others write that it was, and still is, forbidden among the Jews for anyone under thirty years of age to read the first and last parts of the Prophet Ezekiel [1:4-28; 40:2–48:35] and the first chapter of Genesis. To be sure, there was no need of this prohibition among the Jews, for Isaiah [29:11-12] prophesies that the entire Holy Scriptures are sealed and closed to the unbelieving Jews. St. Paul says as much in 2 Corinthians 8:14-16, that the veil of Moses remains over the Scriptures, so long as they do not believe in Christ. A NEW PREFACE TO THE PROPHET EZEKIEL.[5]

THE NEED FOR EZEKIEL. JOHN CALVIN: Now we must consider God's purpose for selecting Ezekiel as his prophet. For thirty-five years Jeremiah had not ceased to cry out, but with little success. Therefore, seeing that the prophet, Jeremiah, had worn himself out, God wanted to give him a helper. And it was certainly no small relief, when Jeremiah, who was in Jerusalem, learned that the Holy Spirit was speaking harmoniously through another mouth. Indeed in this way the truth of his teaching was confirmed. . . . Still this was his bitter duty, to announce loudly and continually for thirty-five years to the deaf, actually even to the insane. Therefore, to minister to his servant, God gave him an companion, who would teach the Babylonians the same things, which Jeremiah had not stopped proclaiming to Jerusalem. . . . But the usefulness of his teaching spread much further, since those in Jerusalem were compelled to listen to the prophecies Ezekiel spoke to the Chaldeans. When they understood that these prophecies agreed with Jeremiah's, they could not but at least ask why this was so. Indeed it is not normal for one prophet in Jerusalem, another in Chaldea, to proclaim their prophecies as if with one voice, like two singers harmonizing. Truly it is not possible to ask for a more pleasant or well-composed melody than what was found between these two servants of God. EZEKIEL 1.[6]

[4]*Vision of the Wheels* 3-4. [5]Lenker 6, 305* (WADB 11,1:394). [6]CTS 22:54-55 (CO 18: 23-24).

1:1-28 THE LIVING CREATURES AND THE GLORY OF THE LORD

1In the thirtieth year, in the fourth month, on the fifth day of the month, as I was among
the exiles by the Chebar canal, the heavens were opened, and I saw visions of God.[a] 2On
the fifth day of the month (it was the fifth year of the exile of King Jehoiachin), 3the word
of the LORD came to Ezekiel the priest, the son of Buzi, in the land of the Chaldeans by
the Chebar canal, and the hand of the LORD was upon him there.

4As I looked, behold, a stormy wind came out of the north, and a great cloud, with
brightness around it, and fire flashing forth continually, and in the midst of the fire, as it
were gleaming metal.[b] 5And from the midst of it came the likeness of four living creatures.
And this was their appearance: they had a human likeness, 6but each had four faces, and
each of them had four wings. 7Their legs were straight, and the soles of their feet were like
the sole of a calf's foot. And they sparkled like burnished bronze. 8Under their wings on
their four sides they had human hands. And the four had their faces and their wings thus:
9their wings touched one another. Each one of them went straight forward, without turning
as they went. 10As for the likeness of their faces, each had a human face. The four had the
face of a lion on the right side, the four had the face of an ox on the left side, and the four
had the face of an eagle. 11Such were their faces. And their wings were spread out above.
Each creature had two wings, each of which touched the wing of another, while two covered
their bodies. 12And each went straight forward. Wherever the spirit would go, they went,
without turning as they went. 13As for the likeness of the living creatures, their appearance
was like burning coals of fire, like the appearance of torches moving to and fro among the
living creatures. And the fire was bright, and out of the fire went forth lightning. 14And the
living creatures darted to and fro, like the appearance of a flash of lightning.

15Now as I looked at the living creatures, I saw a wheel on the earth beside the living
creatures, one for each of the four of them.[c] 16As for the appearance of the wheels and
their construction: their appearance was like the gleaming of beryl. And the four had the
same likeness, their appearance and construction being as it were a wheel within a wheel.
17When they went, they went in any of their four directions[d] without turning as they
went. 18And their rims were tall and awesome, and the rims of all four were full of eyes
all around. 19And when the living creatures went, the wheels went beside them; and when
the living creatures rose from the earth, the wheels rose. 20Wherever the spirit wanted to
go, they went, and the wheels rose along with them, for the spirit of the living creatures[e]
was in the wheels. 21When those went, these went; and when those stood, these stood; and
when those rose from the earth, the wheels rose along with them, for the spirit of the living
creatures was in the wheels.

22Over the heads of the living creatures there was the likeness of an expanse, shining
like awe-inspiring crystal, spread out above their heads. 23And under the expanse their
wings were stretched out straight, one toward another. And each creature had two wings
covering its body. 24And when they went, I heard the sound of their wings like the sound of

many waters, like the sound of the Almighty, a sound of tumult like the sound of an army. When they stood still, they let down their wings. [25]*And there came a voice from above the expanse over their heads. When they stood still, they let down their wings.*

[26]*And above the expanse over their heads there was the likeness of a throne, in appearance like sapphire;*[f] *and seated above the likeness of a throne was a likeness with a human appearance.* [27]*And upward from what had the appearance of his waist I saw as it were gleaming metal, like the appearance of fire enclosed all around. And downward from what had the appearance of his waist I saw as it were the appearance of fire, and there was brightness around him.*[g] [28]*Like the appearance of the bow that is in the cloud on the day of rain, so was the appearance of the brightness all around.*

Such was the appearance of the likeness of the glory of the LORD. *And when I saw it, I fell on my face, and I heard the voice of one speaking.*

a Or *from God* **b** Or *amber;* also verse 27 **c** Hebrew *of their faces* **d** Hebrew *on their four sides* **e** Or *the spirit of life;* also verse 21 **f** Or *lapis lazuli* **g** Or *it*

OVERVIEW: Our commentators begin this lengthy and difficult chapter by considering the identity of Ezekiel and his location in Babylon. Attention is also given to the peculiar beginning of the book, which is often overlooked by translators and commentators. After one difficulty comes another. What is meant by "in the thirtieth year"? Some suggest that the date proceeds from a jubilee; others reckon it from the discovery of the Law by Josiah.

Although a review of historical opinion is given on who the four living creatures are, our commentators agree that they are to be understood as four angels or cherubim. Less agreement is found with the four wheels. Some understand this generally as representing change; some see the four parts of the world represented; and others, understanding the whole prophecy to be about the kingdom of Christ, suggest that the four wheels, pointing to the New Testament, represent the Word of God, baptism, the Lord's Supper, and the office of the keys. Finally, all the commentators are agreed that Ezekiel beheld the person of Christ, the very Son of God.

Two general meanings of the vision are put forward by our commentators. For some, it is a vision about the sovereignty of God; he alone directs all things to his glory. For others, it is a vision about Christ and his kingdom; here great agreement exists between Ezekiel and Jeremiah 31.

1:1-3 *Ezekiel in Babylon*

EZEKIEL. JOHN MAYER: Ezekiel is said to be the son of Buzi and a priest in order to purchase him the greater authority, as being none of the vulgar sort, but a priest. Ezekiel signifies the strength of God; Buzi, contempt; whereon Origen gathers that he was a figure of Christ, who was the mighty power of God but despised by the Jews. . . .

The time of his prophesying and the place where is exactly set down, that we might know that he prophesied in the land of the Chaldeans in some part of the time when Jeremiah prophesied in the land of Judah. . . . In this time then they prophesied both together, Ezekiel, being by the Lord, was stirred up to confirm that which Jeremiah said. COMMENTARY UPON ALL THE PROPHETS.[1]

A PECULIAR BEGINNING. WILLIAM GREENHILL: "Now." The word in the original is "and." "And it came to pass." It seems a strange

[1]*Prophets*, 365.

beginning of a book, especially when it refers to nothing said or written before. Many books of sacred Writ begin in this manner, as Exodus, Leviticus, Numbers, Joshua, Ruth, Samuel, Kings, and many others show. In historical books, it may note the series and connect things antecedent with things consequent. But in prophetical books, it cannot note or make a connection with things foregoing. Jonah begins his prophecy so, and what was the antecedent to make up the connection? Here is the query, and difficulty, why the prophet should begin his book in this manner, "And it came to pass."

Some satisfy the issue this way. They make it an idiom or propriety of the Hebrew tongue to begin books with this particle, *and*, or *now*. And so they make nothing of it. But surely this is not all. There is something wrapped up in this *now*, or *and*, which may be of instruction and use to us.

"Now," or, "and it came to pass." The prophet doubtless was meditating on the condition he was in; meditating on the condition he had been in. There was a time when we were at Jerusalem, that we went with joy to the temple and to the solemn assemblies. A time that we heard the voice of God, that we saw his glory, his beauty, his power and his strength there. A time when we had communion with the saints and sang songs of Sion together with cheerfulness and with joy. We had precious ordinances, honorable sabbaths, sacrifices that did cheer our hearts, seal up pardon of our sins to us and intimate the good will of God in Christ to our souls. We sat under our vines and our fig trees and were in safety. But now, now we eat the bread of mourners, we drink our own tears. Now we are deprived of all ordinances, stripped of all our comforts. We are sold into the hands of enemies. We are become captives to a heathen prince. Our bondage is grievous and must continue seventy years. It is the fruit of our sin. God is righteous in all his judgments, and if we willingly accept the punishment of our iniquity, he will in wrath remember mercy and regard us in our low estate. He will sweeten and sanctify our captivity to us. Such thoughts as these were in the breast of the prophet. AN EXPOSITION OF EZEKIEL.[2]

THE THIRTIETH YEAR. JOHN CALVIN: We see that our prophet was called to the teaching office in the fifth year after Jehoiachin had voluntarily surrendered himself to the King of Babylon, and had been dragged into exile along with his mother. He says, however, that it was the thirtieth year. Most commentators follow the Chaldean paraphraser, understanding this date to refer to the rediscovery of the Book of Law. It is clear enough, that this year was the nineteenth of King Josiah's rule, but according to my calculations I do not agree with those who think the date refers to the rediscovery of the Book of Law. Truly this phrase, the thirtieth year, would be too obscure and forced. Nowhere do we read authors who started counting from there. Besides there is no doubt that the usual method among the Jews was to start counting from a year of Jubilee, which truly was the start pointing for the next era. Thus, I do not doubt that the thirtieth year followed a Jubilee. Nor is this a new argument. For example, Jerome also mentions this same method, although he incorrectly rejects it, because he is misled by another opinion. However, it is certain that the Jews used this method of counting, starting from a Jobel, that is, a Jubilee. This best explains the thirtieth year. If someone objects that nowhere do we read that the eighteenth year of King Josiah's rule was that festival year when everyone returned to their own field, slaves were given their freedom, and the restoration of the entire people took place, the answer is simple. Although nothing is found about which year the Jobel happened, it is still enough for us, that the Jubilee was a festival year. The Israelites

[2]*Exposition*, 8.

followed this tradition of counting years. Just like the Greeks had their Olympiads, the Romans had their Consuls, and calculated their festivals from that time. So also the Hebrews were accustomed to begin counting from a Jobel year to the next restoration, as I said. Ezekiel 1.[3]

In the Thirtieth Year. William Greenhill: "In the thirtieth year." This time troubles interpreters very much. It is not said in the thirtieth year of what, or of whom, but only in the thirtieth year. Here is an uncertain chronology, which makes a difficulty in the prophet.

1. "In the thirtieth year." Not the thirtieth year from the jubilee, as some make it, for the fifth year of Jehoiachin's captivity corresponds not with the thirtieth from the jubilee. As Franciscus Junius and some others (that take pains in searching out the truth here stated) observe that falls during the ninth year from the jubilee. Therefore we let that pass.

2. "In the thirtieth year." Some make this to be the thirtieth year of his age. The prophet was thirty years old and then he began to prophesy. But this is not the practice of the penmen of Scripture to compute the prophecies from their own age and birth. And there is good reason for it, because prophecies, and things that concern the good of the church so nearly and so much, receive witness and strength from the time wherein they are extant. Those times must not be particular times, times of particular men that are not known, but the times must be such as are known to the world, that all may be convinced the thing was done at such a time. Now the birth of one that afterward was to be a prophet is not likely to be a time so noted in the world that the world then should take notice that Ezekiel was born. Therefore, they would not begin the computation of his prophecy from that point. It is not likely that this should be the meaning of the thirtieth year. If so, he would have said, "In the thirtieth year of my life."

3. "In the thirtieth year." That is, in the thirtieth year since the law was found in Josiah's days, and since that great Passover that was kept by him. In 2 Kings 22, there is mention of finding the Book of the Law. And in 2 Kings 23, of the great Passover, and this was in the eighteenth year of Josiah's reign [2 Kings 23:33].

Now if we compute the time from the eighteenth year of Josiah, it amounts even to the thirtieth year, in which our prophet had his vision and began his prophecy. An Exposition of Ezekiel.[4]

The Heavens Were Opened. William Greenhill: "The heavens were opened, and I saw visions of God." The word *opening,* among the Jews, denotes sometimes not the reality, but the effect of a thing. Genesis 3:7, "Their eyes were opened." They were not shut before, and so their eyes are said to be opened. In the gospel, Christ is said to open the eyes of the blind, the ears and mouth of the deaf and dumb. It is not that their mouths were absolutely so closed that they could not stir their eyelids, but Christ opened them so, as he made them to see, hear and speak, to do that which they could not do before. For that reason, in regard of the effect, they are said to be opened. Sometimes again it denotes the truth of a thing. So Stephen saw heaven opened and Christ standing at the right hand of God. Peter saw heaven opened and a sheet coming down to him.

The question is, which of these ways it is to be taken here? Origen says that the heavens were open to the eyes of his body, there was a division of the heavens, and so in a literal sense he saw the visions and the things presented to him. Jerome says the heavens were opened, not by the rending of the firmament, but by

[3]CTS 22:51-52 (CO 18:21-22). [4]*Exposition,* 9.

the faith of the believer. You may take it in the literal sense, and according to the truth of the thing. The inconvenience objected against it is not considerable. For it is said, if the heavens were literally opened, how could Ezekiel see so far, as to see things in heaven? The strength of his eyes could not reach it. For if the sun, and fixed stars that are far above the sun, are greater bodies than the earth and seem so little to us, how little would anything in heaven seem to the eye, when it is exceedingly beyond both these?

Answer: When it says the heavens were opened, it does not follow that Ezekiel must see the visions in heaven. The things he saw might be nearer than the stars or sun. The dove came down and lighted on Christ, and the sheet was let down from heaven to Peter. As such the visions might be nearer to Ezekiel than the highest heavens. "The heavens were opened, and he saw visions of God." It is not said that he saw visions of heaven. And grant it to be heaven, Stephen saw Christ there, and so might Ezekiel see the object of his vision there. Yet neither did Stephen by his natural strength see Christ, nor Ezekiel these visions, but he that opened heaven did open their eyes, strengthened them to see at such a distance. An Exposition of Ezekiel.[5]

The Word of Yahweh. John Calvin: He says *the word of Yahweh was given to him*, for we know God alone should be heard. The prophets should only be listened to, if they proclaim what is from God alone. It is necessary, therefore, that all teachers of the church have first been students, so that God alone maintains his right as the sole leader and teacher, and accordingly the authority rests in God alone. Whenever prophets demand to be heard, they also add that they do not carry their own words, but faithfully deliver a word from God. And so it was with our prophet. . . . Now he adds *the hand of the Lord was on him*. Some explain "hand" to mean "prophecy," however, to me this seems trivial and watered-down. I myself understand "hand" to mean "power," as if Ezekiel were saying that he had been clothed in the power of God. In this way he made clear that he himself was chosen to be a prophet. The hand of the Lord, then, was evidence of a new grace, so that Ezekiel could place all the captives under himself, since he carried the authority of God.

This could also mean the effectiveness of his teaching. Indeed the Lord not only provides the words for his servants, but also he works by the secret inspiration of his Spirit. He will not allow their labors to be for nothing. And so this passage should be understood in this way. But since the prophet here merely takes for himself what was necessary, thus claiming for himself the rank and office of prophet, I do not doubt that when he speaks of the "hand," that he means an internal working of the Holy Spirit. Ezekiel 1.[6]

God Manifests Himself to the Prophets. William Greenhill: God has manifested himself to his prophets several ways.

1. By speaking immediately to them without interposition of any medium, even mouth to mouth and face to face. So he spoke to Adam in paradise; to Moses, "The Lord spoke to Moses face to face, as a man speaks to his friend" (Ex 33:11). This manner of God's manifesting himself was peculiar to Moses above any, or all the prophets besides, as you may read (Deut 34:10).

2. God manifested himself to his people by dreams, which was in the night season. There was some representation of something to them when they were asleep. Thus God manifested himself to Jacob (Gen 28:12). And Jacob said that "the angel of God spoke to him in a dream" (Gen 31:11).

3. God has manifested himself to his people by visions: "You spoke in vision to your holy

[5]*Exposition*, 16-17. [6]CTS 22:61 (CO 18:28-29).

one" (Ps 89:19). And Genesis 15:1, "The word of the Lord came to Abraham in a vision." These three you have together in two verses (Num 12). And part of the eighth, "If there is a prophet among you, I the Lord will make myself known to him in a vision and speak to him in a dream; and to Moses will I speak mouth to mouth." Here in the text it is by way of vision that God speaks or appears to Ezekiel, "I saw visions of God." An Exposition of Ezekiel.[7]

1:4-14 *The Four Creatures*

God's Judgment. Johannes Oecolampadius: That God is the just judge of the world, such that he himself protects the elect and punishes the reprobate, is plainly stated; indeed, his glory is declared throughout both Testaments. Mention of judgment occurs many times in the Scriptures; often he is angry but, on account of his covenant, he turns to mercy. . . . Now it is Christ through whom God judges the world, as it is stated, "To the Son he gave the authority to execute judgment" (Jn 5:27). Therefore it is proved that he judges the world, beginning with his death, to which pertains his whole life in the flesh, all his words and deeds, and then with his resurrection, by which he was exalted in glory by the Holy Spirit, according to the Father's promise, after being condemned by people, according to the flesh, to death, he was raised by the Spirit, according to the Father, to eternal life. . . . Therefore, in this opening verse, the prophet makes us aware of the terrible judgment of the Lord against Jerusalem. Commentary on the Prophet Ezekiel.[8]

A Revelation of Christ. Martin Luther: This vision in the first part of Ezekiel [1:4-28], however, is nothing else than a revelation of the kingdom of Christ in faith here upon earth, in all four corners of the whole world as said in Psalm 19:4, *In omnem terram.* This is how I understand it (let someone else improve on it). For no one can be a prophet, as St. Peter testifies, unless he has the Spirit of Christ [2 Pet 1:21]. But to give an interpretation of the entire vision is too long a matter for an introduction. To put it briefly: this vision is the spiritual chariot of Christ in which he rides here in the world, meaning thereby his entire holy church. A New Preface to the Prophet Ezekiel.[9]

The Four Creatures. John Calvin: Now as to the vision itself, some understand the four animals to be the four seasons of the year, supposing that here the power of God in the management of the entire world is celebrated. But that is too far-fetched. Others believe four virtues are depicted, for, they say, the image of justice is inherent in humanity, wisdom in the eagle, courage in the lion, and self-control in the ox. Despite how cleverly this is devised, still it is not trustworthy.

Others take yet another view, thinking "obviously four passions are denoted: fear and hope, sorrow and joy." While others find three aspects of the soul to be indicated here: to be sure in the soul, *to logikon,* is the seat of reason, *thymikon* is the office of the emotions, *epithymētikon* is the desires, they add *synteresis* as the fourth, that is the conscience. But these all are merely childish babblings.

For a long time it was the accepted view that the four evangelists were portrayed by this image. They believed that Matthew was compared to a human, because he starts with the genealogy of Christ. Mark was compared to a lion, because he begins with John the Baptist's preaching. Luke, they believed to resemble an ox, because he begins by talking about the priesthood. While John was compared to an eagle, because he pierces through the secrets of heaven. But also in this fable there is noth-

[7]*Exposition,* 17. [8]*Commentarius in Ezechielem* (1553), 4, 6. [9]Lenker 6, 305* (WADB 11,1:394).

ing sturdy, in fact all of this disappears, if it is examined closer.

Others find the glory of God in the church described, therefore they believe the animals are to be taken as the saints who have already passed on in the faith, while the wheels are for the weak and the undisciplined. After this they continue stacking up even more nonsense, which is better buried at once, rather than wasting a lot of time refuting it. Therefore, I reject all of these. EZEKIEL 1.[10]

THE FOUR LIVING CREATURES. WILLIAM GREENHILL: Now we come to that part of the vision that concerns the living creatures [Ezek 1:5-15], where God's glory and government of the world are set out from superior causes, namely, celestial things. . . .

What these living creatures are is the great dispute among expositors. Some make them to be the four covenants of God: Adamic, Noahic, Mosaic and apostolic. Some make them to be all the creatures. Some, the four cardinal virtues: justice, wisdom, fortitude, temperance. Some, the four faculties in the soul: the rational, irascible, concupiscible and conscience. Some, the four chief passions: joy, grief, hope and fear. Some, the four monarchies: Assyrian, Persian, Grecian and Roman. Some, the twelve tribes of Israel, in their stations, east, west, north, south, when in the wilderness. Some, the four elements, of which the human body consists. Some, the four Evangelists: Matthew, Mark, Luke, John. And this, being the opinion of Jerome and Gregory the Great, prevailed much but now is deserted. Others understand by these four creatures those who are complete and more perfect in the church. Others expound them to be Christ. But Christ is brought in, in the latter end of the chapter, sitting on the throne. These creatures are distinct from him and inferior to him. By them then we are to understand the angels, which have a great part under God in the government of the world. . . .

"Four living creatures." These were four angels in particular. Some conceive Michael, Gabriel, Raphael and Uriel, which were chief over the rest of the whole host of angels. But that is not the sense. It is also not true that God only uses four angels in his service, for many thousands are employed. "There was a multitude of the heavenly host" (Lk 2:13), and there was an army with the prophet (2 Kings 6:17). But it relates to the object, namely, the world, which is distinguished into four parts: east, west, north and south. The work of these angels laid in all those parts, and none of them were exempt from the presence, observation and operation of the angels. AN EXPOSITION OF EZEKIEL.[11]

ON THE FOUR CREATURES. JOHN MAYER: By these four animals, the angels of God or cherubim are set forth, who were of old made by Solomon at God's direction, like to young men having wings, and placed in the Holy of Holies over the mercy seat. Now four appear to Ezekiel (Is 6). He sees seraphim about God's throne, but not telling how many, yet it may be conceived that they were but two, for one cried to another, Holy, Holy, Holy. But why do four appear now? To this Calvin says well (who holds the cherubim and seraphim to be the same) that the Jews being degenerated to idolatry, and so from the way of worship prescribed in the sanctuary, the Lord would not now set forth his ruling by his providence, by two cherubim only. Rather he does this by four, whereby they might know that his providence was not cooped up within the limits of Canaan but extended itself to all the four parts of the world, in which he had his angels both to govern as presidents over all countries, as is expressed elsewhere of Persia and Greece (Dan 10:20), and to bring them against, and to arm them with power, for the destruction of any that rebelled against him. These four came out

[10]CTS 22:63-64 (CO 18:29-30). [11]*Exposition*, 27-28.

of the midst of the fire, and amber representing the Lord, who is a consuming fire, to show that no power should be able to stand against him, as the fire consumes all things. Commentary upon All the Prophets.[12]

The Four Living Creatures. Matthew Meade: In Ezekiel 1:5 you read of four living creatures, every one of which had four faces (Ezek 1:6). He does not say who, or what these living creatures are in that vision, but in the tenth chapter he does. He tells you they are the angels: "The living creatures that I saw, under the God of Israel, I knew that they were the cherubim, every one had four faces apiece" (Ezek 10:20-21). The vision in Ezekiel 1 was at Chebar; the vision in Ezekiel 10 in the temple. God discovers himself more in the temple than at Chebar. Visions in Babylon are not as clear as visions in Zion. "In his temple everyone speaks of his glory" (Ps 29:9).

. . . Wisdom and Prudence typed out by the face of a man; courage and boldness by the face of a lion; diligence and industry by the face of an ox; and expedition and dispatch by the face of an eagle. These were the likenesses of the four faces. . . . The angels, called here the four living creatures, are the great ministers of Christ in the government of the world, not because Christ uses that number and no more, but the number relates to the object, namely, the world, which is constantly divided into four parts: east, west, north and south. These are called the four quarters of the earth (Rev 20:8). And the four quarters of heaven (Jer 49:36). The Vision of the Wheels.[13]

The Faces. William Greenhill: The face of a man represents to us the understandings of angels, and that their administrations are with knowledge and equity. Of this we have already spoken. This face is put first to show the excellence of reason, which must have the introduction into and managing of all actions, else they are neither human nor angelical. By this face also is noted their love to humankind. . . .

The face of a lion signifies the strength of angels. . . . The next face is that of an ox; and it shows the willing obedience, faithfulness, patience and usefulness of angels in their ministrations. For an ox accustomed to the yoke is very tractable, not stubborn, as untamed heifers are. . . . The last face is of an eagle, and in it, as in a glass, we may see the perspicaciousness, swiftness and vivacity of the angels. These three things are observable in eagles. An Exposition of Ezekiel.[14]

The Living Creatures Ran. Matthew Meade: "The living creatures ran—as the appearance of a flash of lightning" (Ezek 1:14), which notes their great speed and swiftness in doing the will of God, and therefore they are described with wings: "Every one had four wings" (Ezek 1:6), which are ascribed to them to express the agility of their nature and the swiftness of their motion in the execution of their office.

. . . There is the return of the living creatures. So it is said, "The living creatures ran and returned" (Ezek 1:14), but this seems to contradict Ezekiel 1:9 and Ezekiel 1:12. There it is said that they turned not when they went. But this receives an easy solution. They turned not from going and doing the work appointed them, but when that work was done, then they returned. They turned not from executing their commission, but then they returned to receive new instructions. They went not back from the work till they had finished what was begun, and then they returned, both to give an account of their work and to watch and wait for a new charge, and hence they are called watchers. "Behold a watcher and a holy one" (Dan 4:13) and "This matter is by the decree of the watchers" (Dan 4:17). They watch for God's orders to execute them for the church's

[12]*Prophets*, 367. [13]*Vision of the Wheels*, 7-8. [14]*Exposition*, 31-32.

good. The Vision of the Wheels.[15]

Christ Rides on Cherubim. Martin Luther: There are the four living creatures, which Ezekiel calls in chapter 10 "cherubim," for Christ sits, rides, and travels on cherubim, as the Scriptures often declare. Each living creature has four faces. They stand foursquare like four horses, but inside and between the wheels. For about the living creatures there are also four perfect wheels, by each beast a wheel. All is so arranged that they can go to the four corners of the world—that is, forward, backward, and to both sides—without needing to turn. Likewise the living creatures go on calves' feet toward the four corners of the world without having to turn. There is no axle, pole, frame, pin, rack, wagon, rope, or trace, but the Spirit drives it all surely from within. Overhead is the firmament, like a saddlecloth, and in it a throne for a saddle. And on the throne sits God, that is, Christ. A New Preface to the Prophet Ezekiel.[16]

The Problem of the Cherub and Ox. John Calvin: Still one question remains, and a difficult one. In chapter ten Ezekiel writes cherub instead of ox. Some think, or at least they say, that at a distance it looked like the face of an ox, but up close it was a cherub. Everyone sees that this is mere banter, because they are not able to avoid, that they have imagined a fable which is not trustworthy. Others judge the cherub and ox to be the same. This is easily disproved by a number of passages, since there is no doubt that cherubim do not have heads of oxen, as is well known.

Therefore I have no doubt that there was some difference in the second vision, when God appeared to his prophet in the temple. It is called the same vision because of its similarity, but it does not follow that all the details were the same. Nor should this interpretation be rejected, since when God revealed himself to his servant in Chaldea, as I have already said, he wanted to deaden the people's stupidity with this complicated image. However, when he appeared in the temple a second time, there was something more heavenly. Therefore the difference, that each animal had the face of a cherub instead of an ox. Consequently, other than the shape of the whole body, there was a remarkable feature, that caused the prophet to recognize these creatures more easily and intimately as cherubim or angels. Ezekiel 1.[17]

The Fire and Lightning. John Calvin: It is not without reason that he says, *fire walked among the creatures.* For the prophet sees what seems to be a burning figure, but he also sees flashing fire everywhere, as if burning torches moved all around the creatures. God wanted to show the power of his Spirit in every deed, so that we do not measure him by our own standard according to the wickedness inherent in us. When we talk about the works of God, we understand what our reason is able to grasp, in this way we try to confine God to our own world. God, however, shows that when he works there is an astonishing power, like fire moving all around. Now, this power is too great for our reason.

Next he says, *the fire was brilliant and lightning came out of it.* When the prophet saw fire radiantly shining in such an unaccustomed manner, this greatly affected his mind. We know that fire is often bright, especially when the flame is near to us. But the prophet here is trying to describe something very unusual, as if he were saying that the fire was not like what comes from wood, but even more brilliant. Consequently it is made clear here that God is displaying his glory visibly. This, too, is why he says, *lightning came out of the fire.* The brilliance just mentioned has to do with the fire being mixed with the lightening. We know that it is not possible for lightning to be seen

[15]*Vision of the Wheels*, 35, 39-40. [16]Lenker 6, 305-306* (WADB 11,1:394-396). [17]CTS 22:74-75 (CO 18:38).

without trembling, for in that moment the heavens seem to be on fire, as if God wanted in some way to swallow up the world. So, the sight of lightning is always terrible to us. In order to frighten the prophet more so by the vision, God showed him this flashing figure, although this was not merely to terrify Ezekiel, but to humble him.

As I already warned, this vision was not given to the prophet for his own private use, but rather for the benefit of all the people. The prophet himself, being merely human, needed this preparation so that he would be humbled. For we are always ignorantly prideful, causing our senses to be dulled, so that we are incapable of God's glory. Whenever God wants to make himself known to us, he strips away all of our pride and security. In the end humility is the beginning of true understanding. Now we understand why lightning came out of the fire. Later this same point is confirmed. EZEKIEL 1.[18]

THE HOLY SPIRIT RULES THROUGH ANGELS. MATTHEW MEADE: Although Christ rules absolutely, yet he does not rule unmediately. He governs the world by the agency of the eternal Spirit. As Christ rules for God, so the Spirit rules for Christ. He is the great administrator of the government throughout the mediatorial kingdom. He sets all a-going; therefore you read, "whither the Spirit was to go, they went" (Ezek 1:12) and again, "whithersoever the Spirit was to go, they went, thither was their Spirit to go" (Ezek 1:20). By the Spirit here no other can be meant but the Holy Ghost, who is coessential, and coequal with the Father and the Son. All the angels of God are under the command and conduct of the Spirit. What great things have angels done, defending, comforting and guarding the people of God, destroying their enemies:

"An angel of the Lord smote a hundred and eighty-five thousand of the Assyrians in one night" (2 Kings 19:35). If angels contend against princes, overturn kingdoms, it is all done by the conduct of the Spirit. He has the great hand in all. THE VISION OF THE WHEELS.[19]

1:15-28 *The Wheels of the Chariot*

ARE THE WHEELS A VISION? MATTHEW MEADE: The wheels are on the earth: "As I beheld the living creatures, behold one wheel on the earth by the living creatures" (Ezek 1:15). He mentions but one wheel because he that saw one, saw all, by reason of their likeness, for they were all as one. But how could the wheel be seen on the earth, when the prophet saw the vision in heaven (Ezek 1:1)? As the wheels were not material wheels but visional, so this earth was not the material earth but earth in a vision, and so it was not the earth beneath but an earth above. "The wheel was on the earth," but that earth was in heaven. So that this earth was in representation only, as it is in landscapes, where you have things in representation but not in reality. There are rivers, and earth, and trees in view, but not in verity.

The wheels are said to be seen on the earth, and not in heaven, to intimate to us the difference between this state and that. This is a state of changes, but that state is unchangeable; the wheels are on the earth, there are none in heaven. As there are no changes in God (I am the Lord, I change not, Mal 3:6) so there are no changes in the glory that results from his presence. All things in that state are durable and permanent. The things of the other world admit of no change, neither in hell nor in heaven. This is the place of changes, which is one difference our Lord Christ puts between treasures on earth and treasures in heaven; those are subject to "the moth, the rust and the thief," but these are not (Mt 6:19-20). THE VISION OF THE WHEELS.[20]

[18]CTS 22:80-81 (CO 18:42). [19]*Vision of the Wheels*, 6. [20]*Vision of the Wheels*, 29.

THE KINGDOM OF CHRIST. MARTIN LUTHER: The four wheels run alike, for all churches in the four corners of the earth, that is, in the whole world, have one and the same harmonious course, in faith, hope, love, the cross, and all spiritual things; they are not driven from without by doctrines of men, but from within by one Spirit, Romans 8:2-27, 1 Corinthians 12:3-13, Ephesians 4:4.

Now the four living creatures go with the wheels—or rather the wheels with them—forward, backward, upward, and to both sides. For the apostles, or the preaching ministry, the word of God, baptism, sacrament, keys, and all that belongs to the spiritual government of the church are also alike and in agreement throughout the world. And the living creatures and the wheels hold firmly and surely together, so that the chariot is one, without any external hitching, fastening, or yoking. Thus, everything is in fours: four living creatures, four faces, feet, hands and wings to each living creature, and four wheels and four spokes to a wheel. This signifies, as said, that Christendom, or the kingdom of Christ in faith, is to go to the four corners, that is, into all the world. A NEW PREFACE TO THE PROPHET EZEKIEL.[21]

THE GOVERNMENT OF WHEELS. MATTHEW MEADE: Christ, who rules all, sends his Spirit; the Spirit acts the angels; the angels rule the world. Therefore you have in the next place a vision of wheels. By these wheels the world is resembled and all the affairs of it. All kingdoms and nations, all countries and cities, all places and people, all actions and affairs are intended and represented by these wheels. Now these wheels are wholly under the conduct and guidance of the living creatures. They acted the wheels. Therefore, it is said, "When the living creatures went, the wheels went by them; and when the living creatures were lifted up from the earth, the wheels were lifted up" (Ezek 1:19). . . . Here you have a short view of the whole subordination of causes in ordering all the affairs of this lower world. God the Father puts the government of all into the hand of Christ. Christ substitutes the Spirit as his viceroy and sends him into the world to manage all things. The Spirit acts the angels, and they all minister to him. The angels act the wheels, and they all are governed by them. THE VISION OF THE WHEELS.[22]

THE FOUR WHEELS. JOHN CALVIN: As to the four wheels, I have no doubt that they signify all the upheavals, which are commonly called changes. For we see the world constantly changing, as if it were putting on a new face. It is like a wheel turning itself or being turned by some external force. We know that there is nothing stable in the world, but everything is in constant upheaval. Therefore the prophet here connects the wheels with angels, as if he were saying that no change happens in the world accidentally, but depends on some external force, namely angels. Not that they move things by their own power, but only to the extent that they are God's hands, like we have already said. EZEKIEL 1.[23]

ON THE FOUR WHEELS. WILLIAM GREENHILL: These wheels, being four, represent to us the four parts of the world (eastern, western, northern, southern) and that in them are great stirs and changes. . . . There are turnings and wheelings in all estates and parts of the world. The four living creatures denote the four parts of the world, and their agencies in them and by them. Now are presented the wheels. Every living creature had a wheel by it. This strongly implies that there are wheeling, turnings and changes in all parts; indeed, the very same that are in one part are at one time or other in another part. The wheels are alike. Are wars, plagues, famine in one country? They are, or will be, in another too. Do people die here?

[21]Lenker 6, 306-307* (WADB 11,1:396). [22]*Vision of the Wheels*, 11-12. [23]CTS 22:67 (CO 18:32).

So they did in all parts. Are people unfaithful now? So they were unfaithful of old. In David's days he said, "Men of high degree are a lie, and men of low degree vanity" (Ps 62:9). Are there unseasonable times here? Such are abroad as well. Are things carried by violence, oppression, injustice here? So they are elsewhere too. Are there designs, plots on our kingdom and church? So there are on others as well. Whatever befalls one state befalls another, internally and externally. The wheels are the same and move alike, though sometimes backward in one part of the world and forward in another. There is no stability anywhere, but all things are changing. In vain then do people travel the world to find certainty and contentment. In vain do we go up and down, here and there, thinking to find settledness and something satisfactory. The world is like itself everywhere. Go east or west, and there is nothing but a wheel, and wheel running. An Exposition of Ezekiel.[24]

The Wheels. John Mayer: From animals the prophet proceeds to wheels, which he also saw, and most probably they portended the same things that the animals did, their number, faces and motions being the same. It is not unusual with the Lord to represent one thing by various things showed in vision. He does this in Jeremiah 1 by an almond rod and a seething pot toward the north.

But what does he mean by saying, one wheel, and later on he speaks of wheels (Ezek 1:16), as of more, indeed, and expressly of four wheels (Ezek 10:9), one wheel by one cherubim, and another by another? Solution. It is meant as there, one wheel by one living creature, and another by another. There being by the four animals, four wheels, near to each of which wheels one stood, as it were to guard it, "with his four faces," each wheel having four faces carved on it, of a man, lion, ox and eagle, as the animal had, showing that this vision tended to the same with the other. Commentary upon All the Prophets.[25]

The Holy Spirit and the Wheels. Matthew Meade: Here is another thing ascribed to these wheels, and that is, the influencing virtue of the same spirit which acted the living creatures. "The spirit of the living creature was in the wheels" (Ezek 1:20). The question is, What Spirit is this? I shall not trouble you with any other sense than that which I take to be the sense of the Holy Spirit, and that is, that by the spirit here is meant the divine Spirit, the eternal Spirit of God; the same Spirit that acts the living creatures acts the wheels also, which in Ezekiel 10:17 is called the Spirit of life, and this is that Spirit who guided all their motions. Therefore it is said, "Whither the Spirit was to go, they went" (Ezek 1:12). There is not an angel in heaven or a wheel on earth, but are all acted and governed by the same Spirit. The Vision of the Wheels.[26]

God Directs All Things. John Calvin: In this verse (v. 19) the prophet teaches that all the upheaval in the world depends on some external force, obviously heavenly power. As we have already said the creatures symbolize to us angels, whom God inspires with secret power, so that he works through their hands. Now consequently when Ezekiel says that the wheels moved through a higher power than their own, it follows that nothing happens accidentally in the world, but God through his own incomprehensible wisdom directs everything, so that nothing happens without his hidden orchestration, which we cannot see with our eyes. . . .

So, we understand that the wheels are moved, although not just because of the creatures' influence over the wheels. For God does not grant to winter or summer, to peace or war, to calm or storm, to death or anything

[24]*Exposition*, 45. [25]*Prophets*, 369. [26]*Vision of the Wheels*, 40-41.

else its own judgment and desire. So, how do these things happen? Truly neither heaven, nor sea, nor earth have any power by themselves, but only to the extent that God, through his angels, directs the earth, or molds the plans of people either to war or to peace.

Now, therefore, we clearly see the meaning of the spirit of the creatures is in the wheels, truly God pours his power into the world through angels, so that not even a sparrow falls to the earth without his providence, as Christ says. For this reason, whenever the stresses of our lives incite us to despair, may this thought come to our minds: the spirit of the creatures indeed is in the wheels. Surely, whenever we tremble due to uncertain circumstances, what else can we do, but find rest in this teaching? It is true that, the end of everything happens as God determines, since nothing happens without his permission. There is no movement, no disturbance under the heavens, unless he himself orchestrates it through his angels. Ezekiel 1.[27]

God's Infinite Wisdom. Matthew Meade: The wheels are said to be lifted up from the earth, and to be high and dreadful (Ezek 1:18-21). This is to teach us that God's wisdom is infinite and unsearchable, and his providences full of mystery. Sometimes they move in an ordinary way, then the wheels move on the earth. Sometimes God goes out of the usual road and acts in extraordinary ways and in unaccountable methods that reason cannot reach or the short line of human wisdom fathom. Then the wheels are said to be high and lifted up from the earth. Who can trace God in his motions, whose ways are far above our sight? The Vision of the Wheels.[28]

The Glory of Christ. William Greenhill: In these verses (Ezek 1:22-25), we have the fourth vision, or fourth part of the general vision, which is concerning the firmament. This vision, as formerly has been shown, holds forth to us the glory of God. . . . There is yet more and higher glory to be spoken of, and that is, the glory of God in the person of Christ. . . .

The scope of Ezekiel 1:23 is to show that the ministry of the angels refers to and sets out the glory of Christ. This is seen in the observations to be given. (1) That where Christ is, there the angels are near to him. He was above the firmament, and they just under it. The firmament was on their heads. There was only a glorious transparent firmament between Christ and them. Distanced from Christ they are, but not far. (2) The angels, wise, strong, serviceable, swift and glorious creatures, attend Christ's throne and are subject to him. They were under the firmament about his throne. . . . (3) They are ready to exercise the will and pleasure of Christ. This further advances the honor of Christ. Their wings were stretched out, and they were willing to move in any service, if their Lord gave out the word. An Exposition of Ezekiel.[29]

Ezekiel Sees Christ. John Calvin: It is worth noting that Ezekiel says, *he saw the likeness of an appearance* (v. 26). From this we gather that he did not actually see heaven, nor was the throne made from any real substance, nor was it a real and natural body of a human. The prophet expresses this clearly, so that no one would imagine that there is anything visible in God, like the fanatics, supposing him to be material. And so no one would ignorantly gather from this passage that God can be seen with the eye, that he is confined in space, and that he is seated like a person. So these false images do not sneak into people's minds, the prophet here testifies that it was not a human body, nor did he see a material throne, but that these shapes and sights were merely presented to him. . . .

---

[27]CTS 22:87-89 (CO 18:46-48). [28]*Vision of the Wheels*, 22. [29]*Exposition*, 54, 56.

Now someone might complain: why did God present himself in the form of a person in this vision, as well as in others? I gladly embrace the opinion of the fathers, who say this is a foretaste of that mystery, which was eventually revealed, and which Paul lifts up so splendidly, when he cries out: "Great is this mystery—at last God is revealed in the flesh." Jerome's view is drastic; he applies the words to the Father himself. We know that the Father never presented himself in human flesh. If he had merely said that God is shown here, nothing would have been out of place. Remove all mention of persons, then it is true: that person seated on the throne was God. . . .

But, considering the passage at hand, it should be enough for us, that the prophet saw God only in the person of Christ, since what is said about the likeness of a person cannot be transferred to the person of Father, or to the Spirit. Indeed neither the Father nor the Spirit were revealed in flesh, but God was revealed in flesh when Christ appeared to us, and the fullness of divinity resides in him. . . .

The point is that the likeness of a body was only so in appearance, as the prophet says, but not in essence. From this we gather that when simple mention is made of God, the whole essence is understood, which is common to the Son and the Holy Spirit, as well as the Father. To be sure it is absurd to understand Christ only under the name Jehovah. It follows, then, that the whole essence of God is here understood. And yet, when the persons are compared together, it only applies to Christ, when it is said "in the form of a human." So, the whole deity appeared to his prophet, and in the form of a human at that. However, neither Father nor Holy Spirit appeared, because the distinction of the persons only begins to appear when the unique attributes of Christ are revealed. Ezekiel 1.[30]

The Vision About Christ. John Mayer: This is now spoken that we might not doubt, but know assuredly, who was before represented sitting on a throne above the firmament, namely, God the Son, who together with the Father is Jehovah, one and the same essence. Here then is a representation of God sitting in great majesty on high, portending his incarnation to come. He is set forth with a chariot going on four wheels, the tops of it reached to the firmament under him, typifying his ministers going out into the four parts of the world, or being in the four parts preaching and publishing his gospel, together with the books of the Old and New Testament, out of which they preach. Therefore here are wheels seen within wheels, the New Testament within the Old, because nothing else is herein set forth but what was before in the Old spoken of and typified.

To the wheels of a chariot they are compared, above which the Lord sits, because they are guided by him. They are said to have the Spirit in them and eyes, because it is both by the Holy Spirit that they are enabled to this blessed work. Moreover, he accompanies their teaching, making it effectual, and enlightens them, making them clearly to discern all things. As it is said, *the spiritual man discerns all things* (1 Cor 2:15). They are eyes or lights to others round about them. Or vigilant bishops, overseers of the Lord's flocks, are intimated by all these eyes.

Let me touch on the Lord appearing like amber, both from his loins upward and from his loins downward. The part upward may well be understood of his divinity, and the part downward of his humanity. By virtue of the union with his divinity, the humanity partakes of the same most resplendent glory. Therefore it is further said to be as fire and brightness round about. It is fire because his day is as a refiner's fire, destructive to dross and purifying to the sons of Levi, who are the elect. And it is brightness for the bright shining of his gospel.

[30]CTS 22:95-100 (CO 18:52-55).

It being now daylight, as when the sun shines, being before as the dark night, for which he is also called the Sun of righteousness. . . .

Now for the living creatures, which were four, I dislike not their exposition who think the four Evangelists to be here set forth. But as they only expound it of Matthew, Mark, Luke and John, I conceive rather both them and the whole New Testament, all books and epistles therein contained, to be by these four figured out also. And as they understand the four faces of them, ascribing the face of a man to one, of a lion to another, of an ox to a third and of an eagle to a fourth, I rather think these faces to agree to all these writings in common. Each one setting him forth, that was as a man, by his taking flesh of the Virgin Mary; as a lion, by his coming of the tribe of Judah, whose emblem was a lion; as an ox, for his being offered up in sacrifice; and as an eagle, for his quick-sightedness, being able to see into the thoughts of people's hearts. Commentary upon All the Prophets.[31]

A Vision of Christ. Matthew Meade: "Above the firmament was the likeness of a throne, and on the throne was the likeness of a man about on it" (Ezek 1:26). Who is this but the Lord Christ in the person of the mediator? Question: But Christ was not as yet come in the flesh. Why then is he here represented in the likeness of a man?

Answer: It was to prefigure his incarnation, his divine nature being in the fullness of time to assume our flesh into the unity of his person. It was to show that the government of the world was put into his hand as Mediator, and that he possessed the throne of the world, not as God only, but according to his human nature. The government of the world was put into the hand of Christ from the time of the fall. . . . Therefore it is said, "By him all things consist" (Col 1:17). And hence it is that God the Father calls him "my king" (Ps 2:6). He has set him up to rule and given him a universal dominion, so that he that is above on the throne, in the likeness of a man, rules all. The Vision of the Wheels.[32]

Meaning of Vision. Martin Luther: This vision, moreover (as Ezekiel himself shows in chapters 8–9), signified the end and destruction of the synagogue, or of Judaism, that is, of the priesthood, the worship, and the [ceremonial] organization instituted and given them by Moses. For all of these were instituted only until Christ should come, as St. Paul says in Romans 8:2-3 and 2 Corinthians 3:6, as Christ himself says in Matthew 11:13, and as the Epistle to the Hebrews says repeatedly. . . .

For this prophecy contains two things. The first is that Israel and Judah shall return to their land after their captivity. This came to pass through King Cyrus and the Persians, before the birth of Christ, at the time when the Jews returned to their land and to Jerusalem from all countries. They also came to Jerusalem every year to the feasts, even from foreign countries where they maintained their residence, drawing many Gentiles with them and to them. . . .

The second thing, and the best thing in this prophecy—that which the Jews will neither see nor heed—is that God promises to create something new in the land, to make a new covenant unlike the old covenant of Moses that they dream about. This is plain from Jeremiah 31:31-32 and from many more passages. No longer are there to be two kingdoms but one kingdom, under their King David who is to come; and his shall be an everlasting kingdom, even in that same physical land.

This, too, has been fulfilled. For when Christ came and found the people of both Israel and Judah gathered again out of all lands so that the country was full, he started something new: he established the promised new covenant. He did this not at a spiritual place,

[31]*Prophets*, 371-72. [32]*Vision of the Wheels*, 5.

or at some other physical place, but exactly in that same physical land of Canaan, and at that same physical Jerusalem—as had been promised—to which they had been brought back out of all lands.

And although the Jews did not want this covenant—or at least not many of them would accept it—it has, nevertheless, remained an everlasting covenant, and not only at Jerusalem and in that land. It has broken forth from there into all the four corners of the world, and remains to the present day, both at Jerusalem and everywhere. For the place, Jerusalem, is still there, and Christ is Lord and King there as he is in all the world. He helps and hears all who are there or who come there, as he does those in all the world. . . . Christ is and remains Lord over all. A New Preface to the Prophet Ezekiel.[33]

Most Important Part of Vision. John Calvin: Now the prophet states the most important part of the vision: God was seated on his throne. If he only went so far as to mention the creatures and wheels, the vision would have been less helpful—incomplete at the least. But since he places God on his throne, we can understand that the angels, who orchestrate movement in other things, do not have any motion or power themselves. Altogether, the prophet is teaching here, that angels cause all things under heaven to be set in motion, so that no motion should be ascribed to those things themselves. And why? Because God presides over all things and directs their actions. That is the main point of the vision, which is now clarified. Ezekiel 1.[34]

The Glory of God Revealed to Ezekiel. William Greenhill: The scope of this vision is to set forth the glory of God. This appears from the last verse of the chapter where it is said, "This was the appearance of the likeness of the glory of the Lord." The Spirit interprets all to be a manifestation of the glory of God. . . . This glory of God is presented to Ezekiel in this vision for these ends:

1. To breed in him a high reverence of divine majesty. The sight of great and glorious things do awaken our dull, heavy, sensual spirits. Naturally we are indifferent to the things of God, and unless something transcendent and glorious is presented to us. . . . Therefore in Exodus 19:16, when the people saw the lightning and heard the thunder, when God came down on the mount in that glorious manner, this awakened them and bred an awful reverence in them of divine majesty: "All the people that were in the camp trembled."

2. To prepare and fit him for entertainment of what God should speak to him. We are not always in a frame to hear God speak. There are great distempers in our spirits. You have all experience enough of the truth of this. Therefore it is said, "Be still, and know that I am God" (Ps 46:10). Be still, let not your spirit be in a rage, taken up with the world, the cares, fears, pleasures and businesses of it. Be not parleying with a lust, but be still, and know that I am God.

3. It is to encourage him to his work and to frame his spirit to a ready execution of it. Ezekiel was to enter on a heavy task. He was to deal with the stubborn Jews, a rebellious people. He knew that Jeremiah had preached thirty-five years, and other prophets in times better than he was in, and little or no good had been done on this hard-hearted people. Therefore lest Ezekiel should be discouraged, that his heart might not faint but be quickened to the work, the Lord shows him his glory in these hieroglyphics, his glory in these creatures, his glory in his Son. That so seeing the glory of God, he might be warmed, oiled and encouraged to run about his work. For the sight of glory is potent with a gracious heart, to make it active for God. "We cannot," say

[33]Lenker 6, 306-307* (WADB 11,1:396-400). [34]CTS 22:90 (CO 18: 49).

Peter and John, in Acts 4:20, "but speak the things that we have seen and heard." Now they had seen his "glory as the glory of the only begotten Son of God" (Jn 1:14). They had been on the mount, seen Christ transfigured and his face shine as the sun (Mt 17:1-2). And having seen his glory and heard his voice, this encouraged them, notwithstanding all difficulties, to be active for him. This was God's way to appear to his servants, to encourage them to the work he would set them about. God appeared to Moses in a burning bush (Ex 3). To Joshua in a vision like a man with a sword in his hand (Josh 5:13). To Elisha by horses and chariots of fire (2 Kings 6:17). Peter, being confirmed by a vision of a sheet let down from heaven, goes and preaches to the Gentiles (Acts 10). And Ezekiel here has vision on vision, that being so strongly confirmed, he might not fear the faces of Jews or Babylonians but proceed with life and spirit about the work he was sent. AN EXPOSITION OF EZEKIEL.[35]

[35]*Exposition*, 21-22.

2:1–3:27 EZEKIEL'S CALL AND A WARNING TO ISRAEL

1And he said to me, "Son of man,[a] stand on your feet, and I will speak with you." 2And as he spoke to me, the Spirit entered into me and set me on my feet, and I heard him speaking to me. 3And he said to me, "Son of man, I send you to the people of Israel, to nations of rebels, who have rebelled against me. They and their fathers have transgressed against me to this very day. 4The descendants also are impudent and stubborn: I send you to them, and you shall say to them, 'Thus says the Lord GOD.' 5And whether they hear or refuse to hear (for they are a rebellious house) they will know that a prophet has been among them. 6And you, son of man, be not afraid of them, nor be afraid of their words, though briers and thorns are with you and you sit on scorpions.[b] Be not afraid of their words, nor be dismayed at their looks, for they are a rebellious house. 7And you shall speak my words to them, whether they hear or refuse to hear, for they are a rebellious house.

8"But you, son of man, hear what I say to you. Be not rebellious like that rebellious house; open your mouth and eat what I give you." 9And when I looked, behold, a hand was stretched out to me, and behold, a scroll of a book was in it. 10And he spread it before me. And it had writing on the front and on the back, and there were written on it words of lamentation and mourning and woe.

3 And he said to me, "Son of man, eat whatever you find here. Eat this scroll, and go, speak to the house of Israel." 2So I opened my mouth, and he gave me this scrollto eat. 3And he said to me, "Son of man, feed your belly with this scroll that I give you and fill your stomach with it." Then I ate it, and it was in my mouth as sweet as honey.

4And he said to me, "Son of man, go to the house of Israel and speak with my words to them. 5For you are not sent to a people of foreign speech and a hard language, but to the house of Israel— 6not to many peoples of foreign speech and a hard language, whose words you cannot understand. Surely, if I sent you to such, they would listen to you. 7 But the house of Israel will not be willing to listen to you, for they are not willing to listen to me: because all the house of Israel have a hard forehead and a stubborn heart. 8 Behold, I have made your face as hard as their faces, and your forehead as hard as their foreheads. 9Like emery harder than flint have I made your forehead. Fear them not, nor be dismayed at their looks, for they are a rebellious house." 10Moreover, he said to me, "Son of man, all my words that I shall speak to you receive in your heart, and hear with your ears. 11And go to the exiles, to your people, and speak to them and say to them, 'Thus says the Lord GOD,' whether they hear or refuse to hear."

12Then the Spirit[c] lifted me up, and I heard behind me the voice[d] of a great earthquake: "Blessed be the glory of the LORD from its place!" 13It was the sound of the wings of the living creatures as they touched one another, and the sound of the wheels beside them, and the sound of a great earthquake. 14The Spirit lifted me up and took me away, and I went in bitterness in the heat of my spirit, the hand of the LORD being strong upon me. 15And I came to the exiles at Tel-abib, who were dwelling by the Chebar canal, and I sat where they were dwelling.[e] And I sat there overwhelmed among them seven days.

16And at the end of seven days, the word of the LORD came to me: 17"Son of man, I have made you a watchman for the house of Israel. Whenever you hear a word from my mouth, you shall give them warning from me. 18If I say to the wicked, 'You shall surely die,' and you give him no warning, nor speak to warn the wicked from his wicked way, in order to save his life, that wicked person shall die for[f] his iniquity, but his blood I will require at your hand. 19But if you warn the wicked, and he does not turn from his wickedness, or from his wicked way, he shall die for his iniquity, but you will have delivered your soul. 20Again, if a righteous person turns from his righteousness and commits injustice, and I lay a stumbling block before him, he shall die. Because you have not warned him, he shall die for his sin, and his righteous deeds that he has done shall not be remembered, but his blood I will require at your hand. 21But if you warn the righteous person not to sin, and he does not sin, he shall surely live, because he took warning, and you will have delivered your soul."

22And the hand of the LORD was upon me there. And he said to me, "Arise, go out into the valley,[g] and there I will speak with you." 23So I arose and went out into the valley, and behold, the glory of the LORD stood there, like the glory that I had seen by the Chebar canal, and I fell on my face. 24But the Spirit entered into me and set me on my feet, and he spoke with me and said to me, "Go, shut yourself within your house. 25And you, O son of man, behold, cords will be placed upon you, and you shall be bound with them, so that you cannot go out among the people. 26And I will make your tongue cling to the roof of your mouth, so that you shall be mute and unable to reprove them, for they are a rebellious house. 27But when I speak with you, I will open your mouth, and you shall say to them, 'Thus says the Lord GOD.' He who will hear, let him hear; and he who will refuse to hear, let him refuse, for they are a rebellious house.

a Or *Son of Adam;* so throughout Ezekiel **b** Or *on scorpion plants* **c** Or *the wind;* also verse 14 **d** Or *sound* **e** Or *Chebar, and to where they dwelt* **f** Or *in;* also verses 19, 20 **g** Or *plain;* also verse 23

Overview: Our commentators begin with the comfort Christ gives Ezekiel in his call. Important to our authors is that the Spirit works through the Word. It is the Spirit who brings us to faith and grants us understanding in the Scriptures. True prophets are called by Christ and endowed with the gift of prophecy, which is symbolized by the eating of the scroll. The question is asked why Ezekiel must eat a scroll instead of reading it. The answer is that by his words he would speak prophecy, so here he is told to eat the scroll. By eating the scroll Ezekiel shows that he speaks only the words given to him by God. It is for this reason he is designated a watchman.

2:1-10 *Word and Spirit*

The Christ Comforts Ezekiel. William Greenhill: The Lord Christ is full of compassion. Ezekiel fell down on his face. The glory of the vision, and greatness of him that sat on the throne, had conquered and felled this our prophet to the earth. There he lay as a man wounded, without strength. Christ leaves him not in this condition but speaks, and that kindly to him. . . .

Those who are humble and struck down with a sense of their own vileness, weakness or worthlessness, through the sight of glory and greatness, Christ quickly raises to comfort again. Our prophet was down at the end of the last chapter, and in the beginning of this he is up again. The humbling from the sight of God, his glory and greatness, is the most effective humbling; and the most speedy, effectual and sweetest comfort does follow it. . . .

The Lord loves to encourage man to his duty. He says not here, "Stand on your feet" only, which might have sufficed, but he makes him a promise, "and I will speak with you." I that am on the throne, compassed with glory, that has the rule of all the world in my hand, I will speak with you. . . . The word of the Christ is a sweet comfort to a soul troubled. An Exposition of Ezekiel.[1]

Word and Spirit. John Calvin: Here the prophet states that God ordered him to stand up. For God never knocks his people down, leaving them on the ground, but always raises them up again. As for when he looks at the wicked, they are so terrified by the sight of God, that they collapse immediately, never to stand up again. However, with those who believe it is different, because the pride of the flesh is corrected in them. Then God extends his hand to them, restoring them, as if to bring them from death to life. . . .

At the same time the prophet teaches, that nothing happened through this voice until the Spirit approached. Indeed God works effectively by his words, but we do not believe that this is accomplished through the noise alone, instead it is caused by the secret orchestration of the Spirit. Therefore the prophet shows both things. On the one hand, he reports that *he heard the voice of God, so he stood on his feet.* Through this God wanted to encourage Ezekiel's confidence. But at the same time he adds, that he was not raised up by that voice, until *the Spirit stood him on his feet.* And so, he here binds together the work of the Spirit with the word of God. Yet still a distinction is made, so that we would know that the outer word is of no importance by itself, unless it is brought to life by the power of the Spirit. . . .

Now this teaching, briefly explained in this way, is sufficient to reject foolish objections, which flit about in the mouths of many who fret about human freewill. They say we can either listen to the word which is offered to us or reject it. However, we see what the prophet says. If any of us is capable of offering obedience to God, the prophet surely was superior in this. And yet the word of God did nothing for him, until the Spirit granted strength, so

[1]*Exposition*, 71-72.

that he rose to his feet. Here we gather, it is not at all in our capability to obey whatever God directs, unless he grants it himself. Ezekiel 1.[2]

Christ and the Spirit. William Greenhill: Those the Lord Christ intends to set up for officers in his church, he gives his Spirit to. The Spirit enters into Ezekiel before he is called; he is filled with the Spirit, the gifts and graces of it. . . . Humankind by natural abilities cannot reach or receive the things of God. Ezekiel must have the Spirit enter into him before he can hear or understand anything to purpose. Reason and discourse are not more above the capacity of the beast than the things of Christ and his Spirit are above the capacity of humanity. . . . The word without the Spirit is inefficacious. When he spoke, the Spirit entered. Had not there been entrance of the Spirit, the word had not prevailed, the prophet had not been raised. . . . It is the Spirit of God that enables us to discern the things of God and assures our spirits of the truth and reality of them. The Spirit entered into the prophet, set him on his feet, that he would hear him that spoke to him. Now, having the Spirit, he was fitted to hear Christ, enabled to judge of what he spoke, to satisfy his soul concerning the truth, reality and excellence of his doctrine. An Exposition of Ezekiel.[3]

The Spirit Alone Brings Us to Faith. John Mayer: Then the Spirit entered into me and set me upon my feet (Ezek 2:2). This was done to show that whoever would hear the Lord speaking must stand on his feet by being intent in his affections to that which he says. But this he cannot do until the Spirit entering into him sets him up. By the Spirit entering he stands up. This is said against all those who attend not to the word of the Lord when he speaks but are remiss in their affections toward it. Let none say, I shall then be set on my feet when the Spirit enters into me, taking no further care hereabout, but ask the Spirit by earnest praying of our heavenly Father, for he will (says the Lord) give his Spirit to them that ask him. Commentary upon All the Prophets.[4]

Proclaiming God's Word. John Calvin: Whenever we undertake what God instructs, we ought to have good expectations, desiring that some fruit from our work would become visible. So, we are able to entertain hopes and desires. And if something other than what we had anticipated happens, then we ought to leave the result in God's hands, and continue to pursue the task we are called to. This is the point of the sentence: you, he says, will make known my words, or recite my words, whether they listen or not. Even if it is just like you were to sing a song to the deaf, as it is said, still you will certainly not cease to make known my words. He also adds the explanation, because they are a rebellious people. However, God warns his servant that there is no reason why he should change his course. Even if he sees absolutely no fruit from his work, because they have no ears, all the same he must speak in the name of God. It is certain, as we mentioned earlier, there were a few, to whom his teaching was useful. Here, however, he discusses the people at large. Consequently we learn, that whenever God calls us to the teaching office, not to be distracted by the kind of people we are to teach. For if it pleases God to use us as we struggle with the rebellious and stubborn, still his word is to be made known, because that is what he commands. Ezekiel 1.[5]

God Uses Signs. Johannes Oecolampadius: "And when I looked, behold, a hand was stretched out to me" (Ezek 2:9). That is, I have understood by a prophetic vision. By certain signs God strengthens weakened consciences. In such a way, the seraph was sent to Isaiah

[2]CTS 22:108-109 (CO 18:61-62). [3]*Exposition*, 73-74. [4]*Prophets*, 378. [5]CTS 22:123 (CO 18:72).

with a burning coal to touch his lip: "Behold, this burning coal has touched your lips; your iniquity is removed and your sins atoned for" (Is 6:7). Likewise the Lord touched the mouth of Jeremiah, saying, "Behold, I have put my words into your mouth" (Jer 1:9). Certainly this is the idea contained in this vision to Ezekiel. For he wishes to say, "Behold, I give into your mouth those words that are bitter and harsh that you might declare these things to this people." . . . A sign was given to Moses that his staff would change into a serpent. For Ezekiel, a scroll of a book was handed to him by the hand of the Lord, that is, a book folded in the eastern custom, which is how they produced their books in those times. COMMENTARY ON THE PROPHET EZEKIEL.[6]

CHRIST CALLS AND SENDS. WILLIAM GREENHILL: It is Christ's prerogative to set up and send officers to the church. . . . Those offices and officers are holy and warrantable, which depend on the will and authority of Christ; not those of which are of the wills and authority of people. . . . He gives gifts and graces to people and then sends them. The Spirit entered into Ezekiel and then said, "I send you." . . . Those that are sent by Christ may not delegate their power and execute the office by others but must do it themselves. The prophet might not appoint another, being sent by Christ to the children of Israel.

. . . The prophet being struck down with the sight of his glory which sat on the throne, in the former chapter [Ezek 1], is lifted up and comforted by the Spirit in the first two verses [Ezek 2:1-2]. He is called to public service in the next three [Ezek 2:3-5], and that among a wretched, rebellious people. In this and the next two verses, the Lord Christ gives him instruction concerning his office. First, negatively, in the sixth verse, "Be not afraid of them." I have made you a prophet, and it is not for a prophet to fear the face of man [Ezek 2:6]. Second, positively, in the seventh verse, where he informs him, whose words he must speak to them, "You shall speak my words to them." It is not for a prophet to speak his own words but the words of him that sends him.

. . . Those who teach others must first hear and be taught themselves. They must hear Christ and learn of him. Ezekiel must hear what Christ says to him, and then he would be fit to speak to others. When the Lord Christ sent out his disciples, he instructed them first. . . . God looks for more from them he calls to any service than from others. And "you, son of man, be not rebellious." I expect other things at your hand; I look for you to be as tractable as they have been intractable, as dutiful as they have been rebellious. . . . We must not follow the examples and ways of sinful people. "Be not you rebellious like that rebellious house." They have set an ill example before you; do not imitate them. They have written a foul copy; do not write after them. They have walked in wrong paths; do not trace their steps. AN EXPOSITION OF EZEKIEL.[7]

3:1-15 *True Prophets of God*

THE SCROLL. WILLIAM GREENHILL: For the signification of this scroll, some make it to signify the secret counsels of God. It is true, they were written in it but not signified by it. The scroll here is a typical sign of the gift of prophecy to be given to the prophet and in that sense we are to take it. . . . The gift of prophecy is from Christ. He reached out his hand and gave the scroll of a book. He is the great Prophet and has all prophecy and prophetical power in himself. Whom he pleases he can make a prophet and inspire with prophetical virtue.

. . . It is the Lord Christ who opens and interprets mystical things efficaciously to the faithful. He spread the scroll before Ezekiel and made him to understand the mysteries of it. What are the Scriptures but a scroll folded

[6]*Commentarius in Ezechielem* (1553), 13. [7]*Exposition*, 80, 83, 92.

up, a book sealed till Christ opens it? The servants of God must not refuse to receive and propound large and sad messages to the people. An Exposition of Ezekiel.[8]

Eating the Scroll. Johannes Oecolampadius: He opened his mouth, which is to say, he received the word of the Lord deep within his soul. He ate the book, and Christ poured into him the gift of wisdom that he might understand what was written in the book. . . . All of these things happened in a vision, and he was entrusted all these things that were written in the book. He ordered that he commit these things to memory, not just to pass quickly over them, but to carefully examine these writings. It is not enough to keep the chewed-up book in the stomach, from which it could easily be vomited forth, but to have it absorbed into your inmost heart, where it becomes nourishment for the soul. In this sense, the Lord responded to the woman who said, "Blessed is the womb that bore you," that it is truly "better for those who hear the word of God and keep it" (Lk 11:27-28). As such he wishes the food to be in the stomach and not only on the lips. "For the kingdom of God is not in word but in power" (1 Cor 4:20). Commentary on the Prophet Ezekiel.[9]

True Servants of God. John Calvin: By this crude symbol God confirms Ezekiel in his calling. He commands *eat the book*, which occurs in a vision. Jeremiah uses the same metaphor in chapter fifteen (v. 16), but with a slight variation, because our prophet sees himself eat this book. While Jeremiah only indicates that he digested the words of God like food, not that he only tasted them with his tongue. Thus, they were deeply rooted in his mind as if he really had cooked and digested them.

But God wished to confirm our prophet in another way. Instead he extended the book to him and commanded him to eat. There is no doubt that this book expressed whatever the Spirit of God later spoke to the prophet. It was just as if God had made an instrument of his Spirit out of a mere human. As if he had said: "Now you will proclaim nothing human or of this world, because you will proclaim what my Spirit has already written in this book."

Here we see the difference between the true servants of God, who perform their duty seriously, and those chattering people, who are filled with their own eloquence or wit. There are many able speakers who vomit what they have never taken to heart, but their teaching is absolutely empty. This is what Paul had in mind when he said that the kingdom of God is not made of words, but power. Those who truly consecrate themselves to God do not just learn what they talk about. Rather like food being eaten, so they receive the word of God in themselves, hiding it in the deepest chamber of their heart, so that they can serve it from there as food properly digested. Ezekiel 1.[10]

True and False Prophets. Hans Denck: The false prophets are not full of the power and spirit of God, full of justice and might to show everyone's faults, be they great or small. Therefore they come on their own authority. They are neither bid nor called by God through his word or spirit.

When they see the wolf approaching they do not remain steadfastly with the sheep, for they do not have the right, living word of God in their vessels. But one who is sent by God does not go about with empty phrases and lies. Rather, he is strong in the Lord and full of God's spirit to speak the truth for everyone, be he of high or low estate. He shows up people's faults with no regard for what a person amounts to in the world. For the gates of hell have to be opened wide for the king of glory, and he alone is able to resist all the forces in his own people. Of this we read in Ezekiel 3:8 as follows, "I (the

[8]*Exposition*, 94-95. [9]*Commentarius in Ezechielem* (1553), 14. [10]CTS 22:126-127 (CO 18:74-75).

Lord) have hardened your face against their faces, your forehead against their foreheads; yes, as hard as adamant can be." [I made] your forehead harder than flint, so that you need not fear them nor be dismayed at their sight and that you might be strong enough to recount everyone's sin without regard of person. Reflections on Micah.[11]

Eating the Scroll. William Greenhill: It is conceived here that the eating was not literal but spiritual, or in vision. Of this Ezekiel 3:10 confirms us, where it is said, "All my words that I shall speak to you, receive into your heart and hear with your ears." This was the eating, to hear, mediate and believe. . . . But why was he bid to eat the scroll? Had not seeing and reading been more suitable? The Scripture attributes excellence to, and places natural and supernatural virtue in, that organ or sense by which it is exercised. Ezekiel is said to "eat the scroll" not to see or hear it, because by the mouth the gift of prophecy which was given to him by the scroll was to be manifested and discovered by the people.

Our obedience to Christ must be absolute and simple. There might have been something unsavory or bitter tendered to the prophet, even that which nature abhors. However, he must eat it, not dispute the case, but yield obedience.

The symbols and truths that Christ gives are the meat that the souls of prophets and ministers must feed on. . . . When ministers and messengers have eaten and digested the truths of God, then they are fit to go and preach them to the people of God. An Exposition of Ezekiel.[12]

Speaking God's Word. John Calvin: Ezekiel continues to say, as we have just seen, that he was given a book, which he ate, because the servants of God should speak from the deepest longing of their heart. We know that many have a tongue sufficiently fluent, but use it for nothing else than to make themselves great. God treats their vanity as a laughingstock, because their work is fruitless. Therefore, we again take note of the passage of Paul cited above "the kingdom of God is made of power." Now the power of the Holy Spirit is not revealed, unless the one called to teach eagerly and sincerely seeks to devote themselves to their office. For this reason Ezekiel is commanded to eat the book.

He then says *it was as sweet as honey.* Only a little earlier, he said it was filled with curses. So either he is without a human nature, or he ought to be overwhelmed with grief when he found himself appointed as the herald of God's vengeance. Elsewhere we see that the servants of God were filled with two kinds of feelings. They were often stern and bitter when need be, but also they grieved with the oppressed. Still this grief did not prevent them from continuing any less bravely in the course of their calling. Now for this reason Ezekiel next says *the book was sweet,* because he rejoiced in God's command. Although he sympathized with his people, still he recognized that no other option was possible, and he agreed to the just judgment of God. Accordingly by the word *sweetness* nothing else is indicated than his approval and acceptance of the office given to him. Thus, he obeyed God, forgetting all the sorrow contained in the book. The justice of God was stronger indeed. Through this he snuffed any excessive empathy, which otherwise would have held him back. . . .

God commands him *to make known,* or *to speak his words.* It is worth noting that these mean the same thing. So, if Ezekiel ought to announce nothing other than what he had received from God, then this rule ought to influence all God's servants. They should not pour out their own thoughts, but, as if from God's own mouth, they should declare what they have learned from him. Ezekiel 1.[13]

[11]*Writings,* 117. [12]*Exposition,* 96. [13]CTS 22:130-132 (CO 18:76-78).

Speak to the House of Israel. Martin Luther: The Jews cling to the name Israel and claim that they alone are Israel and that we are Gentiles. Now this is true so far as the first part of the prophecy and the old covenant of Moses are concerned, though this has long since been fulfilled. But according to the second part of the prophecy and the new covenant, the Jews are no longer Israel, for all things are to be new, and Israel too must become new. Those alone are the true Israel who have accepted the new covenant which was established and begun at Jerusalem. A New Preface to the Prophet Ezekiel.[14]

Trust in God Alone. John Calvin: Ezekiel was warned about the people's stubbornness, actually even their hopeless depravity. Now God strengthens him, so he would not lose heart, when he saw that he was about to battle with such a reckless and lost people. . . .

If he had hoped for more fruit from his work, perhaps that attitude would have caused laziness. For confidence makes us more relaxed when the work in hand is neither arduous nor difficult. Certainly then the prophet would have been more indifferent. If he were convinced that the people were ready to listen, he would have addressed them carelessly. So, God stirs him up when he speaks of their stubbornness. And just as it was helpful that the prophet perceive how difficult the undertaking of his appointed task was, so also it is fitting that he was armed with the power of God, otherwise he would have yielded too easily to the difficulty of his task. . . .

In this way he was warned that strength was to be expected from somewhere else, and that he should not consider his own strength, but instead allow himself to be governed by the Spirit of God. To be sure whenever we reflect on the kind and number of our own abilities, it can happen that we melt and lose strength, or at least wither a bit, so that we do not courageously carry out our office. Therefore God revives his prophet when *he says he had given him a face*. As if he said that Ezekiel would not go to war in his own strength, but instead would be armed with heavenly power.

Even though this seems to have been spoken only once and only for Ezekiel's own benefit, it actually belongs to all of us. Consequently we should know that when God calls us to the teaching office, we ought never to measure our work by the small stature of our own ability, or consider what we are able to do, instead we ought to rest in the promised power, which God here holds up with no empty words. Therefore, whoever acknowledges that God is enough to overcome all barriers prepares bravely for work. But whoever dwells on estimating their own strength, not only is weakened, but already is defeated.

We see here that we are encouraged to humility and modesty, so that we do not attribute anything to our own strength. . . . Thus, we should learn to ask God alone for the courage we lack. We are not superior to Ezekiel. If it was fitting for him to be strengthened by the Spirit of God, how much more do we need it today. Ezekiel 1.[15]

The Spirit Lifted Me. William Greenhill: By spirit here we should understand, not the wind, as if some great wind should take up the prophet, or an angel, as if he had been lifted up by angelic virtue, or his own spirit, as Jerome would have it. But that Spirit who was in the living creatures and the wheels (Ezek 1:12, 20) and led them. That Spirit who entered into Ezekiel and set him on his feet. That Spirit who led Christ into the wilderness, even the eternal Spirit of God. . . .

Those that are called to employment in the church of Christ have need not only of Christ's Word, but Christ's Spirit also. Christ had spoken largely to Ezekiel, and here the Spirit

[14]Lenker 6, 307* (WADB 11,1:400). [15]CTS 22:136-137 (CO 18:81).

lifts him up, and does so in an especial manner and arms him to the work. An Exposition of Ezekiel.[16]

The Spirit Comforts. John Mayer: And the Spirit took me up, and I heard behind me the voice of a great rushing, saying, Blessed be the glory of the Lord from his place (Ezek 3:12). As the Lord had by words, and the sign of the scroll of a book given to Ezekiel to eat confirmed and comforted him, so now he strengthened him to his office by taking him up by his Spirit above all earthly things, that he might not be troubled or have his mind distracted by these, but he might be wholly intent to the heavenly business in which the Lord was about to employ him. So likewise his Spirit takes up other prophets and ministers of his, insomuch as they pass not for worldly losses, dangers or indignities, offered to them, as rejoicing to do the work to which they are appointed to the end. Commentary upon All the Prophets.[17]

Ezekiel's Conflict. John Calvin: But what follows seems to contradict a verse above. First he said that the book was as sweet as honey, but now *he departed in the bitterness of his spirit*. But as I briefly clarified earlier this is easily reconciled. Naturally the prophet was not stripped of all reason. Although he was entirely dedicated to God, and he neglected nothing due to his diligence and eagerness, still he kept some of his humanity. And so, the spirit of bitterness, which he mentions, calling it *his own spirit*.

We see an unstated contrast between that task he had been seized by and this feeling, which was not wicked, but still differed in some way from the grace of the Spirit, since the prophet burned with such devotion that he carried out the commands of God neglecting himself. At the same time, he felt something human in himself, since the power of the Spirit had not snuffed out all sorrow. Therefore, we hold that the prophet was in some way seized by the Spirit, but also had *his own bitter spirit*. He adds, and *the hand of the Jehovah was strong upon me*. By "hand" some understand prophecy, but in my opinion ignorantly. I do not doubt that in fact it signifies power or absolute authority. He says, *the hand of God was strong*, because it was fitting to obey God, even though the bitterness that he mentioned would have lured him in the opposite direction. Just like Paul said, that he was controlled by devotion for God, so also the prophet indicates that he was controlled by the secret orchestration of the Spirit, so that he did not act out of human motives, nor did he obey the desires of his own heart, nor did he follow his own plan. Instead he only aimed to display obedience to God. Ezekiel 1.[18]

3:16-27 *A Watchman for Israel*

God Speaks Through His Watchmen. John Calvin: Now the prophet shows more clearly why he continued in silence for seven days. This was because he had been appointed as a teacher, but the right time had not yet arrived for him to deliver God's commands. . . . So it seems that God works gradually in his servants, so that he claims them for his own. In general, he next reveals to them what tasks and duties they must complete. Lastly, he sends them out to this work and to the performance of their office. . . .

What Ezekiel heard belongs to all teachers of the church, that is those who are divinely appointed and established, like watchmen in watchtowers, to look out for the common safety of everyone. From the beginning it has been proper for those appointed as ministers of heavenly teaching to be watchmen. . . .

What I have said must be upheld, when God chose prophets, it was as if they were

[16]*Exposition*, 101. [17]*Prophets*, 378. [18]CTS 22:145 (CO 18:86-87).

placed in watchtowers to look out for the safety of the entire church. Even today this image ought to be powerful, so pastors recognize that they have been charged to be watchful. This is one point. Now no one is able to do this, unless they are blessed with exceptional gifts. At the very least they must be stronger in the grace of the Spirit than the common person. It is not enough for pastors to live just like any other person. It is good for them to be much more mindful, as if they had been lifted up into a lofty watchtower, which demands keen eyes and shrewd skill. This is the second point.

Now it is added, *you will hear words from my mouth and you will announce them to the people from me*. Here a general rule is ordained for all prophets and pastors of the church: they should hear the word from the mouth of God. By this rule God wants to exclude whatever people might invent or allege themselves. For it is clear, when God claims the right to speak for himself that he orders all people to be silent, not offering anything of their own. Ezekiel 1.[19]

Two Sorts of Watchmen. William Greenhill: There were two sorts of watchmen God set in his church. Those who were extraordinary: prophets, apostles, evangelists. And those who were ordinary: pastors and teachers. These latter continue to this day and watch for the good of souls (Heb 13:17). Their office is, as the prophets, to learn of Christ and to warn the people. The others have ceased. An Exposition of Ezekiel.[20]

Watchman. John Mayer: What manner of man is Ezekiel made? A watchman, a bishop, as such are called in the New Testament. But how must he acquit himself according to this office? By taking his words from God's mouth, and so speaking to the people and not bringing forth any of his own, as Paul did (1 Thess 2:13, Acts 20). But the Pharisees did not do this, or the papists at this day. Therefore although they have the title of bishops, they are indeed nothing less by reason of their ignorance, which keeps them from seeing, and of the traditions of people and legends, which they teach, and not the words coming from God's mouth only. Neither can ignorant preachers among us, or such as preach themselves, venting their spleen against particulars or going in high strains of human eloquence, philosophical discourses or rhapsodies of many quotations out of human writings, better acquit themselves for such watchmen. Commentary upon All the Prophets.[21]

When Prophecies Cease. John Calvin: This passage (vv. 25-26) teaches that it is an omen of God's judgment, when all prophecies cease and the benefit of his teaching is taken away. Just as God shining on us through his word, grants us a guarantee of his fatherly grace and favor. So also when his teaching is withdrawn, it is just as if God were to hide his face, actually, even as if he were to turn his back on us. . . .

Therefore God stops, when he sees that he is dealing with the senseless and the deaf. This does not happen only after the first irritation. In fact he is able to wrestle with human thanklessness. And as we see in Jeremiah, he never ceases to rise each morning and keep watch even during the night. He never ceases to call himself even to those who are slow and lazy, even those who are completely rebellious. But in the end, if he sees that he does not succeed after great patience, then he snatches away his word, as we have said. Therefore the church complains bitterly that it is barren of prophets, recognizing that loss among the extreme signs of God's anger: "We do not see our signs, and prophets do not appear among us."

In this way they understand that they are separated from God, and that there is no com-

[19]CTS 22:148-149 (CO 18:89-90). [20]*Exposition*, 109. [21]*Prophets*, 379.

fort left to them when God no longer gives any taste of his goodness through prophets. This is actually what the wicked long for, because nothing is more troubling to them than to hear God continually proclaiming his word. Therefore, as much as possible, they search for lairs to hide in, thinking nothing is better than to be in a stupor surrounded by their sins, and to be deaf to every voice of correction. And yet nothing is more deadly to them, because, as long as God encourages us to repent, he presents himself as a doctor, who cures our diseases. However, when he is silent, it is as if he is abandoning us to destruction. For this reason I said nothing is more deadly than when no voice of correction rings in our ears. Instead we are sweetly lulled, because in this way Satan tears away our guard. His last poisoning is when he soothes us with his charm, putting a stop to all correction which would shake loose our false sense of security. Ezekiel 1.[22]

Ezekiel Bound Metaphorically. William Greenhill: Literally thus: They seeing the prophet sad seven days, and now astonished at what he had seen and heard, and observing some strange looks and carriages from him, they thought he was or would be beside himself, and therefore they bound him. . . . In the metaphorical sense take it thus: The Jews cannot endure you or your prophecy; they are so bitter, so rebellious, obstinate and set against you that they will not suffer you. . . . Not that he had any material bands on him, but was bound up in this sense. Their sins were the prophet's bonds.

. . . I conceive the words are not to be taken in their literal sense because the prophet is bid in the next chapter (Ezek 4:9) to prepare meat and to eat it, which he could not do if his tongue had cleaved to the roof of his mouth. . . . The Lord has the power over prophet's lips to shut and open them at his pleasure. If God forbids the prophets to speak, they must be dumb. An Exposition of Ezekiel.[23]

A True Messenger. Hans Denck: A true messenger of Christ can present his Master's best message so that it appears hateful to all flesh for as long as it is unwilling to accept it in truth. One who presents it in such a fashion that it becomes pleasant to pigs and dogs is a steward who does not greatly value the Master's treasures and has no intention of investing his talent as long as he gets away without great harm. One who rightly proclaims God's wrath may also proclaim his grace fruitfully (Ezek 3:17; 33:1). But one who is silent about just one or reduces it can neither speak of nor proclaim the other. The Law of God.[24]

God Alone Judges and Condemns. John Calvin: In the first place, God affirms what we saw earlier. No person is granted the freedom to convict or acquit according to their own judgment. Therefore, when God sends his servants out, he does not forfeit that power. Truly, the ultimate authority remains with him, because, as James says, there is one lawgiver who is able to save and to destroy. . . .

From this we understand that all are ungodly who tether consciences to their own laws, principles and beliefs—commanding this, forbidding that—because they tear away from God what he here wants only to be his. It is only for God alone to proclaim judgment; the prophets are merely messengers.

At the same time the fanatics, who manipulate this passage, are to be rejected. They want freedom to sin to be granted, as well as for there to be no difference between good and evil, because "it is not for us to find fault." However, properly speaking, we do not assume any authority for ourselves when we repeat what has been proclaimed by the mouth of God. God convicts adulterers, thieves, drunks, murderers, those who covet, gossips, and the greedy. If someone admonishes an adulterer,

[22]CTS 22:167-168 (CO 18:102-103). [23]*Exposition*, 123, 125. [24]*Writings*, 233-34.

someone else corrects a thief, a third reproves a drunk, should we say that they rashly assumed more authority than is right? Not at all, because they do not proclaim their own words, as we have already said, but God spoke it. They are only witnesses and messengers of his judgment. . . .

Here [*if you give him no warning, nor speak to warn the wicked*] the office which was placed on Ezekiel is referred to. This does not apply to common people without the prophetic name. So, we note that this is not a general statement aimed at all people without distinction, rather it only concerns a prophet, who had already been called to be a watchman. . . .

As I have recently mentioned, this passage shows how dangerous a task it is for those who are called to the teaching office. Nothing is more precious to God than souls that he created in his image and of whom he is Redeemer and Father.

Therefore, since our souls and their salvation are so dear to God, we understand how diligently all prophets and pastors ought to be dedicated to their office. Just as if God had entrusted souls to their care, asking for an account of each to be given. And it is not enough if they only warn this one or that, unless they strive with great effort to call each one from death back to life and salvation. Otherwise we hear what God proclaims here. . . .

So, we see that carelessness in prophets and pastors is a result of their unfaithfulness, when they knowingly and willingly allow souls to perish because of their own silence. EZEKIEL I.[25]

ADMONISHING SINS. JOHN MAYER: *Also when a righteous man turns from his righteousness. . .* Here another part of the minister's office is set forth, namely, as to admonish the wicked, so to seek the turning of the righteous, in case they have fallen into sin or error. But how is it that such a case is put, seeing the righteous have the seed of God in them and cannot sin? Solution: This is either spoken of such as never had anything else but seeming righteousness. About such people the Lord says, *I came not to call the righteous, but sinners to repentance.* That is to say, the truly righteous, who are subject to fall into sin, though not to fall away so as to delight in any evil way that they formerly hated, trading now in it. For all are to be admonished of their sins, being otherwise in the way of death, and the minister of God seeing one or another of these righteous persons gone from his righteousness to sin, he cannot distinguish between them and therefore must warn both. Indeed, by this means, it pleases God to turn his elect servants again that they may come to the life to which he has predestinated them. COMMENTARY UPON ALL THE PROPHETS.[26]

[25]CTS 22:152-157 (CO 18:91-95). [26]*Prophets*, 379-80.

4:1-17 THE SIEGE OF JERUSALEM SYMBOLIZED

1"And you, son of man, take a brick and lay it before you, and engrave on it a city,
even Jerusalem. 2And put siegeworks against it, and build a siege wall against it, and cast
up a mound against it. Set camps also against it, and plant battering rams against it all
around. 3And you, take an iron griddle, and place it as an iron wall between you and the
city; and set your face toward it, and let it be in a state of siege, and press the siege against
it. This is a sign for the house of Israel.
4"Then lie on your left side, and place the punishment[a] of the house of Israel upon it.
For the number of the days that you lie on it, you shall bear their punishment. 5For I
assign to you a number of days, 390 days, equal to the number of the years of their pun-
ishment. So long shall you bear the punishment of the house of Israel. 6And when you
have completed these, you shall lie down a second time, but on your right side, and bear
the punishment of the house of Judah. Forty days I assign you, a day for each year. 7And
you shall set your face toward the siege of Jerusalem, with your arm bared, and you shall
prophesy against the city. 8And behold, I will place cords upon you, so that you cannot
turn from one side to the other, till you have completed the days of your siege.
9"And you, take wheat and barley, beans and lentils, millet and emmer,[b] and put them
into a single vessel and make your bread from them. During the number of days that you
lie on your side, 390 days, you shall eat it. 10And your food that you eat shall be by weight,
twenty shekels[c] a day; from day to day[d] you shall eat it. 11And water you shall drink by
measure, the sixth part of a hin;[e] from day to day you shall drink. 12And you shall eat it as
a barley cake, baking it in their sight on human dung." 13And the Lord said, "Thus shall
the people of Israel eat their bread unclean, among the nations where I will drive them."
14Then I said, "Ah, Lord God! Behold, I have never defiled myself.[f] From my youth up
till now I have never eaten what died of itself or was torn by beasts, nor has tainted meat
come into my mouth." 15Then he said to me, "See, I assign to you cow's dung instead of
human dung, on which you may prepare your bread." 16Moreover, he said to me, "Son
of man, behold, I will break the supply[g] of bread in Jerusalem. They shall eat bread by
weight and with anxiety, and they shall drink water by measure and in dismay. 17I will
do this that they may lack bread and water, and look at one another in dismay, and rot
away because of their punishment."

a Or *iniquity;* also verses 5, 6, 17 **b** A type of wheat **c** A *shekel* was about 2/5 ounce or 11 grams **d** Or *at a set time daily;* also verse 11 **e** A *hin* was about 4 quarts or 3.5 liters **f** Hebrew *my soul* (or *throat*) *has never been made unclean* **g** Hebrew *staff*

Overview: Ezekiel is told to take a brick and lay it before himself. The use of a material brick or tile to convey divine things invites from our commentators comparison with sacraments. As God uses common and ordinary things like bread and wine in the Lord's Supper and water in baptism, here he uses a brick or tile on which a city and army are portrayed against the house of Israel. What makes the sacraments of the New Testament sacramental and what makes this brick or tile significant is that the Word of God was added to them.

Ezekiel is told to lie on his side. Our commentators do not understand the text to mean that Ezekiel was literally on his side for 390 days. He does this in a vision. God here signifies that the sack of Jerusalem is inviolable.

GOD'S SACRAMENTAL USE OF THE MATERIAL. WILLIAM GREENHILL: God's appointment and authority make things and actions mean and ridiculous in the eyes of the world to be weighty and of great use. It seems to carnal reason a childish thing that the prophet should take a tile, draw the city on it, make forts, mounts, warlike engines to batter it, indeed, to take "a pan of iron" and set it between him and the city. People of the world are apt to look at this as ridiculous, much like the practice of boys in snow, who make forts, mounts, etc., in sport. But be not deceived. What the infinitely wise God commands is of great concernment, however mean the things and actions about those things appear. If you look on it in itself, the worship demanded by the law seems strange. That they should kill so many beasts and burn them to ashes; that the tabernacle and things belonging to it should be sprinkled with blood; that they must refrain from such meat, be unclean if they touch such things; be circumcised, eat a paschal lamb, etc. I say, if we look at them externally, they seem irrational things, but if we eye God commanding them, they had an excellence and were of great use to them, and instruments of much good. Now bread, wine, water in baptism and the supper of the Lord seem mean things, and such they are as are common to the world. But Christ's appointment to use these makes the difference that gives dignity and weight, so that they are of great virtue to them that rightly partake of them. AN EXPOSITION OF EZEKIEL.[1]

GOD'S WORD AND SACRAMENTS. JOHN MAYER: Here the Lord bids Ezekiel by signs to foretell the siege and destruction of Jerusalem. He must portray a city on a tile and an army besieging it. Lyra says that the tile to be taken must be one unburned, and so fit to portray anything on, and this must be done to make that which was to come on the Jews for their sins the more plain, as was then the manner of God's teaching. But all this, says Calvin, might seem to be childish and ridiculous, only being done at the Word of the Lord it was a matter of great moment. By this was showed that Jerusalem should most certainly be so dealt with by the Chaldeans. And this is that which makes the sacraments instituted by God to be reverend, because they are done at his Word, although there appears nothing in them but contemptible materials—in respect of the ends for which they were ordained. There being nothing in the one but water, and in the other bread and wine. But God's Word coming, they are most excellent and heavenly means of sanctification and salvation, although no such thing appears outwardly to the eye of the beholder. He that commanded baptism cleanses the soul invisibly from the filthiness of sin. And by our receiving that bread and wine, he strengthens and refreshes our souls to eternal life. COMMENTARY UPON ALL THE PROPHETS.[2]

EZEKIEL ON HIS SIDE. JOHN CALVIN: But we know that this is the usual manner of Scripture, because God judges sins to the third and fourth generations. So, when God wanted the ten tribes to be dragged into exile, he punished them for their evil deeds for 390 years. . . .

I move on to the words: *you,* he says, *will lie on your left side.* It should be noted that this did not really happen, because Ezekiel did not lie on his side for 390 days. This really only happened in the vision, so later he could tell the people what God had revealed. As to the opinion of some commentators who think the left side signifies the ten tribes, because Samaria was located to the left, I do not see how this is applicable.

[1]*Exposition,* 128. [2]*Prophets,* 381.

I do not doubt that God wanted to prefer the tribe of Judah over the kingdom of Israel . . . Therefore the right side signifies the honor that God always wanted to give the kingdom of Judah. The ten tribes, however, are marked as the left side, because, as I have said, they did not enjoy the same glory as the kingdom of Judah, even though they were more populous, more courageous, and even though they were superior in all good things.

Now it should be noted that the burden of carrying their sins was placed on the prophet. Not because God shifted the sins of the people to him, as some invent through allegory, saying that the prophet was a type of Christ who willingly carried the sins of the people on himself. But an atonement is not protrayed here. Instead we know that God used his servants for many different purposes. . . .

Then he adds, *see I will place cords on you so that you do not turn from side to side, until you have fulfilled the days of your siege*. God signifies that his decree about the plunder of Jerusalem is absolute. By having his servant so securely bound he showed his decree was unwavering, although the Judeans thought that they would be able to shake free through deceit. We know that they always deceived themselves with flattery whenever they were threatened by the prophets. So God shows that the siege of the city was certain until it was plundered, because the prophet was bound with cords, and would not move himself or turn from side to side. Ezekiel 1.[3]

Ezekiel Lies on His Side. William Greenhill: Did our prophet, in the literal sense, lie so many days on his side, or was it only in vision? Some make it real and say, Ezekiel did lie on his side all the days that are mentioned. Although he slept not all the time, yet he lay in that posture. This occurred by special help of God, since nature could not of itself accomplish it. . . . This opinion has many and great authors. Yet I must join with those who are for the prophet's visional lying on his side.

The prophet lay on his left side. By this posture of the prophet is typed out to us the different respect of God to the house of Israel and Judah. The ten tribes were less dear to God than the other. They had grievous sins, and God would show them less mercy, dealing with them as those at his left side. An Exposition of Ezekiel.[4]

God Alone Nourishes Us. John Calvin: God returns to the citizens of Jerusalem, and announces that they will be so destroyed by famine, that they will be reduced to the last hope, and all but consumed by want. . . . I said different forms of punishment, because even if bread was sufficient, God often breaks its staff, as he calls it. . . . We see then that God breaks the staff of bread, when a sufficiently plentiful supply exists, but those who eat are not satisfied.

That this may appear more clearly, we must assume the principle that "men do not live by bread only, but by every word which proceeds from the mouth of God." For here God shows that we are not nourished by virtue of the bread, properly speaking. How can bread be life giving when it lacks both mind and power? We see then that there is no power in bread to nourish except for the hidden grace of God. For we live by the word of God.

The subject here is not the word of doctrine nor spiritual life. Moses understands that we are sustained not by bread and wine and other food, or by any kind of drink. Instead by a hidden power of God, he grants strength to the bread for our nourishment. Bread then is our nourishment, but not by any particular or intrinsic power. This it has from another source, that is, the favor and ordination of God. . . . God, therefore, breaks the staff of bread when he causes people to be famished, even when

[3]CTS 22:179-181 (CO 18:110-112). [4]*Exposition*, 129.

they have an abundance of bread. No matter how much they gorge themselves, they are not satisfied, because the food burdens instead of refreshes them. This is the first punishment with which God threatens the Jews.

Another is added, that is, *"that they shall be destitute of bread."* We see then that there is a bipartite fashion by which God punishes us through hunger. For although bread is sufficient, still he breaks and destroys its staff, so that it cannot prop us up nor bring back our lost strength. At length he takes away our bread, because he either strikes our fruits with blight or hail, or makes us suffer under other disasters. EZEKIEL 1.[5]

[5]CTS 22:187-98 (CO 18:116-117).

5:1-17 JERUSALEM WILL BE DESTROYED

1"And you, O son of man, take a sharp sword. Use it as a barber's razor and pass it over your head and your beard. Then take balances for weighing and divide the hair. 2A third part you shall burn in the fire in the midst of the city, when the days of the siege are completed. And a third part you shall take and strike with the sword all around the city. And a third part you shall scatter to the wind, and I will unsheathe the sword after them.
3And you shall take from these a small number and bind them in the skirts of your robe.
4And of these again you shall take some and cast them into the midst of the fire and burn them in the fire. From there a fire will come out into all the house of Israel.

5"Thus says the Lord GOD: This is Jerusalem. I have set her in the center of the nations, with countries all around her. 6And she has rebelled against my rules by doing wickedness more than the nations, and against my statutes more than the countries all around her; for they have rejected my rules and have not walked in my statutes. 7Therefore thus says the Lord GOD: Because you are more turbulent than the nations that are all around you, and have not walked in my statutes or obeyed my rules, and have not[a] even acted according to the rules of the nations that are all around you, 8therefore thus says the Lord GOD: Behold, I, even I, am against you. And I will execute judgments[b] in your midst in the sight of the nations. 9And because of all your abominations I will do with you what I have never yet done, and the like of which I will never do again. 10Therefore fathers shall eat their sons in your midst, and sons shall eat their fathers. And I will execute judgments on you, and any of you who survive I will scatter to all the winds. 11Therefore, as I live, declares the Lord GOD, surely, because you have defiled my sanctuary with all your detestable things and with all your abominations, therefore I will withdraw.[c] My eye will not spare, and I will have no pity. 12A third part of you shall die of pestilence and be consumed with famine in your midst; a third part shall fall by the sword all around you; and a third part I will scatter to all the winds and will unsheathe the sword after them.

13"Thus shall my anger spend itself, and I will vent my fury upon them and satisfy

myself. And they shall know that I am the Lord—that I have spoken in my jealousy—
when I spend my fury upon them. 14*Moreover, I will make you a desolation and an*
object of reproach among the nations all around you and in the sight of all who pass by.
15*You shall be*[d] *a reproach and a taunt, a warning and a horror, to the nations all around*
you, when I execute judgments on you in anger and fury, and with furious rebukes—I
*am the Lord; I have spoken—*16*when I send against you*[e] *the deadly arrows of famine,*
arrows for destruction, which I will send to destroy you, and when I bring more and
more famine upon you and break your supply[f] *of bread.* 17*I will send famine and wild*
beasts against you, and they will rob you of your children. Pestilence and blood shall pass
through you, and I will bring the sword upon you. I am the Lord; I have spoken."

a Some Hebrew manuscripts and Syriac lack *not* b The same Hebrew expression can mean *obey rules, or execute judgments,* depending on the context c Some Hebrew manuscripts *I will cut you down* d Dead Sea Scroll, Septuagint, Syriac, Vulgate, Targum; Masoretic Text *And it shall be* e Hebrew *them* f Hebrew *them*

Overview: God had bestowed innumerable blessings on Jerusalem. These blessings, which were meant for their salvation and the glory of God, were turned to sacrilegious purposes. And so God now declares that he is against Jerusalem. Through their sin, they defiled all the good things that God had bestowed on them. Our commentators agree that Jerusalem is to blame for its fall into sin and its contempt for God.

"This Is Jerusalem" Like "This Is My Body." Racovian Catechism: Explain to me, then, the true and genuine sense of these words, "This is my body."

This you will easily understand, if you only bear in mind that, in the sacred writings, and indeed in common practice, figures, images and commemorating signs are called by the names of those things of which they are the figures, images and memorials. Wherefore, when Christ designed that in this rite his bloody death should be declared by us, under a kind of shadow or representation, he said that this bread that is broken is his body, delivered for us. That is to say, it is a commemorating sign, a kind of emblem of his body to be shortly, on our account, broken; that is, lacerated, pierced, wounded and tortured. And also, in like manner, that the cup, or the wine contained in it, was for the same reason his blood, to be shortly shed for us. For the wine is not otherwise in the cup than as it is poured out of his vessel, or at least drawn from his grapes. It is by way of figure or emblem only that it is said in Ezekiel (Ezek 5:1-5) concerning the hair, whereof a part was to be cut, a part burned, a part scattered and a part preserved, to be afterwards consumed: "This is Jerusalem." That is, this is an emblem of Jerusalem, or a shadow of what it is to become. As to what is stated in the account of Luke and Paul—that this cup is the new testament in the blood of Christ—this must be understood as if they had said, This is a certain memorial, or commemorating sign, of the New Covenant confirmed by the blood of Christ. Racovian Catechism.[1]

Why God Punishes Jerusalem. John Calvin: Now God shows the reason why he determined to act so severely and harshly towards that holy city that he had selected as the royal residence. Despite that he had adorned that city with many kindnesses, its repulsive and wicked ingratitude was far greater. . . .

Let us learn from this passage, that unless we use God's blessings with purity the charge of ingratitude will always be against us. Whatever God grants us, he sanctifies for our

[1]*RC* 272-73.

salvation and also for the glory of his name. Thus, we are filled with sin whenever we corrupt those things which were destined for his glory. We are totally corrupted whenever we contort what God has granted for our salvation into our own ruin. . . . Therefore, when God entrusts the treasure of heavenly teaching to us, we must diligently take care that we do not turn aside to impiety, because there is no excuse for error once we have been taught what is right, especially from the mouth of God himself. . . .

[He] says that they had not fallen through ignorance but through pride and contempt. When the will of God is made known to us, there is no room for ignorance. So, we do not sin lightly, rather our minds are unavoidably infected with pride and contempt for God. Ezekiel 1.[2]

God Against Jerusalem. John Mayer: I, even I am against you (Ezek 5:8). That is, not people who shall come of themselves seeking to destroy you, for so you might hope from such to escape. But I will come with them against you, and they shall be but my instruments to do execution on you. For that he meant not by this that he would immediately by his judgments from heaven destroy them, appears, because he did it by the Chaldeans, so that they are much mistaken that expound it of his immediate judging of them, as some do. And these his judgments he says shall be so great that the like has not been before, nor shall be done hereafter. Commentary upon All the Prophets.[3]

Sin Defiles Holy Things. William Greenhill: "You have defiled my sanctuary" (Ezek 5:11). Sin defiles the holy things of God. They defiled not only themselves but also the sanctuary and worship of God in it. The land of Canaan was holy, and sin defiled that (Jer 16:18); the temple was holy, and sin defiled that (Ezek 23:38); the altar was holy, and sin polluted that (Mal 1:7); the sabbaths were holy, and sin profaned them (Neh 13:17); the priesthood and covenant were holy, and sin defiled them (Neh 5:29); God's name is holy, and sin pollutes that (Ezek 20:39). An Exposition of Ezekiel.[4]

[2]CTS 22:195-197 (CO 18:121-123). [3]*Prophets*, 381. [4]*Exposition*, 149.

6:1-14 A Prophecy Against the Mountains of Israel

1The word of the Lord came to me: 2"Son of man, set your face toward the mountains
of Israel, and prophesy against them, 3and say, You mountains of Israel, hear the word of
the Lord God! Thus says the Lord God to the mountains and the hills, to the ravines and
the valleys: Behold, I, even I, will bring a sword upon you, and I will destroy your high
places. 4Your altars shall become desolate, and your incense altars shall be broken, and I
will cast down your slain before your idols. 5And I will lay the dead bodies of the people

*of Israel before their idols, and I will scatter your bones around your altars. 6Wherever
you dwell, the cities shall be waste and the high places ruined, so that your altars will be
waste and ruined,[a] your idols broken and destroyed, your incense altars cut down, and
your works wiped out. 7And the slain shall fall in your midst, and you shall know that I
am the Lord.*

*8"Yet I will leave some of you alive. When you have among the nations some who
escape the sword, and when you are scattered through the countries, 9then those of you
who escape will remember me among the nations where they are carried captive, how I
have been broken over their whoring heart that has departed from me and over their eyes
that go whoring after their idols. And they will be loathsome in their own sight for the
evils that they have committed, for all their abominations. 10And they shall know that I
am the Lord. I have not said in vain that I would do this evil to them." 11Thus says the
Lord God: "Clap your hands and stamp your foot and say, Alas, because of all the evil
abominations of the house of Israel, for they shall fall by the sword, by famine, and by
pestilence. 12He who is far off shall die of pestilence, and he who is near shall fall by the
sword, and he who is left and is preserved shall die of famine. Thus I will spend my fury
upon them. 13And you shall know that I am the Lord, when their slain lie among their
idols around their altars, on every high hill, on all the mountaintops, under every green
tree, and under every leafy oak, wherever they offered pleasing aroma to all their idols.
14And I will stretch out my hand against them and make the land desolate and waste, in
all their dwelling places, from the wilderness to Riblah.[b] Then they will know that I am
the Lord."*

a Or *and punished* **b** Some Hebrew manuscripts; most Hebrew manuscripts *Dibla*

Overview: Ezekiel directs his prophecy against the mountains of Israel. Here God shows that the Israelites are deaf and unworthy of Ezekiel's teaching. The inanimate has more understanding than the senseless Israelites. God's vengeance is directed toward the idols and incense altars of the people. Despite this judgment, God would preserve a remnant. This remnant is saved because of God's faithfulness and mercy, not because they were better than the others.

The Prophecy. William Greenhill: The prophecy itself has three parts. (1) A threatening of desolation to the land of Judea, the idols, altars and people thereof (Ezek 6:3-7). (2) A promise of mercy to them in their scattered condition (Ezek 6:8-10). Some should escape the judgments, repent of their evil ways and know the Lord. (3) A prefiguration of the grief they should have for the judgments to come on them, which are repeated (Ezek 6:11-14).

Junius observes this prophecy to have been on the sabbath day, the one and twentieth of the fifth month, in the sixth year of their captivity. An Exposition of Ezekiel.[1]

Prophecy to the Mountains. John Calvin: Ezekiel is not ordered to urge the Israelites to repentance, or to threaten them with the punishment that still remained, but he is ordered to turn his proclamation *to the hills and mountains and valleys*. Thus God indirectly demonstrates first that the Israelites were deaf, and then unworthy of the trouble that Ezekiel would spend in teaching them. . . . God, therefore, requires the mountains to listen, to show people that an inanimate object

[1] *Exposition*, 154.

can be given understanding, causing them to examine their own stupidity. EZEKIEL 1.[2]

PROPHECY TO ISRAEL'S MOUNTAINS. JOHN MAYER: Calvin, because Israel is here named, will have this prophecy understood to be against the ten tribes long before carried away by the Assyrians. And although this seems not to agree, since a prophecy is not of things past but things to come, he says that it may be taken as doctrinal, or understood as being against those of the ten tribes that still remained in the land and went on in the same sins. But all these are mere imaginations, for Judah is by this prophet before commonly called Israel (Ezek 2; 3). By a general name of all the tribes, because many of the other tribes were mingled with Judah. And it is plainly said that he was bidden to prophesy against the mountains of Israel, so that it must be understood of things to come. And lastly, it is said that all Israel was carried away captive by Shalmanesar (2 Kings 17), and not that any were left, as afterwards it is said of Judah, that the poor of the land were left to till the ground. Leaving this therefore, Lyra says, that Ezekiel, having spoken against Jerusalem in the two previous chapters, now comes to prophesy against other parts of the kingdom of Judah. He directs his prophecy not to the people but to the mountains, hills, valleys and rivers, to intimate the stupidity and unworthiness of the Jews the more, who were passed by for this, as more dull of hearing than the earth itself that has no ears. COMMENTARY UPON ALL THE PROPHETS.[3]

ATTRIBUTION AND PROPHECY. MATTHEW MEADE: Nothing is more frequent in Scripture than to ascribe sense to things without sense. "Give ear, O ye heavens, and I will speak, and hear, O earth, the words of my mouth" (Deut 32:1). "Hear ye, O mountains, and foundations of the earth" (Mic 6:1-2). "Thus says the Lord to the mountains and to the hills, to the rivers and to the valleys" (Ezek 6:3). Now this speaking of God to the inanimate creatures and calling them to hear is very emphatic. (1) It is to set out the great importance and weight of the thing spoken, and the general concernment is to be heard and attended to. (2) This way of attributing sense to dumb creatures is very usual in Scripture, thereby to convince people of their stupidity and insensibleness, and that flocks and stones, hills and mountains, would as soon hear as they. (3) This speaking or crying to dumb creatures and inanimate beings is to show how absolutely they are acted by God. THE VISION OF THE WHEELS.[4]

THE CORRUPTION OF WORSHIP. JOHN CALVIN: In other words, the prophet indicates that God will exact punishment on the ten tribes for their superstitions everywhere. So, it is clear that no nook was free from corruption. By saying all dwelling places he means that every place fit to live is polluted. . . . .

Finally he adds, *your works will be destroyed*. Here he meaningfully uses a general word to point out the difference between the pure worship of God and all corruptions. There is no need of a long discussion if we desire to know how God is to be worshiped. He rejects and excludes our works. Therefore, if we do not force our works into worship, but only follow what God demands, our worship will be pure. But if we add anything of our own, it is detestable.

Therefore, we see that useful instruction can be gathered from one word: all worship is perverse and rejected by God when people bring anything forward of themselves. By works Ezekiel does not here indicate only idols made of wood, stone, brass, gold, or silver, but he also includes whatever people have fashioned, and whatever can be credited to them. This is because, they have not listened to the

[2]CTS 22:219-220 (CO 18:137-138). [3]*Prophets*, 386. [4]*Vision of the Wheels*, 43.

mouth of God and the commands of the law. Ezekiel 1.[5]

God's Mercy. William Greenhill: God's wrath is never so hot against his people, but he will show mercy to some. God would bring a sweeping judgment, lay mountains, hills, rivers, valleys, cities, high places, altars, idols, images, waste and desolate; yet he would have a remnant, preserve some, when they dwelled in the midst of their enemies, among Babylonians and other nations.

. . . It was great wrath to be driven out of their country, to be in banishment, which lawyers call a civil death, because people in it are divided from their friends, liberties and comforts, which sweeten their lives. But to have the sword at their heels added to the weight of wrath and threatens all their lives. Yet notwithstanding this condition, God reserved some from the sword in their banishment. They might on this severe prophecy think, What will become of the church, shall all perish and God's faithfulness fail? No, God would have a care of that; a remnant he would save. An Exposition of Ezekiel.[6]

A Remnant Preserved. John Calvin: Now if the difference is sought for between the few allowed to escape and the many who perished, none other will be found, except that it pleased God to preserve a seed. All deserved death. He consumed almost all of the people; although he wanted a small number to remain safe.

Therefore, we see that the safety of those of whom the prophet now speaks flowed from the pure mercy of God. Besides, what I have said needs to be remembered: no one repented but those to whom it was given . . .

It follows *that he was broken down,* or worn down, *by their heart.* There may be a double meaning of the words. The first is, that God was finally conquered by their wickedness, after he had found that he did accomplished nothing by bearing them patiently. Whenever he sees that his grace has become a laughingstock, he is even angrier, and rightly so. . . .

So, we gather that those who seriously repent do not acknowledge their fault lightly, but think over in what ways, and how long, and how stubbornly they have provoked God's wrath. . . .

Those who pollute the worship of God with their inventions think that they offer acceptable obedience. Since the blind and unbelieving so please themselves by their corruptions, Scripture compares them to adulterers. . . . [A]s it has often been said, the prophets allude to a sacred and spiritual marriage in which God has bound himself to his Church. For the fidelity of the soul is the pure worship of God. Ezekiel 1.[7]

[5]CTS 22:224-226 (CO 18:141-143). [6]*Exposition,* 157. [7]CTS 22:228-231 (CO 18:144-146).

7:1-27 THE END HAS COME

1 The word of the LORD came to me: 2 "And you, O son of man, thus says the Lord GOD to the land of Israel: An end! The end has come upon the four corners of the land.[a] 3 Now the end is upon you, and I will send my anger upon you; I will judge you according to your ways, and I will punish you for all your abominations. 4 And my eye will not spare you, nor will I have pity, but I will punish you for your ways, while your abominations are in your midst. Then you will know that I am the LORD.

5 "Thus says the Lord GOD: Disaster after disaster![b] Behold, it comes. 6 An end has come; the end has come; it has awakened against you. Behold, it comes. 7 Your doom[c] has come to you, O inhabitant of the land. The time has come; the day is near, a day of tumult, and not of joyful shouting on the mountains. 8 Now I will soon pour out my wrath upon you, and spend my anger against you, and judge you according to your ways, and I will punish you for all your abominations. 9 And my eye will not spare, nor will I have pity. I will punish you according to your ways, while your abominations are in your midst. Then you will know that I am the LORD, who strikes.

10 "Behold, the day! Behold, it comes! Your doom has come; the rod has blossomed; pride has budded. 11 Violence has grown up into a rod of wickedness. None of them shall remain, nor their abundance, nor their wealth; neither shall there be preeminence among them.[d] 12 The time has come; the day has arrived. Let not the buyer rejoice, nor the seller mourn, for wrath is upon all their multitude.[e] 13 For the seller shall not return to what he has sold, while they live. For the vision concerns all their multitude; it shall not turn back; and because of his iniquity, none can maintain his life.[f]

14 "They have blown the trumpet and made everything ready, but none goes to battle, for my wrath is upon all their multitude. 15 The sword is without; pestilence and famine are within. He who is in the field dies by the sword, and him who is in the city famine and pestilence devour. 16 And if any survivors escape, they will be on the mountains, like doves of the valleys, all of them moaning, each one over his iniquity. 17 All hands are feeble, and all knees turn to water. 18 They put on sackcloth, and horror covers them. Shame is on all faces, and baldness on all their heads. 19 They cast their silver into the streets, and their gold is like an unclean thing. Their silver and gold are not able to deliver them in the day of the wrath of the LORD. They cannot satisfy their hunger or fill their stomachs with it. For it was the stumbling block of their iniquity. 20 His beautiful ornament they used for pride, and they made their abominable images and their detestable things of it. Therefore I make it an unclean thing to them. 21 And I will give it into the hands of foreigners for prey, and to the wicked of the earth for spoil, and they shall profane it. 22 I will turn my face from them, and they shall profane my treasured[g] place. Robbers shall enter and profane it.

23 "Forge a chain![h] For the land is full of bloody crimes and the city is full of violence.

[24]*I will bring the worst of the nations to take possession of their houses. I will put an end*
to the pride of the strong, and their holy places[i] *shall be profaned.* [25]*When anguish comes,*
they will seek peace, but there shall be none. [26]*Disaster comes upon disaster; rumor fol-*
lows rumor. They seek a vision from the prophet, while the law[j] *perishes from the priest*
and counsel from the elders. [27]*The king mourns, the prince is wrapped in despair, and*
the hands of the people of the land are paralyzed by terror. According to their way I will
do to them, and according to their judgments I will judge them, and they shall know that
I am the Lord."

a Or *earth* **b** Some Hebrew manuscripts (compare Syriac, Targum); most Hebrew manuscripts *Disaster! A unique disaster!* **c** The meaning of the Hebrew word is uncertain; also verse 10 **d** The meaning of this last Hebrew sentence is uncertain **e** Or *abundance;* also verses 13, 14 **f** The meaning of this last Hebrew sentence is uncertain **g** Or *secret* **h** Probably refers to an instrument of captivity **i** By revocalization (compare Septuagint); Hebrew *and those who sanctify them* **j** Or *instruction*

Overview: The prophesied destruction is at hand, and nothing can prevent it. The end has come. Ezekiel repeats the word *end* not in vain but to reinforce the certainty of God's judgment. Our commentators disagree on the identity of the "rod" or "staff" that will be used for this destruction. Some suggest Nebuchadnezzar; others understand it allegorically as Judah. We are to learn from this chapter to cherish the Word of God and to receive it with gratitude.

The End. John Calvin: This prophecy is distinguished from the earlier one, but still the subject is the same, without any difference, as it seems to weave into the same discourse. This, indeed, is true. Still it was necessary for him to be sent twice, so that the people would understand that what he heard from God's mouth was to be repeated not only once, but a second time and continually. This made it quite clear, that God was concerned about their salvation, since he never ceased to exhort them. . . .

Therefore, he uses the word *end,* as if he said, until now I have treated you restrainedly. And surely God had displayed remarkable evidence of his mercy in punishing the Israelites so lightly when he could have destroyed them entirely. . . .

"The end," he says, *"the end is coming,"* that is, "after this you will no longer be able to hope for any restraint. I see there is no hope of repentance in you. Therefore I will totally destroy you." . . . Again, therefore, he teaches that no part of the earth will be free from the carnage that he prophesies. . . .

He uses the word *end* a third time, and repeats it even a fourth and fifth time. From this we gather that those miserable people were like wild animals, even though they were warned more than enough both by teaching and experience, so that they continued to promise themselves a remnant, and were not driven away by the fear that the prophet strikes them with. They did not think that the end was really coming, but said, "Oh! Something will remain, some will escape." This was their arrogance. Ezekiel 1.[1]

Now is the End. William Greenhill: The word *end* is doubled in the first verse and mentioned again in the third, "Now is the end," and repeated in the sixth, "An end is come, the end is come." These repetitions are not in vain. They set out, first, the zeal, intention and speed of the speaker; second, the evidence, certainty and weight of the thing spoken of; third, they serve to make the deeper impression.

. . . Kingdoms and churches have their peri-

[1]CTS 22:241-243 (CO 18:153-154).

ods. They may continue for some hundreds of years, but at length they expire. The kingdom and church of Judah flourished many years. From Saul, their first king, to Zedekiah, their last, were 480 years. But then you see an end is come, the end is come. An end of the state, an end of their church, an end of all comforts, of all glory and greatness. An Exposition of Ezekiel.[2]

Nebuchadnezzar is the Staff. John Calvin: There is no doubt that by the rod he means Nebuchadnezzar. However, interpreters disagree on the context. Many look to the following verse, thinking it is about the king of Babylon. Others rightly, in my opinion, apply it to the Israelites themselves. As to his saying *the rod has blossomed,* he is observing God's patience. Since the Israelites had sinned for a long time without punishment, they thought, as I said earlier, that their peace with God would be uninterrupted.

However, the opposite is what Ezekiel proclaims here. It was as if God had a hidden root. Just like when someone plants a tree they look forward to the time when it will grow to its proper height, in the same way he compares Nebuchadnezzar to a rod, one that was growing. . . .

In summary, when it is said that *the rod has blossomed,* it refers to those steps that God takes to execute his judgments. He does not act rashly like people do, rather he is just like a farmer who sows and plants. Thus, for his own purpose God determines ministers of his vengeance, and allows them to grow and to reach maturity. Ezekiel 1.[3]

Nebuchadnezzar Is Not the Rod. William Greenhill: "The rod has blossomed" (Ezek 7:10). By rod, some interpreters understand Nebuchadnezzar, whom they conceive so called (Jer 1:11; Is 10:5). A rod in the Scripture sense denotes, first, power, strength (Ps 2:9). Second, it denotes afflictions, heavy judgments (Ps 89:32). Third, it denotes rigid and harsh government (Is 14:5). Nebuchadnezzar had great strength, sorely afflicted the land of Judah, he was an iron rod that broke them in pieces and ruled them rigidly in Babylon.

. . . Others by rod understand the state of Judah and Jerusalem. So the word *rod* is used in Scripture (Jer 48:17): "How is the strong staff broken, and the beautiful rod!" That is, the state and dignity of Moab; and thus we may understand it. The word *rod* signifies a tribe (Num 1), either because they grew out of the stock of Jacob, as branches do out of a tree, or because the names of the twelve tribes were written on rods (Num 17:2). And the word being *hammatteh,* the tribe, "the rod" carries me to conceive it is meant of Judah rather than of Nebuchadnezzar. And the sense runs in a continued allegory: Judah is compared with a tree that blossoms, buds and brings forth its fruit; it had blossomed or flourished, and now the fruit was growing ripe, their sins were great, the measure of them full, and punishment grew near and weighty. An Exposition of Ezekiel.[4]

Destruction Cannot Be Avoided. John Mayer: *They have blown the trumpet, but none makes ready to the battle* (Ezek 7:14). Their destruction being showed in the former words, here he begins to show that they shall not be able by any means to keep it away. It will not be avoided by them arming themselves, set forth by blowing the trumpet, for so they might gather company together, but all in vain, for they should not have the courage to go forth to battle. Neither by keeping within the walls of the city, for the famine and pestilence should destroy them there. Then in amplifying their misery further, he says, *they that escape of them shall flee as the doves to the mountains* (Ezek 7:16). That is, being full of fear and

[2]*Exposition,* 163. [3]CTS 22:250-251 (CO 18:159-160). [4]*Exposition,* 167-68.

trembling, to save their lives they shall flee to dry and barren places, and there mourn as doves in the want of all things necessary for the sustentation of life. As such, their lives shall be to them more grievous than death. They shall pine away in desert places, through grief, want and poverty. Commentary upon All the Prophets.[5]

Disaster Comes Upon Disaster. John Calvin: In this way he warns the Jews that they grasp for security in vain, as if after merely one disaster they were already done. For as soon as God withdraws his hand the wicked think that they have escaped all trouble. Therefore they despise God more carelessly.

For they imagine that they have settled the debt. Just like a debtor who has been granted credit again after paying a small sum to his creditor is untroubled, so the reprobate harden themselves when God grants them some respite. They think that they have an bargain with him that he should not trouble them more. However, the prophet warns that there will be such a heap of evils *that one calamity will have many companions,* because God will not stop adding evils to evils. . . .

As to the prophets, he says that in vain the Jews will ask them what the will of God is. The point is that although God had always governed that people, their dispersion will be tragic. No longer will his teaching light their way, instead they will be submerged in the darkness of ignorance.

This was the gravest threat, because in extreme evil it is no small consolation when the Lord shines his word on us. For by this we are encouraged to be patient. Our sorrows are alleviated when we taste some hope of pardon, and God testifies that he will favor us. But when this comfort is withdrawn, we are easily overwhelmed by even the smallest evils. . . .

When God can be found nowhere, the lightest trial buries us in the deepest abyss. Therefore this was the sign of God's terrible vengeance when the gift of prophecy was snuffed out among the Jews, and the priests and elders had no counsel to give. . . .

So, let us learn from this passage that the gift of prophecy and all teaching is God's remarkable gift. Let us learn that this gift is taken away when God wishes to execute punishment for man's thanklessness. Ezekiel 1.[6]

Mourning for Iniquity. William Greenhill: The fruit of sin is sorrow: "all of them mourning, every one for his iniquity." Before they sported in their sins; now they should sigh for them. Their consciences were asleep through custom of sinning. God's judgments had now awakened them, and they brought their sins so to mind, that they wept and sorrowed sorely for them. They had gone on in their idolatrous, oppressing and provoking ways long. They saw no cause to be sorry. All was well with them. But when trouble came, their sins appeared, their souls were sad and filled with apprehensions. Such things drew bitter tears from them. An Exposition of Ezekiel.[7]

---

[5]*Prophets*, 389. [6]CTS 22:271-274 (CO 18:173-175). [7]*Exposition*, 173.

8:1–9:11 IDOLATRY IN THE TEMPLE

1In the sixth year, in the sixth month, on the fifth day of the month, as I sat in my house, with the elders of Judah sitting before me, the hand of the Lord GOD fell upon me there. 2Then I looked, and behold, a form that had the appearance of a man.[a] Below what appeared to be his waist was fire, and above his waist was something like the appearance of brightness, like gleaming metal.[b] 3He put out the form of a hand and took me by a lock of my head, and the Spirit lifted me up between earth and heaven and brought me in visions of God to Jerusalem, to the entrance of the gateway of the inner court that faces north, where was the seat of the image of jealousy, which provokes to jealousy. 4And behold, the glory of the God of Israel was there, like the vision that I saw in the valley.

5Then he said to me, "Son of man, lift up your eyes now toward the north." So I lifted up my eyes toward the north, and behold, north of the altar gate, in the entrance, was this image of jealousy. 6And he said to me, "Son of man, do you see what they are doing, the great abominations that the house of Israel are committing here, to drive me far from my sanctuary? But you will see still greater abominations."

7And he brought me to the entrance of the court, and when I looked, behold, there was a hole in the wall. 8Then he said to me, "Son of man, dig in the wall." So I dug in the wall, and behold, there was an entrance. 9And he said to me, "Go in, and see the vile abominations that they are committing here." 10So I went in and saw. And there, engraved on the wall all around, was every form of creeping things and loathsome beasts, and all the idols of the house of Israel. 11And before them stood seventy men of the elders of the house of Israel, with Jaazaniah the son of Shaphan standing among them. Each had his censer in his hand, and the smoke of the cloud of incense went up. 12Then he said to me, "Son of man, have you seen what the elders of the house of Israel are doing in the dark, each in his room of pictures? For they say, 'The LORD does not see us, the LORD has forsaken the land.'" 13He said also to me, "You will see still greater abominations that they commit."

14Then he brought me to the entrance of the north gate of the house of the LORD, and behold, there sat women weeping for Tammuz. 15Then he said to me, "Have you seen this, O son of man? You will see still greater abominations than these."

16And he brought me into the inner court of the house of the LORD. And behold, at the entrance of the temple of the LORD, between the porch and the altar, were about twenty-five men, with their backs to the temple of the LORD, and their faces toward the east, worshiping the sun toward the east. 17Then he said to me, "Have you seen this, O son of man? Is it too light a thing for the house of Judah to commit the abominations that they commit here, that they should fill the land with violence and provoke me still further to anger? Behold, they put the branch to their[c] nose. 18Therefore I will act in wrath. My eye will not spare, nor will I have pity. And though they cry in my ears with a loud voice, I will not hear them."

9 Then he cried in my ears with a loud voice, saying, "Bring near the executioners of the city, each with his destroying weapon in his hand." 2And behold, six men came

from the direction of the upper gate, which faces north, each with his weapon for slaughter
in his hand, and with them was a man clothed in linen, with a writing case at his waist.
And they went in and stood beside the bronze altar.
[3]Now the glory of the God of Israel had gone up from the cherub on which it rested to
the threshold of the house. And he called to the man clothed in linen, who had the writing
case at his waist. [4]And the Lord said to him, "Pass through the city, through Jerusalem,
and put a mark on the foreheads of the men who sigh and groan over all the abominations
that are committed in it." [5]And to the others he said in my hearing, "Pass through the city
after him, and strike. Your eye shall not spare, and you shall show no pity. [6]Kill old men
outright, young men and maidens, little children and women, but touch no one on whom
is the mark. And begin at my sanctuary." So they began with the elders who were before
the house. [7]Then he said to them, "Defile the house, and fill the courts with the slain. Go
out." So they went out and struck in the city. [8]And while they were striking, and I was left
alone, I fell upon my face, and cried, "Ah, Lord God! Will you destroy all the remnant of
Israel in the outpouring of your wrath on Jerusalem?"
[9]Then he said to me, "The guilt of the house of Israel and Judah is exceedingly great.
The land is full of blood, and the city full of injustice. For they say, 'The Lord has for-
saken the land, and the Lord does not see.' [10]As for me, my eye will not spare, nor will I
have pity; I will bring their deeds upon their heads."
[11]And behold, the man clothed in linen, with the writing case at his waist, brought back
word, saying, "I have done as you commanded me."

a By revocalization (compare Septuagint); Hebrew *of fire* **b** Or *amber* **c** Or *my*

Overview: Ezekiel has a vision of the abominations in the temple. Christ assumes the appearance of man before Ezekiel. Christ shows the idolatrous acts committed in the temple. He orders Ezekiel to dig in the wall. Ezekiel finds more abominations being committed in secret and in places obscured from sight. Such wickedness, however, is never concealed from God, even if it is from our fellow human beings.

At the beginning of Ezekiel 9, a man clothed in linen appears. Some commentators think this man is an angel; most, however, understand this man to be the Son of God. It is suggested that in this appearance of Christ we see his kingly, priestly and prophetic office.

8:1-18 *Abomination in the Temple*

The Appearance of Christ. William Greenhill: Our prophet, being in an ecstasy, the Lord Jesus Christ appears to him as a man and is described, generally, and that is by a likeness of fire (Ezek 8:2). He seemed to Ezekiel to be a man of fire, or as the appearance of fire. More particularly, and from his loins downward, and the appearance thereof was of fire. From his loins upward, the appearance was as brightness, as the color of amber. Christ being presented here as a man of fire, it is worthy of consideration to examine the grounds of it.

The Jews had sinned exceedingly, provoked God by their idolatry to great jealousy, and being now resolved on their destruction, he gives out a fiery vision of Christ to the prophet, whose appearance was suitable to the work now intended.

There have been appearances in fire before. Christ appeared to Moses in a flame of fire (Ex 3:2); the angel there, interpreters made to be Christ. And God led the Jews in the wilderness by a pillar of fire (Ex 13:21).

He was in that pillar (Ex 14:24).

Christ is also likened to fire. It is a shining, glorious thing; so Christ is glorious. "We beheld his glory" (Jn 1:14). And his appearing will be glorious, and so glorious as to lighten the world (Tit 2:13). When men come to judgment, they come with some glory and majesty.

He is likened to fire, to set out his knowledge and discovery of things. Fire is of a disclosing nature that makes things manifest. Christ's eyes are like a flame of fire, they see into every place (Rev 1:14). And here Christ discloses to the prophet the sins of Jerusalem, the hidden abominations there.

It also shows the active virtue that is in Christ. Fire is a lively and purging thing, separating dross from the precious metals. Christ is of infinite virtue; he distinguishes between the precious and the vile. "He is like a refiner's fire" (Mal 3:2), exceedingly active and decretive; he burns with zeal and jealousy. An Exposition of Ezekiel.[1]

A Vision of the Temple. John Calvin: There is no doubt that a prophetic vision is told here. The prophet was not carried to Jerusalem, nor had he moved, nor were the elders of Judah before him. Instead, it seemed to him that he was seized by the Spirit of God, so that he could see the pollutions with which the Jews had profaned the temple. . . .

A year and two months elapsed between the first vision, that was just explained, and this one, that will now be discussed. Since, therefore, fourteen months had elapsed, God appeared again to his prophet. . . .

Accordingly God appeared to his servant under some image. It is not inappropriate that it is a human figure. If it had been any other figure the prophet certainly would not have left it unmentioned.

But we have already seen that God had put on human form, and so depicted himself in the person of his only begotten Son, as we have said and will see again in chapter ten. This is the likeness the prophet is talking about. He uses this word on purpose, so we would know that it was not the real, solid and substantial thing called a body. Therefore, what the prophet saw was a figure or a likeness. This happened only in a mere vision, God did not actually put on a body at that time. . . .

Therefore, in the splendor God's majesty was revealed, humbling the prophet and all the faithful, so that they would receive the vision reverently. In the fire God's vengeance was revealed, so that the Jews would not make a shield out of God's name for them to hide behind falsely and deceptively. Ezekiel 1.[2]

The Abominations. John Calvin: Now the prophet was ordered *to dig in the wall* (v. 8). We gather from this that superstitions are sometimes so hidden in secret places, that they escape our eyes even while we look at them. This is the weakness of the human mind, that it does not easily understand how hateful it is to corrupt the worship of God. . . .

Here the prophet reports how the temple was profaned in another way. The chief citizens of Jerusalem and those who should have pointed out the way to others, prostituted themselves to ungodly forms of worship. . . .

[N]ot only did they worship the sun in their own homes, but in the temple itself, and not without great and pointed contempt of God. When they turned their back on the sanctuary, they mocked God. So, it seems that they were so defiant that they openly boasted in their superstitions, intentionally polluting God's temple. . . .

Now he reports another even greater dishonor done to God, when *they turned their backs on the sanctuary.* As I have said, they could have polluted themselves with such defilements at home in secret. But instead they came voluntarily into the temple as if they wanted to challenge God openly and violently.

[1]*Exposition*, 194. [2]CTS 22:276-279 (CO 18:177-179).

Now, when they turn their back, this is not merely a repugnant denial but an outrageous contempt of God. As if they had said, that God is unworthy of their respect. Ezekiel 1.[3]

A Hole in the Wall of Idolatry. William Greenhill: Idolaters oftentimes act closely and cover up their works from the eyes of the world. They had their imagery in chambers and secret places; it was walled up and unobvious to most eyes. Some covers and pretences such persons always have for their superstitions and idolatries. They cover them with their good intentions, great devotion, religion of their ancestors, such as have some pomp and state; there are in them such objects as help their memories and affections. There is, they say, some truth, some good, and the rest may be borne with; those who worship so, prosper and are at ease in their way. They meet not with those temptations and troubles that others do.

Such ways of wickedness cannot be carried so close, but there will be some notice of them. Let them make walls to cover them up, yet Providence will order it so, that there will be a hole in the wall, some crevice to look through and discern their doings; the mystery of iniquity could not work so closely, but it was discerned. An Exposition of Ezekiel.[4]

God Sees All. Matthew Meade: Why is it that people are so daring, impudent and resolute in sinning, but because they never consider that God sees and takes notice of all they do. . . . What wickedness will not a person commit when the sense of God's omniscience is blotted out? "Son of man," says God, "have you seen what the elders of the house of Israel do in the dark, for they say, the Lord sees us not" (Ezek 8:12). That made them bold in sin. Oh, that you would but much and often think of this all-knowledge of God. Keep the sense of it always on your minds. Wherever you are, remember this, that God sees you and observes all your actions. Sermons.[5]

Prayers Without Faith. John Calvin: If any one were to object that God always hears prayers, then I reply that he never turns away prayers born from faith. Here by the loud voice it is shown what hard times force out of unbelievers. Even though they try to seek refuge in God, as their common sense impels them, still they do not do this with settled minds. They do not even rely on the promises of God. But because their tormented minds do not allow them to rest, they instinctively turn to prayer, offering themselves to God, crying out loudly to him. Nevertheless they do this without faith and an honest heart (v. 18). Ezekiel 1.[6]

9:1-11 *Idolaters Killed*

The Man Clothed in Linen. John Calvin: Now he says that among them there was *a man clothed in linen* (v. 2). He is not placed in the crowd, as if he were just like the others, but he is separated, because he is different. Therefore, this *man* certainly was an angel. It is indeed common enough in Scripture, that whenever angels assume visible form they are called humans. Not because they really are humans, but because God clothes them with whatever form he sees fit. Ezekiel 1.[7]

Christ the Man Clothed in Linen. William Greenhill: Who this one man should be is questionable. Some make him to be an angel. . . . Others by this one man understand the Lord Christ, the angel of the covenant; and those contend that in the letter here is meant an angel and make that angel representative of Christ, so that the difference is not much. I join them that make this one man to be Christ, and that, because he is brought in as mediator here with an adjunct of oneness, as in 1 Timothy 2:5, "One media-

[3]CTS 22:287, 294-295 (CO 18:184, 189-190). [4]*Exposition*, 200. [5]*Sermons*, 199. [6]CTS 22:299 (CO 18:193). [7]CTS 22:302 (CO 18:195).

tor." The godly Jews had no other mediator.

Here are implied the three offices of Christ. His kingly office, whereby he rules and commands all creatures. That is couched in the words "among them," or in the midst of them. . . . His priestly office, implied in his linen clothing. . . . His prophetical office, shadowed out by the inkhorn he had by his side. An Exposition of Ezekiel.[8]

Christ the Man in White. John Mayer: Immediately six men armed to destruction appear coming from the north, and entering go to the temple and stand by the brazen altar. By these six men, Jerome understands six devils. Theodoret, who has it better, thinks them to be six angels since one among them was clothed with linen and had a charge to mark the servants of God in their foreheads. Devils never appear to do such things. But one of them only is said to be clothed with linen, who was not one of these six, but another singularly appointed to the office of marking. He was chief among them and best knew who were to be marked, as one mourning for sin out of hatred for it, and not to seem pious and zealous to people. And therefore it is most commonly held that this was Christ the Son of God, who is called an angel (Mal 3) and appeared like a man sitting on a throne in Ezekiel 1. He appears in white linen, as also other angels sometimes have done, to show his purity. Linen that is fine and white is also, or was then, accounted the best sort of clothing and fittest to be used about the service of God, for which the priests had their linen ephods and linen breeches. Now one of the company being so clothed to demonstrate his purity, it is not probable but that the rest who came with him were holy angels of God also and not devils? Commentary upon All the Prophets.[9]

Set a Mark on the Foreheads. William Greenhill: What this was is much disputed (Ezek 9:4). Popish expositors say it was the letter *tau*, which prefigured the cross of Christ. Some Hebrews by that mark (*tau*) understand those who have perfect knowledge of the law. Some, those who kept the law, *tau* standing for *torah*, signifying the law. Others understand believers in the Messiah, *tau* noting a cross. Jerome and some with him think the Hebrew was originally like the Greek *tau*, representing the cross; and that Ezra, returning from the captivity, found out new characters, which are those we use. . . .

This sign was no corporal sign, as if the Lord had made some impression in their foreheads, whereby to distinguish them from others. For this was a vision, not to be taken really, but in a spiritual sense. The Lord Christ took special notice of these and distinguished them by special providence from those who were to perish in the destruction of the city. He did not go up and down from house to house and set a mark on their foreheads. He applied his blood and merits and sealed them by his Spirit—not that they were not washed in the blood of Christ before, but now there was a new and special evidence of it. An Exposition of Ezekiel.[10]

Sigh and Weep Over Your Sins. Martin Luther: When the nation was compelled to spend the entire seventy years of exile in Babylon among the heathen, there was no lack of complaints, tears, sighs and prayers. But what do the prophets say, yes, even God through the prophets? "I," he says (Jer 7:25; 35:15), "sent prophets, cried aloud and wept to call you back on the way, but you killed them. Therefore I shall let you, too, weep in vain."

Thus today Germany has so far not cried, not wept and not grieved over the awful sins we are committing. But now that punishments are coming, we are beginning to moan and wail, although this should have been done long ago.

[8]*Exposition*, 211. [9]*Prophets*, 394-95. [10]*Exposition*, 215.

For when the punishments are being inflicted, we cry out and wail in vain. But those who wail before punishment comes—by their sighs the Lord is moved, and he mitigates the punishments, as is promised in Ezekiel 9:4-6, where God, who is about to inflict punishments on the priests and the people, commands that those who are sobbing because of idolatry be picked out and saved, lest they perish together with the ungodly. LECTURES ON GENESIS.[11]

CHILDREN OF GOD MOURN OVER THE ABOMINATIONS. JOHN CALVIN: God here shows what he wants his children to be like. Consequently if we act as though we approve of the sins of the wicked, and try to win their favor, and congratulate them, then it is in vain that we pride ourselves to be God's children. Anyone who does not groan over these abominations God does not count as his own. . . .

When we see on one hand the name of God trampled under foot and all justice violated, and on the other we see the church of God miserably and cruelly afflicted, and we laugh untroubled, we clearly show that we have nothing in common with God, and in vain we call him Father.

Accordingly these marks must be inscribed, with which the prophet distinguishes all God's elect, when he says, *whoever groans over the abominations*. Then he adds *crying out* to express better the severity and intensity of their zeal. This is as if he said that groaning was not enough, since many groan in a corner when they see the whole order of God so corrupted. Yet when they come to the light and the sight of people, they do not dare to show any sign of the smallest disapproval, because they are unwilling to experience hostility and hatred. Therefore, the prophet here exacts more from the children of God than secret groaning. He wants them to groan openly and cry out loudly, so that they bear witness that they detest what God has condemned in his law. EZEKIEL 1.[12]

[11]LW 3:60. [12]CTS 22:307-308 (CO 18:198-199).

10:1-22 THE GLORY DEPARTS FROM THE TEMPLE

1Then I looked, and behold, on the expanse that was over the heads of the cherubim there appeared above them something like a sapphire,[a] in appearance like a throne. 2And he said to the man clothed in linen, "Go in among the whirling wheels underneath the cherubim. Fill your hands with burning coals from between the cherubim, and scatter them over the city."

And he went in before my eyes. 3Now the cherubim were standing on the south side of the house, when the man went in, and a cloud filled the inner court. 4And the glory of the LORD went up from the cherub to the threshold of the house, and the house was filled with the cloud, and the court was filled with the brightness of the glory of the LORD. 5And the sound of the wings of the cherubim was heard as far as the outer court, like the voice of God Almighty when he speaks.

6 And when he commanded the man clothed in linen, "Take fire from between the whirling wheels, from between the cherubim," he went in and stood beside a wheel. 7 And a cherub stretched out his hand from between the cherubim to the fire that was between the cherubim, and took some of it and put it into the hands of the man clothed in linen, who took it and went out. 8 The cherubim appeared to have the form of a human hand under their wings.

9 And I looked, and behold, there were four wheels beside the cherubim, one beside each cherub, and the appearance of the wheels was like sparkling beryl. 10 And as for their appearance, the four had the same likeness, as if a wheel were within a wheel. 11 When they went, they went in any of their four directions[b] without turning as they went, but in whatever direction the front wheel[c] faced, the others followed without turning as they went. 12 And their whole body, their rims, and their spokes, their wings,[d] and the wheels were full of eyes all around—the wheels that the four of them had. 13 As for the wheels, they were called in my hearing "the whirling wheels." 14 And every one had four faces: the first face was the face of the cherub, and the second face was a human face, and the third the face of a lion, and the fourth the face of an eagle.

15 And the cherubim mounted up. These were the living creatures that I saw by the Chebar canal. 16 And when the cherubim went, the wheels went beside them. And when the cherubim lifted up their wings to mount up from the earth, the wheels did not turn from beside them. 17 When they stood still, these stood still, and when they mounted up, these mounted up with them, for the spirit of the living creatures[e] was in them.

18 Then the glory of the Lord *went out from the threshold of the house, and stood over the cherubim. 19 And the cherubim lifted up their wings and mounted up from the earth before my eyes as they went out, with the wheels beside them. And they stood at the entrance of the east gate of the house of the* Lord, *and the glory of the God of Israel was over them.*

20 These were the living creatures that I saw underneath the God of Israel by the Chebar canal; and I knew that they were cherubim. 21 Each had four faces, and each four wings, and underneath their wings the likeness of human hands. 22 And as for the likeness of their faces, they were the same faces whose appearance I had seen by the Chebar canal. Each one of them went straight forward.

a Or *lapis lazuli* b Hebrew *to their four sides* c Hebrew *the head* d Or *their whole body, their backs, their hands, and their wings* e Or *spirit of life*

Overview: In this vision, Ezekiel shows that God will not remain where idolatry is found. Instead, God's glory would depart the temple. Since the vision here is so similar to the one in Ezekiel 1, our commentators are struck by the differences between the two visions. Why cherubim here instead of living creatures? Why do the wheels precede the cherubim here but do not in the first vision?

Our commentators end with a consideration of God leaving the temple. Although the physical structure of the temple is removed, for the faithful God still remains amid the rubble. This is seen in Daniel's prayers toward Jerusalem and the temple. Finally, how are we to understand God's departure from the temple and his promise elsewhere to dwell forever in the temple (Ps 132:14)?

The Purpose of This Vision. John Calvin: Here the prophet teaches the purpose of the vision. The Jews thought that they would always be safe and secure under God's presence. They thought that the sacred fire on the altar had power to atone for all wickedness. However, God showed that he was seated in the temple so that he could prepare his vengeance against them, and that the cherubim were guardians of the weapons that would finally destroy them. So, here we see the false and twisted boasting that intoxicated the Jews torn apart, even though they thought that God was bound to them in some special way. Ezekiel 1.[1]

Why Cherubim and Not Living Creature? William Greenhill: Our prophet had already seen many visions. Being again by the Spirit in a vision, yet at Jerusalem (Ezek 8:3), he has in this chapter [Ezek 10] a vision much like that mentioned in the first chapter [Ezek 1], yet with some difference, as will appear in the opening. . . . This word, "cherubim," is not in the first vision in chapter one. There they are called the living creatures, here cherubim, which is evidence that they are the same, and may strengthen the interpretation given to be of the angels. . . . [In Ezekiel 1], it is living creature and heads; here it is cherubim and head, which may remind us of their oneness and consent in judgment and operations. If there are heads, it is but as one living creature acts from those heads. If there are cherubim, they have all but as one head.

Why are they called cherubim here, and not living creatures, as before? I suppose the reason is this. The former vision was at Chebar, in the open field by a river's side; this was in the temple, where the cherubim were (1 Kings 8:6-7), and so that notion suited with them there. In Babylon, a profane land, the prophet sees living creatures, he had a general and confused apprehension of them; but when he is in the temple, he has a more clear and distinct knowledge of them. Hence you have this note, the Lord did more clearly make known himself and mysteries in the holy land than in other places. "In Judah is God known" more fully and familiarly than elsewhere (Ps 76:1). A vision in Babylon is not so clear as a vision in Zion. An Exposition of Ezekiel.[2]

Cherubim and Living Creatures. Matthew Meade: The wheels are acted on by the living creatures: "When the living creatures went, the wheels went by them, and when the living creatures were lifted up from the earth, the wheels were lifted up" (Ezek 1:19). And you have it again in the tenth chapter: "When the cherubim went, the wheels went by them, and when the cherubim lifted up their wings to mount up from the earth, the wheels turned not from beside them. When they stood, they stood, and when they were lifted up, these lifted up themselves also" (Ezek 10:16-17). The living creatures in the first chapter are the cherubim in this chapter, and they are the angels that are intended by both. And that which is the design of the Holy Spirit in these expressions, again and again repeated, is to confirm this truth that all inferior causes are acted and governed by causes superior. No creature moves below without a guide above: "When the cherubim went, the wheels went." The angels have a great hand in the government of the world; they stand next to the Spirit of God in the administration of all things here below. There is nothing that falls out in the world but the angels have a hand in it. The wheels do in all things follow the motions of the angels. The Vision of the Wheels.[3]

God Uses Angels to Protect and Destroy. John Calvin: Now it must be observed that the angel commanded to mark the elect now assumes a new role. Thus, we gather that the angels were the ministers of God's favor to the faithful, nevertheless whenever they were commanded to, they executed his vengeance. The steward placed over a large

[1]CTS 22:372 (CO 18:212). [2]*Exposition*, 230. [3]*Vision of the Wheels*, 41.

family, is not only responsible for supporting the family by nourishing them, that is, supplying them with food and clothing, but also correcting those who conduct themselves wickedly and sinfully. The role of God's angels is just like this.

When God wants to brand sinners with two portions of shame, he often hands them over to the devil as his executioner. As soon as we are delivered into the devil's hand, this is a sign of extreme vengeance. But God by his angels often administers judgment against the wicked . . .

The same thing is now *delivered* by the prophet. We saw the angel clothed in linen as the protector of the faithful, removing them from all harm. Now, however, he is sent *to scatter coals over the whole city,* (v. 2) to destroy the stones and the wood, as well as the people. Ezekiel 1.[4]

The Fire. Matthew Meade: The coals that must be scattered over the city must come from between the cherubim (Ezek 10:2), in the house of the Lord, by which we are taught that the sins that do so highly provoke God are the sins of his own people, corrupt worship, Lord's day profaneness, human invocations, looseness, pride, luxury, uncleanness and worldliness. These found under a profession of religion will kindle the fire of God's wrath, and who shall quench it? The Vision of the Wheels.[5]

The Glory of the Lord. William Greenhill: "The glory of the Lord" (Ezek 10:4) was Christ, say expositors, who was in his glorious apparition, and now in the temple but going out of it. He had once before done thus, gone off from the cherub to the threshold (Ezek 9:3), but was returned again, and here the second time does it. He was now in a judiciary way and would leave the temple, if they did not presently prevent it by repentance.

Christ standing thus on the threshold, and being on terms of departure, behind him was the cloud that filled the house, there was darkness, but before the Lord Christ was light and brightness, the court, which he stood looking into, was full of the brightness of the Lord's glory. The glory was now gone out of the sanctuary into the court. An Exposition of Ezekiel.[6]

The Wheels. William Greenhill: In Ezekiel 1, mention is made, first, of the living creatures, and then, of the wheels. Here, the wheels are first set down (Ezek 10:9-14), and after them the cherubim, or living creatures (Ezek 10:15-22). Why there is a great inversion and change made in the vision, I find no reason given, neither do I conceive any satisfactory reason can be given, but the will of the Lord. It pleased him to represent the vision in that way to the prophet, and that may suffice us. Yet if we may conjecture, the wheels are set first here, for that changes and motions of second causes in the world are more obvious to our eyes, we observe them first, and that virtue that acts in them is more out of sight. An Exposition of Ezekiel.[7]

The Turning of the Wheels. Matthew Meade: These wheels are said "to go on their four sides" (Ezek 10:11). I told you before that the four wheels answer to the four parts of the world, and when it is said they went on their four sides, the meaning is, that look what quarter of the world was appointed to them, there they went, and there they moved. And then it shows their motion was constant and settled, answering to the immutable purpose of him with whom there is no shadow of change. God is not as a human being, who is fickle and inconstant, and does not know his own mind, turning from one side to another, now for this, anon for that, today for pulling down what yesterday he set up. Such mutable beings

[4]CTS 22:322-323 (CO 18:209). [5]*Vision of the Wheels,* 50. [6]*Exposition,* 234. [7]*Exposition,* 238.

we are, actions change, affections change and principles change too, but it is not so with God. There is no altering the course of providence, no art, no power, no policy, can turn him out of the way. His providence is settled in its motion. The wheels go on their four sides, and therefore to confirm this, it is said, there is no going back: "They turned not as they went but to the place where the head looked they followed it, they turned not as they went" (Ezek 10:11). The expression is doubled (like Pharaoh's dream) for the greater confirmation of the truth that we may be sure there are no retrograde motions in the course of providence. THE VISION OF THE WHEELS.[8]

THE IMAGE OF THE WHEELS. JOHN CALVIN: Here the prophet, as in the first chapter, says that wheels were added to each creature. I have previously explained what the wheels mean. I will now only allude to them. I will clarify the creatures more fully in a little bit. The wheels are images of all the upheavals that are seen in the world. No more suitable figure can be chosen, because indeed nothing is stationary in the world, since changes, as they are commonly called, are incessantly taking place. Therefore, because things are constantly being altered, even whirling haphazardly, unbelievers are not able to know that the world is governed by the sure plan of God. Instead they imagine for themselves random fortune. As a concession to us, the upheavals of all things, all "accidents," as they are called, all events God portrayed under the form of wheels. As if he were saying, that all things in the world are revolving and changing, not just that all the elements are jostled up and down, but especially human affairs. . . . The prophet saw that the wheels did not turn on their own, but were connected to the angels, because all events depend on a first cause. Of course, it is the secret orchestration and inspiration of God that moves the angels and also grants them their power. EZEKIEL 1.[9]

THE WHEELS ARE FULL OF EYES. MATTHEW MEADE: It is said the wheels are full of eyes: "The wheels were full of eyes round about" (Ezek 10:12). This implies the omniscience of Christ and his exact notice of all matters in the world. Though many things may be hidden from us, yet there is nothing hidden from him. "People may dig deep to hide their counsels from the Lord, and say, Who sees us?" (Is 29:15). But "there is no darkness or shadow of death where the workers of iniquity may hide themselves, for his eyes are on the way of man, and he sees all his goings" (Job 34:21-22). If we could suppress anything done by people that is unknown to God, why then, in that particular thing the knowledge of people would be superior to God. A human being would know something more than God knows, which is impossible, for "the eyes of the Lord are in every place, beholding the evil and the good" (Prov 15:3). There is not the closest corner or the darkest deep, not the most covered contrivances or the most hidden project, or the most secret wickedness, but it is open to the eye of God, for "all things are naked and opened to the eyes of him with whom we have to do" (Heb 4:13). There are secrets of government, secrets of state, secrets of the heart, secret contrivances, secret aims and intentions, but none of them are secrets of God. As nothing can be hard to an omnipotent arm, so nothing can be hidden from an omniscient eye. God cannot but know all the offenses, qualities, inclinations and activities of the creature, since all those several principles and qualities so far as without sin were wrought in them by him. "Known to God are all his work, from the beginning of the world" (Acts 15:8). Thus, the wheels are full of eyes. THE VISION OF THE WHEELS.[10]

THE FOUR FACES. JOHN CALVIN: There is motion in a man, in an ox, in an eagle, and in a

[8] *Vision of the Wheels*, 20. [9] CTS 22:329-330 (CO 18:214). [10] *Vision of the Wheels*, 18-19.

lion (v. 14). In this image these creatures represent each part of the universe. At the same time since the creatures are angels we must observe how God attributes to angels the head of a lion, an eagle, and a man. This certainly does not seem to relate to them in the least. But he could not better express the inseparable connection between the motion of the angels and the motion of all creatures. . . .

A difficult question remains: why does Ezekiel say here that the first head was a cherub, while in chapter one he said it was that of an ox. Some avoid the difficulty by saying that from a distance it looked like an ox, but a closer look proved it was a cherub. But this is too forced. Conesquently I have no doubt that there is some difference in this vision. Still, that he then adds that this creature was what he saw by the river Chebar does not contradict this. Indeed whatever is related and has the same purpose he calls the same. Paul says (1 Cor 10:3-4) the fathers in the desert ate the same spiritual food and drank the same spiritual drink. Yet we know the symbol of manna and the water flowing from the rock are very different from the holy supper that Christ left for us. Still, as I have already said, because there is a relationship between the sacred symbols, they refer to the same purpose. For this reason Paul says "the same drink and the same food," and Ezekiel says, *it was the same creature*. . . .

Earlier the face of an ox was presented to the prophet near the river Chebar. Now the face of a cherub is presented to him, so that he would understand that they were angels or living cherubs, and that the four heads would not distract him. Reminded by this evidence he understands that each creature is nothing other than an angel or a cherub, even though it differs from the accepted form that God had presented to Moses on the mountain. EZEKIEL I.[11]

WHEN WHEELS AND CHERUBIM STOP. MATTHEW MEADE: The wheels are sometimes at a stop, they stand still. "When the cherubim stood, the wheels stood" (Ezek 10:18). This sometimes is really so. God suspends the ordinary operation of the creatures. The lions' mouths are shut so long as Daniel is in the den. The first has no power on the three martyrs. God can stop the motions of all secondary causes as he pleases. The sun stands still on Gibeon, and the moon in the valley of Ajalon, if God will have it so (Josh 10:12). The sea divides and the waters stand as a wall to fence out a passage for Israel. God can put a stand to the greatest wheels.

. . . And as the wheels do sometimes really stand, so sometimes though they do not stand, yet to us they seem as if they did, and this is from a sentence of death that God usually puts on a mercy before it is accomplished. Abraham begs a son, God promises he shall have his desire, but Abraham waits and hopes, and yet no son, till his body was now dead and Sarah past childbearing, for "it ceased to be with her after the manner of women" (Gen 18:11). How do the wheels seem to be at a stand? Israel in Egypt cries for deliverance, God promises the thing and sends Moses to effect it, but instead of being delivered, their bondage is increased and their task doubled. The wheels seemed to stand. So when in Babylon, the church cries for a redemption, God promises to redeem them, but first they must be as dead and dry bones, and past hope. "Behold, they say, Our bones are dried, our hope is lost, we are cut off for our parts" (Ezek 37:11). O what a stand is here! "Can these dry bones live" (Ezek 37:3)? THE VISION OF THE WHEELS.[12]

THE SPIRIT ACTS IN THE WHEELS. WILLIAM GREENHILL: We should not terminate our thoughts on second causes but look up to the supreme overruling Cause. Here the prophet is led up to the Spirit; he does not

[11]CTS 22:334-335 (CO 18:217-218). [12]*Vision of the Wheels*, 26-28.

look at the cherubim and wheels standing or moving only, but his eye is higher, it is on the Spirit of life that was in them. We are apt to look at that instrument or cause that is next to us, in present view, and there to terminate. This is a great evil, to eye the creature and forget God. It is his Spirit that acts in the wheels, and if we take not notice of it, how can we be thankful when the creature is the instrumental cause of good to us, how patient when it is instrumental of hurt to us? If the creature strikes and hurts you, it is the Spirit of life in that creature that set it on its work; and if it profits and pleases you, it was the same Spirit that moved it to do so. Many are so blind that they see nothing of the Spirit in any wheel or in any motion. AN EXPOSITION OF EZEKIEL.[13]

GOD LEAVES THE TEMPLE. JOHN CALVIN: Here the prophet teaches us the main point of the vision: God has abandoned the temple. We know with what great confidence the Jews boasted that they will always be safe and secure under the protection of God. Because of the promise that had been given, that God's temple will be his dwelling place, they did not believe it was possible that God would ever leave them. So, they sinned without restraint. Although they drove him far away by their evil deeds, nevertheless they wanted to keep him tightly bound to them. This foolishness is mocked by Isaiah (66:1): "Heaven is my throne, and the earth is my footstool. What house would you build for me?" . . . When his angels abandoned the temple, God abandoned the Jews, so that in the future they will boast in vain that they are securely under his protection. . . .

The visible form of the temple was taken away, but nevertheless, because the temple was established on the promise of God, it stood among those ruins, as I have said. For this reason, although loneliness and devastation should have turned away his eyes and thoughts from Judea, Daniel prayed in that direction, as if the temple had remained untouched. Why? He remembered the promise.

And for this reason, after the return from captivity the prophets said that the glory of the second temple surpassed the glory of the first, as the prophet Haggai says in chapter two. And we know how lavishly and splendidly Isaiah describes the splendor of the second temple and its unfathomable glory. We will see a similar teaching at the end of this book. Therefore, since the temple stood before God, because it was established on his promise, this temporary desertion was not able to destroy what I have said about God's continual watch. . . . Now then we understand how God left his temple, but did not break his steadfast promise at all. EZEKIEL 1.[14]

GOD AND THE TEMPLE. JOHN MAYER: Now the prophet proceeds again to tell what became of the glory of God, which was said before to have gone from off the cherubim and to have stood on the threshold. And this was done to show God's departing from his earthly house among the Jews to his heavenly house. By this was shown that they now were destitute of his help and the help of his angels. They were now exposed to the fury of their heathen enemies. And this was done to humble their pride and their carnal confidence in the temple, by which they thought themselves safe against all the forces of the world.

But it may be doubted here how the promise formerly made was verified, *This is my house, and here will I dwell forever* (Ps 132:14). Solution: When God made this promise he propounded a condition. If his people kept his law, worshiping him purely, as he prescribed, he would dwell forever with them. But they in confidence of this left him to worship false gods, and so corrupted most foully his worship and waxed bold also to oppress and steal, to swear falsely, to commit adultery and to wal-

[13]*Exposition*, 242. [14]CTS 22:340-343 (CO 18:221-223).

low in the swinish sin of drunkenness, wherefore that promise now held no longer (cf. Jer 7; 18:10). But, despite the fact that the same material house was still among them, it was just with God to leave them destitute of his help, and to be gone up to his heavenly throne afar from them and so to make that house no more than another building. Although the building was most sumptuous, there was no help to be had in time of need. And it was necessary to show this beforehand, lest when afterwards they should see the temple and sanctuary burned with the city, they should conceive anything unworthy concerning God, as if he also had suffered in these flames. Yet it is to be understood that the Lord did not now so leave his temple, but that the place was still sacred. Indeed, on this very place, a temple should after seventy years be built again and be filled with more glory than this present house. And therefore Daniel still prayed toward this place, and the Jews spared out of captivity brought offerings here even when this house lay in the ruins. COMMENTARY UPON ALL THE PROPHETS.[15]

[15]*Prophets*, 398-99.

11:1-25 JUDGMENT ON ISRAEL'S LEADERS AND RETURN

*1The Spirit lifted me up and brought me to the east gate of the house of the LORD,
which faces east. And behold, at the entrance of the gateway there were twenty-five men.
And I saw among them Jaazaniah the son of Azzur, and Pelatiah the son of Benaiah,
princes of the people. 2And he said to me, "Son of man, these are the men who devise in-
iquity and who give wicked counsel in this city; 3who say, 'The time is not near[a] to build
houses. This city is the cauldron, and we are the meat.' 4Therefore prophesy against them,
prophesy, O son of man."*

*5And the Spirit of the LORD fell upon me, and he said to me, "Say, Thus says the LORD:
So you think, O house of Israel. For I know the things that come into your mind. 6You
have multiplied your slain in this city and have filled its streets with the slain. 7Therefore
thus says the Lord GOD: Your slain whom you have laid in the midst of it, they are the
meat, and this city is the cauldron, but you shall be brought out of the midst of it. 8You
have feared the sword, and I will bring the sword upon you, declares the Lord GOD. 9And
I will bring you out of the midst of it, and give you into the hands of foreigners, and ex-
ecute judgments upon you. 10You shall fall by the sword. I will judge you at the border of
Israel, and you shall know that I am the LORD. 11This city shall not be your cauldron, nor
shall you be the meat in the midst of it. I will judge you at the border of Israel, 12and you
shall know that I am the LORD. For you have not walked in my statutes, nor obeyed my
rules, but have acted according to the rules of the nations that are around you."*

13And it came to pass, while I was prophesying, that Pelatiah the son of Benaiah died.

Then I fell down on my face and cried out with a loud voice and said, "Ah, Lord God! Will you make a full end of the remnant of Israel?"

[14]And the word of the Lord came to me: [15]"Son of man, your brothers, even your brothers, your kinsmen,[b] the whole house of Israel, all of them, are those of whom the inhabitants of Jerusalem have said, 'Go far from the Lord; to us this land is given for a possession.' [16]Therefore say, 'Thus says the Lord God: Though I removed them far off among the nations, and though I scattered them among the countries, yet I have been a sanctuary to them for a while[c] in the countries where they have gone.' [17]Therefore say, 'Thus says the Lord God: I will gather you from the peoples and assemble you out of the countries where you have been scattered, and I will give you the land of Israel.' [18]And when they come there, they will remove from it all its detestable things and all its abominations. [19]And I will give them one heart, and a new spirit I will put within them. I will remove the heart of stone from their flesh and give them a heart of flesh, [20]that they may walk in my statutes and keep my rules and obey them. And they shall be my people, and I will be their God. [21]But as for those whose heart goes after their detestable things and their abominations, I will[d] bring their deeds upon their own heads, declares the Lord God."

[22]Then the cherubim lifted up their wings, with the wheels beside them, and the glory of the God of Israel was over them. [23]And the glory of the Lord went up from the midst of the city and stood on the mountain that is on the east side of the city. [24]And the Spirit lifted me up and brought me in the vision by the Spirit of God into Chaldea, to the exiles. Then the vision that I had seen went up from me. [25]And I told the exiles all the things that the Lord had shown me.

a Or *Is not the time near... ?* b Hebrew *the men of your redemption* c Or *in small measure* d *Hebrew To the heart of their detestable things and their abominations their heart goes; I will*

Overview: Ezekiel begins by prophesying against the perverse and wicked leaders of the people. Our commentators note the susceptibility of corruption and wickedness among those charged with authority as they begin to think of their own interests and greed. Moreover, the people are not excused and may not claim ignorance when their leaders drag them into ruin. Ezekiel pronounces judgment and ruin on the city. The people are not excused but held accountable.

The second part of the chapter offers comfort to those in captivity. Here is the promise of a new heart and spirit that God will give to the people he gathers from captivity. As observed in Ezekiel 2, that the Spirit alone brings us to faith and understanding, so likewise here our commentators emphasize that God alone changes our heart and regenerates us.

11:1-15 *Leaders*

Perverse Leaders. John Calvin: Here the prophet warns all the people that wicked leaders will be the cause of their destruction. "If the blind lead the blind both will fall into the ditch." Therefore, because the princes of the city were such wicked apostates, they dragged the whole body of people into the same ruin. Now, therefore, the prophet shows that the condition of the city was so corrupt that no hope of pardon remained, since those who should have been the eyes of the whole people were covered in darkness. . . .

Common people are accustomed to using their leaders as a shield, just as we today see happening in the papacy. This is their last refuge, objecting that they themselves are guilty of no fault when they obey holy mother church. Such also formerly was the stubbornness of the people.

To sum up, people always and with pleasure drive away all blame from themselves under the cloak of error or ignorance. For this reason the prophet now shows that the city will not be free from God's wrath, because it was corrupted by its leaders and rulers. On the contrary, this will be the cause of its destruction, because the people too easily turned away to wicked examples. . . .

But here the prophet shows, that however illustrious those who are granted power over the people are, nevertheless they are not inviolable nor are they released from the law by any special right, since God freely judges them by his Spirit, and reproves them by his prophets. So, if we want to execute our office well, especially when the role of teaching is entrusted to us, we should set aside all *prosopolempsia*. Those who boast that they are greater than others are still subject to God's punishments. EZEKIEL I.[1]

CORRUPT LEADERS. WILLIAM GREENHILL: People chief in dignity and place are for the most part corrupt. Here the twenty-five, who bore the sway in the city and had great power, were all joined together in wickedness. Isaiah (Is 1:10) calls their rulers "rulers of Sodom," because of their extreme wickedness. And he excepts none, they were generally such. . . . The prophet thought the great ones, who had great obligations on them to honor God, who knew what pertained to worship and justice, that they would hearken to him. They cast off all respect, subjection and obedience to the law of God. They followed their own wills, lusts, humors; they regarded neither equity nor honesty. They were far worse than the poorer sort, whom the prophet had tried also. Luke (Lk 18:1-6) mentions but one judge, and he was an unjust one. Are not too many of the great ones among us corrupt, loose and enemies to Christ and his kingdom? AN EXPOSITION OF EZEKIEL.[2]

THE FACE AND HAND OF GOD. JOHN CALVIN: [L]et us note that when God has tolerated us a long time, if we stand firm in our stubbornness, that nothing else is left except for the light of teaching to be extinguished so that God can reveal himself in another way. The prophet's sermon is like a mirror in which God displays himself. But when we shut our eyes and throw the mirror to our feet and shatter it, then God reveals himself to us in another way. That is, he no longer thinks it right to show us his face, but teaches us by his hand, and through the display of his power he demonstrates our wicked stubbornness, because we were unwilling to submit to his teaching. EZEKIEL I.[3]

11:16-25 *Promised Return of Israel*

COMFORT FOR GOD'S PEOPLE. WILLIAM GREENHILL: At this verse (Ezek 11:16) begins comfort for the captives. They were cast out, rejected and insulted by their brethren, filled with sad thoughts of their condition. But here heaven opens, and light breaks out in sweet promises; and they are these: (1) A promise of mercy to them in Babylon (Ezek 11:16); (2) Of returning from Babylon to Zion (Ezek 11:17); (3) Of purifying them from their pollution in the land of Canaan (Ezek 11:18); (4) Of regeneration of conversion (Ezek 11:19-20); (5) A threat to those whose hearts should cleave to their detestable things, which is comfortable to the godly. AN EXPOSITION OF EZEKIEL.[4]

[1]CTS 22:347-348 (CO 18:226). *Prosopolempsia* is a Greek word that occurs in Rom 2:11, Eph 6:9, and Col 3:25. The KJV renders this as "respect of persons" and the ESV "partiality". [2]*Exposition*, 251. [3]CTS 22:360 (CO 18:235). [4]*Exposition*, 258.

Sincere Worshipers of God. John Calvin: Here he adds something more important. When the Israelites have returned to their country they will be sincere worshipers of God, who not only offer sacrifices in the temple, but also purge the land of all its defilements. Here also the prophet warns how great and detestable the wickedness of the ten tribes was, because they had contaminated the land with idols. He does not mention here the idols of the nations, but instead reproves the Israelites because they had contaminated the land that had been dedicated to God with their filth. So then, the prophet urged his people to repentance, making clear that they were not thrown out of the land until it had been defiled. For this reason they were justly punished for their ungodliness. This is one point.

Now it should be noted, that we truly and purely enjoy God's blessings, when we direct their use to the purpose that is here set before us, of course, to worship purely and rightly. Nothing confronts us more frequently than this teaching: it is certain that we have been redeemed by God to celebrate his glory. The church was planted so that in it he would be glorified, and we would make known his mighty works. . . .

Thirdly, it should be noted, that we do not rightly perform our duty to God, unless we cleanse his worship from all filth and defilement. Many worship God in a way that they corrupt with vile poisons whatever obedience they believe to fulfill. Ezekiel 1.[5]

God Alone Changes Our Heart. John Calvin: Now let us consider more carefully the whole matter that the prophet discusses. When God speaks of a heart of stone, without a doubt he condemns all humans of stubbornness. This is not a matter of a few people whose nature differs from others. But just as in a mirror he places the Israelites next to us, so that we would know what our condition is, when after being abandoned by God we follow our own inclinations. So, we gather from this passage that everyone has a heart of stone, that is, everyone is so corrupted that they cannot stand to obey God. And so, they would rather be carried off by stubbornness. . . .

But as we have said, in the beginning the will of Adam was upright, at least it was receptive to following the righteousness of God. However, when Adam corrupted himself, we also were ruined with him. Consequently, the heart of stone, because we were stripped of that original wholeness that God had granted us in the beginning. Whatever Adam lost became our loss, because he was not created for himself alone, but in him God had revealed what would be the condition of the human race. . . .

In short, we see what the beginning of regeneration is, when God sweeps away that depravity that we were sold to. But it should be noted that there are two parts of regeneration that the prophet handles. God announces that *he gives his elect one heart and a new spirit.* It follows, therefore, that the whole soul is damaged, from reason even to the emotions. . . .

We see therefore that regeneration is constantly taking place, so that we strive for its result. This is just like Paul teaches (Phil 2:12), saying, "Work out your salvation with fear and trembling." Here he urges the faithful to struggle. Truly God does not want us to be like stones. Therefore, let us struggle, exerting every muscle, putting to practice our zeal to conduct ourselves rightly. But Paul urges this to be done with fear and trembling, that is, by abandoning all reliance in our own strength. If we are intoxicated with that devilish arrogance that we are colaborers with God, and by the action of our free will his grace is helped, we will burst apart, and eventually God will show how great our blindness was. . . . [H]umans always wickedly devise how they might diminish the grace of God. With ungodly boldness

[5]CTS 22:369-370 (CO 18:241-242).

they try to claim for themselves what belongs to him. Therefore, so that the prophet might better remove all pride, he says that our walking in God's precepts, guarding his statutes, and obeying the entire law must be attributed to God.

Therefore let us learn to leave entirely to God his own praise, and thus acknowledge that in our good works nothing is our own. Ezekiel 1.[6]

One Heart. William Greenhill: Some think by one heart is meant the mutual consent to hasten to Jerusalem to build the temple. As they were one people, of one language and spirit, in building Babel, so these should be one people, of one mind and language, in rebuilding Jerusalem. But if it should be confined to this sense, it were no spiritual mercy, and here God is promising spiritual mercies. This sense may be included, but there is something beyond it. We will inquire what heart was antecedently in this people, which will give us light for the better understanding of this oneness of heart.

They had a backsliding, apostatizing heart in them. . . . They had a slippery, unfaithful heart. . . . They had a deceitful, hypocritical heart. . . . They had a divided, forward, bitter heart. . . . Now this one heart here mentioned is opposite all these. God would give them "one heart," and that is, a heart that should be for himself, and not for idols; a heart that should not withdraw or turn back to any false ways but cling to himself only. After they came out of Babylon, they never could endure idols anymore; God had separated their hearts from them. Therefore on their return God promised they should take away all detestable things (Ezek 11:18). . . . They should look at God as the only and adequate object of their heart, they should be content with him alone; they should not ask counsel, confide in, fetch comfort from or worship any other. He only had made covenant with that people, and they should own him only for their God. An Exposition of Ezekiel.[7]

A New Heart. John Mayer: That an upright heart is meant by one heart, or a single heart, which is opposed to a double, is the gift of God. We have this not of ourselves. So too, we have not unanimity of ourselves, by which is meant to walk together consentingly in one way of righteousness (cf. Ps 12:3; Acts 4:32).

2. That our hearts are changed from stony, or being like stones that yield not to any beating, to be as flesh, that is, soft by the power of his grace and spirit only.

3. Because he says, not only a new heart, but a spirit, by the one denoting the will, by the other the understanding and judgment of the soul, that whatever is good in us comes only from God, both to will and to do, we having of ourselves, since the fall of Adam, no liberty of will left to us to do good, but to this we attain, as God is pleased to work it in us, that he may have the praise of all.

4. They only have this blessed work wrought in them that walk in God's statutes. It is vain for others to talk of their good hearts, it being certain, that as a good tree cannot be without good fruit, so a good heart cannot be without good works. Commentary upon All the Prophets.[8]

Sacraments as Visible Word. John Calvin: The prophet calls us back to the power of the Spirit which we are unable to measure on our small scale. Therefore, since the operation of the Spirit is incomprehensible, we should not be surprised that the prophet was carried to Jerusalem in a vision, then brought back to exile. . . .

Augustine says that a sacrament is a visible word. And he speaks correctly, because in baptism God speaks to our eyes, when he brings

[6]CTS 22:374-380 (CO 18:244-249). [7]*Exposition*, 265-66.
[8]*Prophets*, 401-2.

forward water as a symbol of our purification and regeneration. In the Supper he also directs his word to our eyes, since Christ reveals his flesh to us as real food, and his blood as real drink, when bread and wine are set before us. For this reason also the prophet now says that *he saw the word of God*, because it was clothed in external symbols. Ezekiel 1.[9]

[9]CTS 22:387 (CO 18:252-253). Cf. Augustine, *Tractates on the Gospel of John*, 80.3 (NPNF, i, VII, 344).

12:1-28 The Exile Symbolized

*1The word of the Lord came to me: 2"Son of man, you dwell in the midst of a rebel-
lious house, who have eyes to see, but see not, who have ears to hear, but hear not, for
they are a rebellious house. 3As for you, son of man, prepare for yourself an exile's bag-
gage, and go into exile by day in their sight. You shall go like an exile from your place to
another place in their sight. Perhaps they will understand, though[a] they are a rebellious
house. 4You shall bring out your baggage by day in their sight, as baggage for exile, and
you shall go out yourself at evening in their sight, as those do who must go into exile.
5In their sight dig through the wall, and bring your baggage out through it. 6In their
sight you shall lift the baggage upon your shoulder and carry it out at dusk. You shall
cover your face that you may not see the land, for I have made you a sign for the house
of Israel."*

*7And I did as I was commanded. I brought out my baggage by day, as baggage for exile,
and in the evening I dug through the wall with my own hands. I brought out my baggage
at dusk, carrying it on my shoulder in their sight.*

*8In the morning the word of the Lord came to me: 9"Son of man, has not the house of
Israel, the rebellious house, said to you, 'What are you doing?' 10Say to them, 'Thus says
the Lord God: This oracle concerns[b] the prince in Jerusalem and all the house of Israel
who are in it.'[c] 11Say, 'I am a sign for you: as I have done, so shall it be done to them.
They shall go into exile, into captivity.' 12And the prince who is among them shall lift
his baggage upon his shoulder at dusk, and shall go out. They shall dig through the wall
to bring him out through it. He shall cover his face, that he may not see the land with his
eyes. 13And I will spread my net over him, and he shall be taken in my snare. And I will
bring him to Babylon, the land of the Chaldeans, yet he shall not see it, and he shall die
there. 14And I will scatter toward every wind all who are around him, his helpers and all
his troops, and I will unsheathe the sword after them. 15And they shall know that I am
the Lord, when I disperse them among the nations and scatter them among the countries.
16But I will let a few of them escape from the sword, from famine and pestilence, that they
may declare all their abominations among the nations where they go, and may know that
I am the Lord."*

*17And the word of the Lord came to me: 18"Son of man, eat your bread with quaking,
and drink water with trembling and with anxiety. 19And say to the people of the land,
Thus says the Lord God concerning the inhabitants of Jerusalem in the land of Israel:
They shall eat their bread with anxiety, and drink water in dismay. In this way her land
will be stripped of all it contains, on account of the violence of all those who dwell in it.
20And the inhabited cities shall be laid waste, and the land shall become a desolation; and
you shall know that I am the Lord."*

*21And the word of the Lord came to me: 22"Son of man, what is this proverb that
you*[d] *have about the land of Israel, saying, 'The days grow long, and every vision comes
to nothing'? 23Tell them therefore, 'Thus says the Lord God: I will put an end to this
proverb, and they shall no more use it as a proverb in Israel.' But say to them, The days
are near, and the fulfillment*[e] *of every vision. 24For there shall be no more any false vision
or flattering divination within the house of Israel. 25For I am the Lord; I will speak the
word that I will speak, and it will be performed. It will no longer be delayed, but in your
days, O rebellious house, I will speak the word and perform it, declares the Lord God."*

*26And the word of the Lord came to me: 27"Son of man, behold, they of the house of
Israel say, 'The vision that he sees is for many days from now, and he prophesies of times
far off.' 28Therefore say to them, Thus says the Lord God: None of my words will be de-
layed any longer, but the word that I speak will be performed, declares the Lord God."*

a Or *will see that* **b** Or *This burden is* **c** Hebrew *in the midst of them* **d** The Hebrew for *you* is plural **e** Hebrew *word*

Overview: Ezekiel continues his prophecy against the rebellious house of God. He prepares for himself an exile's baggage. By day and night he is to go about from place to place as those do who must go into exile. And yet the rebellious house fails to believe what they see. Our commentators observe that this is the mark of the hypocrite who closes his eyes and ears to the light and truth around him. The hypocrite's defiance renders him ignorant. Furthermore, Ezekiel's actions are judgment against those who remain in Jerusalem but comfort for those who reside in Babylon.

There is also a pastoral lesson to be learned from Ezekiel's example. He receives the word of the Lord and obediently proclaims it. Even if there appears little or no fruit for our labors, we are called to be faithful and obedient to God's word.

Finally, our commentators agree that the "prince" spoken against is Zedekiah; a prophecy fulfilled in Jeremiah 52.

Israel's Defiance. John Calvin: Here God shows that the Israelites were not able to hide their error, as if they had sinned unintentionally. Instead that they could neither hear nor see he attributes to their stubbornness. And this should be noted carefully, because most hypocrites, when found guilty, grasp for this hiding place, that they slipped through error or ignorance. On the contrary, however, God here proclaims that the Israelites were blind and deaf, showing that their blindness was voluntary. So, when unbelievers claim that they have not been enlightened by the Lord, it will indeed be conceded that they are blind and deaf. Still often it is necessary to go beyond this, since their stubbornness is the fountain of their blindness and deafness. And God does blind them, because they refuse to accept the light offered to them. In fact they plug their ears. Ezekiel 1.[1]

[1]CTS 22:389 (CO 18:254).

A Rebellious House. William Greenhill: Ezekiel, having been in a vision at Jerusalem, saw and heard many remarkable things, which he declared to them of the captivity. Here the word of the Lord came afresh to him, and he is put on doing those things that might convince Zedekiah and others of the sad judgments coming on them.

. . . It is a question to whom these words of the Lord do refer, "You dwell in the midst of a rebellious house." Our prophet was in Babylon, and before the captives there; he was to remove in their sight, and this was not to give them hopes of any speedy return out of Babylon but to quiet their disturbed minds. For these typical actions of the prophet in carrying out his stuff and digging through the wall, etc., have a double aspect, one toward them at Jerusalem, to evidence to them that their captivity was at hand, another toward those already in captivity, which was to comfort them, in letting them see what heavy judgments they had escaped, being safe there in Babylon, though burdened with some difficulties. An Exposition of Ezekiel.[2]

Preachers Must Trust God Always. John Calvin: [L]et us learn from this passage, that even if the outcome does not show our labor that we devoted to God, still we must go on. This lesson is extremely helpful, because when God charges us with some task, we argue with ourselves about what its result will be. And so all our enthusiasm is spent up, for unless we determine a favorable result, it is hardly pleasing to us to even lift a finger. Accordingly, because we are always too conscientious about the fruit of our labor, this passage should be carefully noted. For when God sends his prophet, he also adds if perhaps they should listen (v. 3). Whatever kind of task it might be, it is subject to God. Even if we accomplish nothing through our labor, still God desires obedience. Ezekiel 1.[3]

The Prince in Jerusalem. William Greenhill: "The prince" (Ezek 12:10). It was Zedekiah, a wicked and timorous king. The Hebrew means either he is "exalted" above the people or should ease and lighten the grievances of the people, as in Exodus 18:22. But if they grow tyrannical and impose heavy burdens on the people, the Lord has a burden for them. As here Zedekiah must dig through the wall, carry forth on his shoulder, flee, etc. This you may see fulfilled in Jeremah 52:7-11, where you have his flight mentioned, the Chaldeans' pursuit and apprehension of him, his carrying to Riblah, where his eyes were put out, and after to Babylon, where he died. An Exposition of Ezekiel.[4]

King Zedekiah. John Mayer: After all things are said to this point and done to awaken the Jews from sleeping securely in their sins, as from whom stupendous judgments were not far off, now because they were nothing moved by all this, the Lord makes his prophet a sign portending their going into captivity. Even the best of them shall go, their prince and King Zedekiah, whom he shows should be glad to dig through the wall in the night, and so to pass away with some of his precious stuff, carrying it on his shoulders, which was a base thing for a king to do, and yet doing so, he should not escape but be taken and his eyes being put out carried into Babylon, which is applied in that he says that he should go into the Chaldeans' country, and yet not see that land, which the history shows to have come to pass accordingly. For he was taken and brought before the king of Babylon, as he was fleeing away, and having his eyes put out he was carried there to end his days in misery. Thus he is said to have been taken in God's snare because the Chaldeans came and took him by the secret moving of them by his

[2]*Exposition*, 288. [3]CTS 22:391 (CO 18:256). [4]*Exposition*, 290.

power to do so. COMMENTARY UPON ALL THE PROPHETS.[5]

GOD'S HAND AND WORD ALWAYS JOINED. JOHN CALVIN: [T]he plunge from this security to open contempt of God is easy. Those who imagine themselves to be at peace and without danger, because God patiently delays his judgments, essentially think he is too caught up with his own leisure to pay attention to human affairs. Therefore, let us guard ourselves against Satan's snares, not only shuddering at the ugly blasphemy that the prophet speaks of, but as soon as God threatens us, let us expect his judgment. We should not promise ourselves a long period of escape, that might paralyze us, so that no fear remains in us. . . . [G]od certainly does not speak in vain, because he does not contradict himself. It will happen that people lie or vainly claim to do something that they are not able to do or change their plans. Nothing of the sort should be imagined of God. His hand is always in agreement with his word. EZEKIEL 1.[6]

[5]*Prophets,* 402. [6]CTS 22:414 (CO 18:271-272).

13:1-23 FALSE PROPHETS CONDEMNED

1The word of the LORD came to me: 2"Son of man, prophesy against the prophets of
Israel, who are prophesying, and say to those who prophesy from their own hearts: 'Hear
the word of the LORD!' 3Thus says the Lord GOD, Woe to the foolish prophets who fol-
low their own spirit, and have seen nothing! 4Your prophets have been like jackals among
ruins, O Israel. 5You have not gone up into the breaches, or built up a wall for the house
of Israel, that it might stand in battle in the day of the LORD. 6They have seen false vi-
sions and lying divinations. They say, 'Declares the LORD,' when the LORD has not sent
them, and yet they expect him to fulfill their word. 7Have you not seen a false vision and
uttered a lying divination, whenever you have said, 'Declares the LORD,' although I have
not spoken?" 8Therefore thus says the Lord GOD: "Because you have uttered falsehood
and seen lying visions, therefore behold, I am against you, declares the Lord GOD. 9My
hand will be against the prophets who see false visions and who give lying divinations.
They shall not be in the council of my people, nor be enrolled in the register of the house
of Israel, nor shall they enter the land of Israel. And you shall know that I am the Lord
GOD. 10Precisely because they have misled my people, saying, 'Peace,' when there is no
peace, and because, when the people build a wall, these prophets smear it with whitewash,[a]
11say to those who smear it with whitewash that it shall fall! There will be a deluge of
rain, and you, O great hailstones, will fall, and a stormy wind break out. 12And when
the wall falls, will it not be said to you, 'Where is the coating with which you smeared it?'
13Therefore thus says the Lord GOD: I will make a stormy wind break out in my wrath,
and there shall be a deluge of rain in my anger, and great hailstones in wrath to make a
full end. 14And I will break down the wall that you have smeared with whitewash, and

bring it down to the ground, so that its foundation will be laid bare. When it falls, you shall perish in the midst of it, and you shall know that I am the Lord. [15]Thus will I spend my wrath upon the wall and upon those who have smeared it with whitewash, and I will say to you, The wall is no more, nor those who smeared it, [16]the prophets of Israel who prophesied concerning Jerusalem and saw visions of peace for her, when there was no peace, declares the Lord God.

[17]"And you, son of man, set your face against the daughters of your people, who prophesy out of their own minds. Prophesy against them [18]and say, Thus says the Lord God: Woe to the women who sew magic bands upon all wrists, and make veils for the heads of persons of every stature, in the hunt for souls! Will you hunt down souls belonging to my people and keep your own souls alive? [19]You have profaned me among my people for handfuls of barley and for pieces of bread, putting to death souls who should not die and keeping alive souls who should not live, by your lying to my people, who listen to lies.

[20]"Therefore thus says the Lord God: Behold, I am against your magic bands with which you hunt the souls like birds, and I will tear them from your arms, and I will let the souls whom you hunt go free, the souls like birds. [21]Your veils also I will tear off and deliver my people out of your hand, and they shall be no more in your hand as prey, and you shall know that I am the Lord. [22]Because you have disheartened the righteous falsely, although I have not grieved him, and you have encouraged the wicked, that he should not turn from his evil way to save his life, [23]therefore you shall no more see false visions nor practice divination. I will deliver my people out of your hand. And you shall know that I am the Lord."

a Or *plaster; also verses 11, 14, 15*

Overview: In the previous chapter, Ezekiel prophesied against the king and the people. He now speaks against the false prophets and prophetesses of Israel who prophesy from their own hearts. These false prophets are led by their own thoughts, seek to deceive the people with their lies and speak always against God's word. The people, however, are not excused for ignorantly following these false prophets. God always sends true prophets, and therefore God's light always remains among the people.

Our commentators make a number of observations to distinguish true and false prophets. False prophets speak the thoughts of their own heart, never preach repentance and always encourage sin. True prophets speak what God speaks to them, always kill with the law and make alive with the gospel.

False Prophets. William Greenhill: The former chapter concerned the king and the people; this concerns only the false prophets and prophetesses, who taking on them that office, were led by their own spirits and deceived the people with vain visions and lying divinations, to accomplish their own ends. Against these does the Lord set our prophet Ezekiel on work to prophesy severely. In the chapter you have two general parts: a prophecy against false prophets in the first sixteen verses [Ezek 13:1-16] and a prophecy against women prophets from the seventeenth verse to the end [Ezek 13:17-23]. An Exposition of Ezekiel.[1]

No Excuse to Follow False Prophets. John Calvin: He speaks of the exiled proph-

[1]*Exposition*, 297.

ets, as will be clear from the context. Among the captives there were those who hid behind the name of God, boasting that they were gifted with the prophetic spirit, while in fact they were forcing themselves into the office, vainly boasting in their lies. However, the end they declared promised the people a swift return, so that they would win favor with the public. So, when the people heard that after three years they will return, they easily allowed themselves to be deceived by such charms. Even though God burns furiously with anger against those impostors, he does not therefore single out their sin, absolving the people or even diminishing their fault. In fact the people are not even able to object that they were deceived by those lies, because they knowingly and willingly threw themselves into the snares. They were not abandoned by the true prophets. God had even distinguished his servants from false prophets by well-known signs, so that no one could have been mistaken except willfully (Deut 13:3). But in the midst of light they were blind. Therefore, God let them be deceived. But that was the just reward of their pride, because they were not able to subject themselves to God and his servants. COMMENTARIES ON EZEKIEL.[2]

FALSE PROPHETS AND FOXES. JOHN MAYER: Of all beasts the fox is the most subtle and dangerous for getting into and hurting the vineyard through any breach he finds in the hedge or wall. For this reason, false prophets among the Jews are compared with foxes, and such they are to the church of God in any place. The breach is made by sin. This the true prophet seeks to make up by exhorting and stirring to repentance. By earnest prayer to God he stands in the day of battle to keep out enemies from coming to destroy it, as Moses by prayer is said to have stood in the gap. But these false prophets, on the contrary, craftily mislead the people, whereby they were brought into danger, and gaps were made instead of being hedged up, for which Ezekiel inveighs against them, as pernicious beasts, and such are also called foxes. COMMENTARY UPON ALL THE PROPHETS.[3]

DISCERNING TRUE AND FALSE PROPHETS. JOHN CALVIN: Here, as I have said, we may readily decide at once who are the true and who the false prophets: the Spirit of God pronounces every one who prophesies from his own heart to be an impostor. Hence nothing else remains but for the prophets faithfully to utter whatever the Spirit has dictated to them. Whoever, therefore, has no sure testimony to his vision and cannot truly testify that he speaks from God's mouth and by the revelation of his Spirit, although he may boast in the title of prophet, yet he is only an impostor. For God here rejects all who speak from their own heart. And hence we also gather the extreme vanity of the human mind: for God puts a perpetual distinction between the human mind and the revelation of his Spirit. If this is so, it follows that what people utter of themselves is a perverse fiction, because the Spirit of God claims to himself alone, as we have said, the office of showing what is true and right. . . .

Hence there is no doubt that these pretenders of whom Ezekiel speaks were held in great esteem, and so, when swollen with bombast, they puffed forth surprising wisdom; but meanwhile the Holy Spirit shortly pronounces them fools: for whatever pleases the world under the mask of wisdom, we know to be mere folly before God. COMMENTARIES ON EZEKIEL.[4]

TRUE AND FALSE PROPHETS. WILLIAM GREENHILL: See here who are true prophets and who are false. The word of the Lord came to Ezekiel; it came not to them. The true prophets saw visions; the false saw nothing.

[2]CTS 23:5-6 (CO 18:272-273). [3]*Prophets*, 403. [4]CTS 23:7-8 (CO 18:274).

The true prophets were moved by the Spirit of God; the false by their own spirits. Out of their own hearts came what the false prophets delivered; out of heaven what the true prophets delivered. God spoke by the true prophets; Satan by the false—he is a lying spirit in the mouth of all the false prophets (1 Kings 22:22). An Exposition of Ezekiel.[5]

False Prophets Do Not Preach Repentance. John Calvin: Hence, when true prophets exhort sinners to hope and predict God's freeness to pardon, they likewise discourse about penitence; they do not indulge sinners but rouse them, nay, wound them sharply with a sense of God's anger, so as in some way to stir them up, since God's mercy is set before us for that end, that by it we may seek life. Hence we must be dead in ourselves; but false prophets sever between the two and divide God, as it were, in half, since they speak only of his freeness to forgive and declare his clemency to be set before all, while they are profoundly silent about repentance. Now, therefore, we see why the prophet here reproves these traitors who abused the name of God, since they made the people to hope (Ezek 13:6). Without hope, indeed, the sinner could not be animated to seek God: but they promised peace, as he will say directly, when there was no peace. Commentaries on Ezekiel.[6]

False Prophets Encourage Sin. William Greenhill: These [false] prophets did not oppose the sins of the people, convince them of their idolatry, oppression, security, hypocrisy, profaneness, etc. But they either sinned with them or winked at their sins and so went not up "into the gap" (Ezek 13:5) to keep out the severe judgments of God from crowding in on them. They should have called the people to repentance, declared the judgments of God to have been at hand, interceded mightily with the Lord for them and if possible have prevented judgment. But these things they did not. An Exposition of Ezekiel.[7]

True Prophets Kill and Make Alive. John Calvin: We have said before that by this mark the true and righteous servants of God were distinguished from impostors. For the servants of God, who faithfully discharge the duty enjoined on them, kill and make alive: for God's word is life and brings health to lost humankind but is a savor of death to death in those who perish, as Paul says (2 Cor 2:15-16). Hence it is true that prophets who faithfully and properly discharge their duty both kill and make alive, but they give life to the souls that are to be freed from death and slay the souls that are devoted to destruction; for they denounce eternal death to all unbelievers unless they repent; and whatever they bind on earth is also bound in heaven (Mt 18:18). Their teaching, therefore, is effective for destruction, as also Paul elsewhere teaches. We have at hand, says he, vengeance against every high thing that exalts itself against Christ (2 Cor 10:5-6). Hence honest teachers are armed by God's vengeance against all unbelievers who remain obstinate, but they convey life to those who repent, since they are messengers of reconciliation; nay, they reconcile people to God when they offer Christ to them as our peace, and by whom the Father is propitious to us (Eph 2:16). When false prophets desire to rival God's servants, they omit the principal part, namely, faith and repentance; hence it happens that they proclaim life to souls already adjudged to destruction; for they give life to the reprobate who are hardened in contempt of God by their flatteries; for they do not require of people either faith or penitence but only a reward. Hence also it happens that they slay the souls that ought not to die, namely, because nothing is prouder or more cruel than

[5]*Exposition*, 298. [6]CTS 23:13 (CO 18:278). [7]*Exposition*, 301.

these false prophets. For they fulminate according to their pleasure and sink the whole world even to the lowest hell when no hope of profit appears. Commentaries on Ezekiel.[8]

Satan Deceives as an Angel of Light. John Calvin: Since, then, certain women were gifted with the prophetic spirit, Satan, according to his custom, abused this under a false pretense (Ezek 13:17-18). We know that he always emulates God and transforms himself into an angel of light, because if he were to show himself openly, all would instantly flee from him: hence he uses God's name deceptively, to ingratiate himself among the simple and incautious. And he not only sends forth false prophets to scatter abroad their lies and impostures, but he turns even females to the same injurious use.

Here we see how anxiously we ought to guard against any corruption that may creep in to contaminate the pure gifts of God. But this contest seems not to have been sufficiently honorable to the servant of God, for it was almost a matter of shame when they engaged with women. We know that those who desire praise for their bravery do not willingly engage with unequal antagonists who have no strength to resist, since there is no praise in a victory when it is too easy; so also Ezekiel could put away from him this undertaking, since it was unworthy of the prophetic office. Hence it appears that God's servants cannot faithfully discharge the duties assigned to them unless they strive to remove all impediments. This then is the condition of all those to whom God assigns the office of teaching, that they may oppose all false doctrines and errors and never consider or wish for great praise from their victory: it should suffice them to assert God's truth against all Satan's devices. Commentaries on Ezekiel.[9]

Prophetesses. William Greenhill: "The daughters of your people" (Ezek 13:17). Some would understand by these women, men prophets who were weak and womanish, without courage, constancy and prudence; but we have no cause to take the words in that sense. Our prophet had spoken of men prophets before and now is directed of God to another distinct subject, and that is, the women prophets, who are called daughters of his people; this cannot belong to the men.

. . . This is an old practice of Satan to trouble the church: as with false prophets, so with false prophetesses. God raised up women prophets to honor that sex and to help his people. The devil raises up women to spread lies, to deceive and hurt the people and to gain by that sex the more to his kingdom. An Exposition of Ezekiel.[10]

[8]CTS 23:34 (10:292-293). [9]CTS 23:28 (CO 18:288-289). [10]*Exposition*, 310-12.

14:1-23 IDOLATERS AND JUDGMENT

1Then certain of the elders of Israel came to me and sat before me. 2And the word of the
Lord came to me: 3"Son of man, these men have taken their idols into their hearts, and
set the stumbling block of their iniquity before their faces. Should I indeed let myself be
consulted by them? 4Therefore speak to them and say to them, Thus says the Lord God:
Any one of the house of Israel who takes his idols into his heart and sets the stumbling
block of his iniquity before his face, and yet comes to the prophet, I the Lord will answer
him as he comes with the multitude of his idols, 5that I may lay hold of the hearts of the
house of Israel, who are all estranged from me through their idols.
6"Therefore say to the house of Israel, Thus says the Lord God: Repent and turn away
from your idols, and turn away your faces from all your abominations. 7For any one of the
house of Israel, or of the strangers who sojourn in Israel, who separates himself from me,
taking his idols into his heart and putting the stumbling block of his iniquity before his
face, and yet comes to a prophet to consult me through him, I the Lord will answer him
myself. 8And I will set my face against that man; I will make him a sign and a byword and
cut him off from the midst of my people, and you shall know that I am the Lord. 9And if
the prophet is deceived and speaks a word, I, the Lord, have deceived that prophet, and
I will stretch out my hand against him and will destroy him from the midst of my people
Israel. 10And they shall bear their punishment[a]—the punishment of the prophet and the
punishment of the inquirer shall be alike—11that the house of Israel may no more go
astray from me, nor defile themselves anymore with all their transgressions, but that they
may be my people and I may be their God, declares the Lord God."
12And the word of the Lord came to me: 13"Son of man, when a land sins against me by
acting faithlessly, and I stretch out my hand against it and break its supply[b] of bread and
send famine upon it, and cut off from it man and beast, 14even if these three men, Noah,
Daniel, and Job, were in it, they would deliver but their own lives by their righteousness,
declares the Lord God. 15"If I cause wild beasts to pass through the land, and they ravage
it, and it be made desolate, so that no one may pass through because of the beasts, 16even
if these three men were in it, as I live, declares the Lord God, they would deliver neither
sons nor daughters. They alone would be delivered, but the land would be desolate.
17"Or if I bring a sword upon that land and say, Let a sword pass through the land,
and I cut off from it man and beast, 18though these three men were in it, as I live, declares
the Lord God, they would deliver neither sons nor daughters, but they alone would be
delivered.
19"Or if I send a pestilence into that land and pour out my wrath upon it with blood,
to cut off from it man and beast, 20even if Noah, Daniel, and Job were in it, as I live,
declares the Lord God, they would deliver neither son nor daughter. They would deliver
but their own lives by their righteousness.
21"For thus says the Lord God: How much more when I send upon Jerusalem my four
disastrous acts of judgment, sword, famine, wild beasts, and pestilence, to cut off from
it man and beast! 22But behold, some survivors will be left in it, sons and daughters who

will be brought out; behold, when they come out to you, and you see their ways and their deeds, you will be consoled for the disaster that I have brought upon Jerusalem, for all that I have brought upon it. [23]*They will console you, when you see their ways and their deeds, and you shall know that I have not done without cause all that I have done in it, declares the Lord God."*

a Or *iniquity;* three times in this verse **b** Hebrew *staff*

Overview: Ezekiel condemns the elders who have set up idols in their hearts. Our commentators note that the heart is the seat of a person's faith or idolatry. Those who cling to idols will be punished. God's strong words of judgment against the rulers, people and prophets through Ezekiel were to bring them to repentance. They were to turn from their idols to God. Our commentators note that God's reason for humbling us and speaking judgment against us is only ever to bring us to repentance and salvation. The question arises if repentance is our work or a gift of God. The answer is that God grants what he commands. Neither repentance nor faith is possible through human industry; they are both the work of the Holy Spirit.

The second part of the chapter continues the unavoidable judgment against Jerusalem. The question arises why God names Noah, Daniel and Job and not others. Although many reasons are proposed, all our commentators agree that the holiness of these men was well known, and yet even they could not prevent the destruction of those around them.

Finally, our commentators seek to explain what is meant by someone being saved on account of his own righteousness. Surely no one is saved on account of his own righteousness; such a claim would stand in opposition to the rest of Scripture (Ps 143:2; Rom 3:10). The answers proposed by our commentators are diverse. One commentator resists suggesting that their righteousness is by faith and looks instead to their works; another affirms their faith but locates their righteousness in sanctification; and another affirms the grace and mercy of God.

14:1-11 *Idolaters*

God, Idols and the Heart. Martin Luther: A god is that to which we look for all good and in which we find refuge in every time of need. To have a god is nothing else than to trust and believe him with our whole heart. As I have often said, the trust and faith of the heart alone make both God and an idol. If your faith and trust are right, then your God is the true God. On the other hand, if your trust is false and wrong, then you have not the true God. For these two belong together, faith and God. That to which your heart clings and entrusts itself is, I say, really your God. Large Catechism.[1]

Idols in Their Heart. John Calvin: First, he says they have set up idols in their hearts; by which words he means that they were addicted to superstition, so that idols obtained a high rank in their hearts; as Paul exhorts the faithful, that the peace of God which passes all understanding may obtain the rule in their hearts (Phil 4:7; Col 3:15); so on the other hand the prophet says that these people had given supreme sway to idols. And again an implied comparison must be remarked between God and idols. For God has erected the seat of his empire in our hearts, but when we set up idols, we necessarily endeavor to overthrow

[1]Tappert 365:2-3.

God's throne and to reduce his power to nothing. Hence the most heinous crime of sacrilege is here shown in those people who caused idols to rise above their hearts. For hence it follows that all their senses were drowned in their superstitions. Commentaries on Ezekiel.[2]

Idolaters Must Be Removed. Hans Denck: Therefore, they must be laid waste totally; like a field which one no longer remembers, they must be forgotten. They must be removed from within as well as from without, as the Lord says to the prophet in Ezekiel 14:2ff. These people who came to you (probably to hear the word of the Lord) carry their idols in their hearts, and they themselves caused the offense of their transgression. Therefore I will turn my face in anger toward them. Anyone, however, who turns about and casts the idols out of his heart pleases God. Reflections on Micah.[3]

God Seeks Our Repentance. John Calvin: Now God shows why he had threatened the false prophets and the whole people so severely, namely, that they should repent (Ezek 14:6); for the object of God's rigor is that, when terrified by his judgments, we should return into the way. Now, therefore, he exhorts them to repentance. Hence we gather the useful lesson, that whenever God inspires us with fear, he has no other intention than to humble us and thus to provide for our salvation, when he reproves and threatens us so strongly by his prophets, and in truth is verbally angry with us, that he may really spare us. Commentaries on Ezekiel.[4]

Repentance. William Greenhill: Is not repentance the work and gift of God? If so, how is it that people are commanded to repent? Answer: Repentance is of the Lord (Acts 11:18). Ministers must meekly instruct those that oppose, if God will give them repentance (2 Tim 2:25). It is also the gift of Christ. He is "exalted to be a prince and savior, to give repentance to Israel" (Acts 5:31). Yet God commands people to repent because they may do something that they may repent; as, first, seriously consider the nature of their sin, what circumstances it is clothed with, what aggravations it admits, how crimson and scarlet it is, against what light, mercies, means, engagements, etc. Apprehension of sin under false notions of profit or pleasure induces to it, and consideration of sin in its own nature helps to repent of it and abhor it. . . .

God gives what he commands. In Ezekiel 11:19, he had promised to "take the stony heart out of their flesh and to give them a heart of flesh," and therefore here might command them to repent. In Mark 1:15, "Repent ye, and believe the gospel." Neither of these were in their power; they might as well create new heavens and new earths as do these acts; but God gives and works them both in the hearts of whom he pleases (2 Tim 2:25; Phil 1:29). Neither repentance nor faith is natural or any acquired habits by the industry and acts of people, but they are the efficacious work of the Spirit in and on the heart. God and Christ do work repentance by the Spirit, and therefore it is attributed to them and denied to be in the power of people (2 Cor 3:5; Phil 2:13). Commands argue no power and free will in people to repent. An Exposition of Ezekiel.[5]

14:12-23 *Judgment Inescapable*

Noah, Daniel and Job. John Calvin: It is sometimes asked why Noah, Daniel and Job are named, rather than Abraham, Jacob or David, or any others. Those who wish to be precise guess various comments; namely, because Noah could not preserve the old world from the deluge, but only his sons and their wives. But this example does not suit; and as to

[2]CTS 23:45-46 (CO 18:300-301). [3]*Writings*, 54-55. [4]CTS 23:50 (CO 18:303). [5]*Exposition*, 317.

the others, they say that Job did not preserve his own sons, since they were all consumed by the lightning. But the same thing happened to others. Thus Abraham was the common father of the people, and even he could not snatch his posterity from the wrath of God; nay, Jeremiah describes Rachel, though dead, weeping for her children and refusing consolation because none of them survived (Jer 31:15). We see, then, that this is cold. Others say that these three men had experienced three different kinds of life; that Noah, living before the deluge, had seen the horrible devastation of the whole earth, and yet the renovation of the world had followed; they say, also, that Job had flourished in prosperity and then was deprived of all his goods and his children, and was so defiled by disease and filth as to be rather a carcass than a living man, and yet he was restored like a captive from the enemy's hand. Daniel, again, had lived at Jerusalem, had been taken captive and had lived there in exile; that he at length saw the beginning of the restoration of the people when that sudden change happened and the Babylonian monarchy passed to the Persians. These things, at the first glance, seem to be clever; but whatever is affected is always cold and tame. Ezekiel here mentions these three men, simply because they first occurred to him. . . . Three men, then, are placed here, whose holiness was celebrated. Daniel was then living; the others had been dead many ages ago, but the integrity of them all was universally manifest. It is then as if he had said, even if those should come who either are or have been most perfect among people, yet they would avail nothing in interceding for a land already devoted to destruction. Commentaries on Ezekiel.[6]

The Naming of Noah, Daniel and Job. John Mayer: It may be inquired why these three are here named more than any other? Calvin says that some give this reason that these three were famous for righteousness at three several times: Noah in the old world, Daniel in the time of captivity, being also now living, and Job being one of another country eminent above all among the nations. Others because Job could not save his sons or daughters by his piety, nor Daniel the Jews, among whom he was carried away captive into Babylon, neither could Noah save the old world from drowning. But he thinks nothing else to be meant in specifying these, but only in general, if some of the most gracious men who ever lived were among them, such as these three were, whom he named rather than others, as they came first to his mind, they should not profit such incorrigible sinners as they were.

I rather conceive because it is the Lord that thus speaks that there was some special reason of this his specification. It might be because these three men more than others of great note lived in times of proving what might be done in that case, which is here in agitation, and yet the old world was not the more delivered for Noah's righteousness, nor Job's children for his, nor the Jews that went into captivity in the third year of Jehoiakim for Daniel's. Commentary upon All the Prophets.[7]

Why Noah, Daniel and Job? William Greenhill: Some make great inquiry why these three men should be mentioned rather than others, and they give in answer the following. It is thought they are named because they could not divert God's wrath from the people of their times by their holiness and prayers. Noah could not keep off the flood, nor Job the sad things that befell himself and his, nor Daniel the captivity. Others think they are named because they freed others in imminent danger in their times. Noah saved his family from the flood; Job prayed for his friends, and they were spared; Daniel preserved the magicians and wise men.

But rather they are named because they were men of great holiness, exercised with

[6]CTS 23:72-73 (CO 18:319-320). [7]*Prophets*, 407-8.

great trials, and so the more fervent in prayer. "And what if these men, who were so acceptable to me, had so much interest in me, and often prevailed with me, should pray for you, yet they should do nothing for your deliverance by their prayers." These were men in great afflictions, and affliction is the whetstone of prayer, the bellows to blow up that fire. AN EXPOSITION OF EZEKIEL.[8]

RIGHTEOUSNESS AND SALVATION. JOHN CALVIN: But the prophet's saying, they should be saved on account of their own righteousness, seems absurd, for no one can be found whose righteousness can stand before God's tribunal; for if God was to reason with people, everyone must be found guilty, as the Scripture also often teaches and experience most fully convinces us. Here the prophet seems to extol too much the merit of works when he attributes the person's freedom to his righteousness. But the solution is easy; namely, this righteousness of which mention is made ought not to be separated from gratuitous pardon that reconciles people to God, so that their sins are not imputed to them, for as to some saying that they were justified by faith, this does not forward the inquiry; and besides that, it is forced. By their own righteousness shall they free their own souls, that is, say they, by their faith. But when God addresses Noah (Gen 7:1) and says that he was found just through his piety, he does not mean that he was endued with faith; this would be of little consequence. There is no doubt, then, that he commends sanctity and integrity in his servant; so also in this passage, under the word righteousness or justice, he implies the fear of God, in which all virtues are founded, and chastity and temperance, and whatever belongs to the rule of living holy and justly. But meanwhile this derogates nothing from the righteousness of faith; for the faithful are reckoned just before God, and their works are also reckoned just—not by any inherent merit—not because they bring any perfection of that kind before God that may conciliate his favor and in which they can stand; but because God pardons them indulgently through his own paternal clemency and so approves their righteousness, which otherwise might be deservedly rejected. COMMENTARIES ON EZEKIEL.[9]

RIGHTEOUSNESS AND SALVATION. JOHN MAYER: But what does he mean by adding, he shall save his own soul by his righteousness? Shall anyone have his soul saved for his own righteousness, or by faith only? Solution: Although a person is saved by faith only, yet no person is truly faithful who is not also upright in his heart and life, which is his righteousness and is by reason of his faith accepted, as if he were perfect. He is therefore worthy to be saved, as it is said of Abraham that he believed and it was counted to him for righteousness. But this does not happen without his being upright, to show that none are thus accepted, although believers, except they also walk before God and be upright, as was said to Abraham, and as James reasons at large. COMMENTARY UPON ALL THE PROPHETS.[10]

HOLINESS NO MERIT TO SALVATION. WILLIAM GREENHILL: You must not think that their holiness or righteousness merited deliverance of themselves. A person's goodness is nothing to God; all he can do is debt, and the best he does is imperfect, which is no motive of God's will. Deliverance and salvation are acts of grace and favor. "By grace are you saved; and that not of yourselves: it is the gift of God, not of works, lest any should boast" (Eph 2:8-9). God has out of his free grace promised to do great things for his elect, for the godly. When he does this for them, it is not because they deserve it or because they are godly, but because he has promised. AN EXPOSITION OF EZEKIEL.[11]

[8]*Exposition*, 325-26. [9]CTS 23:73-74 (CO 18:320). [10]*Prophets*, 408. [11]*Exposition*, 326.

15:1-8 JERUSALEM, A USELESS VINE

[1]And the word of the Lord came to me: [2]"Son of man, how does the wood of the vine surpass any wood, the vine branch that is among the trees of the forest? [3]Is wood taken from it to make anything? Do people take a peg from it to hang any vessel on it? [4]Behold, it is given to the fire for fuel. When the fire has consumed both ends of it, and the middle of it is charred, is it useful for anything? [5]Behold, when it was whole, it was used for nothing. How much less, when the fire has consumed it and it is charred, can it ever be used for anything! [6]Therefore thus says the Lord God: Like the wood of the vine among the trees of the forest, which I have given to the fire for fuel, so have I given up the inhabitants of Jerusalem. [7]And I will set my face against them. Though they escape from the fire, the fire shall yet consume them, and you will know that I am the Lord, when I set my face against them. [8]And I will make the land desolate, because they have acted faithlessly, declares the Lord God."

Overview: The destruction of Jerusalem is foretold again in this chapter but this time through the parable of the useless vine. Our commentators note the fittingness of the vine to represent Israel. The vine compared with other trees is a lowly thing, unable to support itself, often trodden underfoot. Likewise is Israel compared with other nations. What made Israel greater than other nations was that God had bestowed privileges and benefits on it. Moreover, the vine is a useless thing when torn from the soil. Its wood is of no value, and therefore it is simply cast into the fire. From this parable about Israel, we gain a lesson for today. We are nothing by nature but only by God's gratuitous grace and mercy.

Parables and Allegories. William Greenhill: In this short chapter, under the similitude of a useless and fruitless vine tree is set forth the condition of the inhabitants of Jerusalem; that is, fit for nothing but the fire, and so are they fit only for judgment. . . .

The ministers of God have warrant to use similitudes in their teaching of the people. God himself does it here. He brings in a parable of the vine tree and allegorizes on it. The Scriptures are frequent in parables and allegories. Christ was much in parables; they help memory, if familiar and known. They convince more fully than plain speeches. An Exposition of Ezekiel.[1]

The Parable. John Mayer: This chapter tends to do nothing else but aggravate the misery of Jerusalem, which should shortly be burned down with fire. This is shown by a comparison taken from a vine, which, after being cut down, is good for nothing else than to be burned. Therefore, outside of being cut down and burned, no good use can be made of it anymore. And the Lord does thus debase Jerusalem and the Jews in opposition to their pride and confidence in this, that they were God's peculiar people.

And he proceeds by comparing them standing yet in the vineyard, as it were with other trees of the wood, that is, with heathen nations. For what is a vine to another tree, either oak or cedar, but only in respect of the

[1]*Exposition*, 329-30.

fruitfulness? Truly it is nothing, for trees grow erect and are beautiful to behold, but the vine is a crooked, low, writhen thing, unable to bear itself up from the ground unless it is supported, and so subject to be trodden underfoot and bitten and torn by cattle. So the Jews were in comparison with other nations most contemptible, especially being, as they now were, without fruit, barren of good works and full of evil. COMMENTARY UPON ALL THE PROPHETS.[2]

OUR WORTH IN GOD ALONE. JOHN CALVIN: It is certain that the vine produces very good fruit and therefore is preferred to other trees: the very flower of the vine has a most delicious scent, but the fruit that it produces proves its excellence. For the wood of the vine is without elegance and shapeless: it does not attain to any thickness; it is slender, pliable and twisted. In looking at a vine, it seems scarcely worth numbering among shrubs; if compared with trees, it clearly has no value, but in the excellence of trees something is easily acknowledged that surpasses all vines. For when we cast our eyes on a branching tree, we are struck with admiration, while the vine lies at our feet. If, therefore, a tree is compared with the wood of the vine, it will be praised for its beauty, while the vine will be despised as a low and insignificant wood. Hence God collects that the Jews were in no respect more excellent than others, unless because they are planted by himself, as he says in many places in Isaiah: "O my vine, I have planted you" (Is 5). Then in Psalm 80, he brought his vine out of Egypt and planted and propagated it even to the sea (cf. Ps 80:9-12; Jer 2:21).

Now we understand the prophet's meaning, namely, that the Jews excelled, indeed, in privileges but not in nature, nor yet by themselves but by the gratuitous kindness of God; and if other nations were compared with them, they had greater dignity than the Jews. And we know that other nations flourished in arts and wealth, in population, in warlike valor, and in other respects: the profane nations were like lofty trees that grow up and attract all eyes to themselves. But the Jews were like a vine that, being planted by God's hand, deserved more praise than the trees of the wood that were fruitless. Ezekiel now carries on the comparison at greater length: *if the vine is torn up, can its wood,* says he, *be fitted to any use?* It will not make beams or tables, or any vessels; it will not make a peg or a hook on which to hang a hat or cloak, or anything of the kind. Since, then, the wood of the vine is useless when torn from the soil and is of no use but for burning, hence the Jews are made acquainted with their condition since their excellence and worthiness depend on the mere good pleasure of God: since, as he planted them, he can pluck them up in a moment; and when they have been torn up, they will be altogether useless and will be cast into the fire, while trees are of some use. But the prophet proceeds another step: if a bundle of twigs were cast into the fire, and the two extreme parts were burned up, and the middle made dry, that scorched part would be much less useful. For since fire penetrates to the very marrow, wood, which is half consumed, is reduced to powder by the touch alone. COMMENTARIES ON EZEKIEL.[3]

A LESSON FOR US TOO. JOHN CALVIN: Now after we understand the prophet's meaning, let us learn that the Holy Spirit so addressed the Jews formerly, that this discourse might profit us in these days. We must perceive, in the first place, that we are superior to the whole world, through God's gratuitous pity, but naturally we have nothing of our own in which to boast. But if we carry ourselves haughtily, through reliance on God's gifts, this arrogance would be sacrilege, for we snatch away from God his own praise and clothe ourselves, as it were, in his spoils. But Paul, when he speaks

[2]*Prophets*, 409. [3]CTS 23:84-86 (CO 18:328-329).

of the Jews, shortly but clearly, defines both sides: Do we excel? says he (for he there makes himself one with the people). Do we excel the Gentiles? says he (Rom 3:1). By no means, for Scripture denounces us all to be sinners—all to be accursed. Since, therefore, we are children of wrath, he says, there is nothing that we can claim to ourselves over the profane Gentiles. After he has so prostrated all the pride of his own nation, he repeats again: What? Are we not superior to others? Yes, we excel in every way. For the adoption, and the worship, and the law of God and the covenant confer on us remarkable superiority, and such as we find nothing like it in the whole world. How do those things agree? That the Jews excel and are to be preferred to others, and yet that they excel in nothing! Namely, since they have nothing in themselves to cause them to despise the Gentiles or boast themselves superior. Hence their excellence is not in themselves but in God. And so, Paul here does not commend their virtues but says that they excel by gratuitous adoption, because God made his covenant with Abraham, and they were to arise from the holy nations, because he instituted a fixed line of piety among them, in promising himself to be a Father to them; nay, he determined that Christ should spring from them, who is the life and light of the world. We see, then, the former privileges of the Jews. Ours is the same in these days. As often as we are favored with God's gifts, by which we approach near him and overcome the world, we ought also to remember what we were before God took us up. Then our origin will prostrate all arrogance and prevent us from being ungrateful to God. Commentaries on Ezekiel.[4]

[4]CTS 23:91 (CO 18:331-332).

16:1-63 An Allegory of Unfaithful Jerusalem

1Again the word of the Lord came to me: 2"Son of man, make known to Jerusalem her
abominations, 3and say, Thus says the Lord God to Jerusalem: Your origin and your birth
are of the land of the Canaanites; your father was an Amorite and your mother a Hit-
tite. 4And as for your birth, on the day you were born your cord was not cut, nor were you
washed with water to cleanse you, nor rubbed with salt, nor wrapped in swaddling cloths.
5No eye pitied you, to do any of these things to you out of compassion for you, but you were
cast out on the open field, for you were abhorred, on the day that you were born.
6"And when I passed by you and saw you wallowing in your blood, I said to you in your
blood, 'Live!' I said to you in your blood, 'Live!' 7I made you flourish like a plant of the
field. And you grew up and became tall and arrived at full adornment. Your breasts were
formed, and your hair had grown; yet you were naked and bare.
8"When I passed by you again and saw you, behold, you were at the age for love, and I
spread the corner of my garment over you and covered your nakedness; I made my vow to
you and entered into a covenant with you, declares the Lord God, and you became mine.

9Then I bathed you with water and washed off your blood from you and anointed you with
oil. 10I clothed you also with embroidered cloth and shod you with fine leather. I wrapped
you in fine linen and covered you with silk.[a] 11And I adorned you with ornaments and
put bracelets on your wrists and a chain on your neck. 12And I put a ring on your nose
and earrings in your ears and a beautiful crown on your head. 13Thus you were adorned
with gold and silver, and your clothing was of fine linen and silk and embroidered cloth.
You ate fine flour and honey and oil. You grew exceedingly beautiful and advanced to
royalty. 14And your renown went forth among the nations because of your beauty, for it
was perfect through the splendor that I had bestowed on you, declares the Lord God.

15"But you trusted in your beauty and played the whore[b] because of your renown and
lavished your whorings[c] on any passerby; your beauty[d] became his. 16You took some of
your garments and made for yourself colorful shrines, and on them played the whore. The
like has never been, nor ever shall be.[e] 17You also took your beautiful jewels of my gold
and of my silver, which I had given you, and made for yourself images of men, and with
them played the whore. 18And you took your embroidered garments to cover them, and set
my oil and my incense before them. 19Also my bread that I gave you—I fed you with fine
flour and oil and honey—you set before them for a pleasing aroma; and so it was, declares
the Lord God. 20And you took your sons and your daughters, whom you had borne to me,
and these you sacrificed to them to be devoured. Were your whorings so small a matter
21that you slaughtered my children and delivered them up as an offering by fire to them?
22And in all your abominations and your whorings you did not remember the days of your
youth, when you were naked and bare, wallowing in your blood.

23"And after all your wickedness (woe, woe to you! declares the Lord God), 24you built
yourself a vaulted chamber and made yourself a lofty place in every square. 25At the head
of every street you built your lofty place and made your beauty an abomination, offering
yourself[f] to any passerby and multiplying your whoring. 26You also played the whore with
the Egyptians, your lustful neighbors, multiplying your whoring, to provoke me to anger.
27Behold, therefore, I stretched out my hand against you and diminished your allotted
portion and delivered you to the greed of your enemies, the daughters of the Philistines,
who were ashamed of your lewd behavior. 28You played the whore also with the Assyrians,
because you were not satisfied; yes, you played the whore with them, and still you were not
satisfied. 29You multiplied your whoring also with the trading land of Chaldea, and even
with this you were not satisfied.

30"How sick is your heart,[g] declares the Lord God, because you did all these things, the
deeds of a brazen prostitute, 31building your vaulted chamber at the head of every street,
and making your lofty place in every square. Yet you were not like a prostitute, because
you scorned payment. 32Adulterous wife, who receives strangers instead of her husband!
33Men give gifts to all prostitutes, but you gave your gifts to all your lovers, bribing them
to come to you from every side with your whorings. 34So you were different from other
women in your whorings. No one solicited you to play the whore, and you gave payment,
while no payment was given to you; therefore you were different.

35"Therefore, O prostitute, hear the word of the Lord: 36Thus says the Lord God,
Because your lust was poured out and your nakedness uncovered in your whorings with
your lovers, and with all your abominable idols, and because of the blood of your chil-
dren that you gave to them, 37therefore, behold, I will gather all your lovers with whom

*you took pleasure, all those you loved and all those you hated. I will gather them against
you from every side and will uncover your nakedness to them, that they may see all your
nakedness. 38And I will judge you as women who commit adultery and shed blood are
judged, and bring upon you the blood of wrath and jealousy. 39And I will give you into
their hands, and they shall throw down your vaulted chamber and break down your lofty
places. They shall strip you of your clothes and take your beautiful jewels and leave you
naked and bare. 40They shall bring up a crowd against you, and they shall stone you and
cut you to pieces with their swords. 41And they shall burn your houses and execute judg-
ments upon you in the sight of many women. I will make you stop playing the whore, and
you shall also give payment no more. 42So will I satisfy my wrath on you, and my jealousy
shall depart from you. I will be calm and will no more be angry. 43Because you have not
remembered the days of your youth, but have enraged me with all these things, therefore,
behold, I have returned your deeds upon your head, declares the Lord GOD. Have you not
committed lewdness in addition to all your abominations?*

*44"Behold, everyone who uses proverbs will use this proverb about you: 'Like mother,
like daughter.' 45You are the daughter of your mother, who loathed her husband and her
children; and you are the sister of your sisters, who loathed their husbands and their chil-
dren. Your mother was a Hittite and your father an Amorite. 46And your elder sister is
Samaria, who lived with her daughters to the north of you; and your younger sister, who
lived to the south of you, is Sodom with her daughters. 47Not only did you walk in their
ways and do according to their abominations; within a very little time you were more
corrupt than they in all your ways. 48As I live, declares the Lord GOD, your sister Sodom
and her daughters have not done as you and your daughters have done. 49Behold, this was
the guilt of your sister Sodom: she and her daughters had pride, excess of food, and pros-
perous ease, but did not aid the poor and needy. 50They were haughty and did an abomi-
nation before me. So I removed them, when I saw it. 51Samaria has not committed half
your sins. You have committed more abominations than they, and have made your sisters
appear righteous by all the abominations that you have committed. 52Bear your disgrace,
you also, for you have intervened on behalf of your sisters. Because of your sins in which
you acted more abominably than they, they are more in the right than you. So be ashamed,
you also, and bear your disgrace, for you have made your sisters appear righteous.*

*53"I will restore their fortunes, both the fortunes of Sodom and her daughters, and
the fortunes of Samaria and her daughters, and I will restore your own fortunes in their
midst, 54that you may bear your disgrace and be ashamed of all that you have done,
becoming a consolation to them. 55As for your sisters, Sodom and her daughters shall
return to their former state, and Samaria and her daughters shall return to their former
state, and you and your daughters shall return to your former state. 56Was not your sister
Sodom a byword in your mouth in the day of your pride, 57before your wickedness was
uncovered? Now you have become an object of reproach for the daughters of Syria[h] and
all those around her, and for the daughters of the Philistines, those all around who despise
you. 58You bear the penalty of your lewdness and your abominations, declares the LORD.*

*59"For thus says the Lord GOD: I will deal with you as you have done, you who have
despised the oath in breaking the covenant, 60yet I will remember my covenant with you
in the days of your youth, and I will establish for you an everlasting covenant. 61Then you
will remember your ways and be ashamed when you take your sisters, both your elder and*

your younger, and I give them to you as daughters, but not on account of[i] the covenant with you. [62]*I will establish my covenant with you, and you shall know that I am the* LORD, [63]*that you may remember and be confounded, and never open your mouth again because of your shame, when I atone for you for all that you have done, declares the Lord* GOD."

a Or *with rich fabric* **b** Or *were unfaithful;* also verses 16, 17, 26, 28 **c** Or *unfaithfulness;* also verses 20, 22, 25, 26, 29, 33, 34, 36 **d** Hebrew *it* **e** The meaning of this Hebrew sentence is uncertain **f** Hebrew *spreading your legs* **g** Revocalization yields *How I am filled with anger against you* **h** Some manuscripts (compare Syriac) *of Edom* **i** Or *not apart from*

OVERVIEW: This lengthy chapter is an allegory against the Jews who were at Jerusalem and their wickedness. Our commentators reflect on the origins of the people, whose birth was in the land of Canaan and whose father was an Amorite and mother a Hittite. Here the sinfulness of the people is shown. Moreover it follows that it is by God's grace alone that we are called to faith.

The allegory continues to discuss the maiden's adornment and demise. The benefits bestowed by God are the maiden's adornment. When he takes a people to himself, he provides for them and cares for them. Nothing is more vain than to boast about God's gifts as if you were the author of those gifts. Woe is spoken to this sinful woman, and judgment is made. The chapter ends with the promise of the Lord's everlasting covenant. Our commentators reflect on the meaning of God's everlasting faithfulness in keeping his covenant and specifically how this covenant points to the atonement made by Christ for our sins.

16:1-7 *The People*

THE CITIZENS OF JERUSALEM. JOHN CALVIN: This chapter contains very severe reproaches against the people of Judea who were left at Jerusalem. For although Ezekiel had been a leader to the Israelites and the Jewish exiles, yet God wished his assistance in profiting others. Hence the office that God had imposed on his prophet is now extended to the citizens of Jerusalem, whose abominations he is ordered to make manifest. The manner is afterwards expressed, when God shows the condition of that nation before he embraced it with his favor. But after recounting the benefits by which he had adorned the people, he reproves their ingratitude and shows in many words and by different figures how detestable was their perfidy in revolting: so far from God after he had treated them so liberally. COMMENTARIES ON EZEKIEL.[1]

PROPHETS PREACH WHAT GOD COMMANDS. WILLIAM GREENHILL: We now come to the longest chapter in the whole prophecy, and it is against the Jews who were at Jerusalem. . . . What God commands the prophets and ministers to do, it matters not how it is taken by the people, they are to do it.

Here God commands Ezekiel to cause the people to know the abominations; it was not for him to excuse himself from this service, to object against it, to say they will mock me, despise me, misuse me, hate me, seek my hurt, ruin me. God commanded, and it was his duty to do it, carefully, conscientiously and faithfully. He must make known their sins to the world, to themselves, let the event be what it will. "Cry aloud, spare not, lift up your voice like a trumpet, and show my people their transgression, and the house of Jacob their sins" (Is 58:1). The prophet must not whisper but cry, and that aloud; it matters not who hears, he must lift up his voice like a trumpet. When people blow trumpets, they do it with all their strength, and the sound of it goes far;

[1]CTS 23:93 (CO 18:334).

so must the prophets, with extension of their voice, utter the sins of the people and show them their transgressions, they must represent them fully and earnestly before their eyes and to their ears. This they must do. An Exposition of Ezekiel.[2]

The Origins of the People. John Calvin: It is not surprising, then, if God here obliquely blames the stupidity and sloth of the Jews when he *commands their abominations to be laid open*, which are already sufficiently known to all. Afterwards, that God may begin to show how improperly the people were behaving, he recalls them to the first origin or fountain of their race. But we must notice that God speaks differently of the origin of the people. For sometimes he reminds them of Abraham's condition before he had stretched forth his hand and dragged them, as it were, from the lowest regions into life, as it is said in the last chapter of Joshua (Josh 24:2-3): Your father Abraham was worshiping idols when God adopted him. But sometimes the beginning is made from the covenant of God, when he chose Abraham with his posterity for himself. But in this passage God takes the time from the period of the small band of people emerging by wonderful increase into a nation, although they had been so wretchedly oppressed in Egypt; for the redemption of the people that immediately followed is called sometimes their nativity. So here God says that the Jews were there born when they increased so incredibly, though when oppressed by the Egyptian tyranny they had scarcely any place among living people. And what he says of Jews applies equally to all the posterity of Abraham: for the condition of the ten tribes was the same as that of Judea. But since the prophet speaks to a people still surviving, he is silent about what he would have said, if he had been commanded to utter this mandate to the exiles and captives, as well as to the citizens of Jerusalem. Whatever its meaning, God here pronounces *that the Jews sprang from the land of Canaan, from an Amorite father and from a Hittite mother* (Ezek 16:3).

A question arises here—When God had adopted Abraham two hundred years previously, why was not that covenant taken into account? For he here seems not to magnify his own faithfulness and the constancy of his promise when he rejects the Jews as sprung from the Canaanites or Amorites; but this only shows what they were in themselves: for although he never departed from his purpose, and his election was never in vain, yet we must hold, as far as the people were concerned, that they are looked on as profane Gentiles. For we know how they corrupted themselves in Egypt. Since, then, they were so degenerate and so utterly unlike their ancestors, it is not surprising if God says *that they were sprung from Canaanites and Amorites.*

. . . That they should not be ignorant of the favor by which God had bound himself to Abraham, the prophet meets them and pronounces them a seed of Canaan, having nothing in common with Abraham, because, as far as they were concerned, according to common usage, God's promise was extinct and their adoption dead and buried. Since they had acted so perfidiously, they could no longer boast themselves to be Abraham's children. Hence he says, *your habitations*, that is, the place of their origin. Jerome translates it "root," but the word *nativity* suits better, or native soil or condition of birth *in the land of Canaan: and your father an Amorite and your mother a Hittite*. Commentaries on Ezekiel.[3]

Amorites and Hittites. John Mayer: In this chapter the prophet lays open from the beginning the baseness of the Jews, that if it were possible he might humble them and pull

[2]*Exposition*, 334-35. [3]CTS 23:94-96 (CO 18:335-336). The reference to Jerome is to the Vulgate, which has *radix tua et generatio tua* ("your root and your birth"). Jerome is following the LXX, which also has root (*riza*).

down the great pride and self-conceitedness. And therefore he begins with their nativity, saying that it was of Canaan, their father being an Amorite and their mother a Hittite. By this is meant that for their wickedness they were so before God reputed, as elsewhere they are said to have been Ethiopians to him, and the Jews are said by our Lord to have been of their father the devil for the same reason. Jerome thinks that he alludes to their speaking too much and bragging in the name Amorite, and to their madness in the name Hittite, as the words signify. Commentary upon All the Prophets.[4]

Imitation of the Nations. William Greenhill: People are their children, whose ways, manners and example they follow. Jerusalem imitated the nations in their worship, fashions, practices, and it is the child of an Amorite, of a Hittite, and its citizens imitated their impiety, they contracted kindred with them and obtained inheritance with them, as the Fathers comment on the words (Origen, Jerome, Theodoret). . . .

Let us look to it whose ways we take up. If we imitate the world, we are children of the world; if Rome, Babylon, we are their children. The church of Rome boasts that its birth is from the apostle, that Peter, Paul laid its foundation. But does it embrace their doctrine, imitate their examples? No, it is like the nations for its idolatry, superstition, whoredom, deceit, pomp, pride, etc. Therefore its father is an Amorite and its mother a Hittite. We say we are of Christ, but are we like to Christ in our worship and lives? An Exposition of Ezekiel.[5]

Our Sinful Race. Johann Gerhard: By nature we are strangers, separated from God by sin (Is 59:2). Our race and our birth is from the Canaanite land, and our father is from the Amorites and our mother from the Hittites (Ezek 16:3). This is to say that our race is of a sinful, alien nation. This is why it is irrefutable truth that the call of the church in general, and of each individual in particular, is an act of God's grace. One's own merit falls by the way, that is, the idea that one must first prepare oneself for God's grace and make oneself worthy of it. Postilla.[6]

God's Abundant Mercy. Matthew Meade: God delivered Israel out of Egypt, notwithstanding all their unworthiness and unfitness, which was very great; they were no ways fit for deliverance, as I showed you at large, when God delivered them; the Holy Spirit sets forth this most appropriately in comparing their case, when God brought them out of Egypt, with that of a newborn infant. "And as for their nativity, in the day that you were born (that is, brought out of Egypt) your navel was not cut, neither were you washed in water to cleanse you; you were not salted at all, nor swaddled at all. No eye pitied you, to do any of these to you, to have compassion on you; but you were cast out in the open field, to the loathing of your person, in the day that you were born" (Ezek 16:4-5). All these allusive expressions are to show what the state of Israel was when God came to deliver them out of bondage, a most wretched state, as polluted as a newborn infant, as unpleasant and loathsome to behold as an unwashed infant in its natural filth; and he goes on, "when I saw you polluted in your blood, in your own blood, I said to you when you were in your blood, Live! I said to you when you were in your blood, Live" (Ezek 16:6).

Here are three things to be taken notice of. (1) Her great unfitness and unworthiness of deliverance. She was polluted in her own blood; great and horrid sins are in Scripture set out by blood, and to show the greatness of her sins, blood is three times mentioned in this verse. (2) This unfitness and unworthi-

[4] *Prophets*, 410. [5] *Exposition*, 336-37. [6] *Postilla* 1:210-11.

ness were not unknown by God or unobserved by him. And he takes a particular notice of all her unworthiness and unfitness: "I saw you polluted in your blood, in your own blood." (3) Here is a deliverance wrought in the midst of all unfitness, seen and discovered. "I said to you when you were in your blood, Live. I said to you when you were in your blood, Live." It was twice repeated to a twofold end: to bring them to a humble sense of their own unworthiness and to show the freeness of grace in delivering of them. . . . Here is mercy, but no manner of fitness for mercy; redemption, but no manner of fitness for redemption; and this makes it wonderful. Now such was the deliverance of the Jews out of Babylon. Their case was like that of Israel in Egypt, a people altogether unworthy of deliverance and unfit for it when God brought it about. Sermons.[7]

16:8-34 *The Maiden's Adornment*

God's Protection. William Greenhill: When God takes a people to be his, he will protect them in a special manner and cover their nakedness and shame. He took this Israelitish woman, spread his skirt over her and covered her nakedness. He protected her forty years in the wilderness, against enemies and evils that threatened her ruin. He took away her reproach of barrenness and servitude in the house of bondage. He made her fruitful and free. When uncircumcision was a reproach to this people, the Lord took that away (Josh 5:9). When Goliath defied the host of Israel, God took him away by David (1 Sam 17). And when the Lord took in the Gentiles, did he not spread his skirt over them and cover their nakedness (Is 54:1-5)? . . . Therefore God would have special care of her, turn her barrenness into fruitfulness and cover her shame, her idolatry and profaneness. An Exposition of Ezekiel.[8]

God's Adornment of His People. John Calvin: Here the prophet, in a metaphor, relates other benefits of God by which he liberally adorned his people; for we know that nothing has been omitted in God's pouring forth the riches of his goodness on the people. And as to the explanations that some give of these female ornaments allegorically, I do not approve of it, as they fruitlessly conjecture many trifles that are at variance with each other. First of all, their conjectures may be refuted by the prophet's words; then, if we suffer the prophet's words to be turned and twisted, what these allegorical interpreters chatter with each other is entirely contrary in their meaning. Let us, therefore, be content with the genuine sense, that God was so generous toward the Israelites that he poured forth all his blessings in enriching them. Now, if one asks how the people were adorned? I answer, in two ways: first, God embraced them with his favor and promised to be their God, and this was their chief honor; as Moses says, they were naked, and their shame was discovered when they set up an idol in the place of God. He now adds a second kind of blessing when God took care of them in the desert: he appeared by day in a cloud and by night in a pillar of fire; the water flowed for them from the rock; daily food was given them from heaven, as if God with his own hands had placed it within their mouths; then in his strength they conquered their enemies and entered the promised land while he slew the nations for them and gave them quiet possession and dominion there; then he blessed the land, so that it nourished them abundantly and made it testify that it was no vain promise that the land should flow with milk and honey. Commentaries on Ezekiel.[9]

Washed with Water. William Greenhill: Some refer this washing to their passing through the Red Sea (Ex 14:21-22), of which the apostle says, "All our ancestors were under

[7]*Sermons*, 55-57. [8]*Exposition*, 348. [9]CTS 23:106 (CO 18:343-344).

the cloud, and all passed through the sea; and were all baptized to Moses in the cloud and in the sea" (1 Cor 10:1-2). Their bringing out of Egypt was a type of redemption by Christ, and their passage through the Red Sea, a figure of baptism or washing in the blood of Christ.

Some here make the water to be heavenly doctrine that the Lord gave them. "My doctrine shall drop as the rain" (Deut 32:2). When the rain falls, it washes away the filth of places; so did the law, the corruptions and pollutions of this people. Others think here to be meant those legal washings, spoken of in several places, begun in Exodus 19:10. . . . Others put it on God's freeing them from their misery and sordid condition, through their poverty and meanness, raising them up to a considerable estate.

We may step over the second and fourth and take the first and third. I washed you in the Red Sea and with legal washings. Now because these were types, and leading to Christ, we must pass from the ceremony to the substance, namely, the blood of Christ and the remission of sins. I led you by those washings and baptisms to the fountain set open for uncleanness (Zech 13:1). Sin defiles, and the blood of Christ cleanses from that defilement. I find interpreters do understand by this washing with water, forgiveness of sins, which in the New Testament is often expressed by the metaphor of washing, sprinkling, cleansing, purging (1 Jn 1:7; 2 Pet 1:9; Rev 1:5; Heb 9:14; 1 Pet 1:2). Water cleanses, cools, comforts; and so does forgiveness of sin through the blood of Christ (Eph 1:7; Heb 10:22; Mt 9:2; Heb 12:24). An Exposition of Ezekiel.[10]

Figurative Use of Washing. Racovian Catechism: But the apostle, in this very passage (Tit 3:5-6), seems to attribute regeneration to the baptism of water, since he speaks of washing. He does indeed mention washing but does not assert that that washing of regeneration is the baptism of water itself, as they also who mostly urge this passage against us are themselves forced to confess; because they contend that infants alone are regenerated by baptism, and that in adults, regeneration, having been made by faith before baptism, is only indicated by baptism. But in this passage, and in others of a similar kind, adults are intended: since, therefore, the apostle speaks here of the washing of regeneration of adult persons, it is evident that he does not treat of the baptism of water but of a certain spiritual ablution. Nor is it unusual in the Scriptures to call that purgation of our minds, that is, that act of God and Christ whereby our minds are cleansed from the filth of our vices, which is effected by the word or doctrine of the gospel, figuratively by the name of washing. For Paul writes to the Ephesians (Eph 5:26) that Christ cleansed the church "by the washing of water by the Word," that is, through the Word, namely, of the gospel, wherein he alludes to the custom of washing new-married women; to which God also refers, in part, in Ezekiel (Ezek 16:9), where, speaking to the people of Jerusalem, he says, "then washed I thee with water," which, the passage itself most clearly shows, is to be understood figuratively. Racovian Catechism.[11]

Why Is Bloods Plural? Matthew Meade: "I entered into a covenant with you, then washed I you with water, yea, I washed away your blood from you" (Ezek 16:8-9) and "I said to you in your bloods, Live" (Ezek 16:6). It is plural in the Hebrew, and why? To show a twofold state of blood she was in, one by reason of sin, another by reason of bondage and suffering; and this saying, Live, is a remedy against both. When you were in bloody bondage, when there was a bloody proclamation gone forth that all you male children should be destroyed, then "I looked on you and said, Live." I brought you out of that death, and you were in a bloody polluted condition,

[10]*Exposition*, 351-52. [11]*RC* 259-60.

not only by nature but by your actual idolatries in Egypt; I said, Live. I bestowed the grace of my covenant on you and brought you out of that death. It was thus in the Babylonian captivity that the Holy Spirit compares that bondage with death, and their long continuance in it to a rotting in the grave. Now when the Lord comes to deliver them, he fits them for the deliverance by giving them not only a civil life but spiritual life too. Both of which you have in Ezekiel 37 plainly diversified one from another. "The bones came together, bone to his bone, but there was not breath in them" (Ezek 37:7-8). Here is the civil life intimated in the coming together of bone to bone, but where is the spiritual life, the breath in them? That you have in the following: "I will put my Spirit in you and you shall live" (Ezek 37:14). The Vision of the Wheels.[12]

Our Abuse of God's Gifts. John Calvin: Nothing was more unworthy or preposterous than for the Jews to be proud through the pretext of God's gifts. But this vice has always been rife in the world, as it is now too prevalent, and especially among handsome women; for, though beauty is God's gift, nine women out of ten who possess it are proud, and fond of men, and unite lust with elegance of form. This is quite unworthy of them, but it was customary in all ages, as it is this day, for we recognize the same in men; for as each excels in anything, so he arrogates to himself more than he ought, when he exults against God and is reproachful toward others. If anyone abounds in riches, he immediately gives himself to luxury and empty pomp; and others abuse them to various perverse and even corrupt uses. If anyone is endowed with ability, he turns his acuteness to cunning and fraud; then he plans many devices, as if he wished to mingle earth and heaven. Thus almost all people profane God's gifts. But here the prophet shows the fountain of this pride when he says that the Jews trusted in their own beauty (Ezek 16:15), for if modesty flourished in us, it would certainly suffice for restraining all insolence; but when that restraint has been once thrown off, there is no moderation before either God or people. This passage, then, is worthy of observation, where God reproves his ancient people for trusting in their beauty, because the figure signifies that they drew their material for pride from the gifts that ought rather to lead them to piety; for the gifts that we receive from God's hand ought to be invitations to gratitude, but we are puffed up by pride and luxury, so that we profane God's gifts, in which his glory ought to shine forth. Commentaries on Ezekiel.[13]

Idolatry. Martin Luther: All idolatry comes from our wisdom, whereby we appear upright to ourselves and have no regard for what God commands. Thus Ezekiel rebuked the people because they made for themselves "images of men" (Ezek 16:17), that is, with their own brain they set up power and magistracy. Therefore this text rebukes all who wish by their own wisdom to undertake a matter and have no regard for the will of God. Hence we must abide by the Word of faith given us by God, since we shall be certain in all external works and circumstances if we stay on this royal road. This Satan cannot bear, to see his ways rejected. Lectures on Isaiah.[14]

Woe, Woe to You! William Greenhill: That when God's own people go in sinful ways, it is grievous to him, it affects, indeed, afflicts, his heart. Here God, taking notice and speaking of this Israelite woman's sinful practices and proceeding on in them, breaks out in the midst of a sentence, saying, "Woe, woe to you" (Ezek 16:23)! He was so full with thoughts of her ingratitude, unkindness, rebel-

[12]*Vision of the Wheels*, 61. [13]CTS 23:111 (CO 18:347-348). [14]LW 17:17.

lion, idolatry, etc. that he opens, empties and eases himself in these expressions. . . .

The end of wickedness is woe. She had been notoriously wicked, and what followed on it? Woe, woe. It is double and denotes intenseness; she had been intense in sinning, and God was intense in threatening. An Exposition of Ezekiel.[15]

God's Chastisements. John Calvin: Now we understand what the prophet means by this verse (Ezek 16:27): he enlarges on the people's wickedness in not turning to God, though they felt by clear experience that they were under a curse. They ought to examine their lives, to groan before God, to acknowledge their fault and to beg for pardon; since no feeling was awakened, the prophet gathers that their obstinacy was desperate. This passage is worthy of our notice, that we may be attentive to God's chastisements. Whenever God even raises his finger and threatens us, let us know that he is anxious for our safety; in our turn, let us rouse ourselves and implore his pity, and especially let us repent of our sins by which we see his anger to have been enflamed. (Jer 2:30.) But if we remain slothful, we see that no excuse for us remains, since God elsewhere complains that he is trifled with, when he has chastised his children in vain. Commentaries on Ezekiel.[16]

Abuse of God's Gifts. John Mayer: You give gifts to all your lovers (Ezek 16:33). The idolatrous Israelites, not being content with the true God, who had married them to himself, bestowed much of their goods, which he of his bounty had given them, on idols. They built them temples, gave rich gifts to them and maintained priests to serve them. They thought in part that they should have more favor with the Egyptians, Assyrians and Chaldeans if they agreed with them in worshiping the same gods. Thus they profusely spent their substance on heathen superstition. Despite these concessions, they never gained even the slightest benefit at their hands but were contemned and derided by them. Moreover, because of their perfidy toward God, he left them to be subdued and utterly spoiled by them. Commentary upon All the Prophets.[17]

Bridle Your Lusts. John Calvin: The sum of the whole is that the Jews were seized with such a furious impulse that they manifested no moderation in their wickedness. For they had not revolted from God once only, or in one direction: but wherever occasion offered, they were accustomed to seize it too eagerly, so that they showed in this way that not even a drop of piety remained in their minds. Let us learn then from this passage to put the bridle on our lusts in time: for when the fire is lighted up, it is not easily extinguished, and the devil is always supplying wood or adding oil to the furnace, as the phrase is. Let us then prevent the evil that is here condemned in the Jews, and let us restrain ourselves, lest the devil seize on us with insane fury. Commentaries on Ezekiel.[18]

16:35-58 *The Maiden's Demise*

God's Judgments Never Too Severe. John Calvin: This passage (Ezek 16:35-37) teaches us that although the reason for God's judgments does not always clearly appear, yet they are never too severe, and when he condescends to afford us a reason, he grants us a gratuitous indulgence. But when he silently executes his judgments, let us learn to acquiesce in his justice and not to cry out if he exceeds moderation; because when he has once explained that his severity is only justice, hence we must gather the general rule that whenever he seems to treat his people too severely and harshly, yet he has just reasons for it. Let us learn, also, that the Jews only suffered a just recompense when

[15]*Exposition*, 374. [16]CTS 23:131 (CO 18:361-362). [17]*Prophets*, 412. [18]CTS 23:133 (CO 18:363).

God so cursed all their counsels. They thought themselves very provident and circumspect when they engaged in alliances with Egyptians and Assyrians. But all their plans turned out unhappily for them, since they consulted their own will contrary to that of God. Let us learn, then, if we wish to promote our own salvation and to obtain a prosperous result, to do nothing without God's permission and not to undertake any deliberations except those which God has dictated and suggested by his word and Spirit. For here every future event is shown to us as in a glass when we wish to be wiser than they ought and than God permits them. Commentaries on Ezekiel.[19]

Like Mother, Like Daughter. William Greenhill: "As is the mother, so is her daughter" (Ezek 16:44). The mother is lewd, idolatrous, bloody, rebellious, and the daughter is such. Look therefore what befell the mother for her sins, what punishment was inflicted on her, the like shall befall and be inflicted on you. Proverbs suitable to this are these: "Ill birds lay ill eggs," . . . "From the wicked proceeds wickedness." Now these are not always true, but sometimes it falls out that wicked parents have good children, and good parents wicked ones. Noah had a Ham, Isaac an Esau, David an Absalom, Hezekiah a Manasseh. And so contrary, Ahaz that wicked king had good Hezekiah for his son; Amon, Josiah; Lamech, Noah. . . .

We must inquire who was her mother, and wherein the likeness between them lies. Her mother is said here to be a Hittite and her father an Amorite. She was so unlike to Sarah and Abraham, out of whose loins by nature she came, and so like to the Amorites and Hittites, as that the Lord calls her the daughter of them.

Her sisters were Samaria, which was the chief city of the ten tribes, the royal city. It was on a hill, built by Omri, king of Israel, who bought the hill of one Shemer, so from him called it Samaria (1 Kings 16:24), afterwards called Sebaste. An Exposition of Ezekiel.[20]

The Sin of Greed. Martin Luther: God permits the very riches in which people trust to bring about the ruin of those who own them. Thus Ezekiel prophesies against the wicked Jews and misers (Ezek 16:49): they did not aid the poor; therefore they will be led away into captivity and will perish along with their riches. . . . This is the reason why the Lord overthrows Sodom and Gomorrah, that they have riches but do not aid the poor (Ezek 16:49). The miser accumulates, but someone else will dissipate what has been accumulated. The miser thinks, "My son will have these riches." But look, God lets in some thieves or robbers to deprive him of all the riches, so that neither he nor his son has anything left. Therefore one should persist in his toil but should look for the blessing of God and should aid the poor. Indeed, all our toil should be like that of those who, in the winepress or in the harvest, sing as they work. In the midst of our labor and sweat we should be happy and have the feeling that we can lose everything with equanimity. This is how we should think to ourselves: "To be sure, I shall work for myself and for my children. If God gives something, we shall use it. If there is something left after me, my son will have it. If there is nothing, God will provide for him as he has provided for me." Lectures on Ecclesiastes.[21]

The Sins of Sodom. John Calvin: Here (Ezek 16:48-50) God shows that Sodom had not at first fallen into those foul and gross crimes that were the cause of its final destruction. We must diligently mark this, for when Satan begins to entice us, we think that we shall be free to retract our steps whenever we please; but we are ensnared, some in one way and some in another. But when we are entangled by Satan's deceits, it is not in our

[19]CTS 23:142 (CO 18:370). [20]*Exposition*, 384. [21]LW 15:90.

power to escape from them; nay, we feel that we are involved in a complete labyrinth. Since, then, people proceed gradually in provoking God's wrath, we must observe this passage, in which God informs us that the Sodomites were not given up at once to enormous lust, but they began with smaller sins and then became luxurious through their abundance and were stupefied by ease and quiet; meanwhile they despised the poor and needy and did not stretch forth their hands to them. For to *seize the hand* means the same as to stretch forth the hand, when we set up again those who have fallen or prop up those who are slipping. Hence God shows that the Sodomites were afterwards so corrupted by luxuries that he at length adds, *they raised themselves up*, that is, that they purposely, and of their own accord, exempted themselves from all fear of punishment, for this is the meaning of the word "raised up"; that is, they buoyed themselves up, since they promised themselves freedom from punishment; and in that fallacious hope *they dared to perpetrate abomination before my face*. Hence we must always fear lest Satan should entangle us by his enticements and at length so fascinate and stupefy our senses that we can no longer distinguish between good and evil, as the Sodomites exceeded the brutes in their abominations, which were the cause of their ruin.

. . . Now, if anyone should ask whether these crimes that Ezekiel relates are worse than those of the Jews, the answer is at hand, that the Sodomites were not under the law; and hence it is no wonder if they wandered and stumbled in darkness. But when the right course of life was pointed out to the Jews, they professedly sought their own destruction, they knowingly and willfully rejected God's yoke and haughtily despised all the prophets who daily desired to recall them into the path of duty. Commentaries on Ezekiel.[22]

Jerusalem and Her Neighbors. William Greenhill: Cities, states, churches, people are their children in the account of the Scripture, whose manners, ways and examples they follow. Jerusalem took up the ways, worship, manners and customs of the nations and cities near to her; hence her mother is said to be a Hittite, her father an Amorite, her sisters Sodom and Samaria; according to their ways she fashioned herself. Those who follow the faith and steps of Abraham are the children of Abraham (Gal 3:7; Rom 4:16). Those who are peaceable and labor to make peace, they are children of God (Mt 5:9). People who mind the world are provident, frugal and saving; they, following courses of the world, are called children of the world (Lk 16:8). So those who do wickedly are the children of the devil (1 Jn 3:8, 10, 12; Mt 13:38). An Exposition of Ezekiel.[23]

16:59-63 *The Lord's Everlasting Covenant*

Covenant Faithfulness. John Calvin: Here, also, God meets the false objection by which the Jews might strive with him; for whatever they were, yet God had entered into covenant with them. They might, therefore, fly to this refuge, that God had bound himself in covenant with them, since he had adopted Abraham with his seed. Although they had provoked God's anger a thousand times, yet this exception remained, that God ought to stand to his agreement and not to look at what they had deserved by their ingratitude but rather to be consistent with his promises. Now, therefore, he returns to this cavil and says that he is free to break the covenant since they have done so first. I will do, says he, to you as you have done. We see, therefore, that the calumny is here repelled by which the Jews could obliquely defame God, as they were accustomed to do, as if he had rendered

[22]CTS 23:159-60 (CO 18:382-383). [23]*Exposition*, 384-85.

his covenant void. He says, then, that in agreement it is customary for a person, when deceived, no longer to be necessarily bound to a perfidious breaker of agreements, for covenanting requires mutual faith, but the Jews had violated their agreement and reduced it to nothing. Hence, through their perfidy and wickedness, God had acquired the liberty of rejecting them and of no longer reckoning them among his people. Commentaries on Ezekiel.[24]

God Keeps Covenant. William Greenhill: The Scripture says that God is a God who keeps covenant (Neh 9:32). Indeed, faithful in keeping covenant (Deut 7:9), and God says he will not suffer his faithfulness to fail, or break his covenant or alter the thing gone out of his lips (Ps 89:33-34). How does the Lord then say here, "I will deal with you as you have done" (Ezek 16:59)? Is he not bound up by his faithfulness and promise to do them good though they fail? According to that in 2 Timothy 2:13, "If we believe not, yet he abides faithful. He cannot deny himself."

Answer: If the covenant were made on conditions, and those not observed, no imputation could be laid on the Lord if he perform not what was his part. You may see how the covenant runs in several places: "The Lord your God, he is God, the faithful God, who keeps covenant and mercy with them that love him and keep his commandments to a thousand generations; and repays them that hate him to their face, to destroy them" (Deut 7:9). All the blessings and cursing, Deuteronomy 28, depend on obedience and disobedience, keeping and breaking covenant, so that the Lord is free to punish if man perform not.

. . . Though God afflicted them very sorely and cut off the body of this people by severe judgments, yet he reserved some, continued his faithfulness, kept covenant with them and manifested his loving-kindness to them. An Exposition of Ezekiel.[25]

God's Everlasting Covenant in Christ. John Calvin: God therefore pronounces that he would be mindful of his covenant which he had made with that people in their youth, by which words he signifies that his pity should not go forth except from the covenant. For God always recalls the faithful, as it were, to the fountain, lest they should claim anything as their right or imagine this or that to be the cause of God's being reconciled to them. He shows, therefore, that this pity has no other foundation than the covenant; and this is the reason why he says, that he would be mindful of his covenant. He now adds, and I will establish a perpetual covenant with you (Ezek 16:60). Here God promises, without obscurity, a better and more excellent covenant than that ancient one already abolished through the people's fault. This passage, then, cannot be understood except of the new covenant that God has established by the hand of Christ. But these two clauses are so mutually united that they ought to be carefully weighed, namely, that God here gives the hope of a new covenant and yet teaches us that it originates in the old one already abolished through the people's fault. Thus we see that the New Testament flows from that covenant that God made with Abraham and afterwards sanctioned by the hand of Moses. That which is promulgated for us in the gospel is called the New Covenant, not because it had no beginning previously but because it was renewed, and better conditions added, for we know that the Law was abrogated by the New Covenant. Whether it is so or not, the excellence of the New Testament is not injured, because it has its source and occasion in the Old Covenant and is founded on it. Commentaries on Ezekiel.[26]

An Everlasting Covenant. William Greenhill: What covenant this was is to be

[24]CTS 23:171 (CO 18:391). [25]*Exposition*, 406-7. [26]CTS 23:173 (CO 18:392-393).

opened. When this people had so grievously sinned as to be in a great part ruined, and the rest sent into captivity, to outward view God seemed to have no people. The promise made to Abraham, Isaac and Jacob, that in their seed all the nations of the earth should be blessed, seemed to be void, and the covenant made between God and them at Mount Sinai wholly dissolved; but however things appeared, it was otherwise. God minded his covenant, and would establish it with the remnant of them and make additions of more grace and mercy to it. Before he gave them the law in tables of stone; now, he would write it in their hearts and give them power to keep it. In Jeremiah 31:31-34, you have the covenant set down that our prophet here means, and it is called a "new covenant" because of the new addition and new administrations, not that the substance of it is altered. It is the same law that is written in the hearts of those God makes his covenant with as was written in the tables of stone. It is again mentioned in Hebrews 8:10-12. That covenant at Mount Sinai some make to be mixed partly of works and partly of grace; some looked for life and justification by it, but therein it was faulty and weak (Rom 9:31-32; Gal 3:21). And so far as it comprehended anything of the covenant of works, it was antiquated, and more grace added, Christ and the gospel brought in more clearly and fully. An Exposition of Ezekiel.[27]

New Covenant? John Mayer: But why is it called the covenant made with her in her youth (Ezek 16:60), seeing it is a new covenant, that is made under the gospel (Jer 31:31)? Solution: It is not called new because of its substance, for that remained the same. It is called new because of the manner in which it was given. The first being confirmed with the blood of beasts; this by the blood of Christ. The first having nothing expressed but doing so to live; this believing and living. The first given with great terror and accompanied with the heavy burdens of many ceremonies; this in all mildness, and no such burden imposed. Yet it is for substance the covenant made with her in her youth; namely, for faith, which was the main thing. The first made their father Abraham so gracious with God and so brought him and his posterity into this covenant that God bound himself to be his God and the God of his seed forever. Commentary upon All the Prophets.[28]

Repentance. John Calvin: Ezekiel again exhorts the faithful to repentance and constant meditation. We have said that these members cannot be divided, namely, the testimony of grace with the doctrine of repentance; we have said, also, that this is the substance of the gospel, that God wishes those to repent whom he reconciles by gratuitous pardon. For he is appeased by us only when he makes us new creatures in Christ and regenerates us by his Spirit; as it is said in Isaiah, God will be propitious to the people who shall have returned from their iniquity (Is 59:20). That promise is restricted to those who do not indulge and revel in sin but humble themselves before God and decide their own salvation to be impossible without their being severe judges to their own condemnation. Therefore Ezekiel follows up this point when he says that you may remember and be ashamed (Ezek 16:63). Commentaries on Ezekiel.[29]

---

[27]*Exposition*, 408-9. [28]*Prophets*, 415. [29]CTS 23:180 (CO 18:398).

17:1-24 TWO EAGLES AND A VINE

1The word of the LORD came to me: 2"Son of man, propound a riddle, and speak a parable to the house of Israel; 3say, Thus says the Lord GOD: A great eagle with great wings and long pinions, rich in plumage of many colors, came to Lebanon and took the top of the cedar. 4He broke off the topmost of its young twigs and carried it to a land of trade and set it in a city of merchants. 5Then he took of the seed of the land and planted it in fertile soil.[a] He placed it beside abundant waters. He set it like a willow twig, 6and it sprouted and became a low spreading vine, and its branches turned toward him, and its roots remained where it stood. So it became a vine and produced branches and put out boughs.

7"And there was another great eagle with great wings and much plumage, and behold, this vine bent its roots toward him and shot forth its branches toward him from the bed where it was planted, that he might water it. 8It had been planted on good soil by abundant waters, that it might produce branches and bear fruit and become a noble vine.

9"Say, Thus says the Lord GOD: Will it thrive? Will he not pull up its roots and cut off its fruit, so that it withers, so that all its fresh sprouting leaves wither? It will not take a strong arm or many people to pull it from its roots. 10Behold, it is planted; will it thrive? Will it not utterly wither when the east wind strikes it—wither away on the bed where it sprouted?"

11Then the word of the LORD came to me: 12"Say now to the rebellious house, Do you not know what these things mean? Tell them, behold, the king of Babylon came to Jerusalem, and took her king and her princes and brought them to him to Babylon. 13And he took one of the royal offspring[b] and made a covenant with him, putting him under oath (the chief men of the land he had taken away), 14that the kingdom might be humble and not lift itself up, and keep his covenant that it might stand. 15But he rebelled against him by sending his ambassadors to Egypt, that they might give him horses and a large army. Will he thrive? Can one escape who does such things? Can he break the covenant and yet escape?

16"As I live, declares the Lord GOD, surely in the place where the king dwells who made him king, whose oath he despised, and whose covenant with him he broke, in Babylon he shall die. 17Pharaoh with his mighty army and great company will not help him in war, when mounds are cast up and siege walls built to cut off many lives. 18He despised the oath in breaking the covenant, and behold, he gave his hand and did all these things; he shall not escape. 19Therefore thus says the Lord GOD: As I live, surely it is my oath that he despised, and my covenant that he broke. I will return it upon his head. 20I will spread my net over him, and he shall be taken in my snare, and I will bring him to Babylon and enter into judgment with him there for the treachery he has committed against me. 21And all the pick[c] of his troops shall fall by the sword, and the survivors shall be scattered to every wind, and you shall know that I am the LORD; I have spoken."

22Thus says the Lord GOD: "I myself will take a sprig from the lofty top of the cedar and will set it out. I will break off from the topmost of its young twigs a tender one, and I myself will plant it on a high and lofty mountain. 23On the mountain height of Israel will

I plant it, that it may bear branches and produce fruit and become a noble cedar. And under it will dwell every kind of bird; in the shade of its branches birds of every sort will nest. [24]*And all the trees of the field shall know that I am the Lord; I bring low the high tree, and make high the low tree, dry up the green tree, and make the dry tree flourish. I am the Lord; I have spoken, and I will do it."*

a Hebrew *in a field of seed* **b** Hebrew *seed* **c** Some Hebrew manuscripts, Syriac, Targum; most Hebrew manuscripts *all the fugitives*

Overview: A parable of two eagles is now given that shows the coming destruction of Jerusalem. Our commentators agree that the first eagle is Nebuchadnezzar and the second eagle represents the faithlessness of Zedekiah, who trusted in the king of Egypt for safety and protection and not in God. The chapter ends with the promise of restoration and the kingdom of Christ. The tender sprig from the lofty cedar is Christ. By saying he is from the top of the high cedar, reference is made to Christ's divinity; by saying he is tender and low, reference is made to his humanity.

17:1-21 *Two Eagles*

Summary of the Chapter. John Calvin: In this chapter the prophet shows that the Jews were utterly foolish in thinking themselves safe, since they had God as their adversary. At the end of the chapter he promises indeed the restoration of the church and heralds the kingdom of Christ; but the principal part of the chapter is consumed with this teaching, that the Jews were utterly foolish in promising themselves safety for the city, the temple and their kingdom, for, as it now appeared, they had violated the covenant of God and he had rejected them. When deprived of God's help, what could they do? This was egregious folly to hope for a prosperous state of their kingdom when their power was diminished and cut off, and they were reduced almost to the very last straits. Commentaries on Ezekiel.[1]

Summary of Chapter. John Owen: This chapter, to verse 22, is taken up in a riddle, a parable, with the exposition of it. The time being come that God would destroy the outward, visible monarchy of the Jews, for their false worship, tyranny, persecution and oppression, he employs the king of Babylon in that work (2 Chron 36:17), who subdues the nation, takes away two kings, one after another, and appoints Zedekiah a titular governor under him (2 Kings 24:1-3). But the wrath of God being to come on them to the uttermost, he also closes with Egypt, rebels against him (Jer 37:1) by whose appointment alone he had any right to be a ruler (Ezek 17:16); so way is made, by his ruin, to put an end to the kingly reign of the house of David in Jerusalem (Jer 29:16-17). Sermon.[2]

The First Eagle. John Calvin: Here the prophet reasons from the greater to the less: for if Nebuchadnezzar was able to subdue the whole kingdom with ease, when as yet the Jews were touched, how much more readily would he overthrow them when wretched and all but ruined, for nothing remained that was not threatened with ruin; and this is the meaning of the prophet. But he compares King Nebuchadnezzar with an eagle, whom he says was great, and then with large or extended wings. There is no doubt that by wings, feathers and plumes he means the regions and peoples over which Nebuchadnezzar presided; for we know that the Chaldeans possessed the monarchy of the East. Since, therefore, so many regions and people obeyed Nebuchadnezzar's sway, it

[1]CTS 23:186 (CO 18:401-402). [2]Owen, *Works* 8:316.

is not surprising that the prophet calls him a great eagle, with ample wings and with numerous feathers or plumes. Commentaries on Ezekiel.[3]

Nebuchadnezzar Called An Eagle. William Greenhill: Nebuchadnezzar, who was a heathen, is called an eagle, who is the chief of all birds, and not simply an eagle but a great eagle, with great and long wings, full of feathers. He had great power, great territories, multitudes of peoples, indeed, kings and princes under him (Dan 2:37-38). He had vast power over people, fowls and beasts; he was the greatest eagle of those times. . . .

No kings or kingdoms are so high or great but that the Lord can bring them down and abase them. A great eagle comes and crops the highest branch of the cedar and the top of his young twigs; Jehoiachin, the princes and nobles, are taken away by him and deprived of all their greatness and glory. The top of this tall cedar was broken off and thrown down to the ground, and it was done by the counsel, appointment and providence of God: "Thus says the Lord, A great eagle came to Lebanon." God sent this eagle to do it. He has means, ways, times, to un-power kingdoms, to un-king kings, to un-noble nobles; he can at his pleasure remove kings and take them and others from all rule and government. An Exposition of Ezekiel.[4]

Lebanon and the Young Twigs. John Calvin: But here Ezekiel means the land and names Lebanon rather than other places, not only because that mountain was the remarkable ornament of the region on account of its lofty cedars and balsam and aromatic trees, but because this was needful to complete his allegory. If he had said that an eagle had come to a city, it would have been absurd. Hence we see that the word *Lebanon* is taken for that part of Judea in which the most beautiful trees spring up and flourish. But he says *that it plucked off a bough, from the top of the cedars,* because Nebuchadnezzar, who is intended by the eagle, took away King Jeconiah, as we said yesterday. Hence King Jeconiah is compared with *a very lofty bough of a cedar,* because at that time all thought that the kingdom was superior to every danger; for the Jews boasted that they were under God's protection and that the city was impregnable; hence that occurrence was incredible. Now the prophet adds, *the eagle plucked off the head* or summit of the boughs, as the Hebrews call the tender shoots; and here the word means the tender branches, and it means, as we shall afterwards see, the elders who were dragged away into exile.

. . . After Ezekiel has narrated that Jehoiachin was carried away with his counselors and the flower of the whole people and was so deprived of his native country as to be without hope of return, he now says, *the eagle took up the seed in Judea and placed it in a fertile land.* . . . The seed, then, that he here means is Zedekiah, the last king. Commentaries on Ezekiel.[5]

The Second Eagle. John Calvin: He now detects, under a figure, the perfidy of Zedekiah, since he very soon applied himself to the king of Egypt and bent his roots and branches toward him, that they might be irrigated. I do not disagree with the opinion of those who think that the prophet alludes to an Egyptian custom, for we know that they dug furrows through which water flowed through the whole region: hence the fruitfulness of the soil, and thus Egypt is elsewhere compared with a garden (Deut 11:10). Whatever the meaning is, the prophet shows that Zedekiah was deceived by a foolish confidence when he thought himself safe under the protection of the king of Egypt; for he had said that the seed was so planted that the vine did not rise to a

[3]CTS 23:188-89 (CO 18:403-404). [4]*Exposition,* 418. [5]CTS 23:190-91 (CO 18:404-405).

great height but spread itself under the wings of the eagle. But Zedekiah despised the king of Babylon, thinking that he should improve his condition by entering into a treaty with the king of Egypt. Commentaries on Ezekiel.[6]

Another Eagle. William Greenhill: Here you have the second part of the parable, where the king of Egypt and Zedekiah's revolting come into consideration. "Another great eagle." This eagle was the king of Egypt [Ezek 17:15, 17]. Kings are called eagles. . . . This eagle was great in power and dominion, but not so great as the other; for though this eagle had great wings, yet it is not said, he had long wings, as the other had. "Many feathers." Much wealth, many people and soldiers. An Exposition of Ezekiel.[7]

The Vine Destroyed. John Calvin: Here (Ezek 17:9-10) God announces that this vine could not flourish any longer and bring forth fruit, for it had been planted to flourish under the shadow of an eagle, and it had removed itself away. Nothing therefore remains than that the former eagle should avenge the injury committed against it. This is the meaning of the passage; hence he says, Shall it prosper? Shall not the eagle tear up its roots and cut off its fruit? Ezekiel assumes this principle, that the vine could not be otherwise preserved than by the power and aid of the eagle that had planted it; for when it passed away from that eagle to another, the prophet says that the end of the ungrateful vine was at hand; all the leaves of its branches shall wither, and so be dried up, and that not in a mighty branch, nor in much people. It is certain that Nebuchadnezzar was accompanied with a great army when he came down upon Judea. But the prophet means, even if Nebuchadnezzar had only brought with him a small band, yet Zedekiah could not remain king, since destruction awaited him through perfidy and revolt, as will afterwards be said. The prophet often speaks by concession, as if he had said that by a singe blast, Zedekiah and all the people would wither away, since he could not remain in safety unless he drew sap from his own root; but he had removed his root elsewhere, and so Ezekiel pronounces that he must immediately wither away. It was not then in the power of much people to tear it from its own roots; for Zedekiah had purposely cut off his own roots, when, through his own levity, he had transferred himself to the king of Egypt. Commentaries on Ezekiel.[8]

17:22-24 *The Kingdom of Christ*

Comfort Added. John Mayer: And from here to the end of the chapter, according to the prophetical manner, comfort is added after the preceding threatening words. This comfort especially concerns Christ, the most high branch to come and to be planted on a high and elevated mountain. He is aptly set forth here as the head of his branches or the principal of the stock of David, of which line he came.

. . . Here in speaking of Christ he calls him the top of the high cedar and yet a tender one. In Isaiah 11, he is set forth, as a branch coming out of the stubble of that tree, that is, Jesse the father of David, which is the lowest branch, and not a branch plucked of the top. But by this is meant first his divinity, in regard of which he was the top and head of all that linage, the crown and greatest glory of it. Second, his humanity, in regard of which he was but a tender one and weak and low, as he is also called (Ezek 17:24).

He was planted on a high mountain, when on Mount Zion, where the temple stood, he sat preaching the gospel, as is further expressed in the next words (Ezek 17:23). Although Mount Zion were not the highest mountain, yet for the excellence in regard of the temples standing there and Christ's preaching there it was

[6]CTS 23:192 (CO 18:406). [7]*Exposition*, 421. [8]CTS 23:193-94 (CO 18:407).

the highest in esteem of all other mountains of the earth, and so it is likewise set forth (Is 2).

And this branch here planted, *branches and fructifies, and here all fowls of every wing dwell and are shadowed, as in the branches of a goodly cedar.* That is, people of all countries and nations, to whom the fruit of Christ's preaching extends, shall dwell in him by faith, when his apostles sent out by him going into all countries shall preach him, and repentance, and faith and salvation in his name. Commentary upon All the Prophets.[9]

Words of Promise. William Greenhill: These verses contain a promise of mercy, which is the last general part of the chapter. And it is no mean promise, but an exceeding great and precious promise, namely, of Christ and his kingdom.

The Lord having resolved and sworn, in the former part of the chapter, to the rooting up of the Jewish vine, namely, the destruction of Zedekiah, his princes, nobles, city, people, and laying all waste. Some among them might say, "What will now become of his promise to Abraham, to David, and others, that out of their loins and seed should come a blessing to all nations, that the Messiah should spring out of their root? If all Judah is rooted up and carried out into Babylon, what truth is there in the promise of God? How will this be made good that has proceeded out of his sacred lips?" What! Will the God of truth be unfaithful and fail now? No, says the Lord, I am mindful of what I have promised. And though you see not how it shall be accomplished, I do. I have ways not thought of by you. An Exposition of Ezekiel.[10]

Restoration of the Nation. John Calvin: Here the prophet begins to treat of the restoration of the nation and kingdom. Thus this prophecy without doubt refers to Christ, because although in some sense God had pity on the people when they enjoyed the liberty of returning under Cyrus and Darius, yet what is here written was never fully exhibited except under Christ. It is indeed true, as I have elsewhere expressed, that when the prophets promise restoration to the church, they do not restrict their discourse to the person of Christ but begin with the return of the people, for that was the beginning of the full and solid liberty that was at length made manifest in Christ. And Christian writers have erred in urging so precisely that anything said about the restitution of the church must be understood of the person of Christ, and thus they make themselves ridiculous to the Jews. But, as it has been said already, as often as the prophets hold out the hope of liberty to the elect and the faithful, they embrace the whole of the time from the return of the people, or from the end of their exile to the end of the kingdom of Christ. When, therefore, the reign of Christ is treated, we must date its commencement from the period of the building of the temple after the people's return from their seventy years' captivity; and then we must take its boundary, not at the ascension of Christ, nor yet in the first or second centuries, but through the whole progress of his kingdom, until he shall appear at the last day. Commentaries on Ezekiel.[11]

Kingdom of Christ. John Calvin: In this verse (Ezek 17:24) the prophet signifies that God's work would be memorable. For when he says that all trees should feel themselves in God's hand and power, to raise what was fallen and to cast down and to prostrate what was elevated, he doubtless expresses no common action. By trees he means all the kings of the earth and all possessed of any dignity. For he follows up his own metaphor: as he called the kingdom of Christ a tree or cedar that grew from a small twig, so he now speaks metaphorically of kings when he says *that all should take*

[9]*Prophets*, 417. [10]*Exposition*, 430. [11]CTS 23:207 (CO 18:417).

notice; for they shall know that Jehovah brings down the high tree. Ezekiel may here seem to be inconsistent with himself, as I have already noticed, because God said that he would take from a lofty cedar a little twig, which he wished to plant; but he now says that God would raise what was low and abject. But we have dissipated this absurdity, because, from the beginning Christ was in the glory of his Father, and thus, as Micah says, his beginning was from eternity (Mic 5:2). This excellence of Christ, therefore, is noticed, because, from the time when God erected David's throne, he at the same time gave a visible sign of the more excellent kingdom that was then secretly hoped for. For this reason Christ was taken from his lofty place, and since he not only put on the form of a slave but emptied himself even to death (Phil 2:7), it is not surprising that the prophet should say, *like a tree cast down.* Although, as I have remarked, this sentence is not to be restricted to the person of Christ but thought to be adapted to his kingdom; that is, to his manner and way of governing, since we know, and it has been lately stated, that the gospel is like a scepter, by which Christ subdues all people and rules them for himself. Now if we reflect on what the preaching of the gospel was, we shall see, as in a glass, the prophet's meaning here, that the low tree was elevated, since no one would have thought that from such slender beginnings the increase that God afterwards bestowed on it could arise. It follows, then, that the height was wonderful, since it could not be comprehended by the human senses. Commentaries on Ezekiel.[12]

Christ's Kingdom. John Owen: In verse 22 of this chapter, he calls them from their thoughtfulness about the destructions, desolations and contentions that were among them in reference to their civil rule, to the consideration of that design that he was secretly and silently carrying on under all these dispensations. "I will also take of the highest branch of the high cedar and will set it; I will crop off from the top of his young twigs a tender one and will plant it on a high mountain and eminent: in the mountain of the height of Israel will I plant it; and it shall bring forth boughs and bear fruit, and be a goodly cedar; and under it shall dwell all fowl of every wing; in the shadow of the branches thereof shall they dwell" (Ezek 17:22-23). As if the Lord should say, There is a great noise in the world about setting up and plucking down of kings, in this their carnal rule; and many of you see nothing else. You will look no farther. But I also have my work in hand; my design is not bounded within these limits and outward appearances; I am setting up a king that shall have another manner of dominion and rule than these worms of the earth. He shall stand (Mic 5:4).

The setting up, then, of this kingdom of Christ, who is "the highest branch of high cedar," and planting it in the church, the "mountain of Israel," with the prosperity thereof, and safety of him that shall dwell therein, is the subject of Ezekiel 17:22-23. Sermon.[13]

Christ's Humble Kingdom. John Calvin: What is the outward appearance of Christ's kingdom? In truth we shall feel nothing but despair if we judge of Christ's kingdom by the present state of affairs. But when we see how the gospel creeps along the ground, this passage should come to our minds that God will raise up the tree that is abject and contemptible. At the same time, let us learn that the changes that happen and are perceived in the world are to be imputed to the pride of those who are blinded by their own boasting; for kings, as we have said, forget that they are men, and so rebel against God; hence they must of necessity fall. If this is not fulfilled immediately, let us learn patiently to await the effect of this prophecy. Whatever happens, God has so established the kingdom of Christ

[12]CTS 23:211-12 (CO 18:420). [13]Owen, *Works* 8:317.

alone, that it shall last as long as the sun and moon, but the other empires of the world shall vanish away with their own splendor, and their loftiness shall fall although at present they overtop the clouds. Commentaries on Ezekiel.[14]

High and Low Trees. John Owen: The tree that is to be cast down and withered, and that is the "high tree" and the "green tree"—a tree that in their eyes had both beauty and vigor, high and green; this was the Judaical kingdom, admired and delighted in by the Jews. This, says God, I will reject; as also he will many a tall Eliab, that even some Samuels may think to be his anointed.

The tree that is to be exalted and made to flourish, and that is the "low tree," the "dry tree," contemptible for growth—it is low, useless for fruit, it is dry. And this is the spiritual kingdom of the Messiah, contemned, despised. This, says God, I will exalt, carry on and make glorious; for though the interest of Christ and the gospel may seem low and dry for a season, in comparison of the glory of other flourishing interests, yet, in the issue, it shall be exalted above them all. Sermon.[15]

[14]CTS 23:212-13 (CO 18:421). [15]Owen, *Works* 8:319.

18:1-32 The Soul Who Sins Will Die

1The word of the Lord came to me: 2"What do you[a] mean by repeating this proverb
concerning the land of Israel, 'The fathers have eaten sour grapes, and the children's teeth
are set on edge'? 3As I live, declares the Lord God, this proverb shall no more be used by
you in Israel. 4Behold, all souls are mine; the soul of the father as well as the soul of the
son is mine: the soul who sins shall die.
5"If a man is righteous and does what is just and right—6if he does not eat upon the
mountains or lift up his eyes to the idols of the house of Israel, does not defile his neigh-
bor's wife or approach a woman in her time of menstrual impurity, 7does not oppress
anyone, but restores to the debtor his pledge, commits no robbery, gives his bread to
the hungry and covers the naked with a garment, 8does not lend at interest or take any
profit,[b] withholds his hand from injustice, executes true justice between man and man,
9walks in my statutes, and keeps my rules by acting faithfully—he is righteous; he shall
surely live, declares the Lord God.
10"If he fathers a son who is violent, a shedder of blood, who does any of these things
11(though he himself did none of these things), who even eats upon the mountains, defiles
his neighbor's wife, 12oppresses the poor and needy, commits robbery, does not restore the
pledge, lifts up his eyes to the idols, commits abomination, 13lends at interest, and takes
profit; shall he then live? He shall not live. He has done all these abominations; he shall
surely die; his blood shall be upon himself.
14"Now suppose this man fathers a son who sees all the sins that his father has done; he

sees, and does not do likewise: 15he does not eat upon the mountains or lift up his eyes to
the idols of the house of Israel, does not defile his neighbor's wife, 16does not oppress any-
one, exacts no pledge, commits no robbery, but gives his bread to the hungry and covers
the naked with a garment, 17withholds his hand from iniquity,[c] takes no interest or profit,
obeys my rules, and walks in my statutes; he shall not die for his father's iniquity; he shall
surely live. 18As for his father, because he practiced extortion, robbed his brother, and did
what is not good among his people, behold, he shall die for his iniquity.

19"Yet you say, 'Why should not the son suffer for the iniquity of the father?' When the
son has done what is just and right, and has been careful to observe all my statutes, he
shall surely live. 20The soul who sins shall die. The son shall not suffer for the iniquity of
the father, nor the father suffer for the iniquity of the son. The righteousness of the righ-
teous shall be upon himself, and the wickedness of the wicked shall be upon himself.

21"But if a wicked person turns away from all his sins that he has committed and
keeps all my statutes and does what is just and right, he shall surely live; he shall not die.
22None of the transgressions that he has committed shall be remembered against him; for
the righteousness that he has done he shall live. 23Have I any pleasure in the death of the
wicked, declares the Lord God, and not rather that he should turn from his way and live?
24But when a righteous person turns away from his righteousness and does injustice and
does the same abominations that the wicked person does, shall he live? None of the righ-
teous deeds that he has done shall be remembered; for the treachery of which he is guilty
and the sin he has committed, for them he shall die.

25"Yet you say, 'The way of the Lord is not just.' Hear now, O house of Israel: Is my
way not just? Is it not your ways that are not just? 26When a righteous person turns away
from his righteousness and does injustice, he shall die for it; for the injustice that he has
done he shall die. 27Again, when a wicked person turns away from the wickedness he has
committed and does what is just and right, he shall save his life. 28Because he considered
and turned away from all the transgressions that he had committed, he shall surely live;
he shall not die. 29Yet the house of Israel says, 'The way of the Lord is not just.' O house
of Israel, are my ways not just? Is it not your ways that are not just?

30"Therefore I will judge you, O house of Israel, every one according to his ways, de-
clares the Lord God. Repent and turn from all your transgressions, lest iniquity be your
ruin.[d] 31Cast away from you all the transgressions that you have committed, and make
yourselves a new heart and a new spirit! Why will you die, O house of Israel? 32For I have
no pleasure in the death of anyone, declares the Lord God; so turn, and live."

a The Hebrew for *you* is plural **b** That is, profit that comes from charging interest to the poor; also verses 13, 17 (compare Leviticus 25:36)
c Septuagint; Hebrew *from the poor* **d** Or *lest iniquity be your stumbling block*

Overview: The sins of the father are not imputed to the son. The father will bear the punishment for his sins; the son also for his own. In this chapter, God declares that he deals justly with all people and that all people bear their own sin. If a person repents, he receives mercy; if he turns from righteousness, judgment. Moreover, all souls belong to God. He is creator and sustainer of all.

Our commentators deal at length with the middle section of this chapter. Three questions are of particular importance. First, what is the relationship between the law and righteousness? Can a person be justified by works of the law? Second, does God wish all to be saved or does he predestine some to damnation? Third, can a righteous person turn from righteousness to sin? Finally, the chapter ends with the reminder that God's ways are not our ways.

Summary of the Chapter. John Mayer: Here, because the prophet had formerly aggravated the sins of the Jews, the people were living by the sins of their ancestors and now complained about this, as if they were unjustly dealt with; for when their ancestors committed the same sins, they escaped, yet the people to whom Ezekiel prophesied were now threatened with destruction. To convince them therefore of their unjust complaining in this regard and so justify the Lord in his proceedings against them, he largely declares in this chapter that neither they nor any other were at any time judged unjustly by the Lord, but in all justice and righteousness. Commentary upon All the Prophets.[1]

18:1-4 *All Souls Belong to God*

Charges Brought Against God. William Greenhill: The Jews in Babylon meeting with much hardship in their captivity, instead of being humbled for their sins, which brought sad miseries on them, took up an unjust complaint against God and charged him to deal unjustly by them; namely, that their ancestors had sinned, and they who were their children suffered for their sins. We being innocent are grievously afflicted for their iniquities. This false charge God clears himself of in this chapter and shows them that he is most just in punishing and rewarding. Everyone shall bear his own sins, and not another's, be rewarded according to what he is and has done, whether he is just or unjust. If the unjust repents of his evil ways, he shall have mercy; if the just turns from his righteousness he shall have judgment. And this is the sum and main argument of this chapter. An Exposition of Ezekiel.[2]

Sinners Distort God's Word. John Calvin: We may collect from this rebuke that the Jews were perverse interpreters of the best teaching; they purposely reviled the prophet's expression and drew it to a contrary meaning. . . . The prophet now convinces them of this unfairness and shows that they had no reason for transferring their faults to others or to thrust them away from themselves, since God was just in taking vengeance on them. We know that people willingly shuffle so as to free themselves from blame and then afterwards accuse God of cruel injustice. Commentaries on Ezekiel.[3]

All Souls Belong to God. John Calvin: Some interpreters explain the beginning of the verse thus: that people vainly and rashly complain when God seems to treat them too severely, since the clay does not rise against the potter. Since God is the maker of the whole world, we are his workmanship: what madness, then, to rise up against him when he does not satisfy us; and we saw this simile used by Jeremiah (Jer 18:6). The sentiment, then, is true in itself, that all souls are under God's sovereignty by the right of creation, and therefore he can arbitrarily determine for each whatever he wishes; and all who clamor against him reap no profit; and this teaching it is advantageous to notice. But this passage ought to be understood otherwise, namely, that nothing is more unworthy than that God should be accused of tyrannizing over people, when he rather defends them as being his own workmanship. When, therefore, God pronounces *that all souls are his own,* he does not merely claim sovereignty and power, but he rather shows that he is affected with fatherly love toward the whole human race since he created and formed it; for, if a workman loves his work because he recognizes in it the fruits of his industry, so, when God has manifested his power and

[1]*Prophets,* 417*. [2]*Exposition,* 433. [3]CTS 23:214 (CO 18:421-422).

goodness in the formation of people, he must certainly embrace them with affection. True, indeed, we are abominable in God's sight, through being corrupted by original sin, as it is elsewhere said (Ps 14:1, 2); but inasmuch as we are people, we must be dear to God, and our salvation must be precious in his sight. We now see what kind of refutation this is: *all souls are mine*, says he; I have formed all and am the creator of all, and so I am affected with fatherly love toward all, and they shall rather feel my clemency, from the least to the greatest, than experience too much rigor and severity. At length he adds, *the soul that sinned shall die*. Now, Ezekiel expresses how God restrains the Jews from daring to boast any longer that they are afflicted undeservedly, since no innocent person shall die; for this is the meaning of the sentence; for he does not mean that every guilty person should die, for this would shut against us the door of God's mercy, for we have all sinned against him; so it would follow that there is no hope of safety, since every person must perish, unless God freed sinners from death. But the prophet's sense is not doubtful, as we have said, since those who perish are not without fault; neither can they bring up their innocence to God or complain of his cruelty in punishing them for the sins of others. Commentaries on Ezekiel.[4]

God the Father of All. William Greenhill: Here the Lord does vindicate himself from that unjust crime they laid to his charge; namely, that he punished one for another, the child for the sin of the parent. You mistake, says God; all souls are mine, I am the common Father of all, I observe the ways of all and render to them all according to their works. I do not accept the persons of any in judgment, but being essentially just, am righteous in all my ways and holy in my works (Ps 145:17). None in heaven or earth has any sufficient warrant to accuse me, and if I should punish the son for the father's sin, I could give you satisfactory grounds for it. An Exposition of Ezekiel.[5]

All Are God's. John Mayer: *As I live, all souls are mine, says the Lord, as the soul of the son, so of the father, the soul that sins shall die* (Ezek 18:4). That is, I have a like interest in all souls, and they are alike dear to me, as I made them all; therefore I will undoubtedly proceed alike against every person, not respecting any relations of one to another, but where I find any wicked they shall die for their wickedness, and they only, not others for them. And this is further amplified by putting forth various cases: (1) Of a person being righteous in all points of righteousness, in this case whether he is parent or child he shall not die but live (Ezek 18:5); (2) Of the child of a righteous parent degenerating to wickedness, he shall not live for his parent's righteousness, but die (Ezek 18:10-11); (3) Of a righteous child of a wicked parent, he shall not die although his parent were wicked, but live assuredly (Ezek 18:14-15); (4) Of the same soul that has done wickedly but repents and turns and fulfills all righteousness now by keeping all God's commandments, he shall live despite his former unrighteousness and therefore not be punished with death (Ezek 18:21-22); (5) Of a righteous person turning from his righteousness to sin, he shall not live but die, his former righteousness standing him in no stead (Ezek 18:24). And these two last cases are repeated again for further confirmation of the same (Ezek 18:26-28). Commentary upon All the Prophets.[6]

The Soul That Sins Shall Die. William Greenhill: If the soul that sins shall die, how is it then that the children suffer for their fathers' sins? . . . We must make an exception here in the point of original sin; for because of the sin of our first parents, death comes on all their posterity (Rom 5:12). For the sin of

[4]CTS 23:216-17 (CO 18:423-424). [5]*Exposition*, 435. [6]*Prophets*, 417-18.

the parent, the child suffers not eternal death. No person is eternally damned for another's sin simply considered. It is a person's own sin which is his everlasting ruin.

Temporal and bodily punishments do often befall the children for their parents' iniquities, and that justly. For indeed they are parts of them, they come out of their loins, too often inherit their corruptions, imitate and live in their sins. They are part of the family. They make the house. Therefore God said he would bring the evil on Ahab's house, and so he suffered in the suffering of his family. An Exposition of Ezekiel.[7]

18:5-20 *Law and Righteousness*

To Live Justly. John Calvin: But this is the Spirit's intention, that God has prepared a reward for each according to their lives, so that he does not permit them to be deprived of their promised blessing or let the impious and despisers of his law escape. Now let us come to the words, if anyone has been just, he shall be just, therefore he shall live. He speaks generally first; he afterwards enumerates certain species under which he embraces the sum of the whole law. The full sentence is, if anyone has been just, he shall live in consequence of his justice. But the prophet defines what it is to be just, and he there chooses certain parts of the law: by putting a part for the whole, as I have said, he signifies, that whoever faithfully observes the law is esteemed just before God. . . . But it is clear from this that we fear God when we live justly with our brethren, for piety is the root of charity. Although many profane persons seem blameless in their life and manifest a rare integrity, yet no one ever loves his neighbor from his heart unless he fears and reverences God. Since, therefore, charity flows from piety and the fear of God, as often as we see the duties of the second table placed before us, we should learn them to be the testimonies to the worship of God, as is this place, but then the prophet also adds certain parts of the first table. Commentaries on Ezekiel.[8]

Seventeen Acts of Righteousness Enumerated. John Mayer: Now in the enumeration of particular sins here putting all the cases together, they are by Jerome noted to be seventeen, as the parts of righteousness are: (1) to execute judgment; (2) to join to judgment righteousness or justice; (3) not to eat on the mountains; (4) not to lift up the eyes to idols; (5) not to go in to another man's wife; (6) not to go in to a menstruous woman, his own wife; (7) not to make sad anyone; (8) to restore the pledge; (9) to take nothing by violence; (10) to give bread to the hungry; (11) to clothe the naked; (12) not to put money to usury; (13) to take nothing again of that which you have given; (14) to turn one's hand from iniquity; (15) to judge truly between person and person; (16) to walk in the precepts of the Lord; (17) to keep his judgments and justifications. Commentary upon All the Prophets.[9]

Justification by Works. John Calvin: The prophet now expresses this, while a difficult question arises from the passage; for he says *that he is just who has kept the law*, and so God will bestow a recompense on him; hence these two things are connected together, and the question that I mentioned arises from the former clause, for the whole Scriptures teach that no one is just and that none can be justified by the law. But these things are contrary to each other; to be just and worthy of reward through keeping the law, since none is just, all are transgressors, all devoid of justice, and so but one remedy remains—that of seeking our safety from the gratuitous mercy of God. But although, at first sight, this kind of inconsistency disturbs the rude and partially exercised commentator, yet this solution is easy, since,

[7]*Exposition*, 436. [8]CTS 23:220-21 (CO 18:426). [9]*Prophets*, 418-19.

strictly speaking, justice is the observance of the law. If anyone asks, then, what justice is, the proper definition is the observance of law. Why so? Because the law, as I said yesterday, lays down the solid rule of justice; whoever observes it will be esteemed just; and thus justification is properly said to be placed in works.

But Scripture pronounces what is very true and entirely confirmed by experience, that no one can satisfy the law, and, on account of this defect, we are all deprived of justification by works. . . . Let it suffice, then, that we are by nature all together rebels against God, so that not the slightest particle of good can be found in us. As far as concerns the faithful, they aspire indeed to righteousness, but lamely and at a great distance from their aim; they often wander from the way, and they often fall, so that they do not satisfy the law and hence require God's pity. Hence we must come to the second kind of righteousness, which is improperly so called, namely, that which we obtain from Christ. He who does righteousness is righteous (1 Jn 3:7). None of us does it; but Christ, who fulfilled the law, is esteemed just before God. Hence it is necessary that we should be approved by God through his righteousness; that is, it is imputed to us, and we are accepted through his righteousness. Hence justification by faith, as it is called, is not properly righteousness; but on account of the defect of true righteousness, it is necessary to fly to this as to a sacred anchor. . . .

Thus it still remains true that faith without works justifies, although this needs prudence and a sound interpretation; for this proposition, that faith without works justifies is true and yet false, according to the different senses that it bears. The proposition, that faith without works justifies by itself, is false, because faith without works is void. But if the clause "without works" is joined with the word *justifies*, the proposition will be true, since faith cannot justify when it is without works, because it is dead and a mere fiction. He who is born of God is just, as John says (1 Jn 5:18). Thus faith can be no more separated from works than the sun from its heat, yet faith justifies without works, because works form no reason for our justification; but faith alone reconciles us to God and causes him to love us, not in ourselves but in his only-begotten Son. Now, therefore, that question is solved, when the prophet teaches that life is reposed in the just, even if they are born of wicked and unholy parents. Commentaries on Ezekiel.[10]

Everyone Must Bear His Own Burden. Hans Denck: God judges the world on account of the sin of unbelief, which has its evil, untimely fruits just as faith has its good fruit. These condemn everyone who does them, as is written in Ezekiel 18:20-21: "The child shall no longer bear the iniquity of his parent, nor shall the parent suffer for the iniquity of the child. Rather everyone shall die on account of his own guilt. Everyone of the house of Israel, says the Lord, I will judge according to his path so that the saying (Our parents have eaten sour grapes, and the children's teeth are set on edge) will be no longer heard in Israel. Israel must suffer penance for its iniquity, and Jacob must personally suffer on account of his sin." This without doubt has been said to us also. Everyone must bear his own burden, and no one can bear it for us. Thus we ought to abstain readily from evil and do what is good, for God well knows each transgression, as we shall see. Reflections on Micah.[11]

We Are All Sinners. John Calvin: When we consider the perishing of the whole human race, it is said with truth that we perish through another's fault, but it is added at the same time that every one perishes through his own iniquity. If then we inquire into the cause of the curse that presses on all the posterity of

[10]CTS 23:235-38 (CO 18:437-439). [11]*Writings*, 46-47.

Adam, it may be said to be partly another's and partly our own: another's, through Adam's declension from God, in whose person the whole human race was spoiled of righteousness and intelligence, and all parts of the soul utterly corrupted. So that everyone is lost in himself, and if he wishes to contend with God, he must always acknowledge that the fountain of the curse flows from himself. For before the child was born into the world, it was corrupt, since its menial intelligence was buried in darkness and its will was perverse and rebellious against God. As soon as infants are born, they contract pollution from their father Adam: their reason is blinded, their appetites perverted and their senses entirely vitiated. This does not immediately show itself in the young child, but before God, who discerns things more acutely than we do, the corruption of our whole nature is rightly treated as sin. There is no one who during the course of his life does not perceive himself liable to punishment through his own works; but original sin is sufficient for the condemnation of all people. When people grow up they acquire for themselves the new curse of what is called actual sin, so that one who is pure with reference to ordinary observation is guilty before God; hence Scripture pronounces us all naturally children of wrath: these are Paul's words in the second chapter of the epistle to the Ephesians (Eph 2:3). If then we are children of wrath, it follows that we are polluted from our birth; this provokes God's anger and renders him hostile to us: in this sense David confesses himself conceived in sin (Ps 51:5). He does not here accuse either his father or his mother so as to extenuate his own wickedness, but when he abhors the greatness of his sin in provoking the wrath of God, he is brought back to his infancy and acknowledges that he was even then guilty before God. We see then that David, being reminded of a single sin, acknowledges himself a sinner before he was born; and since we are all under the curse, it follows that we are all worthy of death. Thus, the child properly speaking shall not die through the iniquity of his parent but is considered guilty before God through his own fault. Commentaries on Ezekiel.[12]

18:21-23 *Does God Wish All to Be Saved?*

The Question. Thomas Manton: "Have I any pleasure at all that the wicked should die, says the Lord God" (Ezek 18:23)? The words are propounded by way of interrogation; in which form of speech there is more evidence, efficacy, life and convincing force. That is to say, "You know it is evident that I have no such desire, no such pleasure. It dare not enter into your thoughts that I should take pleasure in the bare destruction of the creature." This pleasure of God is expressed negatively, what he delights not in: "Have I any pleasure at all that the wicked should die?" It is also expressed positively, what he does delight in: "That he should turn from his ways and live." God had rather his conversion. In both are implied two great truths; namely, the connection between sin and death, repentance and life, wicked and die, return and live. God does not obscurely nullify or disown his judgment and execution according to that law or give you any hopes that his law shall not be executed, but he tells you what he takes pleasure in; rather in the conversion than in the destruction of the creature. Sermons upon Ezekiel.[13]

The Sweetest Comfort. Martin Luther: It is an evangelical word and the sweetest comfort in every way for miserable sinners, where Ezekiel says, "I desire not the death of a sinner, but rather that he may turn and live" (Ezek 18:23, 32), like Psalm 29:6: "For his anger is but for a moment, and his favor is for a lifetime." Then there is Psalm 108:21 (Vg): "How sweet is thy mercy, O Lord" and "For

[12]CTS 23:241-42 (CO 18:441). [13]Manton, *Works* 21:463-64.

I am merciful" (Jer 3:12), and Christ's saying in Matthew 11:28: "Come to me, all you who labor, and I will give you rest," and that in Exodus 20:6: "I show mercy to many thousands, to those who love me." What, indeed, does almost more than half of holy Scripture contain but sheer promises of grace, in which mercy, life, peace and salvation are offered by God to people? And what else do words of promise have to say but this: "I desire not the death of a sinner"? Is it not the same thing to say, "I am merciful," as to say, "I am not angry, I do not want to punish, I do not want you to die, I want to pardon, I want to spare"? And if these divine promises were not there to raise up consciences afflicted with the sense of sin and terrified with the fear of death and judgment, what place would there be for pardon or hope? What sinner would not despair? But just as free choice is not proved by other words of mercy or promise or comfort, so neither is it proved by this one: "I desire not the death of a sinner," etc. The Bondage of the Will.[14]

Does God Wish All to Be Saved? John Calvin: It follows, then, that what the prophet now says is very true, that God wills not the death of a sinner, because he meets him of his own accord and is not only prepared to receive all who fly to his pity, but he calls them toward him with a loud voice when he sees how they are alienated from all hope of safety. But the manner must be noticed in which God wishes all to be saved, namely, *when they turn themselves from their ways*. God thus does not so wish all people to be saved as to renounce the difference between good and evil; but repentance, as we have said, must precede pardon. How, then, does God wish all people to be saved? By the Spirit's condemning the world of sin, of righteousness and of judgment at this day, by the gospel, as he did formerly by the law and the prophets (Jn 16:8). God makes manifest to humankind their great misery, that they may betake themselves to him; he wounds that he may cure and slays that he may give life. We hold, then, that God wills not the death of a sinner, since he calls all equally to repentance and promises himself prepared to receive them if they only seriously repent.

If anyone should object—then there is no election of God, by which he has predestinated a fixed number to salvation, the answer is at hand: the prophet does not here speak of God's secret counsel but only recalls miserable people from despair, that they may apprehend the hope of pardon, and repent and embrace the offered salvation. If anyone again objects—this is making God act with duplicity, the answer is ready, that God always wishes the same thing, though by different ways and in a manner inscrutable to us. Although, therefore, God's will is simple, yet great variety is involved in it, as far as our senses are concerned. Besides, it is not surprising that our eyes should be blinded by intense light, so that we cannot certainly judge how God wishes all to be saved and yet has devoted all the reprobate to eternal destruction and wishes them to perish. . . .

God is said *not to wish the death of a sinner*. How so? since he wishes all to be converted. Now we must see how God wishes all to be converted, for repentance is surely his peculiar gift; as it is his office to create people, so it is his province to renew them and restore his image within them. For this reason we are said to be his workmanship, that is, his fashioning (Eph 2:10). Since, therefore, repentance is a kind of second creation, it follows that it is not in people's power; and if it is equally in God's power to convert people as well as to create them, it follows that the reprobate are not converted because God does not wish their conversion; for if he wished it he could do it, and hence it appears that he does not wish it. But again they argue foolishly, since God does not wish all to be converted, he is himself deceptive, and nothing can be certainly stated

[14]LW 33:136 (WA 18:683).

concerning his paternal benevolence. But this knot is easily untied, for he does not leave us in suspense when he says that he wishes all to be saved. Why so? for if no one repents without finding God propitious, then this sentence is filled up. But we must remark that God puts on a twofold character, for he here wishes to be taken at his word. As I have already said, the prophet does not here dispute with subtlety about his incomprehensible plans but wishes to keep our attention close to God's word. Now, what are the contents of this word? The law, the prophets and the gospel. Now all are called to repentance, and the hope of salvation is promised them when they repent. This is true, since God rejects no returning sinner. He pardons all without exception. Meanwhile, this will of God that he sets forth in his word does not prevent him from decreeing before the world was created what he would do with every individual. And as I have now said, the prophet only shows here that when we have been converted we need not doubt that God immediately meets us and shows himself propitious. Commentaries on Ezekiel.[15]

God Desires None to Perish. John Mayer: *Have I any pleasure at all, that the wicked should die, but that he should turn from his ways and live* (Ezek 18:23)? The case of a wicked person turning and living, despite his former wickedness being laid open in the premises, now he infers on this ground: that the Lord wills not, neither delights in, anyone's death, but in his conversion and salvation. Indeed, that none, however far he has gone in sin, might despair, but by hope in his mercy be drawn to turn to him who is so gracious.

But against this it is objected both that he has foreordained some to damnation and that it is not in people to will, but he works to will and to do of his own good pleasure. If then he takes no pleasure in the death of the wicked, why does he not turn him? Answer: He offers him grace and pardon for all that is past to turn him; indeed, he counsels him to turn, and entreats him, by his benefits seeks to lead him to repentance. Indeed, more than all this, he knocks at the door of his heart by his Spirit. Who can say then, but that it is true, which is here said, he delights not in his dying?

Objection: But all this is nothing if either he has foreordained him to death or works not effectually with the means by which he may be converted.

Answer: He foreordains none to damnation but such as he foresees will be impenitent, when he has used all the means of reclaiming them that may be, and therefore Christ speaking of the cursed going into hell fire, says, not prepared for you, but *for the devil and his angels*, whereas, on the contrary, to the blessed he says, *come into the kingdom prepared for you from the beginning*, so that impenitent sinners come into condemnation by their preferring of the pleasures of sin before the joy of salvation. For his effectual working on his will, he works so by his Word and Spirit that he may, if there is not an aversion in his will, turn himself being thus helped, as it is said here, *Turn yourselves and live* (Ezek 18:32). For if God, who bids us thus to do, stood not ready to help and enable us, this were but a delusion. But doing all that can be expected to be done on his part, indeed that he could do, as he says (Is 5), the impenitent sinner is unreasonable in charging God as the cause of his nonconversion, when as indeed he is the sole cause of it himself and consequently of his own damnation. As a man in the water held up by the chin that thrusts away his hand that holds him up that he might swim out, if he sinks and is drowned, is the sole cause of his own death. And so the sinner is the cause of his own damnation, because he is not only held up, as it were, but exhorted over and over to turn and live (Ezek 18:30-32). Therefore, unless God would save him against his will or take and carry him to heaven as a

[15]CTS 23:246-48 (CO 18:445-446).

block or dead thing, he never putting on to do anything tending to salvation, and so do more for him, than for any that are saved, he can never attain life but must die and perish everlastingly. COMMENTARY UPON ALL THE PROPHETS.[16]

OUR DEATH IS OUR FAULT. RICHARD BAXTER: The Lord here swears that he has no pleasure in your death, but rather that you would turn and live; if yet you will go on and die, rather than turn, remember if was not to please God that you did it, it was to please the world and to please yourselves. And if people will damn themselves to please themselves, and run into endless torments for delight and have not the wit, the heart, the grace to hearken to God or person that would reclaim them, what remedy is there? But they must take what they get by it and repent in another manner, when it is too late. A CALL TO THE UNCONVERTED.[17]

WHY MORE ARE NOT SAVED. THOMAS MANTON: If God has more pleasure in the conversion of sinners than their destruction, why are there not more converted than we find to be? The greatest part of humankind is perishing in their unbelief and impenitency. Answer: I might answer that this text speaks not absolutely but comparatively. God rejoices in the execution of his justice, as well as in all his other works; but if you compare things with things, he rejoices rather in acts of mercy than in acts of vengeance. His disposition inclines him to mercy rather to wrath: "Mercy pleases him" (Mic 7:18); and mercy rejoices over judgment in the conflict. Justice is *alienum opus*, "his strange work" (Is 28:21). "He does not afflict willingly, nor grieve the children of men" (Lam 3:33), not with his heart. Mercy, like live honey, drops of its own accord. He is forced to the other; it is wrested from him. Though the properties are equally infinite in God, yet they do diversely exert themselves toward people as to the effects. Now the world is on its trial. God's primary end is the conversion of the sinner; his secondary end the honor of his vindictive justice. SERMONS UPON EZEKIEL.[18]

18:24-32 *Righteousness and God's Ways*

CAN THE RIGHTEOUS FALL? JOHN CALVIN: As in the last lecture the prophet offered to sinners a sure hope of pardon if they heartily repented and promised that God would be propitious to them as soon as they shall seek reconciliation with him, so now, on the other hand, he pronounces, *if the just shall decline from his justice*, whatever he has so far done shall not come into the account before God. . . . But here a question arises, Can a truly just person deflect from the right way? for one who is begotten of God is so free from the tyranny of sin that he devotes himself wholly to righteousness, and then if any do turn aside, they prove that they were always strangers to God. If they had been of us, says John, they would never have gone out from us (1 Jn 2:19). And regeneration is an incorruptible seed, so we must determine that the faithful who are truly regenerate never fall away from righteousness but are retained by God's unconquered power, for God's calling in the elect is without repentance (Rom 11:29). Hence he continues the course of his grace even to the end. Nor are they to be listened to, who, in contradiction to Scripture, teach that faith is extinct in the elect, when, through its barrenness, they bring forth no fruit. In what sense, then, does Ezekiel mean that the just fall away? That question is easily answered, since he is not here treating of the living root of justice but of the outward form or appearance, as we commonly say. Paul reminds us that God knows us but adds that this seal remains (2 Tim 2:19). God therefore claims to himself alone the difference between the elect and the reprobate, since

[16]*Prophets*, 421-22. [17]*Practical Works* 2:521. [18]Manton, *Works* 21:465.

many seem to be members of his church who are only outwardly such. Commentaries on Ezekiel.[19]

The Righteous Turning to Sin. William Greenhill: Having laid down the case of a wicked person, repenting of and turning from his sins, and so cleared the proceedings of God, that such a one finds mercy and suffers not for his own sin, much less for his parent's, he comes here to the use of a righteous person, who if he turns from his righteousness and falls to wicked courses, his former righteousness shall not advantage him, but he shall be dealt with according to his present sin. The sin of the wicked repenting shall not hinder him from mercy and eternal life; and the righteousness of the righteous sinning shall not keep him from justice and eternal death. Old sins shall not burden a returning sinner, and old righteousness will not help a revolting saint. . . .

Johann Gerhard brings this verse to prove that a person by his sins may put away faith and the Holy Spirit. Bellarmine brings it to prove that a person may lose a new heart and makes use of this verse to show that faith may be lost. The Arminians also say; hence it is evident that everyone may see it, that a righteous person may totally and finally fall away.

For answer to these, know that it is said when the righteous person does turn away, he shall be so dealt with as if he had never been righteous. It is a caution to prevent a righteous person's falling, rather than an implication that he will or shall turn from his righteousness. Second, the prophet speaks here of a righteous person considered in himself, not in relation to God or Christ; and so he may turn from his righteousness, as angels and Adam did. Third, the scope of the chapter is not to prove falling away from grace but to clear the Lord's justice. An Exposition of Ezekiel.[20]

Repentance. Matthew Meade: Fitness for deliverance supposes repentance for sin, especially for those sins that procured the judgment: a people who are under judgment for sin and do not repent of sin but continue in it notwithstanding the judgment are not fit for deliverance; and thus it was with this people. Sin pulled down the judgment, but there was no repentance to remove it; sin had dug their graves and buried them, but there was no repentance to roll away the stone and bring them out. God calls them to repent before the judgment is come, to prevent it: "I will judge you, O house of Israel, every one according to his own way, says the Lord God. Repent, and turn yourselves from all your transgressions; so iniquity shall not be your ruin" (Ezek 18:30). . . . They are called to repent before judgment comes that they might prevent it, but they repented not. Sermons.[21]

God's Ways Are Not Our Ways. John Calvin: [The hypocrites] say *that God's ways are not equal*. . . . We know with how much greater clearness the angels are able reverently to adore God's wisdom than the human race. What, therefore, must we do? Not only is God's wisdom incomprehensible, but his justice is the most perfect rule of all justice. Now, if we desire to pass opinions on God's works according to our own perceptions and to weigh them in our balance, what else are we doing but passing judgment on him? But we must remember that passage of Isaiah: "As I live," says Jehovah, "every knee shall bend before me, and every tongue shall swear by me" (Is 45:23). Paul, too, is a faithful interpreter of this sentiment when he forbids mortals to judge arrogantly by saying, We shall all stand before the judgment seat of Christ (Rom 14:10-11). Since, then, it will be necessary for us to render an account before Christ's heavenly tribunal, we must now acquiesce in God's judgments; because, when at length our license has entirely spent itself

[19]CTS 23:249-50 (CO 18:447). [20]*Exposition*, 459. [21]*Sermons*, 57.

and our petulance has had its full scope, God will be our judge. We see, therefore, that when people claim to themselves the right of daring to pronounce their own opinions on God's work, they first subject his wisdom to their own fictions and then feel too much hostility and contempt toward his justice. But this one thing ought to be sufficient, that people are too forgetful of their own condition when they dare to open their mouth against their Maker, not only to murmur but openly to condemn him, as if they were his superiors. Let us then obey the contrary rule; let us with sobriety and modesty learn to look on those works of God that are unknown to us and to concede to him the praise of supreme wisdom, although his counsels seem at first sight contradictory. Commentaries on Ezekiel.[22]

[22]CTS 23:253-54 (CO 18:449-450).

19:1-14 A Lament for Israel's Prince

[1]And you, take up a lamentation for the princes of Israel, [2]and say:

What was your mother? A lioness!
Among lions she crouched;
in the midst of young lions
she reared her cubs.
[3]And she brought up one of her cubs;
he became a young lion,
and he learned to catch prey;
he devoured men.
[4]The nations heard about him;
he was caught in their pit,
and they brought him with hooks
to the land of Egypt.
[5]When she saw that she waited in vain,
that her hope was lost,
she took another of her cubs
and made him a young lion.
[6]He prowled among the lions;
he became a young lion,
and he learned to catch prey;
he devoured men,
[7]and seized[a] their widows.
He laid waste their cities,
and the land was appalled and all who were in it
at the sound of his roaring.
[8]Then the nations set against him
from provinces on every side;
they spread their net over him;
he was taken in their pit.
[9]With hooks they put him in a cage[b]
and brought him to the king of Babylon;
they brought him into custody,
that his voice should no more be heard
on the mountains of Israel.

[10]Your mother was like a vine in a vineyard[c]
planted by the water,
fruitful and full of branches
by reason of abundant water.
[11]Its strong stems became rulers' scepters;
it towered aloft
among the thick boughs;[d]
it was seen in its height

with the mass of its branches.
[12]*But the vine was plucked up in fury,*
cast down to the ground;
the east wind dried up its fruit;
they were stripped off and withered.
As for its strong stem,
fire consumed it.
[13]*Now it is planted in the wilderness,*
in a dry and thirsty land.
[14]*And fire has gone out from the stem of its shoots,*
has consumed its fruit,
so that there remains in it no strong stem,
no scepter for ruling.

This is a lamentation and has become a lamentation.

a Hebrew *knew* **b** Or *in a wooden collar* **c** Some Hebrew manuscripts; most Hebrew manuscripts *in your blood* **d** Or *the clouds*

Overview: A lament for Israel's princes follow according to two parables. The first parable is about a lioness and her cubs. Our commentators agree that the nation of Israel is the lioness, the first lion is king Jehoahaz and the second lion king Jehoiakim. The second parable is about a vine. The vine is Israel, and it was destroyed by the Egyptians and Babylonians. The chapter ends with lamentation, which concerns the prophecy of Jerusalem's destruction and the abandonment of God by his people. It should bring mourning to all the faithful as they see and ponder what happened to the princes of Israel and Jerusalem, the temple and the people.

The Nation Is a Lioness. John Calvin: Here the prophet, under the image of a lion, informs us that whatever evils happened to the Israelites could not be imputed to others. We must understand then his intention: it is not surprising that the Spirit of God insists on a matter not very obscure, since nothing is more obstinate than the pride of people, especially when God chastises them, although they pretend to humility and modesty yet swell with pride and are full of bitterness, and, lastly, they can scarcely be induced to confess God to be just, and that they deserve chastisement at his hand. For this reason, therefore, Ezekiel confirms what we formerly saw, that the Jews were not afflicted without deserving it. But he uses, as I have said, a simile taken from lions. He calls *the nation itself a lioness,* for when he treats of the mother of the people, we know that the offspring is considered. He says, therefore, that the people were full of insolence. Commentaries on Ezekiel.[1]

The Lioness and Lions. John Mayer: In this chapter, under the similitude of a lioness and her whelps, the kings who were in Judea as of late are set forth. The one was Jehoahaz, the first son of Josiah, whom Pharaoh Neco took and carried into Egypt; another was Jehoiakim, whom he made king in his stead, who was taken and carried into Babylon. The state is represented by the lioness; it consisted of rich people addicted to making of the poor, as a lioness makes a prey of other beasts. For the two whelps taken and brought up until they became lions, the first, Jehoahaz, was made king by the people, after Josiah his father was slain by Pharaoh Neco. But when Jehoahaz had reigned three months, in which time he is said to have done evil, that is, as is here expressed, by oppressing the people, Pharaoh was displeased at their boldness to set him up for king without his consent; therefore Pharaoh came and took him away into Egypt, where he died. Commentary upon All the Prophets.[2]

Another Lion. John Calvin: The prophet says that Judea produced another lion after the

[1]CTS 23:267-68 (CO 18:460). [2]*Prophets,* 422*.

former had been captured and led into Egypt. Now this ought to be referred to King Jehoiakim, who was appointed by King Nebuchadnezzar, when he had laid waste a part of Egypt, possessed the whole of Judea and imposed laws by establishing a king, according to the rights of conquest. But since he also acted perfidiously, he was led away into captivity. The prophet, therefore, means that the nation did not repent through this single chastisement, nor did it change its disposition, since its mother was a lioness: and not only did it bring forth young lions but also taught them to seize on their prey till they became grown up. He says, therefore, *that she saw what she had hoped, and her hope was futile*. Some think that the noun "hope" is here repeated by the prophet—she saw that her hope was lost; lost hope, I say. But the other reading is better—*she saw that she had hoped*; that is, she saw that her hope had not produced any fruit for some time, because the royal throne remained deserted; *therefore she took another of her whelps, says he, and made him a lion*. The prophet again briefly teaches that the whole royal offspring was like young lions. Although, therefore, the lion alone is called king, yet he is said to be taken from a number of whelps; and hence it follows that this denotes the depraved and cruel nature of all. Thus we see that the Jews are indirectly reproved for not returning to soundness of mind when God punished them severely and King Jehoahaz was taken. COMMENTARIES ON EZEKIEL.[3]

VINE, BRANCHES AND RODS. WILLIAM GREENHILL: God lays waste, destroys flourishing and potent kingdoms when they provoke him by their sinful and grievous courses. This kingdom of Judah did flourish like a vine, had many branches, strong rods, much wealth and power, but it trespassed grievously (Ezek 14:13), and here God plucks it up in fury; he spares neither branches, body nor roots. The quiet, happiness and flourishing condition of earthly kingdoms is not perpetual; God has ways to weaken them, to ruin and root them up. By the Egyptians he lopped this vine, and by the Babylonians he pulled it up. AN EXPOSITION OF EZEKIEL.[4]

A LAMENTATION. JOHN CALVIN: *This is a lamentation, and it shall be a lamentation* (Ezek 19:14). Some think this to be said of the Jews, that is, of all the Israelites, since they should all be lamentable, because God would not cease to inflict his judgments on them until he had utterly consumed them. But I had rather refer it to the prophecy, and this is the more correct sense. *This lamentation*: thus the prophet designates this sad and mournful prophecy because it contains the last slaughter of the people. Second, he adds, *it shall be for a lamentation*, because it suggests material for wailing, since remarkable miseries are accustomed to being more celebrated. If anything usual occurs, people soon forget it; but if any slaughter happens worthy of notice and of remembrance it is everywhere spread abroad, nay, it supplies posterity with material for their poems. Hence the prophet signifies not only that this prophecy was mournful but also that God's wrath would fly about in common conversation through so rare and memorable an example. COMMENTARIES ON EZEKIEL.[5]

LAMENTATION FOR ISRAEL. WILLIAM GREENHILL: This prophecy is a matter of mourning to me at present. To hear and speak of such sad things coming on Judah and Jerusalem "is a lamentation," and when they shall be accomplished, they will be "for a lamentation" to posterity. They will lament for the princes of Israel, for Jerusalem, for the temple and for this vine plucked up by the roots. AN EXPOSITION OF EZEKIEL.[6]

[3]CTS 23:271 (CO 18:462). [4]*Exposition*, 479. [5]CTS 23:281 (CO 18:470). [6]*Exposition*, 479.

20:1-49 REBELLIOUS ISRAEL

1In the seventh year, in the fifth month, on the tenth day of the month, certain of the elders of Israel came to inquire of the LORD, and sat before me. 2And the word of the LORD came to me: 3"Son of man, speak to the elders of Israel, and say to them, Thus says the Lord GOD, Is it to inquire of me that you come? As I live, declares the Lord GOD, I will not be inquired of by you. 4Will you judge them, son of man, will you judge them? Let them know the abominations of their fathers, 5and say to them, Thus says the Lord GOD: On the day when I chose Israel, I swore[a] to the offspring of the house of Jacob, making myself known to them in the land of Egypt; I swore to them, saying, I am the LORD your God. 6On that day I swore to them that I would bring them out of the land of Egypt into a land that I had searched out for them, a land flowing with milk and honey, the most glorious of all lands. 7And I said to them, Cast away the detestable things your eyes feast on, every one of you, and do not defile yourselves with the idols of Egypt; I am the LORD your God. 8But they rebelled against me and were not willing to listen to me. None of them cast away the detestable things their eyes feasted on, nor did they forsake the idols of Egypt.

"Then I said I would pour out my wrath upon them and spend my anger against them in the midst of the land of Egypt. 9But I acted for the sake of my name, that it should not be profaned in the sight of the nations among whom they lived, in whose sight I made myself known to them in bringing them out of the land of Egypt. 10So I led them out of the land of Egypt and brought them into the wilderness. 11I gave them my statutes and made known to them my rules, by which, if a person does them, he shall live. 12Moreover, I gave them my Sabbaths, as a sign between me and them, that they might know that I am the LORD who sanctifies them. 13But the house of Israel rebelled against me in the wilderness. They did not walk in my statutes but rejected my rules, by which, if a person does them, he shall live; and my Sabbaths they greatly profaned.

"Then I said I would pour out my wrath upon them in the wilderness, to make a full end of them. 14But I acted for the sake of my name, that it should not be profaned in the sight of the nations, in whose sight I had brought them out. 15Moreover, I swore to them in the wilderness that I would not bring them into the land that I had given them, a land flowing with milk and honey, the most glorious of all lands, 16because they rejected my rules and did not walk in my statutes, and profaned my Sabbaths; for their heart went after their idols. 17Nevertheless, my eye spared them, and I did not destroy them or make a full end of them in the wilderness.

18"And I said to their children in the wilderness, Do not walk in the statutes of your fathers, nor keep their rules, nor defile yourselves with their idols. 19I am the LORD your God; walk in my statutes, and be careful to obey my rules, 20and keep my Sabbaths holy that they may be a sign between me and you, that you may know that I am the LORD your God. 21But the children rebelled against me. They did not walk in my statutes and were not careful to obey my rules, by which, if a person does them, he shall live; they profaned my Sabbaths.

"Then I said I would pour out my wrath upon them and spend my anger against them

in the wilderness. 22But I withheld my hand and acted for the sake of my name, that it
should not be profaned in the sight of the nations, in whose sight I had brought them out.
23Moreover, I swore to them in the wilderness that I would scatter them among the na-
tions and disperse them through the countries, 24because they had not obeyed my rules,
but had rejected my statutes and profaned my Sabbaths, and their eyes were set on their
fathers' idols. 25Moreover, I gave them statutes that were not good and rules by which
they could not have life, 26and I defiled them through their very gifts in their offering up
all their firstborn, that I might devastate them. I did it that they might know that I am
the LORD.

27"Therefore, son of man, speak to the house of Israel and say to them, Thus says the
Lord GOD: In this also your fathers blasphemed me, by dealing treacherously with me.
28For when I had brought them into the land that I swore to give them, then wherever
they saw any high hill or any leafy tree, there they offered their sacrifices and there they
presented the provocation of their offering; there they sent up their pleasing aromas, and
there they poured out their drink offerings. 29(I said to them, What is the high place to
which you go? So its name is called Bamah[b] to this day.)

30"Therefore say to the house of Israel, Thus says the Lord GOD: Will you defile
yourselves after the manner of your fathers and go whoring after their detestable things?
31When you present your gifts and offer up your children in fire,[c] you defile yourselves
with all your idols to this day. And shall I be inquired of by you, O house of Israel? As I
live, declares the Lord GOD, I will not be inquired of by you.

32"What is in your mind shall never happen—the thought, 'Let us be like the nations,
like the tribes of the countries, and worship wood and stone.'

33"As I live, declares the Lord GOD, surely with a mighty hand and an outstretched arm
and with wrath poured out I will be king over you. 34I will bring you out from the peoples
and gather you out of the countries where you are scattered, with a mighty hand and an
outstretched arm, and with wrath poured out. 35And I will bring you into the wilderness
of the peoples, and there I will enter into judgment with you face to face. 36As I entered
into judgment with your fathers in the wilderness of the land of Egypt, so I will enter into
judgment with you, declares the Lord GOD. 37I will make you pass under the rod, and I
will bring you into the bond of the covenant. 38I will purge out the rebels from among you,
and those who transgress against me. I will bring them out of the land where they sojourn,
but they shall not enter the land of Israel. Then you will know that I am the LORD.

39"As for you, O house of Israel, thus says the Lord GOD: Go serve every one of you his
idols, now and hereafter, if you will not listen to me; but my holy name you shall no more
profane with your gifts and your idols.

40"For on my holy mountain, the mountain height of Israel, declares the Lord GOD,
there all the house of Israel, all of them, shall serve me in the land. There I will accept
them, and there I will require your contributions and the choicest of your gifts, with all
your sacred offerings. 41As a pleasing aroma I will accept you, when I bring you out from
the peoples and gather you out of the countries where you have been scattered. And I
will manifest my holiness among you in the sight of the nations. 42And you shall know
that I am the LORD, when I bring you into the land of Israel, the country that I swore to
give to your fathers. 43And there you shall remember your ways and all your deeds with
which you have defiled yourselves, and you shall loathe yourselves for all the evils that you

have committed. 44*And you shall know that I am the* Lord, *when I deal with you for my*
name's sake, not according to your evil ways, nor according to your corrupt deeds, O house
of Israel, declares the Lord God."
45[d]*And the word of the* Lord *came to me:* 46"*Son of man, set your face toward the*
southland;[e] *preach against the south, and prophesy against the forest land in the Negeb.*
47*Say to the forest of the Negeb, Hear the word of the* Lord: *Thus says the Lord* God,
Behold, I will kindle a fire in you, and it shall devour every green tree in you and every
dry tree. The blazing flame shall not be quenched, and all faces from south to north shall
be scorched by it. 48*All flesh shall see that I the* Lord *have kindled it; it shall not be*
quenched." 49*Then I said, "Ah, Lord* God! *They are saying of me, 'Is he not a maker of*
parables?'"

a Hebrew *I lifted my hand;* twice in this verse; also verses 6, 15, 23, 28, 42 b *Bamah* means *high place* c Hebrew *and make your children pass through the fire* d Ch 21:1 in Hebrew e Or *toward Teman*

Overview: Ezekiel recounts at length the numerous episodes of idolatry in the history of Israel. The elders of Israel who came to Ezekiel pretended piety but were filled with hypocrisy. Their desire was to imitate the nations, not follow the Lord. Some consideration is given by our commentators to God's statement that if they follow the statutes or the sabbaths he gave them, then they would live. One commentator argues that the statutes, the laws, were not for life but to show us our sins and imperfections. This brings us to repentance and justification by faith. Another commentator sees a close relationship between the sabbaths and sacraments. The Spirit is promised in both if they are received by faith.

The chapter ends with judgment and restoration. The house of Israel is judged because of mixing the worship of God with idolatrous worship. Moreover, this rebellious house falsely claims the name Israel; true Israel, those who believe and follow the Lord, will dwell on God's holy mountain and serve him all their days. This faithful remnant alone shall be preserved.

20:1-29 *Salvation and Idolatry*

Hypocrisy. William Greenhill: Hypocrisy is a hidden sin and is in those we oftentimes would not think it of. It is found where it was not expected, in "the elders of Israel," those who here came to Ezekiel, pretended piety, sat before him, as if they would hearken to whatsoever the Lord should say, and do it. Yet they intended no such thing but were resolved to go on in their own ways and to be as the Babylonians and heathens, as you may see in Ezekiel 20:32, so that they might enjoy peace and safety. They did here like many that are on marriage, who will go to two or three to inquire and have counsel but are resolved to go on, whatever is said to them; so whatever counsel they should have had given them from the Lord, they meant to go on in their wicked ways. And this was profound hypocrisy, whose wont it is to veil the foulest things with the fairest pretenses. An Exposition of Ezekiel.[1]

Salvation Not Earned. John Mayer: Some people demand to know whether people by keeping God's command may attain everlasting life, because it is said, *I gave them statutes by which he that does them shall live* (Ezek 20:11)? Some answer that living and prospering in this world only is meant because it is our

[1]*Exposition*, 482.

duty to obey God's precepts. Therefore having done so we merit nothing but are unprofitable servants. But according to this rule we should not in obeying have our lives prolonged here, since even that is more than we are worthy of. This does not mean, then, that we shall be worthy of having such a promised life if we obey. Rather, it is out of God's kindness, who might, without this condition, require all due obedience at our hands. Wherefore out of his grace he makes this covenant with us, "Do this and live." Such covenant means both here by being saved from judgments, which if we sin will come on our land and hasten death, and in the world to come, from which we shall surely be rejected, if we happen to live long here, as a sinner may do according to that saying, *If a sinner lives a hundred years and God prolongs his days.* Now because no one can perfectly keep the commandments and so attain to life, to the law of doing is added the law of believing. Because of our imperfections, we should repent of our sins with the uttermost of our power, turn from them and believe in Christ so that perfect justification and salvation may be attained. And so it is not in vain that God bids us to do this and live, which he knows we cannot exactly do. But, we who repent of our failings and do what we can, the Son of God puts to his helping hand and both obeys perfectly for us and pays his blood for a ransom of our failings, whereby we come undoubtedly to live indeed. Commentary upon All the Prophets.[2]

The Sabbath and Sacraments. John Calvin: What he had said generally concerning the commandments he now applies again to the sabbath, and not without reason. For, as we said yesterday, God not only wished by that day of rest to exact from the people what was due to him, but he rather commands it for another purpose, namely, *that his sabbaths should be sanctified.* But the manner of keeping it holy was formerly explained, since mere rest was insufficient. God was not satisfied by the people's resting from their occupations, but the inward sanctification was always the chief end in view. And for this reason he also repeats again, *that they may be a sign between me and you to show you that I Jehovah am your God.* In this passage God bears witness, that if the Jews rightly observed their sabbaths they should feel the effects of that favor that he wished to be represented thereby. For we said that the sabbath was a sacrament of regeneration; now therefore he promises the efficacy of his Spirit if they did not shut the door by their own impiety and contempt. Hence we see that sacraments are never destitute of the virtue of the Spirit unless when people render themselves unworthy of the grace offered them.

When papists speak of the sacraments they say that they are efficacious, if we only remove the obstacle of mortal sin; they make no mention of faith. If a person is neither a thief nor an adulterer nor a murderer, they say that the sacraments produce their own effect; for example, if anyone without a single particle of faith intrudes himself at the table of Christ, they say that he receives not only his body and blood but also the fruit of his death and resurrection, and only because he has not committed mortal sin, that is, cannot be convicted of theft or homicide. We see how they are steeped in blindness, according to God's just judgment. We must hold, therefore, that there is a mutual relation between faith and the sacraments, and hence that the sacraments are effective through faith. People's unworthiness does not detract anything from them, for they always retain their nature. Baptism is the laver of regeneration, although the whole world should be incredulous (Tit 3:5); the Supper of Christ is the communication of his body and blood (1 Cor 10:16), although there were not a spark of faith in the world; but we

[2]*Prophets*, 425-26.

do not perceive the grace that is offered to us; and although spiritual things always remain the same, yet we do not obtain their effect or perceive their value unless we are cautious that our want of faith should not profane what God has consecrated, our salvation. Commentaries on Ezekiel.[3]

Two Kinds of Idolatry. John Calvin: But this passage, like many others, teaches that not only is God's worship corrupted when his honor is transferred to idols but also when people heap up their own fictions and contaminate God's commands by the mixture. We must remember, then, that there are two kinds of idolatries; the one being grossest when idols are worshiped openly, and Moloch, or any Baal, is substituted for the living God: that is a palpable superstition, because God is in some sense cast down from his throne. But the other kind of idolatry, although more hidden, is abominable before God, namely, when, under the disguise of a name, people boldly mingle whatever comes into their minds and invent various modes of worship; as at present we see in the papacy statues adored, and dead people invoiced and God's honor violated in various ways. Hence, however, the papists chatter, they are self-convicted, and the wonder is that they are not utterly silenced, since their superstitions are so gross that even children perceive them. But there are other superstitions more specious and refined; for when they have invented many things in honor of God, they will not bring forward the names of either Saint Barbara or Saint Christopher, but the name of God covers all those abominations. But we see that this excuse is frivolous, when people assert that they have nothing else in their mind than the worship of God. Not only does God wish worship to be offered to himself alone, but that it should be without any dependence on human will; he wishes the law to be the single rule of true worship, and thus he rejects all fictitious rites. Commentaries on Ezekiel.[4]

20:30-49 *Judgment and Restoration*

Worshiping Wood and Stone. John Mayer: Now the prophet comes to discover their hypocrisy (Ezek 20:32). They pretended piety toward God when they come to him to make inquiry. They came, however, with wicked thoughts in their minds. If they could not have a good answer of present comfort from him, they would make an utter defection to the heathen and worship as they did. They would serve wood and stone, supposing that hereby they should get more favor among them, since they were presently maligned by all nations for serving one God, who differed from all others and who was worshiped in a different way. By revolting to the heathen, though, they should be incorporated among them as one people. Likewise, some carnal professors of true religion at this day, when they see the worldly felicity of others and their own poor and afflicted estate, begin to think of falling to them. Commentary upon All the Prophets.[5]

The Hypocrisy of the Elders. William Greenhill: Hypocrisy so displeases God that he will have nothing to do with hypocrites. These elders, this house of Israel, they polluted themselves in their ancestors' sins, they took up ways of false worship and lived in the same to the day they came to inquire. And what says God? "Shall I be inquired of by you, O house of Israel?" You dissemble, act the hypocrite's part, and you provoke me not only to refuse to hear you but also to swear against you: "As I live, I will not be inquired of by you." You come not in sincerity but in subtlety; you pretend to walk in my ways, but you intend to follow your ancestors' ways; you make as if you would worship me, but you mean to worship idols. Ah! you old hypocrites, painted sepulchers, why do you come to me? I will not

[3]CTS 23:311-12 (CO 18:492). [4]CTS 23:320 (CO 18:497).
[5]*Prophets*, 428.

hear, answer or have anything to do with you.

. . . Labor, therefore, to be sincere, for the upright are his delight. Those who regard iniquity in their hearts, whoever they are, whatever they inquire and seek for at the hands of God, God will not hear them but discover them and give them the reward of hypocrites. AN EXPOSITION OF EZEKIEL.[6]

THE PARTIAL WORSHIP OF GOD. JOHN CALVIN: This passage (Ezek 20:39) is peculiarly remarkable, since at this time many are deceived while they rest on their own inventions and think that they best discharge their duty toward God when they partially obey his commandments, and then they pile up a great heap of superstitions, partly received from their ancestors and partly fabricated by themselves. Again, scarcely one in a hundred will be found who does not think it better partially to worship God than entirely to devote themselves to idols; and this indeed is true as far as people are concerned, for the impiety is more foul and detestable when people openly reject God, and divorce themselves from him and devote themselves to idols, than if they partly worshiped God and partly idols. But in the meantime, we see that God pronounces that he cannot bear this profanation; and we must diligently notice the reason that is added, for when gross and palpable impiety is indulged in, God's name is not so profaned as when clever people reconcile the pure worship of God with superstitions. And for this reason, that monstrous Interim [of Emperor Charles V] was in God's sight worse than the papacy; and why so? For although the papists profane God's name, yet their madness is at present so detected, that it openly appears that they are idolaters; but that invention mingled darkness with light and infected the pure doctrine with its leaven. But God here exclaims that he could not endure this deception when people profess to worship him, for they defile themselves with superstitions, since profaneness is added to impiety, and both are the result of hypocrisy. COMMENTARIES ON EZEKIEL.[7]

THE NAME ISRAEL. MARTIN LUTHER: The Jews make a point of the name Israel and claim that they alone are Israel and that we are Gentiles. Now this is true so far as the first part of the prophecy and the old covenant of Moses are concerned, though this has long since been fulfilled. But according to the second part of the prophecy and the new covenant, the Jews are no longer Israel, for all things are to be new, and Israel too must become new. Those alone are the true Israel who have accepted the new covenant which was established and begun at Jerusalem.

For according to the old covenant I am no Israelite, or Jew. But I claim now that I am the son of St. Paul, and an Israelite or Benjamite. For Paul is my father, not the old Paul but the new Paul. He is still the old Paul, but out of the old Paul there has arisen a new Paul in Christ; and he has begotten me in Christ by the gospel [1 Cor 4:15], so that I am in his likeness according to the new covenant. Thus all the Gentiles who are Christians are the true Israelites and new Jews, born of Christ, the noblest Jew. Everything, therefore, rests in the new covenant, which the Messiah was to found, making all things new, as he has done.

And this rule is to be noted well: when the prophets say of Israel that it is to return or to be gathered in its entirety, as in Mic 2:12, Ezek 20:40, etc., they are certainly speaking of the new covenant, and of the new Israel from which no one will be excluded, the everlasting kingdom of Christ. It cannot possibly be understood to mean the old Israel, for the majority of them remained in Assyria and Babylonia, both living and dead, and only a very few returned; Ezra [2:1-65] numbers them all. A NEW PREFACE TO THE PROPHET EZEKIEL.[8]

[6]*Exposition*, 508-9. [7]CTS 23:334-35 (CO 18:507-508). The "monstrous Interim" was the Augsburg Interim of 1548. See "Interims," *OER* 2:319-21. [8]Lenker 6, 307-308* (WADB 11,1:400).

Preservation of the Elect. John Calvin: God now directs his address to the elect, or the remnant in whom he wished his church to survive. Thus far he has spoken of the whole body of the people; he says, although he should free them from the hand of the Gentiles, yet that redemption would be but partial, because they should perish in the desert and never enjoy the promised land. On the whole, he shows that those to whom a free return to their own country was given were no less strangers than if they had been exiles at the time and always remained outlaws, since their impiety prevented their restoration. God now addresses the true Israelites, who were not only naturally descended from their ancestors but also were genuine and spiritual children, as Paul distinguishes between those sons of Abraham born according to the flesh and to promise (Rom 9:7-9). For this reason also it is said in Psalm 73—And surely God is good to Israel—to those who are upright in heart: for the prophet here asserts that God is gracious toward the Israelites; but since many hypocrites boast themselves to be members of the church, for the sake of correcting them, he restricts the sentence and does not reckon any as true Israelites except the upright in heart. Commentaries on Ezekiel.[9]

The Threshold of Our Eternal Salvation. John Calvin: *And you shall know that I am the Lord, when I have wrought with you for my name's sake* (Ezek 20:39). . . . Let us learn that we cannot otherwise worship God with acceptance unless we adopt whatever pleases him as pertaining to our salvation. For if we wish to come to a debtor and creditor account or to consider that he is in the slightest degree indebted to us, we in this way diminish his glory, and as far as lies in our power we despoil ourselves of that inestimable privilege that the prophet now commends. Hence let us desire to acknowledge God in this way, since he treats us with amazing clemency and pity out of regard for his own name, and not according to our sins. And since that was said to his ancient people because they returned to the land of Canaan, how much more ought God's gratuitous goodness be extolled by us, when his heavenly kingdom is at this day open to us, and when he openly calls us to himself in heaven and to the hope of that happy immortality that has been obtained for us through Christ? Commentaries on Ezekiel.[10]

Maker of Parables. John Owen: In the preaching and prophesying of Ezekiel, this one thing among others is eminent, that he was *artifex parabolarum*—a wonderful "framer of similitudes and parables" (Ezek 20:49); a way of teaching attended with much evidence, clearness and power.

In particular, he frequently compares the world with a field or a forest, and the inhabitants of it to the trees therein—an allusion exceedingly proper, considering the great variety and difference of condition both of the one and the other. The trees of the field are some high, some low; some green, some dry; some strong, some weak; some lofty, some contemptible; some fruitful, some barren; some useful, some altogether useless: so that you have all sorts of persons, high and low, of whatever condition, relation or interest clearly represented by the trees of the field. Sermon.[11]

[9]CTS 23:336 (CO 18:508-509). [10]CTS 23:345 (CO 18:514-515). With this paragraph, Calvin ends his commentary on Ezekiel. [11]Owen, *Works* 8:316.

21:1-32 BABYLON, GOD'S SWORD OF JUDGMENT

1[a]The word of the LORD came to me: 2"Son of man, set your face toward Jerusalem and preach against the sanctuaries.[b] Prophesy against the land of Israel 3and say to the land of Israel, Thus says the LORD: Behold, I am against you and will draw my sword from its sheath and will cut off from you both righteous and wicked. 4Because I will cut off from you both righteous and wicked, therefore my sword shall be drawn from its sheath against all flesh from south to north. 5And all flesh shall know that I am the LORD. I have drawn my sword from its sheath; it shall not be sheathed again.

6"As for you, son of man, groan; with breaking heart and bitter grief, groan before their eyes. 7And when they say to you, 'Why do you groan?' you shall say, 'Because of the news that it is coming. Every heart will melt, and all hands will be feeble; every spirit will faint, and all knees will be weak as water. Behold, it is coming, and it will be fulfilled,'" declares the Lord GOD.

8And the word of the LORD came to me: 9"Son of man, prophesy and say, Thus says the Lord, say:

"A sword, a sword is sharpened
and also polished,
10sharpened for slaughter,
polished to flash like lightning!

(Or shall we rejoice? You have despised the rod, my son, with everything of wood.)[c] 11So the sword is given to be polished, that it may be grasped in the hand. It is sharpened and polished to be given into the hand of the slayer. 12Cry out and wail, son of man, for it is against my people. It is against all the princes of Israel. They are delivered over to the sword with my people. Strike therefore upon your thigh. 13For it will not be a testing—what could it do if you despise the rod?"[d] declares the Lord GOD.

14"As for you, son of man, prophesy. Clap your hands and let the sword come down twice, yes, three times,[e] the sword for those to be slain. It is the sword for the great slaughter, which surrounds them, 15that their hearts may melt, and many stumble.[f] At all their gates I have given the glittering sword. Ah, it is made like lightning; it is taken up[g] for slaughter. 16Cut sharply to the right; set yourself to the left, wherever your face is directed. 17I also will clap my hands, and I will satisfy my fury; I the LORD have spoken."

18The word of the LORD came to me again: 19"As for you, son of man, mark two ways for the sword of the king of Babylon to come. Both of them shall come from the same land. And make a signpost; make it at the head of the way to a city. 20Mark a way for the sword to come to Rabbah of the Ammonites and to Judah, into Jerusalem the fortified. 21For the king of Babylon stands at the parting of the way, at the head of the two ways, to use divination. He shakes the arrows; he consults the teraphim;[h] he looks at the liver. 22Into his right hand comes the divination for Jerusalem, to set battering rams, to open the mouth with murder, to lift up the voice with shouting, to set battering rams against

the gates, to cast up mounds, to build siege towers. 23*But to them it will seem like a false*
divination. They have sworn solemn oaths, but he brings their guilt to remembrance, that
they may be taken.
24*"Therefore thus says the Lord God: Because you have made your guilt to be re-*
membered, in that your transgressions are uncovered, so that in all your deeds your sins
appear—because you have come to remembrance, you shall be taken in hand. 25*And you,*
O profane[i] *wicked one, prince of Israel, whose day has come, the time of your final punish-*
ment, 26*thus says the Lord God: Remove the turban and take off the crown. Things shall*
not remain as they are. Exalt that which is low, and bring low that which is exalted. 27*A*
ruin, ruin, ruin I will make it. This also shall not be, until he comes, the one to whom
judgment belongs, and I will give it to him.
28*"And you, son of man, prophesy, and say, Thus says the Lord God concerning the*
Ammonites and concerning their reproach; say, A sword, a sword is drawn for the slaugh-
*ter. It is polished to consume and to flash like lightning—*29*while they see for you false*
visions, while they divine lies for you—to place you on the necks of the profane wicked,
whose day has come, the time of their final punishment. 30*Return it to its sheath. In the*
place where you were created, in the land of your origin, I will judge you. 31*And I will*
pour out my indignation upon you; I will blow upon you with the fire of my wrath, and I
will deliver you into the hands of brutish men, skillful to destroy. 32*You shall be fuel for*
the fire. Your blood shall be in the midst of the land. You shall be no more remembered,
for I the Lord have spoken."

a Ch 21:6 in Hebrew **b** Some Hebrew manuscripts, compare Septuagint, Syriac *against their sanctuary* **c** Probable reading; Hebrew *The rod of my son despises everything of wood* **d** Or *For it is a testing; and what if even the rod despises? It shall not be!* **e** Hebrew *its third* **f** Hebrew *many stumbling blocks* **g** The meaning of the Hebrew word rendered *taken up* is uncertain **h** Or *household idols* **i** Or *slain;* also verse 29

Overview: Ezekiel again prophesies against Jerusalem. Now we are told that a sword will be brought against the city and the righteous and the wicked alike. The temple will provide no sanctuary for the wicked. God will strike against it. The prophet is told to sigh before the people that they might know the coming disaster. The sword that is coming is the king of Babylon, Nebuchadnezzar. The profane and wicked prince of Israel is Zedekiah. One point of concern in this chapter is the suggestion that Nebuchadnezzar's use of divination determined his course for Jerusalem (Ezek 21:21). This was not the case, however. The prophecy given by Ezekiel revealed God's will and determined Nebuchadnezzar's actions.

Summary of the Chapter. Jakob Raupius: Two prophecies are contained in this chapter. One is against the Jews, who remain in the land under the rule of Zedekiah, whom the prophet has already spoken about. The other is against the Ammonites, whom the Lord also threatens through Ezekiel with the sword of the Babylonians. Commentary on Ezekiel.[1]

Who Are the Righteous? Jakob Raupius: *I will cut off from you both the righteous and the wicked* (Ezek 21:3). Piscator understands by the "righteous" the one who is not entirely unrighteous. But the Lord compares the righteous with the wicked. We understand here those who were certainly righteous. Surely and truly those who are righteous, that is, those reborn and in grace with God, were accustomed

[1]*Commentarius Synopticus* (1655), 153.

to stand against public wickedness, even if they are reprimanded because of their ancestors' sins. They learn from the example of the wicked that God severely punishes the sins of people. Commentary on Ezekiel.[2]

The Prophet's Sigh. William Greenhill: The goodness of the Lord toward a stubborn, willful, perishing people, in that he will have the prophet to see what prophetical signs will do, when prophetical threats did nothing. "Sigh, son of man, with the breaking of your loins and with bitterness" (Ezek 20:6). These were prophetical sighs, representing to them the great evils that were coming upon them, so that they might consider, sigh in like manner for their sins and prevent their destruction, or else certainly expect the same. God laid a heavy burden on the prophet, to sigh so. An Exposition of Ezekiel.[3]

Prophesying in Sackcloth. William Greenhill: It is no new thing for the prophets of the Lord to prophesy in sackcloth (Ezek 21:14). Ezekiel must prophesy and strike his hands together, in token of mourning and heaviness; our prophet was in sackcloth, being a captive in Babylon, seeing the sad judgments that were coming on Jerusalem. So Jeremiah, Hosea, Joel, Amos had mournful spirits and prophesied in sackcloth, they struck their hands together and dropped out sad things. The times were black in their days; they are not clear now. Is not the sword coming the third time? Is it not putting on for slaughter? Shall not the prophets mourn and strike their hands together?

Where the word prevails not to reform a people, there the judgments of God will come in, one after another, to the destruction of a people. "Prophesy, and let the sword be doubled the third time." He had often prophesied, but there appeared no repentance, no returning to God; therefore let the sword come again and again. Had they repented of their sins, God would have repented of the evils intended (Jer 18:7-8), but when people go on in their sins, God will go on in his judgment, even to destruction. An Exposition of Ezekiel.[4]

The King of Babylon and Divination. John Mayer: *The king of Babylon stood at the head of the way . . . and mingled arrows.* According to Jerome, he took two arrows. On one he wrote Jerusalem and on the other Rabbath. He put them into a quiver and removed one blindfolded. He removed the one saying Jerusalem and divined that he should go with success against Jerusalem. And this the prophet speaks, not as if he had already done so, but that he would shortly do so. Then, his hand being guided by the Lord, although to him unknown, it should happen in this way and he should come and prevail. But by this he meant not to set up the credit of such divinations used by heathens, but only that the divination made concurred with his prophecy. It should more fully appear that this must occur. Since they were superstitious in the same way as the heathen, this would terrify them the more. And it was no new or strange thing that God should declare the coming destruction of the wicked by wicked means, seeing he revealed such great mysteries by Balaam, and by a counterfeit Samuel raised up by the witch of Endor to the terror of Saul, foretelling his terrible ruin. Commentary upon All the Prophets.[5]

Nebuchadnezzar's Way Foreseen in the Past Tense. William Greenhill: Here the past tense is put for the future (Ezek 21:21). The king of Babylon had not yet stood there, but he shall stand at the parting of the way, at the mother of the way; when a way di-

[2]*Commentarius Synopticus* (1655), 155. Johannes Piscator (1546–1625), a Reformed theologian, prepared summaries and detailed notes for the entire Old and New Testament and published a German translation of the Bible. [3]*Exposition*, 522. [4]*Exposition*, 527. [5]*Prophets*, 428.

vides into or begets two ways, the Hebrew calls the first way, the mother of the other, and head of them, as here: "the head of the two ways."

. . . The Lord knows things to come most certainly, indeed, as certainly as if done already. He knew that Nebuchadnezzar would come out of Babylon, what way he would come and where he would make a stand and consult, which he shows to the prophet and speaks of as done already (Ezek 21:24). The Lord sees things afar off and knows what shall be in ages to come. Hereby he confounds all idol gods and proves himself to be the true God. An Exposition of Ezekiel.[6]

Zedekiah the Last King Before Christ. John Mayer: And you profane wicked prince of Israel, whose day is come, when iniquity shall have end, remove the diadem, take off the crown, this shall not be the man; exalt him that is low, and abase him that is high (Ezek 21:25-26). . . . Zedekiah is called the profane prince for his impiety toward God, and wicked for his injustice towards people. . . . And the speech is directed only to the king, and therefore against him only is this spoken to show his deposing and so the cessation of the kingdom in him. And profaneness is laid to his charge, because he broke his oath to Nebuchadnezzar. Moreover, it is here showed that there should be no more king after him until Christ should come. For although after the captivity there was a prince, and the principality coming to the priest, Alexander made himself king and some others after him, yet those kings were not worthy to be spoken of. At that time, the state was in such confusion, and in the time of the princes, they ruled as inferior persons at the will of other kings. The low one to be exalted was Christ, who was poor and humble, the high one to be brought down was wicked Zedekiah, to whom no respective terms are given, because the speech comes, as it were, from God, with whom is no respect of persons. Commentary upon All the Prophets.[7]

Profane and Wicked Prince of Israel. William Greenhill: This prince was Zedekiah, and the titles given him are not Your sacred majesty or Your excellency's highness, but "You profane and wicked prince" (Ezek 21:25). His profaneness and wickedness were doubtless great, though much is not specified in the word; yet something is set down in 2 Chronicles 36. . . .

The prophet may seem here to forget himself in speaking so opprobriously of the prince, which the law forbade (Ex 22:28). They might neither think nor speak evil of the ruler, nor wish evil to him (Eccles 10:20). And here Ezekiel calls Zedekiah the prince of Israel, profane and wicked. And in so doing he sinned not. For being a prophet, he was to give out what the Spirit of God gave in and moved him to. So dealt Jeremiah with Coniah, when he called him "a despised broken idol, a vessel wherein was no pleasure" (Jer 22:28). They would not flatter princes by being false to truth. When it is done from a private and depraved spirit, then it is ill.

. . . Of all princes in the world, the princes of Israel had cause to be holy and just. They were seated where the worship of the true God was. They had the law of Moses and were commanded to read it continually and not to depart from it to the right hand or to the left (Deut 17:18-20). They had the Sanhedrin, the priests and prophets to counsel and advise them. Yet princes of Israel were profane; they minded not the law of Moses or the worship of God; they despised priests and prophets; they were wicked, they persecuted good people and were perfidious to other princes—both Jehoiakim and Zedekiah were so to Nebuchadnezzar (2 Kings 24). An Exposition of Ezekiel.[8]

[6]*Exposition*, 528-29. [7]*Prophets*, 433-34. [8]*Exposition*, 531.

22:1-31 JERUSALEM'S SINS

1And the word of the LORD came to me, saying, 2"And you, son of man, will you judge, will you judge the bloody city? Then declare to her all her abominations. 3You shall say, Thus says the Lord GOD: A city that sheds blood in her midst, so that her time may come, and that makes idols to defile herself! 4You have become guilty by the blood that you have shed, and defiled by the idols that you have made, and you have brought your days near, the appointed time of[a] your years has come. Therefore I have made you a reproach to the nations, and a mockery to all the countries. 5Those who are near and those who are far from you will mock you; your name is defiled; you are full of tumult.

6"Behold, the princes of Israel in you, every one according to his power, have been bent on shedding blood. 7Father and mother are treated with contempt in you; the sojourner suffers extortion in your midst; the fatherless and the widow are wronged in you. 8You have despised my holy things and profaned my Sabbaths. 9There are men in you who slander to shed blood, and people in you who eat on the mountains; they commit lewdness in your midst. 10In you men uncover their fathers' nakedness; in you they violate women who are unclean in their menstrual impurity. 11One commits abomination with his neighbor's wife; another lewdly defiles his daughter-in-law; another in you violates his sister, his father's daughter. 12In you they take bribes to shed blood; you take interest and profit[b] and make gain of your neighbors by extortion; but me you have forgotten, declares the Lord GOD.

13"Behold, I strike my hand at the dishonest gain that you have made, and at the blood that has been in your midst. 14Can your courage endure, or can your hands be strong, in the days that I shall deal with you? I the LORD have spoken, and I will do it. 15I will scatter you among the nations and disperse you through the countries, and I will consume your uncleanness out of you. 16And you shall be profaned by your own doing in the sight of the nations, and you shall know that I am the LORD."

17And the word of the LORD came to me: 18"Son of man, the house of Israel has become dross to me; all of them are bronze and tin and iron and lead in the furnace; they are dross of silver. 19Therefore thus says the Lord GOD: Because you have all become dross, therefore, behold, I will gather you into the midst of Jerusalem. 20As one gathers silver and bronze and iron and lead and tin into a furnace, to blow the fire on it in order to melt it, so I will gather you in my anger and in my wrath, and I will put you in and melt you. 21I will gather you and blow on you with the fire of my wrath, and you shall be melted in the midst of it. 22As silver is melted in a furnace, so you shall be melted in the midst of it, and you shall know that I am the LORD; I have poured out my wrath upon you."

23And the word of the LORD came to me: 24"Son of man, say to her, You are a land that is not cleansed or rained upon in the day of indignation. 25The conspiracy of her prophets in her midst is like a roaring lion tearing the prey; they have devoured human lives; they have taken treasure and precious things; they have made many widows in her midst. 26Her priests have done violence to my law and have profaned my holy things. They have made no distinction between the holy and the common, neither have they taught the difference between the unclean and the clean, and they have disregarded my Sabbaths, so that

I am profaned among them. 27 Her princes in her midst are like wolves tearing the prey,
shedding blood, destroying lives to get dishonest gain. 28 And her prophets have smeared
whitewash for them, seeing false visions and divining lies for them, saying, 'Thus says
the Lord God,' when the Lord has not spoken. 29 The people of the land have practiced
extortion and committed robbery. They have oppressed the poor and needy, and have
extorted from the sojourner without justice. 30 And I sought for a man among them who
should build up the wall and stand in the breach before me for the land, that I should not
destroy it, but I found none. 31 Therefore I have poured out my indignation upon them.
I have consumed them with the fire of my wrath. I have returned their way upon their
heads, declares the Lord God."

a Some Hebrew manuscripts, Septuagint, Syriac, Vulgate, Targum; most Hebrew manuscripts *until* **b** That is, profit that comes from charging interest to the poor (compare Leviticus 25:36)

Overview: The sins of Jerusalem are enumerated. Her iniquities have hastened her end. The root cause of her sins is the forgetfulness of God. No regard was given to what God had declared, commanded, bestowed on them or promised; their thoughts were consumed only with their rebellion and sin. Jerusalem's punishment is likened to the dross that must be removed from a furnace. Dross is deceptive. It gives the appearance of metal, but it is not metal. Likewise the house of Israel was deceitful and hypocritical. The Lord looked about the people for a righteous hedge (Ezek 22:30) to stand in the gap that the land should not be destroyed. None was found.

The Sins of Israel Enumerated. John Mayer: In this chapter the sins of the Jews inhabiting Jerusalem, which were laid open in Ezekiel 20, for which the Lord asked the prophet saying, *Will you judge them?*, are, with the same question, further declared. They were first idolatry and bloodshed (Ezek 22:3-6), making the holy city infamous among the heathen, for which the princes are especially accused. 2. Dishonoring parents and oppressing strangers and widows (Ezek 22:7). 3. Despising God's holy things, that is, his sacrifices, . . . and profaning his sabbaths (Ezek 22:8). 4. Eating on the mountains and carrying tales to shed blood (Ezek 22:9); of eating on the mountains enough has been spoken before (Ezek 18) and of tale bearing (Lev 19:16). 5. Incest with a man's father's wife, after the manner of Reuben, and going in to a menstruous woman (Ezek 22:10). 6. Adultery, incest with daughter-in-law and with sister (Ezek 22:11), of which see Leviticus 18. 7. Taking bribes, usury and extortion (Ezek 22:12). Commentary upon All the Prophets.[1]

The Sins of Israel. Johannes Oecolampadius: "You have become guilty by the blood you have shed" (Ezek 22:4). You will not be punished on account of another's sins, but you will be punished because of your murders and injustices and your many idolatries. Read "you have sinned" where the text has "you have neglected" or "you have become guilty"; that is, you are the guilty party, and you are openly and manifestly found with the pollution of sin. By your evil deeds, you have hastened your years and your visitation, the time of your departure, captivity and destruction. Your total wickedness calls forth a severe judgment. Commentary on the Prophet Ezekiel.[2]

Forgetfulness of God. William Greenhill: The forgetfulness of God is the cause of all the sins in a city or people. Jerusalem's sins

[1] *Prophets*, 433-34. [2] *Commentarius in Ezechielem* (1553), 116.

are here reckoned up: cruelty, idolatry, slighting of parents, oppression of strangers, vexing of fatherless and widows, despising of holy things, profanation of sabbaths, tale carrying to shed blood, eating on the mountains, devising wickedness, incest, adultery, bribery, usury, extortion. And what is the root of all these? "'You have forgotten me,' says the Lord God" (Ezek 22:12). When people mind not what God commands, forbids, what he threatens, what he approves, when they acknowledge not his eye, his power, his judgments, the account they must give to him, they fall into all manner of sins, lewdnesses and transgressions. An Exposition of Ezekiel.[3]

God's Punishment. John Mayer: *You shall know that I am the Lord* (Ezek 22:16). You, polluted city, having in you so much sin, and punished accordingly by being given over into the hands of the heathen and made to dwell in misery in a heathen country shall be made by experience to know that I am the Lord. I justly judge you who would not by any means be brought to repentance and amendment of life.

Having showed what they should suffer in the land of the heathens, now he shows what they should suffer in their own land before their going into captivity during the time of the siege. They should be as lead, brass and iron, in the midst of the ardent fire of God's wrath burning, and kept here until they were as silver and these baser metals melted together by the famine, pestilence and sword, and the burning of the city and the temple. Commentary upon All the Prophets.[4]

A Hedge. William Greenhill: "That should make up a hedge." The Hebrew is "hedging a hedge." The words are metaphorical, and the metaphor is taken from vineyards, gardens and places enclosed, which used to have fences and hedges about them to preserve them from everything that might harm them, both people and beasts. The Jews were God's vineyard (Is 5:1), and he had fenced and hedged them; they were God's garden, and he had enclosed them (Song 4:12). The fence, "hedge" or wall about this people was God's protection of them. He had a special care of them, being his church and people, above all others; as the city of Jerusalem had a wall about it (Neh 1:3), so God was a wall to the citizens of it. . . .

Those things and means that God had given them to be a hedge or wall for them were the following: (1) Sound doctrine; which was a "hedge" to keep out all errors, corrupt and heathenish opinions, which they were in danger of, having the nations round about them. But God had given them good doctrine (Prov 4:2), right words (Ps 33:4), lively oracles (Acts 7:38), faithful commands (Ps 33:4), sure testimonies (Ps 93:5), such as they were to try all doctrines and opinions (Is 8:20); (2) Pure worship, which was a "hedge" between them and the heathens. . . . (3) Good laws. . . . (4) God had given them good prophets, priests and princes for their safety, to be a "hedge" to them. The prophets were to preserve the doctrine sound, the priests to keep the worship pure, and the princes to see justice impartially executed.

The hedge was broken and gaps were made. The doctrine was corrupted. . . . The worship was greatly corrupted. The sanctuary was defiled with detestable things. . . . The laws were wrested and perverted, so that there was no justice. . . . For the people, who should have been as strong stakes to keep up the "hedge," they were rotten. The prophets were lions (Jer 23:14), the priests corrupters and wicked (Lam 4:13), the princes were rebellious and companions of thieves (Is 1:23), and all of them broke the covenant with God (Ezek 16:59), so that it is evident the "hedge" was broken and gaps made. An Exposition of Ezekiel.[5]

A Righteous Hedge. John Mayer: Here

[3]*Exposition*, 542. [4]*Prophets*, 436. [5]*Exposition*, 557-58.

the Lord shows how, despite so many great sins abounding in Jerusalem, if he could have found some righteous persons there who had by fervent prayer sought to make up the hedge, as Moses who stood in the gap, that sin had made there, by earnestly opposing themselves against evil, seeking the reformation of the city, he would not have proceeded to bring the judgments threatened. If there had been but one godly prophet more besides Jeremiah, a few priests, one or two godly princes, and some few godly people among those many thousands who were so grossly tainted with sin, according to the four sorts mentioned before (Ezek 22:25-30), he would not have proceeded. It is not likely that he meant precisely one, as also Lyra says, for there was Jeremiah and Baruch, and some godly persons more, that were marked in their foreheads (Ezek 9:4). . . . Wherefore I assent rather to him holding that by one a competent number is meant, as in Sodom, the Lord said, if there had been found ten righteous, he would spare Sodom for their sakes.

From this, note that sin makes a gap or breach in the hedge of God's providence about a state. When it is thus, God looks to his faithful servants to make it up by prayer and by opposing sinful courses. By being himself righteous, he makes up the breach. There must yet, for the saving of a state from utter ruin, be a competent number of such people there, and then God's mercy is such that for their sakes, the whole shall be saved in the most dangerous times. Yet none wicked shall for another's sake be saved eternally, but only temporally. There is for all another time of reckoning when they shall not escape everlasting destruction, both of soul and body, which may make us still to live in hope, that England shall stand, wherein I doubt not, but that there be some in every place, and many in populous places throughout the land, who fear God and pray and labor earnestly against sin daily, the number of whom God increase. COMMENTARY UPON ALL THE PROPHETS.[6]

[6]*Prophets*, 437.

23:1-49 TWO ADULTEROUS SISTERS

1The word of the LORD came to me: 2"Son of man, there were two women, the daugh-
ters of one mother. 3They played the whore in Egypt; they played the whore in their youth;
there their breasts were pressed and their virgin bosoms[a] handled. 4Oholah was the name
of the elder and Oholibah the name of her sister. They became mine, and they bore sons
and daughters. As for their names, Oholah is Samaria, and Oholibah is Jerusalem.
5"Oholah played the whore while she was mine, and she lusted after her lovers the As-
syrians, warriors 6clothed in purple, governors and commanders, all of them desirable
young men, horsemen riding on horses. 7She bestowed her whoring upon them, the choic-
est men of Assyria all of them, and she defiled herself with all the idols of everyone after
whom she lusted. 8She did not give up her whoring that she had begun in Egypt; for in her
youth men had lain with her and handled her virgin bosom and poured out their whoring

lust upon her. 9Therefore I delivered her into the hands of her lovers, into the hands of
the Assyrians, after whom she lusted. 10These uncovered her nakedness; they seized her
sons and her daughters; and as for her, they killed her with the sword; and she became a
byword among women, when judgment had been executed on her.
11"Her sister Oholibah saw this, and she became more corrupt than her sister[b] in her
lust and in her whoring, which was worse than that of her sister. 12She lusted after the As-
syrians, governors and commanders, warriors clothed in full armor, horsemen riding on
horses, all of them desirable young men. 13And I saw that she was defiled; they both took
the same way. 14But she carried her whoring further. She saw men portrayed on the wall,
the images of the Chaldeans portrayed in vermilion, 15wearing belts on their waists, with
flowing turbans on their heads, all of them having the appearance of officers, a likeness
of Babylonians whose native land was Chaldea. 16When she saw them, she lusted after
them and sent messengers to them in Chaldea. 17And the Babylonians came to her into
the bed of love, and they defiled her with their whoring lust. And after she was defiled
by them, she turned from them in disgust. 18When she carried on her whoring so openly
and flaunted her nakedness, I turned in disgust from her, as I had turned in disgust from
her sister. 19Yet she increased her whoring, remembering the days of her youth, when she
played the whore in the land of Egypt 20and lusted after her paramours there, whose mem-
bers were like those of donkeys, and whose issue was like that of horses. 21Thus you longed
for the lewdness of your youth, when the Egyptians handled your bosom and pressed[c] your
young breasts."
22Therefore, O Oholibah, thus says the Lord God: "Behold, I will stir up against you
your lovers from whom you turned in disgust, and I will bring them against you from
every side: 23the Babylonians and all the Chaldeans, Pekod and Shoa and Koa, and all
the Assyrians with them, desirable young men, governors and commanders all of them,
officers and men of renown, all of them riding on horses. 24And they shall come against
you from the north[d] with chariots and wagons and a host of peoples. They shall set them-
selves against you on every side with buckler, shield, and helmet; and I will commit the
judgment to them, and they shall judge you according to their judgments. 25And I will
direct my jealousy against you, that they may deal with you in fury. They shall cut off
your nose and your ears, and your survivors shall fall by the sword. They shall seize your
sons and your daughters, and your survivors shall be devoured by fire. 26They shall also
strip you of your clothes and take away your beautiful jewels. 27Thus I will put an end to
your lewdness and your whoring begun in the land of Egypt, so that you shall not lift up
your eyes to them or remember Egypt anymore.
28"For thus says the Lord God: Behold, I will deliver you into the hands of those whom
you hate, into the hands of those from whom you turned in disgust, 29and they shall deal
with you in hatred and take away all the fruit of your labor and leave you naked and bare,
and the nakedness of your whoring shall be uncovered. Your lewdness and your whoring
30have brought this upon you, because you played the whore with the nations and defiled
yourself with their idols. 31You have gone the way of your sister; therefore I will give her
cup into your hand. 32Thus says the Lord God:

"You shall drink your sister's cup
that is deep and large;
you shall be laughed at and held in
derision,

for it contains much;
[33]*you will be filled with drunkenness and sorrow.*
A cup of horror and desolation,
the cup of your sister Samaria;
[34]*you shall drink it and drain it out,*
and gnaw its shards,
and tear your breasts;

for I have spoken, declares the Lord God. [35]*Therefore thus says the Lord God: Because you have forgotten me and cast me behind your back, you yourself must bear the consequences of your lewdness and whoring."*

[36]*The Lord said to me: "Son of man, will you judge Oholah and Oholibah? Declare to them their abominations.* [37]*For they have committed adultery, and blood is on their hands. With their idols they have committed adultery, and they have even offered up*[e] *to them for food the children whom they had borne to me.* [38]*Moreover, this they have done to me: they have defiled my sanctuary on the same day and profaned my Sabbaths.* [39]*For when they had slaughtered their children in sacrifice to their idols, on the same day they came into my sanctuary to profane it. And behold, this is what they did in my house.* [40]*They even sent for men to come from afar, to whom a messenger was sent; and behold, they came. For them you bathed yourself, painted your eyes, and adorned yourself with ornaments.* [41]*You sat on a stately couch, with a table spread before it on which you had placed my incense and my oil.* [42]*The sound of a carefree multitude was with her; and with men of the common sort, drunkards*[f] *were brought from the wilderness; and they put bracelets on the hands of the women, and beautiful crowns on their heads.*

[43]*"Then I said of her who was worn out by adultery, Now they will continue to use her for a whore, even her!*[g] [44]*For they have gone in to her, as men go in to a prostitute. Thus they went in to Oholah and to Oholibah, lewd women!* [45]*But righteous men shall pass judgment on them with the sentence of adulteresses, and with the sentence of women who shed blood, because they are adulteresses, and blood is on their hands."*

[46]*For thus says the Lord God: "Bring up a vast host against them, and make them an object of terror and a plunder.* [47]*And the host shall stone them and cut them down with their swords. They shall kill their sons and their daughters, and burn up their houses.* [48]*Thus will I put an end to lewdness in the land, that all women may take warning and not commit lewdness as you have done.* [49]*And they shall return your lewdness upon you, and you shall bear the penalty for your sinful idolatry, and you shall know that I am the Lord God."*

a Hebrew *nipples;* also verses 8, 21 **b** Hebrew *than she* **c** Vulgate, Syriac; Hebrew *bosom for the sake of* **d** Septuagint; the meaning of the Hebrew word is unknown **e** Or *have even made pass through the fire* **f** Or *Sabeans* **g** The meaning of the Hebrew verse is uncertain

Overview: Here follows the parable of two adulterous sisters, Aholah and Aholibah, who are Jerusalem and Samaria. The content is similar to Ezekiel 16. The sisters prostituted themselves with the idolatrous practices of the neighboring nations and now must bear the consequences of their iniquity. These adulteresses would be judged by righteous people, that is, the Babylonians. They were righteous not in themselves but in the sentence they executed against the sisters. Here we are to learn that any contamination of the worship of God is like defiling the marriage bed.

Summary of the Chapter. Jakob Raupius: There are other prophecies against the

Jews in this chapter who at that time remained in the land under the rule of Zedekiah. The chapter is conveniently divided into three parts. The first contains the complaint against the idolaters. The second part is the announcement of their destruction. The third is an embellishment in which their idolatries and destruction are repeated, elucidated and amplified. Commentary on Ezekiel.[1]

Aholah and Aholibah. Johannes Oecolampadius: "Aholah was the name of the elder and Aholibah the name of her sister" (Ezek 23:4). The Lord himself explains lest anyone distort by another word these names created for occasion. He specifically named each kingdom by the tabernacle. Samaria is called the kingdom of the ten tribes because the city of Samaria is the head of the kingdom. "Aholah," that is, her tabernacle, as if he had said, that very tabernacle that you have does not have me. Jerusalem is truly "Aholibah," that is, my tabernacle is in her; which is to say, the one in which I dwell and has my holy things in it. Commentary on the Prophet Ezekiel.[2]

Parable of Aholah and Aholibah. John Mayer: In this chapter the prophet sets forth at God's direction the same that he did in Ezekiel 16 but with this difference—there he plainly without any parable laid open their sins, here he does so by a parable of Aholah and Aholibah. To the first name he compares Samaria, the head city of the kingdom of Israel, and to the other the kingdom of Judah. These names served most aptly to set forth these nations, for Aholah signifies a tent, and Aholibah, a tent, or tabernacle in her, or the one her tabernacle, the other my tabernacle in her. Samaria being so called, because her tabernacle, to which she resorted to worship her golden calf, was at Bethel, and likewise at Dan, and in Jerusalem was the tent of God where Judah worshiped.

Both of these are said to have fornicated in Egypt, because their idolatry had originated from there, where both had of old been idolaters, as has been showed in Ezekiel 20, and they learned to worship an ox or calf. But this was not all their sin. Aholah went further in committing idolatry with the gods of the Assyrians, for which and for other foul sins she was destroyed by the same Assyrians. Then Aholibah was so far from being amended by her punishment that she did worse, in that she served idols and burned her sons and daughters to them in sacrifice, and from this abominable sin, she came to the house of God to worship him, who abhors more those that do so than such as serve idols altogether (1 Kings 18:37-39). Commentary upon All the Prophets.[3]

The Two Women Aholah and Aholibah. William Greenhill: "There were two women, the daughters of one mother." The Jews were at first one people, till the days of Rehoboam, and then they were divided. Ten tribes fell off to Jeroboam, which frequently after were called Ephraim, and Israel, or the children of Israel, the house of Israel. The other two tribes were called Judah, and the house of Judah: one was the kingdom of Israel, the other the kingdom of Judah. These two were the two women here mentioned. . . . "They committed whoredoms in Egypt." They, being in the loins of their "mother," forsook the God of Abraham, Isaac and Jacob and fell in love with the Egyptian gods.

. . . "The names of them were Aholah, the elder." The name of the one was Aholah, and this Aholah was Samaria, the chief city of the ten tribes, where the kings of Israel had their chief residency. Aholah is from the Hebrew word for tent or tabernacle; and Aholah is his own, or their own, tabernacle; that is, Samaria,

[1]*Commentarius Synopticus* (1655), 175. [2]*Commentarius in Ezechielem* (1553), 122. [3]*Prophets*, 437.

or the ten tribes, have not me, or my worship, among them; they have devised a worship of their own, set up golden calves at Dan and Bethel; they have forsaken my temple, and set up their own tabernacle and dwell by themselves, separate from me.

. . . "Aholibah her sister." Thus is the name of the other woman. Aholah's sister was Aholibah, which signifies my tabernacle, or dwelling in her; and this was Jerusalem, where the temple and worship of the Lord were; what was done there the Lord himself appointed, and that was the place he chose. An Exposition of Ezekiel.[4]

Bruised Breasts. Martin Luther: Ezekiel 23:21 rebuked the synagogue for shamelessness of the heart, for the fact that her breasts were bruised in Egypt. The devil attempts with all his power to bruise the breasts of the soul, that is, to defile it with evil thoughts. It means, similarly, that the church does not, like the heretics who teach their own doctrine, have independent breasts with which she feeds milk to the weak, but she is captive to the authority of Scripture and does not teach anything but the Word of God. The breasts of the church are the teachers of the weak, whom they instruct with the milk of more pleasant doctrine. First Lectures on the Psalms.[5]

Profaning God. William Greenhill: To profane holy things is to wrong God. . . . When they had sinned, and so came into the sanctuary and profaned that and the sabbath, God says, "This they have done to me. Lo, thus have they done in the midst of my house" (Ezek 23:38). God takes the wrong done to his house, worship and day as done to himself; for he dwelled in the temple, instituted the worship and day, had stamped holiness on them. Therefore the defiling and profaning of them he counted as the defiling and profaning of his name and of himself, and it did so sorely offend him that he sets a double mark or brand thereon: "This they have done to me. Thus have they done in my house." An Exposition of Ezekiel.[6]

Righteous Men. John Mayer: *The righteous men shall judge them after the manner of adulteresses* (Ezek 23:45). That is, the Chaldeans, into whose hands they should come. But how are they called righteous? Answer: For their executing of the sentence of the righteous judge on them without any partiality, and not for any righteousness that was in themselves, for they were wicked idolaters, as the Jews were, and lived in many other sins. It is probable, however, that they kept covenants, to which they were sworn, better than the Jews, and were more morally righteous. As the greater ones, they were not so oppressive to the inferior people under their dominions. To this we may also add that they were altogether addicted to the religion of which they were and were not a compound of linsy-woolsy, halting between two opinions, as the Jews did, neither did they enjoy such means, living in darkness and without the light of the word, which the Jews enjoyed. And therefore in comparison with the Jews they were righteous. . . .

And therefore whatever nation professes the truth and lives under the teaching of it, but is wicked, may justly fear to be given over into the hands of heathen, Turks, infidels and papists, to be by them judged as they deserve, that is, with stoning, as adulterers and adulteresses ought by the law of God to be served, and having their houses burned and others of them slain with the sword together with their children (Ezek 23:47). Commentary upon All the Prophets.[7]

[4]*Exposition*, 561. [5]LW 10:219. [6]*Exposition*, 568. [7]*Prophets*, 439.

24:1-27 THE COOKING POT

1 In the ninth year, in the tenth month, on the tenth day of the month, the word of the
LORD came to me: 2 "Son of man, write down the name of this day, this very day. The king
of Babylon has laid siege to Jerusalem this very day. 3 And utter a parable to the rebellious
house and say to them, Thus says the Lord GOD:

"Set on the pot, set it on;
  pour in water also;
4 put in it the pieces of meat,
  all the good pieces, the thigh and the shoulder;
  fill it with choice bones.
5 Take the choicest one of the flock;
  pile the logs[a] under it;
boil it well;
  seethe also its bones in it.

6 "Therefore thus says the Lord GOD: Woe to the bloody city, to the pot whose corrosion
is in it, and whose corrosion has not gone out of it! Take out of it piece after piece, without
making any choice.[b] 7 For the blood she has shed is in her midst; she put it on the bare rock;
she did not pour it out on the ground to cover it with dust. 8 To rouse my wrath, to take
vengeance, I have set on the bare rock the blood she has shed, that it may not be covered.
9 Therefore thus says the Lord GOD: Woe to the bloody city! I also will make the pile great.
10 Heap on the logs, kindle the fire, boil the meat well, mix in the spices,[c] and let the bones
be burned up. 11 Then set it empty upon the coals, that it may become hot, and its copper
may burn, that its uncleanness may be melted in it, its corrosion consumed. 12 She has
wearied herself with toil;[d] its abundant corrosion does not go out of it. Into the fire with
its corrosion! 13 On account of your unclean lewdness, because I would have cleansed you
and you were not cleansed from your uncleanness, you shall not be cleansed anymore till
I have satisfied my fury upon you. 14 I am the LORD. I have spoken; it shall come to pass;
I will do it. I will not go back; I will not spare; I will not relent; according to your ways
and your deeds you will be judged, declares the Lord GOD."

15 The word of the LORD came to me: 16 "Son of man, behold, I am about to take the
delight of your eyes away from you at a stroke; yet you shall not mourn or weep, nor shall
your tears run down. 17 Sigh, but not aloud; make no mourning for the dead. Bind on your
turban, and put your shoes on your feet; do not cover your lips, nor eat the bread of men."
18 So I spoke to the people in the morning, and at evening my wife died. And on the next
morning I did as I was commanded.

19 And the people said to me, "Will you not tell us what these things mean for us, that
you are acting thus?" 20 Then I said to them, "The word of the LORD came to me: 21 'Say
to the house of Israel, Thus says the Lord GOD: Behold, I will profane my sanctuary, the
pride of your power, the delight of your eyes, and the yearning of your soul, and your sons

and your daughters whom you left behind shall fall by the sword. [22]*And you shall do as I have done; you shall not cover your lips, nor eat the bread of men.* [23]*Your turbans shall be on your heads and your shoes on your feet; you shall not mourn or weep, but you shall rot away in your iniquities and groan to one another.* [24]*Thus shall Ezekiel be to you a sign; according to all that he has done you shall do. When this comes, then you will know that I am the Lord GOD.'*

[25]*"As for you, son of man, surely on the day when I take from them their stronghold, their joy and glory, the delight of their eyes and their soul's desire, and also their sons and daughters,* [26]*on that day a fugitive will come to you to report to you the news.* [27]*On that day your mouth will be opened to the fugitive, and you shall speak and be no longer mute. So you will be a sign to them, and they will know that I am the LORD."*

a Compare verse 10; Hebrew *the bones* **b** Hebrew *no lot has fallen upon it* **c** Or *empty out the broth* **d** The meaning of the Hebrew is uncertain

OVERVIEW: Ezekiel directs his attention to the fulfillment of the prophecies that he had spoken before about the destruction of Jerusalem. The siege of the city had begun, and the final destruction was near. Once again Ezekiel uses a parable. The city is likened to a boiling pot, and the inhabitants of the city are the contents of the pot. The second part of the chapter deals with the death of Ezekiel's wife. He is told she will be taken from him, and his grief for her is a lesson for Jerusalem. As the desire of Ezekiel's eyes is taken from him, likewise the temple and city, so dear to the Jews, would be taken from them.

SUMMARY OF THE CHAPTER. JAKOB RAUPIUS: This chapter sets forth two prophecies against the Jews who are living in the land under the rule of Zedekiah. Each of them announces the destruction of the city of Jerusalem. The first does this through the image of a boiling pot; the other by the image of the unexpected death of Ezekiel's wife. COMMENTARY ON EZEKIEL.[1]

24:1-14 *The Siege of Jerusalem*

NEBUCHADNEZZAR. WILLIAM GREENHILL: This chapter is conceived to be the last prophecy against the kingdom of Judah, before its final destruction, which, with its great calamity, is set out under the type of a boiling pot and the death of the prophet's wife. . . .

"In the ninth year, the tenth month, and the tenth day thereof." Our prophet, being in Babylon, reckons from the ninth year of the captivity, the time that Jehoiachin, himself and others were brought into Babylon, and not from the time of Zedekiah's reign. . . .

"The king of Babylon set himself against Jerusalem this same day." Here was the occasion, or cause, of his writing down the day and so prophesying on it. Nebuchadnezzar was that "day" sitting down before Jerusalem, as you may clearly see (2 Kings 25:1; Jer 39:1; 52:4). When Nebuchadnezzar was on a warlike expedition, he knew not whether he should go to Rabbath or Jerusalem, but he was ordered by a divine hand to lay siege to Jerusalem, the tenth day of the tenth month, in the ninth year, which Ezekiel could not possibly know, had the Lord not revealed it. This was a business of high concern to the Jews in Judea and those in Babylon.

The Lord takes notice of what people do and can make known the same to whom he pleases, at whatever distance. Nebuchadnezzar and his forces were in Judea, sitting down before Jerusalem, and this the Lord revealed to Ezekiel, being in Babylon. AN EXPOSITION OF EZEKIEL.[2]

[1]*Commentarius Synopticus* (1655), 188. [2]*Exposition*, 570-71.

A Boiling Pot. John Mayer: The miserable case of the Jews is here set forth under the similitude of a pot, where flesh and bones chopped in pieces are set over a hot burning fire. They are boiled until they are consumed and wasted (cf. Jer 1:13). The pot here spoken of was Jerusalem. The parts or pieces of flesh to be sodden away in it were the Jews, flocking here from all parts for the defense of the city. The bones were the stoutest and most expert warriors. The boiling of them all, that they might be consumed, intimated a long continued siege, and for this reason they should be wasted, some after, others by famine and pestilence. The fire made under with much wood served to set forth the Chaldean army, which was to them as this fire, and finally with fire burned down the city.

But what does he mean by saying "burn the bones under it"? Not as some expound it, says Lyra, because bones make a more ardent fire than wood, for the contrary is true. But as Rabbi Salomon has it, the putting of the bones under was the putting of them under the pieces of flesh, the flesh being laid on them and borne up by them lying at the bottom of the pot. By this was set forth how the strong and valiant should bear the greatest brunt of this war, but yet their strength and valor should not save them. The stronger they were, the more fiery heat should come nearer to them to consume them. Commentary upon All the Prophets.[3]

The Cooking Pot. William Greenhill: "Set on a pot, set it on." It is for cooks to set on pots, put in water, then the meat. Ezekiel, he must bid them "set on the pot." A strange work for a prophet, and because strange, it would make the people mind it the more and search out the mystery. By this pot is meant Jerusalem. . . . So Jerusalem was strong, comprehended much and was more durable than other places when besieged: not Jerusalem simply, but under judgment, was the "pot."

"And also pour water into it." When pots are set over the fire, they put in and fill them with "water," so that whatever they please may be boiled in it. By this "water" is meant the afflictions and judgments in which, as in "water," God would boil Jerusalem. Now the king of Babylon was set down round about it, had besieged it, and a variety of calamities were on it, and the waters of affliction began to be hot.

. . . "Even every good piece, the thigh and the shoulder." Here the people, or commonwealth of Israel, is likened to a body dissected. They must take the good or principal pieces, those that were the strength and support of the body and head, as the thighs and shoulders; that is, the nobles, counselors, priests and chief soldiers among them. An Exposition of Ezekiel.[4]

Bring It Out Piece by Piece. William Greenhill: Jerusalem's sins did cling close to her; the more she boiled in the judgments of God, the more fast she held to her sins; her scum and filth stuck to every side of her. . . . "Bring it out piece by piece." He persists in the allegory of the pot, and orders how they should all be dealt with who were in the city. They should be brought out severally, not all at once, but as pieces are taken out of the pot, one after another, till there is no more. So it should be done with this city: one piece of it should be brought out and consumed with famine, another piece of it with the plague, with the sword, should be carried away into captivity, so that it should be emptied of all. . . . This city was emptied somewhat under Jehoiakim, when he was carried to Babylon (2 Chron 36:6-7); it was emptied more when Jehoiachin was taken, and many with him also carried there (2 Kings 24:15); but it was wholly emptied when Zedekiah was taken and carried away (2 Kings 25). An Exposition of Ezekiel.[5]

[3]*Prophets*, 440. [4]*Exposition*, 571. [5]*Exposition*, 572.

God's Purifying Punishment. Martin Luther: These matters should be carefully meditated on . . . that we may be able to understand the cause of our afflictions. For even though we are not lacking in deeds and works and in one way or another retain external discipline, nevertheless the flesh which we carry around with us is impure, and we understand neither how great our sin is nor our wretchedness, which must be removed. To be sure, all sins have been remitted and covered, but they have not yet been completely cleansed away. Not only do the dregs of lust, pride, hatred, wrath, and other desires cling to us, but also inner evils and hidden stains, doubts about God, unbelief, impatience and murmuring, which do not come out into the open until the conscience is troubled by the law and by the terrors of sin. Although we pay no attention to these things and do not sob because of such a disgraceful fall, yet God sees them. Therefore he tries to purge our impure nature. This is what he thinks: "You have been enlightened and baptized, but you still stink, and your flesh is full of many great vices. Therefore I must cleanse it, for that which is unclean and polluted shall not enter the kingdom of heaven" (cf. Rev 21:27). This is where God's game begins, not that we may be destroyed, but that he may examine us and lead us to a knowledge of our foulness, yet not in such a way that we despair, but rather that we cry to him, invoke his mercy and learn that he shows his mercy wondrously, as Psalm 17:7 says. For this is what he has meant with his game.

. . . In Hosea 6:5 we read: "Therefore I have hewn them by the prophets, I have slain them by the words of my mouth." And, in Ezekiel 24, God calls Jerusalem a pot covered with rust that cannot be cleansed unless it is melted anew. Here there is a description of God's game by which we are troubled and mortified until we return to the earth from which we were taken and are buried. But why does God deal so harshly with us? In Ezekiel 24, he replies, "Its thick rust does not go out of it by fire" (Ezek 24:12). It is burned in too deep. Therefore he says that he will melt it in the fire, that it may be boiled out and purified. Lectures on Genesis.[6]

24:15-27 *Ezekiel's Wife Dies*

Ezekiel's Wife. John Mayer: *I will take away the desire of your eyes with a stroke* (Ezek 24:16). Here the Lord further shows in the example of Ezekiel that the destruction of the people should be so great and the danger still so continuing to the survivors that they should be so overwhelmed with grief that they should not make any mourning, as they had in times past used to do for the death of their dearest friends.

For this end his wife was struck by death and he was forbidden to mourn for her. When he is asked the reason, his is to tell them that so it should be with them (Ezek 24:20-22). As his wife was the desire of his eyes, whom he dearly loved, so was the sanctuary to them, as taking their chief glory to lie in it. And if any of them were not so much affected to it, yet surely they were to their sons and daughters, but their sanctuary should be burned and their children die, yet they should be as people so overcome with sorrow that they should have no more tears to shed for this, all the mourning that they could now make, being little enough for their mutual miseries, who were still living in comparison of whom they should think the dead happy. Commentary upon All the Prophets.[7]

Ezekiel's Wife and the Temple. William Greenhill: "Behold, I will profane my sanctuary." By Ezekiel's wife was typed out the temple and what was desirable. By her sudden death, the destruction of the same. The temple was as dear to the Jews as Ezekiel's wife was to

[6]LW 7:229. [7]*Prophets*, 441-42.

him. God would bring the Chaldeans into it, and they should profane it with the blood of those they found in it (for many fled to it for refuge) and then set it on fire. The Jews had profaned it with idols and idolatrous worship (Ezek 8) by coming into it with the guilt of notorious sins on them (Jer 7:9-10). Now heathens should enter into it, defile and destroy it. The thought of this made the psalmist long before to complain, saying, "O God, the heathen are come into your inheritance; thy holy temple have they defiled; they have laid Jerusalem on heaps" (Ps 74:1). The defiling of the temple was grievous to prescience, to remote apprehensions. What was it then to those who had the present sight of it! AN EXPOSITION OF EZEKIEL.[8]

THE WIFE OF EZEKIEL. JOHANNES OECOLAMPADIUS: As the wife of the prophet was very much loved by him, and from whom he hoped for much future happiness, so too the temple was the dearest love for the people, in which they had placed their great trust. Now by this sign of the prophet they were roused. They showed more regard for the beauty of ceremonies than for the truth of worship. Thus the temple was called "the pride of your power, the tenderness of your soul" (Ezek 24:21), that is, what should never be dishonored. "The delight of your eyes," what is most pleasing to behold, which God himself shall profane by giving entry to the heathen enemy, sparing none of the sacred things. COMMENTARY ON THE PROPHET EZEKIEL.[9]

EZEKIEL A SIGN. WILLIAM GREENHILL: God may and does put his own faithful servants on hard and unwanted things, thereby to declare what shall be the condition of the wicked. "Thus Ezekiel is to you a sign" (Ezek 24:24). He has had his dearest comfort taken away by an extraordinary stroke; he has not been allowed to mourn or weep therefore. And why so? That he may be a sign to you. You would not be taught by my doctrine; now you must be taught by my example, "according to all that he has done shall you do." The things are harsh and unnatural that I have done, but it is for your sakes that I am put upon them. You shall do as I have done. Thus Isaiah was put on to walk naked and barefoot three years, which was hard and reproachful. And why? That he might be "for a sign and wonder on Egypt and Ethiopia" (Is 20:3). Some may think God deals ill with his servants in putting them on harsh, reproachful, unnatural, ridiculous things. But know all souls are the Lord's, and he may command them what he please. They have comfort in their obedience, whatever people think or say of them. Whereas those they are made signs to have nothing but bitterness and terrors. AN EXPOSITION OF EZEKIEL.[10]

[8]*Exposition*, 582. [9]*Commentarius in Ezechielem* (1553), 131. [10]*Exposition*, 584.

25:1–27:36 JUDGMENTS AGAINST THE NATIONS

[1]The word of the Lord came to me: [2]"Son of man, set your face toward the Ammonites
and prophesy against them. [3]Say to the Ammonites, Hear the word of the Lord God:
Thus says the Lord God, Because you said, 'Aha!' over my sanctuary when it was pro-
faned, and over the land of Israel when it was made desolate, and over the house of Judah
when they went into exile, [4]therefore behold, I am handing you over to the people of the
East for a possession, and they shall set their encampments among you and make their
dwellings in your midst. They shall eat your fruit, and they shall drink your milk. [5]I will
make Rabbah a pasture for camels and Ammon[a] a fold for flocks. Then you will know
that I am the Lord. [6]For thus says the Lord God: Because you have clapped your hands
and stamped your feet and rejoiced with all the malice within your soul against the land
of Israel, [7]therefore, behold, I have stretched out my hand against you, and will hand you
over as plunder to the nations. And I will cut you off from the peoples and will make you
perish out of the countries; I will destroy you. Then you will know that I am the Lord.
[8]"Thus says the Lord God: Because Moab and Seir[b] said, 'Behold, the house of Judah
is like all the other nations,' [9]therefore I will lay open the flank of Moab from the cities,
from its cities on its frontier, the glory of the country, Beth-jeshimoth, Baal-meon, and
Kiriathaim. [10]I will give it along with the Ammonites to the people of the East as a pos-
session, that the Ammonites may be remembered no more among the nations, [11]and I will
execute judgments upon Moab. Then they will know that I am the Lord.
[12]"Thus says the Lord God: Because Edom acted revengefully against the house of
Judah and has grievously offended in taking vengeance on them, [13]therefore thus says the
Lord God, I will stretch out my hand against Edom and cut off from it man and beast.
And I will make it desolate; from Teman even to Dedan they shall fall by the sword.
[14]And I will lay my vengeance upon Edom by the hand of my people Israel, and they shall
do in Edom according to my anger and according to my wrath, and they shall know my
vengeance, declares the Lord God.
[15]"Thus says the Lord God: Because the Philistines acted revengefully and took ven-
geance with malice of soul to destroy in never-ending enmity, [16]therefore thus says the
Lord God, Behold, I will stretch out my hand against the Philistines, and I will cut off
the Cherethites and destroy the rest of the seacoast. [17]I will execute great vengeance on
them with wrathful rebukes. Then they will know that I am the Lord, when I lay my
vengeance upon them."
26 In the eleventh year, on the first day of the month, the word of the Lord came to
me: [2]"Son of man, because Tyre said concerning Jerusalem, 'Aha, the gate of the
peoples is broken; it has swung open to me. I shall be replenished, now that she is laid
waste,' [3]therefore thus says the Lord God: Behold, I am against you, O Tyre, and will
bring up many nations against you, as the sea brings up its waves. [4]They shall destroy the
walls of Tyre and break down her towers, and I will scrape her soil from her and make
her a bare rock. [5]She shall be in the midst of the sea a place for the spreading of nets, for I
have spoken, declares the Lord God. And she shall become plunder for the nations, [6]and

her daughters on the mainland shall be killed by the sword. Then they will know that I
am the Lord.
⁷"For thus says the Lord God: Behold, I will bring against Tyre from the north Nebu-
chadnezzar[c] king of Babylon, king of kings, with horses and chariots, and with horsemen
and a host of many soldiers. ⁸He will kill with the sword your daughters on the mainland.
He will set up a siege wall against you and throw up a mound against you, and raise a roof
of shields against you. ⁹He will direct the shock of his battering rams against your walls,
and with his axes he will break down your towers. ¹⁰His horses will be so many that their
dust will cover you. Your walls will shake at the noise of the horsemen and wagons and
chariots, when he enters your gates as men enter a city that has been breached. ¹¹With the
hoofs of his horses he will trample all your streets. He will kill your people with the sword,
and your mighty pillars will fall to the ground. ¹²They will plunder your riches and loot
your merchandise. They will break down your walls and destroy your pleasant houses.
Your stones and timber and soil they will cast into the midst of the waters. ¹³And I will
stop the music of your songs, and the sound of your lyres shall be heard no more. ¹⁴I will
make you a bare rock. You shall be a place for the spreading of nets. You shall never be
rebuilt, for I am the Lord; I have spoken, declares the Lord God.
¹⁵"Thus says the Lord God to Tyre: Will not the coastlands shake at the sound of
your fall, when the wounded groan, when slaughter is made in your midst? ¹⁶Then all
the princes of the sea will step down from their thrones and remove their robes and strip
off their embroidered garments. They will clothe themselves with trembling; they will sit
on the ground and tremble every moment and be appalled at you. ¹⁷And they will raise a
lamentation over you and say to you,

" 'How you have perished,
you who were inhabited from the seas,
O city renowned,
who was mighty on the sea;
she and her inhabitants imposed their terror
on all her inhabitants!
¹⁸Now the coastlands tremble
on the day of your fall,
and the coastlands that are on the sea
are dismayed at your passing.'

¹⁹"For thus says the Lord God: When I make you a city laid waste, like the cities that
are not inhabited, when I bring up the deep over you, and the great waters cover you,
²⁰then I will make you go down with those who go down to the pit, to the people of old,
and I will make you to dwell in the world below, among ruins from of old, with those who
go down to the pit, so that you will not be inhabited; but I will set beauty in the land of
the living. ²¹I will bring you to a dreadful end, and you shall be no more. Though you be
sought for, you will never be found again, declares the Lord God."

27 *The word of the Lord came to me: ²"Now you, son of man, raise a lamenta-*
tion over Tyre, ³and say to Tyre, who dwells at the entrances to the sea, merchant
of the peoples to many coastlands, thus says the Lord God:

"O Tyre, you have said,
'I am perfect in beauty.'
4Your borders are in the heart of the seas;
your builders made perfect your beauty.
5They made all your planks
of fir trees from Senir;
they took a cedar from Lebanon
to make a mast for you.
6Of oaks of Bashan
they made your oars;
they made your deck of pines
from the coasts of Cyprus,
inlaid with ivory.
7Of fine embroidered linen from Egypt
was your sail,
serving as your banner;
blue and purple from the coasts of Elishah
was your awning.
8The inhabitants of Sidon and Arvad
were your rowers;
your skilled men, O Tyre, were in you;
they were your pilots.
9The elders of Gebal and her skilled men were in you,
caulking your seams;
all the ships of the sea with their mariners were in you
to barter for your wares.

10"Persia and Lud and Put were in your army as your men of war. They hung the
shield and helmet in you; they gave you splendor. 11Men of Arvad and Helech were on
your walls all around, and men of Gamad were in your towers. They hung their shields
on your walls all around; they made perfect your beauty.
12"Tarshish did business with you because of your great wealth of every kind; silver,
iron, tin, and lead they exchanged for your wares. 13Javan, Tubal, and Meshech traded
with you; they exchanged human beings and vessels of bronze for your merchandise.
14From Beth-togarmah they exchanged horses, war horses, and mules for your wares.
15The men of Dedan[d] traded with you. Many coastlands were your own special mar-
kets; they brought you in payment ivory tusks and ebony. 16Syria did business with
you because of your abundant goods; they exchanged for your wares emeralds, purple,
embroidered work, fine linen, coral, and ruby. 17Judah and the land of Israel traded
with you; they exchanged for your merchandise wheat of Minnith, meal,[e] honey, oil, and
balm. 18Damascus did business with you for your abundant goods, because of your great
wealth of every kind; wine of Helbon and wool of Sahar 19and casks of wine[f] from Uzal
they exchanged for your wares; wrought iron, cassia, and calamus were bartered for your
merchandise. 20Dedan traded with you in saddlecloths for riding. 21Arabia and all the
princes of Kedar were your favored dealers in lambs, rams, and goats; in these they did
business with you. 22The traders of Sheba and Raamah traded with you; they exchanged
for your wares the best of all kinds of spices and all precious stones and gold. 23Haran,
Canneh, Eden, traders of Sheba, Asshur, and Chilmad traded with you. 24In your mar-
ket these traded with you in choice garments, in clothes of blue and embroidered work,
and in carpets of colored material, bound with cords and made secure. 25The ships of
Tarshish traveled for you with your merchandise. So you were filled and heavily laden
in the heart of the seas.

26"Your rowers have brought you out
into the high seas.
The east wind has wrecked you
in the heart of the seas.
27Your riches, your wares, your merchandise,

your mariners and your pilots,
your caulkers, your dealers in merchandise,
and all your men of war who are in you,
with all your crew
that is in your midst,
sink into the heart of the seas
on the day of your fall.
28*At the sound of the cry of your pilots*
the countryside shakes,
29*and down from their ships*
come all who handle the oar.
The mariners and all the pilots of the sea
stand on the land
30*and shout aloud over you*
and cry out bitterly.
They cast dust on their heads
and wallow in ashes;
31*they make themselves bald for you*
and put sackcloth on their waist,
and they weep over you in bitterness of soul,
with bitter mourning.
32*In their wailing they raise a lamentation for you*
and lament over you:
'Who is like Tyre,
like one destroyed in the midst of the sea?
33*When your wares came from the seas,*
you satisfied many peoples;
with your abundant wealth and merchandise
you enriched the kings of the earth.
34*Now you are wrecked by the seas,*
in the depths of the waters;
your merchandise and all your crew in your midst
have sunk with you.
35*All the inhabitants of the coastlands*
are appalled at you,
and the hair of their kings bristles with horror;
their faces are convulsed.
36*The merchants among the peoples hiss at you;*
you have come to a dreadful end
and shall be no more forever.' "

a Hebrew *and the Ammonites* **b** Septuagint lacks *and Seir* **c** Hebrew *Nebuchadrezzar;* so throughout Ezekiel **d** Hebrew; Septuagint *Rhodes* **e** The meaning of the Hebrew word is unknown **f** Probable reading; Hebrew *wool of Sahar, Vedan, and Javan*

Overview: With this chapter begins the second major division of Ezekiel. The prophet directs his attention to the judgment of the nations surrounding Israel, especially Tyre. The judgment against the nations is because they rejoiced at Jerusalem's destruction and hated their religion. It was principally their hatred of the truth that evoked the wrath of God. The wealth and magnificence of Tyre gave it the appearance of security. Compared with the other nations it seemed invincible and impregnable. And yet nothing in nature or art shall hinder the judgment of God.

25:1–26:21 *Prophecy Against the Nations*

The Second Major Division of Ezekiel. William Greenhill: In this prophecy of Ezekiel are four things chiefly to be considered. The first is the destruction of the Jewish state by the Babylonians, which our prophet having declared in the twenty-one chapters preceding, he comes now to the second general head, which is, threatening of judgment to other nations for their pride and insulting over the Jews in their misery. This he does in the eight next chapters from the beginning of this to chapter thirty-three. An Exposition of Ezekiel.[1]

The Nations Hate the Truth. John Mayer: The prophet having to this point

[1] *Exposition*, 586.

declared the judgments to come on Israel and having touched a little on the Ammonites (Ezek 21:28), now prophesies again, against the Ammonites, Moabites, Edomites and Philistines, because they rejoiced at the destruction of Jerusalem and the temple, as bearing always a deadly hatred against the Jews because of their religion. From this note how great a sin it is for the wicked and those seduced by error in religion to hate the professors of the truth. For this the wrath of God shall burn against them until they be destroyed, and likewise it shall be to all wicked people who rejoice at the fall of God's people. Commentary upon All the Prophets.[2]

Aha! Johannes Oecolampadius: "Aha!" is the expression of joy and congratulations. As if they had said, "You worship the one God for no purpose and separate yourselves from the rest of people for no reason. Your temple is useless. It is profaned and occupied by Gentiles. The land of the ten tribes is devastated; the people have been carried into captivity." Therefore, God declares, "Lest you rejoice, Ammonites, the fate that befell Jerusalem will be the same for you from the sons of the East. . . . They will take your camels, drink your milk and eat your fruit; that is to say, they will seize every good thing in your land. . . . Thus they will know that I am the Lord." Commentary on the Prophet Ezekiel.[3]

The Scoffing of the Nations. William Greenhill: That when God's people are severely dealt with by the Lord for their sins, others do impiously and inhumanely scoff at and insult them. When Jerusalem was sacked by the Babylonians, the Tyrians cried, "Aha, she is broken." So too the Ammonites (Ezek 25:3); they had their "Aha" against the sanctuary and land of Israel. So in Ezekiel 36:2 the enemy said "Aha" against the Jews. Nature teaches people to sympathize with those who are in misery, not to multiply their miseries by scoffs and mocks. But the nations showed themselves impious and unnatural in dealing so with the Jews. Similar things may God's people expect now from the world. If they meet with breaking for their sins, the people of the world will say, "Aha," so would we have it; others' mourning is their music, others' tears are their wine. An Exposition of Ezekiel.[4]

27:1-36 *A Lament for Tyre*

Who Are the Gammadims? John Mayer: In Ezekiel 27, that the ruin of Tyre might appear to be the greater, the prophet sets forth at large the wealth and magnificence of that city and the great command of it over other places, so that it might seem to be of incomparable strength and invincible. There is nothing here that needs exposition until we come to verse 11: *Gammadims were upon your towers* (Ezek 27:11). Because the word signifies a cubit, some, says Junius, understand men but one cubit tall; namely, the pygmies. But how probable this is, let the reader judge, for they are said to be part of the forces that stood to defend Tyre. He therefore conjectures that the word is not proper but appellative, by Gammadim cubit men, strong armed men being understood to draw the bow and shoot most mightily. Yet there were a people of this name, who, as Pliny says, inhabited a region in Phoenicia lying on the sea in the form of a cubit, being for that reason called Gammadim, which region was devoured long ago by the sea. Commentary upon All the Prophets.[5]

The Gammadims. Jakob Raupius: "The Gammadims were in your towers" (Ezek 27:11). Junius believes the Gammadim come from the region of Phoenicia. The Vulgate has "pygmies." The Hebrew word derives from "cubit" (Judg 3:16). As if you were using "cubit" to

[2]*Prophets*, 443. [3]*Commentarius in Ezechielem* (1553), 132. [4]*Exposition*, 597. [5]*Prophets*, 445.

identify the part from the elbow to the tip of the finger or the forearm because these people had powerful arms and were physically robust. So long as it is agreed that the "Gammadim" did not have the height of a cubit. COMMENTARY ON EZEKIEL.[6]

THE PRIDE OF TYRE. WILLIAM GREENHILL: No situation, strength or outward advantage can secure proud cities. The borders of Tyre were in the heart of the seas, it was compassed about with great waters, judged by all to be impregnable. God's design was to ruin Tyre for its pride, and he found out a way and means to do it. Let cities be built where they will, in the deeps, on rocky mountains, wherever, if they glory in their strength, beauty, situation, God can bring destruction on them; nothing shall hinder in nature or art.

. . . Nothing human can protect a sinful city and people from the judgments of God. Tyre was as strong a place as the world had; its walls, towers, ships, wise, strong men, could not do it. Tyre was as rich a place as any under heaven; it had a multitude of all riches. Yet these kept it not from being brought into great waters. What power or art of humankind can keep off the wind from a ship when it is at sea? It is not in the power of all the seamen or mariners in the world to do it. Neither can any number of people, or all people, keep off a judgment of God when it is coming on a sinful place. Let us not confide in human things. AN EXPOSITION OF EZEKIEL.[7]

[6] *Commentarius Synopticus* (1655), 209. [7] *Exposition*, 604, 611.

28:1-26 A PROPHECY AGAINST TYRE AND SIDON

1The word of the LORD came to me: 2"Son of man, say to the prince of Tyre, Thus says the Lord GOD:

"Because your heart is proud,
and you have said, 'I am a god,
I sit in the seat of the gods,
in the heart of the seas,'
yet you are but a man, and no god,
though you make your heart like the heart of a god—
3you are indeed wiser than Daniel;
no secret is hidden from you;
4by your wisdom and your understanding
you have made wealth for yourself,
and have gathered gold and silver
into your treasuries;
5by your great wisdom in your trade
you have increased your wealth,
and your heart has become proud in your wealth—
6therefore thus says the Lord GOD:
Because you make your heart
like the heart of a god,
7therefore, behold, I will bring foreigners upon you,
the most ruthless of the nations;
and they shall draw their swords against the beauty of your wisdom
and defile your splendor.
8They shall thrust you down into the pit,
and you shall die the death of the slain
in the heart of the seas.
9Will you still say, 'I am a god,'
in the presence of those who kill you,
though you are but a man, and no god,

in the hands of those who slay you?
10You shall die the death of the
uncircumcised
by the hand of foreigners;
for I have spoken, declares the Lord
GOD."

11Moreover, the word of the LORD came to me: 12"Son of man, raise a lamentation over
the king of Tyre, and say to him, Thus says the Lord GOD:

"You were the signet of perfection,[a]
full of wisdom and perfect in beauty.
13You were in Eden, the garden of God;
every precious stone was your covering,
sardius, topaz, and diamond,
beryl, onyx, and jasper,
sapphire,[b] emerald, and carbuncle;
and crafted in gold were your settings
and your engravings.[c]
On the day that you were created
they were prepared.
14You were an anointed guardian
cherub.
I placed you;[d] you were on the holy
mountain of God;
in the midst of the stones of fire you
walked.
15You were blameless in your ways
from the day you were created,
till unrighteousness was found in you.
16In the abundance of your trade
you were filled with violence in your
midst, and you sinned;
so I cast you as a profane thing from the
mountain of God,
and I destroyed you,[e] O guardian
cherub,
from the midst of the stones of fire.
17Your heart was proud because of your
beauty;
you corrupted your wisdom for the sake
of your splendor.
I cast you to the ground;
I exposed you before kings,
to feast their eyes on you.
18By the multitude of your iniquities,
in the unrighteousness of your trade
you profaned your sanctuaries;
so I brought fire out from your midst;
it consumed you,
and I turned you to ashes on the earth
in the sight of all who saw you.
19All who know you among the peoples
are appalled at you;
you have come to a dreadful end
and shall be no more forever."

20The word of the LORD came to me: 21"Son of man, set your face toward Sidon, and
prophesy against her 22and say, Thus says the Lord GOD:

"Behold, I am against you, O Sidon,
and I will manifest my glory in your
midst.
And they shall know that I am the LORD
when I execute judgments in her
and manifest my holiness in her;
23for I will send pestilence into her,
and blood into her streets;
and the slain shall fall in her midst,
by the sword that is against her on
every side.
Then they will know that I am the LORD.

24"And for the house of Israel there shall be no more a brier to prick or a thorn to hurt
them among all their neighbors who have treated them with contempt. Then they will
know that I am the Lord GOD.

[25]*"Thus says the Lord GOD: When I gather the house of Israel from the peoples among whom they are scattered, and manifest my holiness in them in the sight of the nations, then they shall dwell in their own land that I gave to my servant Jacob.* [26]*And they shall dwell securely in it, and they shall build houses and plant vineyards. They shall dwell securely, when I execute judgments upon all their neighbors who have treated them with contempt. Then they will know that I am the LORD their God."*

a The meaning of the Hebrew phrase is uncertain **b** Or *lapis lazuli* **c** The meaning of the Hebrew phrase is uncertain **d** The meaning of the Hebrew phrase is uncertain **e** Or *banished you*

OVERVIEW: The judgments against the nations continue. The focus of this chapter remains on Tyre but adds Sidon. In the previous chapter, the pride of Tyre, the city, was denounced. Here the pride of the prince of Tyre, who considered himself a god, who boasted in an imaginary wisdom, is denounced. The self-deification of princes and rulers should not surprise us. When our natural endowments exceed those of others, endowments that are gifts from God, we are often led to self-conceit and self-importance. Our pride leads us to a false sense of security. Such pride is of the devil. The faithful lament when they see a person claim as his own accomplishment the blessings God has bestowed. The chapter ends with comfort. God will protect his faithful who dwell amid briers and thorns, which are the nations.

28:1-23 *Prophecy Against Tyre and Sidon*

SUMMARY OF THE CHAPTER. JAKOB RAUPIUS: This chapter contains four prophecies. The first and the second are against the king of Tyre and the city of Tyre. The third is against the city of Sidon. The fourth concerns the restoration of the church. In the first part he declares the destruction of the king of Tyre and the reason that moved God against this king, which was his pride (Ezek 28:2-6). . . . The administering cause, which God was to use to destroy the king of Tyre, was the Babylonians or Chaldeans, who are signified by the word *foreigners* (Ezek 28:7). . . . The third part of the chapter recites the destruction of Sidon. The efficient cause of this destruction is God (Ezek 28:20-22). The final cause is the twofold glory of God and the liberation of his people (Ezek 28:22-24). The cause of their destruction will be pestilence and murder (Ezek 28:23). . . . The fourth part of the chapter addresses the restoration of the church, which is set forth in three parts: the first is God's gathering of the people; second, the people shall dwell in the land of Canaan (Ezek 28:25); and third, they will dwell securely (Ezek 28:26). COMMENTARY ON EZEKIEL.[1]

WHO IS THE PRINCE OF TYRE? JOHN MAYER: Having spoken against the whole city of Tyre in the two previous chapters, here he comes in particular to charge the prince with intolerable pride and self-conceit in respect of his great riches and imaginary wisdom, by which he regarded himself to be a god. Because no man is so mad, or ever was, to say this about himself, some understand it as spoken of the devil under the name of the prince of Tyre (Jerome, Augustine, Ambrose, Isidore and Tertullian). But Isaiah speaks similarly of Belshazzar, as his speech is mixed, something being said of the devil properly and some things of the king of Babylon in allusion to him (Is 14). So the same is here. His heart was so proud that he thought there was no God above him or more excellent than he, so did he dote on his own wit and wealth, and he was confident that God would not bring him down from his

[1]*Commentarius Synopticus* (1655), 214, 220.

high honor. Indeed, if we shall say, that that man spoke so of himself, it is no more than Caius Caligula, a Roman emperor, did, and Elagabalus and Julius Caesar suffered divine honors to be done to them, and Nebuchadnezzar set up his image to be worshiped by all. Optatus of Milevis applies this prince of Tyre to Donatus, a bishop, who thought himself in holiness to excel all other men, and therefore he would not suffer any to come to him but with most low reverence, and he would have them called by his name Donatists. This man was bishop of Tyre, a colony of Carthage, and so a spiritual prince. Commentary upon All the Prophets.[2]

Self-Deification by Princes. William Greenhill: Princes and great ones are prone not only to be proud but also to deify themselves. The prince of Tyre puffed up his heart, and he said, "I am a god" (Ezek 28:2). This is the height of pride, to make oneself a god, to arrogate that which is due to the Lord. God had said it: "I am God, and there is none else; I am God, and there is none like me" (Is 46:9). Now what pride, what blasphemy was it for this prince to say, "I am a god!" There are two things that God claims to himself, "vengeance" (Deut 32:35) and godship (Is 44:8). This prince robbed God of one, making himself God. Various heathen emperors would either be called or worshiped as gods. Caligula made himself a god, erecting a temple with his image in it, ordaining priests and most costly sacrifices to be offered there to himself. Domitian by a public edict ordained that in all writings where he was mentioned, he should be called *Dominus Deus*, Lord God.

. . . Haughtiness and pride of spirit do precede and presage the destruction of people. This prince was near to utter ruin, and before it his heart was puffed up. He said, "I sit in the seat of God," I punish and I spare whom I please. But quickly after this he was thrust out of his seat and made an example of divine vengeance for his pride and presumption. . . . Whatever thoughts and conceits princes or others have of themselves, yet they are but dust and ashes, poor, inconsiderable things in respect of God. An Exposition of Ezekiel.[3]

Wiser Than Daniel. Martin Luther: We must not think that everything someone understands in a subtle way even in the Scriptures or thinks up and finds in an extraordinary way is from God or pleasing to God. For thus Ezekiel says to the devil under the name of the prince of Tyre (Ezek 28:3): "Behold, you are wiser than Daniel" (that is, wiser than all speculative thinkers). The devil now knows all mysteries, because they were revealed throughout the world, and he is more brilliant than we. Therefore, by God's permission, he can suggest remarkable things to the mind for the purpose of seducing the proud. This is what he is now doing for the heretics and what he did in the past. They have abounded with a remarkable understanding in the Scriptures, even though they might be blinded with heretical darkness. First Lectures on the Psalms.[4]

Wiser Than Daniel? John Mayer: Here he seeks to make him ashamed of his most insipid boasting by deriding him and ironically telling him, Ah, you are wiser than Daniel? As if he had said, although you are not ashamed to compare yourself with God, I will name to you a man, who by the consent of Nebuchadnezzar was the wisest of men. If you think yourself a god, you must then think yourself much wiser than he was, which is most ridiculous, for he, as wise as he was, attributed nothing to himself but all his understanding to God alone. Commentary upon All the Prophets.[5]

God Looks at the Heart. William Greenhill: The Lord takes notice of people's

[2]*Prophets*, 445-46. [3]*Exposition*, 613. [4]LW 10:347. [5]*Prophets*, 446.

hearts, in what frame they are. "Your heart is lifted up." People cannot look into the heart, being shut up in a house of clay, but the eyes of the Lord pierce through our mud walls and behold our hearts and the workings of them. "The Lord looks on the heart" (1 Sam 16:7). We look on actions, faces, outward appearances, but God looks inward and fixes his eye on the heart; and so, that he knows what is in the heart and how it works, he understands all the thoughts of it and the imaginations of those thoughts (1 Chron 28:9). He knows people's minds exactly and can tell you whose hearts are proud and whose are humble, whose are forward and whose are meek, whose are chaste and whose unclean. AN EXPOSITION OF EZEKIEL.[6]

LAMENTATION FOR THE KING. WILLIAM GREENHILL: When people have natural or acquired excellences beyond others and abuse them, it is a matter of mourning. "Take up a lamentation on the king of Tyre." He had more wisdom, beauty, blessing, prosperity and abundance than others, but he abused all. His heart was puffed up. He honored not God with what he had, and therefore Ezekiel must lament, he must lament for the princes of Israel (Ezek 19:1), who abused their power, places, parts and blessings they had.

Choice accomplishments, with outward glory and greatness, are no arguments of God's grace or God's special favor toward people. Heathens, and the worst of people, have had these. The prince of Tyre, who blasphemously said he was a god, sealed up the sum. He was a complete prince, he had choice endowments, he was full of wisdom, perfect in beauty, he had outward glory and greatness as much as any, he was seated in a paradise, he glistened with pearls and precious stones, and he had as choice music as was to be had. Yet, notwithstanding all these, he was a wretched man, under the curse of God, and was to die the death of the uncircumcised. What vanity is it, therefore, to pride ourselves in any human excellences, to set our hearts on, or confide in, any outward glory or greatness! AN EXPOSITION OF EZEKIEL.[7]

LUCIFER AND THE KING OF TYRE. JOHN MAYER: *You were in Eden, the garden of God; every precious stone was your covering* (Ezek 28:13). Here another point of felicity, like that of Adam in the state of innocence, is mentioned. Because of his pride, he thought himself most happy for being prince of so rich and magnificent a city, and therefore he adorned himself with all manner of precious stones. It is to be noted that the stones here named are the same that were in the place of the high priest, but in number they came short, there being in it twelve, in his crown but nine. Gregory argues that nine is set forth for Lucifer, the most glorious one among the angels, of whom there were nine orders, for he, as others, applies all this to the devil. But it is better, as I said before, to understand it, as was spoken, in way of allusion to the devil, but properly of the king of Tyre, who was so like to him in pride, vaunting himself as a god, as he did, and a pattern of perfection to other kings and princes, and equal to Adam in paradise, and to the high priest in the precious stones of his diadem, no more yet being reckoned up than nine, and the rest left to be understood. COMMENTARY UPON ALL THE PROPHETS.[8]

TYRE AND SIDON. MARTIN LUTHER: About Tyre and Sidon, these very rich cities (for they were coastal cities overflowing with every kind of fine merchandise), we must consult the history books. These cities were destroyed twice, once by Nebuchadnezzar, king of Babylon. Ezekiel recalls in great detail the destruction he caused: "Nebuchadnezzar, king of Babylon, made his army labor hard against Tyre" (Ezek 29:18). The second destruction occurred

[6]*Exposition*, 613. [7]*Exposition*, 618. [8]*Prophets*, 446.

at the hands of King Alexander, who was called Alexander the Great. This account the historians of the Gentiles write. Mention of this overthrow we find also in the accounts of the Gospels, when Christ says, "Woe to you, Chorazin! Woe to you, Bethsaida! for if such mighty works done in you had been done in Tyre and Sidon" (Mt 11:21). In this passage Christ bears witness that those cities had been overthrown and completely destroyed. That happened in the more recent destruction at the hand of Alexander the Great. Then, after Alexander had died, there was perpetual discord, very bitter hatred and armed conflict between the kings of Egypt and Syria. They were often involved in bitter warfare with each other—not without great disaster and destruction for those cities that were lying between them. For whoever would win, to him they would become subject and by him they would be plundered. See the histories of the Maccabees and Josephus. Lectures on Zechariah.[9]

28:24-26 *Restoration of the Church*

Deliverance from Briers and Thorns. William Greenhill: The church and people of God shall not always be among briers and thorns. They shall have a time of freedom: "There shall be no more a pricking brier and a grieving thorn" (Ezek 28:24). Again, "They shall no more be a prey to the heathen" (Ezek 34:28). This was made good to the Jews in the letter after their return; the nations, which had been thorns to them, the Lord destroyed. This promise refers also to the gospel times; the Lord is making way for it now. When enemies have power, strength, counsel, are active and successful, then they are thorny and grievous; but the Lord is disappointing his church's enemies and consuming them as briers and thorns (Is 27:4).

This is a matter of comfort to the church. Although it has been long among briers and thorns and has been much offended by them, indeed, wounded, yet there is a time when it shall be freed from them. It is approaching, and makes haste (Lk 18:7-8). The Israelites were freed from the Egyptians, and Lot from the Sodomites, who were thorns, indeed, terrible ones, to them.

This should draw out our spirits in prayer to the Lord, to hasten the time, that he would make good what he has promised. "Instead of the thorn shall come up the fir tree, and instead of the brier shall come up the myrtle tree" (Is 55:13). Let us pray earnestly that God would give us fir trees and myrtle trees, in the room of our briers and thorns; good magistrates and good ministers, instead of those who have been no better than thorns and briers to us. An Exposition of Ezekiel.[10]

Restoration of the Church. Johannes Oecolampadius: On the one hand God punishes the wicked heathen and on the other elects his faithful children. He denies hope to those left behind. All of those people are punished so that they do not return. The children of Israel, however, are promised a return. They are promised to dwell securely, without doubt being at peace with the Father through the Son. And so they shall dwell, build houses and plant vineyards; that is to say, continuing in safety, which certainly did not entirely come to pass in the return from Babylon. For many were hindered at that time by Sidon and others. This promise was fully brought about by Christ, as Zachariah says, "that we, being delivered from the hands of our enemies, might serve him without fear, in holiness and righteousness before him, all the days of our life" (Lk 1:75-76). This is signified by the building of houses; such is a prelude of eternal salvation. Commentary on the Prophet Ezekiel.[11]

[9]LW 20:89. [10]*Exposition*, 626-27. [11]*Commentarius in Ezechielem* (1553), 142.

29:1–30:26 A Prophecy Against and Lament for Egypt

1In the tenth year, in the tenth month, on the twelfth day of the month, the word of the Lord came to me: 2"Son of man, set your face against Pharaoh king of Egypt, and prophesy against him and against all Egypt; 3speak, and say, Thus says the Lord God:

"Behold, I am against you,
Pharaoh king of Egypt,
the great dragon that lies
in the midst of his streams,
that says, 'My Nile is my own;
I made it for myself.'
4I will put hooks in your jaws,
and make the fish of your streams stick
to your scales;
and I will draw you up out of the midst of
our streams,
with all the fish of your streams
that stick to your scales.
5And I will cast you out into the
wilderness,
you and all the fish of your streams;
you shall fall on the open field,
and not be brought together or
gathered.
To the beasts of the earth and to the birds
of the heavens
I give you as food.

6Then all the inhabitants of Egypt shall know that I am the Lord.

"Because you[a] have been a staff of reed to the house of Israel, 7when they grasped you with the hand, you broke and tore all their shoulders; and when they leaned on you, you broke and made all their loins to shake.[b] 8Therefore thus says the Lord God: Behold, I will bring a sword upon you, and will cut off from you man and beast, 9and the land of Egypt shall be a desolation and a waste. Then they will know that I am the Lord.

"Because you[c] said, 'The Nile is mine, and I made it,' 10therefore, behold, I am against you and against your streams, and I will make the land of Egypt an utter waste and desolation, from Migdol to Syene, as far as the border of Cush. 11No foot of man shall pass through it, and no foot of beast shall pass through it; it shall be uninhabited forty years. 12And I will make the land of Egypt a desolation in the midst of desolated countries, and her cities shall be a desolation forty years among cities that are laid waste. I will scatter the Egyptians among the nations, and disperse them through the countries.

13"For thus says the Lord God: At the end of forty years I will gather the Egyptians from the peoples among whom they were scattered, 14and I will restore the fortunes of Egypt and bring them back to the land of Pathros, the land of their origin, and there they shall be a lowly kingdom. 15It shall be the most lowly of the kingdoms, and never again exalt itself above the nations. And I will make them so small that they will never again rule over the nations. 16And it shall never again be the reliance of the house of Israel, recalling their iniquity, when they turn to them for aid. Then they will know that I am the Lord God."

17In the twenty-seventh year, in the first month, on the first day of the month, the word
of the LORD came to me: 18"Son of man, Nebuchadnezzar king of Babylon made his army
labor hard against Tyre. Every head was made bald, and every shoulder was rubbed bare,
yet neither he nor his army got anything from Tyre to pay for the labor that he had per-
formed against her. 19Therefore thus says the Lord GOD: Behold, I will give the land of
Egypt to Nebuchadnezzar king of Babylon; and he shall carry off its wealth[d] and despoil it
and plunder it; and it shall be the wages for his army. 20I have given him the land of Egypt
as his payment for which he labored, because they worked for me, declares the Lord GOD.
21"On that day I will cause a horn to spring up for the house of Israel, and I will open
your lips among them. Then they will know that I am the LORD."

30 The word of the LORD came to me: 2"Son of man, prophesy, and say, Thus says
the Lord GOD:

"Wail, 'Alas for the day!'
3For the day is near,
the day of the LORD is near;
it will be a day of clouds,
a time of doom for[e] the nations.
4A sword shall come upon Egypt,
and anguish shall be in Cush,
when the slain fall in Egypt,
and her wealth[f] is carried away,
and her foundations are torn down.

5Cush, and Put, and Lud, and all Arabia, and Libya,[g] and the people of the land that is
in league,[h] shall fall with them by the sword.

6"Thus says the LORD:
Those who support Egypt shall fall,
and her proud might shall come down;
from Migdol to Syene
they shall fall within her by the sword,
declares the Lord GOD.
7And they shall be desolated in the midst
of desolated countries,
and their cities shall be in the midst of
cities that are laid waste.
8Then they will know that I am the
LORD,
when I have set fire to Egypt,
and all her helpers are broken.

9"On that day messengers shall go out from me in ships to terrify the unsuspecting
people of Cush, and anguish shall come upon them on the day of Egypt's doom;[i] for, be-
hold, it comes!
10"Thus says the Lord GOD:

"I will put an end to the wealth of Egypt,
by the hand of Nebuchadnezzar king of
Babylon.
11He and his people with him, the most
ruthless of nations,
shall be brought in to destroy the land,
and they shall draw their swords against
Egypt
and fill the land with the slain.
12And I will dry up the Nile
and will sell the land into the hand of
evildoers;
I will bring desolation upon the land and
everything in it,
by the hand of foreigners;
I am the LORD; I have spoken.

13"Thus says the Lord GOD:

"I will destroy the idols
and put an end to the images in Memphis;
there shall no longer be a prince from the land of Egypt;
so I will put fear in the land of Egypt.
14*I will make Pathros a desolation*
and will set fire to Zoan
and will execute judgments on Thebes.
15*And I will pour out my wrath on Pelusium,*
the stronghold of Egypt,
and cut off the multitude[j] *of Thebes.*
16*And I will set fire to Egypt;*
Pelusium shall be in great agony;
Thebes shall be breached,
and Memphis shall face enemies[k] *by day.*
17*The young men of On and of Pi-beseth*
shall fall by the sword,
and the women[l] *shall go into captivity.*
18*At Tehaphnehes the day shall be dark,*
when I break there the yoke bars of Egypt,
and her proud might shall come to an end in her;
she shall be covered by a cloud,
and her daughters shall go into captivity.
19*Thus I will execute judgments on Egypt.*
Then they will know that I am the Lord."

20*In the eleventh year, in the first month, on the seventh day of the month, the word of*
the Lord came to me: 21*"Son of man, I have broken the arm of Pharaoh king of Egypt, and*
behold, it has not been bound up, to heal it by binding it with a bandage, so that it may be-
come strong to wield the sword. 22*Therefore thus says the Lord God: Behold, I am against*
Pharaoh king of Egypt and will break his arms, both the strong arm and the one that was
broken, and I will make the sword fall from his hand. 23*I will scatter the Egyptians among*
the nations and disperse them through the countries. 24*And I will strengthen the arms of*
the king of Babylon and put my sword in his hand, but I will break the arms of Pharaoh,
and he will groan before him like a man mortally wounded. 25*I will strengthen the arms*
of the king of Babylon, but the arms of Pharaoh shall fall. Then they shall know that I am
the Lord, when I put my sword into the hand of the king of Babylon and he stretches it
out against the land of Egypt. 26*And I will scatter the Egyptians among the nations and*
disperse them throughout the countries. Then they will know that I am the Lord."

a Hebrew *they* **b** Syriac (compare Psalm 69:23); Hebrew *to stand* **c** Hebrew *he* **d** Or *multitude* **e** Hebrew lacks *doom for* **f** Or *multitude;* also verse 10 **g** With Septuagint; Hebrew *Cub* **h** Hebrew *and the sons of the land of the covenant* **i** Hebrew *the day of Egypt* **j** Or *wealth* **k** Or *distress* **l** Or *the cities;* Hebrew *they*

Overview: Judgment is now spoken against Egypt. Issues of chronology are a special concern here. The prophecy against Tyre precedes the prophecy against Egypt, but the chronology is reversed. The prophecy against Egypt came in Zedekiah's tenth year; the prophecy against Tyre in his eleventh. The reason for the chronological disorder is that Tyre was destroyed first. The wicked pride of the king of Egypt was no different from that of the other kings surrounding Israel. God would destroy the Egyptians, and the lands would remain desolate for forty years. After this time of captivity, God promised to gather the Egyptians and return them to their land. Here we see the goodness and mercy of God extending even to the heathen. Ezekiel 29 ends with comfort and the promised horn of salvation, who is Christ. Finally, this section ends with lamentation. Idolatry brings destruction. Although much prosperity and rejoicing had been found in Egypt, now days of sorrow would come on the nation.

29:1-26 *Prophecy Against Egypt*

God's Punctuality. William Greenhill: "In the tenth year, in the tenth month, in the twelfth day of the month." The Lord would have people mind the time when he sets his prophets on work, and that punctually. The year, month and day are here recorded when he gave out his word to Ezekiel that the same might be observed by all it concerned. The Jews trusted much to Egypt and its kings. The Egyptians were haughty and self-confident. Now God records the time of his commissioning Ezekiel to prophesy against the king of Egypt and the Egyptians that the Jews, hearing of their ruin, designated from such time, might rely no longer on them; and that the Egyptians might consider what to do, being in such imminent danger, for their treachery to the Jews and confidence in what they had. An Exposition of Ezekiel.[1]

The Chronology. John Mayer: For time, it was *the tenth year, the tenth month, the twelfth day,* that is, of Jehoiachin's captivity, and so the tenth year of Zedekiah's reign. But the prophecy against Tyre was in the eleventh year (Ezek 26), which was after this, but the order of time most probably was thus, because although Tyre was last prophesied against, yet it was first destroyed by Nebuchadnezzar. This appears in Ezekiel 29:17, where Egypt is said to be given to him as a reward for his executing judgment on Tyre. This prophecy also (if we compare it with Ezekiel 24) was a year after the siege at Jerusalem began, and therefore proof was by this time made of the king of Egypt failing to help the king of Judah in his straits. Commentary upon All the Prophets.[2]

Judgment Against Pharaoh. William Greenhill: God is an open and professed enemy to wicked kings. He proclaims war against them, be they never so great. "Behold, I am against you, Pharaoh king of Egypt" (Ezek 29:3). Few are the kings who abuse not their authority; they lift up themselves, oppress the people, oppose the interest of God, and therefore he is a declared adversary to them. In Jeremiah 25:18-26, you may see what a multitude of kings the Lord sends the cup of fury to and draws out the sword against. There was scarcely one good king at that time on the face of the earth. God was against them all. It is a dreadful thing for any king to have God denounce war against him, he must be conquered and brought to nothing, for God is the Lord of hosts, armed with such power and majesty as that there is no withstanding him. . . .

Wicked kings are resemblances of Satan. Pharaoh is here called "the great dragon" (Ezek 29:3), and so is Satan. . . . "But I will put hooks in your jaws" (Ezek 29:4). Here begin God's judgments on this confident king. God would deal with him as people do with some great fish. When the hook is in his jaws, they draw him out of the waters to the dry land, where he dies. So God would, by an occasion, draw Pharaoh out of Egypt into another land, and with him a great army of the Egyptians, where they should all perish. An Exposition of Ezekiel.[3]

The Wounded Dragon. Martin Luther: Very freely the prophets refer to ancient history to show that the wonderful deeds of God hitherto can still be brought to bear on his proud enemies, such as anciently the kings of Egypt. He calls that kingdom "Rahab" (Is 51:9), that is, "proud," and he also calls it a wounded dragon. Ezekiel does the same thing (Ezek 29:3). Thus he depicts the feeling of the king of Egypt so that it appears to be

[1]*Exposition*, 628. [2]*Prophets*, 447. [3]*Exposition*, 629.

happening in the same way in our times in the case of our tyrants. They despise our Christ in such a way that they make a mockery of him. They say, "What kind of God is the God of the Lutherans? I wouldn't want to be his creature. Let the devil be his creature; I want nothing to do with his gospel!" Lectures on Isaiah.[4]

Destruction of Egypt. John Mayer: *No foot of man or beast shall pass through it, neither shall it be inhabited forty years* (Ezek 29:11). Of the fulfilling of this no history makes mention. But at the expiration of this time after the destruction of Jerusalem, the state of the king of Babylon beginning to decline, it is most probable that the Egyptians began to gather together again into their own land, which all this time lay in desolation. It now began to be peopled again; that is, after about sixty years of Judah's captivity. Commentary upon All the Prophets.[5]

Return of the Egyptians. William Greenhill: These verses are a promise of mercy to the Egyptians. "At the end of forty years will I gather the Egyptians" (Ezek 29:13). The Egyptians being notorious idolaters, confiding in their own strength, were scattered among the nations, where they wandered and lived without hope of seeing their own country and becoming a people or kingdom again; but the Lord out of his abundant goodness, beyond theirs and others' expectation, promised that after forty years expired he would gather them, wherever they were scattered. Forty years he would exercise them with captivity and those hard things that accompanied the same, but at the end of this he would show them mercy. . . .

The goodness and mercy of God extend to heathens. He has a care of them in their captivity, and after they have suffered his appointed time, he will show kindness to them. . . . God sometimes deals more favorably with heathens than with his own people. "At the end of forty years will I gather the Egyptians." But it was the end of seventy years before he gathered the Jews out of Babylon. His own people were thirty years, or near on, longer under the Babylonian yoke than the Egyptians. There was just cause for this. God's people had sinned worse than the heathens and so provoked him above them. An Exposition of Ezekiel.[6]

Does God Reward Evil Works? Martin Luther: [T]he king of Babylon is called the servant of God, because he laid waste Tyre and Sidon. For God wanted this to be done by the Babylonian king, that he should take Tyre and Sidon. For so God says, "I will destroy Tyre and Sidon. But where shall I find a man who will do this?" There the godless king is made a servant of God so that he will destroy Tyre and Sidon and he receives Egypt for a reward. Therefore, that work which God himself rewarded was a good and pleasing work. For that reason I reply that one must not here look at the excellence of his justice, but one must consider the tremendous divine goodness and the mercy of God, who rewards even sins and does good even to hypocrites. As Augustine says, vices are conquered by vices. The king of Babylon is damned in God's eyes, and yet he receives Egypt as a reward. But as the service is, so is the reward. The service is temporal, the reward is temporal. Although the righteousness of the king of Babylon was not worthy of such rewards, for it was sin, nevertheless, God rewarded the work of a hypocrite for the sake of civil peace. The Disputation Concerning Justification.[7]

Horn of Salvation. John Mayer: As he

[4]LW 17:200. [5]*Prophets*, 447. [6]*Exposition*, 634-35. [7]Lenker 4, 169 (WA 39,1:100-101). Cf. Augustine, *City of God* 21.16 (PL 41, 730).

concluded Ezekiel 28 with comfort for the Israelites, so he does this by the horn budding forth (Ezek 29:21), understanding something to come long after, bringing far greater spiritual and everlasting comfort by Christ. Wherefore Christ and not Zerubbabel, as some say, is this horn, for so he is called, "the horn of salvation" raised up for Israel (Lk 1:69). Although the time seems not to agree, for it is said "in that day," but Christ came not until five hundred years after. I answer he came in that day when Egypt was a base kingdom yet. This was before threatened, that it should be, for it was then under the Romans more than ever, Anthony and Cleopatra being overcome by Augustus Caesar. And if not so, yet if by a day we understand a day with the Lord, which is as a thousand years, this horn budded in that day. Commentary upon All the Prophets.[8]

A Textual Question. William Greenhill: This chapter, according to Franciscus Junius, ended at the seventeenth verse, where he begins the thirtieth chapter. But, according to our translation, this is the last verse of this chapter, and it is a precious promise of mercy to the house of Israel and to the prophet.

. . . After the destruction of enemies, God shows mercy to the Jews. Egyptians were no friends to the house of Israel. When Egypt therefore should be spoiled and brought under the Babylonians, then would he make the horn of Israel to bud. In that day, or after that time, when his justice had fallen on Egyptians, then his mercy should be extended to Israel. An Exposition of Ezekiel.[9]

30:1-26 *A Lament for Egypt*

Sorrow Follows Mirth. William Greenhill: After days of mirth come days of sorrow. Egypt had seen many days of prosperity and rejoicing, and now, "Wail, alas for the day!" Its summer was over, and winter coming on it, black, cloudy, stormy, terrible days were at hand. As there is a change in things, so in times: "There is a time to weep and time to laugh; a time to mourn and a time to dance" (Eccles 3:4). These succeed each other, and neither keeps possession long. Mirth and jollity are thrust out the door, after a few days, by their contrary. Babylon had its days of delight. It was given to pleasure (Is 47:8), but suddenly there was a change (Jer 51:8). An Exposition of Ezekiel.[10]

God as Enemy. William Greenhill: It is a dreadful thing to have the Lord declare himself to be an enemy to a king, to a state, to any. "Behold, I am against Pharaoh." Therefore what was broken could not be healed, and what was whole should be broken; he should be more and more disabled. His princes became fools, his wise counselors brutish, a perverse and seducing spirit was in the midst of them. Egypt was as women, fearful and weak like women (Is 19:11-16). God being against Pharaoh, all his counsels, enterprises were blasted, all his forces broken, all his cities made desolate and all his people consumed or carried into captivity. Better he had had all the princes of the world against him than God, for whomever he is against must be ruined. An Exposition of Ezekiel.[11]

[8]*Prophets*, 448. [9]*Exposition*, 640. [10]*Exposition*, 642. [11]*Exposition*, 649.

31:1–32:32 DESTRUCTION OF EGYPT AND LAMENT

1In the eleventh year, in the third month, on the first day of the month, the word of the LORD came to me: 2"Son of man, say to Pharaoh king of Egypt and to his multitude:

"Whom are you like in your greatness?
3Behold, Assyria was a cedar in Lebanon,
with beautiful branches and forest shade,
and of towering height,
its top among the clouds.[a]
4The waters nourished it;
the deep made it grow tall,
making its rivers flow
around the place of its planting,
sending forth its streams
to all the trees of the field.
5So it towered high
above all the trees of the field;
its boughs grew large
and its branches long
from abundant water in its shoots.
6All the birds of the heavens
made their nests in its boughs;
under its branches all the beasts of the field
gave birth to their young,
and under its shadow
lived all great nations.
7It was beautiful in its greatness,
in the length of its branches;
for its roots went down
to abundant waters.
8The cedars in the garden of God could not rival it,
nor the fir trees equal its boughs;
neither were the plane trees
like its branches;
no tree in the garden of God
was its equal in beauty.
9I made it beautiful
in the mass of its branches,
and all the trees of Eden envied it,
that were in the garden of God.

10"Therefore thus says the Lord GOD: Because it[b] towered high and set its top among the clouds, and its heart was proud of its height, 11I will give it into the hand of a mighty one of the nations. He shall surely deal with it as its wickedness deserves. I have cast it out. 12Foreigners, the most ruthless of nations, have cut it down and left it. On the mountains and in all the valleys its branches have fallen, and its boughs have been broken in all the ravines of the land, and all the peoples of the earth have gone away from its shadow and left it. 13On its fallen trunk dwell all the birds of the heavens, and on its branches are all the beasts of the field. 14All this is in order that no trees by the waters may grow to towering height or set their tops among the clouds, and that no trees that drink water may reach up to them in height. For they are all given over to death, to the world below, among the children of man,[c] with those who go down to the pit.

15"Thus says the Lord GOD: On the day the cedar[d] went down to Sheol I caused mourning; I closed the deep over it, and restrained its rivers, and many waters were stopped.

I clothed Lebanon in gloom for it, and all the trees of the field fainted because of it. 16 I
made the nations quake at the sound of its fall, when I cast it down to Sheol with those
who go down to the pit. And all the trees of Eden, the choice and best of Lebanon, all that
drink water, were comforted in the world below. 17 They also went down to Sheol with
it, to those who are slain by the sword; yes, those who were its arm, who lived under its
shadow among the nations.

18 "Whom are you thus like in glory and in greatness among the trees of Eden? You
shall be brought down with the trees of Eden to the world below. You shall lie among the
uncircumcised, with those who are slain by the sword.

"This is Pharaoh and all his multitude, declares the Lord God."

32 In the twelfth year, in the twelfth month, on the first day of the month, the word
of the Lord came to me: 2 "Son of man, raise a lamentation over Pharaoh king of
Egypt and say to him:

"You consider yourself a lion of the
nations,
but you are like a dragon in the seas;
you burst forth in your rivers,
trouble the waters with your feet,
and foul their rivers.
3 Thus says the Lord God:
I will throw my net over you
with a host of many peoples,
and they will haul you up in my
dragnet.
4 And I will cast you on the ground;
on the open field I will fling you,
and will cause all the birds of the
heavens to settle on you,
and I will gorge the beasts of the whole
earth with you.
5 I will strew your flesh upon the
mountains
and fill the valleys with your
carcass.[e]
6 I will drench the land even to the
mountains
with your flowing blood,
and the ravines will be full of you.
7 When I blot you out, I will cover the
heavens
and make their stars dark;
I will cover the sun with a cloud,
and the moon shall not give its light.
8 All the bright lights of heaven
will I make dark over you,
and put darkness on your land,
declares the Lord God.

9 "I will trouble the hearts of many peoples, when I bring your destruction among the
nations, into the countries that you have not known. 10 I will make many peoples appalled
at you, and the hair of their kings shall bristle with horror because of you, when I bran-
dish my sword before them. They shall tremble every moment, every one for his own life,
on the day of your downfall.

11 "For thus says the Lord God: The sword of the king of Babylon shall come upon you.
12 I will cause your multitude to fall by the swords of mighty ones, all of them most ruth-
less of nations.

"They shall bring to ruin the pride of
Egypt,
and all its multitude[f] shall perish.
13 I will destroy all its beasts
from beside many waters;
and no foot of man shall trouble them
anymore,
nor shall the hoofs of beasts trouble them.

14Then I will make their waters clear,
and cause their rivers to run like oil,
declares the Lord God.
15When I make the land of Egypt
desolate,
and when the land is desolate of all that
fills it,
when I strike down all who dwell in it,
then they will know that I am the
Lord.

16This is a lamentation that shall be chanted; the daughters of the nations shall chant it;
over Egypt, and over all her multitude, shall they chant it, declares the Lord God."
17In the twelfth year, in the twelfth month,[g] on the fifteenth day of the month, the word
of the Lord came to me: 18"Son of man, wail over the multitude of Egypt, and send them
down, her and the daughters of majestic nations, to the world below, to those who have
gone down to the pit:

19'Whom do you surpass in beauty?
Go down and be laid to rest with the
uncircumcised.'

20They shall fall amid those who are slain by the sword. Egypt[h] is delivered to the
sword; drag her away, and all her multitudes. 21The mighty chiefs shall speak of them,
with their helpers, out of the midst of Sheol: 'They have come down, they lie still, the un-
circumcised, slain by the sword.'
22"Assyria is there, and all her company, its graves all around it, all of them slain,
fallen by the sword, 23whose graves are set in the uttermost parts of the pit; and her com-
pany is all around her grave, all of them slain, fallen by the sword, who spread terror in
the land of the living.
24"Elam is there, and all her multitude around her grave; all of them slain, fallen by the
sword, who went down uncircumcised into the world below, who spread their terror in the
land of the living; and they bear their shame with those who go down to the pit. 25They
have made her a bed among the slain with all her multitude, her graves all around it, all
of them uncircumcised, slain by the sword; for terror of them was spread in the land of
the living, and they bear their shame with those who go down to the pit; they are placed
among the slain.
26"Meshech-Tubal is there, and all her multitude, her graves all around it, all of them
uncircumcised, slain by the sword; for they spread their terror in the land of the living.
27And they do not lie with the mighty, the fallen from among the uncircumcised, who went
down to Sheol with their weapons of war, whose swords were laid under their heads, and
whose iniquities are upon their bones; for the terror of the mighty men was in the land of
the living. 28But as for you, you shall be broken and lie among the uncircumcised, with
those who are slain by the sword.
29"Edom is there, her kings and all her princes, who for all their might are laid with
those who are killed by the sword; they lie with the uncircumcised, with those who go down
to the pit.
30"The princes of the north are there, all of them, and all the Sidonians, who have gone
down in shame with the slain, for all the terror that they caused by their might; they lie

uncircumcised with those who are slain by the sword, and bear their shame with those who go down to the pit.

[31]*"When Pharaoh sees them, he will be comforted for all his multitude, Pharaoh and all his army, slain by the sword, declares the Lord God.* [32]*For I spread terror in the land of the living; and he shall be laid to rest among the uncircumcised, with those who are slain by the sword, Pharaoh and all his multitude, declares the Lord God."*

a Or *its top went through the thick boughs;* also verses 10, 14 **b** Syriac, Vulgate; Hebrew *you* **c** Or *of Adam* **d** Hebrew *it* **e** Hebrew *your height* **f** Or *wealth* **g** Hebrew lacks *in the twelfth month* **h** Hebrew *She*

Overview: The downfall of Egypt is here told by the allegory of a great cedar that was chopped down. The king of Egypt thinks himself the equal of God, and yet he is much less than the king of Assyria, whose power, dignity and greatness far exceeded him. And yet, the king of Assyria was utterly destroyed because of his pride and arrogance. In this chapter, we see that God humbles proud kings and destroys their kingdoms.

The Eleventh Year. John Mayer: *The eleventh year, the third month* (Ezek 31:1). The same argument of threatening Pharaoh and his land with destruction is here further prosecuted at another time the same year, but three months after. This time, however, by the example of the king of Assyria, his greatness and fall are set forth. For his pride he was as a most high cedar cut down, and so he shows Pharaoh should not be spared. That if he would not be moved by anything yet spoken by way of a formal denunciation, he might by the example of his peer, who was yet superior to him in dominion by far, be moved, humble himself and repent. Commentary upon All the Prophets.[1]

Whom Are You Like? William Greenhill: This was the question Ezekiel must propound to him, and it was an upbraiding question, taxing him for his pride, arrogance and vain confidences. He had, like most kings, many flatterers, who flattered him into a conceit that he was greater than other kings, indeed, so great in power that he might encounter God himself. The Lord therefore thought it proper to take down his spirit by this question, "Whom are you like in your greatness?" What! Like me? You are far from that. Indeed, you are not even comparable to some mortals. What do you say to the king of Assyria? Are you greater and stronger than he? No. He went far beyond you in power, dignity and greatness, yet for his pride, arrogance and confidences in what he had, he was utterly destroyed. And you, who are inferior, think to stand and avoid the judgments of God when they come? You deceive yourself. An Exposition of Ezekiel.[2]

God Humbles Proud Kings. William Greenhill: Pride and wickedness cause God to bring dreadful judgments on kings and their kingdoms. Because the king of Assyria's heart was lifted up in his height, therefore God delivered him into the hand of a mighty enemy and drove him out for his wickedness. When princes are in the seat of honor, have great means coming in, then they look big, begin to deify themselves, to do what they like, not minding him who exalted them but confiding in their own strength, power and greatness, which makes way for their speedy ruin. Solomon tells us that a person shall not be established by wickedness (Prov 12:13). Kings, by their wicked policies and practices, cannot establish themselves; their wickedness overthrows them, their pride provokes God against them (Dan 4:25). It is good for kings and oth-

[1]*Prophets*, 449. [2]*Exposition*, 650.

ers to be humble in the midst of their enjoyments, and the greater abundance that they do possess, to carry it still the more humbly, for he that is of a humble mind is worthy of honor and has God dwelling with him. An Exposition of Ezekiel.[3]

32:1-32 *A Lament for Pharaoh*

Destruction of Egypt. John Mayer: Here the prophet proceeds in the same argument. First he stirs up to lamentation for the horrible destruction of Egypt in the twelfth year, the twelfth month, the first day. Then he diversely sets forth the destruction of it by mentioning other nations likewise destroyed the fifteenth day of the same month, as Assyria and Elam, Meshech and Tubal, the princes of the North and Sidon, who not only fell but now are lying in the pit, intimating their continuing in desolation. Commentary upon All the Prophets.[4]

The Time of the Calamity. William Greenhill: This was not the time of Zedekiah, who reigned but eleven years. It was in the twelfth year of Jehoiachin's captivity, the twelfth month and first day, not long after the taking of Jerusalem and burning it with fire. The Lord gave out this prophecy then, that the Jews might be taken from trusting in the Egyptians, having cause sufficient to believe that Ezekiel's prophecies against them should be made good, as well as Jeremiah's against them, for it was the same Spirit who breathed in them both.

. . . That times of public calamities are especially to be noted. Ezekiel sets down the year, month and day when the Lord told him what dreadful things should befall Pharaoh and the Egyptians: "In the twelfth year, the twelfth month, the first day of the month, he must take up a lamentation." God's judgments sometimes are lasting, and the duration of them cannot be known unless the beginning of them is taken notice of. An Exposition of Ezekiel.[5]

[3]*Exposition*, 653-54. [4]*Prophets*, 449. [5]*Exposition*, 656.

33:1-33 EZEKIEL A WATCHMAN AND JERUSALEM

1The word of the Lord came to me: 2"Son of man, speak to your people and say to
them, If I bring the sword upon a land, and the people of the land take a man from among
them, and make him their watchman, 3and if he sees the sword coming upon the land
and blows the trumpet and warns the people, 4then if anyone who hears the sound of the
trumpet does not take warning, and the sword comes and takes him away, his blood shall
be upon his own head. 5He heard the sound of the trumpet and did not take warning; his
blood shall be upon himself. But if he had taken warning, he would have saved his life.
6But if the watchman sees the sword coming and does not blow the trumpet, so that the
people are not warned, and the sword comes and takes any one of them, that person is

taken away in his iniquity, but his blood I will require at the watchman's hand.
[7]"So you, son of man, I have made a watchman for the house of Israel. Whenever you
hear a word from my mouth, you shall give them warning from me. [8]If I say to the wicked,
O wicked one, you shall surely die, and you do not speak to warn the wicked to turn from
his way, that wicked person shall die in his iniquity, but his blood I will require at your
hand. [9]But if you warn the wicked to turn from his way, and he does not turn from his
way, that person shall die in his iniquity, but you will have delivered your soul.
[10]"And you, son of man, say to the house of Israel, Thus have you said: 'Surely our
transgressions and our sins are upon us, and we rot away because of them. How then can
we live?' [11]Say to them, As I live, declares the Lord GOD, I have no pleasure in the death
of the wicked, but that the wicked turn from his way and live; turn back, turn back from
your evil ways, for why will you die, O house of Israel?
[12]"And you, son of man, say to your people, The righteousness of the righteous shall not
deliver him when he transgresses, and as for the wickedness of the wicked, he shall not
fall by it when he turns from his wickedness, and the righteous shall not be able to live by
his righteousness[a] when he sins. [13]Though I say to the righteous that he shall surely live,
yet if he trusts in his righteousness and does injustice, none of his righteous deeds shall be
remembered, but in his injustice that he has done he shall die. [14]Again, though I say to the
wicked, 'You shall surely die,' yet if he turns from his sin and does what is just and right,
[15]if the wicked restores the pledge, gives back what he has taken by robbery, and walks in
the statutes of life, not doing injustice, he shall surely live; he shall not die. [16]None of the
sins that he has committed shall be remembered against him. He has done what is just
and right; he shall surely live.
[17]"Yet your people say, 'The way of the Lord is not just,' when it is their own way that
is not just. [18]When the righteous turns from his righteousness and does injustice, he shall
die for it. [19]And when the wicked turns from his wickedness and does what is just and
right, he shall live by this. [20]Yet you say, 'The way of the Lord is not just.' O house of
Israel, I will judge each of you according to his ways."
[21]In the twelfth year of our exile, in the tenth month, on the fifth day of the month, a
fugitive from Jerusalem came to me and said, "The city has been struck down." [22]Now
the hand of the LORD had been upon me the evening before the fugitive came; and he
had opened my mouth by the time the man came to me in the morning, so my mouth was
opened, and I was no longer mute.
[23]The word of the LORD came to me: [24]"Son of man, the inhabitants of these waste
places in the land of Israel keep saying, 'Abraham was only one man, yet he got possession
of the land; but we are many; the land is surely given us to possess.' [25]Therefore say to
them, Thus says the Lord GOD: You eat flesh with the blood and lift up your eyes to your
idols and shed blood; shall you then possess the land? [26]You rely on the sword, you commit
abominations, and each of you defiles his neighbor's wife; shall you then possess the land?
[27]Say this to them, Thus says the Lord GOD: As I live, surely those who are in the waste
places shall fall by the sword, and whoever is in the open field I will give to the beasts to
be devoured, and those who are in strongholds and in caves shall die by pestilence. [28]And
I will make the land a desolation and a waste, and her proud might shall come to an end,
and the mountains of Israel shall be so desolate that none will pass through. [29]Then they
will know that I am the LORD, when I have made the land a desolation and a waste be-

cause of all their abominations that they have committed.
30"As for you, son of man, your people who talk together about you by the walls and
at the doors of the houses, say to one another, each to his brother, 'Come, and hear what
the word is that comes from the Lord.' 31And they come to you as people come, and they
sit before you as my people, and they hear what you say but they will not do it; for with
lustful talk in their mouths they act; their heart is set on their gain. 32And behold, you
are to them like one who sings lustful songs with a beautiful voice and plays[b] well on an
instrument, for they hear what you say, but they will not do it. 33When this comes—and
come it will!—then they will know that a prophet has been among them."

a Hebrew *by it* **b** Hebrew *like the singing of lustful songs with a beautiful voice and one who plays*

Overview: The chapters against the nations are concluded, and Ezekiel turns again to the Jews. With this chapter begins the third major division of Ezekiel, which extends to Ezekiel 39. Ezekiel 33 begins with a description of a watchman appointed by God to speak his word and warn his people. A word of caution is also given that some watchmen are unfaithful in their calling and therefore false watchmen or prophets.

The middle section of the chapter elicits the most comment and disagreement among our commentators. What does God mean when he declares that he takes no pleasure in the death of the wicked (Ezek 33:11)? The question immediately touches on the teaching of predestination and whether God predestines the reprobate as well as the elect. The Calvinists say yes; the Lutherans no.

The chapter ends with the news of Jerusalem's destruction. What Ezekiel prophesied had come to pass. Now the prophet directs his words to those who escaped the destruction of the city. These people remain in their hypocrisy and sin. They still held with vain confidence that they would possess the land.

Summary of the Chapter. William Greenhill: Our prophet having finished his prophecy against the nations in eight chapters. Ezekiel 25–32, which was the second general part of his whole prophecy, comes here again to prophesy to the Jews and begins the third general part of his prophecy, which extends to the end of Ezekiel 39. In this chapter are these things laid down: a renovation of the prophet's call to his office, with the description (Ezek 33:1-9); a confirmation of the prophet against the calumnies of the Jews (Ezek 33:10-20); a denunciation of judgment against those that were not struck at the taking of Jerusalem (Ezek 33:21-29); a reproof of those that were captives in Babylon for their hypocrisy and covetousness (Ezek 33:30-33). An Exposition of Ezekiel.[1]

Four Parts of the Chapters. Jakob Raupius: There are four parts to this chapter. The first part is paranesis. Here God exhorts the prophet to remain faithful amid the impious people. The second part is apologetic. God defends himself against the accusation of the Jews. The third part is prophetic, which foretells the coming destruction of the Jews at Jerusalem. The fourth part is historical, narrating the people's hypocrisy when Ezekiel lived among them. Commentary on Ezekiel.[2]

33:1-9 *Watchman*

The Office of Watchman. William Greenhill: Ezekiel 33:6 sets out the office of

[1]*Exposition*, 663. [2]*Commentarius Synopticus* (1655), 244.

the watchman, which is (1) To look diligently about him, whether there is any danger approaching, any enemy near at hand, coming to invade or make attempts against the land. (2) If so, he is to blow the trumpet presently and to give warning by it, stirring up all to procure public safety. The blowing of the trumpet was a warning to the people to look to themselves. But this warning was not only by the voice of the trumpet but also by the voice of the watchman; for having blown the trumpet on the discovery and approach of an enemy, the watchman was to shift for his life and liberty, by returning to his people, and so to call on them to provide for public safety.

. . . Not all watchmen are faithful. Some are sleepy and careless; they see not the sword coming. Some are perfidious; they see it coming but blow not the trumpet. They warn not the people and what then? Here is the punishment laid down of an unfaithful watchman. Through his sleepiness, negligence or treachery, a soul is taken away, a person is slain by the adversary, who, if the watchman had given warning, might have lived. And therefore, because he did not, he is guilty of the person's blood and must answer for it, at his hands will God require it. An Exposition of Ezekiel.[3]

The Watchmen. Johannes Oecolampadius: Watchmen of the people . . . are appointed to call back the ungodly from their sins and to preach repentance, as the axe positioned at the root of the tree. The principal sin of the people is that they did not listen to the prophets God sent to their ancestors but instead banished them. God the Father commands that we are to listen to Christ (Mt 17:5), for outside the knowledge of Christ there is nothing but hypocrisy and godlessness—whatever the name of the religion. Indeed, as Saint Paul says, "the righteous of God is revealed from faith for faith. The righteous live by faith. For the wrath of God is revealed against all ungodliness and unrighteousness of people, who by their unrighteousness suppress the truth" (Rom 1:17-18). Commentary on the Prophet Ezekiel.[4]

False Prophets. Johann Gerhard: Each and every Christian must be on guard against false prophets. First and foremost, church teachers must be alert and warn the gullible against them. This is why the Lord God has placed the teachers as shepherd and watchmen (Acts 20:28; Ezek 3:17). If a shepherd lets his poor, incautious sheep fall into the wolf's jaws, one can rightly demand the sheep from such an unfaithful shepherd. *But when the watchmen sees the sword approach and does not blow the trumpet or warn the people, and the sword comes and takes some of them, even though they are taken away because of their sins, I will demand their blood from the watchmen's hand* (Ezek 33:6). Thus, God will demand the souls of the pupils from the teachers. Those who, in their silence and negligence, are seduced by false teachers will end in eternal destruction. Postilla.[5]

33:10-20 *God and the Death of the Wicked*

Punishment of the Wicked. Richard Baxter: It has been the astonishing wonder of many a person, as well as me, to read in holy Scripture how few will be saved, and that the greatest part even of those who are called will be everlastingly shut out of the kingdom of heaven and tormented with the devils in eternal fire. Infidels believe not this when they read it, and therefore must feel it. Those that do believe it are forced to cry out with Paul, "Oh, the depth of the riches both of the wisdom and knowledge of God! How unsearchable are his judgments, and his ways past finding out" (Rom 11:13)! But nature itself

[3]*Exposition*, 664. [4]*Commentarius in Ezechielem* (1553), 157. [5]*Postilla* 1:89.

does teach us all to lay the blame of evil works on the doers; and therefore when we see any heinous thing done, a principle of justice does provoke us to inquire after him who did it, that the evil of the work may return the evil of the shame on the author. . . . It is indeed confessed by all that Satan is the cause, but that does not resolve the doubt because he is not the principal cause. He does not force people to sin but tempts them to it and leaves it to their own wills, whether they will do it or not. He does not carry people to an alehouse and force open their mouths and pour in the drink; nor does he hold them that they cannot go to God's service; nor does he force their hearts from holy thoughts. It lies, therefore, between God and the sinner: one of them must be the principal cause of all this misery, whichever it is; for there is no other to cast it on. And God disclaims it. He will not take it on him. And the wicked disclaim it usually, and they will not take it on them. This is the controversy that is here managed in this text (Ezek 33:11). A Call to the Unconverted.[6]

Does God Will the Death of the Wicked? John Calvin: But our opponents are in the habit of quoting in opposition a few Scripture passages in which God seems to deny that the wicked perish by his ordination, except in so far as by their clamorous protests they of their own accord bring death on themselves. . . . A passage of Ezekiel's is brought forward, that "God does not will the death of the wicked but wills that the wicked turn back and live" (Ezek 33:11). If it pleases God to extend this to the whole human race, why does he not encourage to repentance the very many whose minds are more amenable to obedience than the minds of those who grow harder and harder at his daily invitations? Among the people of Nineveh and of Sodom, as Christ testifies, the preaching of the gospel and miracles would have accomplished more than in Judea. If God wills that all be saved, how does it come to pass that he does not open the door to repentance to the miserable people who would be better prepared to receive grace? Hence we may see that this passage is violently twisted if the will of God, mentioned by the prophet, is opposed to his eternal plan, by which he has distinguished the elect from the reprobate. Now if we are seeking the prophet's true meaning, it is that he would bring the hope of pardon to the penitent only. The gist of it is that God is without doubt ready to forgive, as soon as the sinner is converted. Therefore, in so far as God wills the sinner's repentance, he does not will his death. But experience teaches that God wills the repentance of those whom he invites to himself, in such a way that he does not touch the hearts of all. Yet it is not on that account to be said that he acts deceitfully, for even though only his outward call renders inexcusable those who hear it and do not obey, still it is truly considered evidence of God's grace, by which he reconciles people to himself. Let us therefore regard the prophet's instruction that the death of the sinner is not pleasing to God as designed to assure believers that God is ready to pardon them as soon as they are touched by repentance but to make the wicked feel that their transgression is doubled because they do not respond to God's great kindness and goodness. Institutes of Christian Religion.[7]

God and the Wicked. Thomas Manton: God is not the cause of a person's destruction, but it is a person's own fault if he is not converted and saved. That people are apt to charge God foolishly appears by that monition: "O Israel, you have destroyed yourself, but in me is your help" (Hos 13:9). But more expressly here: "The foolishness of a person perverts his way, and his heart frets against the Lord" (Prov 19:3). But the blame cannot lie in God; he does all that seems fit to be done as

[6]*Practical Works* 2:508. [7]*Inst.* 2:982-83.

a lawgiver and governor of the world. There is nothing wanting on his part. "What could I have done more to my vineyard that I have not done to it? Wherefore, when I looked that it should bring forth grapes, brought it forth wild grapes" (Is 5:4). From first to law we may plead the cause of God with you. God made people upright, gave them a righteous law, which, when broken, that all hopes might not be cut off, he sent his Son (Rom 8:3) to be the foundation of a new covenant. He offered you grace in him, pardon of all your sins past, to help you in the course of obedience for time to come. He moved you by powerful arguments, not by low and cheap considerations but those of the greatest weight, the joys of heaven, the torments of hell. He called on you often by the ministry, knocked at your hearts as well as your ears by his Spirit. He waited for your amendment for many years, tried you by mercies if they could melt you, by afflictions if they would reduce you to a sense of your duty. But all this will not do; yet you are still alive, and these means continued. What shall God do more? Now why are you not converted? Others are wrought on by the same means and turned to the Lord, and have entered in by the straight gate and framed their desire to walk in the narrow way. They have not offers more rich or free or particular. God has not told them of a hotter hell or a better heaven, or another gospel. God speaks to you and them in the same terms, with the same grace and favor, and makes the door wide enough to get in. Why are you not converted? Did God cut off all hopes from you and tell you that your repentance would do you no good? No; certainly the fault is in your own obstinacy and impenitence. SERMONS UPON EZEKIEL.[8]

GOD DOES NOT WANT THE DEATH OF ONE SINNER. JOHANN GERHARD: The Calvinists teach that Adam fell into sin by the Lord God's sovereign will and decree. This is contrary to Scripture, which states that the Lord God created Adam in his own likeness, solemnly forbade him to eat from the tree of the knowledge of good and evil and punished him for his fall; hence in the catechism we call God "Father." But it would not be a true, fatherly heart that with full knowledge and intent would lead his children to destruction. This also runs counter to God's glory, for it is cruel mercy that would impoverish a person in order later to do him well.

The Calvinists teach that from all eternity the Lord God's counsel has been to bring thousands of people into condemnation, people whom he never loved, for whom Christ did not die and whom he did not wish to convert by his Word. This is contrary to Scripture, which states that the Lord God has certified by oath that he does not wish the death of one sinner (Ezek 33:11). And our catechism teaches that Christ sent his disciples out into all the world to preach the gospel to all creatures. For the gospel offers to everyone the beneficence of Christ, and in his beneficence God's grace, and in God's grace eternal salvation.

This teaching also takes away the glory of God's truth, as if in his Word he proclaims something other than what he has determined from eternity. It deprives people of all consolation as well, for how can a person have consolation if in his heart he begins to wonder if he may not be consigned to the great throng of those damned by God through his unalterable decree? POSTILLA.[9]

GOD TAKES PLEASURE IN THE CONVERSION OF THE SINNER. WILLIAM GREENHILL: Now here it is said, God has no pleasure in the death of the wicked. This is not an absolute negative, denying God wholly to have delight in death or in the death of sinful, wicked humanity, or of any sinful person. For God took delight in the destruction of Pharaoh and his host in the Red Sea, which Moses shows. . . . The words

[8]Manton, *Works* 21:471-72. [9]*Postilla* 2:93-94.

are not to be taken as an absolute negative, but comparatively, thus, I have pleasure in the turning of the wicked from his ways, rather than in his death. Or, it is more pleasing to me that a wicked person should turn and live than that he should continue and die. . . .

Sinners, in whatever condition they may be, have no cause to despond or despair of mercy, so that they turn from their evil ways. Let them be great sinners, old sinners, sinners under judgments, ready to be destroyed and cut off by the hands of enemies, as these were, yet if they turn from their sins, there is hope for them. For God takes pleasure rather in their conversion and salvation than in their death and destruction: "I have no pleasure in the death of the wicked, but that the wicked turn from his way and live." AN EXPOSITION OF EZEKIEL.[10]

TURN TO GOD. THOMAS MANTON: Let us consider what this turning is. . . . We shall know that by three propositions that contain the whole sum of the Christian faith. (1) That God is humanity's chief good and last end; and unless he is so to every one of us, we cannot be saved (Ps 4:6-7). (2) That there is no way of coming to God, and enjoying him everlastingly, but by Christ (Jn 14:6). (3) There is no way of enjoying communion with Christ but in a constant uniform course of holiness and obedience (1 Jn 1:6-7; Heb 12:14). Therefore this turning that we may live everlastingly consists in three things: in a turning from the creature to God; from self to Christ; and from sin to holiness. And herein lies the great work of grace. SERMONS UPON EZEKIEL.[11]

BUT I CANNOT CONVERT MYSELF. RICHARD BAXTER: Objection: But we cannot convert ourselves until God converts us; we can do nothing without his grace. It is not in him that wills or in him that runs, but in God who has mercy. Answer: God has two degrees of mercy to show: the mercy of conversion first, and the mercy of salvation last. The latter he will give to none but those who will and run, and he has promised it to them only. The former is to make them willing that were unwilling; and though your own willingness and endeavors deserve not his grace, yet your willful refusal deserves that it should be denied to you. Your disability is your very unwillingness itself, which excuses not your sin but makes it the greater. You could turn, if you were but truly willing; and if your wills themselves are so corrupted that nothing but effectual grace will move them, you have the more cause to seek for that grace, and yield to it, and do what you can in the use of the means and not neglect it or set against it. Do what you are able first, and then complain of God for denying you grace, if you have cause.

Objection: But you seem to intimate, all this while, that people have free will. Answer: The dispute about free will is beyond your capacity; I shall, therefore, now trouble you with no more but this about it. Your will is naturally a free, that is, a self-determining faculty, but it is viciously inclined and backward to do good; and therefore, we see by sad experience that it has not a virtuous, moral freedom. But that is the wickedness of it which deserves the punishment. And I pray you let us not befool ourselves with opinions. Let the case be your own. If you have an enemy so malicious that he falls on you and beats you every time he meets you, and takes away the lives of your children, will you excuse him because he says, "I have not free will, it is my nature, I cannot choose, unless God give me grace." If you have a servant who robs you, will you take such an answer from him? Might not every thief and murderer who is hanged at the assize give such an answer: "I have not free will, I cannot change my own heart. What can I do without God's grace?" And shall they, therefore, be acquitted? If not, why, then, should you think to be acquitted for a course of sin against the

[10]*Exposition*, 668-69. [11]Manton, *Works* 21:476.

Lord? A Call to the Unconverted.[12]

God's Comforting Promise. Johann Gerhard: We should direct our hearts toward Ezekiel 33:11 and strengthen our faith with its universal promise: *As sure as I live, says the Lord of lords, I have no pleasure in the death of the godless.* . . . Our faith should lock in on this word of promise and trust it more than the thoughts in one's heart. This promise, because it is divine, never fails. However, the thoughts of our hearts frequently betray us. Our faith should cling to the word of this universal promise like a baby clings to its mother's bosom. Thus our soul will become calm, filled and saturated. Postilla.[13]

33:21-33 *Jerusalem's Fall*

The Destruction of Jerusalem. John Mayer: From Ezekiel 33:1-21, the prophet is again told that he was set for a watchman to the house of Israel as in Ezekiel 3, and he is bidden to speak as he had done before in Ezekiel 18. In Ezekiel 33:21, it is shown how what spoken of before (Ezek 24:27) was in him fulfilled at the coming of one from Jerusalem in the twelfth year, the tenth month, the fifth day, telling him of the destruction of Jerusalem. His mouth was now opened again, which had been silent for speaking to the Jews a long time, that is, almost three years, as may be gathered from comparing the time here spoken of with Ezekiel 24:1. And what does he say now that his mouth is again opened to speak to Israel? Truly that for their sins, in which they persisted, who dwelled yet in the waste of Judah, they should also be carried away from there. The whole land should lie desolate, although they thought that they being many in comparison of Abraham, who was but one, should still be permitted to inhabit there. Commentary upon All the Prophets.[14]

Destruction of Jerusalem. William Greenhill: Here the third general part of the chapter takes place and is a denunciation of judgment against those that escaped at the destruction of Jerusalem. . . . Many perished in Jerusalem by the famine and plague in the time of the siege; many were slain at the taking of it, yet some escaped, and it is probable they hid themselves in holes and woods, among the mountains, or fled to Egypt. One of which, after so long a time as a year, five months and sixteen days, came to Ezekiel and told him the city was smitten. An Exposition of Ezekiel.[15]

Jerusalem's Sins. John Mayer: Finally Ezekiel concludes the chapter by laying open the people's gross hypocrisy, among whom he lived, who spoke and agreed together to come and hear the word of God at his mouth and did so, but because their hearts still went after covetousness, he censures this as a conspiring against the prophet and no honor doing to him. And such are all they in these days that pretend zeal to the word do greatly frequent it, but despite this they are mean worldlings. Commentary upon All the Prophets.[16]

Reasons Why Jerusalem Fell. William Greenhill: These words contain the causes that occasioned and moved God to denounce judgment against the Jews, who escaped the Babylonian sword when Jerusalem was smitten. The cause occasioning God to threaten them with destruction was their vain confidence that they should possess the land still (Ezek 33:24); the causes moving God to destroy them were their sins that are mentioned (Ezek 33:25-26). An Exposition of Ezekiel.[17]

---

[12]*Practical Works* 2:533. [13]*Postilla* 1:236. [14]*Prophets*, 450. [15]*Exposition*, 673. [16]*Prophets*, 450. [17]*Exposition*, 674.

34:1-31 SHEPHERDS AND SHEEP

*[1]The word of the LORD came to me: [2]"Son of man, prophesy against the shepherds of
Israel; prophesy, and say to them, even to the shepherds, Thus says the Lord GOD: Ah,
shepherds of Israel who have been feeding yourselves! Should not shepherds feed the sheep?
[3]You eat the fat, you clothe yourselves with the wool, you slaughter the fat ones, but you do
not feed the sheep. [4]The weak you have not strengthened, the sick you have not healed, the
injured you have not bound up, the strayed you have not brought back, the lost you have
not sought, and with force and harshness you have ruled them. [5]So they were scattered,
because there was no shepherd, and they became food for all the wild beasts. [6]My sheep
were scattered; they wandered over all the mountains and on every high hill. My sheep
were scattered over all the face of the earth, with none to search or seek for them.*

*[7]"Therefore, you shepherds, hear the word of the LORD: [8]As I live, declares the Lord
GOD, surely because my sheep have become a prey, and my sheep have become food for all
the wild beasts, since there was no shepherd, and because my shepherds have not searched
for my sheep, but the shepherds have fed themselves, and have not fed my sheep, [9]there-
fore, you shepherds, hear the word of the LORD: [10]Thus says the Lord GOD, Behold, I am
against the shepherds, and I will require my sheep at their hand and put a stop to their
feeding the sheep. No longer shall the shepherds feed themselves. I will rescue my sheep
from their mouths, that they may not be food for them.*

*[11]"For thus says the Lord GOD: Behold, I, I myself will search for my sheep and will
seek them out. [12]As a shepherd seeks out his flock when he is among his sheep that have
been scattered, so will I seek out my sheep, and I will rescue them from all places where
they have been scattered on a day of clouds and thick darkness. [13]And I will bring them
out from the peoples and gather them from the countries, and will bring them into their
own land. And I will feed them on the mountains of Israel, by the ravines, and in all the
inhabited places of the country. [14]I will feed them with good pasture, and on the mountain
heights of Israel shall be their grazing land. There they shall lie down in good grazing
land, and on rich pasture they shall feed on the mountains of Israel. [15]I myself will be the
shepherd of my sheep, and I myself will make them lie down, declares the Lord GOD. [16]I
will seek the lost, and I will bring back the strayed, and I will bind up the injured, and
I will strengthen the weak, and the fat and the strong I will destroy.[a] I will feed them in
justice.*

*[17]"As for you, my flock, thus says the Lord GOD: Behold, I judge between sheep and
sheep, between rams and male goats. [18]Is it not enough for you to feed on the good pasture,
that you must tread down with your feet the rest of your pasture; and to drink of clear
water, that you must muddy the rest of the water with your feet? [19]And must my sheep eat
what you have trodden with your feet, and drink what you have muddied with your feet?*

*[20]"Therefore, thus says the Lord GOD to them: Behold, I, I myself will judge between
the fat sheep and the lean sheep. [21]Because you push with side and shoulder, and thrust*

at all the weak with your horns, till you have scattered them abroad, [22]*I will rescue*[b] *my flock; they shall no longer be a prey. And I will judge between sheep and sheep.* [23]*And I will set up over them one shepherd, my servant David, and he shall feed them: he shall feed them and be their shepherd.* [24]*And I, the* Lord*, will be their God, and my servant David shall be prince among them. I am the* Lord*; I have spoken.*

[25]*"I will make with them a covenant of peace and banish wild beasts from the land, so that they may dwell securely in the wilderness and sleep in the woods.* [26]*And I will make them and the places all around my hill a blessing, and I will send down the showers in their season; they shall be showers of blessing.* [27]*And the trees of the field shall yield their fruit, and the earth shall yield its increase, and they shall be secure in their land. And they shall know that I am the* Lord*, when I break the bars of their yoke, and deliver them from the hand of those who enslaved them.* [28]*They shall no more be a prey to the nations, nor shall the beasts of the land devour them. They shall dwell securely, and none shall make them afraid.* [29]*And I will provide for them renowned plantations so that they shall no more be consumed with hunger in the land, and no longer suffer the reproach of the nations.* [30]*And they shall know that I am the* Lord *their God with them, and that they, the house of Israel, are my people, declares the Lord* God*.* [31]*And you are my sheep, human sheep of my pasture, and I am your God, declares the Lord* God*."*

a Septuagint, Syriac, Vulgate *I will watch over* **b** Or *save*

Overview: Ezekiel now directs his words against the shepherds of Israel. He recites the sins of the shepherds. They pursued their own desires and neglected their care of the people. These shepherds were both political and ecclesiastical. They were the princes and rulers and the priests and prophets. They were appointed by God to protect the people. They were to feed the people God's word, and instead they starved them, leading them into destruction.

The chapter ends with hope and comfort. God will gather his scattered sheep into the church and feed them with his word and sacraments. Here a description of the pastoral office is given. The faithful pastor, the faithful shepherd, is to feed, protect, care for and encourage the sheep entrusted to him. God promises to raise up a single Shepherd, who is Christ, described under the figure of David. Those who take this prophecy of the one shepherd to be Zerubbabel are wrong. It points only to Christ. The chapter ends with a discussion of the plant of renown. Some take this to be about Christ; others see a double reference to Christ and the church.

Summary of the Chapter. William Greenhill: Ezekiel, having reproved and threatened the judgments of God against the people for their sins, comes in this chapter to deal with the governors and rulers of them, through whose default they became so wicked and suffered the Babylonian yoke. In this chapter are these things to be considered: a reproof of the shepherds and judgment threatened against them (Ezek 34:1-10); God's care of and comfortable provision for his flock (Ezek 34:11-22); a sweet prophecy of Christ and his kingdom, under the figure of David (Ezek 34:23-31). An Exposition of Ezekiel.[1]

34:1-10 *The Shepherds of Israel*

[1]*Exposition*, 681.

The Shepherds of Israel. Martin Luther: "Should not the shepherds feed the sheep? You eat the fat, and you clothe yourselves with the wool, you kill the fatlings . . . and so forth (Ezek 34:2-6). God reproves the shepherds who do not keep the sheep. And now mark well what he has written. His earnest intent in this paragraph is that the weak, sick, broken, those who are driven away and the lost, are to be strengthened, bound up, healed, and sought again, and that they are not to be torn to pieces and scattered. This you should have done, says he to the shepherds, but you have not done it; therefore, I will do it myself. As he says further on, in verse 16: "I will seek that which was lost, I will bring back that which was driven away, and will bind up that which was broken, and will strengthen that which was sick."

Here you see that Christ's kingdom is to be concerned about the weak, the sick, the broken, that he may help them. That is, indeed, a comforting declaration. The only trouble is that we do not realize our needs and infirmities. If we realized them, we would soon flee to him. But how did those shepherds act? They ruled with rigor, and applied God's Law with great severity; and, moreover, they added their own commandments, as they still do, and when these were not fulfilled, they raved and condemned, so that they were driving and driving and exhorting and exacting, continually. That is no proper way to tend and keep souls, says Christ. He is no such shepherd as that; for no one is benefited, but is rather wholly undone, by such a course, as we shall presently hear. Sermon on John 10.[2]

Israel's False Prophets. John Mayer: Here the prophet inveighs against the false prophets of Israel by the name of shepherds, but they are evil ones (cf. Jer 23). Only that which Jeremiah spoke briefly about is here more largely set forth.

He lays open their wickedness. (1) They ate the fat and clothed themselves with the wool, that is, took largely for their maintenance, although they did not the work, but on the contrary killed them and starved them, which is done when they minister not the sincere milk of the word to them but instead the poison of false and erroneous doctrine. (2) They healed not the diseased and sick, nor bound up the broken, that is, endeavored not the conversion of sinners, who were as persons sick and diseased, for which the Lord says, *The whole need not the physician, but the sick.* Nor did they comfort consciences distressed for their sins.(3) They sought not that which was lost, that is, to bring into the fold such as were out, either being carried away by the deceit of heretics seducing them and making them to separate from the church, or profaneness making them to neglect to come to that place. (4) *They ruled with force and cruelty,* that is, not seeking by exhortations and loving persuasions to reduce them but hardening their hearts by their spiteful proceedings.

By these means he shows that they were scattered because they had no shepherd. That is, although they had many, yet none to do to them as was before said, by means of which negligence and the shepherds seeking themselves and not the good of the flock, they became so full of sin that their enemies were for this brought on them, who carried them away captive into other lands to their unspeakable misery. Commentary upon All the Prophets.[3]

The Characteristics of a Shepherd. William Greenhill: The shepherds of Israel were the chief rulers, both political and ecclesiastical, princes, magistrates, prophets, priests and Levites. . . . They are called shepherds because they are to govern, protect, provide for and feed the people. . . . Here was their sin: they fed themselves, not the flock. Those who

[2]CSML 2.1, 21-22 (WA 12:531-532). [3]*Prophets*, 451.

are shepherds in state or church are set up for the good of the people to benefit and advantage them. They are not to seek themselves, to draw from the people what they can to make themselves great. They should be content with their allowance and lay out themselves fully and wholly for the good of them that are committed to their trust. An Exposition of Ezekiel.[4]

The Failure of Israel's Shepherds. Jakob Raupius: *The weak you have not comforted,* because you have not comforted, it then follows, *the sick you have not healed.* He calls the weak those members who are afflicted over something; the sick are those whose whole body was seized by illness. *The injured you have not bound up, the strayed,* those abandoned in a cave, ditch or some deep cavity in the ground, *you have not brought back, the lost,* the spiritually depraved, *you have not sought. With violence,* vehemently, strongly, violently, see Judges 8:1, *you ruled them, and with harshness,* either harshness or harshly. In Exodus 5:13-14, Moses nearly uses the same words to describe the Egyptian tyrants against the Israelites. So here God indicates that the shepherds of Israel are no better when it comes to the care of the sheep. They are as far removed from their office as can be. Instead of mercy, gentleness, readiness and tolerance, which are especially used in the care of the weak, they claim for themselves a harsh and violent dominance. Commentary on Ezekiel.[5]

Strengthen the Weak. Martin Luther: The sheep that are weak are to be strengthened (v. 4); that is, consciences weak in faith and troubled in spirit and of tender disposition are not to be driven and told: You must do this. You must be strong. If you are weak, you are lost. That is not strengthening the weak. . . . Accordingly, they should not be driven with rigor, but should be comforted, even though they are weak, lest they be driven to despair; and in time they will grow stronger. Sermon on John 10.[6]

Heal the Sick. Martin Luther: "Neither have ye healed the sick" (v. 4). Who are the sick? They are those who are manifestly deficient in certain of their works. The first clause has reference to tender consciences; the second, to outward conduct. As, for instance, when one growls and sulks, and now and then lapses, and in anger and other foolish ways oversteps the bounds; even as the apostles, at times, grievously stumbled. But even those who in their outward works before men manifest their shortcomings, so that people are offended at them and say that they are rude and peculiar, he will not cast away; for his kingdom here below is not so constituted as to embrace only the strong and the whole, as it will be in the life to come. Christ is sent here that he might receive and help just such people.

Therefore, even though we are weak and sick, we must not despair and say we are not in the kingdom of Christ. But the more we realize our sickness, all the more should we turn to him; for that is what he is here for, to heal and make us whole. Accordingly, if you are sick and a sinner, and realize your condition, you have all the more reason to go to him and say: Dear Lord, I come just because I am a sinner; that you may help me, and make me good. Thus, necessity drives you to him; for the greater your ailment, the more imperative it is that you seek relief. And that is what he wants; therefore, he tenderly bids us to be of good cheer, and to come unto him. They who are not good shepherds, however, expect to make people good by hatefully scolding and driving them, whereas they are thereby only making matters worse. And this may be seen when we look upon present conditions, brought about by this wrong method, when everything is so piteously

[4]*Exposition,* 682. [5]*Commentarius Synopticus* (1655), 254.
[6]CSML 2.1, 22 (WA 12:532-533).

scattered, even as the prophet has here said. Sermon on John 10.[7]

Bind Up the Broken. Martin Luther: "Neither have ye bound up that which was broken" (v. 4). To be broken is as though one had a bone fractured or were otherwise wounded. As when a Christian is not only weak and infirm, so that he makes a misstep at times, but when he falls into such great temptation that he breaks his leg; for instance, if he should fall and deny the Gospel, as St. Peter did, when he denied Christ. Well, even though one should make such a misstep as to be impeded or overthrown—even then you should not cast him away, as though he no more belonged to this kingdom. For you must not rob Christ of his characteristic, that in his kingdom abounding grace and mercy alone prevail, so that he helps those who realize their misery and wretchedness, and desire to be helped, and that his kingdom is wholly one of consolation, and that he is a comforting, friendly shepherd, who tenderly invites, and would induce, all men to come unto him.

Now, all this is effected through the Gospel alone, by means of which we are to strengthen all the weak and heal all the sick; for this Word will satisfy every want of those whose consciences are troubled, and will give full consolation to all, so that no one, no matter how great a sinner he has been, need despair. Hence, Christ alone is the good shepherd, who heals all our infirmities and raises up again those who have fallen. He who does not do that is no shepherd. Sermon on John 10.[8]

Bring Back the Strayed. Martin Luther: "Neither have you brought back that which was driven away." What is meant by "that which was driven away?" It is that despised soul that is fallen so low that all efforts to reclaim it seem to be in vain. Nevertheless, Christ would not have even such dealt with rigorously. He would not have his kingdom narrowed down so as to include only such as are strong and healthy and perfect.

. . . Therefore, we should so preach Christ as one who will reject nobody, however weak he may be, but will gladly receive and comfort and strengthen everybody; that we may always picture him to ourselves as a good shepherd. Then hearts will turn to him of their own accord, and need not be forced and driven. The Gospel graciously invites and makes men willing, so that they desire to go, and do go, to him with all confidence. Sermon on John 10.[9]

34:11-19 *God Gathers*

God Gathers His Sheep. John Mayer: The Lord promises to the comfort of the faithful that he will take the pastoral office on him and do all these things, which were needful for their good and neglected to be done by their former shepherds. Whereas by their means they were scattered, he promises to gather them from all parts to their own land again; and whereas they healed not the sick, he promises to strengthen them, to bind up the broken, to seek up those driven away and to feed them all. These are duties of every faithful pastor to do. Commentary upon All the Prophets.[10]

God Gathers His Sheep. William Greenhill: God, finding his sheep wscattered into several nations, where they met with hardships, graciously promises to bring them out of those nations. They should not always be among their enemies, who were no better than wild beasts to them. . . . God would bring them into their own land, namely, into Canaan, a type of church. They should both possess their land and be put into a church condition again, and he would feed them with his word and ordinances and put them into a

[7]CSML 2.1, 23-24 (WA 12:533-534). [8]CSML 2.1, 24 (WA 12:534). [9]CSML 2.1, 24-25 (WA 12:534-535). [10]*Prophets*, 452.

better state than ever. This refers to the times of Christ and the gospel; then especially did God gather his sheep out of Babylon and bring them to Zion, then did he feed them on the mountains of Israel by the rivers. AN EXPOSITION OF EZEKIEL.[11]

THE PASTORAL OFFICE. MARTIN CHEMNITZ: And in Ezekiel 34:15-17 the office of a good and faithful pastor is well described, namely, that he feed the sheep, seek the lost, lead back the erring, care for the wounded and the weak, encourage the strong, distinguish sheep from goats, etc. MINISTRY, WORD AND SACRAMENTS.[12]

34:20-28 *One Shepherd*

THE SHEPHERD AND THE SHEPHERDS. JOHANN GERHARD: *And I will raise up for them one shepherd,* says the Lord, *who shall graze them, namely, my servant David,* that is, Christ, who shall be born from the lineage of David. *He shall graze them and be their shepherd. And I, the Lord, shall be their God. However, my servant David shall be the prince among them. I, the Lord, say this* (Ezek 34:23-24). Each individual Christian today should let this entire chapter be read to him, because it speaks so gloriously and comfortingly about Christ's office of being a shepherd!

. . . God the Lord promised in this chapter that as the shepherds of Israel shall feed themselves, they shall gobble up the fat. They will clothe themselves with their wool, slaughter the fattened ones, not look after the weak ones, not heal the sick, not bind up the wounded ones, not bring back errant sheep, not search for the lost ones. Instead, they shall strenuously run roughshod over them. So when this shall occur with the shepherds of Israel, then God the Lord will personally receive his sheep to himself, and he shall *raise up for them the one true shepherd who shall graze them.* POSTILLA.[13]

THE GOOD SHEPHERD. JOHANNES OECOLAMPADIUS: Christ, the Good Shepherd (Jn 10), who lays down his life for the sheep, feeds by his Word and by his flesh for eternal life. He is called David because he is from the seed of David. And he repeats *he shall feed* to show earnestness. . . . We acknowledge the Lord to be our God, and as he feeds us, we know the Father to be the true God and Jesus Christ, whom he sent (Jn 17:3). Nothing diminishes God's divinity. Before God said he would feed his sheep (Ezek 34:13-14), and now this is bestowed on the man Christ, who because of his humanity is prince of the church, the firstborn of all creatures, who has been given the name about every name and is anointed above his companions. COMMENTARY ON THE PROPHET EZEKIEL.[14]

I WILL SET UP ONE SHEPHERD. HANS DENCK: [God] always desires to redeem what has been corrupted and does not intend to extinguish the smoking wick. For this he gave us his Son and made him a king and shepherd over us. This is indicated severally in Scripture in David's name and was also spoken by the Father in Ezekiel 34:23, "I will raise up from among them one shepherd who shall lead them to pasture, my servant David. He will feed them and be their shepherd. I the Lord will be their God, and David shall be their prince. I the Lord have spoken it." Thus, God makes something of that which was nothing, creating for himself a people of many heirs (the word must always bear fruit). He makes a mighty nation of one that was a defeated one and no people at all. This happens not because of our own might but because God receives us again. REFLECTIONS ON MICAH.[15]

CHRIST THE ONE SHEPHERD. WILLIAM GREENHILL: "And I will set up one shepherd

[11]*Exposition*, 686. [12]*Ministry, Word and Sacraments*, 46. [13]*Postilla* 1:371-72. [14]*Commentarius in Ezechielem* (1553), 168. [15]*Writings*, 129.

over them." Some make this shepherd to be Zerubbabel, who came of the race of David and brought the Jews out of Babylon into their old pastures again, namely, into the land of Canaan, where they had their temple, worship and ordinances, as in former days. But if we consult Ezekiel 37:24-25, where he speaks of the same person, you shall find things there incompetent to Zerubbabel, and must refer to Christ. . . . By "shepherd" is meant the Lord Christ, who is frequently so called in Scripture. AN EXPOSITION OF EZEKIEL.[16]

ONE SHEPHERD FOR ISRAEL. JOHN MAYER: *I will set one shepherd over them, David.* That is, the promised successor of David in his kingdom, in whom it should be made everlasting, for he is called David after the name of him that first began that line. That David was the greatest and most eminent king of Israel. The name is here used in a manner similar to the Roman emperors after Julius Caesar who had the name of Caesars, and the kings of Egypt, who were called Ptolemies after Ptolemy, who first raised the kingdom of Egypt from baseness to magnificence. And it is said that he shall be their shepherd and feed them, so in John 10, the Lord speaks at large of himself as feeding and saving his sheep and fraying away the evil beasts from them, as here it is further promised (Ezek 34:25). This prophecy indeed first relates to the time of the Jews' return out of Babylon, when Zerubbabel and Nehemiah and other godly princes succeeding them ruled over the Jews. Although they had much trouble by reason of their enemies for many years, yet evil beasts after that ceased in the land, there being none that tyrannically oppressed as before. Moreover, those enemies who opposed their building of the temple and city were at length confounded by the king's favor toward them. But most fully it was accomplished in the time of Christ, by whom his sheep were so fed with heavenly doctrine and protected by his power. Although they were at the first apprehended and imprisoned, they came out safe again and were filled with joy for their very sufferings. Above all they rejoiced in their being saved from sin and the power of Satan, the most terrible wild beast, that roaring lion, that sought to devour them. And finally in the days of Constantine the Great they might without fear of persecuting enemies rest in quietness, as sheep in the fields, where there are no wolves or foxes, bears or lions to devour them or their lambs. COMMENTARY UPON ALL THE PROPHETS.[17]

CONVERSION OF THE JEWS. MATTHEW MEADE: A certain scholar thinks it not probable that the Jews shall return again to their own land, because, says he, it is very hard to give an account where the ten tribes are. A strange reason of a learned man, as if the fulfilling of the promise depended on his knowledge. Indeed, if God knew not where they were, it were something, but if he does, it is no hindrance of the promise, though we do not. And that God does know is plain from Jeremiah 30:10-11. In Ezekiel we read, "I will set up one shepherd over them, even my servant David shall be a prince over them; I the Lord have spoken it" (Ezek 34:23). This is spoken of Christ, and it refers to the time, when he shall reign over the Jews. It is the same with what the angel told Mary: "You shall bring forth a son and call his name Jesus; he shall be great, and the Lord shall give him the throne of his father David, and he shall reign over the house of Jacob forever; and of his kingdom there shall be no end" (Lk 1:31). This is a kingdom that Christ is to possess at the conversion of the Jews. So that here is a plain promise, nay, promise on promise, of their settlement again in their own land, as a peculiar blessing of Christ's times. The Scriptures are very plain that prove this truth. SERMONS.[18]

[16]*Exposition*, 690. [17]*Prophets*, 453. [18]*Sermons*, 89-90.

34:29-30 *A Renowned Plant*

A Plant of Reknown. John Mayer: *And I will raise up for them a plant of renown* (Ezek 34:29). Here the same Christ before called David is set forth by another name, as in Isaiah 11:1 and in many other places, where it has been showed why he was so called, namely, for similitude of his springing up out of the house of Jesse. This house had decayed as the stub of a tree standing long without any shoots, but in the end beyond expectation branching forth. The branch coming forth growing above the height and greatness of any other tree, for such a branch is a renowned branch indeed, and so was our Lord Jesus coming forth out of that house. At that time, this house was so poor, but no family has since flourished so much as that did in him, who became a vine covering the whole earth. Commentary upon All the Prophets.[19]

A Plant of Peace. William Greenhill: This verse speaks about the goodness of God to his flock abundantly, in positive and negative mercies; he would raise up for it a plant, and that of renown, and he would free it from hunger and shame. . . . "Plant of renown." The Septuagint is a "plant of peace"; the Aramaic, a plantation that they may remain; the Vulgate, a noble sprint, or plant. This "plant of renown" is, by some expositors, interpreted to be the Christian church, gathered out of all nations and planted in Christ. . . . Others expound it of Christ. We may take both: Christ and the church, which springs up out of him. An Exposition of Ezekiel.[20]

[19]*Prophets*, 453. [20]*Exposition*, 696.

35:1-15 A PROPHECY AGAINST EDOM

[1]The word of the Lord came to me: [2]"Son of man, set your face against Mount Seir,
and prophesy against it, [3]and say to it, Thus says the Lord God: Behold, I am against
you, Mount Seir, and I will stretch out my hand against you, and I will make you a desolation and a waste. [4]I will lay your cities waste, and you shall become a desolation, and
you shall know that I am the Lord. [5]Because you cherished perpetual enmity and gave
over the people of Israel to the power of the sword at the time of their calamity, at the time
of their final punishment, [6]therefore, as I live, declares the Lord God, I will prepare you
for blood, and blood shall pursue you; because you did not hate bloodshed, therefore blood
shall pursue you. [7]I will make Mount Seir a waste and a desolation, and I will cut off
from it all who come and go. [8]And I will fill its mountains with the slain. On your hills
and in your valleys and in all your ravines those slain with the sword shall fall. [9]I will
make you a perpetual desolation, and your cities shall not be inhabited. Then you will
know that I am the Lord.
[10]"Because you said, 'These two nations and these two countries shall be mine, and we

will take possession of them'—although the LORD *was there—*[11]*therefore, as I live, declares the Lord* GOD, *I will deal with you according to the anger and envy that you showed because of your hatred against them. And I will make myself known among them, when I judge you.* [12]*And you shall know that I am the* LORD.

"I have heard all the revilings that you uttered against the mountains of Israel, saying, 'They are laid desolate; they are given us to devour.' [13]*And you magnified yourselves against me with your mouth, and multiplied your words against me; I heard it.* [14]*Thus says the Lord* GOD: *While the whole earth rejoices, I will make you desolate.* [15]*As you rejoiced over the inheritance of the house of Israel, because it was desolate, so I will deal with you; you shall be desolate, Mount Seir, and all Edom, all of it. Then they will know that I am the* LORD."

OVERVIEW: After the words of great comfort that ended the previous chapter, Ezekiel is directed to speak against the enemies of the church. The principal enemy here addressed is Edom, who especially hated the children of Israel and their religion. They blasphemed God and despised his word. Now they would be laid waste.

THE EDOMITES' HATRED. JOHN MAYER: In this chapter, the prophecy against Edom, which was very briefly uttered above (Ezek 25:12), is again resumed and prosecuted more largely, as the Edomites for their inveterate hatred against the children of Israel and their helping the Chaldeans in destroying them were well worthy. . . . The Edomites most probably stirred up Nebuzaradan, the king of Babylon's steward (2 Kings 25:8), who came after this to burn the city and temple with fire, which was a most horrible sin, to such as are extremely miserable to add more misery. Therefore the vengeance here threatened must come on them to the full, and so all they must expect that it should be done to them that sin in like manner hardening their hearts to oppress their oppressed brethren. COMMENTARY UPON ALL THE PROPHETS.[1]

HATRED AND EVIL AFFECTIONS. WILLIAM GREENHILL: One sinful affection sets others to work. The Edomites' hatred set their anger and envy to work. They used these out of their hatred of the Jews; they hated them, and that hatred stirred up their anger to do them harm, and their envy to persecute them to death.

God will deal with people not only according to their evil actions but according to their evil affections also. . . . The Lord takes notice of all the bitter, reproachful and provoking speeches that wicked ones do utter against the church and people of God. AN EXPOSITION OF EZEKIEL.[2]

EDOMITES OPPOSE GOD'S WORD. JOHN MAYER: *You shall know that I have heard all your blasphemies* (Ezek 35:12). Hence note that it is blasphemy to derogate from the tenth of God's word in anything, for he had promised restitution within seventy years to his people and threatened desolation to their land only so long a time. But the Edomites, to discredit the word of God, said contrariwise, that their land should always lie desolate in respect of them, and that they, the Edomites, should consume henceforward the increase of them as the owners. They had hoped to consume it by fire and sword to this end, that it should never come into their possession any more, for this was an intolerable affront given to God, who had so often promised the contrary. COMMENTARY UPON ALL THE PROPHETS.[3]

[1]*Prophets*, 453-54. [2]*Exposition*, 703-4. [3]*Prophets*, 454.

36:1-38 A PROPHECY TO THE MOUNTAINS OF ISRAEL

*1“And you, son of man, prophesy to the mountains of Israel, and say, O mountains of
Israel, hear the word of the LORD. 2Thus says the Lord GOD: Because the enemy said of
you, ‘Aha!’ and, ‘The ancient heights have become our possession,’ 3therefore prophesy,
and say, Thus says the Lord GOD: Precisely because they made you desolate and crushed
you from all sides, so that you became the possession of the rest of the nations, and you
became the talk and evil gossip of the people, 4therefore, O mountains of Israel, hear
the word of the Lord GOD: Thus says the Lord GOD to the mountains and the hills, the
ravines and the valleys, the desolate wastes and the deserted cities, which have become a
prey and derision to the rest of the nations all around, 5therefore thus says the Lord GOD:
Surely I have spoken in my hot jealousy against the rest of the nations and against all
Edom, who gave my land to themselves as a possession with wholehearted joy and utter
contempt, that they might make its pasturelands a prey. 6Therefore prophesy concerning
the land of Israel, and say to the mountains and hills, to the ravines and valleys, Thus
says the Lord GOD: Behold, I have spoken in my jealous wrath, because you have suffered
the reproach of the nations. 7Therefore thus says the Lord GOD: I swear that the nations
that are all around you shall themselves suffer reproach.*

*8“But you, O mountains of Israel, shall shoot forth your branches and yield your fruit
to my people Israel, for they will soon come home. 9For behold, I am for you, and I will
turn to you, and you shall be tilled and sown. 10And I will multiply people on you, the
whole house of Israel, all of it. The cities shall be inhabited and the waste places rebuilt.
11And I will multiply on you man and beast, and they shall multiply and be fruitful. And
I will cause you to be inhabited as in your former times, and will do more good to you than
ever before. Then you will know that I am the LORD. 12I will let people walk on you, even
my people Israel. And they shall possess you, and you shall be their inheritance, and you
shall no longer bereave them of children. 13Thus says the Lord GOD: Because they say to
you, ‘You devour people, and you bereave your nation of children,’ 14therefore you shall
no longer devour people and no longer bereave your nation of children, declares the Lord
GOD. 15And I will not let you hear anymore the reproach of the nations, and you shall
no longer bear the disgrace of the peoples and no longer cause your nation to stumble,
declares the Lord GOD.”*

*16The word of the LORD came to me: 17“Son of man, when the house of Israel lived in
their own land, they defiled it by their ways and their deeds. Their ways before me were
like the uncleanness of a woman in her menstrual impurity. 18So I poured out my wrath
upon them for the blood that they had shed in the land, for the idols with which they had
defiled it. 19I scattered them among the nations, and they were dispersed through the
countries. In accordance with their ways and their deeds I judged them. 20But when they
came to the nations, wherever they came, they profaned my holy name, in that people said*

of them, 'These are the people of the Lord, and yet they had to go out of his land.' [21]But I had concern for my holy name, which the house of Israel had profaned among the nations to which they came.

[22]"Therefore say to the house of Israel, Thus says the Lord God: It is not for your sake, O house of Israel, that I am about to act, but for the sake of my holy name, which you have profaned among the nations to which you came. [23]And I will vindicate the holiness of my great name, which has been profaned among the nations, and which you have profaned among them. And the nations will know that I am the Lord, declares the Lord God, when through you I vindicate my holiness before their eyes. [24]I will take you from the nations and gather you from all the countries and bring you into your own land. [25]I will sprinkle clean water on you, and you shall be clean from all your uncleannesses, and from all your idols I will cleanse you. [26]And I will give you a new heart, and a new spirit I will put within you. And I will remove the heart of stone from your flesh and give you a heart of flesh. [27]And I will put my Spirit within you, and cause you to walk in my statutes and be careful to obey my rules.[a] [28]You shall dwell in the land that I gave to your fathers, and you shall be my people, and I will be your God. [29]And I will deliver you from all your uncleannesses. And I will summon the grain and make it abundant and lay no famine upon you. [30]I will make the fruit of the tree and the increase of the field abundant, that you may never again suffer the disgrace of famine among the nations. [31]Then you will remember your evil ways, and your deeds that were not good, and you will loathe yourselves for your iniquities and your abominations. [32]It is not for your sake that I will act, declares the Lord God; let that be known to you. Be ashamed and confounded for your ways, O house of Israel.

[33]"Thus says the Lord God: On the day that I cleanse you from all your iniquities, I will cause the cities to be inhabited, and the waste places shall be rebuilt. [34]And the land that was desolate shall be tilled, instead of being the desolation that it was in the sight of all who passed by. [35]And they will say, 'This land that was desolate has become like the garden of Eden, and the waste and desolate and ruined cities are now fortified and inhabited.' [36]Then the nations that are left all around you shall know that I am the Lord; I have rebuilt the ruined places and replanted that which was desolate. I am the Lord; I have spoken, and I will do it.

[37]"Thus says the Lord God: This also I will let the house of Israel ask me to do for them: to increase their people like a flock. [38]Like the flock for sacrifices,[b] like the flock at Jerusalem during her appointed feasts, so shall the waste cities be filled with flocks of people. Then they will know that I am the Lord."

a Or *my just decrees* **b** Hebrew *flock of holy things*

Overview: The chapter begins with a prophecy to the mountains of Israel, which represents both the land of Judea and the people contained in the land. After passing judgment on the nations, Ezekiel explains why Israel was taken into captivity and prophesies their restoration. The comfort spoken to the people is not to be understood temporally in terms of their return from Babylon but rather spiritually as pointing to the gospel of Christ. Moreover, the reason for their return from captivity is not because of their repentance in Babylon. Quite the contrary, they increased in their sins and caused the name of God to be profaned by the heathen. For this reason, God spares them for the sake of his holy name.

God promises to "sprinkle clean water" on them and purify them of their idolatry when they are brought out of captivity. Our commentators question what this water means. Suggestions are given that it points to the purifying waters of baptism. Suggestions are given that it points to the purifying waters of baptism, the blood of Christ, which cleanses us from all sin, or both.

SUMMARY OF THE CHAPTER. WILLIAM GREENHILL: The Jews, being deprived of their comforts, were carried into captivity, suffered hard things and lay under great reproach among the nations; therefore the Lord here in this chapter does the following. He denounces judgment against the heathen, setting out the causes that moved him to this (Ezek 36:1-7); he promises mercy to the land of Israel, which is specified in several particulars (Ezek 36:8-15); he shows the causes why the Jews were driven out of their country (Ezek 36:16-20); he sets out the ground of their restoration (Ezek 36:21-24); he multiplies promises of spiritual and temporal things on them and their land (Ezek 36:25-38).

In the former chapter he prophesied against Mount Seir; in this he is to prophesy to the "mountains of Israel." Against that he prophesied judgment, to these he prophesies mercies. These "mountains of Israel," by a synecdoche, are put for the whole land of Judea, and by a metonomy, for the people contained there or who had lived there. AN EXPOSITION OF EZEKIEL.[1]

WORDS OF COMFORT. JOHN MAYER: In this chapter, the prophet returns again to the children of Israel, comforting them by renewing the promise of their restitution in many more words than he had done before. He begins by speaking to the mountains and valleys, as the prophets have done at many other times, intimating by this that the Lord can give ears to hear to senseless things and to do as he wills them, either for the good or hurt of people, concerning whom he speaks to them.

But whereas he promises in Ezekiel 36:11 to do better for his people of Israel than in former times, this is not to be understood of that which should be done temporally for them on their return out of the Babylonian captivity but spiritually in the time of the gospel by Christ, for that good, which is done for the faithful now, is far greater than any worldly benefit before bestowed on them. COMMENTARY UPON ALL THE PROPHETS.[2]

GOD'S FURY AND RIGHTEOUSNESS. WILLIAM GREENHILL: *Wherefore I poured my fury on them* (Ezek 36:18). They had committed heinous sins and continued long in them without repentance. This is evident from the Lord's fury. He is not in fury for small sins, nor presently furious for great sins; but when people go on from day to day in them, his anger grows hotter and at last rises up into fury. This being increased the Lord would not let it out in petty judgments, as it were drop by drop, but pour it out in greater judgments, as the sea pours out water when a breach is in the banks, it pours out water with violence and drowns all the adjacent country.

. . . Whatever judgments God brings on sinners, he is just and righteous in so doing. God poured fury on them, he drove them out of their own country, he scattered them up and down among heathens, whose language they understood not, who were bitter and harsh toward them. And all this was not more, no, not so much as their sins deserved: *According to their way and their doings, I judged them*, says the Lord. I did them no wrong, they had not any cause to complain of me, the fault was their own. Whatever God's proceedings are with any nation, family or person, he is right-

[1]*Exposition*, 706. [2]*Prophets*, 454.

eous. AN EXPOSITION OF EZEKIEL.[3]

GOD'S MERCY NOT EARNED. MATTHEW MEADE: Consider the subject of mercy, a people fit to be delivered and yet in danger of being undone and ruined, utterly unworthy of redemption and yet on the very brink of destruction. As to our fitness for such a mercy, never was a people more unfit or more unworthy, but it is the way of divine goodness to act by prerogative, and that is the reason of mercy, when no other reason can be given. "I do not this for your sakes but for my holy name's sake" (Ezek 36:22). When God had a purpose to show mercy, he never wants a reason in himself, though there can be none found in us why he should. The deliverances he works for his people are on the account of the covenant. THE VISION OF THE WHEELS.[4]

GOD'S GLORY AND THE PEOPLE'S SINS. JOHANNES OECOLAMPADIUS: Everywhere Scripture vindicates the glory of God, especially in these verses (Ezek 36:16-21). He very clearly demonstrates that the reason for our ruin comes from us and is incurred because of our sins. Moreover, salvation comes not because of our worthiness but only from the mercy of God. "Son of man," he says, "the sons of Israel have become contemptible and this did not happen because of my severity. I brought them to dwell in their own land, and they sinned most grievously." They are compared with menstruating women because of their two abominable sins: idolatry and murder, on account of their lack of faith and love. COMMENTARY ON THE PROPHET EZEKIEL.[5]

GOD IS HOLY AND GREAT. WILLIAM GREENHILL: These verses (Ezek 36:21-24) contain the ground of the Jews' restoration, which is the fourth general part of the chapter. They, being in captivity and sinning there greatly, caused the name of God to be profaned by the heathens. Deserving nothing but confusion, he pitied them and for his name's sake delivered them. The name of God is set out by two adjuncts, or epithets: holy and great.

The Hebrew is, "And I spared them on the account of my holiness." That is, I spared them on the account of my holy name. I would not suffer it to be profaned by the heathen and therefore did deliver them. The Septuagint is, "I spared them for my holy name's sake." I had a tender respect to my name, which being holy, I would not suffer to lie under heathenish obloquies.

. . . The name of the Lord is holy. His essence, his will, his attributes, his works, his word are his name. All these set out God, make him known, and so are his name, even the name of his holiness, or "his holy name." There is no name under heaven like the Lord's. It is a holy name, and so glorious; a great name, and so dreadful. We should sanctify the name of God, which is done by believing. AN EXPOSITION OF EZEKIEL.[6]

DELIVERANCE AND REPENTANCE. MATTHEW MEADE: It was the mercy of their deliverance that melted down their hard hearts into a mournful and penitent frame. "Then shall you remember that I had pity, for my holy name that the house of Israel had profaned among the heathen, wherever they went" (Ezek 36:21). What does this point to? Ezekiel 36:24 tells you: "For I will take you from among the heathen and gather you out of all countries, and I will bring you into your own land." . . . Deliverance and repentance came together. They were so far from repenting of sin in their captivity that they continued in their wickedness to the great reproach of God among the heathen. . . . They had no expectation of deliverance, and where there is no faith there can be no fitness for it. There-

[3]*Exposition*, 710-11. [4]*Vision of the Wheels*, 58. [5]*Commentarius in Ezechielem* (1553), 173. [6]*Exposition*, 712-13.

fore when God does deliver them he tells them it was not for their sakes. As if he had said, I do it not because of your worthiness for it, but for the glory of my own name. "I do not this for your sakes, O house of Israel, but for my holy name's sake" (Ezek 36:22). Sermons.[7]

Baptism and Legal Purifications. Johannes Oecolampadius: "To sprinkle" alludes to baptism and ritual purifications, most especially to the water mixed with the ashes of a red heifer, which was a particular rite of purification (Num 19). Such purifications of water are appointed for sins and ritual impurities. David pleads for this purging: "Purge me, Lord, with hyssop, and I shall be clean" (Ps 51:7). . . . This also pertains to the sacrament of baptism, in which water and the words of Christ are bestowed through the ministry of the church on those admitted to the grace of adoption, as we have reformed it. Commentary on the Prophet Ezekiel.[8]

The Water Is the Blood of Christ. John Mayer: The prophet indeed spends most words from the beginning of the chapter to verse 25 in speaking of their deliverance from Babylon [Ezek 36:1-25], but in this verse he enlarges himself in brief to the evangelical times, and Ezekiel 36:25 speaks more fully of that exceeding great good that should come by Christ for the cleansing away of sin and the grace of regeneration by his spirit.

By sprinkling with clean water he means the blood of Christ cleansing from all sin, alluding here to the sprinkling of old appointed with water made of the ashes of a red heifer and running water, the sprinkling of which cleansed from legal uncleanness. Of taking away the heart of stone from them and giving them a new heart, see Jeremiah 32:30.

From Ezekiel 30–38 he both amplifies the benefit of their deliverance from captivity and planting them in their own country again. For that reason and for the deliverance by Christ, he teaches that neither of them were for their own sakes but for his grace and mercy, that none might boast themselves but acknowledge all the good that they enjoy, both temporal and spiritual, to come from him and to give him all the praise and glory forever. Commentary upon All the Prophets.[9]

Water is the Blood of Christ. William Greenhill: "Then will I sprinkle clean water on you." When they were called and came out of Babylon, then the Lord would sprinkle clean water on them. The Jews by "water" mean the abundance of outward things. Some others interpret it as the water in baptism. But neither does the abundance of outward things or the water of baptism cleanse from the pollution of idols. . . . Some other sense of the word therefore must we seek out. By "water" the blood of Christ is intended, say the best expositors. Some make grace the thing; but that is too general, unless we limit it to the blood of Christ, which of grace is given to wash sinners with. These words, "I will sprinkle clean water on you," have some allusion to the waters mingled with the ashes of the red cow, which being sprinkled by a branch of hyssop on the unclean party, he was cleansed. . . . This red cow figured Christ in his afflictions and sufferings; and the water mingled with the ashes of it, the blood of Christ, which is called "the blood of sprinkling" (Heb 12:24).

The water they used in sprinkling was clean water, running or spring water, free from all filth. So the blood of Christ is pure; he was without sin and blemish, or spot. His blood was precious and pure (1 Pet 1:19), and here it is called "clean water."

This sprinkling of clean water on them is the application of the blood of Christ by the Spirit

[7]*Sermons*, 58. [8]*Commentarius in Ezechielem* (1553), 174. [9]*Prophets*, 454-55.

of God. As the priest was to take the blood of the red heifer with his finger and to sprinkle it, so God by the hand and finger of his Spirit does take and sprinkle the blood of Christ, that is, apply the fruit and benefit of it to the hearts of people. An Exposition of Ezekiel.[10]

Baptized with the Blood of Christ. Jakob Raupius: *I will sprinkle clean water on you*, that is, the blood of Christ. Some expound this concerning holy baptism. Among the best expositors both of these thoughts are able to stand, since in baptism itself we are sprinkled with the blood of Christ. Commentary on Ezekiel.[11]

[10] *Exposition*, 714. [11] *Commentarius Synopticus* (1655), 269.

37:1-28 The Valley of Dry Bones and Two Sticks

*1The hand of the Lord was upon me, and he brought me out in the Spirit of the Lord
and set me down in the middle of the valley;[a] it was full of bones. 2And he led me around
among them, and behold, there were very many on the surface of the valley, and behold,
they were very dry. 3And he said to me, "Son of man, can these bones live?" And I an-
swered, "O Lord God, you know." 4Then he said to me, "Prophesy over these bones, and
say to them, O dry bones, hear the word of the Lord. 5Thus says the Lord God to these
bones: Behold, I will cause breath[b] to enter you, and you shall live. 6And I will lay sinews
upon you, and will cause flesh to come upon you, and cover you with skin, and put breath
in you, and you shall live, and you shall know that I am the Lord."*

*7So I prophesied as I was commanded. And as I prophesied, there was a sound, and
behold, a rattling,[c] and the bones came together, bone to its bone. 8And I looked, and
behold, there were sinews on them, and flesh had come upon them, and skin had covered
them. But there was no breath in them. 9Then he said to me, "Prophesy to the breath;
prophesy, son of man, and say to the breath, Thus says the Lord God: Come from the
four winds, O breath, and breathe on these slain, that they may live." 10So I prophesied
as he commanded me, and the breath came into them, and they lived and stood on their
feet, an exceedingly great army.*

*11Then he said to me, "Son of man, these bones are the whole house of Israel. Behold,
they say, 'Our bones are dried up, and our hope is lost; we are indeed cut off.' 12Therefore
prophesy, and say to them, Thus says the Lord God: Behold, I will open your graves and
raise you from your graves, O my people. And I will bring you into the land of Israel.
13And you shall know that I am the Lord, when I open your graves, and raise you from
your graves, O my people. 14And I will put my Spirit within you, and you shall live, and
I will place you in your own land. Then you shall know that I am the Lord; I have spo-*

ken, and I will do it, declares the Lord."

15The word of the Lord came to me: 16"Son of man, take a stick[d] and write on it, 'For Judah, and the people of Israel associated with him'; then take another stick and write on it, 'For Joseph (the stick of Ephraim) and all the house of Israel associated with him.' 17And join them one to another into one stick, that they may become one in your hand. 18And when your people say to you, 'Will you not tell us what you mean by these?' 19say to them, Thus says the Lord God: Behold, I am about to take the stick of Joseph (that is in the hand of Ephraim) and the tribes of Israel associated with him. And I will join with it the stick of Judah,[e] and make them one stick, that they may be one in my hand. 20When the sticks on which you write are in your hand before their eyes, 21then say to them, Thus says the Lord God: Behold, I will take the people of Israel from the nations among which they have gone, and will gather them from all around, and bring them to their own land. 22And I will make them one nation in the land, on the mountains of Israel. And one king shall be king over them all, and they shall be no longer two nations, and no longer divided into two kingdoms. 23They shall not defile themselves anymore with their idols and their detestable things, or with any of their transgressions. But I will save them from all the backslidings[f] in which they have sinned, and will cleanse them; and they shall be my people, and I will be their God.

24"My servant David shall be king over them, and they shall all have one shepherd. They shall walk in my rules and be careful to obey my statutes. 25They shall dwell in the land that I gave to my servant Jacob, where your fathers lived. They and their children and their children's children shall dwell there forever, and David my servant shall be their prince forever. 26I will make a covenant of peace with them. It shall be an everlasting covenant with them. And I will set them in their land[g] and multiply them, and will set my sanctuary in their midst forevermore. 27My dwelling place shall be with them, and I will be their God, and they shall be my people. 28Then the nations will know that I am the Lord who sanctifies Israel, when my sanctuary is in their midst forevermore."

a Or *plain;* also verse 2 **b** Or *spirit;* also verses 6, 9, 10 **c** Or *an earthquake* (compare 3:12, 13) **d** Or *one piece of wood;* also verses 17, 19, 20 **e** Hebrew *And I will place them on it, the stick of Judah* **f** Many Hebrew manuscripts; other Hebrew manuscripts *dwellings* **g** Hebrew lacks *in their land*

Overview: Words of comfort are given the people of Israel in this chapter under the image of the valley of dry bones. The reunification of Israel and Judah is promised in the second part of the chapter under the image of two sticks. For our commentators, the valley of bones represents either the general resurrection of humankind or the restoration of Israel from captivity. There is some question if this is a real valley of dry bones or a vision that the prophet has. Ezekiel prophesies to these bones that they are to hear the word of the Lord, which alone is life-giving and sustaining. By his word alone, dry trees flourish and barren wombs conceive. So too bodies are raised from the dead.

The second part of the chapter promises the reunification of the house of Israel and Judah. The name Ephraim is put for Israel because Jeroboam was of Ephraim. These two houses will become one kingdom. God promises that his servant David, who is Christ, will shepherd them together. They will be one people with one God. The question remains whether this prophecy has been fulfilled in the days of Christ when Jew and Gentile were brought together as one people in Christ or if this prophecy points to the ultimate conversion of the Jews. In either case, our commentators emphasize that this unity is found in Christ alone.

37:1-2 *Valley of Bones*

The Purpose of the Vision. Johannes Oecolampadius: With the city and temple destroyed, the very place that signified the promises and held the people's hope, an event is seen in these verses concerning the Jews in Babylon. This vision, which is a type of the future resurrection, the Lord puts before them to strengthen their faith and to show what will follow the time of their salvation when their corruptible bodies die. As he declares, "Why do you doubt your restoration? It is I who promise a return to you that bring the dead back to life." Commentary on the Prophet Ezekiel.[1]

Only a Vision. Matthew Meade: In this prophecy, you have a description of the sad and deplorable condition of the Jews in their present captivity in Babylon, and a prophecy of their wonderful and unexpected deliverance out of that thralldom. Both these are couched under the type of dry bones [Ezek 37:1-11], and there he explains the meaning of the bones—these are the whole house of Israel, that is, these bones are the emblem or hieroglyphic of the house of Israel; so that these dry bones are not to be looked on as a thing real, but only visional; not true in the history of the thing, but true in the signification of the emblem; for this you have intimated in the first verse: "The hand of the Lord was on me, and carried me out in the Spirit and set me down in the midst of the valley that was full of bones." He was carried out in the Spirit, not corporally, but visionally, as he says elsewhere: "The Spirit lifted me up by a lock of my head between the earth and the heavens and brought me in the visions of God to Jerusalem" (Ezek 8:3). He was then in Babylon, and it is not likely that the Spirit of God carried him by the hair of the head to Jerusalem. No! It was a vision. Sermons.[2]

Dry Bones. John Mayer: In this chapter the Lord bids the prophet to teach by similitudes the gracious acts promised to be done in the former chapter. First, of dry bones to which he is bidden to prophesy and say, "Live you," which he doing they lived and became men and women. By this a demonstration was made of the living of the children of Israel again in their own land, whereas now they lay dead, as it were, in Babylon. This should so continue for many years, until, according to human reasoning, there was no more hope of this than of their rising again, who have lain so long dead that the flesh is all rotted off their bones. Commentary upon All the Prophets.[3]

The Valley of Bones. William Greenhill: "Which was full of bones." This valley or plain was no burying place, for then the bones would not have lain on the face of the earth and been exposed to view. Some make these bones to be the bones of all humankind being dead and to be about the general resurrection; but they are wrong as nothing of that is here intended. Some make them to be the bones of the Babylonians, but the prophet's scope here is not to comfort them. It is the Jews' condition he points at, and therefore by "bones" are meant the Jews, as is clear in Ezekiel 37:11. These bones were visional also, not real, for then they should not have lain unburied, suffering reproach. . . . These bones were not clothed with flesh, juicy and full of marrow, which had been more easily raised to life if so. They were dry; all the moisture was out of them. They had lain long, for nearly seventy

[1]*Commentarius in Ezechielem* (1553), 176. [2]*Sermons*, 1-2. [3]*Prophets*, 455.

years, in that condition, and had almost become earth. An Exposition of Ezekiel.[4]

Valley of Dry Bones. Matthew Meade: These bones were in the open valley, and this is a further expression of their misery; for valleys, being low bottoms, are often put to express a low and afflicted state. And they are not only said to be in the valley, but in the open valley, exposed to all violence and injury of wind and weather. Such was their state in Babylon. How sad was their condition; they were very many, and what they felt lay very heavy, till they were past hope, the bones were very many, very dry and in the open valley. Sermons.[5]

37:3-14 *Prophesy*

The Prophet's Answer. William Greenhill: This verse is a dialogue between God and the prophet. "Son of man, can these bones live?" Ezekiel, you have had a full view of them, you see how dry they are, in what condition they lie. Tell me your thoughts. What is your judgment of them? I am desirous to know your mind. . . . "And I answered, O Lord God, you know." The prophet's answer is suitable to the Lord's question, which was concerning the present life of these bones, not future life at the general resurrection, which he doubted not of; therefore he confesses his ignorance: I do not know, O Lord, what your pleasure is; you are able to put life into these dry bones in a moment, though neither myself nor any other creature can do it; our power is finite, yours is infinite. An Exposition of Ezekiel.[6]

Prophesy on These Bones. Johannes Oecolampadius: *And I prophesied* (Ezek 37:7). First, the prophet heard from the Lord, next he spoke the very thing he heard, and finally the effect followed. Similarly, what our Lord Jesus Christ has heard from the Father he has made known to us through his servants, from whom you will hear about God and Christ, until your life completes its course. The saints, who have lived well, will have the resurrection of their bodies. Indeed, there is no perfect blessedness unless they are raised together with their bodies. Commentary on the Prophet Ezekiel.[7]

O Lord, You Know. Matthew Meade: Now to this question the prophet gives his answer to God in the next words: "O Lord, you know." In which answer there are three things included. (1) An exclusion of all natural power of living. As if the prophet should say, It is manifest that these bones, so dried and scattered, so exposed, cannot live again by any power in themselves to live, or by any act or power in any creature to quicken them. (2) It implies the hesitancy of his own thoughts about the event of the thing in question, whether they should live again or not. O Lord, you know, but as for me, I know not; as I see no hope, so I do not know what to think. (3) The answer is such as refers all to God; who is infinite in power, wonderful in counsel and excellent in working. O Lord, you know, as if he should say, "You are omniscient and know what you shall do; and omnipotent, and can do whatever you have a mind to do. Though I do not know what will become of this your poor people that are dead and past hope, and cannot say whether you will ever restore and relieve them again, yet, O Lord, you know." Sermons.[8]

God's Mighty, Efficacious Word. William Greenhill: This seems an absurd thing, that the prophet should prophesy to creatures insensible, unintelligible, void of life; it was as if God should bid a man preach to a heap of stones, or dry chips, which are incapable of hearing. But though these bones were inca-

[4]*Exposition*, 738. [5]*Sermons*, 3. [6]*Exposition*, 739. [7]*Commentarius in Ezechielem* (1553), 177. [8]*Sermons*, 4-5.

pable of hearing Ezekiel's voice, yet they were not incapable of hearing God's voice, for all creatures, even the most senseless, hear the Lord when he speaks. The stormy winds fulfill his word (Ps 148:8); the heavens and the earth (Is 1:2); whales and ravens (Jon 2:10; 1 Kings 17:4). The Lord intended to bestow life on these bones, and, that they may have life, they must hear his word, which had enlivening power in it. There is an obedient virtue in every creature to yield to the will and command of the Creator, and when it does so, then it is said to hear the voice of the Lord.

. . . How low, deplorable or desperate so ever the creature is, God can alter it, and that easily. These dry bones were almost dust and had almost come to nothing. Their condition was very deplorable and desperate. The prophet himself could not tell what to think of them. Did not God alter their condition quickly and with ease? He bids the prophet prophesy and say, "Hear the word of the Lord, you dry bones." And that being done, presently the bones shake, come together, are clothed with sinews, flesh and skin, receive breath, live and stand up. Here was a wonderful sudden change wrought with great facility. God can make the dry tree to flourish (Ezek 17:24), Aaron's rod to bud and blossom, Sarah's dead womb to conceive, rivers in high places and springs of water in dry lands (Is 41:18). If God speaks but the word, these things are done. . . . There is a mighty efficacy in God's word. An Exposition of Ezekiel.[9]

The Opening of Their Graves. Matthew Meade: What is meant by opening their graves and causing them to come out of their graves? I answer, as the graves are metaphorical and allusive, so is the opening and bringing them out. Now this may be explained particularly with respect to the Jews, or more generally with respect to the whole church of God.

As it respects the Jews—so the opening of their graves is the destroying the power of their enemies. For what was this grave but the power and wrath of the enemy; this brought them down, this kept them under. Therefore, when God breaks the power of Babylon and recompenses this wrath on them, then he is said to open the graves of his people and cause them to come out. And this was done literally by Cyrus's proclamation (2 Chron 36:23).

As it respects the church of God—(as doubtless it does) both Jews and Gentiles. So God may be said to open their graves in two cases especially. (1) When he does deliver them out of their sufferings, by removing insuperable difficulties that cannot otherwise be removed. . . . (2) When God vindicates the names of his people from the reproach and ignominy that is cast on them—for great sufferings are attended with great reproaches. Therefore when God gives his people into the hand of his enemies, he is said to give them to be a hissing and reproach among the people. Now when God vindicates their name and cause and rolls away the reproach in which their names lay buried, this is opening their graves and bringing them out. Sermons.[10]

The Resurrection of the Dead. Jakob Raupius: Before we turn to the analysis of this chapter, it is necessary to say something briefly about its content. Some interpreters think that the prophet's vision represents no more than the liberation from captivity in Babylon and restitution to the land in Canaan. And certainly we do not deny that by this vision is confirmed the promise of Israel's liberation from Babylonian captivity and a return to their former condition, since this fits well with what is said to the prophet himself (Ezek 37:11-12). But we deny that the liberation from Babylonian captivity is alone to be considered. For indeed the universal resurrection of the dead is also put forth in this vision as a certain

[9]*Exposition*, 740-41. [10]*Sermons*, 37-38.

prelude and picture.

. . . This reading is proved in the following ways. First, it is proved by the emphatic description of the vision. There is hardly any other place of Scripture in which the form and mode of the resurrection is emphasized so clearly by words and phrases.

Second, it is proved from the broader subject matter. It is said that the dry bones are brought to life by the breath that comes from the four winds (that is, from the four corners of the world) and this breath breathes on these slain that they may live (Ezek 37:9). But the Jews who returned to the land of Canaan were not collected from the four corners of the world—this is only true of the universal resurrection at the end of time (Mt 24:31; Mk 13:37). Furthermore, of those resuscitated, it is said that they were an exceedingly great army (Ezek 37:10). But the Israelites returning to Canaan from Babylon were not such a great number. . . .

Third, it is proved by comparing other Old and New Testament statements in which nearly the same phrases are used to describe the resurrection of the dead. Fourth, it is proved from the unanimous testimony of the Fathers. For such testimonies see the sayings collected by the blessed Johann Gerhard in his *Theological Commonplace* on the resurrection. Fifth, it is proved by the even older confessions of the rabbis. Commentary on Ezekiel.[11]

The Resurrection of the Body. William Greenhill: In the resurrection people shall have their own bodies and souls again. This vision of the dry bones is, by the Fathers and others, held to be a lively representation of the resurrection. And see here, the bones came together, bone to his bone, the same bones that were united before were united again in this resurrection; and the sinews, the flesh, the skin that belonged to them formerly, the same came and covered them again; so the same souls, the same breath, came and entered them, and they lived. The father had not the soul or body of the son, or the daughter the soul or body of the mother, but everyone had their own bodies and souls. Job was of this faith, saying, "Though after my skin worms destroy this body, yet in my flesh shall I see God: whom I shall see for myself, and my eyes shall behold" (Job 19:26-27).

The souls of people do not sleep with their bodies in the dust or vanish into nothing. The prophet calls for the soul of everybody here to come from the "four winds," that is, from those parts where they were. Had they been in the bones or dust of the earth or vanished into nothing, the Lord would not have directed the prophet to have called for them from all parts of the world. An Exposition of Ezekiel.[12]

Redemption of the Jews? Matthew Meade: "And you shall know that I am the Lord, when I have opened your graves and brought you of your graves" (Ezek 37:14). This signifies their redemption. "And shall put my spirit in you and you shall live" (Ezek 37:15). This signifies their conversion. Now that this looks beyond their redemption out of Babylon is most plain from the next prophecy after this, which is nothing else but an explanation of this of the bones by the metaphor of two sticks made one; a metaphor that shows that Israel and Judah shall be forever united together under Christ. I will make the stick of Ephraim and Judah one stick, and they shall be one stick in my hand, that is, when they come under my government. And this is when the aforementioned things shall come to pass, when they shall be gathered out of all nations, and settled in their own land and converted to the Lord. Sermons.[13]

37:15-23 *One People, One Lord*

[11] *Commenatius Synopticus* (1655), 271. Raupius's explanation is taken directly from Johann Gerhard, *Locorum Theologicorum Tomus Octavus* (Jena, 1621), 996-1003. [12] *Exposition*, 742. [13] *Sermons*, 95-96.

Two Sticks. John Mayer: By the similitude of two sticks, on one of which he must write the name of Judah, on the other the name of Ephraim. After this, he must join them together and then prophesy of the joining together of the two kingdoms of Judah and Israel, which were divided to Rehoboam and Jeroboam but will be reunited under David, who, again, is Christ set forth by this name (Ezek 34:24). After this he says that they shall be divided no more forever but continue as one people in a prosperous and happy estate, having the Lord's sanctuary in the midst of them.

Here the name of Ephraim is put for the kingdom of Israel because Jeroboam was of Ephraim. That this prophecy was not touching their estate under Zerubbabel, or the princes succeeding him after their return, is apparent because he was no king like David, neither were they of the ten tribes united to Judah under him, or any other succeeding him. But, indeed, they still remain in an excised estate in expectation of the time, when the Lord by converting them to Christ will make them thus blessed and happy, according to Romans 11:25, as has been discussed elsewhere in the prophets. Commentary upon All the Prophets.[14]

Two Sticks United. William Greenhill: The vision of the dry bones, and interpretation of them, being ended, here the typical work of two sticks, and the uniting of them, succeeds. . . . God would make these two sticks one, not one tribe but one kingdom. They had been two kingdoms, at great enmity, and were at this time scattered abroad among the nations. But the Lord promises to gather them together and to unite them, so that there shall not be a kingdom of Israel and a kingdom of Judah, but the stick of Ephraim shall be united to the stick of Judah. They should be but one stick, one kingdom and one king, and that in the hand of the Lord. The Septuagint says in the hand of Judah. An Exposition of Ezekiel.[15]

Two Kingdoms One. John Mayer: The two kingdoms, says Jerome, are not precisely to be understood of the children of Israel according to the flesh but according to the spirit. As such it is meant, whereas the division was before into Jews and Gentiles, now here should no more be any such division, but all should be one in Christ, the old partition wall being broken down. Whereas he speaks of their dwelling in their own land again after this, it is to be understood only by way of allusion to that which was done in the days of David. For as then their happiness lay in part in this, that they dwelled not in a strange land, but their own, which God in mercy had given them. So now the happiness of Christians should likewise lie in this, that in whatever land they dwell, it should be to them no more as profane but holy and sanctified by their faith, whereby they should become as God's sanctuary in the midst of it, as the land of Canaan of old was, in which peculiarly the Lord had then his sanctuary and temple. Commentary upon All the Prophets.[16]

Two Become One in Christ. Johannes Oecolampadius: The prophecy refers to the person of Christ and those who in the distant future would be added to the promises of Judah. . . . The people shall be one, that is, since the dividing wall has been destroyed by Christ, the two are brought together apart from the law by the gift of faith. We are first called by his grace in order to be one people, since there is one God, one Lord, one Spirit, one King and one Priest. In whichever hand is held each stick (for it is a single kingdom of grace extended to all), they are joined as one; they are one kingdom from two. There is no distinction—to the Jew first and then the Greek. . . . All are reconciled by the one Christ, who has been given as our propitiation from the Father, outside of whom there is no salvation. Com-

[14]*Prophets*, 455. [15]*Exposition*, 745-46. [16]*Prophets*, 455.

mentary on the Prophet Ezekiel.[17]

God's Gracious Promises. William Greenhill: In this verse (Ezek 37:21) is promised the return of the twelve tribes, comprehended under these words, "the children of Israel," out of all countries where they were scattered into their own land. Not only Judah and Benjamin should be gathered up and brought into Canaan again, but the rest of the tribes also. This is a great and gracious promise.

... Being brought into their land, here God adds three great promises more. The first is uniting them into one nation, who had some hundreds of years been divided and were at bitter enmity, one against another.

After the division made by Jeroboam, you read of several kings they had, kings of Judah and kings of Israel. There were two kingdoms, and different kings of them both; but the kingdoms being united into one, the Lord promises them not a succession of kings over them, but one king to rule over them both. They should be one kingdom and have one king. This is the second great promise.

"And they shall be no more two nations, neither shall they be divided into two kingdoms any more at all." This is the third promise, and it is a great one also, namely, they shall continue as a kingdom, one kingdom, and never be torn in pieces anymore. There shall be no Rehoboams or Jeroboams to cause divisions in it. An Exposition of Ezekiel.[18]

God's People. Jakob Raupius: Ezekiel 37:22: *And I will make them one nation* (that is to say, I will bring about from them one nation) *in the land, on the mountains of Israel, and one king* (this king, of course, is Christ, as gathered from Ezekiel 37:24) *shall be king over them all* (that is to say, their king will be king of all); *and they will no longer be in two nations* (nor will they any longer be of two nations) *nor any longer divided into two kingdoms anymore.* "Anymore" is added to intensify the expression. Piscator changes the verse to say *nor any longer divided into two kingdoms hereafter.*

Paul expresses these same sentiments at Ephesians 2:14. And it is noted that the some of the Samaritans in the time of Christ are freed from the superstition of the heathen. Thus this verse (Ezek 37:22) indicates that the gathering of the church is from the Jews, Samaritans, heathen, etc. Commentary on Ezekiel.[19]

Conversion of the Jews. William Greenhill: It is the opinion, if not the faith, of many that the two sticks representing the two houses of Judah and Israel are yet to be united and made one. The great reason for it is because they have not had one king, one shepherd, namely, David, by whom is meant the Messiah, to reign over them.

... The conversion of the Jews we may with warrant expect and pray for. God has promised to gather the children of Israel and to bring them to David their king, that is, Christ: *I will gather them out of every side; I will take the children of Israel from among the heathen whither they be gone; and one king shall rule over them* (Ezek 37:21-22). Seeing God has promised to do it, we may believe and pray for the same. An Exposition of Ezekiel.[20]

The Jews Converted. Matthew Meade: Three things you have asserted by the Holy Spirit in the following parts of this prophecy to put it [the conversion of the Jews] out of all doubt. First, that they shall be gathered out of all nations. "I will take the children of Israel from among the heathen, and will gather them on every side and bring them into their own land" (Ezek 37:21), which is the second. "And I will make them one nation in the land, on the mountains of Israel" (Ezek 37:22). He adds in Ezekiel 37:25, "they shall dwell in the

[17]*Commentarius in Ezechielem* (1553), 180. [18]*Exposition*, 747. [19]*Commentarius Synopticus* (1655), 276. [20]*Exposition*, 747.

land that I gave to Jacob my servant, wherein your ancestors have dwelled. They shall dwell therein, even they and their children, and their children's children." Third, they shall be converted to the Lord. That you have in Ezekiel 37:23, "They shall not defile themselves anymore with their idols, nor with any of their transgressions." Then it follows, "I will cleanse them, so shall they be my people, and I will be their God." Here is their conversion, which is further confirmed from Ezekiel 37:26: "I will make an everlasting covenant with them, and I will set my sanctuary in the midst of them forevermore." This is not meant of their worldly sanctuary but a gospel sanctuary, a glorious gospel temple that shall never be destroyed, as their first and second temple was. SERMONS.[21]

WHY BELIEVE IN THE CONVERSION OF THE JEWS? MATTHEW MEADE: You will say, what does such a doctrine as this of the Jews returning to their own land concern us, what is it to us whether they ever return or not? I answer, this doctrine is very instructive and teaching to us, and especially in these four or five things.

1. It shows us what a wonderful efficacy there is in the electing love of God; not one of the objects of it shall ever miscarry. The Jews are a great proof of this. . . . God will not utterly cast them off; though he cast them out, he will not cast them off, because God has a seed among them that must be converted. The election shall obtain, though the rest are blinded and hardened. So we may see here reason to admire the electing love of God, what the virtue of it is through all ages and times.

2. This doctrine is of great use to confirm our faith in the great attribute of God's faithfulness, both to his people, and to his promise. . . .

3. We may learn from this return of this people to their own land, what use to make of lesser blessings, and do not let us slight them, for they are the forerunners of greater mercy. . . .

4. Let us all have faith in this truth, that the poor Jews shall be converted. Let us believe for a people that cannot believe for themselves.

Does God require us to preach it? Then he requires you to believe it. "Hear the word of the Lord, o ye nations, and declare it in the isles afar off, and say, He that scattered Israel will gather them and keep them" (Jer 31:10). SERMONS.[22]

37:24-28 *David and Christ*

MY SERVANT DAVID IS CHRIST. WILLIAM GREENHILL: By "David" Zerubbabel cannot be meant, for he was not a king. Had he been so, yet he was not their prince forever, as it is said of this "David." "David" is here put for Christ, which the holy Scripture does frequently (Ezek 34:23; Hos 3:5; Is 37:35; 2 Kings 19:34; Jer 30:9). And that you may clearly see it is so, compare Isaiah 55:3, where mention is made of "the sure mercies of David," with Acts 13:34, where it is interpreted of Christ. Likewise, in Amos 9:11, "the tabernacle of David" refers to Christ (Acts 15:16). So then, this "David" is the Lord Christ, who is so called both because he descended from his loins (Rom 1:3), whereupon he is called "the Son of David" (Mt 1:1; 15:22; Mk 12:35), and because David was a type of him in his slaying Goliath and in his kingly and prophetical office. AN EXPOSITION OF EZEKIEL.[23]

CHRIST AND DAVID. JOHANN GERHARD: First Samuel 22:2 recounts that when David was wandering about in exile and forced to flee from King Saul, numerous men had joined him who were in distress, humiliation and despair. David was in this respect, as in many other respects as well, a prototype of our Lord Jesus Christ. In Scripture Christ is not only called at times the Son of David, but also the name David itself is ascribed to him (Ezek 34:23; 37:24). Before his exile, David had been anointed king over all Israel. However, he did

[21]*Sermons*, 96. [22]*Sermons*, 97-99. [23]*Exposition*, 750.

not come immediately to rule, but first, by the wondrous providence of God, had to wander about in poor and humble station. This is how it was with Christ, who, according to his human nature, was anointed king and high priest by the Holy Spirit. Yet he did not immediately implement his eternal kingdom but emptied himself of it and wandered in servitude on the earth until, at his victorious ascension into heaven, he finally received all power in heaven and on earth (Mt 28:18) and was made Lord over all creation; and everything was placed beneath his feet (Ps 8:7). Postilla.[24]

David Is Christ. Matthew Meade: To set out the truth of their conversion [that is, the Jews] to Christ, Ezekiel adds, they shall not only seek the Lord their God but David their king. This is not David the son of Jesse, for he was dead and rotten long before this promise was made; nor can it be Zerubbabel, for this is spoken of a time that is to be two thousand years after his time. There is nothing plainer than that by David is meant the Lord Christ. He is often called David in the Scriptures. "They shall serve the Lord their God and David their king," that is, Christ (Jer 20:9). "I will be their God and my servant David a prince among them" (Ezek 34:24). And, "My servant David shall be their prince forever" (Ezek 37:24). Now who can this be but Christ? What David is a prince forever, but he that was David's Son and David's Lord? He is therefore called the root and the offspring of David. He is his Root as God, his Offspring as man descending from him. That by David is meant Christ is plain. Sermons.[25]

An Everlasting Covenant. Johannes Oecolampadius: This covenant will be established by Christ, through whom we have peace with the Father, forever and ever. "And I will give them such an excellent mediator, who is my blessing for the nations and who will multiply his own by his word, and he will be my temple and dwelling in their midst." . . . And in this temple, which through the resurrection has been rebuilt and glorified, we find our peace, and whatever we seek in prayer, we shall find. Now in this temple God dwells forever and responds to our prayers. In this way, God brings relief and help to us, for we are his people, following him by faith. Commentary on the Prophet Ezekiel.[26]

The Covenant of Peace. William Greenhill: The meaning is that they shall no more live after the courses of people or imaginations of their own hearts, but they should consult with the word of God and frame their lives according to it. They shall trust no longer in their legal performances but look at David their king and call him "the Lord our righteousness."

Some look on this promise of David to be king over the Jews as accomplished in the reign of Christ the Messiah when here on earth because he gave out his commands then and required obedience to them. . . . Others are of a different judgment and believe that this great promise made here to the two houses of Judah and Israel remains yet to be performed: (1) Because the two houses are not yet united into one. . . . (2) Because the Jews do not own Christ; neither one house nor the other do it; neither Judah nor Israel acknowledged Christ to be the Messiah. . . . (3) The Jews have been, and are still, under many kings and shepherds. . . . (4) They shall then walk in the ways of Christ, not the ways of Moses. . . .

From Ezekiel 37:26- 27 I shall only give you this observation that there are great and precious promises that concern the Jews, yet unperformed. The everlasting covenant of peace, Christ being their king and temple, with many others, the Jews expect the fulfilling of. And so may we, for God is faithful and will make good his word. An Exposition of Ezekiel.[27]

[24]*Postilla* 1:38-39. [25]*Sermons*, 104-5. [26]*Commentarius in Ezechielem* (1553), 181. [27]*Exposition*, 750-51, 753.

38:1–39:29 THE PROPHECY AGAINST GOG

1The word of the LORD came to me: 2"Son of man, set your face toward Gog, of the land of Magog, the chief prince of Meshech[a] and Tubal, and prophesy against him 3and say, Thus says the Lord GOD: Behold, I am against you, O Gog, chief prince of Meshech[b] and Tubal. 4And I will turn you about and put hooks into your jaws, and I will bring you out, and all your army, horses and horsemen, all of them clothed in full armor, a great host, all of them with buckler and shield, wielding swords. 5Persia, Cush, and Put are with them, all of them with shield and helmet; 6Gomer and all his hordes; Beth-togarmah from the uttermost parts of the north with all his hordes—many peoples are with you.

7"Be ready and keep ready, you and all your hosts that are assembled about you, and be a guard for them. 8After many days you will be mustered. In the latter years you will go against the land that is restored from war, the land whose people were gathered from many peoples upon the mountains of Israel, which had been a continual waste. Its people were brought out from the peoples and now dwell securely, all of them. 9You will advance, coming on like a storm. You will be like a cloud covering the land, you and all your hordes, and many peoples with you.

10"Thus says the Lord GOD: On that day, thoughts will come into your mind, and you will devise an evil scheme 11and say, 'I will go up against the land of unwalled villages. I will fall upon the quiet people who dwell securely, all of them dwelling without walls, and having no bars or gates,' 12to seize spoil and carry off plunder, to turn your hand against the waste places that are now inhabited, and the people who were gathered from the nations, who have acquired livestock and goods, who dwell at the center of the earth. 13Sheba and Dedan and the merchants of Tarshish and all its leaders[c] will say to you, 'Have you come to seize spoil? Have you assembled your hosts to carry off plunder, to carry away silver and gold, to take away livestock and goods, to seize great spoil?'

14"Therefore, son of man, prophesy, and say to Gog, Thus says the Lord GOD: On that day when my people Israel are dwelling securely, will you not know it? 15You will come from your place out of the uttermost parts of the north, you and many peoples with you, all of them riding on horses, a great host, a mighty army. 16You will come up against my people Israel, like a cloud covering the land. In the latter days I will bring you against my land, that the nations may know me, when through you, O Gog, I vindicate my holiness before their eyes.

17"Thus says the Lord GOD: Are you he of whom I spoke in former days by my servants the prophets of Israel, who in those days prophesied for years that I would bring you against them? 18But on that day, the day that Gog shall come against the land of Israel, declares the Lord GOD, my wrath will be roused in my anger. 19For in my jealousy and in my blazing wrath I declare, On that day there shall be a great earthquake in the land of Israel. 20The fish of the sea and the birds of the heavens and the beasts of the field and all creeping things that creep on the ground, and all the people who are on the face of the earth, shall quake at my presence. And the mountains shall be thrown down, and the cliffs shall fall, and every wall shall tumble to the ground. 21I will summon a sword against Gog[d] on all my mountains, declares the Lord God. Every man's sword will be against his brother. 22With pestilence and bloodshed I will enter into judgment with him, and I will rain upon him and his hordes and the many peoples who are with him torrential rains and hailstones, fire and sulfur. 23So I will show my greatness and my holiness and make myself known in the eyes of many nations. Then they will know that I am the Lord.

39 "And you, son of man, prophesy against Gog and say, Thus says the Lord God: Behold, I am against you, O Gog, chief prince of Meshech[e] and Tubal. 2And I will turn you about and drive you forward, and bring you up from the uttermost parts of the north, and lead you against the mountains of Israel. 3Then I will strike your bow from your left hand, and will make your arrows drop out of your right hand. 4You shall fall on the mountains of Israel, you and all your hordes and the peoples who are with you. I will give you to birds of prey of every sort and to the beasts of the field to be devoured. 5You shall fall in the open field, for I have spoken, declares the Lord God. 6I will send fire on Magog and on those who dwell securely in the coastlands, and they shall know that I am the Lord.

7"And my holy name I will make known in the midst of my people Israel, and I will not let my holy name be profaned anymore. And the nations shall know that I am the Lord, the Holy One in Israel. 8Behold, it is coming and it will be brought about, declares the Lord God. That is the day of which I have spoken.

9"Then those who dwell in the cities of Israel will go out and make fires of the weapons and burn them, shields and bucklers, bow and arrows, clubs[f] and spears; and they will make fires of them for seven years, 10so that they will not need to take wood out of the field or cut down any out of the forests, for they will make their fires of the weapons. They will seize the spoil of those who despoiled them, and plunder those who plundered them, declares the Lord God.

11"On that day I will give to Gog a place for burial in Israel, the Valley of the Travelers, east of the sea. It will block the travelers, for there Gog and all his multitude will be buried. It will be called the Valley of Hamon-gog.[g] 12For seven months the house of Israel will be burying them, in order to cleanse the land. 13All the people of the land will bury them, and it will bring them renown on the day that I show my glory, declares the Lord God. 14They will set apart men to travel through the land regularly and bury those travelers remaining on the face of the land, so as to cleanse it. At[h] the end of seven months they will make their search. 15And when these travel through the land and anyone sees a human bone, then he shall set up a sign by it, till the buriers have buried it in the Valley of Hamon-gog. 16(Hamonah[i] is also the name of the city.) Thus shall they cleanse the land.

17"As for you, son of man, thus says the Lord God: Speak to the birds of every sort and to all beasts of the field, 'Assemble and come, gather from all around to the sacrificial feast that I am preparing for you, a great sacrificial feast on the mountains of Israel, and you shall eat flesh and drink blood. 18You shall eat the flesh of the mighty, and drink the blood of the princes of the earth—of rams, of lambs, and of he-goats, of bulls, all of them fat beasts of Bashan. 19And you shall eat fat till you are filled, and drink blood till you are drunk, at the

sacrificial feast that I am preparing for you. 20And you shall be filled at my table with horses
and charioteers, with mighty men and all kinds of warriors,' declares the Lord God.
21"And I will set my glory among the nations, and all the nations shall see my judg-
ment that I have executed, and my hand that I have laid on them. 22The house of Israel
shall know that I am the LORD their God, from that day forward. 23And the nations shall
know that the house of Israel went into captivity for their iniquity, because they dealt so
treacherously with me that I hid my face from them and gave them into the hand of their
adversaries, and they all fell by the sword. 24I dealt with them according to their unclean-
ness and their transgressions, and hid my face from them.
25"Therefore thus says the Lord God: Now I will restore the fortunes of Jacob and
have mercy on the whole house of Israel, and I will be jealous for my holy name. 26They
shall forget their shame and all the treachery they have practiced against me, when they
dwell securely in their land with none to make them afraid, 27when I have brought them
back from the peoples and gathered them from their enemies' lands, and through them
have vindicated my holiness in the sight of many nations. 28Then they shall know that I
am the LORD their God, because I sent them into exile among the nations and then as-
sembled them into their own land. I will leave none of them remaining among the nations
anymore. 29And I will not hide my face anymore from them, when I pour out my Spirit
upon the house of Israel, declares the Lord God."

a Or *Magog, the prince of Rosh, Meshech* b Or *Gog, prince of Rosh, Meshech* c Hebrew *young lions* d Hebrew *against him* e Or *Gog, prince of Rosh, Meshech* f Or *javelins* g Hamon-gog means *the multitude of Gog* h Or *Until* i Hamonah means *multitude*

Overview: The next two chapters discuss a future battle with Gog and Magog. Some confusion exists regarding the identity of Gog. Does Gog represent antichrist and the future battle with antichrist? Does Gog represent a king or nation in Ezekiel's day that would rise up against God's people? The prophecy indicates that the people of God will suffer at the hands of others but God will protect and deliver them.

Ezekiel 39 ends with the promised restoration of the house of Israel. The question is whether this is taken historically of those in Babylon or spiritually of all believers of all time. If historically of the Jews in captivity, then a problem arises with the destruction of Jerusalem by the Romans. Did God abandon his promise to protect them forever? Again the question of the future salvation of the Jews is raised and confirmed. A time will come when God will lavish his abundant mercy on the Jews, gathering them together and pouring his Spirit on them.

Gog and Magog. William Greenhill: This chapter and the next treat of Gog and Magog, who were nations against the people of God. . . . Lest the Jews should presently have looked for the fulfilling of those great promises in the former chapter, concerning the uniting of the two houses, and Messiah to be their King and the great privileges they should have thereby, he tells them here of great calamities that they must look for, of sad times and heavy judgments that should befall their enemies. An Exposition of Ezekiel.[1]

Gog and Magog. John Mayer: By Gog Lyra understands antichrist, who should arise and persecute the church of Christ toward the end of the world, for which it is said, *After many days in the latter years you shall come into the land, that is brought back from the sword* (Ezek 38:8). And he says that he is called Gog

[1]*Exposition*, 754.

signifying "covered" because he should be the devil in the shape of a man, and in the land of Magog, signifying "of the covered" as if he had said of his retinue or family, that is, such as took part with him. To prove this he cites Revelation 20, where Gog and Magog setting forth antichrist are again spoken of after the thousand years, in which time Satan was shut up and expired (2 Thess 2:8).

But Franciscus Junius takes that which is here prophesied of to be about the enemies, by whom the Jews should suffer after their return out of captivity, when they are living again in prosperity for a time in their own land. By Gog he understands a people in Asia Minor. . . . Lyra's opinion is most generally received. Junius, however, speaks more probably that Gog may be understood as the king of Syria, who should afterward reign, since the empire of the Medes and Persians is at an end, and the Grecian monarch, ending after the death of Alexander. For this was after many days and years; namely, about three hundred years after the Jews returned again to live in Judea. Commentary upon All the Prophets.[2]

Gog and Magog. Jakob Raupius: Since there is a great discrepancy of opinions concerning the subject of Ezekiel 38–39, it is first necessary to investigate these opinions and to bring to bear as much light as we can concerning the subject before we interpret the text. What is signified by the names Gog and Magog has little agreement. Jerome interprets it all as allegory concerning the conflict between the flesh and the spirit (cf. Rom 7) and thinks the devil, world, heretics, and finally all the enemies of the church come by the name Gog, Magog, Tubal and Mashech (Gen 10:2). . . . Ambrose derives the meaning from this own time and identifies them with the Goths who devastated the Roman Empire. . . . Junius, following Piscator, understands them concerning the kings of Asia Minor and Syria who lived during the time of the Maccabees and with their armies overtook Judea. Let us set aside these several conjectures and stand with Dr. Luther that the Turks, who harass the church throughout the entire world, are noted by Gog and Magog. Commentary on Ezekiel.[3]

Unwalled Villages. William Greenhill: "I will go up to the land of unwalled villages" (Ezek 38:11). This was the wicked thought Gog had in his mind. He purposed in his heart to go and invade the land of the Jews, and that which invited and encouraged him to do so was their unfortifiedness. They had no walls about their villages. Gog thought, I shall easily conquer and subdue the Jewish nation and add it to my territories, for they have no places of strength. . . . The second reason was their security. The Jews were wearied with their seventy years' captivity and had come again to their land, had rest and safety, according to what God had promised them. An Exposition of Ezekiel.[4]

Security of Christ's Kingdom. Johannes Oecolampadius: The greatest promise is the security of the kingdom of Christ. Zechariah says that Jerusalem will be inhabited as villages because of the people and the livestock that is in it. "And I will be to her, declares the Lord, a wall of fire all around" (Zech 2:5). They are villages without walls where they live freely without fear of the enemy. Commentary on the Prophet Ezekiel.[5]

God's Judgment on Gog. William Greenhill: God takes occasion, from the attempts of the wicked, to execute his just judgments on them and so to get glory for his name even from heathens. Gog took occasion, from the Jews' weakness (they were in unwalled villages), to invade and destroy them. Now God takes occasion from his unjust invading of the

[2]*Prophets*, 456. [3]*Commentarius Synopticus* (1655), 278. [4]*Exposition*, 757. [5]*Commentarius in Ezechielem* (1553), 185.

Jews to inflict dreadful judgments on Gog and his people, that the heathen might know him when he should be sanctified in Gog. They, seeing such just judgments on Gog, should fear the God of Israel and learn righteousness. God is known by executing his judgment (Ps 9:16). Thereby he is known to be the Most High over all the earth. An Exposition of Ezekiel.[6]

God's Holy Name. Johannes Oecolampadius: *Any my holy name I will make known* (Ezek 39:7). Christ is the holy name of God, in whom alone there is salvation, in whom there is all the riches of the wisdom and knowledge of God and great glory, because he abolished all principalities and powers. Commentary on the Prophet Ezekiel.[7]

Comfort Amid Tribulation. John Mayer: This prophecy is of great troubles to come to the Jews. It then tells of deliverance from this trouble by judging their enemies. This was very useful for them that when they should afterwards be thus tried, they might not despair or be discomforted, as thinking that all promises of happiness after their deliverance out of captivity would now come to naught. As it is here said, although their sufferings should be great, yet they should not be but by divine dispensation, and that they should in a short time be delivered from them again. Commentary upon All the Prophets.[8]

The Sacrifice. William Greenhill: The Hebrew word for "sacrifice" signifies a sacrifice of a slain beast. When a beast was killed and to be offered up to God, that was a sacrifice properly. Sometimes it notes the killing of people and beasts, as here, which metaphorically is called a sacrifice. Gog with his men and horses were slain, and these God calls a sacrifice, a great sacrifice that he prepared for the fowls and beasts, a great feast or supper. The place where this should be is "on the mountains of Israel."

. . . By these metaphorical expressions are set out the dead carcasses of men, who were of several dispositions and qualities. Some were like rams and lambs, others like goats and bullocks; some were sweeter and more tender flesh than others. Rams and goats, or great goats, as the Hebrew word signifies, were leaders; lambs and bullocks were those under the leaders. All of them were well-fleshed and fat like the cows of Bashan. Bashan was a high hill, beyond Jordan, which yielded strong oaks and fat cattle.

. . . The fowls of heaven and beasts of the field are likened to people at a feast, where having meat and drink [that pleases them], they eat and drink plentifully. The fat, flesh and blood of people is sweet, and so pleasing to fowls and beasts, which should cram and fill themselves with it.

. . . The mountains of Israel were the table here, the carcasses of men were the dishes, the fowls of heaven and beasts of the field the guests. Such plenty and variety of dishes they should have as had not been seen at any table before. Every guest should be filled. An Exposition of Ezekiel.[9]

39:25-29 *Restoration of Israel*

The Identity of the People. William Greenhill: If we refer these words to the captive Jews in Babylon, the time was drawing near of their deliverance, and therefore the Lord says, "Now will I bring again the captivity of Jacob," that is, the posterity of Jacob being in captivity. But if we refer these words to what went before in the chapter, the sense is, Gog and Magog being destroyed and their funeral over, "now will I bring again the captivity of Jacob," the dispersed Jews, or believers, who were the seed of Jacob. A spiritual reduction is here understood by some. An Exposition of Ezekiel.[10]

[6]*Exposition*, 759. [7]*Commentarius in Ezechielem* (1553), 189. [8]*Prophets*, 458. [9]*Exposition*, 769. [10]*Exposition*, 772.

Chastisement and Reformation. John Mayer: From here to the end of the chapter, it is showed how manifest it should be made by judgments executed on the enemies of God's people that they were not formerly given into the hands of the Chaldeans, as if God had then quite rejected them, but for their chastisement and reformation. Moreover, he continued in his promises perpetually to favor and protect them. They falling again into sin, as they did before their destruction by the Romans, and that more notoriously than ever before, the Lord did not bind himself by this promise. But that he might justly root them out again with more severity than ever, according to the rule of his doings laid down (Jer 18:10), it came to pass at that their fatal overthrow by the Romans. Commentary upon All the Prophets.[11]

The Jews Will Be Saved. William Greenhill: God hid his face seventy years from them in Babylon; and since their crucifying of Christ, he has hid it from them sixteen hundred years. But he has a time to let them see his face again, and never more to hide it from them. They shall have his favor, his counsel, his help and protection. They shall not be under severe judgments but enjoy sweet mercies.

. . . There is a time when the Jews shall not only have mercy but abundant and lasting mercy. God will gather them, pour out his Spirit on them and never hide his face from them anymore. This time will be a happy and glorious time. For the house of Israel to be enriched with the gifts and graces of God's Spirit, which are excellent, and to have the light of God's countenance shining on them, and that always, what can be more desirable? An Exposition of Ezekiel.[12]

[11]*Prophets*, 459. [12]*Exposition*, 773-74.

40:1-47 The New Temple Area and the Gates

1In the twenty-fifth year of our exile, at the beginning of the year, on the tenth day of the month, in the fourteenth year after the city was struck down, on that very day, the hand of the Lord was upon me, and he brought me to the city.[a] *2In visions of God he brought me to the land of Israel, and set me down on a very high mountain, on which was a structure like a city to the south. 3When he brought me there, behold, there was a man whose appearance was like bronze, with a linen cord and a measuring reed in his hand. And he was standing in the gateway. 4And the man said to me, "Son of man, look with your eyes, and hear with your ears, and set your heart upon all that I shall show you, for you were brought here in order that I might show it to you. Declare all that you see to the house of Israel."*

5And behold, there was a wall all around the outside of the temple area, and the length of the measuring reed in the man's hand was six long cubits, each being a cubit and a handbreadth[b] in length. So he measured the thickness of the wall, one reed; and the height, one reed. [6]Then he went into the gateway facing east, going up its steps, and measured the threshold of the gate, one reed deep.[c] [7]And the side rooms, one reed long and one reed broad; and the space between the side rooms, five cubits; and the threshold of the gate by the vestibule of the gate at the inner end, one reed. [8]Then he measured the vestibule of the gateway, on the inside, one reed. [9]Then he measured the vestibule of the gateway, eight cubits; and its jambs, two cubits; and the vestibule of the gate was at the inner end. [10]And there were three side rooms on either side of the east gate. The three were of the same size, and the jambs on either side were of the same size. [11]Then he measured the width of the opening of the gateway, ten cubits; and the length of the gateway, thirteen cubits. [12]There was a barrier before the side rooms, one cubit on either side. And the side rooms were six cubits on either side. [13]Then he measured the gate from the ceiling of the one side room to the ceiling of the other, a breadth of twenty-five cubits; the openings faced each other. [14]He measured also the vestibule, twenty cubits. And around the vestibule of the gateway was the court.[d] [15]From the front of the gate at the entrance to the front of the inner vestibule of the gate was fifty cubits. [16]And the gateway had windows all around, narrowing inwards toward the side rooms and toward their jambs, and likewise the vestibule had windows all around inside, and on the jambs were palm trees.

[17]Then he brought me into the outer court. And behold, there were chambers and a pavement, all around the court. Thirty chambers faced the pavement. [18]And the pavement ran along the side of the gates, corresponding to the length of the gates. This was the lower pavement. [19]Then he measured the distance from the inner front of the lower gate to the outer front of the inner court,[e] a hundred cubits on the east side and on the north side.[f]

[20]As for the gate that faced toward the north, belonging to the outer court, he measured its length and its breadth. [21]Its side rooms, three on either side, and its jambs and its vestibule were of the same size as those of the first gate. Its length was fifty cubits, and its breadth twenty-five cubits. [22]And its windows, its vestibule, and its palm trees were of the same size as those of the gate that faced toward the east. And by seven steps people would go up to it, and find its vestibule before them. [23]And opposite the gate on the north, as on the east, was a gate to the inner court. And he measured from gate to gate, a hundred cubits.

[24]And he led me toward the south, and behold, there was a gate on the south. And he measured its jambs and its vestibule; they had the same size as the others. [25]Both it and its vestibule had windows all around, like the windows of the others. Its length was fifty cubits, and its breadth twenty-five cubits. [26]And there were seven steps leading up to it, and its vestibule was before them, and it had palm trees on its jambs, one on either side. [27]And there was a gate on the south of the inner court. And he measured from gate to gate toward the south, a hundred cubits.

[28]Then he brought me to the inner court through the south gate, and he measured the south gate. It was of the same size as the others. [29]Its side rooms, its jambs, and its vestibule were of the same size as the others, and both it and its vestibule had windows all around. Its length was fifty cubits, and its breadth twenty-five cubits. [30]And there were vestibules all around, twenty-five cubits long and five cubits broad. [31]Its vestibule faced the outer court, and palm trees were on its jambs, and its stairway had eight steps.

32 Then he brought me to the inner court on the east side, and he measured the gate. It
was of the same size as the others. 33 Its side rooms, its jambs, and its vestibule were of the
same size as the others, and both it and its vestibule had windows all around. Its length
was fifty cubits, and its breadth twenty-five cubits. 34 Its vestibule faced the outer court,
and it had palm trees on its jambs, on either side, and its stairway had eight steps.
35 Then he brought me to the north gate, and he measured it. It had the same size as the
others. 36 Its side rooms, its jambs, and its vestibule were of the same size as the others,[g]
and it had windows all around. Its length was fifty cubits, and its breadth twenty-five
cubits. 37 Its vestibule[h] *faced the outer court, and it had palm trees on its jambs, on either*
side, and its stairway had eight steps.
38 There was a chamber with its door in the vestibule of the gate,[i] *where the burnt offer-*
ing was to be washed. 39 And in the vestibule of the gate were two tables on either side, on
which the burnt offering and the sin offering and the guilt offering were to be slaughtered.
40 And off to the side, on the outside as one goes up to the entrance of the north gate, were
two tables; and off to the other side of the vestibule of the gate were two tables. 41 Four
tables were on either side of the gate, eight tables, on which to slaughter. 42 And there were
four tables of hewn stone for the burnt offering, a cubit and a half long, and a cubit and
a half broad, and one cubit high, on which the instruments were to be laid with which the
burnt offerings and the sacrifices were slaughtered. 43 And hooks,[j] *a handbreadth long,*
were fastened all around within. And on the tables the flesh of the offering was to be
laid.
44 On the outside of the inner gateway there were two chambers[k] *in the inner court, one*[l]
at the side of the north gate facing south, the other at the side of the south[m] *gate facing*
north. 45 And he said to me, This chamber that faces south is for the priests who have
charge of the temple, 46 and the chamber that faces north is for the priests who have charge
of the altar. These are the sons of Zadok, who alone[n] *among the sons of Levi may come*
near to the Lord *to minister to him. 47 And he measured the court, a hundred cubits long*
and a hundred cubits broad, a square. And the altar was in front of the temple.

a Hebrew *brought me there* **b** A *cubit* was about 18 inches or 45 centimeters; a *handbreadth* was about 3 inches or 7.5 centimeters **c** Hebrew *deep, and one threshold, one reed deep* **d** Text uncertain; Hebrew *And he made the jambs sixty cubits, and to the jamb of the court was the gateway all around* **e** Hebrew *distance from before the low gate before the inner court to the outside* **f** Or *cubits. So far the eastern gate; now to the northern gate.* **g** One manuscript (compare verses 29 and 33); most manuscripts lack *were of the same size as the others* **h** Septuagint, Vulgate (compare verses 26, 31, 34); Hebrew *jambs* **i** Hebrew *at the jambs, the gates* **j** Or *shelves* **k** Septuagint; Hebrew *were chambers for singers* **l** Hebrew lacks *one* **m** Septuagint; Hebrew *east* **n** Hebrew lacks *alone*

Overview: With this chapter, the final part of Ezekiel begins. It is also here that great difficulties arise. These final chapters, like the first chapter of Ezekiel, are filled with types and figures of the restoration of the church of God under the gospel.

Our commentators begin with the time of Ezekiel's vision. Twenty years had elapsed since his first vision and fourteen years since the destruction of Jerusalem. Ezekiel had now been in captivity for twenty-five years. In a vision, Ezekiel is taken to the city of God, and a man, whose appearance was like bronze, spoke to him. This man is Christ, the Son of God, and this city is his church.

Our commentators devote a great deal of attention to the particulars of the temple seen by Ezekiel. They all agree that it is not a third temple for the Jews under some future messiah. The temple is either the Christian church or the heavenly paradise that awaits all believers. The wall of the temple shows God's protection. The gate refers to Christ, through whom all must pass for entrance. The steps point to either sanctification or the deepening knowledge of divine things by believers. Finally, the two orders of priests show the double work of ministers of the gospel who preach and pray.

Types, Figures and Similitudes. John Bunyan: I may say that God did in a manner tie up the church of the Jews to types, figures and similitudes; I mean, to be butted and bounded by them in all external parts of worship. Indeed, not only the Levitical law and temple, but as it seems to me the whole land of Canaan, the place of their lot to dwell in, was to them a ceremonial or a figure. Their land was a type of heaven, their passage over Jordan into it a similitude of our going to heaven by death. The fruit of their land was said to be uncircumcised, as being at their first entrance unclean; in which their land was also a figure of another thing, even as heaven was a type of grace and glory. Again, the very land itself was said to keep sabbath, and so to rest a holy rest even then when it lay desolate and not possessed of those to whom it was given for them to dwell in. Indeed, many of the features of the then church of God were set forth, as in figures and shadows, so by places and things in that land. Solomon's Temple Spiritualized.[1]

Meaning of Temple. Martin Luther: Therefore this building of Ezekiel is not to be understood to mean a physical building, but like the chariot at the beginning [1:4-28] so this building at the end [40–48] is nothing else than the kingdom of Christ, the holy church or Christendom here on earth until the last day.

As to how all the parts of the prophecy are to be interpreted and arranged, we will leave that until that life in which we shall see the whole building finished and complete. We cannot see it all now, since it is still under construction, and much of the stone and wood that belong to it is not yet born, let alone prepared for use in building. It is enough that we know it to be the house of God, his own building in which we all are.

Whoever has the leisure and the inclination can look into it and investigate it extensively, if he will take up the word of God and the sacraments, with their powers and the effects which the Holy Spirit works in the church through them, and bring these things into agreement. The Revelation of John can also be of help in this regard. A New Preface to the Prophet Ezekiel.[2]

The Final Chapters. William Greenhill: That there are things hard to understand in the sacred Scriptures, these nine last chapters, as well as the beginnings of Ezekiel, do abundantly testify. Such difficult things are in these last chapters that they have made many people of the greatest parts to tremble at the thought of interpreting them. The rabbis say that the first of Ezekiel, and these last chapters, are inexplicable secrets and understood by none. Therefore they forbid their disciples to read them, adding, "Elijah shall come, he will explain all things." . . . I feel the weakness of my own understanding, yet silently I adore its mysteries. It is good to tremble at the Word of God, both what we understand and what we understand not, for all is of equal authority. And to him that trembles at the Word of God, the Lord looks and will let in light. An Exposition of Ezekiel.[3]

The Meaning of the Final Chapters. John Mayer: In this chapter and the rest to the end of this prophecy, the restoration of the

[1]*Temple*, 271. [2]Lenker 6, 310* (WADB 11,1:408). [3]*Exposition*, 774.

church of God under the gospel is by types and figures accommodated to those times, that all might the better be understood, abundantly represented. In Ezekiel 40–42, as Franciscus Junius has it, the state of the church being set forth, Ezekiel 43–44 of the ministry and worship of God, Ezekiel 45–46, etc. to the end of the Christian commonwealth. Commentary upon All the Prophets.[4]

The Meaning of the Final Chapters. Jakob Raupius: From here to the end of the book is described the restoration of the church, the kingdom and people of Christ, whose restoration is signified by types, reckoned as the new temple, the new city of Jerusalem, the new worship, the new people and the form of the church. . . . This whole description and the structure of the temple and city, and the division and distribution of the holy land, did not exist in reality but in the prophetic vision and revelation, as indicated by the prophetic text itself (Ezek 40:2). Commentary on Ezekiel.[5]

40:1-3 *The Man of Ezekiel's Vision*

Ezekiel's Vision. William Greenhill: Here the time is pointed out when this vision was presented to Ezekiel, which was in the twenty-fifth year of his captivity; so long it was since he, with Jehoiakim, was carried into Babylon and kept there. His first vision was in the fifth year of his captivity, and this his last vision was twenty years after, in the beginning of the year, the tenth day of the month. Some make this to be in the autumn, others in the spring. After Jehoiakim had been eleven years in captivity, the city was smitten and utterly laid waste, which was in the eleventh year of Zedekiah. . . . From this period, or epoch, is the vision reckoned. Fourteen years after the desolation of the city, Ezekiel had it.

. . . Here the author of the vision is specified and described from his appearance, the instruments he had and the place where he stood. This "man" is made by some an angel, by others, Christ. It was the Son of God who appeared in the first vision to Ezekiel, and so he does in this last. He was a master builder and appointed by God to build the house. . . . And that this man was Christ his appearance declares, for it "was like the appearance of brass." And so Christ (Rev 1:15) is said to appear, and here his countenance, or whole body, appeared like brass, that is, free from spot, beautiful, bright and shining. Christ was without blemish or spot (1 Pet 1:19); he was holy, harmless, undefiled (Heb 7:26); he was "fairer than the children of men" (Ps 45:2). An Exposition of Ezekiel.[6]

The Vision of Ezekiel. John Mayer: Now Ezekiel had this vision in the land of Judea, where he was by the spirit transported, as he had been before (Ezek 8), to see the abominations there committed. And being brought there and placed on a high mountain he saw as it were the frame of a *City on the South* (Ezek 40:2), which city is further described afterwards, Ezekiel 45 and following. Being here he saw a man who was like shining brass, who stood in the gate of the city with a flaxen line and a reed in his hand to measure it all. He was like a master builder being about to build who should first plot out the ground by measure, on which he would build. Therefore the man here appearing must be Christ, who is here represented building his church, when he should come into the world and preach salvation to all who repent and believe in his name. And he well appears in the likeness of a man, because by this his being made man in time was prefigured, although he were the eternal Son of God the Father, and as shining brass, because that after his resurrection and ascension into heaven he thus appeared to John, showing his glory. Commentary upon All the Prophets.[7]

[4]*Prophets*, 459. [5]*Commentarius Synopticus* (1655), 291. [6]*Exposition*, 775-76. [7]*Prophets*, 460.

40:4 *The New Temple*

Not a Third Temple. Martin Luther: He would understand this building of the temple, altar, city, and land, which Ezekiel [40–48] describes, must take up Lyra, with his figures and glosses; otherwise he will toil and labor on the matter in vain. Since we have not known how better to put the figures on paper, we have not attempted it but refer the reader to Lyra. Besides it is not possible to plot out a building on paper, but a carved model would have to be constructed.

About the significance of it, one scholar has thought one way, another a different way. But the understanding of it that is held by the Jews and others like them is most certainly to be rejected. They think it is supposed to be the third temple, which must be built by their Messiah who is to come; in their foolish and vain hope they claim for it much great glory. The blind and ignorant people do not see that the text does not admit of their fanciful interpretation, as Lyra too has impressively shown. For Ezekiel says neither that this city shall be called Jerusalem, nor that it shall stand at the place where Jerusalem was situated. Jerusalem was situated on the northern slope of the mountain with the temple standing in the midst of it on the hill of Mount Moriah, and the stronghold of Zion on the height south of it. A New Preface to the Prophet Ezekiel.[8]

Not Zerubbabel's Temple. William Greenhill: Some would have this temple, represented to Ezekiel, to be that built by Zerubbabel and the Jews after the captivity. But there is much to be said to prove it not to be so: (1) That temple was built in Jerusalem, in the place where Solomon's temple stood; but this temple Ezekiel saw was to be without the city, as interpreters observe from the Ezekiel 45 and Ezekiel 48; (2) That temple was for the two tribes of Judah and Benjamin. This of Ezekiel is for the whole body of the Jews, all the tribes are mentioned; (3) In Zerubbabel's temple there was no such river or trees yielding new fruit every month; (4) God promised to dwell among the Israelites of this temple forever, which cannot be verified of Zerubbabel's temple and city; for the Lord forsook both and delivered them up to the Romans, who destroyed them; (5) The temple our prophet speaks of was not to be defiled, nor the holy name of God, by the house of Israel; (6) The twenty-five thousand reeds, being the length of the holy portion offered to the Lord, and the breadth of ten thousand reeds, cannot be understood of any city or temple that the Jews should build after their captivity. . . .

It is conceived, therefore, that in this vision is represented the restitution of the Jewish church, their temple, city and worship after the captivity, not simply, but as they were types of the church under the gospel. For, as we must not exclude these, so we must know, this is not the principal thing intended. That which the vision does chiefly hold out to us is the building of the Christian temple, with the worship thereof, under Jewish expressions, which began to be accomplished in the apostles' days (Acts 15:16). . . . There is one thing more also intended, namely, the restoring of the Christian church after its apostasy and suffering in spiritual Babylon under antichrist. An Exposition of Ezekiel.[9]

The Temple. John Mayer: Details of the temple and the whole compass of the wall from gate to gate is set forth from Ezekiel 41 to Ezekiel 42:15. . . . Gregory, a most learned doctor of the church, speaking of the mystical sense of this place says that it might be counted presumption in him to attempt the explanation of it, which none ever yet has attempted to do, neither could, when he studied in private on it. But to explain it publicly being

[8]Lenker 6, 310-311* (WADB 11,1:406). [9]*Exposition*, 774, 775.

helped by the prayers of his hearers he says that he was enlightened to the understanding of it. By the wall round about the house he says that Christ is meant, who is as a wall about his house the church, to protect it and every faithful person—for either is called the house of God, the church (1 Tim 3:15) and the believer (1 Cor 6:19).

The reed of a cubit and a hand breadth, in the cubits sets forth the practical part of the life of the believer, and in the palm the contemplative, which is much less than our practical while we live here. . . . By this must be meant that much more time is spent in action, or doing things that pertain to this life, than in meditation on divine things that pertain to the life to come. Those who know the will of God and are sanctified, do live in proportionate obedience, otherwise their knowledge is but foolishness, and indeed obedience, or the fear of God, which make a person live in obedience to God's laws, is the beginning of wisdom and true knowledge. Therefore the breadth is first spoken of, then the height, and to approve this our Lord says, *if you obey, you shall know, and they that fear the Lord know his secrets* (Jn 7:17; Ps 25:14), wherefore to attain the height of knowledge. Let us lay a foundation by getting humble and obedient hearts ready to submit to the doing of anything commanded by God, as he shall be pleased to show it to us. Commentary upon All the Prophets.[10]

God Cares for His Persecuted Church. William Greenhill: When the church is low, in the worst, most desperate and deplorable condition, even then the Lord has a care of his church. Now the temple, city and land of Canaan were utterly laid waste, many of the people destroyed, the rest in Babylon without hope of ever seeing their own country. In this condition the Lord appears to Ezekiel and gives him a most singular and excellent vision concerning the restoration of the church, the extent, dignity and glory of it, whereby he showed both the prophet and the people, whose hearts were filled with sorrow. When the church is in the wilderness, under persecution, in Egypt or Babylon, the Lord is solicitous for it. . . .

The church is Mount Zion, or Mount Zion is the church, wherein God makes known his mind for the comfort of his people. Ezekiel was carried in Spirit into the land of Israel and set there on a very high mountain, namely, Mount Zion, which typed the church of God. There he had this glorious vision; there sweet consolation was given forth for the afflicted. An Exposition of Ezekiel.[11]

40:5-16 *The East Gate to the Outer Court*

The Wall. William Greenhill: By this wall we may understand the wall of God's protection, which is round about the church. This wall was in height and thickness alike, six cubits high and six cubits thick; it was strong, securing the house Ezekiel saw. God, who is stronger than all, is the defense of the church. . . . The church of God, having such a wall, is secure and invincible. An Exposition of Ezekiel.[12]

The East Gate. Martin Luther: Moses implies that Paradise had a road or a gate toward the east through which there was an access to the garden (Gen 3:24). Likewise, in connection with the temple structure in Ezekiel (40:6) mention is made of the gate of the sanctuary which faced toward the east, obviously to have us realize that the temple was a figure of Paradise; for if nature had remained perfect, Paradise would have been the temple of the entire world. And so, on the road toward the east, which alone led to Paradise, cherubim or angels were placed, to guard that way so that neither Adam nor any of his descendants

[10]*Prophets*, 460-61. [11]*Exposition*, 776. [12]*Exposition*, 777.

could enter Paradise. Lectures on Genesis.[13]

The Gates. John Mayer: He that came to the gate, and the gate, here says Gregory, was all one, namely, Christ Jesus, who says, *I am the door, he that enters by me* (Jn 10). If anyone shall doubt how this can be, he answers, he is both the door and the shepherd entering in by the door, as he himself explains in the Gospel of John. Gregory also says the preacher is the door, because by his preaching people enter into the kingdom of heaven, having the way to heaven opened to them, and the holy Scripture is the door for the same reason. Lastly, the door is faith because by this, as by a door, we enter. But I rest in the first, Christ is the gate, and he himself entered into heaven, as by a gate, when by the merit of his low debasing himself he ascended above the heavens and had a name above all names. Commentary upon All the Prophets.[14]

The Temple Gates. William Greenhill: These gates do hint to us the readiness in Christ and God to receive comers, and the confluence of them from all parts. This temple has many gates, and those looking to the several quarters of the world. If people come from any of them, there is a gate before them and admittance for them. An Exposition of Ezekiel.[15]

The Threshold. John Mayer: *The threshold of the gate* was double as must be acknowledged, because he speaks of a threshold and a threshold, each of which was measured in breadth one reed. That is, the outward threshold and the inner, the one served to set forth the most famous of the faithful progenitors of Christ, Abraham, Isaac and Jacob, etc., of whom he came according to the flesh, and the other the holy apostles, who were of equal virtue with them for their propagating of his gospel into all nations. By this Christ was formed, as it were, again through their travel in the hearts of their hearers by faith in his name. For as the holy patriarchs were like to a threshold without, by whom it was then ascended to Christ, when others seeing their faith and other shining virtues were drawn likewise to believe, and love virtue, so the apostles were like a threshold within, whereby believers of all countries and nations came up to him since the time of his incarnation, when hearing them preach and seeing their holy conversation and miracles, which they wrought, they were converted to him. Commentary upon All the Prophets.[16]

The Steps. John Mayer: The gate, which is said to stand eastward the more aptly, because our Lord is called the east, and sometimes the Sun, which rises in the east. But what is meant by the degrees, by which this man ascended to this gate? Solution: Christ ascends by degrees, when grace begun by his word and spirit is increased daily more and more, for grace is not at the highest pitch in anyone at the first, but this is come to by degrees. As in Peter himself, who had grace at the first, but in much weakness, yet afterwards he attained to so high a degree that he feared not the higher powers or anything that they could do to him. No more did the rest of the apostles, whereas before they all fled from Christ, and Peter's pusillanimity was such that he would not stand to the confession of him before a silly maid. But when the faithful are grown to this height of grace and Christian resolution, Christ is ascended up the stairs in them being thus the more glorified. Wherefore the same Peter exhorts us to *desire the sincere milk of the word to grow thereby*, and *to grow in grace and the knowledge of Jesus Christ* (1 Pet 2:2; 2 Pet 3:18). Commentary upon All the Prophets.[17]

The Temple Steps. William Greenhill: The knowledge of divine things is not attained

[13]LW 1:229 (WA 42:171-172). [14]*Prophets*, 461. [15]*Exposition*, 778. [16]*Prophets*, 461. [17]*Prophets*, 461-62.

without labor and difficulty. There are steps and stairs in this temple, and those who will behold the glory and understand the mysteries of it must go upward, first one step, and then another, and it is difficult to go up stairs and steps. AN EXPOSITION OF EZEKIEL.[18]

ASCENDING TO THE HOUSE OF THE LORD. JOHN BUNYAN: This porch also had certain steps, by which they went up into the house of the Lord. . . . One then who enters into the house of the Lord is an ascending person; as it is said of Moses, he went up into the mount of God. It is ascending to go into the house of God. The world does not believe this; they think it is going downward to go up to the house of God, but they are in a horrible mistake. The steps then by which people went up into the temple are, and ought to be, opposed to those which people take to their lusts and empty glories. Hence such steps are said not only to decline from God, but to take hold of the path to death and hell (Ps 44:18; Prov 2:18; 5:5; 7:25-27). The steps, then, by which people went up to the house of the Lord signified those steps that people take when they go to God, to heaven and glory, for these steps were the way to God, to God in his holy temple. SOLOMON'S TEMPLE SPIRITUALIZED.[19]

THE WINDOWS. WILLIAM GREENHILL: "Of the windows." By these windows is signified the spiritual light that should be in the church of Christ. He is called "the Sun," "a great light" and "the light of the world." By those windows, which are the apostles, prophets, evangelists, pastors and teachers, he has, and still does, let light into the church. AN EXPOSITION OF EZEKIEL.[20]

40:17-37 *The Outer Court, Gates and Inner Court*

THE TWO COURTS. JOHN BUNYAN: I perceive that there are two courts belonging to the temple. The first was called the outward court. This was that into which the people of necessity first entered, when they went to worship in the temple; consequently that was it in and by which the people did first show their desires to be the worshipers of God. . . . In this, though there may sometimes be truth, yet more often lies and dissimulation. Wherefore commonly an outward appearance is set in opposition to faith and truth, as the outward is in opposition to the inner court, and outward to the inner person.

. . . But as there was an outward, so there was an inner court, a court that stood nearer the temple; and so to the true practical part of worship than that outward court did (Ezek 10:3; 46:1; 1 Kings 6:36). This inner court is that which is called "the court of the priests," because it was it in which they boiled the trespass offerings and in which they prepared the sin offering for the people (2 Chron 4:9; Ezek 46:20). This court, therefore, was the place of practice and of preparation to appear before God, which is the first true token of a sincere and honest mind. Wherefore here, and not in the outward court, stood the great brazen altar, which was a type of Christ, by whom alone the true worshipers make their approach with acceptance to God. SOLOMON'S TEMPLE SPIRITUALIZED.[21]

THE OUTER COURT. WILLIAM GREENHILL: In "the outward court" the people stood; and it represented the nations, which are out of the church. In "the inward court," where was the candlestick, the showbread and altar of perfumes, were the Levites and priests. This court represented the church, where the Word of God enlightens and nourishes us. Christ is our altar of perfumes. The holy of holies represented heaven; into it the high priest only entered, typifying our high priest, the Lord

[18]*Exposition*, 778, 779. [19]*Temple*, 285. [20]*Exposition*, 780. [21]*Temple*, 278.

Christ. He entered in there alone by his own power, to bring us there. AN EXPOSITION OF EZEKIEL.[22]

THE CHAMBERS AND TREASURIES. JOHN MAYER: *Then he brought me to the outward court, and lo, there were chambers, and a pavement round about, and on the pavement thirty chambers.* To this point the Lord has been showing Ezekiel the inner court and the chambers, gates, porches and fronts; now he shows the outward court with its appurtenances. For chambers here the Vulgate has "treasuries," and the Hebrew word signifies either. And what can we better understand, says Gregory, by treasuries than the ministers of Christ, who are treasurers of divine learning and knowledge? By this he speaks well, *for every scribe,* says our Lord, *instructed to the kingdom of heaven is like to a householder, that out of his treasury brings forth things both new and old* (Mt 13:52).

But why are treasuries placed in the outer court, when the common manner is to place them more inwardly, where they may be safest from thieves, and if the treasure of a minister is knowledge, it is chiefly within? Solution: This is not done to show their inward knowledge, which is in their breasts, but that which they bring forth by preaching outwardly to the enriching of their hearers with knowledge and understanding. O that people would thus make account of knowledge, then would they dig and search for it, as for gold, as is commanded, and such earthen vessels, as bring this treasure, should be highly accepted among them for their preaching and writing, especially that bend their studies to the enriching of their souls most in that knowledge. This happens by reading the holy Scriptures or hearing them, and preaching on places plain and easy they cannot attain to, their feet surely should be beautiful on the mountains, whereby they go not only into particular congregations, as when they preach thus, but into all parts of the kingdom to make a more universal distribution of his treasure, as when they write. O how lightly are the labors of such teachers esteemed of by most people, and therefore their books lie still neglected as superfluous things. COMMENTARY UPON ALL THE PROPHETS.[23]

THE GATES. JOHN BUNYAN: There belonged to this court several gates, an east, a south and a north gate; and when the people of the land went into this court to worship, they were not to go out at that gate by which they came in, but out of the gate over against it, to show that true Christians should persevere right on and not turn back, whatever they meet with in the way. "He that enters in by the way of the north gate to worship shall go out by the way of the south gate; and he that enters in by the way of the south gate shall not return by the way of the gate whereby he came in but shall go forth over against it" (Ezek 46:9). SOLOMON'S TEMPLE SPIRITUALIZED.[24]

40:38-47 *Rooms for Sacrifices and the Priests*

WASHING OF THE BURNT OFFERING. WILLIAM GREENHILL: Some, by this washing of the burnt offering (Ezek 40:38), think baptism to be prefigured, which denotes washing away the filthiness of sin by the blood of Christ. It may denote to us the purity of that which is to be presented to the Lord. Nothing unclean will be acceptable to him. AN EXPOSITION OF EZEKIEL.[25]

THE BURNT OFFERING. JOHN BUNYAN: This altar seems to be placed about the middle of this court over against the porch of the house and . . . was called "the altar of burnt offering," and therefore it was a type of Christ in his divinity. For Christ's body was our true burnt

[22]*Exposition*, 780. [23]*Prophets*, 468. [24]*Temple*, 278. [25]*Exposition*, 781.

offering, of which the bodies of the sacrificed beasts were a type; now that altar on which his body was offered was his Divinity or Godhead; for that, and that only, could bear up that offering in the whole of its suffering; and that therefore, and that only, was to receive the fat, the glory. SOLOMON'S TEMPLE SPIRITUALIZED.[26]

TWO ORDERS OF PRIESTS. JOHN MAYER: And these priests or ministers are of two sorts (Ezek 40:44): some keepers of the house and some of the altar. Here there is an allusion to the distinction of the priests of old, some of whom were such as kept the watch of the Lord's house in their course, and some offered the sacrifices. Those who offered are said to be the sons of Zadok of Levi, because Abiathar was dismissed from the priest's office by Solomon and Zadok was set up in his stead to be high priest. Therefore his sons as the superior priests served at the altar; the other priests kept the house, that no unclean persons might enter. But by this it was showed that under the gospel the ministers of Christ should have a double work to do, one to preach and pray, which was as an offering of sacrifice to God, according to that, *Offer to God the sacrifice of praise* (Ps 50:14), and to that of the apostle, *We are everywhere a sweet smelling savor to God* (2 Cor 2:15). And well may this be compared with that which was done on the altar; namely, burning and consuming flesh by fire, because by the Spirit going along with their preaching what is carnal and fleshly in their hearers is consumed. The other of ruling by censuring gross offenders, and absolving the penitent and suppressing and stopping the mouths of heretics, for thus the church of God, which is his house, is kept, as it were, with watch and ward. COMMENTARY UPON ALL THE PROPHETS.[27]

[26]*Temple*, 279. [27]*Prophets*, 474-75.

40:48–42:20 THE TEMPLE

48Then he brought me to the vestibule of the temple and measured the jambs of the
vestibule, five cubits on either side. And the breadth of the gate was fourteen cubits, and
the sidewalls of the gate[a] were three cubits on either side. 49The length of the vestibule was
twenty cubits, and the breadth twelve[b] cubits, and people would go up to it by ten steps.[c]
And there were pillars beside the jambs, one on either side.
41 Then he brought me to the nave and measured the jambs. On each side six cu-
bits[d] was the breadth of the jambs.[e] 2And the breadth of the entrance was ten cu-
bits, and the sidewalls of the entrance were five cubits on either side. And he measured
the length of the nave,[f] forty cubits, and its breadth, twenty cubits. 3Then he went into
the inner room and measured the jambs of the entrance, two cubits; and the entrance, six
cubits; and the sidewalls on either side[g] of the entrance, seven cubits. 4And he measured
the length of the room, twenty cubits, and its breadth, twenty cubits, across the nave. And
he said to me, "This is the Most Holy Place."

5Then he measured the wall of the temple, six cubits thick, and the breadth of the side
chambers, four cubits, all around the temple. 6And the side chambers were in three stories,
one over another, thirty in each story. There were offsets[h] all around the wall of the temple
to serve as supports for the side chambers, so that they should not be supported by the wall
of the temple. 7And it became broader as it wound upward to the side chambers, because
the temple was enclosed upward all around the temple. Thus the temple had a broad area
upward, and so one went up from the lowest story to the top story through the middle story.
8I saw also that the temple had a raised platform all around; the foundations of the side
chambers measured a full reed of six long cubits. 9The thickness of the outer wall of the side
chambers was five cubits. The free space between the side chambers of the temple and the
10other chambers was a breadth of twenty cubits all around the temple on every side. 11And
the doors of the side chambers opened on the free space, one door toward the north, and an-
other door toward the south. And the breadth of the free space was five cubits all around.

12The building that was facing the separate yard on the west side was seventy cubits
broad, and the wall of the building was five cubits thick all around, and its length ninety
cubits. 13Then he measured the temple, a hundred cubits long; and the yard and the build-
ing with its walls, a hundred cubits long; 14also the breadth of the east front of the temple
and the yard, a hundred cubits.

15Then he measured the length of the building facing the yard that was at the back and
its galleries[i] on either side, a hundred cubits.

The inside of the nave and the vestibules of the court, 16the thresholds and the nar-
row windows and the galleries all around the three of them, opposite the threshold, were
paneled with wood all around, from the floor up to the windows (now the windows were
covered), 17to the space above the door, even to the inner room, and on the outside. And
on all the walls all around, inside and outside, was a measured pattern.[j] 18It was carved of
cherubim and palm trees, a palm tree between cherub and cherub. Every cherub had two
faces: 19a human face toward the palm tree on the one side, and the face of a young lion
toward the palm tree on the other side. They were carved on the whole temple all around.
20From the floor to above the door, cherubim and palm trees were carved; similarly the
wall of the nave.

21The doorposts of the nave were squared, and in front of the Holy Place was something
resembling 22an altar of wood, three cubits high, two cubits long, and two cubits broad.[k]
Its corners, its base,[l] and its walls were of wood. He said to me, "This is the table that is
before the Lord." 23The nave and the Holy Place had each a double door. 24The double
doors had two leaves apiece, two swinging leaves for each door. 25And on the doors of the
nave were carved cherubim and palm trees, such as were carved on the walls. And there
was a canopy[m] of wood in front of the vestibule outside. 26And there were narrow win-
dows and palm trees on either side, on the sidewalls of the vestibule, the side chambers of
the temple, and the canopies.

42 Then he led me out into the outer court, toward the north, and he brought me
to the chambers that were opposite the separate yard and opposite the building on
the north. 2The length of the building whose door faced north was a hundred cubits,[n] and
the breadth fifty cubits. 3Facing the twenty cubits that belonged to the inner court, and
facing the pavement that belonged to the outer court, was gallery[o] against gallery in three
stories. 4And before the chambers was a passage inward, ten cubits wide and a hundred

cubits long,[p] and their doors were on the north. 5Now the upper chambers were narrower,
for the galleries took more away from them than from the lower and middle chambers of
the building. 6For they were in three stories, and they had no pillars like the pillars of the
courts. Thus the upper chambers were set back from the ground more than the lower and
the middle ones. 7And there was a wall outside parallel to the chambers, toward the outer
court, opposite the chambers, fifty cubits long. 8For the chambers on the outer court were
fifty cubits long, while those opposite the nave[q] were a hundred cubits long. 9Below these
chambers was an entrance on the east side, as one enters them from the outer court.
10In the thickness of the wall of the court, on the south[r] also, opposite the yard and
opposite the building, there were chambers 11with a passage in front of them. They were
similar to the chambers on the north, of the same length and breadth, with the same exits[s]
and arrangements and doors, 12as were the entrances of the chambers on the south. There
was an entrance at the beginning of the passage, the passage before the corresponding wall
on the east as one enters them.[t]
13Then he said to me, "The north chambers and the south chambers opposite the yard
are the holy chambers, where the priests who approach the LORD shall eat the most holy
offerings. There they shall put the most holy offerings—the grain offering, the sin offer-
ing, and the guilt offering—for the place is holy. 14When the priests enter the Holy Place,
they shall not go out of it into the outer court without laying there the garments in which
they minister, for these are holy. They shall put on other garments before they go near to
that which is for the people."
15Now when he had finished measuring the interior of the temple area, he led me out
by the gate that faced east, and measured the temple area all around. 16He measured the
east side with the measuring reed, 500 cubits by the measuring reed all around. 17He
measured the north side, 500 cubits by the measuring reed all around. 18He measured
the south side, 500 cubits by the measuring reed. 19Then he turned to the west side and
measured, 500 cubits by the measuring reed. 20He measured it on the four sides. It had a
wall around it, 500 cubits long and 500 cubits broad, to make a separation between the
holy and the common.

a Septuagint; Hebrew lacks *was fourteen cubits, and the sidewalls of the gate* **b** Septuagint; Hebrew *eleven* **c** Septuagint; Hebrew *and by steps that would go up to it* **d** A *cubit* was about 18 inches or 45 centimeters **e** Compare Septuagint; Hebrew *tent* **f** Hebrew *its length* **g** Septuagint; Hebrew *and the breadth* **h** Septuagint, compare 1 Kings 6:6; the meaning of the Hebrew word is uncertain **i** The meaning of the Hebrew term is unknown; also verse 16 **j** Hebrew *were measurements* **k** Septuagint; Hebrew lacks *two cubits broad* **l** Septuagint; Hebrew *length* **m** The meaning of the Hebrew word is unknown; also verse 26 **n** A *cubit* was about 18 inches or 45 centimeters **o** The meaning of the Hebrew word is unknown; also verse 5 **p** Septuagint, Syriac; Hebrew *and a way of one cubit* **q** Or *temple* **r** Septuagint; Hebrew *east* **s** Hebrew *and all their exits* **t** The meaning of the Hebrew verse is uncertain

OVERVIEW: The following two chapters continue the description of the temple. Our commentators offer spiritual interpretations of all aspects of the temple, which is here described not as a physical building. It is the place of God or where God is. The measurements of the parts of the temple indicate such things as the Ten Commandments, the holy Trinity and baptism. The righteousness of faith and holy living is set forth by the measurement of the porch. Others see here signified the body of Christ. Finally, the holy offerings given by the priests represent what Christ offers for us and to us. Here a figure of the Lord's Supper is observed.

40:48–42:12 *Spiritual Understanding of the Temple*

A Wide or Narrow Gate? John Bunyan: The porch, at which was an ascent to the temple, had a gate belonging to it. This gate, according to the prophet Ezekiel, was six cubits wide. The leaves of this gate were double, one folding this way, the other folding that (Ezek 40:48). Now here some may object and say, Since the way to God by these doors were so wide, why does Christ say the way and gate is narrow? Answer: The straightness, the narrowness, must not be understood of the gate simply, but because of that cumber that some people carry with them, that pretend to be going to heaven. Six cubits! What is six cubits to one who would enter in here with all the world on his back? The young man in the gospel, who made such a noise for heaven, might have gone in easily enough; for in six cubits' breadth there is room: but, poor man, he was not for going in there, unless he might carry in his houses on his shoulder too, and now the gate was narrow (Mk 10:17-27). Wherefore he that will enter in at the gate of heaven, of which this gate into the temple was a type, must go in by himself, and not with his bundles of trash on his back. Solomon's Temple Spiritualized.[1]

Not a Physical Building. Martin Luther: But this city of Ezekiel is supposed to lie to the south [of the temple] and he says, "It shall be called *Dominus ibi*," "There God," or "God there," that is, "Where God himself is" [Ezek 48:35]. The temple shall not be in the city but—as the reckoning shows—seven good, big German miles to the north of it. And the city on the high mountain shall be about nine good, big German miles both in length and breadth, so that the encircling wall shall be approximately thirty-six German miles around. We may call that a little city, and the hill on which it lies, a little hill!

If a townsman living at the southern end of the city wanted to go to church, or to the temple, he would have to walk sixteen [German] miles, nine through the city and seven to the temple. . . . This cannot be any physical building; still less can it be at the place where Jerusalem was situated. A New Preface to the Prophet Ezekiel.[2]

Spiritual Understanding of the Porch. John Mayer: That the length of the porch was twenty cubits is showed by Ezekiel 40:49. That there were posts, although not here expressed, is showed there also, and steps by which to go up to the porch, as standing on the top of Mount Zion. For the measures of this side and the other, each being five cubits, they together make ten. By this the Ten Commandments may not inaptly be understood, and by the three and three cubits of the gates, the one the faith of the blessed Trinity, the Father, Son and Holy Spirit, the other the three applications of the commandment against murder, against adultery and against swearing. For whoever will enter into life must keep the commandments both of the Old Testament and of the New, and he who believes shall be saved. True believing is in the Father, in the Son and in the Holy Spirit, as in the form of baptizing (Mk 16:16).

For the length of the porch is twenty cubits and the breadth eleven. Jerome will have corruption here set forth in the best of God's saints in this life, indeed even in those who carry a treasure in earthen vessels, the ministers of Christ. He does this because twenty is two tens, and the number two is never put to express good, but only the number one or three, and the number eleven comes one short of twelve, a perfect number, and therefore the apostle Paul accordingly speaks of himself, as is common to the least: *In me, that is, in my flesh dwells no good*, and *miserable man that I am, who shall deliver me from the body of this death?* But ten is a number of perfection, and,

[1]*Temple*, 286. [2]Lenker 6, 310-311* (WADB 11,1:406-408).

in the number of twenty, ten is doubled and eleven includes ten in it, and one more; and in him that had two talents, we find that the number two sets forth good. In those also that were called in the eleventh hour of the day, the number eleven is commended to us. I cannot subscribe to Jerome but rather conceive that double perfection is hereby set forth to be in those that are in the porch for a double righteousness: (1) Of imputation through faith in Christ; (2) Of sanctification, which is righteousness inherent by virtue of our regeneration, because of such as be regenerate, it is said, *He that is born of God sins not, neither can he*. And by the number eleven perfect righteousness with the author thereof one God, unity in Trinity, of whom we have it, and not of our selves, *Who cannot of ourselves think a good thought*. Commentary upon All the Prophets.[3]

The Temple Porch. John Bunyan: We come next to the porch of the temple that is commonly called Solomon's. (1) This porch was in the front of the house and so became the common way into the temple (1 Kings 6:3; 2 Chron 3:4). (2) This porch therefore was the place of reception in common for all, whether Jews or religious proselytes, who came to Jerusalem to worship (Acts 3:11; 5:12). (3) This porch had a door or gate belonging to it, but such as was seldom shut, except in declining times or when people put themselves into a rage against those better than themselves (2 Chron 29:7; Acts 21:28-30). (4) The gate of this porch was called Beautiful, even the Beautiful gate of the temple, and was that at which the lame man lay to beg for an alms of those who went in to worship (Acts 3).

Now, then, since this porch was the common place of reception for all worshipers, and the place also where they laid the beggars, it looks as if it were to be a type of the church's bosom for charity. Here the proselytes were entertained, here the beggars were relieved and received alms. These gates were seldom shut; and the houses of Christian compassion should be always open. This therefore beautified this gate, as charity beautifies any of the churches. Solomon's Temple Spiritualized.[4]

Spiritual Understanding of the Inner Temple. William Greenhill: "Of the signification of this temple." Some make the court belonging to it to represent the world and the temple to represent heaven. It may be considered whether the porch does not point out the common professor of the faith, the temple, the true saints, who are temples of the Spirit, and the holy of holies, the saints in glory, the condition of those made perfect. The true representation of this temple, I take it, is the body of our Lord Jesus Christ; both his body natural and his body mystical, namely, the church. An Exposition of Ezekiel.[5]

Spiritual Understanding of the Altar. John Mayer: *The altar of wood was three cubits high, and the length two cubits, and the corners, length and walls were of wood, and he said, this is the Table which is before the Lord* (Ezek 41:22). . . . This place seems to me to represent the turning of a golden altar that was under the Old Testament (where all outward glory was in the temple, by such glory to draw people in the nonage of the church to it, as children are drawn by goodly things) into an wooden table for the communion, that then should be celebrated at it, being metaphorically only called an altar. Now it is for the precious body and blood of Christ set thereon in remembrance of his sacrificing of himself once for our sins. It was three cubits high to show the great mystery of the elements there propounded, bread and wine, hiddenly exhibiting to the faithful Christ's body and blood to be truly received, which is a threefold mystery, the bodily eye seeing nothing but bread and wine,

[3]*Prophets*, 476. [4]*Temple*, 284. [5]*Exposition*, 783.

to the feeling there being nothing else felt, and to the taste of the palate, there being nothing else tasted. The length is two cubits denoting two things only given us, which are all that are necessary for our sustentation, meat and drink, not any object to be looked at and adored or to this end to be elevated or carried in procession as a remedy against any bodily evil, it being altogether a spirit. It is good, and to be used accordingly, yet with all due reverence, as Christ has ordained. COMMENTARY UPON ALL THE PROPHETS.[6]

THE PILLARS OF THE TEMPLE. WILLIAM GREENHILL: The strength of this temple was not everywhere alike. Some parts had pillars, some had none, or not equal to others. The chambers had not pillars, as the pillars of the court. So in the church of Christ, some parts of it have strong pillars, eminent teachers, whereas other parts are destitute wholly or have such as are weak. The church at Jerusalem had strong pillars in it, all the apostles, who were full of the Spirit, and taught infallibly. Other churches had no such pillars. AN EXPOSITION OF EZEKIEL.[7]

THE FOLDING DOORS. JOHN BUNYAN: These doors or gates were folding, and they opened by degrees. First, a quarter, and then a half, after that three quarters, and last of all the whole. These doors also hanged on hinges of gold and on posts made of the goodly olive tree (1 Kings 6:33-34; Ezek 41:23-24). These doors did represent Christ, as he is the way to the Father, as also did the door of the tabernacle, at which the people stood when they went to inquire of God. Wherefore, Christ says, "I am the door" (Jn 10:9).

. . . The leaves of this gate or door, as I told you before, were folding, and so, as was hinted, has something of signification in them. For by this means a person, especially a young disciple, may easily be mistaken, thinking that the whole passage, when yet but a part was open, whereas three parts might be yet kept undiscovered to him. For these doors, as I said before, were never yet set wide open. I mean, in the antitype. Never yet did a mortal see all the riches and fullness that is in Christ. So that I say, a newcomer, if he judged by present sight, especially if he saw but little, might easily be mistaken. . . . So, then, whoever you are that are come to the door, of which the temple door was a type, trust not to your first conceptions of things, but believe there is grace abundant. You know not yet what Christ can do; the doors are folding doors. He can "do exceeding abundantly above all that we can ask or think" (Eph 3:20). SOLOMON'S TEMPLE SPIRITUALIZED.[8]

42:13-20 *Holy Offerings*

THE MOST HOLY OFFERINGS. JOHN MAYER: The north and south chambers that are before the separate place are holy, where the priests that approach to the Lord shall eat the most holy things. Having spoken so much of the treasuries or chambers before, now he proceeds to tell for what use they served. Namely, it was for the priests attending in their courses to eat those parts of the offerings that were theirs by God's ordinance.

To put off and lay up their garments, wherein they ministered to the Lord, putting on other garments when they went out to the people to minister to them. Eating holy things in the holy place represented the eating at the Lord's Supper, not in any place indifferently, but in the place dedicated to his worship. So it was done even in the apostle's days, who says, *when you come together into one place, this is not to eat the Lord's body,* intimating by this, that it was there a custom then to congregate to one known public place, which was called the house of God. COMMENTARY UPON ALL THE PROPHETS.[9]

[6]*Prophets,* 484. [7]*Exposition,* 787. [8]*Temple,* 288. [9]*Prophets,* 487.

The Offerings a Type of Christ. William Greenhill: These offerings were types of Christ, who is our true meat offering, the bread of life, the nourishment of every hungry and thirsty soul. His flesh and his blood are meat and drink indeed. At his table we feed on him crucified, and so our meat offering. He is our sin offering and trespass offering. An Exposition of Ezekiel.[10]

[10]*Exposition*, 788.

43:1-27 The Glory Returns to the Temple

[1]*Then he led me to the gate, the gate facing east.* [2]*And behold, the glory of the God of*
Israel was coming from the east. And the sound of his coming was like the sound of many
waters, and the earth shone with his glory. [3]*And the vision I saw was just like the vision*
that I had seen when he[a] *came to destroy the city, and just like the vision that I had seen*
by the Chebar canal. And I fell on my face. [4]*As the glory of the* Lord *entered the temple*
by the gate facing east, [5]*the Spirit lifted me up and brought me into the inner court; and*
behold, the glory of the Lord *filled the temple.*

[6]*While the man was standing beside me, I heard one speaking to me out of the temple,*
[7]*and he said to me, "Son of man, this is the place of my throne and the place of the soles*
of my feet, where I will dwell in the midst of the people of Israel forever. And the house of
Israel shall no more defile my holy name, neither they, nor their kings, by their whoring
and by the dead bodies[b] *of their kings at their high places,*[c] [8]*by setting their threshold by*
my threshold and their doorposts beside my doorposts, with only a wall between me and
them. They have defiled my holy name by their abominations that they have committed,
so I have consumed them in my anger. [9]*Now let them put away their whoring and the*
dead bodies of their kings far from me, and I will dwell in their midst forever.

[10]*"As for you, son of man, describe to the house of Israel the temple, that they may be*
ashamed of their iniquities; and they shall measure the plan. [11]*And if they are ashamed*
of all that they have done, make known to them the design of the temple, its arrangement,
its exits and its entrances, that is, its whole design; and make known to them as well all
its statutes and its whole design and all its laws, and write it down in their sight, so that
they may observe all its laws and all its statutes and carry them out. [12]*This is the law of*
the temple: the whole territory on the top of the mountain all around shall be most holy.
Behold, this is the law of the temple.

[13]*"These are the measurements of the altar by cubits (the cubit being a cubit and a*
handbreadth):[d] *its base shall be one cubit high*[e] *and one cubit broad, with a rim of one*
span[f] *around its edge. And this shall be the height of the altar:* [14]*from the base on the*
ground to the lower ledge, two cubits, with a breadth of one cubit; and from the smaller

*ledge to the larger ledge, four cubits, with a breadth of one cubit; [15]and the altar hearth,
four cubits; and from the altar hearth projecting upward, four horns. [16]The altar hearth
shall be square, twelve cubits long by twelve broad. [17]The ledge also shall be square, four-
teen cubits long by fourteen broad, with a rim around it half a cubit broad, and its base
one cubit all around. The steps of the altar shall face east."*

*[18]And he said to me, "Son of man, thus says the Lord God: These are the ordinances
for the altar: On the day when it is erected for offering burnt offerings upon it and for
throwing blood against it, [19]you shall give to the Levitical priests of the family of Zadok,
who draw near to me to minister to me, declares the Lord God, a bull from the herd for
a sin offering. [20]And you shall take some of its blood and put it on the four horns of the
altar and on the four corners of the ledge and upon the rim all around. Thus you shall
purify the altar and make atonement for it. [21]You shall also take the bull of the sin of-
fering, and it shall be burned in the appointed place belonging to the temple, outside the
sacred area. [22]And on the second day you shall offer a male goat without blemish for a
sin offering; and the altar shall be purified, as it was purified with the bull. [23]When you
have finished purifying it, you shall offer a bull from the herd without blemish and a
ram from the flock without blemish. [24]You shall present them before the Lord, and the
priests shall sprinkle salt on them and offer them up as a burnt offering to the Lord.
[25]For seven days you shall provide daily a male goat for a sin offering; also, a bull from
the herd and a ram from the flock, without blemish, shall be provided. [26]Seven days shall
they make atonement for the altar and cleanse it, and so consecrate it.[g] [27]And when they
have completed these days, then from the eighth day onward the priests shall offer on the
altar your burnt offerings and your peace offerings, and I will accept you, declares the
Lord God."*

a Some Hebrew manuscripts and Vulgate; most Hebrew manuscripts *when I* **b** Or *the monuments*; also verse 9 **c** Or *at their deaths* **d** A *cubit* was about 18 inches or 45 centimeters; a *handbreadth* was about 3 inches or 7.5 centimeters **e** Or *its gutter shall be one cubit deep* **f** A *span* was about 9 inches or 22 centimeters **g** Hebrew *fill its hand*

Overview: In the first part of this chapter, Ezekiel sees the glory of God. Although our commentators agree that Ezekiel seeing the glory of God when looking eastward is significant and has something to do with Christ, they are not in agreement on exactly what this means. It may have reference to the greater glory of Christ or that Christ is the Sun of righteousness. Ezekiel is told that this spiritual temple is the place where Christ will dwell forever with all the faithful. This eternal habitation is the new Jerusalem and heaven itself.

The chapter ends with a description of the altar. Luther is struck by the dimensions of the altar. These dimensions would require a priest who is at least twenty-seven feet tall. The other commentators understand the altar as a type of Christ, who is our only altar for the atonement of sins.

Summary of the Chapter. Jakob Raupius: There are four things treated in this chapter. First, Ezekiel narrates how he saw the glory of the Lord enter into the temple, which he had described in earlier chapters, and how the Lord spoke from the temple itself. . . . Second, he indicates the holiness of the temple (Ezek 43:12). Third, he describes the altar of sacrifice in the temple (Ezek 43:13-18). Finally, God instructs how he ought to sanctify the altar and how it ought to be used for the worship of God (Ezek 43:18-27). COMMENTARY ON EZEKIEL.[1]

EZEKIEL SEES THE GLORY OF GOD. JOHN MAYER: Here for twelve verses the prophet, before he proceeds any further to describe other things about this temple, shows that he saw the glory of God again, as he had done when he went out to destroy, of which see Ezekiel 9–10 and as by the river Chebar. But as then his glory went out of the house, so now it went in and filled the house, and it went in by the gate looking eastward, to show that in the time of the gospel the church should through Christ set forth by the east be made more glorious than ever Solomon's temple was, in alluding to which Haggai says, *The Lord shall come and fill this house with more glory than the former* (Hag 2:7). COMMENTARY UPON ALL THE PROPHETS.[2]

THE GLORY SEEN FACING EAST. WILLIAM GREENHILL: The place was at the east gate. He was brought from the west side of the temple to the east gate, where he had this vision coming out of the east. Christ is the Sun of righteousness; and the sun's motion is from east, westward. So here, this glorious vision came out of the east and entered by the east gate, which led directly to the most holy place. It is the Lord Christ who brings us out of darkness to light and shows us the way into the temple and most holy place.

. . . From where did it come? "from the way of the east." Christ's star was seen in the east (Mt 2:2); his coming was from there (Zech 3:8; 6:12). Christ is called *anatole* by the Septuagint and *oriens* by the Vulgate, which is the east, because Christ should come from heaven and enlighten the dark world, as the sun does, when it rises in the east. Luke (Lk 1:78) calls Christ *anatole*, which we render "the dayspring," and may be rendered the east, for the day springs in the east first. Whether it is east or dayspring, it is from on high. Christ came from heaven to bring light into the blind world. Hence says Christ, "I am the light of the world" (Jn 8:12), the great light, the sun of it, which rising in the east, shines into the utmost parts of the west. AN EXPOSITION OF EZEKIEL.[3]

THE SPIRITUAL TEMPLE. JOHN MAYER: *The place of my throne, and the place of the soles of my feet, where I will dwell forever, in the midst of the children of Israel.* The prophet, having seen the house of God or church that should be under the gospel before represented, and the glory of God filling it, now hears the man who had led him about and measured all parts of it telling him for the comfort of all faithful Christians that here he would rule as king and dwell here among the faithful called the children of Israel forever. Daniel had before spoken about this in the spirit, saying, *This is my habitation, and here will I dwell.* By this he shows a difference between the material, and this spiritual temple, because he so dwelled in that that he left it again for their gross abominations among whom it was placed. But in this he promised to dwell and never to depart from here anymore. COMMENTARY UPON ALL THE PROPHETS.[4]

THE HOUSE OF GOD. WILLIAM GREENHILL: This house was to be the habitation of God's throne; a representation of new Jerusalem and heaven itself. Therefore it is styled not only holy but "most holy." The church of God has a good foundation. It is a house on a mountain, and that is strong (Job 39:28). Rocks and mountains are strong places; they stand immovable. The rock, or mountain, on which the church is founded and built is the Lord Christ (1 Cor 3:11), who is called "a mountain" (Dan 2:35); "a precious cornerstone, a sure foundation" (Is 28:16); a "rock" (1 Cor 10:4); "the

[1]*Commentarius Synopticus* (1655), 320. [2]*Prophets*, 489. [3]*Exposition*, 790. [4]*Prophets*, 489.

strength of Israel" (1 Sam 15:29); "the root of David" (Rev 22:16); and the upholder of all things (Heb 1:3). He upholds the world and the church.

The church of God is eminent and conspicuous. It is on the top of a mountain, and that mountain was very high (Ezek 40:2), where he saw this temple, which holds forth the visibility and eminency of the church under the gospel. An Exposition of Ezekiel.[5]

43:13-27 *The Altar*

A Mighty Tall Priest. Martin Luther: The altar shall be eleven cubits high and fourteen cubits wide at the top [Ezek 43:13–17], so that even if a priest manages to mount the steps, he must have an arm seven cubits long to reach onto the altar and arrange the sacrifice. That would have to be a pretty small priest too, to be fifteen or sixteen good, big cubits tall! [Luther's hypothetical priest would be about 27 feet tall with arms 12 feet long]. A New Preface to the Prophet Ezekiel.[6]

The Altar a Type of Christ. William Greenhill: This altar for burnt offerings was a type of Christ, as those of Moses and Solomon were (Ex 27:1; 2 Chron 4:1). This altar was but one. So Christ is our altar, and our only altar (Heb 13:10). The Christian church knows no other. An Exposition of Ezekiel.[7]

The Spiritual Understanding of the Altar. John Meyer: This altar sets forth Christ, of whom by the name of an altar it is spoken (Heb 13:10). And as of this altar, there is first one part but a cubit high and a cubit broad. So Christ at the first was but a poor despicable infant born of a poor virgin, yet set forth by a border to grace him. That is, shepherds coming out of the field, who were Jews, by the instigation of angels, to publish what they had seen and heard on the one side, and magi coming out of the east country, that were Gentiles, on the other side, to proclaim him king by the conduct of a star miraculously appearing to them.

Then there is a second part two cubits high and but one still broad. So Christ arising somewhat more in height in his youth, when he was but twelve years old, by the taste that he gave of his understanding among the doctors in the temple, yet kept at the same breadth, none were hereby won to him.

3. There was here another part four cubits higher, but yet one cubit only broad. So Christ being baptized, and beginning to preach and to work miracles, could yet win few or none to him but was as a poor despicable man still in the account of the great ones of this world.

4. Here was a hearth twelve cubits square; so Christ having not only wrought miracles in his life but at his death spread himself by his twelve apostles into all four parts of the world, so that they came from the east, west, north and south, as our Lord speaks, *To sit down with* Abraham, Isaac and Jacob in the kingdom of heaven.

5. As here were four horns, so the invincible strength of Christ was such that no opposition, when he went out by his apostles conquering, could withstand him. But he broke in pieces the four monarchies of the world, as the stone, of which Daniel speaks, falling out of the mountain and filling all the earth, broke all the parts of the image in pieces.

6. As the ledge next to the hearth was yet fourteen cubits larger square, so after a long time of persecution by heathen emperors there rose up a Christian, Constantine the Great, by whose means, and the Christian emperors succeeding him, Christ was enlarged more, all heathens being put down and idolaters not suffered anymore. Rabanus indeed in showing the spiritual meaning here

[5]*Exposition*, 797. [6]Lenker 6, 311* (WADB 11,1:408). [7]*Exposition*, 798.

agrees in the main about Christ set forth; but when he comes to this square of fourteen he says that the fourteen generations from Abraham to David, and fourteen from David to Jehoiakin and fourteen from him to Christ are set forth, endeavoring to make it hold thus according to the square here spoken of. Let whoever wishes to follow him; I rest in the sense above. And finally for the border last spoken of, this is the grace in which our Lord Jesus now is all over the Christian world set forth. He is by all people adored as a king, whose head and crown has a border about it of all manner of rich and precious stones. Commentary upon All the Prophets.[8]

The Sacrifices. William Greenhill: Here are three sorts of sacrifices mentioned, the burnt offering, the sin offering and the peace offering (Ezek 43:18-19, 27). Concerning these and their different rites, you may read (Lev 1; 6:24; 7:11-22). These sacrifices were not sufficient to expiate sin, but they were means of worship, leading them to Christ. An Exposition of Ezekiel.[9]

[8]*Prophets*, 491. [9]*Exposition*, 799.

44:1-31 The Prince, the Levites and the Priests

[1]Then he brought me back to the outer gate of the sanctuary, which faces east. And it was shut. [2]And the Lord said to me, "This gate shall remain shut; it shall not be opened, and no one shall enter by it, for the Lord, the God of Israel, has entered by it. Therefore it shall remain shut. [3]Only the prince may sit in it to eat bread before the Lord. He shall enter by way of the vestibule of the gate, and shall go out by the same way."

[4]Then he brought me by way of the north gate to the front of the temple, and I looked, and behold, the glory of the Lord filled the temple of the Lord. And I fell on my face. [5]And the Lord said to me, "Son of man, mark well, see with your eyes, and hear with your ears all that I shall tell you concerning all the statutes of the temple of the Lord and all its laws. And mark well the entrance to the temple and all the exits from the sanctuary. [6]And say to the rebellious house,[a] to the house of Israel, Thus says the Lord God: O house of Israel, enough of all your abominations, [7]in admitting foreigners, uncircumcised in heart and flesh, to be in my sanctuary, profaning my temple, when you offer to me my food, the fat and the blood. You[b] have broken my covenant, in addition to all your abominations. [8]And you have not kept charge of my holy things, but you have set others to keep my charge for you in my sanctuary.

[9]"Thus says the Lord God: No foreigner, uncircumcised in heart and flesh, of all the foreigners who are among the people of Israel, shall enter my sanctuary. [10]But the Levites

who went far from me, going astray from me after their idols when Israel went astray, shall bear their punishment.[c] *11They shall be ministers in my sanctuary, having oversight at the gates of the temple and ministering in the temple. They shall slaughter the burnt offering and the sacrifice for the people, and they shall stand before the people, to minister to them. 12Because they ministered to them before their idols and became a stumbling block of iniquity to the house of Israel, therefore I have sworn concerning them, declares the Lord GOD, and they shall bear their punishment. 13They shall not come near to me, to serve me as priest, nor come near any of my holy things and the things that are most holy, but they shall bear their shame and the abominations that they have committed. 14Yet I will appoint them to keep charge of the temple, to do all its service and all that is to be done in it.*

15"But the Levitical priests, the sons of Zadok, who kept the charge of my sanctuary when the people of Israel went astray from me, shall come near to me to minister to me. And they shall stand before me to offer me the fat and the blood, declares the Lord GOD. 16They shall enter my sanctuary, and they shall approach my table, to minister to me, and they shall keep my charge. 17When they enter the gates of the inner court, they shall wear linen garments. They shall have nothing of wool on them, while they minister at the gates of the inner court, and within. 18They shall have linen turbans on their heads, and linen undergarments around their waists. They shall not bind themselves with anything that causes sweat. 19And when they go out into the outer court to the people, they shall put off the garments in which they have been ministering and lay them in the holy chambers. And they shall put on other garments, lest they transmit holiness to the people with their garments. 20They shall not shave their heads or let their locks grow long; they shall surely trim the hair of their heads. 21No priest shall drink wine when he enters the inner court. 22They shall not marry a widow or a divorced woman, but only virgins of the offspring of the house of Israel, or a widow who is the widow of a priest. 23They shall teach my people the difference between the holy and the common, and show them how to distinguish between the unclean and the clean. 24In a dispute, they shall act as judges, and they shall judge it according to my judgments. They shall keep my laws and my statutes in all my appointed feasts, and they shall keep my Sabbaths holy. 25They shall not defile themselves by going near to a dead person. However, for father or mother, for son or daughter, for brother or unmarried sister they may defile themselves. 26After he has become clean, they shall count seven days for him. 27And on the day that he goes into the Holy Place, into the inner court, to minister in the Holy Place, he shall offer his sin offering, declares the Lord GOD.

28"This shall be their inheritance: I am their inheritance: and you shall give them no possession in Israel; I am their possession. 29They shall eat the grain offering, the sin offering, and the guilt offering, and every devoted thing in Israel shall be theirs. 30And the first of all the firstfruits of all kinds, and every offering of all kinds from all your offerings, shall belong to the priests. You shall also give to the priests the first of your dough, that a blessing may rest on your house. 31The priests shall not eat of anything, whether bird or beast, that has died of itself or is torn by wild animals.

a Septuagint; Hebrew lacks *house* **b** Septuagint, Syriac, Vulgate; Hebrew *they* **c** Or *iniquity;* also verse 12

Overview: Ezekiel is shown the east gate and told that it will remain closed. No one will ever enter through it because the Lord, the God of Israel, has entered through it. The modern reader may be somewhat surprised by what our commentators discuss with respect to this closed gate through which the Lord has passed. The issue for them is whether or not this is a reference to the perpetual virginity of Mary. Some argue that it is; others dismiss this as an improper reading of the text. The closed gate may be a reference to the gate of heaven through which no person could pass, except Jesus Christ, our high priest, who was without sin. The closed gate may be a figure of our hearts that must be opened only by the Lord and closed to all others. The rest of the chapter addresses the appearance and conduct of priests.

Summary of the Chapter. Jakob Raupius: In this chapter the prophet discusses the ministry of the religious rites to be performed in the new temple. Four general things are stated concerning this. First, he shows a certain privilege of the high priest (Ezek 44:1-3). Second, foreigners are excluded from the priesthood (Ezek 44:4-9). Third, he discusses the demotion of the rest of the Levites (Ezek 44:10-15). Fourth, he confirms the sons of Zadok in the priesthood and prescribes certain laws for them and gives them certain privileges (Ezek 44:15-31). Commentary on Ezekiel.[1]

44:1-2 *The Closed Gate and the Virgin Mary*

The Closed Gate and Mary. Johann Gerhard: Mary, the mother of the Lord, is a virgin and the closed gate; so also, Christ is born in virginal hearts that do not cling to the world or live in sin with it. All believing souls are closed gates on the living temple of God, through which only the Lord and no one else enters. For true faith opens the door of the heart for no one except for Christ alone and clings to no one except to Christ alone. That is why Christ did not want to find any room in this world, so that he might find room in our hearts; our heart is to be his cradle, and our faith is to be his swaddling clothes. Postilla.[2]

The Closed Gate and Perpetual Virginity. William Greenhill: What is meant by the gate shut is necessary to inquire. It was not the womb of the virgin, which was shut up after the birth of Christ, as popish interpreters expound it. Some of the ancients make it to be heavenly mysteries, which none know but the Father and the Son; some make it the Scripture, or the "book sealed with seven seals," which none could open but Christ. This shut gate rather notes the gate or entrance into heaven, which Adam by his fall had shut, so that no one, being sinful, could open it or enter. Only Jesus Christ our high priest has opened it and entered. An Exposition of Ezekiel.[3]

Mary and the Closed Gate. John Mayer: In the shutting of this gate, by reason of the Lord's entering in at it, so that none but the Prince might ever enter through it, has been commonly understood by antiquity to represent the mystery of Christ's incarnation. That is to say, his entering, by his divinity, into the Virgin Mary's womb, being with child by the Holy Spirit, and being born of her, after which her womb was ever shut up, so that no man else ever knew her, but she remained always a pure virgin. Jesus the King only entering in here, and thus putting a bar to all others for coming in, she never bearing another child. Indeed, it was a gross error of some to hold that they who are called the brethren of our Lord were by Joseph begotten of the Virgin Mary. They were his kinsmen only, as I have

[1] *Commentarius Synopticus* (1655), 326. [2] *Postilla* 1:112. [3] *Exposition*, 800.

showed in my exposition on the Gospels, and called his brethren according to the manner of the Hebrews.

Augustine writes the following about this gate being shut: "What is it, but that the Virgin Mary ever remained a virgin? And what that no man shall pass through it, but that Joseph should never go in to her? He has filled my belly with the Deity, but he has not evacuated it of chastity; I was not found in my conception without shame, but I was found in my childbearing without pain, might she well say."[4] The Greek Scholiast says that Christ supernaturally opened this gate never before opened, and being shut, kept it so naturally. Likewise Jerome, Ambrose and Chrysostom say. The shut gate was her virginity, and a closed garden and sealed fountain. The east gate might well set this forth for the reason before said, because Jesus was the east, the sun arising there. Zwingli says this. And this for the thing, by so many learned men agreed on, I believe to be true, that the womb of the Virgin Mary was always shut and that Joseph never knew her. COMMENTARY UPON ALL THE PROPHETS.[5]

THE CLOSED GATE IS A CLOSED GATE. JAKOB RAUPIUS: *And he brought me back,* that is, the man who spoke to him above (Ezek 40:3), *to the way of the gate of the outer sanctuary,* which is a peculiar way of naming the sacred place, just as the inner sanctuary is named the holy of holies, *that faces east, and it was closed. And the Lord said to me,* that is, he was speaking from the temple, as stated above (Ezek 43:6), *this gate shall remain shut, not to be opened, and no man shall enter by it,* which is to say no one shall walk through it, *for the Lord, the God of Israel, has entered in by it,* that is, he entered through it, *and is shall be shut,* that is, it will remain closed. COMMENTARY ON EZEKIEL.[6]

44:3-31 *Priests*

PRIESTLY VESTMENTS. WILLIAM GREENHILL: Here, and in the following verses (Ezek 44:17-31), are certain rules and instructions given forth for the priests. The first concerns their vestures and attire. When the sons of Zadok come to minister to the Lord, they must be clothed all in linen; no woolen garments must be on them, as it was in Moses' days (Ex 28:42-43; 29:27-29; Lev 16:4). They had linen bonnets, linen breeches, linen girdles and linen coats; woolen was not permitted them, because it is less pure than linen. And as those linen garments that Aaron and his sons had denoted the purity and innocence of Christ, so these, which the sons of Zadok had, denoted the purity and innocence of the ministers under Christ and the gospel. The twenty-four elders were clothed in white raiment (Rev 4:4); and those who served the Lord in his temple were arrayed with white robes (Rev 7:13, 15). The ministers of Christ ought to be holy, chaste, unblamable and patterns of virtue to others (1 Tim 4:12; 2 Tim 2:22; Tit 1:7-8). When they savor the things of the flesh, they are brutish and have on woolen garments, which should not be. They are to avoid all things that may make them infamous and to hear ill. Sweat is an unsavory thing. They must not wear anything that causes that, signifying they must do nothing that may justly cause an ill savor. Their loins must be girded with sincerity, and their conversations such as may be inoffensive before God and people. AN EXPOSITION OF EZEKIEL.[7]

PRIESTLY MARRIAGE. WILLIAM GREENHILL: A fourth rule is touching their marriage. They are not forbidden to marry but are cautioned about the same and shown whom they must not marry, not a widow or one divorced. And Moses mentions two more (Lev 21:14), a profane one and a harlot, which they might not

[4]Cf. Augustine *Sermon* 184.1 (*WSA* III/6, 17). [5]*Prophets*, 493. [6]*Commentarius Synopticus* (1655), 326. [7]*Exposition*, 804.

take; a virgin or a priest's widow they might, and these must "be of the seed of the house of Israel." Strange virgins or strange widows they might not join themselves to. The scope of the words is that they should marry them who were modest, chaste, pious, sober and well-educated, so that they might be a comfort and an honor to their husbands in that office. The priests were a type of Christ, and the ministers of the gospel are in Christ's stead to the people. Marriage represents the mystical union and marriage between Christ and his church. Therefore, of all men, they should see to it what wives they take, even such as will be subject in all things, as the church is to Christ (Eph 5:24); and so remind others of their duty. AN EXPOSITION OF EZEKIEL.[8]

[8]*Exposition*, 804-5.

45:1–46:24 DIVISION OF THE LAND AND HOLY DAYS

1"When you allot the land as an inheritance, you shall set apart for the LORD a portion of the land as a holy district, 25,000 cubits[a] long and 20,000[b] cubits broad. It shall be holy throughout its whole extent. 2Of this a square plot of 500 by 500 cubits shall be for the sanctuary, with fifty cubits for an open space around it. 3And from this measured district you shall measure off a section 25,000 cubits long and 10,000 broad, in which shall be the sanctuary, the Most Holy Place. 4It shall be the holy portion of the land. It shall be for the priests, who minister in the sanctuary and approach the LORD to minister to him, and it shall be a place for their houses and a holy place for the sanctuary. 5Another section, 25,000 cubits long and 10,000 cubits broad, shall be for the Levites who minister at the temple, as their possession for cities to live in.[c]

6"Alongside the portion set apart as the holy district you shall assign for the property of the city an area 5,000 cubits broad and 25,000 cubits long. It shall belong to the whole house of Israel.

7"And to the prince shall belong the land on both sides of the holy district and the property of the city, alongside the holy district and the property of the city, on the west and on the east, corresponding in length to one of the tribal portions, and extending from the western to the eastern boundary 8of the land. It is to be his property in Israel. And my princes shall no more oppress my people, but they shall let the house of Israel have the land according to their tribes.

9"Thus says the Lord GOD: Enough, O princes of Israel! Put away violence and oppression, and execute justice and righteousness. Cease your evictions of my people, declares the Lord GOD.

10"You shall have just balances, a just ephah, and a just bath.[d] 11The ephah and the bath shall be of the same measure, the bath containing one tenth of a homer,[e] and the ephah one tenth of a homer; the homer shall be the standard measure. 12The shekel shall be twenty gerahs;[f] twenty shekels plus twenty-five shekels plus fifteen shekels shall be your mina.[g]

13"This is the offering that you shall make: one sixth of an ephah from each homer of wheat, and one sixth of an ephah from each homer of barley, 14and as the fixed portion of oil, measured in baths, one tenth of a bath from each cor[h] (the cor, like the homer, contains ten baths).[i] 15And one sheep from every flock of two hundred, from the watering places of Israel for grain offering, burnt offering, and peace offerings, to make atonement for them, declares the Lord God. 16All the people of the land shall be obliged to give this offering to the prince in Israel. 17It shall be the prince's duty to furnish the burnt offerings, grain offerings, and drink offerings, at the feasts, the new moons, and the Sabbaths, all the appointed feasts of the house of Israel: he shall provide the sin offerings, grain offerings, burnt offerings, and peace offerings, to make atonement on behalf of the house of Israel.

18"Thus says the Lord God: In the first month, on the first day of the month, you shall take a bull from the herd without blemish, and purify the sanctuary. 19The priest shall take some of the blood of the sin offering and put it on the doorposts of the temple, the four corners of the ledge of the altar, and the posts of the gate of the inner court. 20You shall do the same on the seventh day of the month for anyone who has sinned through error or ignorance; so you shall make atonement for the temple.

21"In the first month, on the fourteenth day of the month, you shall celebrate the Feast of the Passover, and for seven days unleavened bread shall be eaten. 22On that day the prince shall provide for himself and all the people of the land a young bull for a sin offering. 23nd on the seven days of the festival he shall provide as a burnt offering to the Lord seven young bulls and seven rams without blemish, on each of the seven days; and a male goat daily for a sin offering. 24And he shall provide as a grain offering an ephah for each bull, an ephah for each ram, and a hin[j] of oil to each ephah. 25In the seventh month, on the fifteenth day of the month and for the seven days of the feast, he shall make the same provision for sin offerings, burnt offerings, and grain offerings, and for the oil.

46 *"Thus says the Lord God: The gate of the inner court that faces east shall be shut on the six working days, but on the Sabbath day it shall be opened, and on the day of the new moon it shall be opened. 2The prince shall enter by the vestibule of the gate from outside, and shall take his stand by the post of the gate. The priests shall offer his burnt offering and his peace offerings, and he shall worship at the threshold of the gate. Then he shall go out, but the gate shall not be shut until evening. 3The people of the land shall bow down at the entrance of that gate before the Lord on the Sabbaths and on the new moons. 4The burnt offering that the prince offers to the Lord on the Sabbath day shall be six lambs without blemish and a ram without blemish. 5And the grain offering with the ram shall be an ephah,[k] and the grain offering with the lambs shall be as much as he is able, together with a hin[l] of oil to each ephah. 6On the day of the new moon he shall offer a bull from the herd without blemish, and six lambs and a ram, which shall be without blemish. 7As a grain offering he shall provide an ephah with the bull and an ephah with the ram, and with the lambs as much as he is able, together with a hin of oil to each ephah. 8When the prince enters, he shall enter by the vestibule of the gate, and he shall go out by the same way.*

9"When the people of the land come before the Lord at the appointed feasts, he who enters by the north gate to worship shall go out by the south gate, and he who enters by the south gate shall go out by the north gate: no one shall return by way of the gate by which he entered, but each shall go out straight ahead. 10When they enter, the prince shall enter with them, and when they go out, he shall go out.

11"At the feasts and the appointed festivals, the grain offering with a young bull shall be an ephah, and with a ram an ephah, and with the lambs as much as one is able to give, together with a hin of oil to an ephah. 12When the prince provides a freewill offering, either a burnt offering or peace offerings as a freewill offering to the Lord, the gate facing east shall be opened for him. And he shall offer his burnt offering or his peace offerings as he does on the Sabbath day. Then he shall go out, and after he has gone out the gate shall be shut.

13"You shall provide a lamb a year old without blemish for a burnt offering to the Lord daily; morning by morning you shall provide it. 14And you shall provide a grain offering with it morning by morning, one sixth of an ephah, and one third of a hin of oil to moisten the flour, as a grain offering to the Lord. This is a perpetual statute. 15Thus the lamb and the meal offering and the oil shall be provided, morning by morning, for a regular burnt offering.

16"Thus says the Lord God: If the prince makes a gift to any of his sons as his inheritance, it shall belong to his sons. It is their property by inheritance. 17But if he makes a gift out of his inheritance to one of his servants, it shall be his to the year of liberty. Then it shall revert to the prince; surely it is his inheritance—it shall belong to his sons. 18The prince shall not take any of the inheritance of the people, thrusting them out of their property. He shall give his sons their inheritance out of his own property, so that none of my people shall be scattered from his property."

19Then he brought me through the entrance, which was at the side of the gate, to the north row of the holy chambers for the priests, and behold, a place was there at the extreme western end of them. 20And he said to me, "This is the place where the priests shall boil the guilt offering and the sin offering, and where they shall bake the grain offering, in order not to bring them out into the outer court and so transmit holiness to the people."

21Then he brought me out to the outer court and led me around to the four corners of the court. And behold, in each corner of the court there was another court—22in the four corners of the court were small[m] courts, forty cubits[n] long and thirty broad; the four were of the same size. 23On the inside, around each of the four courts was a row of masonry, with hearths made at the bottom of the rows all around. 24Then he said to me, "These are the kitchens where those who minister at the temple shall boil the sacrifices of the people."

a A *cubit* was about 18 inches or 45 centimeters **b** Septuagint; Hebrew *ten* **c** Septuagint; Hebrew *as their possession, twenty chambers* **d** An *ephah* was about 3/5 of a bushel or 22 liters; a *bath* was about 6 gallons or 22 liters **e** A *homer* was about 6 bushels or 220 liters **f** A *shekel* was about 2/5 ounce or 11 grams; a *gerah* was about 1/50 ounce or 0.6 gram **g** A *mina* was about 1 1/4 pounds or 0.6 kilogram **h** A *cor* was about 6 bushels or 220 liters **i** See Vulgate; Hebrew *(ten baths are a homer, for ten baths are a homer)* **j** A *hin* was about 4 quarts or 3.5 liters **k** An *ephah* was about 3/5 bushel or 22 liters **l** A *hin* was about 4 quarts or 3.5 liters **m** Septuagint, Syriac, Vulgate; the meaning of the Hebrew word is uncertain **n** A *cubit* was about 18 inches or 45 centimeters

Overview: The next two chapters deal with the division of the land, specifically where the priests are to reside, and the sacrifices to be offered by the people. The division of the land should be understood spiritually, not literally, as pointing to the eschatological completion of the church of Christ. The sacrifices all point to Christ and were fulfilled in him. We also see in these oblations a reference to infant baptism and the Lord's Supper. Finally, a distinction is made between the duties of the prince and the priests. Here a separation between church and state is observed. The prince protects the state but does not interfere with worship, which belongs to the office of priest.

A Description of the Holy Land. John Mayer: From here to the end of this prophecy is a description of the Holy Land, its dimensions and the divisions of it among the twelve tribes of Israel. And he begins with a part first to be divided from the whole for the priests and Levites, which is in the midst of the temple and courts before described. Commentary upon All the Prophets.[1]

A Difficult Passage. William Greenhill: Having laid down the platform and measures of the temple, he comes now to the division and measuring of the land, wherein things are dark, difficult and deep, not to be attempted by human strength but by the help of Christ's Spirit, which makes dark things light, difficult things easy and sounds the greatest depths.

. . . There was a distinction of the land of Canaan in Moses' and Joshua's days (Num 34, 35; Josh 13, 21). But this division differs much from the same, and when the Jews returned from Babylon, there was no such division made of the land. Had it been, Ezra or Nehemiah would have made mention of it. This division, therefore, is not to be understood literally but spiritually, and the completing of it to be looked for in the church of Christ, not in the Jewish state or temple. Here, then, seems to be a spiritual lotting, and bringing people out of Judaism and heathenism into the kingdom of Christ and fellowship of the gospel. . . . The work of grace, and bringing of people into the church, is free; nothing in people, or from people, procures it. An Exposition of Ezekiel.[2]

The City and the Church. John Mayer: For the city, which is said to be for the whole house of Israel, next to this holy portion, it must likewise be 25,000 long but 5,000 broad, and so less by half than it. From this is shown the following.

1. We see that where Christ sets up his ministry in any country, it is first and chiefly to be taken care of by his faithful people and to be provided for in respect of maintenance, as here is enjoined, that provision should be made out of the whole land of Canaan, for the temple and priests first, dividing a proportion of ground for this use, and then for the city, Jerusalem and the king, and all the other tribes of Israel, as hereafter follows. And as the first fruits of old were first taken and brought to the house of the Lord, like to which this proportion of ground is showed to be by saying, *You shall offer a heave offering to the Lord,* such a length and breadth, because the first fruits are often called a heave offering.

2. We see that the maintenance of Christ's ministers ought to be very large. As here there is so much more ground allotted to the priests and Levites, as to the whole city of Jerusalem, which was so populous, and the rendezvous of all the tribes at sundry times to resort to and to continue many days together, there in the worship and service of God. For this reason, it needed to have large precincts.

3. We see that of Christ's ministers, as well as of the old temple, there should be two sorts, presbyters or bishops and deacons.

4. We see that as the temple, so the church,

[1]*Prophets*, 499. [2]*Exposition*, 805.

in the time of the gospel, is but one true catholic and apostolic, although the countries where it is planted be many, and the particular congregations in each country many, and therefore the Lord showed Ezekiel no more but one.

5. We see that a proportion of lands and houses near to the sanctuaries or places dedicated to meet in about the worship of God should be laid out for the ministers that they may be near the place where they ought to officiate. Commentary upon All the Prophets.[3]

45:13–46:24 *The Sacrifices*

The Sacrifices. William Greenhill: All the oblations here, and sacrifices, were types of Christ. The wheat, barley, the oil, the lamb, the sin offering, the meat offering, the burnt offering and the peace offering all represented Christ and were fulfilled by him. An Exposition of Ezekiel.[4]

The Lord's Supper and Infant Baptism. John Mayer: For the oblation on the seventh day . . . I take it to mean that before the Passover, which follows (Ezek 45:21), we must be sanctified. That is, before the taking of holy communion, for *Christ is our passover,* whose flesh and blood is there eaten and drunk, and this sanctifying is likewise by prayer for any to be admitted into the Christian congregation, which is God's house, that has formerly gone astray, as he was blindly led in the way of superstition or other gross sins but is now converted. Or that is simple and ignorant, as little children are, for sanctifying whom by prayer and blessing them, our Lord gave us an example; when being brought to him he took them in his arms and blessed them, and that this may be done to little ones at a week old is showed by saying, *it shall be done for the simple the seventh day,* and so he says, *you shall reconcile the house* or *make good propositions to the house,* using the word *house* in another sense, namely, for those that were contained in the house of God. . . .

Something then must be done by God's minister, as to sanctify a building, so a soul, which till it is done, God is not reconciled. For by nature we are children of wrath and so need reconciliation with him so soon as we are born, and how is this to be made but by his minister's prayers, the infant being brought to him, as they were to his Master, by his prayers to be blessed and to be to God reconciled. Now the church of God under the New Testament never brought infants to his priests to be thus blessed, but when to be baptized, knowing well that if there is no regeneration, there can be no reconciliation, from that saying of his, *Unless one be born again of water and the Holy Spirit he cannot enter into the kingdom of heaven* (Jn 3:5). It is then of no force when it is argued that the apostles were not commanded to baptize infants and therefore they ought not to be baptized. It is enough that they must be sanctified and reconciled by sacrifice, which none can be but by being regenerate; therefore they must come to the water and blessing of the minister both, since regeneration for infants is inseparable from water, and baptizing there with it in the name of the Father, Son and Holy Spirit.

They that are able to believe are, when they believe through the preaching of the Word, hereby regenerate (Jas 1:17; 1 Pet 1:23). Infants are not thus capable of regeneration, and so of reconciliation, but only by baptism accompanied with faithful prayers. It is well noted by Lyra that these two ordinances for the cleansing of the sanctuary, and the erroneous and simple on the first and seventh day are new and here first made, neither of them being in the canon of the ordinances made by Moses, and therefore everyone must be here convinced that they properly concern the time of the New Testament. If so, then we must inquire who are meant by the simple, that must be reconciled? And who by those that have erred, for that they are not both one is plain, because he that has erred but is

[3]*Prophets,* 500. [4]*Exposition,* 809.

now turned from his error is not simple but wise to salvation; little ones then must be meant by the simple, and therefore it is most true that has been already said touching them. COMMENTARY UPON ALL THE PROPHETS.[5]

CHURCH AND STATE. WILLIAM GREENHILL: The second verse (Ezek 46:2) tells us of the prince, his entering by the way of the porch and standing by the post of the gate. It tells us where he was to worship, but also that he might not come into the court. If we understand this of the secular prince, four things are here to be considered:

1. That the prince must not enter into the inner court; he must not meddle with the priestly office or things of God. Princes may not change anything in the worship of God, abrogate or institute aught by their wills or power. . . .

2. They are to countenance and maintain the worship of God. The prince must stand at the post of the gate and see that the priests do their office. . . .

3. That princes must worship the Lord publicly on sabbath days and when there are special occasions, like all other people do. . . .

4. They must not impede the worship of God. The prince shall go forth, but the gate shall not be shut where he has worshiped; he must not hinder others. . . .

If we take the prince here to be Christ, as Oecolampadius and Polanus do, then his coming to and standing by the post of the gate, his sacrificing and worshiping, prefigure his coming in the flesh and his standing at the gate of heaven for us, offering up prayers and supplications for us. AN EXPOSITION OF EZEKIEL.[6]

[5]*Prophets*, 504-5. [6]*Exposition*, 811.

47:1–48:29 THE RIVER FROM THE TEMPLE AND DIVISON OF LAND

[1]Then he brought me back to the door of the temple, and behold, water was issuing
from below the threshold of the temple toward the east (for the temple faced east). The
water was flowing down from below the south end of the threshold of the temple, south
of the altar. [2]Then he brought me out by way of the north gate and led me around on the
outside to the outer gate that faces toward the east; and behold, the water was trickling
out on the south side.

[3]Going on eastward with a measuring line in his hand, the man measured a thousand
cubits,[a] and then led me through the water, and it was ankle-deep. [4]Again he measured
a thousand, and led me through the water, and it was knee-deep. Again he measured a
thousand, and led me through the water, and it was waist-deep. [5]Again he measured a
thousand, and it was a river that I could not pass through, for the water had risen. It
was deep enough to swim in, a river that could not be passed through. [6]And he said to
me, "Son of man, have you seen this?"

Then he led me back to the bank of the river. [7]As I went back, I saw on the bank of the
river very many trees on the one side and on the other. [8]And he said to me, "This water

flows toward the eastern region and goes down into the Arabah, and enters the sea;[b] when the water flows into the sea, the water will become fresh.[c] 9And wherever the river goes,[d] every living creature that swarms will live, and there will be very many fish. For this water goes there, that the waters of the sea[e] may become fresh; so everything will live where the river goes. 10Fishermen will stand beside the sea. From Engedi to Eneglaim it will be a place for the spreading of nets. Its fish will be of very many kinds, like the fish of the Great Sea.[f] 11But its swamps and marshes will not become fresh; they are to be left for salt. 12And on the banks, on both sides of the river, there will grow all kinds of trees for food. Their leaves will not wither, nor their fruit fail, but they will bear fresh fruit every month, because the water for them flows from the sanctuary. Their fruit will be for food, and their leaves for healing."

13Thus says the Lord God: "This is the boundary[g] by which you shall divide the land for inheritance among the twelve tribes of Israel. Joseph shall have two portions. 14And you shall divide equally what I swore to give to your fathers. This land shall fall to you as your inheritance.

15"This shall be the boundary of the land: On the north side, from the Great Sea by way of Hethlon to Lebo-hamath, and on to Zedad,[h] 16Berothah, Sibraim (which lies on the border between Damascus and Hamath), as far as Hazer-hatticon, which is on the border of Hauran. 17So the boundary shall run from the sea to Hazar-enan, which is on the northern border of Damascus, with the border of Hamath to the north.[i] This shall be the north side.[j]

18"On the east side, the boundary shall run between Hauran and Damascus; along the Jordan between Gilead and the land of Israel; to the eastern sea and as far as Tamar.[k] This shall be the east side.

19"On the south side, it shall run from Tamar as far as the waters of Meribah-kadesh, from there along the Brook of Egypt[l] to the Great Sea. This shall be the south side.

20"On the west side, the Great Sea shall be the boundary to a point opposite Lebo-hamath. This shall be the west side.

21"So you shall divide this land among you according to the tribes of Israel. 22You shall allot it as an inheritance for yourselves and for the sojourners who reside among you and have had children among you. They shall be to you as native-born children of Israel. With you they shall be allotted an inheritance among the tribes of Israel. 23In whatever tribe the sojourner resides, there you shall assign him his inheritance, declares the Lord God.

48 "These are the names of the tribes: Beginning at the northern extreme, beside the way of Hethlon to Lebo-hamath, as far as Hazar-enan (which is on the northern border of Damascus over against Hamath), and[m] extending from the east side to the west,[n] Dan, one portion. 2Adjoining the territory of Dan, from the east side to the west, Asher, one portion. 3Adjoining the territory of Asher, from the east side to the west, Naphtali, one portion. 4Adjoining the territory of Naphtali, from the east side to the west, Manasseh, one portion. 5Adjoining the territory of Manasseh, from the east side to the west, Ephraim, one portion. 6Adjoining the territory of Ephraim, from the east side to the west, Reuben, one portion. 7Adjoining the territory of Reuben, from the east side to the west, Judah, one portion.

8"Adjoining the territory of Judah, from the east side to the west, shall be the portion which you shall set apart, 25,000 cubits[o] in breadth, and in length equal to one of the tribal portions, from the east side to the west, with the sanctuary in the midst of it. 9The

portion that you shall set apart for the LORD shall be 25,000 cubits in length, and 20,000[p]
in breadth. 10These shall be the allotments of the holy portion: the priests shall have an
allotment measuring 25,000 cubits on the northern side, 10,000 cubits in breadth on the
western side, 10,000 in breadth on the eastern side, and 25,000 in length on the southern
side, with the sanctuary of the LORD in the midst of it. 11This shall be for the consecrated
priests, the sons of Zadok, who kept my charge, who did not go astray when the people of
Israel went astray, as the Levites did. 12And it shall belong to them as a special portion
from the holy portion of the land, a most holy place, adjoining the territory of the Levites.
13And alongside the territory of the priests, the Levites shall have an allotment 25,000
cubits in length and 10,000 in breadth. The whole length shall be 25,000 cubits and the
breadth 20,000.[q] 14They shall not sell or exchange any of it. They shall not alienate this
choice portion of the land, for it is holy to the LORD.

15"The remainder, 5,000 cubits in breadth and 25,000 in length, shall be for common
use for the city, for dwellings and for open country. In the midst of it shall be the city,
16and these shall be its measurements: the north side 4,500 cubits, the south side 4,500,
the east side 4,500, and the west side 4,500. 17And the city shall have open land: on the
north 250 cubits, on the south 250, on the east 250, and on the west 250. 18The remain-
der of the length alongside the holy portion shall be 10,000 cubits to the east, and 10,000
to the west, and it shall be alongside the holy portion. Its produce shall be food for the
workers of the city. 19And the workers of the city, from all the tribes of Israel, shall till
it. 20The whole portion that you shall set apart shall be 25,000 cubits square, that is, the
holy portion together with the property of the city.

21"What remains on both sides of the holy portion and of the property of the city shall
belong to the prince. Extending from the 25,000 cubits of the holy portion to the east
border, and westward from the 25,000 cubits to the west border, parallel to the tribal por-
tions, it shall belong to the prince. The holy portion with the sanctuary of the temple shall
be in its midst. 22It shall be separate from the property of the Levites and the property
of the city, which are in the midst of that which belongs to the prince. The portion of the
prince shall lie between the territory of Judah and the territory of Benjamin.

23"As for the rest of the tribes: from the east side to the west, Benjamin, one portion.
24Adjoining the territory of Benjamin, from the east side to the west, Simeon, one por-
tion. 25Adjoining the territory of Simeon, from the east side to the west, Issachar, one
portion. 26Adjoining the territory of Issachar, from the east side to the west, Zebulun,
one portion. 27Adjoining the territory of Zebulun, from the east side to the west, Gad,
one portion. 28And adjoining the territory of Gad to the south, the boundary shall run
from Tamar to the waters of Meribah-kadesh, from there along the Brook of Egypt[r] to
the Great Sea.[s] 29This is the land that you shall allot as an inheritance among the tribes
of Israel, and these are their portions, declares the Lord GOD."

a A *cubit* was about 18 inches or 45 centimeters **b** That is, the *Dead Sea* **c** Hebrew *will be healed;* also verses 9, 11 **d** Septuagint, Syriac, Vulgate, Targum; Hebrew *the two rivers go* **e** Hebrew lacks *the waters of the sea* **f** That is, *the Mediterranean Sea;* also verses 15, 19, 20 **g** Probable reading; Hebrew *The valley of the boundary* **h** Septuagint; Hebrew *the entrance of Zedad, Hamath* **i** The meaning of the Hebrew is uncertain **j** Probable reading; Hebrew *and as for the north side* **k** Compare Syriac; Hebrew *to the eastern sea you shall measure* **l** Hebrew lacks *of Egypt* **m** Probable reading; Hebrew *and they shall be his* **n** Septuagint (compare verses 2-8); Hebrew *the east side the west* **o** A *cubit* was about 18 inches or 45 centimeters **p** Compare 45:1; Hebrew *ten* **q** Septuagint; Hebrew *10,000* **r** Hebrew lacks of *Egypt* **s** That is, *the Mediterranean Sea*

OVERVIEW: Ezekiel is shown a life-giving river that flows out of the city. These are spiritual waters. Our commentators suggest either the waters of baptism or the doctrine of the gospel to be here signified. Either way the significance is that water cleanses and quenches thirst, as does the gospel of forgiveness and life found in Jesus alone. The fountain and source of these spiritual waters is Christ.

Ezekiel was shown the abundance of flourishing trees along the river. Here are signified the flourishing people of God who embrace the true faith. These faithful are rooted along the river, which is Christ, and bear much fruit. Ezekiel also sees the abundance of fish in the river. If the trees are the mature believers rooted in Christ, then these small fish are the baptized infants of believers.

The end of Ezekiel 47 and the whole of Ezekiel 48 return to the issue of the division of the land. This time the land is divided according to the tribes of Israel and the priests. Once again our commentators give a spiritual interpretation of this division.

SUMMARY OF THE CHAPTER. JOHN OWEN: This prophecy contains a vision of the glorious, holy, gospel state of the church, under the representation of a most glorious temple, incomparably excelling that built of old by Solomon; an exposition whereof we have (2 Cor 3:6-8, etc.).

The beginning of this chapter sets out the way and means of the calling and gathering of the gospel churches, whose worship is to be so glorious; and this is under the vision of "waters issuing out of the sanctuary," to heal and quicken all places to which they come. SERMON.[1]

47:1-5 *The River*

WATER BELOW THE THRESHOLD. WILLIAM GREENHILL: "And behold, water issued out from under," Vilalpandus makes these waters to be those subterranean waters that were carried in pipes underground and issued forth into the priests' court, to wash the sacrifices and purge away the blood, excrements and filth occasioned by the slaying of so many sacrifices. Certainly had there not been aqueducts about Solomon's temple to have cleansed the places where the sacrifices were slain and prepared, it would have been an unsavory and unhealthful place. These waters issued forth, some from the threshold, some from the south side of the altar, and so ran away. From these waters, the Lord takes occasion to speak of spiritual waters. AN EXPOSITION OF EZEKIEL.[2]

WATER BELOW THE THRESHOLD. JOHN BUNYAN: Although in the holy relation of the building of the temple no mention is made of these waters but only of the mount on which and the materials with which the king did build it, yet it seems to me that in that mount, and there too where the temple was built, there was a spring of living water. This seems more than probable, by Ezekiel 47:1, where he says, "He brought me again to the door of the house, and behold, waters issued out from under the threshold of the house eastward, for the forefront of the house stood toward the east, and the waters came down from under, from the right side of the house, at the south side of the altar." So again, "And a fountain shall come forth of the house of the Lord and shall water the valley of Shittim" (Joel 3:18). Nor was the spring, wherever was the first appearance of these holy waters, but in the sanctuary, which is the holiest of all (Ezek 47:12), where the mercy seat stood, which in Revelation is called "the throne of God, and of the Lamb" (Rev 22:1-2).

. . . This water is said in Ezekiel and Revelation to have the tree of life grow on the

[1]Owen, *Works* 9:179. [2]*Exposition*, 815. Juan Baptista Vilalpandus (1552–1608) was a Spanish Jesuit scholar who published works on exegesis and architecture. He is best known for his commentary on Ezekiel (1596), which he coauthored with Jerome Prado.

banks of it and was a type of the Word and Spirit of God, by which Christ himself sanctified himself, in order to worship as high priest (Ezek 47; Rev 22). And also this water is that which heals all those that shall be saved and by which, they being sanctified thereby also, do all their works of worship and service acceptably, through Jesus Christ our Lord. This water therefore is said to go forth into the sea, the world, and to heal its fish, the sinners therein; indeed, this is that water of which Christ Jesus our Lord says, "Whoever shall drink thereof shall live forever" (Ezek 47:8-10; Zech 14:8; Jn 4:14). Solomon's Temple Spiritualized.[3]

The Waters. John Owen: By the waters here mentioned is the preaching of the gospel intended. And we may observe of them, first, their rise, which was from the sanctuary; second, their progress, they increased until they became a river than none could pass over; third, their effects or efficacy, for they healed all waters where they came and quickened, or cause to live, the fishes that were in them. I must not long insist on these particulars.

First. The house, or temple, from which these waters issues may be taken two ways: (1) Mystically, to denote only the presence of God. God dwelled in his temple; from there come these waters, from his presence. He sends out the word of the gospel for the conversion and healing of the nations (Ps 110:2). (2) Figuratively, and that either for the place where the temple of old stood, that is, Jerusalem, as the preaching of the gospel was to go forth from Jerusalem, and the sound of it from there to proceed to all the world (Is 41:27, 52:7; Acts 1:4, 8); or for the church of Christ and his apostles, the first glorious, spiritual temple to God, from where these waters issued.

Second. Their progress, which is described by degrees, it being at first small—few people preaching it, and to a few—but afterward increasing until it filled the whole earth. Third. The effects mentioned or ascribed to these waters are two—quickening and healing, which I shall not in general speak farther to. Sermon.[4]

The Waters Signify Baptism. John Mayer: Touching these waters, it is said according to the letter that from the temple of old did issue waters in abundance to wash away the blood of the sacrifices, and all the dust and ashes and filth of the temple in a wonderful manner continually, which otherwise, by reason of the abundance of beasts brought there from time to time, could not have been kept sweet. But by these waters the Lord showed the waters of baptism and the doctrine of the gospel issuing out of the temple, at Jerusalem, where Christ taught in great abundance to the watering of all nations. Touching these waters also it is spoken (Zech 14:8), running towards the east and the west, to show the eastern and western churches, whereby this doctrine the countries and nations are watered. Commentary upon All the Prophets.[5]

Christ Reveals What Is Necessary to Know. William Greenhill: The scholars of Christ ought to be content with what it pleases the Lord Christ to make known to them and to rest satisfied therewith. Ezekiel troubles not himself or Christ about the depth of the river, the multitude of waters and several measurements. But being set down on the bank of the river, he is content to see and hear what the Lord should show him and speak to him. There is an itch in people to know things kept secret and hidden. Many, through curiosity, prying into such things, have prejudiced themselves and others. In Genesis 3:6 Eve did so. Let us acquiesce in what Christ reveals and not thirst after hidden secrets, lest we believe lies. An Exposition of Ezekiel.[6]

[3]*Temple*, 316. [4]Owen, *Works* 9:179-80. [5]*Prophets*, 512. [6]*Exposition*, 819.

47:6-8 *The Trees*

The Trees. John Mayer: By this river were many trees on the one side and on the other. Here the flourishing estate of men and women embracing the true faith is set forth, who are now like to trees planted by the river's side, growing and bringing forth fruit in due season, the Word of God and the knowledge communicated to them, being as waters moistening the roots of trees and making them thus to do. Commentary upon All the Prophets.[7]

The Trees Signify the Saints. William Greenhill: As the waters were mystical, so are these trees. They have a mystical and spiritual signification. They signify the saints under the gospel, those who are true Christians. Such are not unfitly compared with trees, for they resemble them in many respects. (1) Trees have life in them; so true Christians have life in them. . . . (2) Trees are rooted in the firm earth, in rocks and mountains; and true Christians are rooted in Christ, who is a firm and solid Rock. An Exposition of Ezekiel.[8]

47:10-12 *The Fishes*

The Fishes and Infant Baptism. John Mayer: He shows that not only the waters of the sea shall be healed by the coming in of this river, but also the fishes, which are of a great number, shall be healed and live. People, among whom the gospel comes, are sometime propounded to us under the notion of trees, sometime of waters and sometime of fishes. According to which our Lord said to his apostles, *Follow me, and I will make you fishers of men.*

And everything where this river comes shall live. That is, the Spirit brought as living water in the preaching of the gospel, shall be vivifying to every man and woman, and in the water of baptism to infants, who have the life of nature before but want reason whereby to live by the Spirit coming in the preaching of the Word. And therefore having said that the fishes should be healed, setting forth men and women capable of reason, which is the mouth, as it were, that opens and swallows the hook of the angler, and so the fish is taken for God, the Author of healing and all good. And so he adds, *Everything where this river comes shall live.* Here he intimates others in the church, or within the pale of preaching the gospel, as infants, the children of believers before spoken of, little fishes newly spawned, who, though they cannot swallow the hook, yet together with the greater are taken in a net, well and close wrought also. Otherwise, after speaking of the fishes being healed and living by these waters, he would certainly not have added this clause further touching every living thing. He that rests not in this, let him give another reason of this addition, if he can. If he cannot, no more impugn the baptizing of infants. Commentary upon All the Prophets.[9]

47:13–48:29 *Division of the Land*

The Temple and the Land. Martin Luther: Besides the tribes and the land of Israel are very differently divided and arranged, so that the city and the temple shall not lie in the land of any tribe of Israel, though Jerusalem was previously located in the land of the tribe of Benjamin [Josh 18:28]. All this and much more is plainly given in the text. A New Preface to the Prophet Ezekiel.[10]

The Spiritual Sense Is of the Church. William Greenhill: Having given you the literal sense of the words (Ezek 47:13-23), now let us see what may be the spiritual sense of them. Indeed, according to the letter, they were not fulfilled after the return from Babylon, but mystically under the gospel they were.

[7]*Prophets*, 513. [8]*Exposition*, 819. [9]*Prophets*, 513. [10]Lenker 6, 311 (WADB 11,1:408).

1. Then here is held out to us the great extent and largeness of the church under Christ and the gospel. The land mentioned signifies the church's state; and the bordering of it out, north, east, south, west, the extent of it into all parts. The Christian church is larger than the Jewish, that was shut up in one nation; now it reaches to all nations (Mt 28:19), neither Asia, Africa, Europe or America is excluded (Mt 24:14; Lk 24:47; Rev 15:4). The church under the gospel is universal and invisible.

2. Those who are subjects or members of this church are not hypocrites but Israelites. Those who were not Israelites, and true Israelites, were not to be in this church. Hypocrites, scandalous, ignorant and unregenerate persons are often in, if not the major part of particular visible churches, but of the universal church of Christ they are not. That consists of true Israelites, such as Nathanael was (Jn 1:47); of Jews inwardly, such as are circumcised in heart and spirit (Rom 2:29); of such as are enrolled in heaven (Heb 12:23); of sealed ones (Rev 7), and these stood with the Lamb on Mount Zion (Rev 14:1). These made up the church and body of Christ.

3. The privileges of this church equally belong to all the members of it. None has preeminence above others in the things of Christ and God. . . .

4. The state of Christians in the church, and all the spiritual blessings they have therein, are of free grace and mere mercy. An Exposition of Ezekiel.[11]

[11]*Exposition*, 823-24.

48:30-35 The Gates of the City

[30]*"These shall be the exits of the city: On the north side, which is to be 4,500 cubits by measure,* [31]*three gates, the gate of Reuben, the gate of Judah, and the gate of Levi, the gates of the city being named after the tribes of Israel.* [32]*On the east side, which is to be 4,500 cubits, three gates, the gate of Joseph, the gate of Benjamin, and the gate of Dan.* [33]*On the south side, which is to be 4,500 cubits by measure, three gates, the gate of Simeon, the gate of Issachar, and the gate of Zebulun.* [34]*On the west side, which is to be 4,500 cubits, three gates,*[a] *the gate of Gad, the gate of Asher, and the gate of Naphtali.* [35]*The circumference of the city shall be 18,000 cubits. And the name of the city from that time on shall be, The Lord Is There."*

a One Hebrew manuscript, Syriac (compare Septuagint); most Hebrew manuscripts *their gates three*

Overview: Ezekiel ends with a discussion of the gates of the new city, which are to be named after the tribes of Israel. The name of this city shall be "the Lord is there." Finally, some consideration is given to the prophet Ezekiel and what became of him after these prophecies. Although we cannot say with certainty, it is agreed by all that Ezekiel, like the other prophets, met with an untimely and unkind end. God's doctrine, delivered by his faithful prophet, Ezekiel, remains. As we consider Ezekiel, we are to be stirred by his example to speak the truth of God's word amid persecution and hostility. We too must stand for the truth, even to death.

THE CITY OF THE CHURCH OF CHRIST. WILLIAM GREENHILL: By this city of Ezekiel I conceive is pointed out to us the glorious state of the Christian church in the latter days. It has been a long time said to war under antichrist and his instruments; the breaches and ruins of it at this day are great, and the face of such a city hardly visible. But when the times of antichrist's destruction and the Jews' conversion do come, then shall this city be built, then shall Zion be in its glory. The Christian church shall be then in a greater glory than formerly.

... There are several things observable concerning this city of the church of Christ: (1) That it is well and strongly founded.... John tells us of this city, the new Jerusalem, that it had twelve foundations, three on every square, which were sure, firm and would never fail. The Lord Christ, the holy Scriptures and the doctrine of the holy prophets and apostles must fall to the ground before the church shall be ruined. (2) It is comely and beautiful.... (3) The greatness and amplitude of this city is described. It had four thousand and five hundred measures eastward, west, north and southward; it was eighteen thousand measures in compass, which sets out the greatness and vast extent of the church of Christ.... (4) The city has access to it from all parts ... which signifies to us the great access that should be to the church of Christ from all parts.... (5) The happiness of this city, which is from the Lord's inhabiting there and giving it its denomination. The name of it shall be Jehovan-shammah, "the Lord is there." AN EXPOSITION OF EZEKIEL.[1]

WHAT BECAME OF EZEKIEL? WILLIAM GREENHILL: Antiquity tells us that his end was very lamentable, and yet like a prophet's. Usually the prophets came to untimely deaths. ... Athanasius tells us he was killed for the people's sake. Epiphanius relates that he was slain by the ruler of the people for reproving his idolatry.... All agree in this that Ezekiel came to an untimely and bloody end, as did most of the prophets and apostles. Whatever people's ends were in killing the prophets, God had other ends: that by their blood and death, the doctrine they delivered, being sealed, might pass the better; that none should look for great matters here in this world when such great worthies were so ill treated; that people might be stirred up by their example to stand for the truth to the death; that it might be a demonstration of the judgment to come, seeing they were used so hardly here. Surely it follows then that there is a time in which God will call over things again and be avenged on those who had done them such wrong. God had such ends as these. AN EXPOSITION OF EZEKIEL.[2]

[1]*Exposition,* 829. [2]*Exposition,* 14-15.

DANIEL

PREFACE

Overview: The first issue addressed is the canonical status of Daniel. A summary is given of rabbinic (ancient and contemporary), pagan and patristic opinions. Decisive for the reformers is Jesus' reference to Daniel (Mt 24:15). After establishing the canonical place of the book of Daniel, consideration is given to the various additions to the book, which are not received as canonical and, for the most part, not commented on by our authors.

Our commentators identify many benefits for those who read Daniel. We find explicit prophecies concerning Christ, the precise time of his coming and the promises of his saving work for us. The histories of the monarchs, the great miracles that occurred in Daniel's day and the comfort of God's fatherly care and watchful providence over his saints are all recorded for the encouragement of our faith.

The book of Daniel has two main divisions. The first six chapters form the historical part; the final six form the prophetical or doctrinal part.

Canonical Status of Daniel. Johann Gerhard: In Hebrew, Daniel is "the judgment of God" or "the man whom God has judged." If what the rabbinic scholars say here and there about Daniel's prophecy is true, it was taken into the canon after the Babylonian captivity but not without some hesitation. After it could not be excluded, however, it was thrown back into the last class of writings of the Old Testament. The Hebrews put Daniel among the kethubim, or hagiographa, and they argue at great length whether one ought to include his prophecy among the immediate works of the Holy Spirit or ascribe it to the common and ordinary gift of prophecy.

. . . In Daniel 9:23 and Daniel 10:11 he is called "a man greatly beloved" or "a much-longed for man," so to him may be attributed a name in proportion to the subject matter that was revealed in him. He is also called "a man who is the heart's great desire," to show that he is especially dear to God. Jerome calls him "the polyhistor of the whole world." Epiphanius mentions that his father was called Sabaea. On the Nature of Theology and Scripture.[1]

Status of Daniel in the Canon. John Mayer: The prophecy of Daniel has been much impugned of old and stiffly denied by many to be canonical Scripture.

First, by Porphyry the disciple of Plotinus, who said that this book was not written by the prophet Daniel but by some other man in his name. Moreover, it was written during the time of Antiochus Epiphanes, that persecuting tyrant, who reigned over Syria and compelled many by punishments to forsake the law of God. It was not written by any prophetical spirit, but under the pretence of prophecy, it related things done in the time of the aforesaid Antiochus. Porphyry says further that the histories written in the first six chapters were true but everything there after that was written in the form of prophecy came from a false and lying spirit. Thus that railer against the

[1]*Theological Commonplaces: Theology and Scripture*, 156-57.

Christian religion, who wrote a treatise against Christianity, in the twelfth book of that work said these things against the prophecy of Daniel.

But that he and not Daniel was a notorious liar is clear from the time when he says this book was written, namely, in the days of Antiochus Epiphanes. For Josephus says that the prophecy of Daniel was shown to Alexander the Great, specifically that vision of the goat (Dan 8:5), representing him in his swift and speedy subduing of all kingdoms and nations. Between Alexander and Antiochus Epiphanes were 140 years. Against this Porphyry wrote Theodoret and Jerome relating such things as these. Second, Celsus also impugned this book as not being canonical Scripture. Against him Origen wrote a treatise in eight books.

Third, many Jewish rabbis have rejected it as not being canonical. This is related by Polanus, who lived for a while in Moravia, where he used the help of some rabbi for the understanding of the Hebrew tongue. He heard them say that they did not acknowledge Daniel to be authentic and therefore seldom read it, especially because Daniel 9 is so clearly about the death and passion of the Messiah. Therefore they did not read it among the people, lest they hereby be turned to Christ and discover that they had been deceived by the rabbis. But the ancient rabbis generally did acknowledge Daniel to be canonical Scripture. . . . And therefore some of them have written commentaries on it, such as Rabbi Solomon, Rabbi Levi, Rabbi Abraham ben David, etc. Some have alleged Daniel as authentic to confirm points of faith, such as Rabbi Moses Maimonides and Rashi.

Christ, whose authority is above all others, speaks of Daniel as a true prophet of God, saying, "When you see the abomination of desolation spoken of by Daniel the prophet" (Mt 24:15). Moreover, experience has abundantly proved Daniel's authority in the fulfillment of the things foretold about the Persian, Grecian and Roman monarchies. This suffices to establish the authority of this prophecy. As for the objections about its canonicity, Jerome argues that Origen and Apollinaris, who wrote against the blasphemer Porphyry, counted these prophecies as fables, and so he too regards them as such. Jerome says that they were written by a certain priest called Daniel, a close friend of Nebuchadnezzar's, and that they are not in Hebrew but in Greek only, and all canonical Scriptures were set forth in Hebrew, which was the holy tongue before the coming of Christ. Therefore, although they and Eusebius adjoin them to Daniel, they do so only with marks in many places to show the uncertainty of the authority of many things found in the book. Commentary upon All the Prophets.[2]

The Apocryphal Additions to Daniel. Andrew Willet: The Romanists would thus persuade us that these histories that are annexed to Daniel and make in the vulgar Latin translation the thirteenth and fourteenth chapters are to be canonical. As such, the Council of Trent has defined them to be regarded as canonical Scriptures. They are used and recited in the Roman liturgy and mass as canonical Scripture. They are cited and alleged by many of the Fathers. Many fathers of the Greek church, such as Origen, Athanasius, Chrysostom and Cyril, do hold these sections to be canonical (Bellarmine, Pintus).

. . . Arguments against the canonical authority of these additions are these which follow. They are not extant in the Hebrew and Chaldean original. They contain some things contradictory to the canonical histories. The apocryphal story says that Daniel was of the tribe of Levi, whereas he is said in the true story to be of the tribe of Judah (Dan 1:6). Josephus making mention of all the other histories recorded in this book, yet omitted these

[2]*Prophets*, 515-16.

two as apocryphal relations.

Jerome touches objections propounded by a Jew against these apocryphal additions. That it is not likely that the three children had so much leisure as to go through all the elements and creatures in their hymn or song. It was no such miraculous thing but a natural work to kill the dragon with gobbets and balls of pitch. And it is without example that any prophet was so transported in body, as Habakkuk was taken up by the hair of the head to go and minister to Daniel. SIXFOLD COMMENTARY UPON DANIEL.[3]

THE AUTHORITY OF DANIEL. JOHANN WIGAND: Great is the authority of the prophet Daniel, which will be shown for the following reasons.

First, because Christ cites his writing as coming from the prophet. He says, "When you see the abomination of desolation spoken of by the prophet Daniel, standing in the holy place, he who reads, let him understand" (Mt 24:15). Therefore, Christ wishes for us to read Daniel and to pay close attention to the things that he records for us about the divine revelation.

Second, he records matters of utmost importance that do not exist in any other book and that so clearly give the events of things, such as the four monarchies in the world and what sort of government will be in place around the time of the end of the world.

Third, he explains so well the prophecies concerning Christ and antichrist. For example, he very plainly designates the time of the Messiah's coming and his passion. He also explains the Messiah's purpose, namely, that he would seal up sin and bring about an eternal righteousness.

Fourth, he also portrays in vivid colors the antichrist. He explains the events in the papacy and his spiritual and worldly reign or rather tyranny.

Fifth, he preserves the witness of the church of God, which renders this book one of the greatest. Although Jews number the book of Daniel among the *hagiographa* (that is, the Writings or Kethubim), he is nevertheless pure, faithful and authoritative. He is never to be doubted among us.

At the same time, the Jews warn that the unfinished works, the Hymn of the Three Youths in the Fiery Furnace, the History of Susanna and Bel and the Dragon are not to be acknowledged as authentic writings but regarded as stories added by others. BRIEF EXPOSITION OF THE PROPHET DANIEL.[4]

THE BENEFIT OF THE BOOK OF DANIEL. MARTIN LUTHER: From this book we see what an excellent and great man Daniel was, before both God and the world. Particularly before God, he above all other prophets had such an extraordinary prophecy. He not only prophesies about Christ, like the others, but also he calculates the time and year, fixing them firmly and certainly. In addition he holds the kingdoms so precisely and tightly in correct order to the same fixed time of Christ, with their ebb and flow, that we certainly cannot miss the future coming of Christ unless we do so deliberately, like the Jews do. From then on to the Last Day he so neatly portrays the rise and existence of the Roman Empire, as well as the general course of the world that one cannot miss the Last Day, too, or suddenly find himself plunged into it, unless one does this deliberately as well, like our Epicureans now do.

Therefore I think St. Peter referred to Daniel in particular when he said in 1 Peter 1 (vv. 10-11): "The prophets searched for when and what kind of time the Spirit of Christ indicates, etc." "When" means that he calculates and determines the time, how long and how many years there ought to be until then.

[3]*Sixfold Commentary* (1610), 9-10. Robert Bellarmine (1542-1621) was one of most learned Jesuit theologians and controversialists of his day. He was the chief Roman Catholic opponent of the Protestants. [4]*Explicatio Brevis* (1571), 2-3.

"What kind of time" means that he precisely depicts how it should be in the world at that time, who should have supreme authority, or where the kingdom should be. So he not only proclaims the time, but also the course, form, and nature of that time. By these means he strengthens our faith in Christ very much, making us firm and sure in conscience, because we see powerfully before our eyes what he long ago described and painted for us clearly and correctly in his book.

Then Daniel prophesies freely and clearly, saying that the future coming of Christ and the beginning of his Kingdom (that is his baptism and preaching office) should happen 510 years after King Cyrus, Daniel 9. And the Persian and Greek Empire will be gone from the world, but the Roman Empire will be in full force, Daniel 7 and 9. So, Christ certainly had to come during the time of the Roman Empire, when it was at its peak, also that it should destroy Jerusalem and the temple, because after this empire no more are to come, rather the end of the world will follow, as Daniel 2 and 7 clearly declare. PREFACE TO THE PROPHET DANIEL.[5]

THE BENEFIT OF READING DANIEL. JOHN CALVIN: For in publishing the lectures that contain my *Interpretation of the Prophecies Of Daniel*, I have the very best occasion of showing you, beloved brethren, in this mirror, how God proves the faith of his people in these days by various trials, and how with wonderful wisdom he has taken care to strengthen their minds by ancient examples, that they should never be weakened by the concussion of the severest storms and tempests, or at least, if they should totter at all, that they should never finally fall away. For although the servants of God are required to run in a course impeded by many obstacles, yet whoever diligently reads this book will find in it whatever is needed by a voluntary and active runner to guide him from the starting post to the goal, while good and strenuous wrestlers will experimentally acknowledge that they have been sufficiently prepared for the contest. COMMENTARIES ON DANIEL.[6]

THE BENEFIT OF READING THE PROPHETS. JOHANN WIGAND: There is a great benefit in reading the prophets. First, because the prophets hand down the same articles of faith that Christ and the apostles explain in the New Testament. Therefore it is useful to examine and understand the great consensus and congruence of these chief teachings for the confirmation of our faith.

Second, they plainly relate the promises concerning Christ and his benefits that Christ himself wishes us to investigate. In the Gospel of John, he says, "Search the Scriptures, for they bear witness about me" (Jn 5:39).

Third, they set forth the history of the church of God, for all times, showing its preservation amid innumerable dangers and adversities. To reflect on and consider such things is a worthwhile endeavor. Although the devil and the world furiously seek to destroy it completely, the church of God is everlasting.

Fourth, the prophetic writings preserve a historical record of all the faithful from the beginning of the world to the time of Christ, the King and Savior of the world. There is no other ancient and more certain historical record extant in the whole world.

Fifth, what was fulfilled in the New Testament was most clearly predicted and handed down in those prophetic books. Consequently, it is of absolute necessity that the church of Christ carefully examine and learn from the prophetic writings. Christ says, "Thus it is written that Christ must suffer and on the third day rise" (Lk 24:46). And Peter says, "To him all the prophets bear witness that everyone who believes in him receives the remission of sins through his name" (Acts 10:43).

[5]WADB 11,2:124-126. [6]CTS 24:lxiv.

Sixth, there are many predictions in the prophets that remain to be completed. For example, the things concerning the fourth monarchy to the destruction of the end of the world, the last days, the judgment of the Son of God and eternal life.

Seventh, many remarkable revelations and miracles of God are recorded in the prophetic writings, which God wishes to be studied by his church for the confirmation of faith, concerning the surrender of idols, divine providence and governance and the preservation of the church.

Eighth, many examples of virtues and vices, rewards and punishments are put before our eyes by the prophets. These are to be considered that the secure repent and that we might rightly imitate the saints of old in their steadfastness, doctrine, faith, and other virtues.

Those who contend that the books of the Old Testament have nothing to do with us because they are old and therefore no longer read them aloud among themselves, these people are stupid. Indeed, the articles of faith, the promises, the history of the church of God, the prophecies concerning the future, the examples of virtues and vices pertain also to all of us. At the very least they should see that there are certain things signified for us by those ceremonies that so clearly confirm the highest articles of our faith, namely, that to be reconciled to God the Father and to be saved is by the Lamb alone or the sacrifice of Christ. BRIEF EXPOSITION OF THE PROPHET DANIEL.[7]

THE BENEFIT OF READING DANIEL. ANDREW WILLET: In this book of Daniel, God's fatherly care and watchful providence over his church are set forth. The use of this book is extended generally to the church of God in all ages, but more especially it concerned the state and condition of the Jews in captivity. For their comfort in captivity, three things especially are declared and foretold. (1) The diverse changes and accidents, calamities and afflictions that should befall the people of God, under the kingdoms of the Chaldeans, Persians and Greeks. First, under Alexander the Great, then under his successors, who divided his empire among them. (2) The coming of the Messiah is pointed out, the time when and the reason why he should come. (3) With such innovations as should follow, as the ceasing of the ceremonies and the abdication of the Jews (Junius). And all to this end, that the people of God might be prepared not to expect any earthly happiness in this life but with patience to await the time of the restoring of all things in the resurrection of the just, which is touched on in Daniel 12. SIXFOLD COMMENTARY UPON DANIEL.[8]

DANIEL AND PROPHECY. JOHN CALVIN: Daniel so prophesies that he describes almost historically events previously hidden. And this was necessary, since in such turbulent convulsions the people would never have tasted that these had been divinely revealed to Daniel unless the heavenly testimony had been proved by the event. This holy man ought so to speak and to prophesy concerning futurity, as if he were relating what had already happened. But we shall see all these things in their own order. I return, then, to what I commenced with, that we may see in few words how useful this book is to the church of Christ. First of all, the matter itself shows how Daniel did not speak from his own discretion, but whatever he uttered was dictated by the Holy Spirit. COMMENTARIES ON DANIEL.[9]

DANIEL'S PROPHECY OF CHRIST. JOHN CALVIN: Now, when Daniel numbers the years till the advent of Christ, how clear and distinct is the testimony that we may oppose against Satan and all the taunts of the impious! And how certain it is that the book of Daniel was famil-

[7]*Explicatio Brevis* (1571), 1-2. [8]*Sixfold Commentary* (1610), 1. [9]CTS 24:78-79 (CO 18:530).

iarly used by people before this event. But when he enumerates the seventy weeks and says that Christ should then come, all profane people may come and boast and swell with increased swaggering, yet they shall fall down convicted, since Christ is that true Redeemer whom God had promised from the beginning of the world. For he was unwilling to make him known without the most certain demonstration, such as all the mathematicians can never equal. First of all, it is worthy of observation that Daniel afterwards discoursed on the various calamities of the church and prophesied the time at which God pleased to show his only-begotten Son to the world. His dissertation on the office of Christ is one of the principal supports of our faith. For he not only describes his advent but also announces the abolition of the shadows of the law, since the Messiah would bring with him its complete fulfillment. And when he predicts the death of Christ, he shows for what purpose he should undergo death, namely, to abolish sin by his sacrifice and to bring in eternal righteousness. Lastly, this also must be noticed: as he had instructed the people to bear their cross, so also he warns them that the church's state would not be tranquil even when the Messiah came. The children of God should be militant until the end and not hope for any fruit of their victory until the dead should rise again and Christ himself should collect us into his own celestial kingdom. Now, we comprehend in few words, or rather only taste how useful and fruitful this book is to us. Commentaries on Daniel.[10]

Christ's Appearances in the Book of Daniel. John Mayer: [Christ appears five times in Daniel's historical section]. First, the vision of the stone cut out of the mountain without hands (Dan 2). Second, of one like the Son of God in the fiery furnace. In this place is set forth the sufferings and burnings of his faithful servants that should occur in the time of persecution, their invincible courage in suffering and his presence with them, changing the nature of the fire, that it seemed no tormenting fire to them but comforting and refreshing (Dan 3). Third, the one cutting down the tree represented to Nebuchadnezzar in another dream, who is called a watchman. Here is set forth for us Christ's cutting down of the devil's kingdom (Dan 4). Fourth, the handwriting seen by Belshazzar on the wall, and then he being by and by cut off, representing the handwriting against us, which Christ took and nailed to his cross, spoiling the principalities and powers (Dan 5). Fifth, Daniel's admirable deliverance out of the lions' den. This prefigured Christ's rising up out of the grave to life again (Dan 6). Commentary upon All the Prophets.[11]

The Contents of Daniel. Johann Wigand: The contents of the book of Daniel are mixed. It is part history and part doctrine. The first part of the book relates the history of what happened to those in Babylon during the exile, beginning first with particular individuals and then the whole church of God. Brief Exposition of the Prophet Daniel.[12]

Division of the Book and Its Place in the Church. Heinrich Bullinger: We will divide the book of Daniel into two parts. The first part will be summed up in the first six chapters, covering six well-known events, full of instruction and usefulness. The first part of the book is discussed in order. Following these events, the book has another six chapters. In these chapters are visions that set forth some of the monarchies and kingdoms of the world, the kingdom of Christ and antichrist and the end of the world. Concerning such things, we shall again discuss them at the proper time and place.

Although the book of Daniel was for-

[10]CTS 24:81-82 (CO 18:532-33). [11]*Prophets*, 527. [12]*Explicatio Brevis* (1571), 9.

merly expounded in the church of Christ and preached to Christians, there are those today who refuse to do this because they are convinced that after the gospel of Christ and apostolic teaching, nothing is to be preached or explained in the church to Christians. Therefore, they exclude the teaching of the prophets, who nevertheless give witness to the gospel and the teaching of the apostles and are repeatedly brought into the discussion by the apostles of the Lord. Therefore, they shamelessly err who do not wish to preach or expound the prophets in the church of Christ.

No one will deny, I suppose, that there is the greatest need in the church of Christ that the kingdom of Christ be made clear and his kingdom delivered from this contemptible world. Daniel beautifully describes through prophecy the kingdom of God and truly shows the kingdom of the world to be false and perishing. These things must be preached to the people of God that they maintain a true faith, be consoled in sad circumstances, and, when depressed, have their spirits raised. When Daniel describes the church of God, it is always having to be preserved amid difficult circumstances, truly having been cut off from the temple in Jerusalem, only then to increase the glory and worship of God among Gentiles. What else does he teach than that the faithful are strengthened in the truth amid trials?

After the advent of Christ, Paul was sent as the apostle to the Gentiles. So too Daniel, in a certain way, was the teacher of the Gentiles in his world. Certainly he propagated the glory of God more broadly and splendidly throughout the world with the people of God scattered and afflicted than if they had been governed and living in peace. But if any one example from so many is able to be highlighted for the learning of the church of God, who, I pray, would prohibit the examples given by Daniel from the history of the world, which are nearly universal truths, to be applied to the church of God? Indeed, why does our Lord Christ himself commend to us the reading of Daniel in Matthew 24? For although he seems to speak about nothing more than the destruction of the city, nevertheless it corresponds to what is said by the Lord concerning the end of the world. With that in mind, who would dispute the great significance and usefulness of Daniel? Saint Peter the apostle does not prohibit us from reading and preaching Daniel when he testifies that the prophet had the spirit of Christ in him and that he searched and inquired carefully about the advent of Christ (1 Pet 1:10-11). Certainly, then, it is useful to read Daniel in the Christian church. DANIEL THE MOST WISE PROPHET OF GOD.[13]

DIVISION OF THE BOOK. ANDREW WILLET: The parts of the book are these. It is partly historical, partly prophetic. The historical part is either concerning certain kings or Daniel and his godly companions. And these things are handled jointly together. The kings whose history is set down were Nebuchadnezzar in the first four chapters, Belshazzar in the fifth and Darius in the sixth. The history of Daniel is continued in all these chapters, only the third excepted, and of his companions in the first and third (Polanus).

And in the first part, three special virtues of Daniel are described: his sobriety and abstinence (Dan 1), his wisdom and divine understanding in the opening and revealing of dreams and hidden mysteries (Dan 2; 4; 5) and his piety toward God (Dan 6). So he is commended for his sobriety, prudence and piety (Hugo).

And by these divine testimonies God gave witness to Daniel that the mystical prophecies following might be received with great authority.

In the second part, the prophetic predictions either concern the enemies of God's church, as of the judgments of God on Nebu-

[13]*Daniel Sapientissimus*, 1-2.

chadnezzar (Dan 4) and Belshazzar (Dan 5), or they belong to the church, either showing their afflictions and calamities (Dan 10; 11) or their deliverance begun in this life by the redemption purchased by the Messiah (Dan 9) and perfected and consummated in the next in the resurrection (Dan 12) (Polanus). Sixfold Commentary upon Daniel.[14]

Summary of the Book. Philipp Melanchthon: Daniel has described so many great, useful and worthy things for the meditations of a good mind that even all of our abilities are not able completely to unfold and explain them. The hard-working student knows there is much to accomplish, if he will have only moderately attended to particular chapters, and by faithful exercises will have learned to translate this book and will have discovered which part teaches the mind about true prayer, which part confirms faith, which refutes the Jews, which attends to penance and which certain virtues. Now it is very useful to refer to the narrative for those doctrinal topics. Therefore, I will enumerate the chief things here contained that will show the benefit of reading this book.

First, you will reflect on the complete work. The entire history of Daniel is a testimony of the preservation of the church and of its adornment with great glory when it seemed nearly extinct. Therefore, Daniel teaches about the punishment of the church and its restoration again amid suffering. He testifies concerning the church not by human judgment, strength or arrangement but by the power of God alone, who has from the beginning continuously defended and increased the church.

Similarly, Daniel teaches about the promises, the promises that God will fulfill, even if he fulfills them not in the manner that we have imagined. For example, he made a promise to the tribe of Judah that he would not remove the scepter or a teacher from Judah until the Savior comes. By relying on this promise the kings of Judah rebelled many times and, as if fighting against the manifest promise of God, boldly condemned the preaching of Jeremiah about the destruction of the kingdom. But Jeremiah knew that God would eventually punish the people and yet not extinguish the royal family or abandon the prophets. And so it happened, contrary to human opinion, the royal family was sent into exile with honor. And God raised up prophets and adorned his church with great glory. Even more, he added Gentiles to the fellowship of the church. The conversion of the Gentiles to God has become a mark of distinction.

Second, you will observe the testimony concerning the Messiah. About this we have been stirred up by the other prophets who also spoke about the promise of the Messiah. Therefore Daniel, who teaches many things, is concerned with this topic. He prophesies concerning the time at which it is right for the Messiah to be born during the final stages of Jewish rule. He very clearly prophesies about the passion of Christ and says that he will be put to death.

Third, you will consider the order of monarchies that was handed down so that the time would be indicated when God wished the Messiah to be born. The time of the resurrection of the dead and judgment was indicated also.

Fourth, the doctrinal topics concerning penance, faith and justification will be observed.

Fifth, the example of good and evil kings will be highlighted.

Sixth, the testimony concerning the resurrection of the dead will be considered.

Seventh, the warning was handed down that wicked kings will attempt to destroy the gospel of God everywhere to the end of the world. Commentary on the Prophet Daniel.[15]

[14]*Sixfold Commentary* (1610), 1. Cardinal Hugo of Florence (c. 1200–1263) was a Dominican theologian and biblical scholar.
[15]*In Danielem Prophetam* (1543), b-b2.

Summary of the Book of Daniel. Giovanni Diodati: Although Daniel never exercised the public calling or function of a prophet, in the quality of an ecclesiastical person to preach to the people and to expound in sacred assemblies the revelations that were sent him by God, yet his book has always been inserted among the number of the other prophets as containing most special and admirable predictions of the state of the world and church from his time to Christ's coming in the flesh. These things have been gathered by him and published in this book, which has two general parts: one historical and the other prophetic.

In the first part, he sets down the notable things that happened to him during the course of his life. He did this so that he would be acknowledged as a true prophet authorized by God. He relates how he was carried away captive to Babylon in his youth and was with others of the same nation, age and condition chosen to be instructed and consequently employed in honorable employments in that empire. But that God took them into his particular care and charge and prevented those humane instructions by an infusion of divine gifts and graces. First, in a spirit of sanctification, zeal and singular piety, Daniel's three companions in their youth were inflicted with cruel torments, and so too was Daniel himself in his old age. As they were remarkable in possessing great understanding and wisdom (spoken of, as it were, by a common proverb), they were promoted to eminent dignities, to the great ease and sustenance of the church in its captivity and sufferings in Babylon.

The spirit of prophecy manifested itself in Daniel in reminding Nebuchadnezzar of the dreams he had forgotten and interpreting them. Also in the miraculous prediction and setting forth of the evils which hung over the head of Belshazzar, Nebuchadnezzar's grandchild. On these occasions, God willed his terrible judgments on the immeasurable pride of the one king and the profane sacrilege and insolence of the other, under whom the people had been carried away and kept in long and cruel slavery, and that these things should be transmitted to the knowledge of posterity. This spirit of prophecy fully shined forth in the incomparable visions set down in the second part of this book. Here we have a vision concerning the four great monarchies of the world until the coming of Christ; a vision that especially touches on the Seleucids, the kings of Syria and other successors of Alexander, under whom the Jewish church should suffer most grievous and mournful accidents. The most cruel, subtle and pestilent persecutor that the church has ever had being Antiochus Epiphanes, whose principal aim and end was to root out God's worship in the church, together with all impression and motion of piety in people's hearts. Under whose figure are also foretold the persecutions of the Roman Empire during its heathen days and of antichrist, the last deadly enemy of the Christian church. Antiochus was against the Jewish church and, against his outrages, the prophet comforted and strengthened the church by the promise of God's help and deliverance in his appointed time. He lifted their hearts to the sovereign comfort of God's promise of everlasting salvation by Christ, who, being established by the Father to be the everlasting King of the world, should from time to time cause ruin to fall on those empires and at the last lay the foundation of his own spiritual and everlasting kingdom, a kingdom established upon the redemption purchased by his death, the prefixed time of this is more clearly shown to Daniel than any other prophet. Pious Annotations.[16]

The Book of Daniel. Geneva Study Bible: The great providence of God and his singular mercy toward his church are set forth here most vividly, who never leaves his own

[16]*Pious Annotations* (1651), pref. to Daniel.

destitute but now in their greatest miseries and afflictions gives them prophets, such as Ezekiel and Daniel, whom he adorned with special graces of his Holy Spirit. And Daniel above all others had most special revelations of such things as would come to the church, even from the time that they were in captivity to the last end of the world and to the general resurrection, as of the four monarchies and empires of all the world, that is, of the Babylonians, Persians, Grecians and Romans. Also of the certain number of the times even until Christ, when all ceremonies and sacrifices would cease, because he would be the accomplishment of them; moreover he shows Christ's office and the reason of his death, which was by his sacrifice to take away sins, and to bring everlasting life. And as from the beginning God always exercised his people under the cross, so he teaches here that after Christ is offered, he will still leave this exercise to his church until the dead rise again and Christ gathers his own into his kingdom in the heavens. Geneva Study Bible.[17]

[17]*Geneva Bible* (1599), 1:1.

1:1-7 Daniel's Training in Babylon

[1]In the third year of the reign of Jehoiakim king of Judah, Nebuchadnezzar king of Babylon came to Jerusalem and besieged it. [2]And the Lord gave Jehoiakim king of Judah into his hand, with some of the vessels of the house of God. And he brought them to the land of Shinar, to the house of his god, and placed the vessels in the treasury of his god. [3]Then the king commanded Ashpenaz, his chief eunuch, to bring some of the people of Israel, both of the royal family[a] and of the nobility, [4]youths without blemish, of good appearance and skillful in all wisdom, endowed with knowledge, understanding learning, and competent to stand in the king's palace, and to teach them the literature and language of the Chaldeans. [5]The king assigned them a daily portion of the food that the king ate, and of the wine that he drank. They were to be educated for three years, and at the end of that time they were to stand before the king. [6]Among these were Daniel, Hananiah, Mishael, and Azariah of the tribe of Judah. [7]And the chief of the eunuchs gave them names: Daniel he called Belteshazzar, Hananiah he called Shadrach, Mishael he called Meshach, and Azariah he called Abednego.

a Hebrew *of the seed of the kingdom*

Overview: The first chapter begins with the occasion that brought Daniel and others to Babylon. Serious thought is given to the chronological questions concerning the time Daniel and Ezekiel began prophesying and how to reconcile the dates of Jehoiakim and Nebuchadnezzar. The point is made that the capture of Jerusalem had less to do with

Nebuchadnezzar and more to do with God's wrath. Here we see at work the providence and judgment of God, who uses a foreign king as his instrument in humbling his people. Finally, consideration is given to the training of the Hebrew youths and the religious significance of changing their names.

MAIN POINTS OF THE CHAPTER. PHILIPP MELANCHTHON: Here are the chief points of the chapter. First, with the punishment of the wicked, one clearly sees the great calamity of the Jewish people. Second, that God to an extraordinary degree provides promises and protects his church, even as he punishes the impious. Third, concerning the moderation of victory, we see the king attend to his duty by preparing the young for service. Fourth, that the faith and perseverance of Daniel and the three youths not fall away from God's law while living among the heathen and that they not be perverted by the practices, enjoyments or wonderful displays of power by the heathen. Fifth, the bodily and spiritual rewards for their faith, perseverance and temperance. Better health, favor with the king and his officials, teaching and prophecy are given. These gifts are granted them because God wanted to give evidence that they serve his church and that his promises are not void. This example teaches that those who publicly confess their faith please God and gain innumerable rewards. Sixth, for what purpose Daniel embraces temperance must be observed. Daniel abstained from the king's food not because of human traditions but because of God's law. Many of the king's foods were prohibited for Jews to eat because they were unclean, contained blood and included many kinds of fish. The use of wine was not prohibited, and Daniel, as we read below, drank wine. Therefore, he abstained from wine at that time not because of their superstitions but because of the youths, and he avoided fellowship with the others. COMMENTARY ON THE PROPHET DANIEL.[1]

THE ARGUMENT OF DANIEL. JOHANN WIGAND: The first chapter explains the occasion on which Daniel was brought to Babylon and when he began to be illumined in doctrine, wisdom and power and to be himself highly valued and a close confidant of the monarchs of the world.

There are five parts to the narrative. First, it tells of the abduction of a certain number of Jews, among whom was Daniel, who is the chief person in this book. Second, it discusses how Daniel and certain others were set apart to be instructed in the disciplines and arts of the Chaldeans. Moreover, God arranged, appointed and directed these things in a miraculous way that Daniel and his associates would comfort and protect the rest of the Jews in exile. Third, it discusses the religion and confession of Daniel and the things he does for his glory. Also the sparks of virtue from the clever and pious youths shoot forth. Fourth, it tells that the success of Daniel and his associates is from the blessing of God alone. When God wishes to raise up mighty people, he provides the occasion for them to learn and to become acquainted with many things. Fifth, it concerns the exploration and manifestation of excellent gifts that God himself furnished and prepared for those youths. This notable testimony God provided for his church, in the midst of hardship, to mercifully grant them some reprieve. BRIEF EXPOSITION OF THE PROPHET DANIEL.[2]

THE BEGINNING OF THE BOOK. HEINRICH BULLINGER: The first deed of the prophet set forth in the first chapter is written concerning true wisdom, and indeed concerning a school or college for the education and discipline of the young and about their actual introduction to true wisdom. In short, it is about the singular grace of God or his excellent gifts,

[1]*In Danielem Prophetam* (1543), 5-6. [2]*Explicatio Brevis* (1571), 10-11.

which God confers on people for the preservation of kingdoms, the commonwealth and true religion. This topic (*locus*) is very memorable and useful. He discusses this with the example of the king of Babylon, who instituted a school in Babylon and cultivated in it bright minds. Among those admitted to study was Daniel, who explains at the outset of his work the occasion of his coming to Babylon in captivity.

. . . The first topic (*locus*) that Daniel discusses is wisdom. It is a knowledge of divine and human things, and of this knowledge there is a true use and right application in human matters, either ecclesiastical or political, either private or public, for the preservation of those in an honest state. This wisdom is bestowed by God alone, from whom it is to be continually and most ardently sought with prayers. He teaches us this with the example of Solomon. He also testifies in Proverbs 2 to acquire and come upon wisdom, which if it be obtained, is equal to gold and silver. These things are obtained with great trouble and effort. Therefore, God requires from us due care and diligence, which he himself supplies (as we have no good thing from ourselves), and he confers this through effort and continual striving for wisdom. Daniel the Most Wise Prophet of God.[3]

Daniel and Ezekiel. John Mayer: It appears that Daniel did not begin to prophesy the year after Ezekiel, as Polanus notes in his preface. Ezekiel did not prophesy until the fifth year of Jehoiakim's captivity, which was thirteen years after Jehoiakim was carried into Babylon, with whom Daniel and his fellows were also carried. Therefore if he ministered to the king of Babylon one year after that and this was the beginning of his prophetic work, he began twelve years before Ezekiel. But to leave this as uncertain it may suffice that he prophesied at the same time with Ezekiel, and so either of them had the more comfort of one another's assistance. Moreover, if he prophesied so long as to the days of Cyrus, as it seems that he did, when the seventy years of captivity were ended, he is placed rightly next after Ezekiel, because he prophesied after him, especially in those things where the greatest burden of his prophecy lies, Daniel 7–8 to the end. And as for his beginning to minister to the king, it was not, as Polanus has it, one year after his coming into Babylon, but three years, as is clear from Daniel 1:5. Commentary upon All the Prophets.[4]

1:1 *Jerusalem and Nebuchadnezzar*

The Fall of Jerusalem. Johannes Oecolampadius: *And the Lord gave* (Dan 1:2). Therefore it is the Jews and not the king of Babylon against whom God himself battles. Indeed that Jehoiakim is captured and the vessels taken away is not to be attributed to the power of Nebuchadnezzar but to the will of God, who, although long-suffering, does not wish to bear with the impiety of his people any longer. Therefore, Nebuchadnezzar was an instrument of God's wrath. Commentary on Daniel.[5]

The Capture of Jerusalem. John Calvin: But Daniel clearly asserts that King Nebuchadnezzar did not possess Jerusalem and was not the conqueror of the nation by his own valor, or counsel, or fortune or good luck, but because God wished to humble his people. Therefore, Daniel here sets before us the providence and judgments of God, that we may not think Jerusalem to have been taken in violation of God's promise to Abraham and his posterity. Commentaries on Daniel.[6]

The Nebuchadnezzars. John Calvin: Here Daniel marks the time in which he was led into captivity together with his compan-

[3]*Daniel Sapientissimus*, 2-3. [4]*Prophets*, 516-17. [5]*In Danielem prophetam libri duo* (1553), 2. [6]CTS 24:86 (CO 18:535-36).

ions, namely, in the third year of Jehoiakim. A difficult question arises here, since Nebuchadnezzar began to reign in the fourth year of Jehoiakim. How then could he have besieged Jerusalem in the third year and then led away the captives according to his pleasure? Some interpreters solve this difficulty by what appears to me a frivolous conjecture, that the four years ought to refer to the beginning of his reign, and so the time may be brought within the third year. But in the second chapter we shall see Daniel brought before the king in the second year of his reign. They explain this difficulty also by another solution. They say the years are not reckoned from the beginning of the reign and this was the second year from the conquest of the Jews and the taking of Jerusalem, but this is too harsh and forced. The most probable conjecture seems to me that the prophet is speaking of the first King Nebuchadnezzar, or at least uses the reign of the second, while his father was yet alive. We know there were two kings of the same name, father and son; and as the son did many noble and illustrious actions, he acquired the surname of Great. Whatever, therefore, we shall afterwards meet with concerning Nebuchadnezzar cannot be understood except of the second, who is the son. COMMENTARIES ON DANIEL.[7]

TWO NEBUCHADNEZZARS. ANDREW WILLET: Pintus thinks that Nebuchadnezzar was a general name of the kings of Babylon, as the kings of Egypt were called by the name of Pharaoh and the kings of the Philistines by Abimelech. And he further is of the opinion that this Nebuchadnezzar had a son of the same name, and that neither of them are the same as that Nebuchadnezzar mentioned in the story of Judith, who sent Holofernes against the Jews. For that was after the return of the Jews out of captivity, as appears (Jdt 5); besides, he thinks that neither Nebuchadnezzar the father nor the son was that Nebuchadnezzar who destroyed Tyre according to the prophecy of Ezekiel 26:7, which he takes to be Cyrus or Alexander. But Pintus is in many things here deceived.

. . . The opinion is to be preferred that makes two Nebuchadnezzars, the father and the son, who was called Nebuchadnezzar the Great (Junius, Calvin, Bullinger, Polanus, so also Josephus, who gives to the reign of the elder twenty-three years and to the other forty-three). SIXFOLD COMMENTARY UPON DANIEL.[8]

1:2-7 *New Names*

NEW EDUCATION AND NEW NAMES. JOHN MAYER: *And the King appointed them a portion of his meat daily, and of the wine that he drank* (Dan 1:5). Polanus says that the king did this not out of any special favor to them as opposed to the other Jews, who fared not as well, but that being delightfully brought up they might be by the pleasures of the court fascinated so as to prefer a Chaldean life and, forgetting their own country and religion, be willing to turn to their superstition. And there he would have them thus fed and instructed a sufficient time; namely, three years, that they might afterwards stand before and minister to him, as other Chaldeans and astrologers did, and be set over the affairs of the kingdom, as the most able and expert of them were. Therefore most probably when he ordered that they should be taught the Chaldean tongue, he meant not only the tongue but the learning and skill of the Chaldeans also.

And to this end their names were changed from Daniel, Hananiah, Azariah and Mishael to Belteshazzar, Shadrach, Meshach and Abednego; that is, from names implying them to be the servants of God to names derived from idols, they being thus, so far as in them lay, that made this change, dedicated to the service of the said idols and false gods of the

[7]CTS 24:83 (CO 18:533-34). [8]*Sixfold Commentary* (1610), 15-16.

Babylonians. For Daniel signifies a judge of God; Hananiah, the grace of God; Azariah, the help of God; and Mishael, one that was of God. In every one of these names there was the name of God. But now, on the contrary, they had names from idols. Daniel from Bel, the great god of the Babylonians, Belteshazzar signifying Bel's treasurer. Hananiah from Rach, signifying king; that is the sun, which they worshiped as the king of the world. Shadrach being as much as the inspiration of the king. Mishael from Shachah, a goddess of pleasure. Meshach being as much as who is Shacah's. Mishael from Nego, the fire that was also worshiped as a god; and therefore Abednego was as much as the servant of the fire.

Thus idolaters endeavor by all means to draw the people of God from his service to the service of idols by carefully instructing them in their ways, providing for their dainty and delicate keeping and giving them names accordingly. . . . And therefore the carelessness of Christian people is here reproved, who have no care what names they give to children, but as their carnal fantasies lead them, and as for their education in godly learning it is set at six and seven, and this redounds to the great shame of this whole land, where no care has been had for educating the children of the papists in the knowledge of the truth, although we have had them in our power above eighty years. Commentary upon All the Prophets.[9]

God and Names. Johannes Oecolampadius: *And among these* (Dan 1:6). As they enticed the youths by the sumptuousness of the food, so also they did with celebrated names. Apollinaris and Chrysostom point out that it is an indication of power and dominion when servants are introduced with new names. One may see this a number of times in the Scriptures. Adam, appointing names for the animals, indicates that he has been established as their lord by God. Christ distinguishes with new names those appointed for his ministry: Simon becomes Peter, sons of Zebedee become sons of thunder, Saul becomes Paul, as had happened formerly when Jacob became Israel and Abram Abraham. Without any doubt they are blessed whom God calls by a new name. Commentary on Daniel.[10]

Concerning the Names of the Four Youths. Heinrich Bullinger: For this there are many reasons given. I will follow what seems to me the simplest explanation. Daniel sounds like "my judge, God" or "the judgment of my God." Therefore, the king himself wished not to call him by the God of Israel but rather Belteshazzar, that is, distinguished guardian of the treasury. Hananiah signifies a person who has the favor of God or who is in the grace of God. Therefore, the king wished for him to have another name and to be called Shadrach, which expresses the tender nipple of another or a pleasing field. Mishael signifies a person who seeks something from God or who calls on God. To this one he gave another name, Meshach, that is, precious or who is exquisite. Azariah signifies a person who has the assistance of God or the help of God. . . . He was called Abednego, that is, servant of Venus for whom the planet is named Nego. . . . These substituted names did not injure their true piety by taking something away from them, in the same way that certain clothes do not induce the body to some idolatry. Your clothes do not change your religion or harm any of your commitments, which contend for true religion. The Lord protects us from all pollution. Amen. Daniel the Most Wise Prophet of God.[11]

[9] *Prophets*, 517-18. [10] *In Danielem prophetam libri duo* (1553), 5. [11] *Daniel Sapientissimus*, 5.

1:8-21 Daniel's Faithfulness

8But Daniel resolved that he would not defile himself with the king's food, or with the wine that he drank. Therefore he asked the chief of the eunuchs to allow him not to defile himself. 9And God gave Daniel favor and compassion in the sight of the chief of the eunuchs, 10and the chief of the eunuchs said to Daniel, "I fear my lord the king, who assigned your food and your drink; for why should he see that you were in worse condition than the youths who are of your own age? So you would endanger my head with the king." 11Then Daniel said to the steward whom the chief of the eunuchs had assigned over Daniel, Hananiah, Mishael, and Azariah, 12"Test your servants for ten days; let us be given vegetables to eat and water to drink. 13Then let our appearance and the appearance of the youths who eat the king's food be observed by you, and deal with your servants according to what you see." 14So he listened to them in this matter, and tested them for ten days. 15At the end of ten days it was seen that they were better in appearance and fatter in flesh than all the youths who ate the king's food. 16So the steward took away their food and the wine they were to drink, and gave them vegetables.

17As for these four youths, God gave them learning and skill in all literature and wisdom, and Daniel had understanding in all visions and dreams. 18At the end of the time, when the king had commanded that they should be brought in, the chief of the eunuchs brought them in before Nebuchadnezzar. 19And the king spoke with them, and among all of them none was found like Daniel, Hananiah, Mishael, and Azariah. Therefore they stood before the king. 20And in every matter of wisdom and understanding about which the king inquired of them, he found them ten times better than all the magicians and enchanters that were in all his kingdom. 21And Daniel was there until the first year of King Cyrus.

Overview: The final part of the chapter concerns Daniel's refusal to defile himself with the king's food. Several reasons are given why Daniel would not eat the king's food. It was against God's law to eat certain foods; it would have meant a loss of religious identity and a concession to the pagan culture of Babylon; it would have scandalized the other Jews in captivity, possibly encouraging the weak to succumb to the Babylonian enticements; and finally, it would have involved them in the false worship of Babylon as is seen at Belshazzar's feast (Dan 5). At the same time, the commentators are adamant that food, in and of itself, does not defile. Rather it is the prohibition of God against such foods that renders them unclean. After refusing the king's food, Daniel and his companions were tested. Here we see that it is God, and not food, that sustains and nourishes us. Moreover, we learn that that those who cling to the word of God are cared for by him. Finally, just as it is God who nourishes Daniel and the youths, so too it is God who grants them learning and wisdom.

1:8-13 *Defilement by Food*

Daniel's Refusal to Defile Himself. Heinrich Bullinger: There are several things to be observed from the example of Daniel and his friends. Daniel firmly resolves in his heart to refuse to be defiled by the king's food. He observes by his resolution no human tradition but the law of God, which prohibits for his Jewish people several beasts and birds (Lev 11). They were held captive in the king's palace and daily brought the king's food. Indeed, the food in itself was not foul, but, when the prohibition of God is added to it, the matter is settled. Since it is so regarded by God, whose will is always good, whoever accepts such food becomes defiled because of disobedience. This very point is evident in the forbidden fruit in paradise, which God prohibited, and for that reason its consumption and use became lethal because of faithlessness and disobedience. In the same way, Eleazar did not wish to eat swine's flesh (2 Macc 6:18-19) and Saint Peter reverently declared that he had never eaten anything common or unclean (Acts 10:14), so Daniel with his friends did not wish to eat the king's food because he knew that several of the items prepared and put forth on the table were prohibited by the law. Since the time of Christ, this law concerning the distinction of foods has been abrogated. In Christian freedom, we are now free to enjoy what the Lord declares according to apostolic doctrine, which is that he prohibits any judgment concerning either food or drink. Indeed, to the pure all things are pure (Tit 1:15). Daniel the Most Wise Prophet of God.[1]

Daniel and Food. Geneva Study Bible: Not that he thought any religion to be in the meat or drink (for afterwards he did eat), but because the king should not entice him by this sweet poison to forget his religion and accustomed sobriety and that in his meat and drink he might daily remember of what people he was from. And Daniel brings this in to show how God from the beginning assisted him with his Spirit and at length called him to be a prophet. Geneva Study Bible.[2]

Daniel and the Ceremonial Law. William Pemble: Why would this defile him? Three reasons: first, it was against the law of God; second, to eat defiled foods is against the Word of God; third, Daniel saw that the king's love and provisions were not single and sincere. The king sought his own profit, which Daniel's companions (Hananiah, Mishael and Azariah) also saw. The king's aim in training them up, that they might stand before him, was that they should attend him as courtiers in his palace. And since they were of royal blood and the seed of the nobility, he might thereby better assure the land of Judah.

But did not Daniel eat after his promotion? He did. When he was in his greatness, he could command the diet he pleased that was neither in nature nor in use against the Levitical law of God. The Jews were bound to the judicial law only within the kingdom of Israel. Daniel and Mordecai were great officers and magistrates in foreign parts; and no question, they ministered justice according to the national laws and customs of those countries and not according to the judicial laws of Moses. But the Jews were most strictly tied all the world over to an exact observance of the ceremonial laws of God. Therefore Daniel, though in exile, dare not eat, lest he defile himself by transgressing the ceremonial law. The Period of the Persian Monarchy.[3]

Daniel and the Food. Giovanni Diodati: [Dan 1:8; *Daniel*, followed here, as it appears,

[1]*Daniel Sapientissimus*, 5-6. [2]*Geneva Bible* (1599), 1:8. [3]*Persian Monarchy* (1659), 373.

by his three companions, did not *defile himself*] either because there might be among that food some flesh that was by the law unclean or had been consecrated to idols. Or because he feared he should damage and corrupt his piety and purity through the allurements and pleasures of the court by not participating sufficiently in the common afflictions of the church. Pious Annotations.[4]

Daniel and the King's Food. John Mayer: *But Daniel purposed in his heart that he would not defile himself with the portion of the king's meat* (Dan1:9). Although Daniel only is named, the other three are also to be understood. None of them would defile themselves. If it is demanded, how could they be defiled with his meat? Polanus gives two answers. First, some of the meats used and served to his table were unclean as determined by God's law. Second, idols were praised. Therefore, as by whose beneficence he enjoyed them, for so it is said touching Belshazzar's feasting and drinking with his princes and concubines, that when they were thus doing, they praised their gods of silver and gold (Dan 5:2-4). And besides all this, the other Jews might have been scandalized by this, if such men as they should have taken liberty against the law of God in this way. The weak being encouraged by their example to do likewise, and others brought to an ill opinion of them, that being fascinated by the pleasures of the king's court, they had bidden adieu to all piety. Lastly, such delicious fare has power by pampering the flesh to corrupt the mind, thus endangering people to be led more by the flesh than the spirit. We see this in the rich man who fared deliciously every day. He was a belly-god and cared not for God or the charge given by him to break his bread to the hungry, to give a portion to six and to seven, to give and lend to the poor and needy. To this we may add that the king's fare was too high for poor captives, who were in the afflicted estate of a people conquered by the enemy and therefore had need to forbear feasting in order to fast and feed themselves with the coarsest meat and slenderest diet, herein choosing, as Moses, to suffer affliction with their brethren, the people of God, rather than to live in excess and fullness. Indeed, at such times the Lord expects that we should humble ourselves by abstinence and reproves it as a great sin in those that do otherwise.

According to this example, it is our duty to avoid anything whereby our weak brethren may be scandalized (Rom 14). Second, to take heed that by things edible, potable and pleasant to the palate, we not be drawn away to sin as gluttons and drunkards are, and such as daily pamper the body. Third, that no favor shown us by great persons or names, whereby people are pleased to designate us according to their hearts, which are wicked, should prevail so far with us to make us such. Fourth, we learn that it is no part of felicity in respect of worldly things to have the wherewithal to eat and drink daily of the best, if we do no unhappiness to be fed poorly and meanly, because the one commonly nourishes the flesh and makes it stronger to rebel against the spirit. For this reason it is said, Woe to them that are full now. The other way is more a means to subdue the flesh to the spirit. Fifth, that there ought to be in us a sympathizing with our brethren in distress, not feasting when they are in adversity, because this is complained of in Amos 6. Sixth, we should show that we are one with them in spirit by weeping with those who weep and abstaining with those who abstain. Commentary upon All the Prophets.[5]

The Three Youths and the Food. Tieleman J. van Braght: Thus, my dear children, follow the example set before you always to walk in the ways of the Lord with sobriety and thankfulness as you have heard me read in Daniel of Shadrach, Meshach and Abednego,

[4]*Pious Annotations* (1651), 1:8. [5]*Prophets*, 518.

who were chosen by the king of Babylon to be fed with the same wine and food that the king ate at his table that they might look fair in order to serve the king but they desired nothing but pulse and water. They would observe with sobriety and thankfulness in the fear of God the law and commands of their ancestors. They were fairer and fatter than they who ate the king's dainties. Thus they faithfully walked in the ways of the Lord. By prayer and supplication they were well pleasing to God. Therefore God did great things by them and delivered them out of the lions' den and out of the fiery furnace. A Martyrology of the Churches of Christ.[6]

1:14-16 *God Alone Sustains Us*

God Nourishes Us. John Calvin: Now this surprising event took place (Dan 1:14-15): Daniel contracted neither leanness nor debility from that mean food, but his face was as bright as if he had continued to feed most delicately; hence we gather, as I have already said, that he was divinely impelled to persist firmly in his own design and not to pollute himself with the royal diet. God, therefore, testified by the result that he had advised Daniel and his companions in this their prayer and proposal. It is clear enough that there is no necessary virtue in bread to nourish us, for we are nourished by God's secret blessing, as Moses says, Man lives not by bread alone (Deut 8:3), implying that the bread itself does not impart strength to people, for the bread has no life in it; how then can it afford us life? As bread possesses no virtue by itself, we are nourished by the Word of God; and because God has determined that our life shall be sustained by nourishment, he has breathed its virtue into the bread—but, meanwhile, we ought to consider our life sustained neither by bread nor any other food but by the secret blessing of God. For Moses does not speak here of either doctrine or spiritual life but says our bodily life is cherished by God's favor, who has endued bread and other food with their peculiar properties. This, at least, is certain: whatever food we feed on, we are nourished and sustained by God's gratuitous power. . . .

For we see that Daniel and his companions were ruddy and plump and even remarkably robust by feeding on nothing but pulse. How could this occur unless the Lord, who nourished his people in the desert on manna alone, when other diet was deficient, even at this day turns our food into manna, which would otherwise be injurious to us (Ex 16:4)? For if anyone asks the medical profession whether pulse and other leguminous plants are wholesome, they will tell us they are very injurious, since they know them to be so. Commentaries on Daniel.[7]

Certainty of Faith. Heinrich Bullinger: To demonstrate their faith, it is related that Daniel and his companions were tested for ten days. They appeared far better in body and more handsome in appearance than the youths who enjoyed the king's table. Therefore, their faith is not mistaken. God does not desert those who firmly cling to the word of God. From this it is apparent that humankind does not live by bread alone but by every word that proceeds from the mouth of the Lord. Moreover, it is the power of the Lord that made the food of those youths efficacious, and without his power it would be worthless and ineffective before the world. Daniel the Most Wise Prophet of God.[8]

God Fills Us with Wisdom. John Mayer: Daniel and his fellows, as they requested, eating pulse and none of the king's meat, and drinking none of his wine, at ten days end were fairer and fatter than those who did. More than this, they increased in understanding and

[6]*Martyrology* 2:291. [7]CTS 24:106-7, 109 (CO 18:550, 552). [8]*Daniel Sapientissimus*, 7.

learning above them all, so much so that the king examined them and found them to excel in these things all the Chaldeans of the land. They were ten times better than any of them. From this we may see another benefit coming through God's blessing on an abstemious course of life: the less the belly is filled, the more is the mind filled with understanding and wisdom; and the more it is forced with delicious meats and drinks, the more stupid and dull it is made in respect of divine understanding. It is as Jerome says, "a fat belly but a lean mind." Therefore Daniel fasted long and prayed to understand divine things. So did Ezra, that perfect scribe, who was so prompt in the law of God. Note also that for the very body, God can by his blessing make such as are poorly fed as thriving, and to be in as good or better plight than those who daily eat and drink of the best and fill their body. Commentary upon All the Prophets.[9]

1:17-21 *Daniel's Wisdom*

The Life of Daniel. Martin Luther: The first chapter sets before us a fine example of the life of Daniel. How holy, how god-fearing he was and what a great and courageous faith in God he had. In the midst of such wild and barbaric living and the many dreadful aggravations that he had to have seen and heard daily in Babylon, he still remained firm and patient, having overcome everything in his heart. For this reason soon afterwards it follows that God shows such great mercy to him, at first honoring him spiritually with wisdom and understanding above all other people. And then God exalts him in the world, doing nothing but mighty and great miracles and works through Daniel. In doing this God shows us all how dearly he loves and values those who fear him and trust in him. With such a great example he amicably calls us to fear of God and faith in God. Preface to the Prophet Daniel.[10]

God Grants Wisdom. Heinrich Bullinger: From the beginning, God, it is said, gave knowledge and intelligence in all literature and wisdom, particularly granting to Daniel understanding of all visions and dreams. By knowledge I understand wisdom, by intelligence a proper use and application of wisdom. He seems to have completed a study of their literary arts and language. Perhaps through wisdom he understood their more refined disciplines such as mathematics, physics, economic and political matters, and insight into their legal system. This text shows that all knowledge and wisdom and progress in discernment are conferred on people by God. He does this to preserve the church and the state, which the example of Solomon and several other testimonies from Scripture confirm. Daniel the Most Wise Prophet of God.[11]

[9] *Prophets*, 519. [10] WADB 11,2:2. [11] *Daniel Sapientissimus*, 8.

2:1-23 NEBUCHADNEZZAR'S DREAM

1In the second year of the reign of Nebuchadnezzar, Nebuchadnezzar had dreams; his
spirit was troubled, and his sleep left him. 2Then the king commanded that the magi-
cians, the enchanters, the sorcerers, and the Chaldeans be summoned to tell the king his
dreams. So they came in and stood before the king. 3And the king said to them, "I had a
dream, and my spirit is troubled to know the dream." 4Then the Chaldeans said to the
king in Aramaic,[a] "O king, live forever! Tell your servants the dream, and we will show
the interpretation." 5The king answered and said to the Chaldeans, "The word from me is
firm: if you do not make known to me the dream and its interpretation, you shall be torn
limb from limb, and your houses shall be laid in ruins. 6But if you show the dream and
its interpretation, you shall receive from me gifts and rewards and great honor. Therefore
show me the dream and its interpretation." 7They answered a second time and said, "Let
the king tell his servants the dream, and we will show its interpretation." 8The king an-
swered and said, "I know with certainty that you are trying to gain time, because you see
that the word from me is firm—9if you do not make the dream known to me, there is but
one sentence for you. You have agreed to speak lying and corrupt words before me till the
times change. Therefore tell me the dream, and I shall know that you can show me its in-
terpretation." 10The Chaldeans answered the king and said, "There is not a man on earth
who can meet the king's demand, for no great and powerful king has asked such a thing of
any magician or enchanter or Chaldean. 11The thing that the king asks is difficult, and
no one can show it to the king except the gods, whose dwelling is not with flesh."

12Because of this the king was angry and very furious, and commanded that all the wise
men of Babylon be destroyed. 13So the decree went out, and the wise men were about to be
killed; and they sought Daniel and his companions, to kill them. 14Then Daniel replied
with prudence and discretion to Arioch, the captain of the king's guard, who had gone
out to kill the wise men of Babylon. 15He declared[b] to Arioch, the king's captain, "Why is
the decree of the king so urgent?" Then Arioch made the matter known to Daniel. 16And
Daniel went in and requested the king to appoint him a time, that he might show the in-
terpretation to the king.

17Then Daniel went to his house and made the matter known to Hananiah, Mishael,
and Azariah, his companions, 18and told them to seek mercy from the God of heaven con-
cerning this mystery, so that Daniel and his companions might not be destroyed with the
rest of the wise men of Babylon. 19Then the mystery was revealed to Daniel in a vision of
the night. Then Daniel blessed the God of heaven. 20Daniel answered and said:

"Blessed be the name of God forever and ever,
   to whom belong wisdom and might.
21He changes times and seasons;

he removes kings and sets up kings;
he gives wisdom to the wise
and knowledge to those who have understanding;
22*he reveals deep and hidden things;*
he knows what is in the darkness,
and the light dwells with him.
23*To you, O God of my fathers,*
I give thanks and praise,
for you have given me wisdom and might,
and have now made known to me what we asked of you,
for you have made known to us the king's matter."

a The text from this point to the end of chapter 7 is in Aramaic **b** Aramaic *answered and said;* also verse 26

Overview: This chapter concerns Nebuchadnezzar's extraordinary dream and Daniel's interpretation of it. This dream was significant not only for the historical details it provides and for the lesson that all wisdom comes from God alone, but also because it repeated God's great promise concerning the Christ to his people who had been carried off into captivity. That the people might be assured that God had not forgotten his promises, the kingdom of Christ is proclaimed from the beginning of their captivity by the prophet Daniel. Before turning to the dream itself, the commentators wrestle again with the chronological relationship between the first chapter and the beginning of the second, the years of Nebuchadnezzar's reign and how Daniel could have so quickly been reckoned among the Babylonian wise men.

The variety of dreams and their causes are discussed. Why it is that Nebuchadnezzar should have such a dream is considered. Here we see a further lesson. In God's providence, the dream was given to Nebuchadnezzar to confound him and his supposed wise men. Wisdom is not to be found in ourselves. Daniel and his companions give us this example by turning to God in prayer before interpreting the dream. God alone provides; he alone nourishes and sustains us; he alone provides us with wisdom. Here we see the great usefulness of prayer. Whether we receive what we seek or not our prayers are always efficacious.

The Main Points of the Chapter. Philipp Melanchthon: Here are the main points of the chapter. First, God reveals in order the four monarchies. He testifies concerning the end of the world and the coming kingdom of the everlasting saints who truly worship God. In this revelation, the first thing put forward for the people is consolation and teaching. They did not consider themselves to be deserted by God when they possessed such prophets like Daniel. They learned that they ought to hope for that perpetual glory as promised to their ancestors. For this reason, the king and many other Gentiles were admonished by this teaching that they might acknowledge the true God and embrace the true worship and true God. Second, we have the example that God hears the prayers of believers and bestows on them the gifts they seek, wisdom and other gifts. Third, we have the testimony that all power is established by God in heaven. Fourth, we have the admonition that little by little power corrupts and destroys the wicked. Commentary on the Prophet Daniel.[1]

[1] *In Danielem Prophetam* (1543), 22-23.

The Argument of the Chapter. Johann Wigand: There are three principal parts to this chapter. The first concerns Nebuchadnezzar's extraordinary dream and prophecy, which the Chaldean wise men were not able to recall for the king, who had forgotten the dream. The second concerns the revelation and interpretation of the dream by Daniel; the clear prophecy of the four principal monarchies of the world; and the advent of Christ. The third point concerns the ascension of Daniel and his companions to the highest dignities and honors in the palace of the mighty king.

The purpose of the chapter also has three points. First, God wanted to confound the skill of the world's so-called bright lights. He permitted them to destroy themselves since they were not able to understand the secret mysteries of God. Second, God wanted to reveal hidden and future things that the true God might be acknowledged and glorified. Third, God wanted to bestow on his church a witness of his presence and truth to lighten their affliction in exile. Brief Exposition of the Prophet Daniel.[2]

The Argument. Heinrich Bullinger: Now it is significant that he expounds [in this chapter] the substance and character of true wisdom and who profits from a true wise man or an education in wisdom. . . . To be sure, true wisdom does not arise from the flesh or the world but from heaven, from God its author. This wisdom acknowledges God as the governor of all things, Christ as our savior and his eternal kingdom. It understands that all things in the world are governed by God, that all these things are transient and passing away and that the kingdom of Christ alone is eternal. Those who belong to this kingdom look on Christ alone, expecting salvation from him alone, honestly and piously living in this world and will live in the world to come forever with the happy and blessed saints. This, I say, is true and divine wisdom, proposed by the dream of Nebuchadnezzar and wisely and clearly explained by Daniel through the Holy Spirit. Therefore Daniel professed this true wisdom as a foreigner in Babylon, regarded by the world with contempt and as a prisoner of war. . . .

He relates this teaching concerning God's providence of all things, Christ's eternal kingdom and the salvation of the faithful first to the confirmation of the divine promise, by which Christ is the promised savior of the world, and then to the consolation of the afflicted people of Judea now in captivity in Babylon. Because the kings and rulers together with the prophets and the people of God were led into captivity, the city with the temple set on fire, the place of worshiping God taken from them, the land promised the ancestors given to another people, it certainly seemed that God was able to forget his promises, no longer wishing to either acknowledge his people or send them a liberator. Because of this, God repeated from the very beginning of the Babylonian captivity the universal promise concerning the Christ. Indeed, he did this so marvelously by using King Nebuchadnezzar for the consolation of the afflicted. Before the captivity is over, as will appear in Daniel 9, he expresses so clearly the whole mystery of redemption by Christ. So the sacred history bears witness that during difficult times and during periods of disturbance the promise of Christ is always repeated and impressed on us. For there is no salvation or consolation outside of Christ. In Christ, there is life, light and the salvation of all people—those who were and those who are to come. Such that they are truly wise who acknowledge him and believe in him; foolish are those who neither acknowledge nor believe in him. Daniel the Most Wise Prophet of God.[3]

2:1 Chronology

[2]*Explicatio Brevis* (1571), 43-44. [3]*Daniel Sapientissimus*, 10.

Chronology Problems. John Calvin: Daniel here says King Nebuchadnezzar dreamed in the second year of his reign. This seems contrary to the opinion expressed in the first chapter. For if Nebuchadnezzar besieged Jerusalem in the first year of his reign, how could Daniel be already reckoned among the wise men and astrologers, while he was as yet but a disciple? Thus it is easily gathered from the context that he and his companions were already brought forward to minister before the king. At the first glance these things are not in accordance, because in the first year of Nebuchadnezzar's reign Daniel and his companions were delivered into training; and in the second he was in danger of death through being in the number of the magi. Some, as we have mentioned elsewhere, count the second year from the capture and destruction of the city, for they say Nebuchadnezzar was called king from the time at which he obtained the monarchy in peace. Before he had cut off the city and temple with the nation, his monarchy could not be treated as united; hence they refer this to the capture of the city, as I have said.

But I rather incline to another conjecture as more probable—that of his reigning with his father, and I have shown that when he besieged Jerusalem in the time of Jehoiakim, he was sent by his father; he next returned to Chaldea from the Egyptian expedition, through his wish to repress revolts, if anyone should dare to rebel. In this, therefore, there is nothing out of place. Nebuchadnezzar reigned before the death of his father, because he had already been united with him in the supreme power; then he reigned alone, and the present narrative happened in the second year of his reign. In this explanation there is nothing forced, and as the history agrees with it, I adopt it as the best. Commentaries on Daniel.[4]

The Issue of Chronology. John Mayer: In this chapter where the dream of Nebuchadnezzar is set forth, Daniel first begins with the time, namely, in his second year, about which many conjecture diversely, because he brought Daniel away captive from Judea, and three years were now expired since that time, in which Daniel and his three fellows were brought up in the learning of the Chaldeans. Now if this were after these three years, how could it be in Nebuchadnezzar's second year? Some say that another Nebuchadnezzar, the son of Nebuchadnezzar the Great, is here meant. But that this cannot stand appears, because there neither was any more Nebuchadnezzars but one, neither could there be if the prophecy of Jeremiah is true, as none will deny. For he says that the Lord had given the nations to serve Nebuchadnezzar and his son and his son's son (Jer 2:7). But if there had been another son of his besides Evil-merodach who had reigned after him, then the time of the nations being kept under by that family had not been only in his, his son's and his grandchild, Belshazzar's time, but also of another son of whom it is nowhere written. Commentary upon All the Prophets.[5]

The Second Year. Giovanni Diodati: Nebuchadnezzar carried away Jehoiakim in the third year of his reign (Dan 1:1), and afterwards those young Jews were brought up for the space of three years (Dan 1:5). Therefore this second year cannot be taken from the time that he came to the crown. But it is likely that after he had subdued the king of Egypt, his greatest emulator, and had by that means established his monarchy, he did then begin a new computation of the years of his reign. Pious Annotations.[6]

2:1b-11 *The King's Dream*

The Reason for Daniel's Captivity. Martin Luther: The second chapter is

[4]CTS 24:115-16 (CO 18:556-57). [5]*Prophets*, 519-20. [6]*Pious Annotations* (1651), 2:1.

concerned with Daniel's honor, beginning with the king's dream which through divine revelation Daniel knows and interprets. Because of this he becomes a prince over the entire land of Babylon, and a bishop or chief minister over all priests and scribes. This also happens for the solace of the entire Jewish people, so that in their misery they should not doubt or become anxious, as if God had rejected them and given up on his promise of Christ. So an imprisoned Jew must rule such a great kingdom, rather than a Babylonian having such an honor. It is as if he had been captured and led into exile so that he should become such a great lord even over those who had captured and imprisoned him. This is how marvelously God guides his faithful. He gives so much more than a person is able even to wish for. Preface to the Prophet Daniel[7]

Natural Causes for Dreams. John Calvin: This verse (Dan 2:2) more clearly proves what I have already said that the dream caused the king to feel God to be its author. Though this was not his first dream, yet the terror that God impressed on his mind compelled him to summon all the magi, since he could not rest even by returning to sleep. He felt as it were a sting in his mind, since God did not suffer him to rest but wished him to be troubled until he received an interpretation of the dream.

Even profane writers very correctly consider dreams connected with divine agency. They express various opinions, because they could not know anything with perfect certainty; yet the persuasion was fixed in their minds relative to some divine agency in dreams. It would be foolish and puerile to extend this to all dreams; as we see some persons never passing by a single one without a conjecture, and thus making themselves ridiculous. We know dreams to arise from different causes, as, for instance, from our daily thoughts. If I have meditated on anything during the daytime, something occurs to me at night in a dream, because the mind is not completely buried in slumber but retains some seed of intelligence, although it be suffocated. Experience also sufficiently teaches us how our daily thoughts recur during sleep, and hence the various affections of the mind and body produce many dreams. If anyone retires to bed in sorrow from either the death of a friend or any loss, or through suffering any injury or adversity, his dreams will partake of the previous preparation of his mind. The body itself causes dreams, as we see in the case of those who suffer from fever; when thirst prevails they imagine fountains, burnings, and similar fancies. We perceive also how intemperance disturbs people in their sleep; for drunken people start and dream in their sleep, as if in a state of frenzy. As there are many natural causes for dreams, it would be quite out of character to be seeking for divine agency or fixed reason in them all; and on the other hand, it is sufficiently evident that some dreams are under divine regulation. Commentaries on Daniel.[8]

Nebuchadnezzar's Dream. John Calvin: I now come to Nebuchadnezzar's dream. In this, two points are worthy of remark. First, all remembrance of its subject was entirely obliterated; and second, no interpretation was found for it. Sometimes the remembrance of a dream was not lost while its interpretation was unknown. But here Nebuchadnezzar was not only perplexed at the interpretation of the dream, but even the vision itself had vanished, and thus his perplexity and anxiety was doubled. As to the next point, there is no novelty in Daniel making known the interpretation; for it sometimes, but rarely, happens that a person dreams without a figure or enigma and with great plainness, without any need of conjurers—a name given to interpreters of dreams. This indeed happens but seldom, since the usual plan of dreams is for God to speak

[7]WADB 11,2:2-4. [8]CTS 24:117-18 (CO 18:558).

by them allegorically and obscurely. And this occurs in the case of the profane as well as of the servants of God. When Joseph dreamed that he was adored by the sun and moon (Gen 37:9), he was ignorant of its meaning; when he dreamed of his sheaf being adored by his brothers' sheaves, he understood not its meaning but related it simply to his brothers. Hence God often speaks in enigmas by dreams, until the interpretation is added. And such was Nebuchadnezzar's dream. COMMENTARIES ON DANIEL.[9]

WHY DID NEBUCHADNEZZAR HAVE THIS DREAM? ANDREW WILLET: The Lord did it for Nebuchadnezzar's sake, that thereby he might be humbled and acknowledge the true God of Israel, and thereon be favorable to his people, whom he held in captivity. It was done also in respect of Daniel that by this means he might be had in reputation and so be exalted for the comfort of the Lord's people. As Joseph for the same cause was advanced in Egypt to be a softer father to his brethren.

The use here also is general concerning the whole church of God, that as these four great monarchies were dissolved by the power of Christ, whose kingdom only is invincible. So God will destroy the mighty kingdoms and potentates of the earth, who shall band themselves against Christ and his church. SIXFOLD COMMENTARY UPON DANIEL.[10]

2:12-17 *The Wise Men of Babylon*

FALSE WISDOM OF THE WORLD. HEINRICH BULLINGER: The wise men of Babylon freely grant the king's request, asking him to recite the dream so that they might add their interpretation to it. Although God is the author of all true wisdom, they make no mention of this fact. Since philosophy or the wisdom of the world is not from the Spirit of God but is derived from the flesh, is puffed up by the flesh, seeks the flesh, to such a degree that it corresponds completely to the flesh and attributes all things to the power of people, in short is presumptuous and boastful, we rightly hear next that this wisdom dismayed the king and was recognized as utter foolishness. DANIEL THE MOST WISE PROPHET OF GOD.[11]

2:17-23 *Daniel Summoned*

WHY DANIEL WAS NOT CALLED IMMEDIATELY. JOHN MAYER: But in as much as Daniel and his three fellows were found by the king to be far more excellent than any of the Babylonian wise men (Dan 1:19-20), it may seem strange that they were not called with the others, since one would think they should have been preferred before them. Here is the explanation. The king by this time had haply forgotten them. It had been about thirty-five years between the time of that special notice that he took of them and the time when the Chaldeans were thus called together. It may also be conceived that they being strangers and the others natives he had not so much confidence in them. Or lastly, they being Jews, although very wise and learned, yet he thought that they did not or would not practice those arts because they were condemned by the law of their God. Thus it may be conceived according to human reason. But certainly it was God's providence that secretly ruled in this matter, ordering it thus, that Daniel should not be first sent for because then the vanity of the astrologers and magicians would not have so much appeared and people might no longer esteem them as worthy to be sought. And as the divine Providence ordered it, he was not first sent for lest he should be among the others and these great secrets should be thought to have come from the skill of the magicians; as it would have been thought, if Daniel appearing among them had disclosed them.

[9]CTS 24:119-20 (CO 18:559-60). [10]*Sixfold Commentary* (1610), 47. [11]*Daniel Sapientissimus*, 11.

Commentary upon All the Prophets.[12]

Daniel and His Companions Pray. Heinrich Bullinger: When the prayer spoken by Daniel and his companions is heard, we are shown clearly the efficacy of the prayer of the faithful in church. Even if God does not always grant that which we seek from him, nevertheless he gives something else far more useful, and therefore our prayers are always efficacious. . . . The young men with Daniel ask for a revelation of the king's secret, and they receive what they seek. Daniel recorded this to display the glory of God and how he cares for those who pray. Therefore, let us always believe that our prayers are heard when we ask for that which is according to the glory of God and for our salvation and the other faithful. Daniel the Most Wise Prophet of God.[13]

Daniel's Prayer. Johannes Oecolampadius: *Blessed be the name of God* (Dan 2:20). That is, God himself is great as he is celebrated everywhere and always proclaimed and glorified. To him, who is the fount and source of all good things, and to none other is glory and honor owed. . . . Daniel blesses the name of God. This is the voice of all the saints of God, those who prosper and those who do not. Job, devoid of all things, declared, "God gives and God takes away, blessed be the name of the Lord." The Lord himself teaches us to pray, "Hallowed be your name." This is the petition of believers that all nations would be led to a knowledge of the one true God and speaking this decently and sublimely, not only with lips but also earnestly praying for a most chaste imitation of the virtuous life. . . .

To you, the God of my fathers (Dan 2:23). Here he gives thanks for the mercy of God, which has been shown to the ancestors, to the chosen people and to whom has been given the greatest promises. Among other people, he says, I acknowledge you to be the God of wisdom and power, bestowing many favors among my ancestors and their posterity, never ceasing to bless us, despite our sins. Commentary on Daniel.[14]

[12]*Prophets*, 520-21. [13]*Daniel Sapientissimus*, 14-15. [14]*In Danielem prophetam libri duo* (1553), 20-22.

2:24-49 Daniel Interprets the Dream

24Therefore Daniel went in to Arioch, whom the king had appointed to destroy the wise men of Babylon. He went and said thus to him: "Do not destroy the wise men of Babylon; bring me in before the king, and I will show the king the interpretation."

25Then Arioch brought in Daniel before the king in haste and said thus to him: "I have found among the exiles from Judah a man who will make known to the king the interpretation."
26The king declared to Daniel, whose name was Belteshazzar, "Are you able to make known to me the dream that I have seen and its interpretation?"
27Daniel answered the king and said, "No wise men, enchanters, magicians, or astrologers can show to the king the

mystery that the king has asked, [28]but there is a God in heaven who reveals mysteries, and
he has made known to King Nebuchadnezzar what will be in the latter days. Your dream
and the visions of your head as you lay in bed are these: [29]To you, O king, as you lay in
bed came thoughts of what would be after this, and he who reveals mysteries made known
to you what is to be. [30]But as for me, this mystery has been revealed to me, not because of
any wisdom that I have more than all the living, but in order that the interpretation may
be made known to the king, and that you may know the thoughts of your mind.

[31]"You saw, O king, and behold, a great image. This image, mighty and of exceeding
brightness, stood before you, and its appearance was frightening. [32]The head of this image
was of fine gold, its chest and arms of silver, its middle and thighs of bronze, [33]its legs of
iron, its feet partly of iron and partly of clay. [34]As you looked, a stone was cut out by no
human hand, and it struck the image on its feet of iron and clay, and broke them in pieces.
[35]Then the iron, the clay, the bronze, the silver, and the gold, all together were broken in
pieces, and became like the chaff of the summer threshing floors; and the wind carried
them away, so that not a trace of them could be found. But the stone that struck the image
became a great mountain and filled the whole earth.

[36]"This was the dream. Now we will tell the king its interpretation. [37]You, O king, the
king of kings, to whom the God of heaven has given the kingdom, the power, and the might,
and the glory, [38]and into whose hand he has given, wherever they dwell, the children of
man, the beasts of the field, and the birds of the heavens, making you rule over them all—
you are the head of gold. [39]Another kingdom inferior to you shall arise after you, and
yet a third kingdom of bronze, which shall rule over all the earth. [40]And there shall be a
fourth kingdom, strong as iron, because iron breaks to pieces and shatters all things. And
like iron that crushes, it shall break and crush all these. [41]And as you saw the feet and
toes, partly of potter's clay and partly of iron, it shall be a divided kingdom, but some of
the firmness of iron shall be in it, just as you saw iron mixed with the soft clay. [42]And as
the toes of the feet were partly iron and partly clay, so the kingdom shall be partly strong
and partly brittle. [43]As you saw the iron mixed with soft clay, so they will mix with one
another in marriage,[a] but they will not hold together, just as iron does not mix with clay.
[44]And in the days of those kings the God of heaven will set up a kingdom that shall never
be destroyed, nor shall the kingdom be left to another people. It shall break in pieces all
these kingdoms and bring them to an end, and it shall stand forever, [45]just as you saw that
a stone was cut from a mountain by no human hand, and that it broke in pieces the iron,
the bronze, the clay, the silver, and the gold. A great God has made known to the king
what shall be after this. The dream is certain, and its interpretation sure."

[46]Then King Nebuchadnezzar fell upon his face and paid homage to Daniel, and com-
manded that an offering and incense be offered up to him. [47]The king answered and said
to Daniel, "Truly, your God is God of gods and Lord of kings, and a revealer of mysteries,
for you have been able to reveal this mystery." [48]Then the king gave Daniel high honors
and many great gifts, and made him ruler over the whole province of Babylon and chief
prefect over all the wise men of Babylon. [49]Daniel made a request of the king, and he ap-
pointed Shadrach, Meshach, and Abednego over the affairs of the province of Babylon.
But Daniel remained at the king's court.

a Aramaic *by the seed of men*

Overview: When Daniel comes before the king, he impresses on him that it is God who gave this dream and God alone who can reveal its meaning. Daniel proceeds to explain the image the king saw and how this is a vision of four monarchies or kingdoms: Babylonian, Persian, Macedonian and Roman. Daniel says more about the fourth kingdom, the Roman, and this is what receives the most attention from our commentators. The final part of the vision concerns Christ's eternal kingdom. A survey of patristic opinion is given that understands the mountain and the stone cut without hands to be a reference to the Virgin Mary and Christ's nativity. The Lutheran authors welcome this interpretation but the Reformed dismiss it. Following Daniel's interpretation, he is praised by the king and promoted. Some authors commend Nebuchadnezzar's confession of God as pious. Others charge Nebuchadnezzar with idolatry. Unstated in the text is Daniel's rebuke of the king. The fruit of that rebuke is seen with Nebuchadnezzar directing his praise rightly to God.

2:24-26 *Daniel Before the King*

No Ordinary Dream. John Calvin: Now, as to Daniel's answer (Dan 2:27-28). He says it was not surprising that the king did not find what he hoped for among the magi, since God had breathed into him this dream beyond the comprehension of human intellect. I know not whether those interpreters are right who think magical arts here simply are condemned, for I rather think a comparison is instituted between the king's dream and the substance of the science of the magi. I always exclude superstitions by which they vitiated true and genuine science. But as far as the principles are concerned, we cannot precisely condemn astronomy and whatever belongs to the consideration of the order of nature. This appears to me the whole intention: the king's dream was not subjected to human knowledge, for mortals have no such natural skill as to be able to comprehend the meaning of the dream, and God manifests those secrets that need the peculiar revelation of the Spirit. When Daniel says the magi, astrologers, and the rest cannot explain to the king his dream and are not suitable interpreters of it, the true reason is because the dream was not natural and had nothing in common with human conjectures but was the peculiar revelation of the Spirit. Commentaries on Daniel.[1]

Daniel's Response to the King. Heinrich Bullinger: There are many worthy things observed with Daniel's response to the king. Most importantly it is free from all flattery and has nothing in common with the smooth talk of the Babylonian wise men. On the contrary, it has his decorum and gravity. He begins by truly acknowledging that human wisdom is not able to explicate the mystery of salvation and true wisdom. . . . Daniel does not fail to mention that true wisdom comes from God. It does not come from any random god, like the several deities worshiped by the Babylonians, but from the true God of heaven. He is plainly the one and true God inhabiting heaven. He, explains Daniel, reveals hidden things; he illumines the mind; and he inspires people with true wisdom. From him such things are to be sought.

Next he explains briefly the substance and end of all mysteries: "To you, O king Nebuchadnezzar, God wishes to show by this mystery what will be in the latter days, that is, at the end of the age." At such time he will clearly turn all to true wisdom. The prophets and apostles called the end of the age chiefly the time of Christ and his eternal kingdom. Now when all of the prophets mentioned this, they intended only a single end, not numerous other ages or kingdoms. Daniel continues with the dream and ends with the mystery of Christ

[1]CTS 24:154-55 (CO 18:584).

the Savior. Daniel the Most Wise Prophet of God.[2]

2:27-30 *Daniel Praises God*

The Glory Belongs to God. John Mayer: Thus holy Daniel showed that by this great gift of knowledge that God had given him he sought not his own but the glory of God. Therefore he impressed the knowledge of God's omniscience on the heart of the king that he might esteem and honor him, as the only true God, abhorring henceforth the service of any other god. Commentary upon All the Prophets.[3]

The Gifts of the Spirit. John Calvin: Here Daniel meets an objection that Nebuchadnezzar might make: If God alone can reveal secrets, how, I pray, can you, a mere mortal, do it? Daniel anticipates this, and transfers the whole glory to God and ingenuously confesses that he has no interpretation of his own to offer but represents himself as led forward by God's hand to be its interpreter, and as having nothing by his own natural talents but acting as God pleased to appoint him his servant for this office and as using his assistance. *This secret*, then, says he, *has been made known to me*. By these words he sufficiently declares how his undertaking to interpret the dream was God's peculiar gift. But he more clearly expresses this gift to be supernatural, as it is called, by saying, *not in the wisdom that belongs to me*. For if Daniel had surpassed the whole world in intelligence, yet he could never divine what the king of Babylon had dreamed! He excelled, indeed, in superior abilities and learning and was endowed, as we have said, with remarkable gifts, yet he could never have obtained this power that he acquired from God through prayer (I repeat it again) through his own study or industry or any human exertions.

We observe how Daniel here carefully excludes not only what people foolishly claim as their own but also what God naturally confers; since we know the profane to be endowed with singular talents and other eminent faculties, and these are called natural, since God desires his gracious gifts to shine forth in the human race by such examples as these. But while Daniel acknowledges himself endowed with no common powers, through the good pleasure and discipline of God, though he confesses this, I say, yet he places this revelation on a higher footing. We observe also how the gifts of the Spirit mutually differ, because Daniel acted in a kind of twofold capacity with regard to the endowments with which it pleased God to adorn him. First of all, he made rapid progress in all sciences and flourished much in intellectual quickness, and we have already clearly shown this to be owing to the mere liberality of God. This liberality puts all things in their proper order, while it shows God's singular favor in the explanation of the dream. Commentaries on Daniel.[4]

God Interprets Through Daniel. Johann Gerhard: Daniel says in Daniel 2:36, "We shall tell our explanation to the king." For how would Daniel speak about himself by way of authority in the plural before the king when he was the king's captive and the king himself would be above all kings? Others say that Daniel is speaking in the plural to attribute the interpretation of the dream to God. On the Nature of God and on the Trinity.[5]

2:31-43 *The Four Kingdoms*

Nebuchadnezzar's Vision of the Four Monarchies. John Calvin: *Nebuchadnezzar then saw an image* (Dan 2:31). All writers endowed with a sound judgment and candidly

[2]*Daniel Sapientissimus*, 16. [3]*Prophets*, 521-22. [4]CTS 24:158-59 (CO 18:587-88). [5]*Theological Commonplaces: God and Trinity*, 365.

desirous of explaining the prophet's meaning understand this, without controversy, of the four monarchies, following each other in succession. The Jews, when pressed by this interpretation, confuse the Turkish with the Roman empire, but their ignorance and unfairness are easily proved. For when they wish to escape the confession of Christ having been exhibited to the world, they seek stale calumnies that do not require refutation, but still something must afterwards be said in its proper place. My assertion is perfectly correct, that interpreters of moderate judgment and candor all explain the passage of the Babylonian, Persian, Macedonian and Roman monarchies, and Daniel himself afterwards shows this sufficiently by his own words. A question, however, arises, why God represented these four monarchies under this image? for it does not seem to correspond throughout, as the Romans had nothing in common with the Assyrians. History has fully informed us how the Medes and Persians succeeded the Chaldeans; how Babylon was besieged by the enemy and how Cyrus, after obtaining the victory, transferred the empire to the Medes and Persians. It may, perhaps, seem absurd that one image only should be proposed. But it is probable—nay, it may be shown—that God does not here regard any agreement between these four monarchies, for there was none at all, but the state of the world at large. God therefore wished, under this figure, to represent the future condition of the world till the advent of Christ. This is the reason why God joined these four empires together, although actually different; since the second sprang from the destruction of the first, and the third from that of the second. COMMENTARIES ON DANIEL.[6]

THE ROMAN EMPIRE. MARTIN LUTHER: The dream and the image are clearly explained in the text by Daniel as four kingdoms, that is, the first is the Assyrian or Babylonian kingdom, the second is the Meden and Persian kingdom, the third is Alexander the Great's and the Greek kingdom, and the fourth is the Roman Empire. The entire world is in agreement in this interpretation and perspective. And events and histories also prove it conclusively. Daniel speaks the most and the longest about the Roman Empire. For this reason we must listen carefully when at the end (2:41-45) the iron legs begin to split into toes at the feet, indicating three things about the Roman Empire.

The first thing is that the toes are divided, although, all the same, they keep their origin in the iron foot. Just as in the human body the toes are also divided but still come from the feet and belong to the feet, in this way the Roman Empire is divided, there is Spain, France, England, and many other pieces that came out of it. And yet it has continued to grow and, just like a plant, has been transplanted (as they call it), *translatum*, from the Greeks to the Germans so that still the iron's nature remained. For it still has its classes, offices, rights, and laws, as it had previously. This is why he here says that even though it will be a divided empire still the root, plant or stem of iron will be in it.

The second thing is that such divided toes are unequal, part iron, part clay, which he interprets to mean that it will be this sort of a divided empire, somewhat mighty, somewhat weak. This has been confirmed to be so. Often there were many mighty emperors, like Charlemagne, the three Ottos, and so on, who were invincible. On the other hand often there were weak and unfortunate emperors, who were conquered often. All of this is said so that we know that the Roman Empire will be the last empire. No one will tear it apart except Christ alone with his own kingdom. Many kings have stood against the German empire, and the Turks also rage against it, and perhaps they all may win several battles, so they must.

[6]CTS 24:162-63 (CO 18:589-90).

However, this iron root or plant will not become weak or be totally stamped out. It must remain until the Last Day, however weak it may be, because Daniel does not lie, and so far experience has also proved this, both to popes themselves and to kings.

The third thing is that such divided, unequal toes are mixed together or switched around. He indicates that it will be such a weak empire that it will sign treaties and make alliances here and there, trying to cobble itself together and strengthen itself by other kings. But nevertheless this will not help, nor will it find any allies. The empire must have its strength and victory through God's provision alone, if it is to last. Preface to the Prophet Daniel.[7]

The Fourth Kingdom and Antichrist. Giovanni Diodati: [Dan 2:40, *The fourth*] This fourth empire is by most people directly referred to the Roman, and even to that of antichrist, with which indeed that is spoken here, and at Daniel 7:7, it may very well be seen by a most agreeable conformity. And perhaps the Holy Spirit's intent was to give a prophetical figure of it in this place. Very often in the prophets many events that happened before the coming of Christ have been made use of to represent and foretell others like it that correspond to them that were to happen afterwards. This is seen by Saint John in many places of his Revelation when he makes a relation of things spoken by Daniel concerning this fourth empire to pagan Rome and antichrist. It is most evident by Daniel where the subject of this vision concerning the empires is reiterated. According to the first proper and literal meaning, this last ought to be understood of Alexander's successors, reigning in Syria and Egypt, who were the last tyrants and oppressors of the church before Christ's coming on earth, and who more than any of the former undertook to overthrow the whole service of God by forcing consciences to consent to them. Pious Annotations.[8]

2:44-45 *Christ's Kingdom and the Virgin Mary*

The Mountain and the Blessed Virgin Mary. Martin Luther: The mountain that the stone was torn from without human hands (2:45) some believe to be the blessed virgin Mary, from whom Christ was born without human assistance. This is not an unchristian thought. However, it may also be that the mountain is the entire Jewish kingdom, from which Christ came who is their flesh and blood, and yet now he has been torn from them, and has come to the nations. He has become a Lord throughout all the world, in each of these four kingdoms. And so he will always be. Preface to the Prophet Daniel.[9]

The Stone Cut from the Mountain. Andrew Willet: Most do understand this of Christ himself, who is signified by this stone, of which opinion are the ancient writers Justin Martyr, Irenaeus, Cyprian, Augustine and Lyra. And of the recent writers, Bullinger by this stone would have Christ understood: as Psalm 118:22, *the stone that the builders refused has become the head stone of the corner,* and Isaiah 28:16, *Behold, I will lay in Sion a stone, a tried stone, a precious cornerstone, a sure foundation.* To the same purpose Melanchthon. Likewise Pererius beside these testimonies of Scripture shows how Christ, this precious stone, was prefigured by certain typical stones in the Old Testament. As by the stone Jacob pitched and anointed it with oil. And the rock that Moses struck with the rod, and water gushed out. By the stone that bore up Moses' hands (Ex 33). Further in these four respects Christ is compared with a stone: (1) for the continuance; (2) for the strength, he is the fun-

[7]WADB 11,2:4-6. The three Ottos refers to three Holy Roman Emperors: Otto the Great, Otto II, and Otto III. They reigned from 962 to 1002 and were all great patrons of art and architecture. [8]*Pious Annotations* (1651), 2:40. [9]WADB 11,2:6.

damental stone; (3) a rock of refuge to them that believe; (4) and a rock of offense for the wicked to stumble at. . . .

How is Christ said to be the stone cut out without hands? Augustine by this mountain understands the people of the Jews. . . . Most interpreters interpret it of the miraculous generation of Christ from the Virgin Mary, so Jerome, Theodoret, Lyra, Vatablus. *Without hands* signifies without the help of man. And the Virgin Mary is compared with a mountain because of the excellence of her virtue (Pintus). Bullinger puts these together understanding by the word *mountain*, partly the high place of heaven, partly the people of the Jews, because he was born of the Virgin Mary.

But this cannot be applied to the Virgin Mary, for she in no sense can be said to be a mountain in respect of Christ, and he to be a small stone in respect of her. Mary was in no way greater than her son. Although Christ was born of Mary without the company of man, yet his natural generation was not altogether without the help of humankind, because he was born of a woman. And therefore Justin Martyr better applies these words to Christ's eternal generation, which was altogether without hands. . . .

Wherefore the meaning is he was cut out of the mountain, he was sent from heaven, from the place of the highest (Polanus). He was sent from God (Calvin). And therefore it is here said the God of heaven shall set him up. SIXFOLD COMMENTARY UPON DANIEL.[10]

CHRIST'S KINGDOM. JOHN MAYER: After the fourth kingdom, a fifth is prophesied of, which is the kingdom of Christ, as both Jews and Christians agree. Only the Jews maintain that Christ is not yet come, because when he comes all earthly monarchies shall be overthrown; whereas the Roman still stands, although much shaken by the Goths and Vandals long ago and impaired both by the Turks in the east and other kingdoms falling from it in the west. Moreover, at the time when we say he came, namely, Augustus Caesar being emperor, the Roman monarchy stood most strongly, and long after till the time of Constantine the Great, which was three hundred years after, and from that time to the Turks' winning of Constantinople. But this is easily answered. It is not meant that Christ at his coming should put down all imperial power and dominion himself, reigning over all nations after the manner of other worldly emperors, but rather spiritually all should be subdued to him, he being by them acknowledged their King and Messiah and therefore doing homage to him by bowing the knee. This was done when Constantine, after a long time of persecution in his predecessor's days, submitted himself and his crown to him. Idolatry was abandoned, for thus truly the stone broke all in pieces, the golden kingdom that was, and the silver and brazen, and the iron then being reduced to the likeness of dust and blown away by the wind, so that no place like that was more to be found, as was said before. Because there was no part of any of these empires that continued in idolatry, but all were Christian, so that he, who should have looked for an idolatrous monarchy now, could nowhere have found it. COMMENTARY UPON ALL THE PROPHETS.[11]

A PROPHECY OF CHRIST. JOHANN GERHARD: It is to be concluded that Christ was born during the time of the fourth monarchy, as previously proclaimed by Daniel 2, where King Nebuchadnezzar saw a huge image, whose head was of gold, the breast and arms of silver, the belly and lumbar region of bronze, the thighs of iron, the feet partly iron and partly clay; ultimately, however, without hands a stone is ripped from the mountain that crushes

[10]*Sixfold Commentary* (1610), 73, 77-78. Theodoret of Cyrus (c. 393–c. 460) was an important theologian of the fifth-century Antiochene school. Francis Vatablus (1485–547) was a noted Hebrew professor at the University of Paris. [11]*Prophets*, 524.

this huge image totally and completely.

This image had symbolized the four great kingdoms or monarchies of the Assyrians, the Persians, the Greeks and the Romans. In the fourth monarchy, a stone is ripped from a mountain without hands; that is, Christ the true rock and cornerstone of our salvation is born from the Virgin Mary without any contribution of any male. He began a kingdom that brings all others into subjection and abides eternally.

However, that Christ wanted to be born during the fourth and last monarchy, and thus toward the end of the world, took place so that he might thereby show that the benefit of his birth applied principally not toward this life but rather to the future life. Thus he also, through the law of Moses, wanted to awaken a longing for his coming within the believers of the Old Testament and to move them to confess their impotent inability before he broke the yoke of their burden and the rod on their shoulder and the stick of their slavedrivers (Is 9:4); that is, before he rescued them from the burden of the law. POSTILLA.[12]

THE KINGDOM OF CHRIST. JOHN CALVIN: The kingdom of Christ is said *to break up all the empires of the world,* not *directly,* but only accidentally, as the phrase is. For Daniel here assumes a principle, sufficiently understood by the Jews; namely, those monarchies were opposed to Christ's kingdom. For the Chaldeans had overthrown God's temple and had endeavored as far as possible to extinguish the whole of his worship and to exterminate piety from the world. As far as concerns the Medes and Persians, although by their kindness a permission to return was granted to the people, yet very soon afterwards the kings of the Medes and Persians raged against that most miserable people, until the greater part of them preferred remaining in exile to returning home. At length came the Macedonian fury, and although the Jews were spared for a short period, we know how impetuously the kings of Syria and Egypt overran Judea, how cruelly they treated the wretched people by rapine and plunder and the shedding of innocent blood. Again, the extreme barbarity of Antiochus in ordering all the prophetic books to be burned and in all but exterminating the religion itself is well ascertained (1 Macc 1:59).

No wonder, then, that Daniel here opposes the reign of Christ to such monarchies! Next, as to the Romans, we know how thoroughly and proudly they despised the name of Christian! They endeavored by all means to root out from the world the gospel and the doctrine of salvation as an abominable thing. With all this we are familiar. Hence, to inform the faithful of their future condition until Christ's advent, Daniel shows how all the empires of the world should be adverse to God and all its most powerful kings and sovereigns should be his very worst and most cruel enemies and should use every means in their power to extinguish true piety. Thus he exhorts them to bear their cross and never to yield to those wretched and sorrowful spectacles but to proceed steadily in the course of their calling until the promised Redeemer should appear. We stated this to be "accidental," since all the kingdoms of this world are clearly founded on the power and beneficence of Christ; but a memorable proof of God's anger ought to exist against them all, because they raised themselves against the Son of God, the supreme King, with such extreme fury and hostility. COMMENTARIES ON DANIEL.[13]

2:46-49 *Daniel's Promotion*

THE KING'S CONFESSION. HEINRICH BULLINGER: The confession of the king that follows is to be praised and commended in every manner. We gather from this that the king acknowledged and worshiped the true God and henceforth sought to imitate him.

[12]*Postilla* 1:47. [13]CTS 24:178-79 (CO 18:601-2).

. . . The confession of Nebuchadnezzar deals with many things. First, with an indisputable certitude of spirit he frankly declares, "In certain truth and without any doubts, the God of Israel is the true God and truly the God of gods." That is, excelling all gods, and alone the true, highest, noblest and greatest God. . . . Then the king acknowledges God of gods to be Lord and King. Therefore with this acknowledgment he places himself under God as a vassal to a lord. He acknowledges God to be lord and governor of all kingdoms, who rules all things by his providence and governs the whole with equity. The same one he confesses to be the revealer of mysteries. Therefore, he acknowledges in him the highest wisdom and infallible foreknowledge. To be sure, if we attribute all these things to God, we rightly confess him. And here is practical use of what we learn from the example of Nebuchadnezzar: when we hear the teaching of truth, we are to confess God sincerely and to believe in him with our whole heart. DANIEL THE MOST WISE PROPHET OF GOD.[14]

DANIEL DIRECTS THE KING'S PRAISE TO GOD. JOHN MAYER: *Then King Nebuchadnezzar fell on his face and worshiped Daniel.* Of Daniel denying to have this honor done to him nothing is said, but it is implied that he refused this honor (Dan 2:47) and bade him worship God, from whom this rare knowledge came, setting him forth to the king as the only true God knowing and foreknowing and ruling over all things. It is said, *the king answered Daniel and said, Of a truth it is that your God is a God of gods and Lord of lords.* This effectively states such, as if it had been said, Daniel refusing that honor and instructing the king better about God, whose wisdom it was and not his to reveal secrets, the king answered, as is here said. For Peter did so toward Cornelius worshiping him, and Paul and Barnabas toward the barbarians worshiping them. Therefore it is not to be doubted that Daniel, being led by the same Holy Spirit, did likewise. And his former speeches, that he had no more wisdom than any other man to reveal such secrets, but that there was a God in heaven who had revealed it, imply no less.

Lastly, if he should not have refused it, he should have sinned terribly, as Herod, indeed even more, and so have provoked God against him for accepting divine honors offered to him. How far he was from sinning in the least appears earlier with his care not to be polluted by the king's meat and drink. Wherefore let no one in the exercise of whatever rare gifts seek himself but rather to seek God's glory, according to that, *Let your light so shine before people, that they may see your good works and glorify your Father who is in heaven.* And let no one by that which was done here to Daniel, or commanded to be done out of blindness, justify the adoration of saints departed. You must consider from time to time what kind of people they were who offered this sort of devotion to any of God's dearest servants. They were blind and superstitious. For this reason abhor from doing the like for fear of becoming like them, who think they are expressing the greatest devotion but will be condemned for blind superstition. COMMENTARY UPON ALL THE PROPHETS.[15]

THE KING'S IDOLATROUS WORSHIP OF DANIEL. WILLIAM PEMBLE: Nebuchadnezzar being amazed with the work of Daniel went about in his person and by his command to make a god of him. Had he only bowed to him in reverence, in that affection that may well be toward a prophet of the Lord (as Alexander did to the high priest, and is indeed lawful to be done), Daniel might have accepted it. But the king went too far. That act of his to command meat offerings and sweet odors to be offered to him was flagrant idolatry. Therefore, it could not stand with the piety of Daniel, who would

[14]*Daniel Sapientissimus*, 22. [15]*Prophets*, 525-26.

not so much as eat of the king's meat, to give the least entertainment to any such idolatry. And though it is not expressed in so many words, yet it is plain enough that Daniel did reprove this effort of the king and thereupon was nothing done. And the words themselves in Nebuchadnezzar's reply give us this meaning, *The King answered unto Daniel* (says the text); therefore Daniel had spoken his mind to the king, though the words are left out *(Of a truth it is, that your God is a God of gods)*. This shows that Daniel had informed the king that there was but one only God and that divine worship was due to that one God only. We may receive prophets and preachers as angels, but we must not receive them as gods. THE PERIOD OF THE PERSIAN MONARCHY.[16]

[16]*Persian Monarchy* (1659), 373.

3:1-18 THE IMAGE OF GOLD

1King Nebuchadnezzar made an image of gold, whose height was sixty cubits[a] and its breadth six cubits. He set it up on the plain of Dura, in the province of Babylon. 2Then King Nebuchadnezzar sent to gather the satraps, the prefects, and the governors, the counselors, the treasurers, the justices, the magistrates, and all the officials of the provinces to come to the dedication of the image that King Nebuchadnezzar had set up. 3Then the satraps, the prefects, and the governors, the counselors, the treasurers, the justices, the magistrates, and all the officials of the provinces gathered for the dedication of the image that King Nebuchadnezzar had set up. And they stood before the image that Nebuchadnezzar had set up. 4And the herald proclaimed aloud, "You are commanded, O peoples, nations, and languages, 5that when you hear the sound of the horn, pipe, lyre, trigon, harp, bagpipe, and every kind of music, you are to fall down and worship the golden image that King Nebuchadnezzar has set up. 6And whoever does not fall down and worship shall immediately be cast into a burning fiery furnace." 7Therefore, as soon as all the peoples heard the sound of the horn, pipe, lyre, trigon, harp, bagpipe, and every kind of music, all the peoples, nations, and languages fell down and worshiped the golden image that King Nebuchadnezzar had set up.

8Therefore at that time certain Chaldeans came forward and maliciously accused the Jews. 9They declared[b] to King Nebuchadnezzar, "O king, live forever! 10You, O king, have made a decree, that every man who hears the sound of the horn, pipe, lyre, trigon, harp, bagpipe, and every kind of music, shall fall down and worship the golden image. 11And whoever does not fall down and worship shall be cast into a burning fiery furnace. 12There are certain Jews whom you have appointed over the affairs of the province of Babylon:

Shadrach, Meshach, and Abednego. These men, O king, pay no attention to you; they do
not serve your gods or worship the golden image that you have set up."
13 *Then Nebuchadnezzar in furious rage commanded that Shadrach, Meshach, and*
Abednego be brought. So they brought these men before the king. 14 *Nebuchadnezzar an-*
swered and said to them, "Is it true, O Shadrach, Meshach, and Abednego, that you do
not serve my gods or worship the golden image that I have set up? 15 *Now if you are ready*
when you hear the sound of the horn, pipe, lyre, trigon, harp, bagpipe, and every kind of
music, to fall down and worship the image that I have made, well and good.[c] *But if you do*
not worship, you shall immediately be cast into a burning fiery furnace. And who is the
god who will deliver you out of my hands?"
16 *Shadrach, Meshach, and Abednego answered and said to the king, "O Nebuchadnez-*
zar, we have no need to answer you in this matter. 17 *If this be so, our God whom we serve*
is able to deliver us from the burning fiery furnace, and he will deliver us out of your
hand, O king.[d] 18 *But if not, be it known to you, O king, that we will not serve your gods*
or worship the golden image that you have set up."

a A *cubit* was about 18 inches or 45 centimeters **b** Aramaic *answered and said;* also verses 24, 26 **c** Aramaic lacks *well and good* **d** Or *If our God whom we serve is able to deliver us, he will deliver us from the burning fiery furnace and out of your hand, O king.*

Overview: The chapter opens with Nebuchadnezzar's rejection of God and fall into idolatry. The desire toward idolatry is common among all people, and our commentators issue numerous warnings about this. We also see how easily the masses obediently follow the godless orders of the king. The question is raised, however, why Daniel did not stop Nebuchadnezzar from building this image of gold. Should Daniel's silence be understood as sin? The king's idolatry leads to pride and cruelty as he seeks to claim himself as a god. Shadrach, Meshach and Abednego are singled out among the faithful Jews for despising the decree of the king. Again questions are raised concerning Daniel. Why was he spared and not also brought before the king? The three youths boldly confessed the one true God. Here we have a model confession for all Christians today; it is clear and certain. All true confessions are spoken openly and courageously.

The Main Points of the Chapter. Philipp Melanchthon: (1) The example is of human moral blindness and audacity, instituting a new form of worship beyond the Word of God. Here Nebuchadnezzar shows that he rejects God. (2) The doctrine is that it is necessary to reject godless worship. (3) That it is necessary to accept the commandment of God before any human or political opinions, human laws, peace, tranquility, or even our lives. (4) Blasphemy must be refuted as the speech of the king is here refuted, Who is the god able to deliver you? (Dan 3:15). (5) What sort of faith one must have for the deliverance of the body. . . . (6) The glorification of believers against blasphemy and the punishment of the impious, especially the accomplices, who serve the fury of another. (7) The witness that amid danger God sends angels to believers. (8) The conversion of the king following the confession and glorification of believers. (9) The edict prohibiting and punishing blasphemy, which extends to the office of the ruler himself. Commentary on the Prophet Daniel.[1]

3:1-3 *Idolatry*

[1] *In Danielem Prophetam* (1543), 40-41.

The Common Desire to Worship a God. John Calvin: We see how Nebuchadnezzar wished to establish among all the nations under his sway a religion in which there should be no mixture of foreign novelty. He feared dissension as a cause of disunion in his empire. Hence we may suppose the king to have consulted his own private ease and advantage, as princes are accustomed to consult their own wishes rather than God's requirements in promulgating edicts concerning the worship of God. And from the beginning, this boldness and rashness have increased in the world, since those who have had supreme power have always dared to fabricate deities and have proceeded beyond this even to ordering the gods that they have invented to be worshiped.

The different kinds of gods are well known as divided into three: the philosophical, the political and the poetical. They called those gods "philosophical" that natural reason prompts people to worship. Truly, indeed, philosophers are often foolish when they dispute about the essence or worship of God, but since they follow their own fancies they are necessarily erroneous. For God cannot be apprehended by human senses but must be made manifest to us by his own word; and as he descends to us, so we also in turn are raised to heaven (1 Cor 2:14). But yet philosophers in their disputes have some pretexts, so as not to seem utterly insane and irrational. But the poets have fabled whatever pleases them and thus have filled the world with the grossest and at the same time the foulest errors. As all theaters resounded with their vain imaginations, the minds of the vulgar have been imbued with the same delusions, for we know human dispositions are ever prone to vanity. But when the devil adds fire to the fuel, we then see how furiously both learned and unlearned are carried away. So it happened when they persuaded themselves of the truth of what they saw represented in their theaters.

Thus, that religion that was founded on the authority of the magi was considered certain by the heathen, as they called those gods "political" that were received by the common consent of all. Those also who were considered prudent said it was by no means useful to object to what the philosophers taught concerning the nature of the gods, since this would tear asunder all public rites, and whatever was fixed without doubt in people's minds. For both the Greeks and Latins, as well as other barbarous nations, worshiped certain gods as the mere offspring of opinion, and these they confessed to have once been mortal. But philosophers at least retained this principle—the gods are eternal; and if the philosophers had been listened to, the authority of the magi would have fallen away. Hence the most worldly-wise were not ashamed, as I have mentioned, to urge the expulsion of philosophy from sacred things.

With regard to the poets, the most politic were compelled to succumb to the petulance of the common people, and yet they taught at the same time what the poets reigned and fabled concerning the nature of the gods was pernicious. This, then, was the almost universal rule throughout the world as to the worship of God and the very foundation of piety—namely, no deities are to be worshiped except those that have been handed down from our ancestors. Commentaries on Daniel.[2]

Why Did Daniel Not Stop Nebuchadnezzar? Andrew Willet: Some think that Daniel being present held his peace seeing that he could prevail nothing, but that the king was resolute in his purpose (Lyra). But Daniel had sinned if he had been silent; he should have used the means available to him and left the success to God.

Osiander thinks that Daniel used what persuasion he could but seeing he was not heard he withdrew himself. But if Daniel had been

[2]CTS 24:205-7 (CO 18:620-21).

present at all, it would have been suspicious if he had now hid himself.

Pappus is of the opinion that Daniel was employed in some remote place of the province at this time. Even if Daniel were now absent, he could not be ignorant of the king's purpose. This great image was not made in a short time.

Wherefore it is not to be doubted but that Daniel did discharge the office of a faithful servant to God and counselor to the king before this, and did use all means to stay this ungodly enterprise, so far as he might go without exasperating the king too much, which would have kindled his anger against the whole nation. Therefore Daniel not prevailing, he gave way to the time, expecting some other means how it should please the Lord to convert the king. Sixfold Commentary upon Daniel.[3]

Nebuchadnezzar's Idolatry. John Mayer: In this chapter Nebuchadnezzar sets up an image of gold sixty cubits high and six cubits broad, commanding all people to worship it. Lyra says the image was his own (being by pride so puffed up) so that he would be worshiped as a god, setting up this image to such an end and purpose, as Gaius Caligula, the Roman emperor, had done. This is a strange turn of events for this man, who on so firm a foundation a little before acknowledged the one and only true God but now falls to this foul sin of exalting himself as a god. Such is the fickleness and inconstancy of carnal people. . . . Nebuchadnezzar did this out of his exceedingly great pride for the exaltation of his dominion. It is also probable that he had accomplices, namely, his princes and lords who envied the Jews for the great favor and authority they had been bestowed. By these means, they thought to work their destruction, as the following part of the history gives us evidence. This is seen with the great penalty threatened to those who would not fall down and worship this image. For none of the nations under the king's dominion were to be suspected for their standing out against this decree but the Jews only. Hence their accusing of Shadrach, Meshach and Abednego and seeking to have them destroyed by the fiery furnace. . . . This is also why the king called his princes and nobles together to see the miracle wrought for those three and why his decree after this said that none should speak evil of their God. For what else did this imply but that they had before spoken spitefully both against Shadrach, Meshach and Abednego and against their God? To prevent these princes and lords from doing this again Nebuchadnezzar wanted them to see this miracle. Commentary upon All the Prophets.[4]

Beware of Idolatry. Menno Simons: Israel is not commanded here to conform themselves to the Gentiles. But when they saw them carry their idols, then they should worship God only and give him the honor. If God had commanded them to conform in all things to the Babylonian idolatry, and only to serve the Lord with their heart secretly, then Schadrach, Meshach and Abednego acted foolishly to refuse worshiping the great golden idol, on account of which they hazarded their lives (Dan 3). Oh no! the miraculous work, shown of God to them, testifies that they acted rightly. All, then, I say, who teach that true believers are not released from Babylon do thereby deny the merits, death and blood of Christ, and faith with its power, and the Holy Spirit with his liberty, and despise wholly the innocent blood of the free witnesses of the free children of God, which is shed so abundantly. Let everyone see well to it what he believes and learns. A Foundation and Plain Instruction.[5]

What Is Idolatry? Johann Wigand: Idolatry is worship, that is, reverence or adora-

[3]*Sixfold Commentary* (1610), 93-94. Johann Pappus (1549–1610) was a conservative Lutheran theologian and church historian. [4]*Prophets*, 526. [5]*Foundation*, 112.

tion of some certain thing other than the true God. Idolatry is against the very Word of God, which points to the only true God. God most severely punishes idolatry.

Idolatry is twofold. One type is spiritual only. The other is also spiritual and at the same time outward. It is said to be spiritual when the heart clings to and is enslaved by some certain thing other than the true God, so that it takes away the fear, faith and love owed to God and transfers it to the creature. Thus wealth consumes the human heart; this trust in wealth and power is called idolatry in Colossians 3 and Ephesians 5.

It is outward idolatry when it adorns the worship of imaginary and fictitious gods with outward things and adds interior feelings. The spiritual is sometimes able to be without the outward. This is not always true though. Brief Exposition of the Prophet Daniel.[6]

Inward and Outward Worship. John Calvin: Respecting the required adoration, nothing but outward observance was needed. King Nebuchadnezzar did not exact a verbal profession of belief in this deity, that is, in the divinity of the statue that he commanded to be worshiped; it was quite sufficient to offer to it merely outward worship. We here see how idolatry is deservedly condemned in those who pretend to worship idols, even if they mentally refrain and act only through fear and the compulsion of regal authority; that excuse is altogether frivolous. We see, then, how this king or tyrant, though he fabricated this image by the cunning of the devil, exacted nothing else than the bending the knees of all the people and nations before the statue. And truly he had in this way alienated the Jews from the worship of the one true God, if this had been extorted from them. For God wishes first of all for inward worship, and afterwards for outward profession. The principal altar for the worship of God ought to be situated in our minds, for God is worshiped spiritually by faith, prayer, and other acts of piety (Jn 4:24). It is also necessary to add outward profession, not only that we may exercise ourselves in God's worship but also offer ourselves wholly to him, and bend before him both bodily and mentally and devote ourselves entirely to him, as Paul teaches (1 Cor 7:34; 1 Thess 5:23). Thus far, then, concerning both the adoration and the penalty. Commentaries on Daniel.[7]

The Obedience of the People to the King's Edict. Johannes Oecolampadius: *Then they were gathered together* (Dan 3:3). Observe the obedience. There is no one who does not obey the king, even if his orders are godless. The chief prefects and governors all stand by the king. The edict was diligently heard, and they all without any doubt worshiped the statue. All are of ignorant breeding. They forsake the true God. They fall down before a dumb and inanimate image from which humans expect neither salvation nor punishment. They stand before the image, made of cheap materials, expectantly, because the king commanded it. Even if some were repulsed by his command, they did not refuse. This is how servile they were. Moreover, the king proclaims his edict with a herald, doubly harassing those who were reluctant with pleasure and torment. To what other end did he employ all kinds of music and gold on the statue than to soften the more stubborn of heart? To what other end did he light the furnace than to frighten the more timid and simple of mind? So also Satan wages battle on the right and the left, so that anyone not caught by his net submits to punishment. Commentary on Daniel.[8]

3:4-15 *The King's Pride and Cruelty*

The King's Pride and Blasphemy. John Calvin: We see, then, in the person

[6]*Explicatio Brevis* (1571), 109. [7]CTS 24:210-11 (CO 18:624). [8]*In Danielem prophetam libri duo* (1553), 42.

of Nebuchadnezzar, how kings swell with pride while they pretend some zeal for piety, since in reality no reverence for God influences them, while they expect all people to obey every command. And thus, as I have said, they rather substitute themselves for God than desire to worship him and promote his glory. This is the meaning of the words *the statue that I have created, and that I have made;* as if he had said, You are not allowed to deliberate about worshiping this image or not; my orders ought to be sufficient for you. I have erected it purposely and designedly; it was your duty simply to obey me. We see then how he claims the supreme power by fashioning a god. Nebuchadnezzar is not now treating matters of state policy; he wishes the statue to be adored as a deity, because he had decreed it and had promulgated his edict. And we must always remember what I have touched on, namely, this example of pride is set before us to show us not to attach ourselves to any religion with rashness but to listen to God and depend on his authority and commands, since if we listen to people, our errors would be endless. Although kings are so proud and ferocious, yet we must be guided by this rule—Nothing pleases God but what he has commanded in his word; and the principle of true piety is the obedience that we ought to render to him alone. With respect to blasphemy, it clearly demonstrates my previous assertion, however kings put forward some desire for piety, yet they despise every deity and think of nothing but extolling their own magnificence. Hence they traffic in the name of God to attract greater reverence toward themselves; but at the same time, if they choose to change their deities a hundred times a day, no sense of religion will hinder them. Religion, then, is to the kings of the earth nothing but a pretext; but they have neither reverence nor fear of God in their minds, as the language of this profane king proves. Commentaries on Daniel.[9]

The King's Cruelty. Hans Denck: Nebuchadnezzar, king of Babylon, had a golden image built, sixty cubits high and six cubits wide. He set it up in the plain of Dura in the province of Babylon. Then he gathered all dukes, lords, earls, judges, etc., together with all who had power in the land that they might come to dedicate the image that Nebuchadnezzar the king had erected [Dan 3:1ff.]. This was done and proclaimed to the people by the prefect: "You peoples, nations and tongues, let it be said to you that whenever you hear the sound of the horns, which will be blown, together with the harps, trigon, psalter, bagpipe and all manner of song, you must fall down and bow before the golden image that Nebuchadnezzar the king had erected. Whoever does not fall down shall be cast into a fiery furnace." Now when the pipes and songs were heard, all the people fell down, bowed before the image that Nebuchadnezzar had erected. At that time there were a few Chaldeans. They came near and betrayed to the king the Jews who had not worshiped the golden image in keeping with the king's commands, saying, "O king, all the people here followed your commandment and bowed before the image except for Shadrach, Meshach and Abednego whom you had appointed over the affairs of the province of Babylon. Therefore, O king, in keeping with your command, throw them into the fiery furnace that one may learn to obey you, serve your god and bow before the image that you erected." The king grew angry and had them cast into the fiery furnace in keeping with his commandment.

Just as Jeroboam oppressed and plundered the people of Israel, tearing away skin and all down to the marrow, with his disobedience, rebellion, commandments and manslaughter, so here the Babylonian king deals with his three prefects. They were part of the establishment, but not for long. Since they refused to worship his image, he had them thrown into

[9]CTS 24:218-19 (CO 18:629).

the fire against all that was fair and just, forgetting the God of Daniel. Similarly, look to Daniel 6 to see what the counselors of Darius undertook against Daniel, who worshiped God in heaven and not the king according to the decree. Since they were at enmity with him, they sought to have him killed, though by right they should have assisted justice. But Daniel was too righteous for their liking, for which reason they would have loved to blow out his candle, as it were. To no avail. Though he had spent some time in the lions' den, they were the ones who were torn to shreds by the lions, for they were not on the side of God's justice since they were idolatrous, nor were they on the side of human justice, for they sought to murder Daniel though he was blameless. But how could those who did not live in the love of God act fraternally toward their neighbor? They had no concern for God's justice and honor! How were they to declare evil evil and the good good, against their own nature? A magpie cannot cease hopping about. Reflections on Micah.[10]

3:16-18 *The Three Youths and True Confession*

The Accusation Against the Three Youths. Heinrich Bullinger: In this part of the history, the church and true religion in the church, which will never be without its accusers and detractors, is clearly signified. If we examine the history of the ancient church and then observe that today there are those who become enemies of the gospel, we will discover that these things happen in the same way. Those who worship Christ are accused at all times of rebellion, disobedience, sedition and being disturbers of all truth, unity, religion and tradition. "These people," they say, "hold in contempt everything that came before them; indeed they despise and ridicule kings and princes, cardinals and bishops, the decrees of the holy fathers, the praiseworthy and ancient traditions, and finally reject the consensus of all the ancient councils, utterly despise and even bestow disgrace and insult on them. Therefore they are ungrateful and show no regard for God and people." Daniel the Most Wise Prophet of God.[11]

Why Only Shadrach, Meshach and Abednego? Andrew Willet: It may seem that the principal and chief men were only or especially called and that the vulgar and common sort of people were not all present. Or at the least, the principal men were most marked and observed, whose example the rest might follow (Pererius). But it seems, by their general accusation of the Jews (Dan 3:8) that there were more Jews present than these three.

It may be also supposed that the vulgar sort of the Jewish people, which were present, did for fear do as the rest did, fall down and worship. Therefore they were not complained of (Pererius). It is very likely indeed that many Jews did fall away in the time of captivity to worship the Chaldean images, because many of them had been idolaters in their own country, for which they were carried into captivity. But that some other of the Jews beside these three refused to fall down may be gathered by the general accusation against the Jews, but principally against these three.

Wherefore this is likely the cause why these three were singled out because they were advanced to honorable place of government and for this cause were envied and maligned of the Chaldeans. And this may be gathered by their manner of accusation (Dan 3:12) wherein they especially urge that point that the king had set them over the province of Babylon, that seemed to be an eyesore and grief to them. The reason Daniel was not accused with the rest was because of his absence. Sixfold Commentary upon Daniel.[12]

[10]*Writings*, 105-6. [11]*Daniel Sapientissimus*, 27. [12]*Sixfold Commentary* (1610), 98.

Why Was Daniel Spared? John Calvin: It is uncertain whether they spoke of the whole nation generally, namely, of all the exiles, or pointed out those three persons only. The accusation was probably restricted to Shadrach, Meshach and Abednego. If these three could be broken down, the victory over the rest was easy. But few could be found in the whole people hardy enough to resist. We may well believe these clamorers wished to attack those whom they knew to be spirited and consistent beyond all others, and to degrade them from those honors that they could not bear them to enjoy. It may be asked, then, why did they spare Daniel, since he would never consent to dissemble by worshiping the statue that the king commanded to be set up? They must have let Daniel alone for the time, since they knew him to be in favor with the king; but they brought the charge against these three, because they could be oppressed with far less trouble. I think them to have been induced by this cunning in not naming Daniel with the other three, lest his favor should mitigate the king's wrath. Commentaries on Daniel.[13]

Daniel Spared. John Mayer: If it is demanded, how it came to pass that Daniel was not now brought into question with his three fellows, it is answered either because he sat in the king's gate, and so as being above all his princes and nobles and as the king's right hand, the proclamation touched not him any more than the king himself, he most probably sitting with the king, as a spectator of that which was done; or by reason of his employments not to be spared to go from the king's gate and judging matters that came before him. And this I take to be the most probable because if he had been there with the king, he certainly would not have held his peace but would have spoken against this gross idolatry and on behalf of his fellows in danger for not conforming to the request. Commentary upon All the Prophets.[14]

The Confession of the True God. John Calvin: In this history it is necessary to observe with what unbroken spirit these three holy men persisted in the fear of God, though they knew they were in danger of instant death. When, therefore, this kind of death was placed straight before their eyes, they did not turn aside from the straightforward course but treated God's glory of greater value than their own life, nay, than a hundred lives, if they had so many to pour forth, and opportunity had been given them.

. . . They imply that the fear of death was set before them in vain, because they had determined and resolved in their inmost souls not to depart a single inch from the true and lawful worship of God. Besides they here give a double reason for rejecting the king's proposal. They say God has sufficient power and strength to liberate them, and then, even if they must die, their life is not of so much value as to deny God for the sake of preserving it. Hence they declare themselves prepared to die, if the king persists in urging his wish for the adoration of the image. This passage is therefore worthy of the greatest attention.

And when they add, *God is sufficiently powerful to preserve us; and if not, we are prepared for death,* they point out to us what ought to raise our minds above all trials, namely, the preciousness of our life in God's sight, since he can liberate us if he pleases. Since, therefore, we have sufficient protection in God, let us not think any method of preserving our life better than to throw ourselves entirely on his protection and to cast all our cares on him. And as to the second clause, we must remark this, even if the Lord should wish to magnify his own glory by our death, we ought to offer up this as a lawful sacrifice; and sincere piety does not flourish in our hearts unless our minds are always prepared

[13]CTS 24:215 (CO 18:627). [14]*Prophets*, 526-27.

to make this sacrifice. Commentaries on Daniel.[15]

God Will Deliver. Johann Wigand: *They answered* (Dan 3:16). Without doubt the king thought that by his own greatness, by his own severe and cruel words, he would repulse and crush these men and that they would beg for pardon, humbly beseeching him on their knees and prostrating before the statue. . . .

No answer necessary (Dan 3:16). They say, "It is not necessary that we respond at length to these words." They conclude that to these very words—that is, blasphemy of the true God—that God himself will respond.

If this is so (Dan 3:17). By no means do they omit their confession with silence. With an eloquent speech they declare the glory of God and profess that this God is true, whom they worship, and that he is able to deliver them. They opposed the blasphemy of the king with an ardent and excellent faith—as if the God of the Jews were not able to liberate them! They knew with certainty that God is omnipotent in all of his works. They knew this from several historical accounts. They knew that he is able to make use of his creation in his own superlative freedom, contrary to or without any secondary causes, to accomplish his free will. Brief Exposition of the Prophet Daniel.[16]

The Faith of the Three Youths. Tieleman J. van Braght: Shadrach, Meshach and Abednego feared God the Lord more than all the torments of the tyrannical king and would rather die a temporal death and abide by their God than forsake him. Daniel rich in spirit and strong in faith was not terrified at the lions' den into which he would be thrown rather than worship any God besides his own. A Martyrology of the Churches of Christ.[17]

The Confession of Faith. Heinrich Bullinger: This is the form of a noble and true confession: it must be clear and certain and not ambiguous or misleading (which could be misconstrued for different purposes) and set forth according to the beliefs of religious people. A genuine confession confesses what is true openly and courageously and denies what is false openly and courageously. Those Christians of old confessed, I believe in Christ, the Son of God, and I do not believe in any other gods. I worship God in spirit, and I do not worship or honor idols. Our religion is from heaven and is certain. Your religion, on the contrary, is superstition and comes from the devil; it is not certain and possesses nothing good. These are the sorts of confessions found in the acts of martyrs in the history of the church. Daniel the Most Wise Prophet of God.[18]

---

[15]CTS 24:219-22 (CO 18:630-32). [16]*Explicatio Brevis* (1571), 104-5. [17]*Martyrology* 1:215. [18]*Daniel Sapientissimus*, 27.

3:19-30 THE FIERY FURNACE AND THE KING'S EDICT

[19]Then Nebuchadnezzar was filled with fury, and the expression of his face was changed against Shadrach, Meshach, and Abednego. He ordered the furnace heated seven times more than it was usually heated. [20]And he ordered some of the mighty men of his army to bind Shadrach, Meshach, and Abednego, and to cast them into the burning fiery furnace. [21]Then these men were bound in their cloaks, their tunics,[a] their hats, and their other garments, and they were thrown into the burning fiery furnace. [22]Because the king's order was urgent and the furnace overheated, the flame of the fire killed those men who took up Shadrach, Meshach, and Abednego. [23]And these three men, Shadrach, Meshach, and Abednego, fell bound into the burning fiery furnace.

[24]Then King Nebuchadnezzar was astonished and rose up in haste. He declared to his counselors, "Did we not cast three men bound into the fire?" They answered and said to the king, "True, O king." [25]He answered and said, "But I see four men unbound, walking in the midst of the fire, and they are not hurt; and the appearance of the fourth is like a son of the gods."

[26]Then Nebuchadnezzar came near to the door of the burning fiery furnace; he declared, "Shadrach, Meshach, and Abednego, servants of the Most High God, come out, and come here!" Then Shadrach, Meshach, and Abednego came out from the fire. [27]And the satraps, the prefects, the governors, and the king's counselors gathered together and saw that the fire had not had any power over the bodies of those men. The hair of their heads was not singed, their cloaks were not harmed, and no smell of fire had come upon them. [28]Nebuchadnezzar answered and said, "Blessed be the God of Shadrach, Meshach, and Abednego, who has sent his angel and delivered his servants, who trusted in him, and set aside[b] the king's command, and yielded up their bodies rather than serve and worship any god except their own God. [29]Therefore I make a decree: Any people, nation, or language that speaks anything against the God of Shadrach, Meshach, and Abednego shall be torn limb from limb, and their houses laid in ruins, for there is no other god who is able to rescue in this way." [30]Then the king promoted Shadrach, Meshach, and Abednego in the province of Babylon.

a The meaning of the Aramaic words rendered *cloaks* and *tunics* is uncertain; also verse 27 **b** Aramaic *and changed*

Overview: The three youths are placed in the fiery furnace and a fourth appears among them. Our commentators are divided on the identity of this fourth person. Is it an angel? Is it the Son of God? The three are delivered by God, who is the protector of life. Following their deliverance, the king confesses the true God and issues an edict prohibiting any people, nation or language to blaspheme the

God of Shadrach, Meshach and Abednego. There is again some debate among our commentators on whether the king truly believed the things he said or not.

3:19-23 *The Fiery Furnace*

Nebuchadnezzar's Fury. John Calvin: With reference to King Nebuchadnezzar, Daniel here shows, as in a glass, the pride and haughtiness of kings when they find their decrees disobeyed. Surely a mind of iron ought to grow soft by the answer that we have just narrated, on hearing Shadrach, Meshach and Abednego committing their lives to God; but when it heard how they could not be drawn aside from their faithfulness by the fear of death, its anger was only increased. In considering this fury, we ought to take into account the power of Satan in seizing and occupying the minds of people. For there is no moderation in them, even if they show some great and remarkable hope of virtues. For, as we have seen, Nebuchadnezzar was endued with many virtues, but as Satan harassed him, we discern nothing but cruelty and barbarity. Meanwhile, let us remember how pleasing our constancy is to God, though it may not produce any immediate fruit before the world. For many indulge in pleasure through thinking they would be rash in devoting themselves to death, without any apparent utility. And on this pretext, they excuse themselves from not contending more boldly for the glory of God, by supposing they would lose their labor and their death would be fruitless. But we hear what Christ pronounces, namely, this sacrifice is pleasing to God, when we die for the testimony of the heavenly doctrine, although the generation before which we bear witness to God's name is adulterous and perverse, nay, even hardened by our constancy (Mt 5:11; 10:32; Mk 8:38). Commentaries on Daniel.[1]

3:24-25 *A Fourth Appeared*

The Fourth Is an Angel. John Calvin: Nebuchadnezzar says, *four men walked in the fire, and the face of the fourth is like the son of a god*. No doubt God here sent one of his angels to support by his presence the minds of his saints, lest they should faint. It was indeed a formidable spectacle to see the furnace so hot, and to be cast into it. By this consolation God wished to allay their anxiety and to soften their grief by adding an angel as their companion. . . .

A single angel was sent to these three men; Nebuchadnezzar calls him a son of God; not because he thought him to be Christ, but according to the common opinion among all people, that angels are sons of God, since a certain divinity is resplendent in them; and hence they call angels generally sons of God. According to this usual custom, Nebuchadnezzar says, *the fourth man is like a son of a god*. For he could not recognize the only-begotten Son of God, since, as we have already seen, he was blinded by so many depraved errors. And if anyone should say it was enthusiasm, this would be forced and frigid. This simplicity, then, will be sufficient for us, since Nebuchadnezzar spoke in the usual manner, as one of the angels was sent to those three men—since, as I have said, it was then customary to call angels sons of God. Commentaries on Daniel.[2]

A Fourth Appeared Among Them. Heinrich Bullinger: The king adds to this account that he saw something extraordinary. There now was a fourth who joined the three, whose appearance is reported as a son of God or gods. The king acknowledges the divine power by which the martyrs are protected. Now according to the Theodotion edition the fourth is named "angel of God." The king himself in his own doxology says, "Blessed be the God who sent his angel and delivered those

[1]CTS 24:226-27 (CO 18:635). [2]CTS 24:230-31 (CO 18:638-39).

who worshiped him." Rightly Apollonaris and several other interpreters think this angel to be a type of Christ, who is Immanuel, that is, he is called God with us, as there is no doubt that he is always present with the Father and he himself always remains with us, to watch over us in all danger and finally to present each and every service not only to the Father but also to us, because Christ is to be present and to be presented. In this exalted way, the king published this wonderful miracle and commended it to the whole world. Daniel the Most Wise Prophet of God.[3]

The Fourth Is the Son of God. Johann Wigand: *The appearance of the fourth is like a son of God* (Dan 3:25). It is disputed among the learned who came into the furnace with these young men, restraining and altering these natural elements, so that he was not destroyed by the fire, which otherwise consumes all things. Some understand "angel," that is, a heavenly spirit, to be a created being sent by God from heaven. This opinion repeats the voice of the angel (cf. Dan 3:49 Vg). Others understand more simply that it is the very Son of God. That he himself joins the martyrs, they marvel at his power, and he delivers them from mortal danger. Now without doubt it is said emphatically that his appearance was the form of the Son of God. And God wished himself to be known by this thing throughout the church. The name "angel" is often assigned the Son of God as he is called "the Angel of Great Counsel" (Is 9:6 LXX). Also, Jacob addressed God, not a creature, when he said, "the angel who redeemed me" (Gen 48:16). I subscribe to the latter opinion. Brief Exposition of the Prophet Daniel.[4]

The Angel of God. Johannes Oecolampadius: It is not surprising if for the consolation of his servants the Lord, Immanuel, appeared, who formerly had shown himself to Abraham, Jacob and Moses, taking for a time some visible and bodily appearance, which is the custom of angels. . . . *Who sent his angel* (Dan 3:28). This truly conveys a type. For as I said, Christ, the Son of God, is the angel. The world of tribulation kindles a fire; it is a furnace in which we are tried. The Angel Christ comes, experiencing with us our miseries, even descending into hell. Commentary on Daniel.[5]

Christ's Appearance in the Furnace. John Mayer: Shadrach, Meshach and Abednego, the most valiant champions of God, cast into the extremely hot fiery furnace, were seen walking in the furnace with a fourth man being among them like the Son of God. . . . This appearance was certainly a prelude of his future incarnation and after that of his continued presence with his people to the end of the world; a presence especially seen in their sufferings, as he showed himself to Stephen before he was to be stoned. Thus it is understood by Tertullian, who says Christ appeared to the king of Babylon in the fiery furnace; the fourth with his martyrs as the Son of God.

But Polanus following the Vulgate translation, which has an account following these words: *they fell down bound in the fiery furnace, and they walked freely in the midst of the fire without any hurt, for the Angel of the Lord descended together with them in the same moment, who shook the flames of the fire out of the furnace and preserved the servants of God safe without any trouble, being cooled as it were with a dew coming on them in a pleasing manner.* . . . From this Polanus argues that the fourth man appearing was an angel, and not a representation of Christ, who should afterwards be made man of a woman. And he argues from the speaker, who was a heathen and therefore knew not any distinction of persons in the

[3]*Daniel Sapientissimus*, 32. Theodotion was a mid-second-century Jewish scholar responsible for the Greek version of the Hebrew Bible. Theodotion's version of Daniel was incorporated into the LXX. [4]*Explicatio Brevis* (1571), 134-35. [5]*In Danielem prophetam libri duo* (1553), 51-53.

Godhead, but spoke here of an angel as the Son of God. Moreover, Polanus says that even the heathen knew that there were angels, and the king says not that he saw one who was the Son of God but one who was like him. From this Polanus concludes that it was not Christ who appeared but an angel in an assumed body, as Nebuchadnezzar himself calls him (Dan 3:28). Therefore Polanus concludes against the testimony of the Fathers. . . .

Note the certainty of the miracles that God performed of old, there being so many made witnesses thereof, that we may not be unbelieving, but believing, as if we had seen them ourselves, and believing our Lord Jesus, the Son of God, to be present, although invisibly, with all his faithful servants in their sufferings, to mitigate them so that they shall be able with comfort to bear them, whatever they be. He was now in the furnace visibly, as the words *Like the Son of God* imply, because we commonly say of a man extraordinary for parts and glory, if he is the king, but never by us seen before, that he is like the king. COMMENTARY UPON ALL THE PROPHETS.[6]

TEXTUAL DIFFERENCE BETWEEN HEBREW AND GREEK OR LATIN. HEINRICH BULLINGER: After these events, follows [the Prayer of Azariah and the Hymn of the Three Youths] in the Latin text, which is taken from Theodotion's Greek edition but is not read in the Hebrew. We have first the prayer of Azariah or Shadrach and then a very eloquent hymn sung by the three martyrs in the middle of the furnace in praise of God and with gratitude. DANIEL THE MOST WISE PROPHET OF GOD.[7]

3:26-27 *The Protection of God*

CROSS AND TRIBULATION. JOHANN GERHARD: God is with us in our cross and tribulation. He comforts, aids and ultimately delivers us (Ps 91:3, 15). If the hellish "King of Babylon" throws us into the fiery oven of cross and tribulation, then God sends his angel to our side to refresh and renew us with the dew of his grace. POSTILLA.[8]

THE GUARDIAN AND PROTECTOR OF LIFE. JOHN CALVIN: Here Daniel relates the miracle by which God liberated his servants. He has two parts: first, these three holy men walked untouched in the midst of the flame; and the fires consumed those attendants who cast them into the furnace. The prophet diligently enumerates whatever tends to prove the power of God.

. . . The sense of the prophet is by no means obscure, since the extremity of the flame consumed those strong attendants by playing round them, while Shadrach, Meshach and Abednego walked through the fuel in the fire and flame. They were not in the extremity of the flame; for it is as if the prophet had said the king's slaves were consumed by the very smoke, and the fire was without the slightest effect on the servants of God. Hence he says *these three fell down in the furnace of fire*. By saying *they fell*, it means they could not take care of themselves or attempt to escape, for he adds, *they were bound*. This might at first naturally suffocate them, till they were immediately consumed, but they remained untouched and then walked about the furnace loose. We hereby see how conspicuous was God's power, and how no falsehood of Satan's could obscure it. And next, when the very points of the flame, or the fiery sparks, devour the servants, here again the deed is proved to be of God. Meanwhile, the result of the history is the preservation of these three holy men, so surprisingly beyond their expectation.

This example is set before us to show us how nothing can be safer than to make God the guardian and protector of our life. For we ought not to expect to be preserved from

[6]*Prophets*, 527-29. [7]*Daniel Sapientissimus*, 31. [8]*Postilla* 1:390.

every danger because we see those holy men delivered; for we ought to hope for liberation from death, if it is useful, and yet we ought not to hesitate to meet it without fear, if God so please it. But we should gather from our present narrative the sufficiency of God's protection, if he wishes to prolong our lives, since we know our life to be precious to him; and it is entirely in his power either to snatch us from danger or to withdraw us to a better existence, according to his pleasure. Commentaries on Daniel.[9]

The Omnipotence of God. Heinrich Bullinger: Furthermore we learn from this history that God is omnipotent, although the might of his omnipotence is not always put forth; that is, he does not always do what he is able to do. But it is not a lack of power or an opportunity to deny his omnipotence when God does not bountifully bestow all that he is able. "We know," say the martyrs, "our God is omnipotent and therefore he is able to deliver us. Whether he wills to deliver us at the present time, we do not assert rashly, but we remain his children and in these circumstances he shall do as he wishes. He shall will from a distance what is profitable for us and what will be to his glory. Certainly if he desires not to deliver us, it is truly appropriate and useful. We will not accuse him of falsehood, and we will never honor your statue." Therefore we must distinguish between the promises of God that are spiritual, eternal and truly promised to us by his grace and those promises of corporeal and temporal benefit. Daniel the Most Wise Prophet of God.[10]

Why Does God Not Always Deliver His Servants? Andrew Willet: If God should do so ordinarily, then the miracle should not seem so great or the power and glory of God so much thereby advanced. It is in God's hand and in his choice whether to deliver his saints from temporal danger or to translate them to immortality. He best knows what is fit for everyone. Sixfold Commentary upon Daniel.[11]

3:28 *The True God Blessed*

Nebuchadnezzar's Confession Worthless and Insincere. John Calvin: This, indeed, is no common confession, but the event proved how suddenly King Nebuchadnezzar was acted on by impulse, without having the living root of the fear of God in his heart. And I repeat this again, to show that repentance does not consist in one or two works but in perseverance, as Paul says, "If you live in the Spirit, walk also in the Spirit" (Gal 5:25). Here he requires constancy in the faithful, by which they may show themselves to be truly born again of God's Spirit. Nebuchadnezzar celebrated the God of Israel as if inspired by an enthusiasm, but at the same time he mingled his idols with the true God, so that there was no sincerity in him. So when the impious feel God's power, they do not dare to proceed with obstinacy against him but wish to appease him by a false repentance, without putting off their natural disposition. Thus we readily conclude Nebuchadnezzar to be always the same, although God extracted from him this confession: *Blessed be the God of Shadrach, Meshach and Abednego!*

Why does he not rather speak of him as his own God? This may be excused had he really devoted himself to the God of Israel and abjured his former superstitions. As he does not act thus, his confession is worthless; not because he wished to obtain people's favor or good opinion by what he said, but he deceived himself after the manner of hypocrites. He pronounces the God of Shadrach, Meshach and Abednego to be blessed; if he really felt this, he must at the same time curse his idols,

[9]CTS 24:228-29 (CO 18:636-37). [10]*Daniel Sapientissimus*, 29. [11]*Sixfold Commentary* (1610), 105.

for the glory of the one true God cannot be extolled without all idols being reduced to nothing. For how can God's praise exist without his being solely conspicuous? If any other deity is opposed to him, his majesty is already buried in complete obscurity. Hence we may collect that Nebuchadnezzar was not touched with true repentance when he blessed the God of Israel.

He adds, *Who sent his angel and delivered his servants.* Here Daniel shows more clearly the absence of conversion in Nebuchadnezzar and his failure to embrace the God of Israel and worship him with sound and complete surrender of his affections. Why so? Because piety is always founded on the knowledge of the true God, and this requires instruction. Nebuchadnezzar knew the God of Israel to be majestic from the display of his power, for he had such a spectacle presented to him as he could not despise, if he wished. Here he confesses that Israel's God was mighty, since he was taught it by a miracle; but this, as I have reminded you, is not sufficient for solid piety, unless instruction is added and occupies the first place. I allow, indeed, that miracles prepare people to believe, but if miracles only occurred without the knowledge of God being added from his Word, faith will vanish away, as the example sufficiently remarkable here sets before us. We term the faith of Nebuchadnezzar to be but momentary because while his senses were fixed on the miracle, he was content with the spectacle, without inquiring into the character of the God of Israel and the bearing of his law. Commentaries on Daniel.[12]

Was Nebuchadnezzar Converted? Andrew Willet: Pererius thinks that Nebuchadnezzar was truly and indeed converted, which he would prove by the effects thereof, namely these four: (1) the confession of his error; (2) the advancing of true religion; (3) the exalting of those that feared God; (4) and severe punishing of all blasphemers and enemies to God. But these were temporary effects. They continued not. They were therefore no signs of a true conversion.

The truer opinion is that Nebuchadnezzar was but moved and affected for a time by the strangeness of this miracle. He was not truly converted. As were the effects of his faith, such was his faith; but the effects were but temporary; they lasted but a while, for presently after in the next chapter, he seeks again his sorcerers for the interpretation of his dream (Junius). He could have not true faith, because he had no true knowledge of God, seeing in the same hour as it were, a little before, he had commanded the golden image to be worshiped. Sixfold Commentary upon Daniel.[13]

God Is Confessed. Martin Luther: In the third chapter Daniel writes about another great and wonderful sign of faith. The three men are kept alive in the fiery furnace, so that God would be confessed and worshiped by the king (Nebuchadnezzar), throughout the entire kingdom, even in public declarations. This also took place for the solace of the exiled Jews, who, along with their God, were disdained and valued as nothing among the tyrants and false gods in Babylon. However, here their God is highly honored above all gods, so that they should firmly believe that he is able and willing to save them, at the right time, and for now they should hold tightly to and comfort themselves with the honor given him and miracles such as these. Preface to the Prophet Daniel.[14]

God Alone Delivers. Heinrich Bullinger: And indeed the king glorifies the true God when he says, "he sent his angel and rescued or delivered his martyrs" (Dan 3:28). In the Vulgate, it says, "the God of Abraham, the God of Isaac and the God of Jacob." In the

[12]CTS 24:236-37 (CO 18:642-43). [13]*Sixfold Commentary* (1610), 105. [14]WADB 11,2:6.

present text, he calls on the God of Shadrach, Meshach and Abednego. Just as he had formerly exhibited his power on behalf of Abraham, Isaac and Jacob, so too now he shows his power and benevolence to Shadrach, Meshach and Abednego. It is a particular power of God to protect, to deliver and to rescue from death and all danger. These powers are not attributed to anyone but the one, true God. I admit that judges and apostles or doctors of the church are called "deliverers" (*servatores*), but for no other reason than that God makes use of them in the office of ministry as "deliverers." As such, in the present text, it is stated about God that he sent his angel and "delivered" the martyrs in the midst of the flames. The angel did not deliver the martyrs; God delivered but through the ministry of the angel. It is of God alone to send angels. These are the spirits and ministers of God. At one time the Evangelist John wanted to worship an angel, but he heard, "See that you do not do this. I am a fellow servant with you and your brothers the prophets, and of them who keep the words of this book" (Rev 22:9). This whole earth is illumined and given life by the light of the sun, but who would worship the sun instead of God? Or who would worship both the sun and God, who established the sun, which gives light and works by means of God? As King Nebuchadnezzar here clearly confesses and glorifies the liberation of God by which he rescued and delivered his martyrs. DANIEL THE MOST WISE PROPHET OF GOD.[15]

3:29-30 *The Edict*

NEBUCHADNEZZAR'S EDICT. JOHN CALVIN: Here Nebuchadnezzar is urged further forward—for we must use this phrase—since he does not take up the worship of one God from his heart and bid his errors finally farewell. Hence it is as if God was thrusting him violently forward while he promulgates this edict. The edict is by itself pious and praiseworthy; but, as we have already said, Nebuchadnezzar is borne along by a blind and turbulent impulse, because piety had no root in his heart. Though he is always intent on this miracle, his faith is only momentary, and his fear of God but partial.

Why then is Nebuchadnezzar now seen as the patron of God's glory? Because he was frightened by the miracle, and thus being acted on by impulse alone, he could not be soundly restrained by the fear of God alone. And finally, this desire that he expresses is nothing but an evanescent movement. It is useful to remark this, since we see many borne along by impetuous zeal and rage to vindicate God's glory; but they lack tact and judgment, so that they deserve no praise. COMMENTARIES ON DANIEL.[16]

NEBUCHADNEZZAR'S EDICT. HEINRICH BULLINGER: Since it is not enough to confess the Lord and to proclaim his name, unless we also prevent or prohibit the insults and blasphemies against the Lord, according to our ability, soon after his confession or doxology the king promulgated a severe edict that forcefully opposed all blasphemy against God. . . . Nebuchadnezzar served God principally as a man but also as a king. When the apostle proclaimed the gospel of God, he served God; likewise when a king mandates and defends the sound doctrine of God, he serves God. Therefore Nebuchadnezzar not only glorified God as a private individual but also as a king by prohibiting anyone from speaking insults or perverse things against the true God. Daniel the Most Wise Prophet of God.[17]

[15]*Daniel Sapientissimus*, 33-34. [16]CTS 24:240-41 (CO 18:645-46). [17]*Daniel Sapientissimus*, 35.

4:1-18 NEBUCHADNEZZAR'S DREAM OF A TREE

1[a]King Nebuchadnezzar to all peoples, nations, and languages, that dwell in all the earth: Peace be multiplied to you! 2It has seemed good to me to show the signs and wonders that the Most High God has done for me.

3How great are his signs,
how mighty his wonders!
His kingdom is an everlasting kingdom,
and his dominion endures from generation to generation.

4[b]I, Nebuchadnezzar, was at ease in my house and prospering in my palace. 5I saw a dream that made me afraid. As I lay in bed the fancies and the visions of my head alarmed me. 6So I made a decree that all the wise men of Babylon should be brought before me, that they might make known to me the interpretation of the dream. 7Then the magicians, the enchanters, the Chaldeans, and the astrologers came in, and I told them the dream, but they could not make known to me its interpretation. 8At last Daniel came in before me—he who was named Belteshazzar after the name of my god, and in whom is the spirit of the holy gods[c]—and I told him the dream, saying, 9"O Belteshazzar, chief of the magicians, because I know that the spirit of the holy gods is in you and that no mystery is too difficult for you, tell me the visions of my dream that I saw and their interpretation. 10The visions of my head as I lay in bed were these: I saw, and behold, a tree in the midst of the earth, and its height was great. 11The tree grew and became strong, and its top reached to heaven, and it was visible to the end of the whole earth. 12Its leaves were beautiful and its fruit abundant, and in it was food for all. The beasts of the field found shade under it, and the birds of the heavens lived in its branches, and all flesh was fed from it.

13"I saw in the visions of my head as I lay in bed, and behold, a watcher, a holy one, came down from heaven. 14He proclaimed aloud and said thus: 'Chop down the tree and lop off its branches, strip off its leaves and scatter its fruit. Let the beasts flee from under it and the birds from its branches. 15But leave the stump of its roots in the earth, bound with a band of iron and bronze, amid the tender grass of the field. Let him be wet with the dew of heaven. Let his portion be with the beasts in the grass of the earth. 16Let his mind be changed from a man's, and let a beast's mind be given to him; and let seven periods of time pass over him. 17The sentence is by the decree of the watchers, the decision by the word of the holy ones, to the end that the living may know that the Most High rules the kingdom of men and gives it to whom he will and sets over it the lowliest of men.' 18This dream I, King Nebuchadnezzar, saw. And you, O Belteshazzar, tell me the interpretation, because all the wise men of my kingdom are not able to make known to me the interpretation, but you are able, for the spirit of the holy gods is in you."

a Ch 3:31 in Aramaic **b** Ch 4:1 in Aramaic **c** Or *Spirit of the holy God;* also verses 9, 18

Overview: The chapter opens with a letter from the king to publish the signs and wonders God has done for him. Despite the edict from the previous chapter, the king had grown arrogant, proud and secure in his own prosperity. He considered his success the product of his own effort and disregarded the blessings of God. A second dream was given to him, and he sought an interpretation. Our commentators discuss a textual variant between the Hebrew and Septuagint in the king's reference to Daniel possessing the spirit of the gods or the Spirit of God. The appearance of a watcher in his dream also elicits comment from our authors; most conclude that this is an angel, but one commentator sees here a reference to the Trinity.

Summary of the Chapter. John Calvin: The contents of this chapter are as follow: Nebuchadnezzar was sufficiently instructed in the worship of the God of Israel as one God and was compelled at the time to confess this; yet he did not depart from his own superstitions; his conceptions of the true God were but momentary, and hence he suffered the punishment due to such great ingratitude. But God intended him to become more and more blinded, as he is accustomed to treat the reprobate and even his elect at times. When people add sin to sin, God loosens his reins and allows them to destroy themselves. Afterwards he either extends his hand toward them, or withdraws them by his hidden virtue or reduces them to order by his rod and completely humbles them. He treated the king of Babylon in this way. We shall afterwards discuss the dream, but we must here briefly notice the king's admonition, that he might feel himself without excuse when he was so utterly broken down. God indeed might justly punish him as soon as he saw he was not truly converted, but before he inflicted the final chastisement—as we shall see in its place—he wished to admonish him, if there were any hope of his repentance. Although he seemed to receive with the greatest modesty what God had manifested by his dream through Daniel's interpretation of it, yet he professed with his mouth what he did not really possess. And he shows this sufficiently, because, when he ought to be afraid and cautious, he does not lay aside his pride but glories in himself as a king of kings and in Babylon as the queen of the whole world! Since, then, he spoke so confidently after being admonished by the prophet, we perceive how little he had profited by his dream. But God wished in this way to render him more inexcusable, and although he did not bring forth fruit immediately, yet a long time afterwards, when God touched his mind, he very properly recognized this punishment to have been divinely inflicted. Hence this dream was a kind of entrance and preparation for repentance, and as seed seems to lie putrid in the earth before it brings forth its fruit, and God sometimes works by gentle processes and provides for the teaching, which seemed for a long time useless, becoming both efficacious and fruitful. Commentaries on Daniel.[1]

4:1-3 *Nebuchadnezzar's Letter*

The Letter's Structure. Andrew Wil-

[1]CTS 24:243-44 (CO 18:647-48).

LET: This epistle of the king consists of the exordium, or beginning in three verses, which some make part of the third chapter, whose opinion is refuted by the narration of this chapter.

The exordium or beginning, which is the general inscription, contains (1) the salutation, (2) the general argument of the whole epistle. The salutation shows the author and writer, Nebuchadnezzar, the persons to whom he writes, to all nations and languages under his kingdom. The salutation itself is *peace be multiplied*.

In the argument three things are declared: (1) what he will set forth, the signs and wonders of God, which are amplified by two adjuncts, of the greatness and strength; (2) what moved him to declare them, because they were showed toward him, he had particular experience of them; (3) to what end, to make known the power of God's everlasting kingdom. SIXFOLD COMMENTARY UPON DANIEL.[2]

NEBUCHADNEZZAR'S LETTER AND THE CANON. HEINRICH BULLINGER: The first part of the letter has the epistolary inscription with salutation (Dan 4:1). King Nebuchadnezzar declares himself to be the author of this epistle. From this we gather that Daniel took the letter from the archives and inserted it into his own work. It was not made canonical either by acceptance or approval of any council or by any opinion or decree of the Fathers. But it is rightly kept in the canon because through Daniel, the prophet and servant of God, indeed by the Holy Spirit, it is passed down to the church. DANIEL THE MOST WISE PROPHET OF GOD.[3]

NEBUCHADNEZZAR'S EDICT AND DOUBTFUL REPENTANCE. JOHN CALVIN: Nebuchadnezzar sends his edict *to all peoples and nations and languages that dwell on the earth*. He afterwards adds, *it seemed to me good to relate the signs and wonders that the mighty God hath wrought with me*. No doubt he feels himself to have paid the penalty of his ingratitude, since he had so punctiliously ascribed the glory to one true God, and yet had relapsed into his own superstitions and had never really said farewell to them. We see how often King Nebuchadnezzar was chastised before he profited by the rod of the Almighty. Hence we need not be surprised if God often strikes us with his hand, since the result of experience proves us to be dull, and, to speak truly, utterly slothful. When God, therefore, wishes to lead us to repentance, he is compelled to repeat his blows continually, either because we are not moved when he chastises us with his hand, or we seem roused for the time, and then we return again to our former torpor. He is therefore compelled to redouble his blows. And we perceive this in the narrative before us, as in a glass. But the singular benefit of God was this, Nebuchadnezzar, after God had often chastised him, yielded at length. It is unknown whether or not this confession proceeded from true and genuine repentance: I must leave it in doubt. COMMENTARIES ON DANIEL.[4]

4:4-7 *The King's Pride and Dream*

NEBUCHADNEZZAR'S ARROGANCE. JOHANNES OECOLAMPADIUS: *I Nebuchadnezzar* (Dan 4:4). I warn all from the beginning, lest anyone trusts in his own prosperity. . . . Do any think they are so holy that they have never sinned? Do any think they are so wise that they have never been deceived? Do any think they are so strong that they have never fallen? This is the wise counsel of the apostle: "Let anyone who thinks that he stands take heed lest he fall" (1 Cor 10:12). Observe how his arrogance is so clearly described: I, Nebuchadnezzar, was prosperous. He did not say, the God of heaven or God on high has blessed me,

[2]*Sixfold Commentary* (1610), 120. [3]*Daniel Sapientissimus*, 37. [4]CTS 24:245 (CO 18:648-49).

but "I" am prosperous, or at peace and prospering. Commentary on Daniel.[5]

Nebuchadnezzar's Pride. Philipp Melanchthon: The text makes clear that the king's sins were security and pride, which are both sins hidden from sight. These sins beset many saints and easily come on a person during favorable times, and especially among excellent people who possess wonderful success, remarkable glory and great gifts of God. These benefits please the soul, which when it does not experience even a hint of the wrath of God, little by little extinguishes the fear of divine wrath and judgment. The soul begins to admire and to love immoderately these good things and forgets about God, never thinking that these successes are from God but regarding his wisdom, his excellence and his power only. . . .

Therefore let us consider the character of his sins so that we learn to fear God and do not nourish security and pride, which give birth to many other sins and punishments: *As it is written, the people sat down to eat and to drink and rose up to play* (1 Cor 10:7). Again, *While people are saying, Peace and security, then sudden destruction will come on them* (1 Thess 5:3). Commentary on the Prophet Daniel.[6]

Nebuchadnezzar's Different Dreams. John Calvin: Doubtless the king often dreamed, and did not always call together the magi and soothsayers, and astrologers, and others who were skilled in the science of divination, or at least professed to be so. He did not consult them on all his dreams; but because God had inscribed in his heart a distinct mark by which he had denoted this dream, hence the king could not rest till he heard its interpretation. As we previously saw the authority of the first dream about the four monarchies and the eternal kingdom of Christ confirmed, so the king perceived this one to have proceeded from heaven. There is another difference between this dream and the one formerly explained. For God blotted out the remembrance of the dream about the four monarchies from King Nebuchadnezzar, so that it became necessary for Daniel to bring his dream before the king and at the same time to add the interpretation. Daniel was then more obscure, for although he proved himself to have excelled all the Chaldeans, yet King Nebuchadnezzar would have wondered at him less if he had only been an interpreter of a dream. God wished, therefore, to acquire greater reverence for his prophet and his doctrine when he enjoined on him two duties; first, the divination of the dream itself, and then the explanation of its sense and purpose. In this second dream Daniel is only an interpreter. God had already sufficiently proved him to be endued with a heavenly spirit, when Nebuchadnezzar not only called him among the rest of the magi but separated him from them all. Commentaries on Daniel.[7]

4:8 *Textual Variant*

Spirit of the Holy God. Johann Wigand: *In whom is the spirit of the holy gods* (Dan 4:8). It seems that Nebuchadnezzar did not understand this expression as pertaining to the third person of the Trinity. Rather it was simply spoken in a customary way that thinks of the divine Spirit as intelligence and wisdom in understanding and interpreting divine matters. Now Gentiles declare innate shrewdness and unusual wisdom in lofty matters to be an instinct of the spirit or the gods. To be sure, it does not matter as long as you understand it concerning the Holy Spirit, whom the king testifies dwells in Daniel and in whom alone resides the light of prophecy. Brief Exposition of the Prophet Daniel.[8]

---

[5]*In Danielem prophetam libri duo* (1553), 56. [6]*In Danielem Prophetam* (1543), 59-61. [7]CTS 24:250 (CO 18:652-53). [8]*Explicatio Brevis* (1571), 141.

Spirit of the Gods. Andrew Willet: The Septuagint reads in the singular, the Holy Spirit of God, thinking to excuse the king and free him from idolatry. But the word in the original is in the plural, *elohim*, gods.

Some think that by gods are here understood the angels, who are sometimes called gods in Scripture (Pintus). But the knowledge of secrets the angels have not, because they know not things to come. And the magicians, who had conference and familiarity with spirits, not being able to tell the king his dream, which he had forgotten, excuse themselves, because none but the gods could declare such things (Dan 2:11).

His meaning then is that the gods above only knew secrets, whose divine spirit Daniel was endued with. He speaks after the manner of the Gentiles, who held that there were many gods (Lyra). And it was a received opinion among them that it was a divine thing to interpret dreams, as Socrates answered the Athenians that he was ignorant of that divine science (Lyra). Sixfold Commentary upon Daniel.[9]

4:13-18 *A Watcher, a Holy One*

A Watcher. John Calvin: No doubt we ought to understand an angel by a watcher. He is called "a holy one," which is only another form of expression for an angel; and they are worthy of this name, because they are perpetually watchful in the performance of God's commands. They are not subject to slumber, they are not nourished by either food or drink but live a spiritual life; hence they have no use for sleep, which is the result of drink and food. Lastly, as angels have no bodies, their very spiritual nature makes them watchful. But this phrase not only expresses their nature but also their duty; because God has them at hand to fulfill his bidding and destines them to the performance of his commands; hence they are called "watchers" (Ps 103:20). In this psalm angels are said to do his bidding, because, by an agility incomprehensible to us, they run about hither and thither and fly directly from heaven to earth, from one end of the world to another—from the rising even to the setting sun. Since, therefore, angels can so easily and promptly fulfill God's orders, they are deservedly called "watchers." They are called "holy ones" because they are not infected by human infirmities. But we are filled with sins, not merely because we are earthly but since we have contracted pollution from our first parents, which vitiates alike the whole body and mind. By this expression, then, Nebuchadnezzar desired to distinguish between angels and mortals. Commentaries on Daniel[10]

The Watching Angel. Giovanni Diodati: That is, an angel, so called, as well by reason of his nature, which being spiritual is incessantly in action and never rests; as also of his office and employment, which is to be always ready to receive God's commands and watch for the safeguard of the church and elect. Pious Annotations.[11]

The Angel Vigilantly Watching. John Mayer: This watcher was an angel of God, so called, because the angels are always vigilant and ready at every command to go about the execution of God's will, as we also ought to be, especially the ministers of God, as it is said to Ezekiel [Ezek 3]. And he says *Cut down the tree* to show that Nebuchadnezzar, set forth by this, should be put down from his kingly dignity and live like a beast a long time. This was the plucking off of his branches, which are ornaments to a tree, and therefore fitly representing a king's royal accommodations making him to appear glorious. Commentary upon All the Prophets.[12]

[9]*Sixfold Commentary* (1610), 123-24. [10]CTS 24:259 (CO 18:659). [11]*Pious Annotations* (1651), 4:13. [12]*Prophets*, 529.

Behold a Watcher, a Holy One. Johann Wigand: *Behold a watcher* (Dan 4:13). Indeed, God himself, or the Son of God, appears here to be called Watcher. The reason is, as he afterwards says, *The sentence is by decree of the watchers*, that in such a manner the tree is chopped down and nevertheless the stump is preserved. Such a thing happens by God, in whom all things have life. So afterwards Daniel clearly says, *It is the decree of the Most High* (Dan 4:24). Therefore "watchers" in the statement, *it is by decree of the watchers*, is to be understood concerning the Trinity. Brief Exposition of the Prophet Daniel.[13]

The Almighty Rules All Things. John Mayer: *This matter is by the decree of the watchers, and the demand by the word of the holy ones*. In the Vulgate: *the sentence is the decree of the watchmen, and this is the speech of the saints and the petition*. The first agrees best with the original, it being meant that it was the decree appointed by God to be published by his watchmen, the angels. At which point, they demand, why it is so, and the answer lies in the next words, *that the living might know that the Most High rules in the kingdoms of mortals and gives them to whom he pleases*. Commentary upon All the Prophets.[14]

[13]*Explicatio Brevis* (1571), 142-43. [14]*Prophets*, 530.

4:19-37 Interpration, Punishment and Praise

[19]*Then Daniel, whose name was Belteshazzar, was dismayed for a while, and his thoughts alarmed him. The king answered and said, "Belteshazzar, let not the dream or the interpretation alarm you." Belteshazzar answered and said, "My lord, may the dream be for those who hate you and its interpretation for your enemies!* [20]*The tree you saw, which grew and became strong, so that its top reached to heaven, and it was visible to the end of the whole earth,* [21]*whose leaves were beautiful and its fruit abundant, and in which was food for all, under which beasts of the field found shade, and in whose branches the birds of the heavens lived—*[22]*it is you, O king, who have grown and become strong. Your greatness has grown and reaches to heaven, and your dominion to the ends of the earth.* [23]*And because the king saw a watcher, a holy one, coming down from heaven and saying, 'Chop down the tree and destroy it, but leave the stump of its roots in the earth, bound with a band of iron and bronze, in the tender grass of the field, and let him be wet with the dew of heaven, and let his portion be with the beasts of the field, till seven periods of time pass over him,'* [24]*this is the interpretation, O king: It is a decree of the Most High, which has come upon my lord the king,* [25]*that you shall be driven from among men, and your dwelling shall be with the beasts of the field. You shall be made to eat grass like an ox, and you shall be wet with the dew of heaven, and seven periods of time shall pass over*

you, till you know that the Most High rules the kingdom of men and gives it to whom he
will. 26And as it was commanded to leave the stump of the roots of the tree, your kingdom
shall be confirmed for you from the time that you know that Heaven rules. 27Therefore,
O king, let my counsel be acceptable to you: break off your sins by practicing righteous-
ness, and your iniquities by showing mercy to the oppressed, that there may perhaps be a
lengthening of your prosperity."

28All this came upon King Nebuchadnezzar. 29At the end of twelve months he was
walking on the roof of the royal palace of Babylon, 30and the king answered and said, "Is
not this great Babylon, which I have built by my mighty power as a royal residence and
for the glory of my majesty?" 31While the words were still in the king's mouth, there fell
a voice from heaven, "O King Nebuchadnezzar, to you it is spoken: The kingdom has
departed from you, 32and you shall be driven from among men, and your dwelling shall
be with the beasts of the field. And you shall be made to eat grass like an ox, and seven
periods of time shall pass over you, until you know that the Most High rules the kingdom
of men and gives it to whom he will." 33Immediately the word was fulfilled against Nebu-
chadnezzar. He was driven from among men and ate grass like an ox, and his body was
wet with the dew of heaven till his hair grew as long as eagles' feathers, and his nails were
like birds' claws.

34At the end of the days I, Nebuchadnezzar, lifted my eyes to heaven, and my reason
returned to me, and I blessed the Most High, and praised and honored him who lives
forever,

for his dominion is an everlasting dominion,
and his kingdom endures from generation to generation;
35all the inhabitants of the earth are accounted as nothing,
and he does according to his will among the host of heaven
and among the inhabitants of the earth;
and none can stay his hand
or say to him, "What have you done?"

36At the same time my reason returned to me, and for the glory of my kingdom, my
majesty and splendor returned to me. My counselors and my lords sought me, and I was
established in my kingdom, and still more greatness was added to me. 37Now I, Nebu-
chadnezzar, praise and extol and honor the King of heaven, for all his works are right and
his ways are just; and those who walk in pride he is able to humble.

Overview: Before Daniel offers the interpretation of the dream, we are told he was greatly dismayed and alarmed. Our commentators note Daniel's regard for the king and the peace of his kingdom. We are to learn from Daniel's example to pray for our enemies, even those tyrants who oppress us. Daniel proceeds with the interpretation and describes the humiliation and judgment of the king. He ends by urging the king to repentance and to the practice of righteousness.

Daniel's final words elicit a great deal of discussion among our commentators. What sort of repentance does Daniel call for? Can we redeem our sins through almsgiving? This particular point was at the center of the Protestant debate with the Roman church. For this reason, there is much to be explained concerning the righteousness, forgiveness and almsgiving mentioned by Daniel.

The king is punished for his sins. The issue that occupies our commentators the most is the nature of this punishment. In what sense was Nebuchadnezzar changed into a beast? Was this a physical change, or did it affect only his mind and soul? Following his seven years of punishment, the king is restored, repents and confesses the true God. Again the question is asked if this confession is sincere and genuine. The commentators agree that it is and seek to reconcile the king's confession with Isaiah's reference to Nebuchadnezzar's everlasting destruction (Is 14:12-16).

4:19 *Daniel's Reaction*

Daniel Was Dismayed. Johann Wigand: *Then Daniel* (Dan 4:19). Three things are recited that grab our attention and highlight the importance of things. The first is the duration of Daniel's deliberation and the depth of his meditation, which without doubt grieved him, as God in his mercy deigned to reveal to Daniel his truth set forth under an image. The second is the severe consternation and disturbance endured by Daniel. He became frightened by the wrath of God, which was set forth by this horrible punishment. The third is the almost abrupt, severe, and ominous beginning of the things narrated for the prosperous king, as Daniel well enough signifies. Brief Exposition of the Prophet Daniel.[1]

Daniel's Prudence. Johannes Oecolampadius: *Then Daniel whose name* (Dan 4:19). Whenever he declares something that is yet to happen, he is slow to speak, lest he seem boastful or like someone rejoicing in the misfortune of the king. Although he is held captive with his people, nevertheless he does not wish to diminish or lessen his regard for the king. Besides, as the ears of the officials are tender and delicate, having been corrupted by the pandering of the flatterers, they would be provoked by sterner words. His hesitation before the king was advantageous, as it made the king more eager to hear the truth. Moreover, seeing his prophet disturbed and filled with sorrow as he reluctantly spoke, the king would not neglect his counsel. At once the king detected by his own keenness the gravity of the dream's interpretation. As the divine judgment terrified the innocent prophet, how great was the king's impiety? Indeed, the courage of the king appeared a second time when he encouraged the prophet and gave him assurance that whatever the interpretation of the dream he wanted it. The prophet, rightly relieved, prayed that these unfortunate things would befall the enemies of the king. By such words he did not contradict the divine will, nor was he feigning this sentiment, but he revealed his concern for the king's well-being. Commentary on Daniel.[2]

Daniel's Sorrow. John Calvin: Here Daniel relates how he was in some sense astonished. And I refer this to the sorrow that the holy prophet had endured from that horrible punishment that God had shown under a figure; nor ought it to seem surprising for Daniel to be grievously afflicted on account of the calamity of the king of Babylon, for although he was a cruel tyrant and had harassed and all but destroyed God's church, yet since he was under his sway, he was bound to pray for him. But God had deafly taught the Jews this, by means of Jeremiah, "Pray for the prosperous state of Babylon, because your peace shall be in it" (Jer 29:7). At the close of seventy years it was lawful for the pious worshipers of God to beg him to free them; but until the time predicted by the prophet had elapsed, it was not lawful either to indulge in hatred against the king or

[1] *Explicatio Brevis* (1571), 145-46. [2] *In Danielem prophetam libri duo* (1553), 59-60.

to invoke God's wrath on him. They knew him to be the executor of God's just vengeance and to be their sovereign and lawful ruler. Since then Daniel was treated kindly by the king when by the rights of warfare he was dragged into exile, he ought to be faithful to his own king, although he exercised tyranny against the people of God. This was the reason why he suffered so much sorrow from that sad oracle. Commentaries on Daniel.[3]

Daniel's Sincerity. Giovanni Diodati: *Was astonished* (Dan 4:19). Both because of the mournful interpretation and because he was to expound it to the king. *Be to them* (Dan 4:19). Namely, would God that the meaning of this dream were directed rather to your enemies than to yourself. A kind of protestation, to show that in this interpretation he was not preoccupied by any hatred or passion against the king. Pious Annotations.[4]

Daniel Praying for His Enemy. John Calvin: *Belteshazzar,* Nebuchadnezzar says, *let not your thoughts disturb you; let not the dream and its interpretation frighten you* (Dan 4:19). Yet Daniel was afraid for his sake. But, as I have already said, while the faithful are afraid though they feel God to be propitious, yet the impious sleep in their security and are unmoved and unafraid by any threats. Daniel adds the cause of his grief. *O my lord,* he says, *may the dream be for your enemies, and its interpretation to your foes!* Here Daniel explains why he was so astonished—because he wished so horrible a punishment to be turned away from the person of the king, for although he might deservedly have detested him, yet he reverenced the power divinely assigned to him. Let us learn, therefore, from the prophet's example, to pray for blessings on our enemies who desire to destroy us, and especially to pray for tyrants if it please God to subject us to their lust; for although they are unworthy of any of the feelings of humanity, yet we must modestly bear their yoke, because they could not be our governors without God's permission; and not only for wrath, as Paul admonishes us, but for conscience's sake (Rom 13:5); otherwise we should not only rebel against them but against God himself. Commentaries on Daniel.[5]

An Example of All Ministers of the Word. John Calvin: Here we see what I have touched on, namely, how Daniel acted respectfully to the king and thus was mindful of his prophetic duty, while he punctually discharged the commands of God. We must notice this distinction, for nothing is more difficult for ministers of the Word than to maintain this middle course. Some are always fulminating through a pretense of zeal and forget themselves to be but human: they show no sign of benevolence but indulge in mere bitterness. Hence they have no authority, and all their admonitions are hateful. Next, they explain God's Word with pride and boasting, when they frighten sinners without either humanity or pain or sympathy. Others, again, who are wicked and perfidious flatterers gloss over the grossest iniquities; they object to both prophets and apostles, esteeming the fervor of their zeal to have driven away all human affections! Thus they delude miserable people and destroy them by their flattery. But our prophet, as all the rest, here shows how God's servants ought to take a middle course. Thus Jeremiah, when prophesying adversity, feels sorrow and bitterness of spirit, and yet he does not turn aside from unsparing reproof of the severest threats, as both sprang from God (Jer 9:1). The rest of the prophets also act in the same manner.

Here Daniel, on the one hand, pities the king, and on the other, through knowing himself to be the herald of God's anger, he is not frightened by any danger while setting before

[3]CTS 24:267-68 (CO 18:665). [4]*Pious Annotations* (1651), 4:19. [5]CTS 24:269 (CO 18:666).

the king the punishment that he had despised. Hence we gather why he was not astonished. He felt no fear of the tyrant, although many do not dare to discharge their duty when an odious message is entrusted to them, which stimulates the impious and the unbelievers to madness. Daniel, however, was not astonished with any fear of this kind; he only wished God to act mercifully toward his king. For he says here, You are king yourself. He does not speak with any doubt or hesitation, neither does he use obscurity or a number of excuses but plainly announces king Nebuchadnezzar to be intended by the tree that he saw. Commentaries on Daniel.[6]

4:20-26 *The Interpretation and Punishment*

The Judgment and Humiliation of the King. Johannes Oecolampadius: *And because the king saw a watcher* (Dan 4:23). Now concerning the judgment and humiliation of the king, Daniel proceeds to explain the dream in detail. The voice of that watcher and holy one, the decree and sentence, is of the Most High God against the king. It is sufficiently established that beyond our understanding he wills through the watcher and holy one, for the decree is of the Most High God, who makes use of his angels in this case. Commentary on Daniel.[7]

The Punishment of the King. Giovanni Diodati: [Dan 4:25] Being (through God's judgment) taken with a disease called lycanthropy, which is a kind of frenzy and madness whereby one loses all humane sense and use of reason, and becomes brutish, fierce and ravenous, like a beast, living in the fields wandering, and to hinder him from doing hurt, he must be kept bound and chained. Wherein without question there is much diabolical operation and possession (as Mt 5:3-4; Lk 8:29).

[Dan 4:26] After you have been quelled by this horrible accident, you shall recover your understanding: having lost all that ambition that you are possessed with, and humbling yourself before God, by whose benefit you reign and to whom you should have given all honor and glory.

[Dan 4:27] *Break off.* It is *redeem* in Italian. Namely, this concerns temporal punishments. Concerning everlasting punishments, a person can give no price sufficient for his redemption, which God has granted his church by the only blood of Christ. The meaning is, prevent God's judgment with repentance, changing your former tyranny into acts of contrary virtues. Pious Annotations.[8]

The Office of Worldy Authority. Mar-tin Luther: For righteous lords and princes this is a comforting and lovely image. That the Lord God models even this tyrannical king after a beautiful tree that nourishes all animals, granting them shade to rest in. By this image God indicates that he grants and sustains through worldly authorities (*Oberkeit*) rest and peace, protection and shelter, nourishment and goods, and this entire worldly life. And it greatly pleases him whenever a lord or prince practices his office diligently. For "it has," he says (Dan 4:21-22), "beautiful fruits, beautiful branches, and beautiful foliage," that is, it has priceless and noble good works. Because it pleases God himself, that he depicts this so finely, commending and adorning [worldly authorities], a lord should indeed carry out his office with joy and gladness, even if it is filled with stress and labor. So, too, we should not consider how wicked tyrants are, but rather we should consider what a priceless and helpful office they have from God, appointed for our own good and well-being. Preface to the Prophet Daniel.[9]

[6]CTS 24:270-71 (CO 18:667). [7]*In Danielem prophetam libri duo* (1553), 60. [8]*Pious Annotations* (1651), 4:25-27. [9]WADB 11,2:8.

4:27 Repentance and Righteousness

DANIEL URGES REPENTANCE. JOHN CALVIN: There is no doubt that Daniel wished to exhort the king to repentance; but he touched on only one kind, which we know was very customary with the prophets. For when they recall the people to obedience by repentance, they do not always explain it fully or define it generally, but they touch on it by a figure of speech and treat only of the outward duties of penitence. Daniel now follows this custom. If inquiry is made concerning the nature of repentance, it is the conversion of a person toward God, from whom he had been alienated. Is this conversion then only in the hands and feet and tongue? Does it not rather begin in the mind and the heart and then pass on to outward works? Hence true penitence has its source in the mind of people, so that he who wished to be wise must set aside his own prudence and put away his foolish confidence in his own reason. Then he must subdue his own depraved affections and submit them to God, and thus his outward life will follow the inward spirit. Besides this, works are the only testimonies to real repentance; for it is a thing too excellent to allow its root to appear to human observation. By our fruits therefore we must testify our repentance. But because the duties of the second table, in some sense, open the mind of people, hence the prophets in requiring repentance only set before us the duties of charity, as Daniel says (Dan 4:27). COMMENTARIES ON DANIEL.[10]

THE REMISSION OF SINS. JOHANN WIGAND: The argument of the papacy rests on this statement in Daniel: Redeem your sins by almsgiving (Dan 4:27, Vg). Therefore, the remission of sins is attributed to good works.

I respond that this is the fallacy of stating as the cause what is not the cause. In the first place, Daniel did not say "by almsgiving" but "by righteousness." But what sort of righteousness releases us from sin he did not explain, as he does in Daniel 9. Besides, any sermon on the amendment of life presupposes conversion to God, which seeks the remission of sins by mercy for the sake of the Messiah. Otherwise no one is able to amend their lives seriously or truly. Good works are, as Paul testifies, the fruits of righteousness made pleasing by faith.

If you state the argument in the following way, the error will appear greater: Whatever redeems from sin justifies. Almsgiving redeems from sin, according to the testimony of Daniel. Therefore, almsgiving justifies. I respond that the major premise is true only of the Son of God, who alone is our Redeemer. BRIEF EXPOSITION OF THE PROPHET DANIEL.[11]

TRUE RIGHTEOUSNESS. JOHN CALVIN: *Redeem*, therefore, *your sins*, says he, or break away or cast them away, but how, namely, by righteousness. Without doubt the word *justice* means here the same as "grace" or "pity." But those who here transfer "grace" to "faith" twist the prophet's words too violently, for we know of nothing more frequent among the Hebrews than to repeat one and the same thing under two forms of speech. As, therefore, Daniel here uses sins and iniquities in the same sense, we conclude justice and pity ought not to be separated, while the second word expresses more fully the sense of justice. For when people see their life must be changed, they feign for themselves many acts of obedience that scarcely deserve the name. They have no regard for what pleases God or for what he commands in his word, but just as they approve of one part or another, they thrust themselves rashly unto God, as we see in the papacy. For what is a holy and religious life with them? To run about here and there; to undertake pilgrimages imposed by vows; to set up a statue; to found masses, as they call it; to fast on certain

[10]CTS 24:279 (CO 18:673-74). [11]*Explicatio Brevis* (1571), 148-49.

days; and to lay stress on trifles about which God has never said a single word. As, therefore, people err so grossly in the knowledge of true righteousness, the prophet here adds the word *pity* by way of explanation; as if he had said, Do not think to appease God by outward pomp, which delight humankind because they are carnal and devoted to earthly things and fashion for themselves a depraved idea of God according to their own imagination; let not then this vanity deceive you, but learn how true justice consists in pity toward the poor. In this second clause, then, only a part of the idea is expressed, since true justice is not restricted simply to the meaning of the word but embraces all the duties of charity. Hence we ought to deal faithfully with humankind, and not to deceive either rich or poor or to oppress anyone, but to render everyone his own. But this manner of speaking ought to be familiar to us, if we are but moderately versed in the prophetic writings. COMMENTARIES ON DANIEL.[12]

FORGIVENESS AND ALMSGIVING. JOHN MAYER: The meaning of this verse (Dan 4:27) is nothing else than where you have been an oppressor do from now on righteously and make restitution to those whom you have wronged. Over and above this be charitable and give abundantly of your goods to the poor. From whence, although no redemption from sin by almsdeeds can be proved, yet it may well be proved that no one is a true convert, or shall find favor at God's hands, who turns not from unjust and deceitful dealings to righteousness in all things, and from hardheartedness to charitableness.

. . . For the last words here, *if it may be a lengthening of your tranquility*, because Daniel speaks doubtfully, the papists, following the Vulgate, gather from this that no one can be certain of his sins being pardoned or consequently of his salvation. But as has been before said, the words are not rightly rendered *it may be God will forgive*, but *if haply there may be a prolonging of your peace or rest*, the temporal judgment threatened against you being prevented. And according to this Jerome notes that a whole year passed before it was executed, and Nebuchadnezzar sinned again by his proud vaunting of himself and of his great Babylon. Thus he says it is probable that he did for a time, as Daniel had counseled him, and so was spared, and had his quiet resting in his palace lengthened to twelve months after this.

. . . From Daniel's example, not only expounding to Nebuchadnezzar his dream but also exhorting him to repentance, note that every minister of God ought to do likewise. They are not to soothe up people in their sins, daubing with untempered mortar, nor are they to expound the word and leave it without application. COMMENTARY UPON ALL THE PROPHETS.[13]

RIGHTEOUS BY FAITH ALONE. HEINRICH BULLINGER: Neither do we read that the saints did simply attribute the benefit of justification or satisfaction to their afflictions. I confess that Daniel, the prophet, gave counsel to the most mighty king Nebuchadnezzar and said, Let your sins be redeemed in righteousness and your iniquities in showing pity to the poor, but in these words the king was taught how to lead the rest of his life that was yet ahead and how to rule the state of his kingdom. The king had till then oppressed many nations and sinned in merciless cruelty, but he persuades him to change his old kind of life to embrace justice and deal well with all people. Therefore he speaks not of the satisfaction of his sins before God but before people. For there is salvation in none other than in Christ alone. But if anyone stubbornly sticks on the letter, we say that the righteousness of Christians is faith by which their sins are properly cleansed and that

[12]CTS 24:279-80 (CO 18:674). [13]*Prophets*, 531-32.

faith is not without good works and charity to which justification is improperly ascribed. The Decades of Henry Bullinger.[14]

Good Works. Philipp Melanchthon: Moreover, as in conversion or repentance, new obedience always ought to follow, as John the Baptist says, "bring forth fruits worthy of repentance" (Lk 3:8). Here Daniel adds the teaching concerning good works. First observe what works he solicits; it is clearly not monkish works or human traditions but the works that God prescribes. And he urges by name that which belongs to vocation. When he tells him to practice righteousness, it is to be understood as universal obedience, such as acknowledgment of God, fear, faith, love of God, exercising authority with justice, restraint, and other virtues, which God requires. By name Daniel adds the particular works of vocation, for Nebuchadnezzar ought especially to practice the works of his vocation. Commentary on the Prophet Daniel.[15]

4:28-31 *Nebuchadnezzar Punished*

The King's Fall and Our Consolation. Martin Luther: In the fourth chapter there is an excellent warning against oppressors and tyrants. There the great and mighty king, robbed of his reason, so raving and mad, that, like a rabid dog, he must be bound with chains and forced into the wilderness so that he might not cause harm to the people. Today, because we read it in a book, this seems to be a minor thing. However, if we should have been there and would have seen it, then we would have witnessed a dreadful and grisly judgment of God. So much so that certainly everyone would have had to have felt pity in his heart for all overlords and wicked tyrants, that such a cruel judgment awaits them if they abuse their power.

However, this also took place, again, as a comfort to the miserable and imprisoned Jews, and also for those who today and forevermore are plagued by tyrants or suffer injustice. This shows them that God is willing and able to take revenge on our enemies, even more than we would wish to desire, as Psalm 58 (v. 10) says, "The righteous person will witness vengeance with joy, and his path will be bathed in the blood of the godless." Therefore, we should not merely patiently suffer such tyrants, but we should have compassion on them because of their future judgment, affectionately interceding for them, just as godly Daniel does here, saddened that the king (who indeed had captured Daniel's people and destroyed their land) should experience such evil, wishing instead this judgment on Nebuchadnezzar's enemies. Preface to the Prophet Daniel.[16]

Nebuchadnezzar Punished or the Devil? John Mayer: Lyra says that some will not have this to be literally understood, but mystically of the devil, who for his pride was the most abased of all others, yet shall hereafter be restored to his pristine glory of an angel of light again. And they argue against the literal understanding of this as Nebuchadnezzar for the following reasons. (1) Because he, retaining his human nature, could not go and live on grass as a beast so long a time; (2) Because being taken with such a disease, as was a kind of madness, they would doubtless rather have shut him up than driven him out into the fields, as is normally to be done to mad people; (3) Because the wild and savage beasts would, when he had come among them, have devoured him; (4) So large an empire would not have been so long without a king, and if another king had been set up, it is not probable that he would have given way to him to return to his throne again. But to believe that the devil shall be restored again to his first glorious condition of an angel of light is most contrary to the holy

[14]*Decades*, 3:92. [15]*In Danielem Prophetam* (1543), 64-65.
[16]WADB 11,2:8.

Scriptures, wherein it is said that hellfire is prepared for the devil and his angels and that it is everlasting, *and the angels, who kept not their first standing he has reserved in everlasting chains of darkness.*

Here are my responses to the objections. (1) No reason can be drawn from the common condition of a man to this man, having this judgment laid on him by the Almighty, who can sustain the life of a person without means as long as he pleases, as he did Moses forty days, and Elijah, and the children of Israel forty years in the barren wilderness. Moreover experience has taught in some, whose bodies have been distempered, that they have used coals and other things, wherein there is no nourishment, for most delectable food, and there is a history of a woman who ate and lived on spiders, and some on locusts. Therefore if God would have Nebuchadnezzar fed with grass, who is he that dares say it was not possible, and likewise on his hands and feet to go about as the beasts; (2) It is not to be doubted, but that when this judgment befell him, Daniel certified the nobles of this, persuading them rather to help put in execution what God had decreed than to hinder it; (3) The same God that appointed his restitution after this fastened the stump of this tree in the mean season, so that as it was not in the power of any creature to pull it up, for which it is said to be bound with bands of brass and iron. Moreover, it is observed in the ordinary course of nature that a mad dog will not bite a fool or a madman, to say nothing of the acquaintance that he got with the beasts by conversing among them, so that they took him going on all fours, and feeding as they did, to be a beast as they were, although in shape differing from them, as a monster among them; (4) It is said that Evil-merodach, the son of Nebuchadnezzar, reigned a while in his stead in this time of his exile, but playing the tyrant was by his subjects shut up in prison, where Jehoiakin, the captive king of Judah, was, with whom he by this means got so good acquaintance that immediately after Nebuchadnezzar's death, he, coming to the throne, lifted up his head and dealt so favorably with him, as is said (2 Kings 25). COMMENTARY UPON ALL THE PROPHETS.[17]

GOD'S DELAYED PUNISHMENT. JOHN CALVIN: Some think Nebuchadnezzar to have been touched with penitence when instructed by God's anger, and thus the time of his punishment was put off (Dan 4:29). This does not seem to me probable, and I rather incline to a different opinion, as God withdrew his hand till the end of the year, and thus the king's pride was the less excusable. The prophet's voice ought to have frightened him, just as if God had thundered and lightened from heaven. He now appears to have been always like himself. I indeed do not deny that he might be frightened by the first message, but I leave it doubtful. Whichever way it is, I do not think God spared him for a time because he gave some signs of repentance. I confess he sometimes indulges the reprobate, if he sees them humbled. An example of this, sufficiently remarkable, is displayed in King Ahab (1 Kings 21:29). He did not cordially repent, but God wished to show how much he was pleased with his penitence by pardoning a king impious and obstinate in his wickedness. The same might be said of Nebuchadnezzar, if Scripture had said so; but as far as we can gather from these words of the prophet, Nebuchadnezzar became prouder and prouder, until his sloth arrived at its height. The king continued to grow proud after God had threatened him so, and this was quite intolerable. Hence his remarkable stupidity, since he would have been equally careless had he lived a hundred years after he heard that threat! Finally, I think although Nebuchadnezzar perceived some dreadful and horrible punishment to be at hand, yet, while frightened for the time, he

[17] *Prophets*, 530-31.

did not lay aside his pride and haughtiness of mind. Meanwhile, he might think this prediction to be in vain, and what he had heard probably escaped from his mind for a long time, because he thought he had escaped; just as the impious usually abuse God's forbearance and thus heap up for themselves a treasure of severer vengeance, as Paul says (Rom 2:5). Hence he derided this prophecy and hardened himself more and more. COMMENTARIES ON DANIEL.[18]

PENITENTIAL BENEVOLENCE. JOHANN WIGAND: *At the end of twelve months* (Dan 4:29). This time of penitence was permitted by God for Nebuchadnezzar. For God is longsuffering. As Paul says, "Do you not know that the kindness of God is meant to lead you to repentance?" (Rom 2:4). However, because he saw his punishment postponed and continued to succeed in all things, the king boasted in his glory and grew in his pride, security and impiety. BRIEF EXPOSITION OF THE PROPHET DANIEL.[19]

4:32-33 *Was Nebuchadnezzar an Actual Beast?*

YOU SHALL EAT GRASS LIKE AN OX. JOHN CALVIN: Some think Nebuchadnezzar to have been changed into a beast; but this is too harsh and absurd. We need not fancy any change of nature, but he was cut off from all intercourse with people, and with the exception of a human form, he did not differ from the brutes; nay, such was his deformity in his exile that, as we shall afterwards see, he became a horrid spectacle. All the hairs of his body stood up and grew like eagles' feathers; his claws were like those of birds. In these points he was like the beasts, in others like the rest of humankind. COMMENTARIES ON DANIEL.[20]

EATING GRASS. JOHANN WIGAND: *To eat grass* (Dan 4:32). These things are to be understood according to the letter because genuine history is being recited. Even if humans are not naturally able to feed on grass as cattle, nevertheless in this punishment God so rules Nebuchadnezzar that he is able to digest it. They are dreaming who see some sort of metamorphosis, as if he had been changed into an ox. This sort of reading opposes the clear text. BRIEF EXPOSITION OF THE PROPHET DANIEL.[21]

NEBUCHADNEZZAR'S PUNISHMENT. WILLIAM PEMBLE: Some have said that Nebuchadnezzar was metamorphosed into a very beast, but it is the truer opinion to say that his malady was in mind, not in body. God struck him with a kind of melancholy madness, insomuch that he lost all judgment, sense and use of reason; living and doing like a beast of the field. His life was a wild kind of life away from the communion of people. And they may as well say, he was turned into an eagle, because it is said that his hairs were grown like eagles' feathers, as to affirm that he was changed into an ox, because he is said to eat grass like an ox. The conclusion would as well be that he was converted into oxen; because as our translator reads it according to the original, it is not said as an ox but as the oxen in the plural number. THE PERIOD OF THE PERSIAN MONARCHY.[22]

NEBUCHADNEZZAR'S TRANSMUTATION. ANDREW WILLET: This then was the transmutation that Nebuchadnezzar had: his man's shape remaining, his human soul was changed to be brutish by his frenzy and madness (Bullinger). Not that the mind of a beast was given him in substance, for he retained his reasonable soul. Nor yet that there was no more understanding in him left than in a brute beast (Osiander). For the reasonable soul remaining, though it became brutish, yet it is

[18]CTS 24:285-86 (CO 18:677-78). [19]*Explicatio Brevis* (1571), 150. [20]CTS 24:289-90 (CO 18:681). [21]*Explicatio Brevis* (1571), 152. [22]*Persian Monarchy* (1659), 373-74.

not altogether as the sense of a brute beast. But as Lyra says, he lost the use of reason by his madness. His mind became brutish. . . . He was somewhat altered and changed in the constitution and sight of his body, being grown misshapen and deformed, though not transformed into the shape of a beast. . . .

As his mind became brutish, so the constitution of his body was much changed and became adaptable to that brutish food by which he lived. He went naked having no care of his clothing, as brute beasts are only covered with their skin. . . . His food and meat was herbs and grass, such as the brute beasts feed on. His habitation was in the fields and woods among the brute beasts. He had no use of his speech living among beasts but made a rude noise like them. And thus he was changed even in respect of his body, that although the fashion of his human shape remained still in his head, hands and feet, yet he was become very deformed. Sixfold Commentary upon Daniel.[23]

Nebuchadnezzar's Humiliation. Menno Simons: Therefore humble yourselves under the almighty hand of God, as Peter teaches (1 Pet 5), and take the prosperous, great king, Nebuchadnezzar, as an example (Dan 3; 4). Observe how grievously he was punished by God, on account of his pride, and how, after being punished, he turned his heart to wisdom and feared the Almighty. He praised his works and adorable name. A Foundation and Plain Instruction.[24]

4:34-37 *The King's Confession*

Gentile Believers and the Law. Martin Luther: So, even the wicked king of Babylon, Nebuchadnezzar, is so strongly converted by Daniel's sermon and God's punishment that he allows a public sermon to be published under his name, ordering that everyone should believe that the God of Israel is the true God, because he is indeed the true God (Dan 4:34-36). See, this king became a believer in God and a righteous man, and without a doubt many others in his kingdom with him. Nevertheless he was not circumcised, and he was not bound by any of the laws of Moses. Daniel certainly would not have neglected to inform and apply the law to him, if he had not known that the law of Moses was imposed on the Jews alone and circumcision on Abraham alone, until the True Master, the Messiah comes forth from the house of Israel. Against the Sabbatarians.[25]

Seven Years Later. John Calvin: The prophet again introduces King Nebuchadnezzar as the speaker. He says, then, *After that time had elapsed, he raised his eyes to heaven* (Dan 4:34). Without doubt, he means those seven years. As to his then beginning to raise his eyes to heaven, this shows how long it takes to cure pride, the disease under which he labored. For when any vital part of the body is corrupt and decaying, its cure is difficult and tedious; so also when pride exists in people's hearts, and gains an entrance within the marrow and infects the inmost soul, it is not easily plucked out; and this is worthy of notice. Then we are taught how God by his word so operated on King Nebuchadnezzar as not immediately and openly to withdraw the effect of his grace. Nebuchadnezzar profited by being treated disgracefully during those seven years or times, and by being driven from the society of humankind; but he could not perceive this at once till God opened his eyes. So, therefore, God often chastises us, and invites us by degrees and prepares us for repentance, but his grace is not immediately acknowledged. Commentaries on Daniel.[26]

Nebuchadnezzar's True Repentance and Salvation. John Mayer: *At the end*

[23]*Sixfold Commentary* (1610), 131-32. [24]*Foundation*, 32. [25]WA 50:327-328. [26]CTS 24:293-94 (CO 18:684).

of these days my understanding returned to me, and I lifted up my eyes to heaven, thus I have translated it, not as the words lie, for his lifting up of his eyes is placed first, and then the returning of his understanding to him. So it is *hysteron proteron,* the last put first, for his understanding must first return to him, and then, and not before, he lifted up his eyes and blessed God. Since the heart of a beast cannot do this, it is hereby plain that the judgment laid unto him was in his mind and not in the transmutation of his body, as this bestial mind made him to go and do like a brute beast. From this relation of Nebuchadnezzar, we learn that man, who is as a tree flourishing by prosperity, is so fascinated hereby, that forgetting God he equalizes himself in his imagination to him, then as pride goes before a fall, God who is very vigilant to look to the swelling heart of such a man cuts him down by sickness or taking his worldly estate away from him, thus making him base and vile, and thus haply he lives and goes on either like a stupid beast a long time, not considering why God's hand is so heavy on him, or murmuring against God. But in fine, if he belongs to God, he considers his former high thoughts and wickedness and repents, and is either lifted up again, as Nebuchadnezzar, and Job in this world, or in the world to come, although after this he be kept always low here. And then what does he do? Bless and praise God to the uttermost of his power, seeking also to make others by his speaking of his praises and wonderful things done for him, to acknowledge him to be the only true God, and therefore to fall to the magnifying of him also, and to living in all holy obedience to his will, to his glory.

And thus, as Lyra says, it is not to be doubted but Nebuchadnezzar after this proceeded to do to his dying day and so was saved. Whereas that which is spoken of him in Isaiah (Is 14:12-16) may seem to argue against this. He answers, no more is there said but what came to pass here, touching his cutting down to the ground and the debasing of him in this world for his pride, he being so left, as a wretched man, suffering still in his body after death. This Isaiah saw should come to him for his intolerable pride, but his final conversion was hidden from him and not revealed, until now in Daniel's time. But forasmuch as after this testimony given of his serious repentance, nothing is more spoken of him, but this his history is concluded. It is to be held that whatever his life had formerly been was forgiven, and in the end he was received to mercy. No penitent sinner, who now turns to do the works of God, may despair of mercy, however foul his life has formerly been. COMMENTARY UPON ALL THE PROPHETS.[27]

NEBUCHADNEZZAR ACKNOWLEDGES GOD. JOHN CALVIN: At the close of the edict, Nebuchadnezzar joins the ingenuous confession of his faults with the praises of God! What he says of the proud, he doubtless applies properly to himself; as if he had said, God wished to constitute me a remarkable monument of his method of humbling the proud for the instruction of all humankind. For I was inflated with pride, and God corrected this by so remarkable a punishment that my example ought to profit the world at large. Hence I said, King Nebuchadnezzar does not simply return thanks to God but at the same time confesses his fault, for though subdued with deserved harshness, yet his haughtiness could not be arrested by any lighter remedy. First of all he says, *I praise, extol and glorify the king of heaven!* This heaping together of words doubtless proceeded from vehement affection. At the same time a contrast must be understood, on the principle formerly mentioned; since God is never rightly praised unless the ignominy of people is detected, he is not properly extolled unless their loftiness is cast down; he is never glorified unless people are buried in shame and

[27]*Prophets*, 533.

prostrate in the dust. Hence, while Nebuchadnezzar here praises, extols and glorifies God, he also confesses himself and all mortals to be nothing—as he did before—to deserve no praise but rather the utmost ignominy. . . .

Since therefore Nebuchadnezzar here confesses God to be just and true in all his works, without any exception, notwithstanding his own severe chastisements, this confession is not feigned; for he necessarily utters what he says from the lowest depths of his heart, through his having experienced the rigor of the divine judgment.

He now adds at last, *He can humble those who walk in pride*. Here Nebuchadnezzar more openly displays his own disgrace, for he is not ashamed to confess his fault before the whole world, because his punishment was known to everyone. As God then wished his folly to be universally detested, by making so horrible an example of him by his punishment, so Nebuchadnezzar now brings his own case forward and bears witness to the justice of the penalty, in consequence of his extreme pride. Here then we see God's power joined with his justice, as we have previously mentioned. He does not attribute to God a tyranny free from all law; for as soon as Nebuchadnezzar had confessed all God's ways to be just, he condemns himself of pride directly afterwards. Hence he does not hesitate to expose his disgrace before humankind, that God may be glorified. And this is the true method of praising God, not only by confessing ourselves to be as nothing but also by looking back on our failings. We ought not only to acknowledge ourselves inwardly guilty before him but also openly to testify the same before all humankind whenever it is necessary. Commentaries on Daniel.[28]

Was Nebuchadnezzar Saved? Andrew Willet: It may be objected that he was not because of that place in Isaiah, *You shall be brought down to hell, to the sides of the pit* (Is 14:15), which, being spoken of Nebuchadnezzar shows his everlasting destruction in hell. And further that in him is set forth and described the fall of Lucifer, who with the rest of the reprobate angels were cast down to hell.

Answer: Though it is admitted and granted that Nebuchadnezzar here is a type of Lucifer, yet it is not necessary that all things that are expressed in such typical predictions should agree to the type. For some things are so spoken that they may fitly agree both to the type and figure, and to the thing prefigured, some to the sign only, some to the thing prefigured only. As in Psalm 2, where David is a type of Christ: *The kings of the earth band themselves, etc.* (Ps 2:2) agrees to both and *I have set my king on Zion* (Ps 2:6). But these words, *You are my son, this day have I begotten you* (Ps 2:7), can only be applied to Christ. So in this place, this casting down to hell may be understood only of Lucifer here prefigured (Pererius). But there are better answers than this.

. . . It may be further and better answered that it is not necessary to understand this prophecy of Nebuchadnezzar but rather it was performed in Belshazzar. For the prophet [Isaiah] prophesied also together of the destruction of Babylon, which continued many years after the death of Nebuchadnezzar. And lastly the word translated *hell* signifies also the grave, and so better interpreted here, because there is mention made of the pit. Wherefore the more probable and certain opinion is that Nebuchadnezzar in the end was saved. Sixfold Commentary upon Daniel.[29]

God's Secret Providence. John Calvin: It now follows: *God does according to his pleasure in the army of the heavens, and among the dwellers on earth* (Dan 4:35). . . . Since this is so, we should remember how extremely unbridled and perverse our rashness is, while we dare object to anything that God does;

[28]CTS 24:302-4 (CO 18:690-91). [29]*Sixfold Commentary* (1610), 150-51.

whence the necessity of this teaching that puts the bridle of modesty on us is proved, since God does all things according to his will, as it is said in Psalm 115:3, *Our God in heaven does what he wishes.* From this sentence we gather that nothing happens by chance, but every event in the world depends on God's secret providence. We ought not to admit any distinction between God's permission and his wish. For we see the Holy Spirit—the best master of language—here clearly expresses two things: first, what God does; and next, what he does by his own will. But permission, according to those vain speculators, differs from will, as if God unwillingly granted what he did not wish to happen! Now, there is nothing more ridiculous than to ascribe this weakness to God. Hence the efficacy of action is added; God does what he wishes, says Nebuchadnezzar. He does not speak in a carnal but in a spiritual sense, or instinct, as we have said; since the prophet must be attended to just as if he had been sent from heaven. Now, therefore, we understand how this world is administered by God's secret providence and that nothing happens but what he has commanded and decreed; while he ought with justice to be esteemed the Author of all things.

Some object here to the apparent absurdity of saying God is the author of sin, if nothing is done without his will; nay, if he himself works it! This calumny is easily answered, as the method of God's action differs materially from that of people. For when any person sins, God works in his own manner, which is very different indeed from that of people, since he exercises his own judgment and thus is said to blind and to harden. As God therefore commands both the reprobate and the evil one, he permits them to indulge in all kinds of licentiousness, and in doing so executes his own judgments. But he who sins is deservedly guilty and cannot implicate God as a companion of his wickedness. And why so? Because God has nothing in common with him in reference to sinfulness. Hence we see how these things that we may deem contrary to one another are mutually accordant, since God by his own will governs all events in the world and yet is not the author of sin. And why so? Because he treats Satan and all the wicked with the strict justice of a judge. We do not always see the process, but we must hold this principle with firmness—supreme power is in God's hands; hence we must not cavil at his judgments, however inexplicable they may appear to us. COMMENTARIES ON DANIEL.[30]

GOD ALMIGHTY. HANS DENCK: You, O God, know how to restore all things, for you are mighty and you have power over all human kingdoms. You give them to one in whom you delight, and you humble another so that he has to eat grass with the beasts of the field for seven years just like an ox, so that you might be known as he who has power over all lords and princes. REFLECTIONS ON MICAH.[31]

[30]CTS 24:297-99 (CO 18:686-88). [31]*Writings*, 129.

5:1-30 THE HANDWRITING ON THE WALL

1 King Belshazzar made a great feast for a thousand of his lords and drank wine in front of the thousand.

*2 Belshazzar, when he tasted the wine, commanded that the vessels of gold and of silver
that Nebuchadnezzar his father[a] had taken out of the temple in Jerusalem be brought,
that the king and his lords, his wives, and his concubines might drink from them. 3 Then
they brought in the golden vessels that had been taken out of the temple, the house of
God in Jerusalem, and the king and his lords, his wives, and his concubines drank from
them. 4 They drank wine and praised the gods of gold and silver, bronze, iron, wood, and
stone.*

*5 Immediately the fingers of a human hand appeared and wrote on the plaster of the
wall of the king's palace, opposite the lampstand. And the king saw the hand as it wrote.
6 Then the king's color changed, and his thoughts alarmed him; his limbs gave way, and his
knees knocked together. 7 The king called loudly to bring in the enchanters, the Chaldeans,
and the astrologers. The king declared[b] to the wise men of Babylon, "Whoever reads this
writing, and shows me its interpretation, shall be clothed with purple and have a chain
of gold around his neck and shall be the third ruler in the kingdom." 8 Then all the king's
wise men came in, but they could not read the writing or make known to the king the
interpretation. 9 Then King Belshazzar was greatly alarmed, and his color changed, and
his lords were perplexed.*

*10 The queen,[c] because of the words of the king and his lords, came into the banqueting
hall, and the queen declared, "O king, live forever! Let not your thoughts alarm you or
your color change. 11 There is a man in your kingdom in whom is the spirit of the holy
gods.[d] In the days of your father, light and understanding and wisdom like the wisdom
of the gods were found in him, and King Nebuchadnezzar, your father—your father the
king—made him chief of the magicians, enchanters, Chaldeans, and astrologers, 12 because
an excellent spirit, knowledge, and understanding to interpret dreams, explain riddles,
and solve problems were found in this Daniel, whom the king named Belteshazzar. Now
let Daniel be called, and he will show the interpretation."*

*13 Then Daniel was brought in before the king. The king answered and said to Daniel,
"You are that Daniel, one of the exiles of Judah, whom the king my father brought from
Judah. 14 I have heard of you that the spirit of the gods[e] is in you, and that light and understanding and excellent wisdom are found in you. 15 Now the wise men, the enchanters,
have been brought in before me to read this writing and make known to me its interpretation, but they could not show the interpretation of the matter. 16 But I have heard that you
can give interpretations and solve problems. Now if you can read the writing and make
known to me its interpretation, you shall be clothed with purple and have a chain of gold
around your neck and shall be the third ruler in the kingdom."*

17Then Daniel answered and said before the king, "Let your gifts be for yourself, and
give your rewards to another. Nevertheless, I will read the writing to the king and make
known to him the interpretation. 18O king, the Most High God gave Nebuchadnezzar
your father kingship and greatness and glory and majesty. 19And because of the greatness
that he gave him, all peoples, nations, and languages trembled and feared before him.
Whom he would, he killed, and whom he would, he kept alive; whom he would, he raised
up, and whom he would, he humbled. 20But when his heart was lifted up and his spirit
was hardened so that he dealt proudly, he was brought down from his kingly throne, and
his glory was taken from him. 21He was driven from among the children of mankind, and
his mind was made like that of a beast, and his dwelling was with the wild donkeys. He
was fed grass like an ox, and his body was wet with the dew of heaven, until he knew that
the Most High God rules the kingdom of mankind and sets over it whom he will. 22And
you his son,[f] Belshazzar, have not humbled your heart, though you knew all this, 23but
you have lifted up yourself against the Lord of heaven. And the vessels of his house have
been brought in before you, and you and your lords, your wives, and your concubines have
drunk wine from them. And you have praised the gods of silver and gold, of bronze, iron,
wood, and stone, which do not see or hear or know, but the God in whose hand is your
breath, and whose are all your ways, you have not honored.

24"Then from his presence the hand was sent, and this writing was inscribed. 25And
this is the writing that was inscribed: MENE, MENE, TEKEL, and PARSIN. 26This is the
interpretation of the matter: MENE, God has numbered[g] the days of your kingdom and
brought it to an end; 27TEKEL, you have been weighed[h] in the balances and found want-
ing; 28PERES, your kingdom is divided and given to the Medes and Persians."[i]

29Then Belshazzar gave the command, and Daniel was clothed with purple, a chain of
gold was put around his neck, and a proclamation was made about him, that he should be
the third ruler in the kingdom.

30That very night Belshazzar the Chaldean king was killed. 31[j]And Darius the Mede
received the kingdom, being about sixty-two years old.

a Or *predecessor;* also verses 11, 13, 18 **b** Aramaic *answered and said;* also verse 10 **c** Or *queen mother;* twice in this verse **d** Or *Spirit of the holy God* **e** Or *Spirit of God* **f** Or *successor* **g** *MENE* sounds like the Aramaic for *numbered* **h** *TEKEL* sounds like the Aramaic for *weighed* **i** *PERES* (the singular of *Parsin*) sounds like the Aramaic for *divided* and for *Persia* **j** Ch 6:1 in Aramaic

OVERVIEW: This chapter introduces us to the impious king Belshazzar, who restores idolatry and profanes the things of God. Some consideration is given to the history and the relationship between Nebuchadnezzar and Belshazzar. The sins of the king displayed at his great feast are discussed, and particularly the right and wrong use of wine is commented on. During this feast, fingers of a human hand appeared and wrote on the plaster wall. Characteristic of his pride the king offers great rewards to the wise man who interprets the handwriting. All fail, and at this point the queen appears. Our commentators remark at length on the identity of this queen and her comments regarding Daniel. The Lutheran commentators are particularly struck by the possible relationship between Daniel, as the chief of the magi, and the magi in the day of Christ. Daniel is brought before the king and begins with a review of history. He then offers his interpretation of the four words. Following his interpretation, the king clothes Daniel in purple and dies an unrepentant tyrant.

5:1a *King Belshazzar*

Historical Considerations. Philipp Melanchthon: Above Daniel showed the king's repentance and propagation of true worship, on whom God bestowed rewards. Now he adds a contrary example of an impious king, restoring idolatry and not repenting, whom God punishes and whom he removed from power.

First, the history must be considered. Nebuchadnezzar reigned for forty-five years. The son, Evil-merodach, who imitated the piety of his father, bestowed royal honor on Jehoiachin, king of Judah, and granted the people of God great benefits. Evil-merodach reigned for twenty-three years.

After this Belshazzar, far different, ruled and fell into idolatry. As it is testified, he was an enemy of true doctrine, sanctioned idolatry, profaned the Jewish vessels and with great contempt insulted God, as Sennacherib and the Rabshakeh did in 2 Kings 18–19, and as the Jews derided Christ, "if you are the Son of God, come down from the cross" (Mt 27:40). Swift punishment follows these blasphemies; according to the law, "the Lord will not hold him guiltless" (Ex 20:7).

This history first admonishes us concerning the horrible power of the devil, who in all ages uses the greatest authorities to sanction idolatry and harass the church. . . . Second, this history urges rulers to piety and warns the impious of punishment. Third, it shows that succession of kings is by God because of various sins. God punishes idolatry and blasphemy, as in Manasseh, and the kings of Israel. With David he punished adultery and his plan of murder. Commentary on the Prophet Daniel.[1]

Nebuchadnezzar and Belshazzar. John Mayer: Touching this Belshazzar the king, some think him to have been the son of Nebuchadnezzar, because he is in this chapter so called, and next after Nebuchadnezzar written of, and although it may seem to make against it, that Evil-merodach succeeded Nebuchadnezzar, it is held by them that Evil-merodach and Belshazzar were all one. This is intimated (Jer 50:2) where it is said, in speaking of the destruction of Babylon, Bel is fallen, Merodach is broken in pieces, which may be taken for Evil-merodach. Although at Jeremiah 27 it is said all nations shall serve Nebuchadnezzar, and his son and his son's son, which was not fulfilled, if Belshazzar were his son, in whose time Babylon was destroyed. They answer that there were two Nebuchadnezzars, touching the former of which Jeremiah says that all nations should serve him and his son and son's son, and so they did, if Belshazzar were son of the second of these Nebuchadnezzars. Others say that Belshazzar was not the son but the grandchild of Nebuchadnezzar and called his son only as the grandchild of any man is commonly and the grandfather the father. According to this, Evil-merodach was Nebuchadnezzar's son and Belshazzar his son. Lastly, others place next to Nebuchadnezzar Evil-merodach, then Niglissar, after him Labosordacus, then Belshazzar, so Josephus whom Jerome follows, but to them he reckons so many years that it agrees not with the years of the Jews captivity: to Evil-merodach eighteen years, to Neglissar forty, to Labosordacus nine months, to Belshazzar seventeen, which together make seventy-five besides the thirty-six years of Nebuchadnezzar after Jerusalem was destroyed. It is therefore rather to be held that Belshazzar was the son of Evil-merodach and that he is omitted by Daniel, as in whose time nothing remarkable fell out, but what was before related (2 Kings 25) and Daniel propounded to himself only to set forth things of greatest note. And thus the prophecy of Jeremiah was fulfilled of all nations serving Nebuchadnezzar, and his son and son's son,

[1]*In Danielem Prophetam* (1543), 78-80.

and we shall not be forced to flee to an uncertain conjecture of another Nebuchadnezzar coming between, of whom neither the Hebrews nor Berosus the Chaldean historiographer makes any mention. Commentary upon All the Prophets.[2]

5:1b-2 *Drinking Wine*

Wine Is God's Good Creation. Heinrich Bullinger: *He drank wine before a thousand of his lords* (Dan 5:1). To drink wine is free of blame. Wine is a good creation of God, given by God for human enjoyment and benefit. And for that reason Belshazzar is here said to drink wine not without censure. It must be understood that he drank immoderately. Daniel the Most Wise Prophet of God.[3]

Wine Drinking. John Calvin: The prophet says *Belshazzar committed this under the influence of wine* (Dan 5:2). Since *tegnem* signifies "to taste," no doubt he here speaks of tasting; and since this may be metaphorically transferred to the understanding, some explain it to mean being impelled by wine, and thus his drunkenness took the place of reason and judgment. Nights and love and wine, says Ovid, have no moderation in them. This explanation I think too forced; it seems simply to mean when Belshazzar grew warm with wine, he commanded the vessels to be brought to him; and this is the more usual view. When, therefore, the savor of the wine prevailed, that is, when it seized on the king's senses, *then he ordered the vessels to be brought*. It is worthwhile to notice this, to induce us to be cautious concerning intemperance in drinking, because nothing is more common than undertaking many things far too rashly when our senses are under the influence of wine. Hence we must use wine soberly, that it may invigorate not only the body but also the mind and the senses, and may never weaken or enervate or stupify our bodily or mental powers. And this is, alas! too common, since the vulgar proverb is well known: pride springs from drunkenness. Commentaries on Daniel.[4]

The Sin of Drunkenness. Johann Wigand: Drunkenness is a sin against the sixth commandment of the Decalogue, in which more drink is consumed than nature requires of persons. The body is weighed down and the mind confused, as one loses control of his mental faculties. I refer to the sixth commandment because it vitiates mind and body, and it produces occasions for illicit desires.

Drunkenness is twofold: Physical drunkenness, which happens by immoderately pouring drink into the human body, creates stupefying feelings that ascend to the head and disturb the brain. Spiritual drunkenness is full of errors and sins, by which the mind and heart are disturbed and bewitched: *Hear this you afflicted and drunken not with wine* (Is 51:21); *Awake, you drunkards, and weep* (Joel 1:5).

The efficient cause of drunkenness is both people and the devil. To be drunk from the devil is well known. John writes, *He who commits sin is of the devil* (1 Jn 3:8). Other sins and condemnation follow drunkenness, they testify. It is from such a spirit that he commits sin. People carry out this sin by free will, extending the hand to the drink, which they are able to draw back, lifting it to their lips, which they are able to turn away, and repeatedly pouring in the drink rather than doing it with moderation. Brief Exposition of the Prophet Daniel.[5]

5:3-4 *Belshazzar's Sins*

Belshazzar's Use of the Sacred Vessels. John Calvin: Here king Belshazzar

[2]*Prophets*, 534. Berosus flourished around 290 b.c. and wrote a history of Babylon. His work survives only in fragments today. [3]*Daniel Sapientissimus*, 50. [4]CTS 24:311 (CO 18:696-97). Ovid (43 b.c—a.d. 17) was one of the most significant Roman poets. Calvin's reference is to Ovid *Amores* 1.6.59. [5]*Explicatio Brevis* (1571), 173.

courts his own punishment, because he furiously stirred up God's wrath against himself, as if he was dissatisfied with its delay while God put off his judgment for so long a period. This is according to what I have said. When the destruction of a house is at hand, the impious remove the posts and gates, as Solomon says (Prov 17:19). God therefore, when he wishes to execute his judgments, impels the reprobate by a secret instinct to rush forward of their own accord and to hasten their own destruction. Belshazzar did this. His carelessness was the sign of his stupidity and of God's wrath, when in the midst of his own pride and crimes he could delight in reveling. Thus his blindness more clearly points out God's vengeance, since he was not content with his own intemperance and excesses but must openly declare war against God. *He ordered, therefore, says he, the gold and silver vessels to be brought to him that he had taken away from Nebuchadnezzar.* These vessels appear to have been laid up in the treasury; hence Nebuchadnezzar had never abused these vessels in his lifetime; we do not read that Evil-merodach did anything of this kind, and Belshazzar now wishes purposely to inflict this insult on God. There is no doubt he brought forth those vessels by way of ridicule, for the purpose of triumphing over the true God, as we shall afterwards see. COMMENTARIES ON DANIEL.[6]

BELSHAZZAR'S SINS. JOHANN WIGAND: Three sins are enumerated by synecdoche, as is the custom of the prophets, which include among many other things extravagance and drunkenness; profanation of sacred vessels; idolatry and blasphemy. The text has, And he drank wine with a thousand, that is, he had eagerness and purpose, drinking with them all the way to drunkenness. Therefore this is the first sin, extravagance in feasting and drunkenness. This sin increases the present danger. Now Babylon was surrounded by enemies. Therefore these things hinder the soundness of your strength and power, they remove the fear of God, they show contempt for your enemies, and they make you secure and impenitent.

The second sin, the profanation of the sacred vessels, which were taken from the temple in Jerusalem, and to this point kept safe. Ephesians 5:18 says wine is followed by debauchery.

. . . The third sin is pagan idolatry and blasphemy, by which the true God is wronged by the greatest dishonor, as if the achievements of Babylon were because of Belshazzar. The king thought he was able to babble foolishly with impunity. He did not realize that God heard that drinking party and the drunk words of his contemptible mouth and was wronged by them. BRIEF EXPOSITION OF THE PROPHET DANIEL.[7]

CONCERNING SACRED THINGS. PHILIPP MELANCHTHON: It is asked concerning sacred things whether or not it is permitted to transfer them to profane use. I respond that whatever is set apart without the Word of God is not to be held back from common use because nothing is made sacred without the Word of God. Indeed, it is impiety to imagine something sacred without the Word of God. In Acts it clearly states, *What God has made clean, do not call common* (Acts 10:15).

. . . Belshazzar profaned things divinely consecrated and added blasphemies. He profaned them to show himself to be an enemy of God. As the text clearly says, *they praised the gods of gold and wood, etc.* Just as Julian the Apostate attempted to restore idolatry, so here Belshazzar had applied himself as an enemy of true doctrine and created the hope of restoring idolatry. COMMENTARY ON THE PROPHET DANIEL.[8]

5:5-9 *The Writing on the Wall*

[6]CTS 24:310 (CO 18:696). [7]*Explicatio Brevis* (1571) 163-64. [8]*In Danielem Prophetam* (1543), 80-81.

THE HANDWRITING. JOHN CALVIN: Here Daniel begins his narration of the change that took place, for at that instant the king acknowledged something sorrowful and disturbing to be at hand. Yet, as he did not at once understand what it was, God gave him a sign as an omen of calamity, according to the language of the profane. In this way God sent him warning when he saw the king and his nobles raging with mad licentiousness. *There appeared*, then, *the hand of a man*, says the prophet, using this expression from its similitude and form. We are sure it was not a man's hand; it had the appearance of one and hence was called so. Scripture often uses this method of expression, especially when treating external symbols. This is, then, a sacramental form of speech, if I may use the expression. God, indeed, wrote the inscription by his own power, but he shows King Belshazzar the figure as if a man had written it on the wall; hence *the fingers of a hand were put forth*. This expression conduces in no slight degree to the reality of the miracle; for if Belshazzar had seen this on the wall from the very first, he might have supposed some artifice had placed the hand there; but when the wall was previously bare, and then the hand suddenly appeared, we may readily understand the hand to have been a sign from heaven, through which God wished to show something important to the king. COMMENTARIES ON DANIEL.[9]

WRITING JUDGMENT ON THE WALL. JOHANNES OECOLAMPADIUS: In that hour, he says, during which impiety swelled beyond measure and he was blaspheming, then God conferred honor on his own name, that all would become aware that the kingdom of Babylon toppled by divine judgment and that it is he who directs kingdoms and times. Therefore, in that hour, which seemed to them free from care, and during which Belshazzar trusted in his gods, it is given and written against such sentiments, afterwards he expressed regret but in vain. . . . Nebuchadnezzar found grace but not Belshazzar; the former sought it, the latter did not. The impenitent neither find nor seek. To the latter, therefore, the hand appeared, as if he had said, I do not send the prophet by whose voice one may recover his senses, but I write the judgment that will be unchangeable that you will fear and not avoid. At first only the king saw what was written and the guests did not, just as Balaam's ass saw the angel but Balaam did not. Opposite the lampstand it wrote so that the writing would be illumined and clearly seen. COMMENTARY ON DANIEL.[10]

EVENTS TYPIFYING THE GOSPEL. JOHN MAYER: To this point the divine spirit that was in Daniel was seen by his interpreting of two dreams of King Nebuchadnezzar. Now a third instance is given of the same in his reading and expounding the strange handwriting on the wall to Belshazzar, in which there is some typifying of things done under the gospel. (1) In the stone cut out of the mountain without hands. (2) In the watcher decreeing the cutting down of the proud king, represented by a huge high and broad tree, for by this was set forth John the Baptist's threatening, that every tree that brings not forth good fruit shall be hewn down and cast into the fire, and our Lord's telling how the barren fig tree should be cut down, which was also fulfilled in the destruction of Jerusalem by the Romans, and for the renewing of the stump still to shoot up again afterwards, it was also true in the Jew, or shall be when converted (Rom 11; 2 Cor 3). In this handwriting setting forth Belshazzar's destruction and loss of his kingdom, because he weighed too light, for by books wherein people's doings are written, all shall at the last by Christ be judged, and then they that are light like chaff and not heavy and substantial like wheat, very husks without

[9]CTS 24:314-15 (CO 18:699). [10]*In Danielem prophetam libri duo* (1553), 67.

grain, shall be destroyed, and the kingdom of heaven given to the solid faithful, who are within, as they show to be outwardly. Commentary upon All the Prophets.[11]

The King's Pride. John Calvin: Now the prophet says, *The king promised the wise men a present of a chain of gold to whoever read the writing;* and besides this, *raiment of purple, and the third rank in the kingdom!* This shows him not to have been sincerely touched by the fear of God. And this repugnance is worthy of observation in the wicked, who dread God's judgments, and yet the pride of their hearts is not corrected and subdued, as we saw in the case of this king. For *his knees struck one against the other, and the joints of his loins were loosened:* he trembles throughout his entire frame and becomes half dead with fear, because God's terror seizes on all his senses. Meanwhile, we see a hidden pride lurking in his mind, which breaks forth in the promise, *whoever shall interpret the writing, shall be the third in rank in the kingdom!* God had already deprived him of his royal dignity; yet he still wishes to raise others on high in defiance of God! What, then, is the meaning of this? We see how often the wicked are terrified, and how deeply they cherish a hidden contumacy, so that God never subdues them. They show, indeed, many signs of repentance; but if anyone carefully weighs all their words and deeds, he will find the prophet's narration concerning King Belshazzar completely verified, because they rage against God and are never teachable or obedient but utterly stupefied. Commentaries on Daniel.[12]

Belshazzar's Pride. Johann Wigand: Pride is the fertile mother of sins. It is opposed to the first and second table of the Decalogue. It attracts and increases the vengeance of God. The pride of the devil and humanity are overthrown. It is the image of the devil, which presses on our foolish mortality. Pride is twofold: spiritual and material. Spiritual pride places confidence in your own works like the hypocrites and Pharisees. Material pride is found in those like Caligula. Brief Exposition of the Prophet Daniel.[13]

5:10-12 *The Queen Intervenes*

The Queen. John Calvin: Here Daniel relates the occasion of his being brought before the king, as the reader and interpreter of the writing. The queen, he says, did this. It is doubtful whether it was the wife of King Belshazzar or his grandmother. She was probably an old woman, as she refers to events in the time of King Nebuchadnezzar. This conjecture has no sufficient foundation, and hence it is better to suspend our judgment than to assert anything rashly; unless, as we before saw, his wife was at table with him. As far as we can gather the words of the prophet with certainty, we must diligently notice them and thus convict the king of ingratitude, because he did not admit Daniel among the magi, Chaldeans and astrologers . . .

Now, when Daniel says *the queen entered the banqueting room;* very probably she was not the king's wife, but his grandmother. I have expressed my intention of not contending the point, since in doubtful cases everyone ought to enjoy his own unbiased judgment. But it is incongruous to say, *The king was feasting with his wife and concubines,* and then to add, *the queen entered the banqueting room.* Hence we suppose her to be called queen through the honor, rank and respect that she still enjoyed, without any power. The testimony of Herodotus confirms this view, for he praises the queen of King Nebuchadnezzar for her singular prudence, calling him Labynetus and her Nitocris. It is far more probable that this matron was absent from a banquet unsuitable to her age and gravity, since she would scarcely

[11]*Prophets*, 533-34. [12]CTS 24:321 (CO 18:703). [13]*Explicatio Brevis* (1571), 171.

be feasting with those who were thus devoting themselves to luxury. When she enters the room, she reminds the king of Daniel. COMMENTARIES ON DANIEL.[14]

ON THE QUEEN. JOHANN WIGAND: *The queen* (Dan 5:11). She offered the occasion for the interpretation. God wished his writing to be known to the king. The queen was either the wife of Nebuchadnezzar or Evil-merodach. She held fast to the pure religion and neither thought like her impious posterity nor had interest in their banquet. BRIEF EXPOSITION OF THE PROPHET DANIEL.[15]

WHO IS THE QUEEN? JOHN MAYER: On this the queen hearing of it came in, about whom it may be questioned what queen she was, seeing his wives and concubines were already with him; but it is answered, most probably she was the wife of Nebuchadnezzar who lived still, or of Evil-merodach his father, who knew what Daniel had formerly done in similar difficult cases, for which reason she commends Daniel to him, and Daniel being sent for came, and read and interpreted the writing. COMMENTARY UPON ALL THE PROPHETS.[16]

THE PRUDENCE OF THE QUEEN. JOHANNES OECOLAMPADIUS: It is said that she was the wife of Nebuchadnezzar; she was more prudent than the others and not drunk. But when she heard all the consternation and the banquet turn to mourning, she hastened with a divine instinct and announced the renown of Saint Daniel. Only one was mindful of all the benefits of Daniel, and she admired his great virtues. COMMENTARY ON DANIEL.[17]

5:11b *Daniel and the Wise Men*

DANIEL AND THE MAGI. MARTIN CHEMNITZ: Because Daniel had been brought up in the school of the magi (Dan 1:6; cf. Dan 4:9, 5:11), some of the magi had undoubtedly been taught the doctrine of the Messiah because of the circumstance of that relationship. Thus, it is very likely on the basis of the background and instruction of Daniel that some seeds of heavenly doctrine had remained among the magi. In Daniel 2:44, he clearly prophesies to the king of Babylon about the coming kingdom of heaven that it will endure forever. Hence it happened that not all the Jews returned to Jerusalem from their Babylonian exile, but many stayed in those places and had renowned synagogues there, just as the rabbinic scholars boast that those wise men taught many things there. Therefore, there were many in various kingdoms at that time who were neither Jews nor proselytes but who were devout, as they are called in Acts; that is, who without circumcision, used to read frequently the prophetic books as they were translated into Greek, and used to worship the God of Israel, just as we read about the Ethiopian eunuch in Acts 8:28. On this account, it will not be absurd if some knowledge of the promises about the Messiah of the Jews whose salvation belonged also to the Gentiles is attributed to the wise men from the rest of the teachings of Daniel or from the Israelite exiles still dwelling in Chaldea or from the reading of the prophets. THE HARMONY OF THE FOUR EVANGELISTS.[18]

DANIEL AND THE WISE MEN. JOHANN GERHARD: One can get on track even better if one considers that the prophet Daniel was reared in the schools of the Persian wise men. As a result, he would have beyond a doubt entrusted to them something about the coming Messiah. This would have continuously been retained by them, especially since these wise men were able to read the holy Scriptures, which had been translated into the Greek language. Be that as it may, one thing is for sure, they would not

[14]CTS 24:324, 326-27 (CO 18:706-07). [15]*Explicatio Brevis* (1571), 167. [16]*Prophets*, 534-35. [17]*In Danielem prophetam libri duo* (1553), 69. [18]*Harmony*, 190.

have been able to recognize the birth of Christ from the appearance of the star alone.

We especially should realize that if we are to come to Christ, then God the Lord also has to lead us through a miraculous, divine Light. With our own understanding, we are in darkness. Thus we are unable to know Christ if God the Lord does not ignite a Light within us. Postilla.[19]

5:13-23 *Daniel Brought Before the King*

Daniel Brought to the King. Heinrich Bullinger: Daniel was not at the immoderate banquet, nor was he with the wise men who were summoned to the king, providing nothing to the king. For the godly separate themselves from the impious and do not mingle with them. Even if the godly and ungodly live in the same city, sometimes making use of the same house and sharing in material things, nevertheless the godly do not communicate with the impious in that which opposes piety. Hence the apostle does not command us to flee from the world, but *Have no fellowship with the unfruitful works of darkness, but rather reprove them* (Eph 5:11). And again he says, *that you may be as children of God blameless in the midst of a crooked and perverse nation, among whom shine as lights in the world, holding forth the word of life* (Phil 2:15-16). Therefore although Daniel lived in Babylon amid a depraved nation, he kept himself pure from the abominations of the Babylonians. Daniel the Most Wise Prophet of God.[20]

Daniel Begins with History. John Calvin: Before Daniel recites the writing and adds its interpretation, he explains to King Belshazzar the origin of this prodigy. He did not begin the reading at once, as he might conveniently have done, saying *Mene, Mene!* as we shall see at the end of the chapter, since the king could not have profited by his abrupt speech. But here Daniel shows it to be by no means surprising if God put forth his hand and showed the figure of a hand describing the king's destruction, since the king had too obstinately provoked his anger. We see then why Daniel begins by this narrative, since King Nebuchadnezzar was a most powerful monarch, subduing the whole world to himself and causing all people to tremble at his word, and was afterwards hurled from the throne of his kingdom. Hence it more clearly appears that Belshazzar did not live in ignorance, for he had so signal and remarkable an example that he ought to have conducted himself with moderation. Since then that domestic admonition did not profit him, Daniel shows the time to be ripe for the denunciation of God's wrath by a formidable and portentous sign. Commentaries on Daniel.[21]

5:24-28 *The Handwriting Interpreted*

Mene, Mene, Tekel, Parsin. Johann Wigand: *Mene* (Dan 5:26). He repeats this word, Mene, Mene, which indicates certainty. The end of your kingdom approaches. Here is set before you the end, look forward to nothing more, your number is complete. This shows that God determines the end of life. *Tekel* (Dan 5:27). This concerns the death of the king. God shows that he does all things by his most just judgment and judges sins severely. He declares Belshazzar unworthy, who delights more in gold. God grants life and ends life, and he punishes the wickedness of humankind. *Peres* (Dan 5:28). The third concerns the transfer of the monarchy and the arrangement of a new kingdom. Brief Exposition of the Prophet Daniel.[22]

The Words on the Wall. John Calvin: First of all, Daniel recites the four words, Mene, Mene, Tekel, Parsin, and then adds

[19]*Postilla* 1:138. [20]*Daniel Sapientissimus*, 53. [21]CTS 24:332-33 (CO 18:711-12). [22]*Explicatio Brevis* (1571), 170-71.

their interpretation. He repeats the word *Mene* twice. Some conjecture this to apply to the numbering of the years of the king's life and to the time of his reign, but the guess seems to be without any foundation. I think the word is used twice for the sake of confirmation, as if the prophet meant the number to be completed, since people usually allow calculations to be liable to error. To impress on Belshazzar that his life and kingdom were at stake, God affirms the number to be complete, meaning, not a moment of time can be added to the boundary already determined. So also Daniel himself interprets it: *God,* says he, *has numbered your kingdom;* implying, God has appointed and prescribed a fixed end to your kingdom; hence it must necessarily come to an end, since its period is fulfilled . . .

The exposition of the word *Tekel, to weigh,* now follows: *Since you have been weighed in the balance, or scale, and found wanting.* Here Daniel shows God so moderating his judgments, as if he were carrying a balance in his hand. The emblem is taken from the custom of humankind, for people know the use of the balance for accurate measurement. So also God is said to treat all things by weight and measure, since he does nothing with confusion but uses moderation; and, according to ordinary language, nothing is more or less than it should be (Wis 11:21). For this reason, Daniel says God *weighed Belshazzar in a balance,* since he did not make haste to inflict punishment but exacted it with justice according to his own uniform rule of government. *Since he was found deficient,* that is, was found light and without weight. As if he had said, You think your dignity must be spared, since all people revere you; you think yourself worthy of honor; you are deceived, says he, for God judges otherwise; God does not use a common scale but holds his own, *and there are found deficient;* that is, you are found a man of no consequence, in any way. From these words there is no doubt that the tyrant was greatly exasperated, but as his last end was approaching, he ought to hear the voice of the herald. And God, without doubt, restrained his fierceness, that he should not rise up against Daniel.

The word *Peres* is added, for the word *Parsin,* meaning *his kingdom was divided* among the Medes and Persians. I have no doubt that by this word God signified the dispersion of the monarchy that was at hand. COMMENTARIES ON DANIEL.[23]

TEKEL AND JESUS CHRIST. HEINRICH BULLINGER: According to the word of this divine statement, *Tekel,* which in Latin is *appendit,* meaning "he weighs out," which Daniel clearly explains saying, "You are in the balance or scales and you are found wanting, without weight or moral value which, it seems, is required by the righteousness and justice of God and must be in you." The scales of justice is a symbol. . . . By this figure the justice of God's judgment toward humankind is beautifully represented. Therefore, we ought to reflect on all our words and deeds gathered together in the balance, and on the opposite scale, these are weighed against the will of God and the righteousness of his law. We will all discover ourselves to be exceedingly light and empty, unless the precious blood of Christ is added to us as our righteous reward and weight. DANIEL THE MOST WISE PROPHET OF GOD.[24]

MORAL APPLICATION OF VISION. ANDREW WILLET: By the hand writing on the wall is signified the justice of God, which both prescribes beforehand the punishments due to people's sins and in due time brings them forth and inflicts them. It also may be applied to the judgment of the conscience. . . . By the three words may be signified the three last things that may come on sinners; the remembrance of which would be most grievous for them: death, final judgment and hell. By the numbering

[23]CTS 24:342-44 (CO 18:718-20). [24]*Daniel Sapientissimus,* 56.

of the days and the fulfilling of them, people are brought to think of their end, as Job says, *are not his days determined, the number of his months are with you* (Job 14:5). By weighing in the balance is signified the most perfect judgment of God in the last day. And by division the punishment of hell, where the wicked and reprobate shall forever be divided and separate from God's presence (Pererius). Sixfold Commentary upon Daniel.[25]

5:29-30 *The King's Reaction*

Belshazzar's Reaction to Daniel. John Calvin: This order of the king (Dan 5:29) may excite surprise, since he had been so sharply reproved by the prophet. He next seemed to have lost all spirit, for he had grown pale a hundred times and would have devoted the holy prophet of God to a thousand deaths! How happens it, then, that he ordered him to be adorned with royal apparel, and next to be proclaimed by his own herald the third person in the kingdom? Some think this was done because the laws of kings were sacred among the Babylonians; nay, their very words were held as binding, and whatever they proclaimed, they desired it to be esteemed firm and inviolable. They suppose King Belshazzar to have acted thus through ambition, that he might keep his promises. My opinion is that he was at first utterly astonished, and through listening to the prophet he became like a stock or a stone! I think he did so to consult his own ease and safety; otherwise he would have been contemptible to his nobles. To show himself unmoved, he commands Daniel to be clothed in these robes, as if his threat had been perfectly harmless. He did not despise what the prophet had said, but he wished to persuade his nobles and all his guests of his perfect indifference to God's threats, as if he did not utter them for the purpose of executing them, but only of terrifying them all. Thus kings, when greatly terrified, are always exceedingly careful not to show any sign of their timidity, since they think their authority would become materially weakened. To continue, therefore, his reverence among his subjects, he is desirous of appearing exceedingly careless and undisturbed; and I do not hesitate to pronounce this to have been the tyrant's intention in ordering Daniel to be clad in purple and in royal magnificence. Commentaries on Daniel.[26]

Unrepentant Tyrant. Martin Luther: In the fifth chapter a warning against tyrants is issued. The earlier example [of Nebuchadnezzar] is still bearable, because the king allowed himself to be punished, and then he returned to God through true repentance, humility, and belief, so that without a doubt he became a great saint out of a tyrant. But now here the stubborn and unrepentant tyrant [Belshazzar], who is secure and joyful in his wickedness, is punished. Without any merely he loses body and soul, his land and his people with one strike. Indeed this is written to frighten all such tyrants. Preface to the Prophet Daniel.[27]

Belshazzar a Warning to Secure Sinners. Johann Gerhard: Just like King Belshazzar was thoroughly carousing in a banquet with his influential people as a hand went up to the wall and wrote of the collapse of his kingdom before his very eyes, so also, when the building of this world and all its kingdoms are soon to be destroyed, it will also happen that people will act secure and will busy themselves with getting drunk. Postilla.[28]

[25]*Sixfold Commentary* (1610), 181. [26]CTS 24:345-46 (CO 18:720-21). [27]WADB 11,2:8-10. [28]*Postilla*, 1:21.

6:1-28 DANIEL AND THE LIONS' DEN

[1]It pleased Darius to set over the kingdom 120 satraps, to be throughout the whole kingdom; [2]and over them three presidents, of whom Daniel was one, to whom these satraps should give account, so that the king might suffer no loss. [3]Then this Daniel became distinguished above all the other presidents and satraps, because an excellent spirit was in him. And the king planned to set him over the whole kingdom. [4]Then the presidents and the satraps sought to find a ground for complaint against Daniel with regard to the kingdom, but they could find no ground for complaint or any fault, because he was faithful, and no error or fault was found in him. [5]Then these men said, "We shall not find any ground for complaint against this Daniel unless we find it in connection with the law of his God."

[6]Then these presidents and satraps came by agreement[a] to the king and said to him, "O King Darius, live forever! [7]All the presidents of the kingdom, the prefects and the satraps, the counselors and the governors are agreed that the king should establish an ordinance and enforce an injunction, that whoever makes petition to any god or man for thirty days, except to you, O king, shall be cast into the den of lions. [8]Now, O king, establish the injunction and sign the document, so that it cannot be changed, according to the law of the Medes and the Persians, which cannot be revoked." [9]Therefore King Darius signed the document and injunction.

[10]When Daniel knew that the document had been signed, he went to his house where he had windows in his upper chamber open toward Jerusalem. He got down on his knees three times a day and prayed and gave thanks before his God, as he had done previously. [11]Then these men came by agreement and found Daniel making petition and plea before his God. [12]Then they came near and said before the king, concerning the injunction, "O king! Did you not sign an injunction, that anyone who makes petition to any god or man within thirty days except to you, O king, shall be cast into the den of lions?" The king answered and said, "The thing stands fast, according to the law of the Medes and Persians, which cannot be revoked." [13]Then they answered and said before the king, "Daniel, who is one of the exiles from Judah, pays no attention to you, O king, or the injunction you have signed, but makes his petition three times a day."

[14]Then the king, when he heard these words, was much distressed and set his mind to deliver Daniel. And he labored till the sun went down to rescue him. [15]Then these men came by agreement to the king and said to the king, "Know, O king, that it is a law of the Medes and Persians that no injunction or ordinance that the king establishes can be changed."

[16]Then the king commanded, and Daniel was brought and cast into the den of lions. The king declared[b] to Daniel, "May your God, whom you serve continually, deliver you!" [17]And a stone was brought and laid on the mouth of the den, and the king sealed it with his own signet and with the signet of his lords, that nothing might be changed concerning

Daniel. [18]Then the king went to his palace and spent the night fasting; no diversions were brought to him, and sleep fled from him.

[19]Then, at break of day, the king arose and went in haste to the den of lions. [20]As he came near to the den where Daniel was, he cried out in a tone of anguish. The king declared to Daniel, "O Daniel, servant of the living God, has your God, whom you serve continually, been able to deliver you from the lions?" [21]Then Daniel said to the king, "O king, live forever! [22]My God sent his angel and shut the lions' mouths, and they have not harmed me, because I was found blameless before him; and also before you, O king, I have done no harm." [23]Then the king was exceedingly glad, and commanded that Daniel be taken up out of the den. So Daniel was taken up out of the den, and no kind of harm was found on him, because he had trusted in his God. [24]And the king commanded, and those men who had maliciously accused Daniel were brought and cast into the den of lions—they, their children, and their wives. And before they reached the bottom of the den, the lions overpowered them and broke all their bones in pieces.

[25]Then King Darius wrote to all the peoples, nations, and languages that dwell in all the earth: "Peace be multiplied to you. [26]I make a decree, that in all my royal dominion people are to tremble and fear before the God of Daniel,

for he is the living God,
enduring forever;
his kingdom shall never be destroyed,
and his dominion shall be to the end.
[27]He delivers and rescues;
he works signs and wonders
in heaven and on earth,
he who has saved Daniel
from the power of the lions."

[28]So this Daniel prospered during the reign of Darius and the reign of Cyrus the Persian.

a Or *came thronging;* also verses 11, 15 **b** Aramaic *answered and said;* also verse 20

OVERVIEW: This well-known chapter opens with Daniel's promotion. Here an example of Daniel's faith, diligence, earnestness, innocence and righteousness is set before us. His elevation is similar to Joseph's in Egypt, performing the functions and duties of a king though not serving as king. The king, Darius, is praised for his wisdom and humility in setting a captive and foreigner over all his satraps. Darius is a person of faith, embracing doctrine and cherishing it but nonetheless allowing himself to succumb to the request of the satraps. Following the king's decree, we see Daniel's boldness of faith as he prays openly. Our commentators ask many questions about what Daniel does. Why was it necessary for him to pray with open windows? Does this conflict with Christ's words that we are to pray in secret (Mt 6)? Why does he pray toward Jerusalem and three times a day? Finally, did Daniel sin by disobeying the king's decree or are believers permitted to disregard the unjust commands of rulers?

The king's response and actions are carefully considered by our commentators, who emphasize a distinction between the sins of the king, who sins out of weakness, and Daniel's accusers, who sin willfully out of jealousy and against the Holy Spirit. Some suggest that Darius likely tried to negotiate for Daniel's release, pleading his importance and usefulness to the nation. In the end, however, it was the king who cast him into the lions' den. Others denounce his sacrilegious pride and false piety in commending Daniel's deliverance to the God he serves.

Daniel is protected and preserved in the lions' den because of his faith. Our commentators dwell on this point, lest some think he was delivered because of his good works and merit. Daniel does say he was found blameless (Dan 6:22), but this blamelessness is explained because he believed in God (Dan 6:23). The king's final decree to all the peoples and nations elicits diverse comments from the reformers. Some praise the king's faith and evangelical statements; others charge the king with unbelief, despite the pious sound of his decree.

THE ARGUMENT OF THE CHAPTER. HEINRICH BULLINGER: To be sure all these things are related to us as in a most excellent picture on a writing tablet, that is the history of Daniel described in this sixth chapter is most elegantly portrayed. First the occasion of the whole history is recited, namely, the arrangement of the kingdom made by Darius, in which Daniel is raised to the highest dignity. For this reason the jealous rulers of the Medes thought to accomplish a guilty, deceitful, destructive plan against him. They tried to take advantage of Daniel's true religion to oppress him. Because as long as Daniel did not wish to hide this, but chose to confess his faith freely and openly, he would fall into the treacherous trap laid by his enemies, and his life would meet with danger. Condemned to the lions he was to die, except God miraculously preserved him. God next, by his own power, brought about the condemnation of Daniel's enemies to the lions, where they were torn to small pieces along with their families. Then the king promulgated a public decree establishing the true religion of God throughout his kingdom. DANIEL THE MOST WISE PROPHET OF GOD.[1]

6:1-5 *Daniel's Promotion*

DANIEL'S INTEGRITY. JOHN CALVIN: Daniel admonishes us by his own example to study to strive after integrity and thus to deprive the malevolent and the wicked of all occasion against us, which they seek. We shall find no better defense against the envious and the slanderous than to conduct ourselves righteously and innocently. Whatever snares they may lay for us, they will never succeed, for our innocence will repel their malice like a shield. Meanwhile we see how Daniel escaped utter ruin, since they sought a pretext against him in something else, namely, his worship of God. Hence let us learn how we ought to esteem piety and an earnest desire for it of more value than life itself. Daniel was faithful and upright in his administration: he discharged his duty so as to close the mouth of his enemies and detractors. Thus, as I have said, integrity is the best of all protectors. Again, Daniel was in danger because he would not leave off the sincere worship of God and its outward profession. Hence we must bravely undergo all dangers whenever the worship of God is at stake. This temporary life ought not to be more precious to us than that most sacred of all things—the preservation of God's honor unstained. We therefore see how we, by these means, are urged to the cultivation of integrity, since we cannot be more secure than when fortified by a good conscience, as Peter in his first epistle exhorts us to the same purpose (1 Pet 3:16). Now, whatever we may fear and what-

[1] *Daniel Sapientissimus*, 59.

ever events await us, even if we become subject to a hundred deaths, we ought never to decline from the pure worship of God, since Daniel did not hesitate to submit to death and enter the lions' den, because he openly professed the worship of Israel's God. Commentaries on Daniel.[2]

Daniel's Elevation. Johannes Oecolampadius: King Darius noticed at once Daniel's faith, diligence, earnestness and righteousness. The king determined that he was deserving of greater honor, truly carrying out what the apostle wrote concerning the magistrate in Romans, "Would you have no fear of the one in authority? Then do what is good and you will have praise from him" (Rom 13:3). . . . Just as Joseph's wisdom was useful to the Egyptian pharaoh, so too Daniel was useful to the Persians and the Medes. Commentary on Daniel.[3]

Daniel Chosen. John Calvin: The Persians, being barbarians, were not naturally more merciful than others; hence God interposed his servant Daniel to succor them. We must notice, in the context of this history, how Daniel alone was chosen by Darius one of these three superior officers. He was the third in rank under King Belshazzar, although for a moment, yet it might occasion envy under the new king that so great an honor was conferred on him. Very probably Darius was informed of the previous predictions of Daniel; how the hand appeared on the wall, how he interpreted the writing and became a heaven-sent messenger to denounce destruction on King Belshazzar. For unless this rumor had reached Darius, Daniel would never have obtained so much authority under him. His own army abounded in numbers, and we know how every conqueror is surrounded in war by many dependents, all of whom wish to share in the spoil. Darius, therefore, would never have noticed a stranger and a captive and admitted him to such great honor and power unless he had understood him to be a known prophet of God and a herald in denouncing destruction against the Babylonian monarchy. Thus we gather how providential it was for him to be among the first satraps, and even third in the kingdom, as this brought him more quickly under the notice of Darius. For if Daniel had been cast down by King Belshazzar he would have remained at home in concealment; but when he appeared clothed in royal apparel, the king inquired who he was. He heard the means of his arriving at so high an honor; hence he acknowledged him as God's prophet and appointed him one of the three prefects. Commentaries on Daniel.[4]

Daniel Like a King. Martin Luther: Even before the world Daniel was an excellent and mighty man. We see here that he ruled as premier magistrate over the first two kingdoms [mentioned in Nebuchadnezzar's dream (Dan 2:31-45)], as if God were saying, "I have to give these kingdoms to someone, even if to do so I have to let my Jerusalem and my people be destroyed." It is quite true that he was not a "king," and he did not receive great treasures or honor, nevertheless he held and discharged the duties, functions and offices of a king. This is how the world works, those who work the most have the least, while those who do nothing receive almost everything, just like the Gospel proverb, "one sows, another reaps" (Jn 4:37). What is even worse is that he must receive hate, jealousy, threats, and persecution as his wages. This is exactly how the world cherishes every service and blessing, showing their thanks with such wages. But this does not trouble Daniel. He is even dearer to God, who rewards him even more abundantly, holding Daniel as a king over Babylon and Persia. For God weighs and judges according to the deed and fruit, not according to the person and

[2]CTS 24:351 (CO 19:5). [3]*In Danielem prophetam libri duo* (1553), 73. [4]CTS 24:349 (CO 19:1-2).

name. Therefore by deed Daniel is the true king of Babylon and Persia, even though he does not have a royal person or name, having not even much treasure, but instead harm and every danger. See, God is able to comfort and honor his captured Jews, making a peasant's son of destroyed Jerusalem into a powerful emperor over Babylon and Persia.

In short, among all the children of Abraham there is no one so exalted in the world as Daniel. There was Joseph, truly great in Egypt with Pharaoh. Also David and Solomon were great in Israel. But they are all minor kings and lords compared to the kings of Babylon and Persia, among whom Daniel was the chief prince, he marvelously won them over to God, and without a doubt Daniel bore great fruit among many people, who through him came to faith in God and became righteous, just as the emperors themselves wrote and commanded that everyone in all lands should honor Daniel's God, as is shown in Daniel 2 and 6. PREFACE TO THE PROPHET DANIEL[5]

SATRAPS. JOHANN WIGAND: Captains, prefects, they are often now called presidents, that is, those who particularly govern, who are the head of provinces by mandate of the king. They administer political justice and collect revenue. Satrap is, in the Persian language, the prefect of a Chaldean province. BRIEF EXPOSITION OF THE PROPHET DANIEL.[6]

6:6-9 *King Darius*

KING DARIUS'S PRUDENCE AND VIRTUE. JOHN CALVIN: Although it was a singular privilege with which God once blessed his people and his prophet, yet we ought to weep over the heartlessness of kings in these days, who proudly despise God's gifts in all good people who surpass the multitude in usefulness and at the same time enjoy the society of the ignorant like themselves, while they are slaves to avarice and rapine and manifest the greatest cruelty and licentiousness. Since, then, we see how very unworthy kings usually are of their empire and their power, we must weep over the state of the world, because it reflects like a glass the wrath of heaven, and kings are thus destitute of counsel. At the last day, King Darius alone will be sufficient to condemn them, for he had discretion enough not to hesitate to set a captive and a foreigner over all his satraps, for this was a royal, nay, a heroic virtue in Darius to prefer this man to all his own friends. But now kings think of nothing else than preferring their own panders, buffoons and flatterers while they praise none but people of low character, whom God has branded with ignominy. Although they are unworthy of being reckoned among humankind, yet they esteem themselves the masters of their sovereigns and treat the kings of these days as their slaves. This happens through their mere slothfulness and their discarding every possible anxiety. Hence they are compelled to deliver up their command to others and retain nothing but the title. This, as I said, is a sure proof of the wrath of heaven, since the world is at this day unworthy of the government that God exercises over it by his hand. COMMENTARIES ON DANIEL.[7]

THE WEAKNESS OF DARIUS'S FAITH. PHILIPP MELANCHTHON: It is necessary to distinguish carefully between those who are weak and the persecutors. The weak one is one who loves and embraces doctrine, desires its propagation, permits himself to be taught and desires to grow in it. He desires teachers to be sound, and he confesses in some manner, he defends it even if he is neither free nor strong and will never deny or attack doctrine.

. . . In this chapter, Darius is weak. He embraces doctrine, desires to defend its confession, cherishes it by his testimony and by his

[5]WADB 11,2:126-128. [6]*Explicatio Brevis* (1571), 181. [7]CTS 24:351 (CO 19:3-4).

confession. These are signs of a pious mind. He never doubts the source but rather questions his own faculties. . . . Although Darius sinned, nevertheless he fell by weakness, and against the fury of the accusers he held onto a scintilla of faith. . . . He exhibited this with his confession saying, "Your God will deliver you." God supports the weak, as is made evident here. The bitter penance of the king follows at once, and from that point forward, he displays a robust faith and great courage, punishing the accusers.

The persecutors are those who neither love nor defend doctrine. They do not permit themselves to be taught. They do not desire to grow in it, neither seeking teachers nor wanting to propagate what they know. They prefer to bury and hide it, showing their hatred for it. Those who have an understanding of doctrine, they fear the judgment of God against blasphemy. Commentary on the Prophet Daniel.[8]

6:10 *Daniel's Faithfulness and Prayer*

Daniel's Piety. John Calvin: Daniel now relates how he was clothed in the boldness of the Spirit of God to offer his life as a sacrifice to God, because he knew he had no hope of pardon left, if his violation of the king's edict had been discovered; he knew the king himself to be completely in shackles even if he wished to pardon him, as the event proved. If death had been before the prophet's eyes, he preferred meeting it fearlessly rather than ceasing from the duty of piety. We must remark that the internal worship of God is not treated here, but only the external profession of it. If Daniel had been forbidden to pray, this fortitude with which he was endued might seem necessary; but many think he ran great risks without sufficient reason, since he increased the chance of death when only outward profession was prohibited. But as Daniel here is not the herald of his own virtue, but the Spirit speaks through his mouth, we must suppose that this magnanimity in the holy prophet was pleasing to God. And his liberation showed how greatly his piety was approved, because he had rather lose his life than change any of his habits respecting the worship of God. We know the principal sacrifice that God requires is to call on his name. For we hereby testify him to be the author of all good things; next we show forth a specimen of our faith; then we fly to him, and cast all our cares into his bosom and offer him our prayers. Since, therefore, prayer constitutes the chief part of our adoration and worship of God, it was certainly a matter of no slight moment when the king forbade anyone to pray to God; it was a gross and manifest denial of piety.

. . . Daniel, therefore, was obliged to persevere in the holy practice to which he was accustomed, unless he wished to be the very foulest apostate! He was in the habit of praying with his windows open; hence he continued in his usual course, lest anyone should object that he gratified his earthly king for a moment by omitting the worship of God. I wish this doctrine was now engraved on the hearts of all people as it ought to be; but this example of the prophet is derided by many, not perhaps openly and glaringly but still clearly enough; the prophet seems to them too inconsiderate and simple, since he incurs great danger, rashly and without any necessity. For they so separate faith from its outward confession as to suppose it can remain entire even if completely buried, and for the sake of avoiding the cross. They depart a hundred times from its pure and sincere profession. We must maintain, therefore, not only the duty of offering to God the sacrifice of prayer in our hearts, but that our open profession is also required, and thus the reality of our worship of God may clearly appear. Commentaries on Daniel.[9]

[8] *In Danielem Prophetam* (1543), 93-96. [9] CTS 24:358-60 (CO 19:8-10).

DANIEL OBEYS GOD. JOHANNES OECOLAMPADIUS: Now this is Daniel's mighty battle against those vipers. He shines forth meanwhile with extraordinary virtue. He gives witness to his faith with an excellent confession, not only not assenting to the impious decree, which without any doubt was contrived against Daniel alone, but also publicly condemning it. Now as soon as he knew that the decree had been established and confirmed by the king, he walked to his house, opened the windows, and as was his custom, he prayed. COMMENTARY ON DANIEL.[10]

THE CIRCUMSTANCES OF DANIEL'S PRAYER. ANDREW WILLET: The occasion is expressed that when he heard of this decree he took himself to prayer, which the children of God most of all use in the time of distress. The place is expressed: he went into his own house, not to any of their idolatrous temples. His own house was his temple. And he prayed in an upper room, not to be more secret, as Pintus gathers, but rather that he might be seen, that he continued constant in his religion (Polanus, Junius). The place is described by the adjunct, the opening of the windows, that he might freely and openly show himself a worshiper of God. The position of the opening of the windows was toward Jerusalem, where he hoped to return. The circumstance of the time is added: he prayed three times a day, in the morning before he went to his business, at noon, when he came home to eat meat, and at night, when he had finished his business. He chose these three times because they were most free from worldly employments and would not be interrupted in his prayer. His gesture is expressed; he kneeled down on his knees. The argument and matter of invocation: prayer, in the petition of a thing necessary; and praise, in giving thanks to God. His constancy is showed as he had done before. SIXFOLD COMMENTARY UPON DANIEL.[11]

DANIEL PRAYS WITH OPEN WINDOWS. JOHN CALVIN: The question arises, Whether it was necessary for Daniel thus to open his windows? For someone may object—he did this under a mistaken opinion; for if God fills heaven and earth, what signified his windows being open toward Jerusalem? There is no doubt that the prophet used this device as a stimulus to his fervor in prayer. For when praying for the liberation of his people, he directed his eyes toward Jerusalem, and that sight became a stimulus to enflame his mind to greater devotion. Hence the opening of the prophet's windows has no reference to God, as if he should be listened to more readily by having the open heaven between his dwelling and Judea; but he rather considered himself and his natural infirmity. Now, if the holy prophet, so careful in his prayers, needed this help, we must see whether or not our sloth in these days has need of more stimulants! Let us learn, therefore, when we feel ourselves to be too sluggish and cold in prayer, to collect all the aids that can arouse our feelings and correct the torpor of which we are conscious. This, then, was the prophet's intention *in opening his windows toward Jerusalem* (Dan 6:10). COMMENTARIES ON DANIEL.[12]

DANIEL PRAYS OPENLY. GIOVANNI DIODATI: [*His windows*] To oppose openly an impious and unlawful law, to overcome the malice of his enemies, who watched his constancy and sought to overthrow it with fear, and to give all believers an example of zeal to God's glory, he was moved by the Holy Spirit not to change or slack anything in his ordinary devotions, which, these respects laid aside, were not absolutely necessary.

[*Toward*] Namely, as toward the place consecrated to the manifestation of God's presence in grace and power: which law stand-

[10]*In Danielem prophetam libri duo* (1553), 76. [11]*Sixfold Commentary* (1610), 180. [12]CTS 24:361 (CO 19:10-11).

ing yet in force, and being very shortly to be re-established in effect, he looked that way, as toward heaven. See 1 Kings 8:48.

[*Three times*] Namely, the morning, noon and evening, which were the three hours of the Jews' daily prayers. See Psalm 55:17. Pious Annotations.[13]

Daniel Prays Toward Jerusalem. Johann Wigand: *Windows opened.* He allows the light of his confession to shine forth. The worship of God should by no means be hidden. Although unrestrained and permitted to pray anywhere in this his private house, nevertheless, because of his confession, Daniel made it publicly. Christ prohibits the false prayers of the hypocrites; he does not forbid public confession (Mt 6:5-6). Daniel opened the windows, turned to heaven and fervently called on the Almighty God of heaven and earth. Then, as his confession went forth, it was a good example for the others. Now the time arrived, for which there was no dissimulation, no false appearance, but the godlessness of the decree had to be shown.

Toward Jerusalem. It was established in 1 Kings 8 that when the exiled peoples made their prayers to God, they were to turn their faces toward that region of the world where the temple of God stood. They did not do this because of some superstition but as a way of remembering the promise of God, especially concerning the sending of the Messiah, and that because of him God would forgive the sins of those who repent. Again, that God would return them to this place at the coming of the Messiah. So Daniel prayed, turning his face to the western meridian. Now having been forgiven in Christ by his perfect redemption of humankind, we are no longer bound to this ceremony. But in all places, we offer our prayers to God by faith in the Mediator. Brief Exposition of the Prophet Daniel.[14]

Daniel at Prayer. John Mayer: All things are here easily to be understood, and therefore I shall speak but little on them. And first of his praying three times a day with his window open toward Jerusalem, as he had used to do. If the reason be demanded, it is answered, God had promised to his people in captivity that if they should pray toward Solomon's temple, he would hear and be merciful, and therefore he set his window open that way, and not to be seen of people, contrary to which it is prescribed, *Enter into your closet, and pray in secret* (Mt 6). . . . But how was he in private, say others, when as the princes by seeing his window open knew of it? Here Polanus enters into a dispute, whether Daniel did well in that he did not for a time pour out his devotions more secretly, where he might not have been seen. And he says, some object against his thus doing, because he might secretly for that time in his mind have worshiped God without using any external gesture, and in so doing have kept a good conscience. 2. If not so, at the least by going in secret, where no mortal eyes might see him. 3. Because the king's decree is to be obeyed in things not contrary to our duty to God. But all this is easily answered. He could not at this time refrain from proceeding externally in his devotion as he used to do, without being reputed a deserter of his piety toward his God, his forbearing to pray, as he had used to do being taken for a relinquishing of him for fear of the king's decree, wherein he knew that he only among all the princes was aimed at, and of what ill consequence this might have been to enemies, who for this would have counted him timorous and without all courage, and to friends, to whom his example might have been a stumbling block to make them to intermit their devotions also. And therefore it was necessary for him to do as he did that his faith, courage and constancy to his first principles might appear to all people,

[13]*Pious Annotations* (1651), 6:10. [14]*Explicatio Brevis* (1571), 188.

and that in the way of piety he feared not people, as his three fellows had done before in Nebuchadnezzar's days. As for obedience to human ordinances, it is no further to be yielded, but as it stands with piety toward God, and doing so as that a good conscience may be kept in all things. Commentary upon All the Prophets.[15]

Prayer. Heinrich Bullinger: Prayer is typically invocation and benediction or thanksgiving. In the present example it seems to be used for invocation. The apostle specifies two kinds of prayers in his letter to the Philippians: invocation and thanksgiving. By the former we ask what we think is necessary for us. By the latter we give thanks for the benefits received. We see that Daniel does both in the present case. It is right that we should always call on God and ask from him what is necessary for soul and body. Finally, we never forget but must always give thanks for the benefits received. Daniel the Most Wise Prophet of God.[16]

Praying Three Times a Day. John Calvin: He says he prayed three times a day. This is worthy of observation, because, unless we fix certain hours in the day for prayer, it easily slips from our memory. Although, therefore, Daniel was constant in pouring forth prayers, yet he enjoined on himself the customary rite of prostrating himself before God three times a day. When we rise in the morning, unless we commence the day by praying to God, we show a brutish stupidity, so also when we retire to rest, and when we take our food and at other times, as everyone finds most advantageous to himself. For here God allows us liberty, but we ought all to feel our infirmities and to apply the proper remedies. Therefore, for this reason, Daniel was in the habit of praying thrice. Commentaries on Daniel.[17]

On Daniel's Prayers. Andrew Willet: Daniel did not choose these hours because he thought them more especially consecrated to prayer, and by the circumstance of the time more holiness and efficacy would be added to them. It is the Romanists who have such a superstitious conceit of their canonical hours. They say the Jews observed these three times with more religious respect. As the third hour because then the Holy Spirit was given, the sixth hour, because then the brazen serpent was lifted up in the wilderness, and the ninth, because then the waters came out of the rock in Kadesh. And so Christians should observe the same three times: the third hour, when the Holy Spirit was given, the sixth, at what time Christ was crucified, and the ninth, when the water gushed out of his side (Pintus).

But this was the reason why Daniel observed these times: he made choice of such times when he had best leisure and was most free from worldly business, which was the morning before he went abroad, at noon when he came home to eat meat, as Joseph also used to do (Gen 43:16), and at night when all his business was ended (Junius). Besides, these are the most suitable times in respect of the benefits received of God, in the morning to give thanks for our deliverance the night past, at noon, when we take our meat, and at night for our preservation that day (Calvin). Sixfold Commentary upon Daniel.[18]

6:11-14 *The King's Response*

The King's Reaction. Johannes Oecolampadius: *When the King heard these words.* There is a great difference between the sins of the king and Daniel's accusers, although he himself, on account of his arrogance and unrighteousness, is not excused. The accusers' jealousy of the servant of God led them to sin

[15]*Prophets*, 535-36. [16]*Daniel Sapientissimus*, 62-63. [17]CTS 24:362 (CO 19:11). [18]*Sixfold Commentary* (1610), 181.

more against the Holy Spirit than the king, who permitted himself to be worshiped, prohibited the worship of God and delivered a just man over to the will of sinners. From this you will see again the diversity of God's judgment, just as with Nebuchadnezzar and Belshazzar. . . . *Then the king commanded and Daniel was brought.* The king considered himself able to accomplish nothing and submitted to the godless accusers, excusing them and condemning Daniel. He acknowledged that Daniel served God, who is able to deliver him, and nonetheless condemned him. Commentary on Daniel.[19]

The King's Selfish Reaction. John Mayer: When the king heard that Daniel was taken in the trap that they had set for him, he was sore displeased with himself and labored to deliver him to the going down of the sun. The king, as it here appears, was merely circumvented, who, when he made his decree, saw not the intentions of the accusers, but now he saw too late and sorrowed fruitlessly. But although he could not see their intentions, yet if he had not been void of all piety, he would never have agreed to make such a decree, no matter how much he had been importuned by them, because even heathens are devout in their kind and know by the light of nature that the worship of the God whom they serve is not to be intermitted so long at any time. His grief for Daniel therefore was not because he was so godly, that for godliness sake he would thus hazard his life, but because he was so wise a man, and so he thought that he should have more loss of him than of all his princes besides. But as great as his grief for Daniel was, and however he labored by speaking for him, seeking some evasion in interpreting his decree made, as Lyra conjectures, or pleading the great usefulness of him for his rare parts to the whole state, he at length caused Daniel to be cast into the lions' den, as Herod afterwards did by John the Baptist, who had hypocritically pretended sorrow, when for his oath he thought himself obliged to do it or was affected with sorrow in some other respect, haply of the hatred of the people, which he should thus incur, because they counted John a prophet. Thus kings sometimes for want of consideration in time entangle themselves in inevitable evils, for which they had need to be very circumspect. Commentary upon All the Prophets.[20]

Darius's Sacrilegious Pride. John Calvin: Daniel now adds, *the king said this to him, Your God, whom you serve,* or worship, *faithfully, he will deliver you!* This word may be read in the optative mood, as we have said. There is no doubt that Darius really wished this; but it may mean, Your God whom you worship will deliver you, as if he had said, "Already I am not my own master, I am here tossed about by the blast of a tempest; my nobles compel me to this deed against my will; I, therefore, now resign you and your life to God, because it is not in my power to deliver you," as if this excuse lightened his own crime by transferring to God the power of preserving Daniel. This reason causes some to praise the piety of King Darius, but as I confess his clemency and humanity to be manifest in this speech, so it is clear that he had not a grain of piety when he thus wished to adorn himself in the spoils of deity! For although the superstitious do not seriously fear God, yet they are restrained by some dread of him; but he here wished to reduce the whole divinity to nothing. What sort of piety was this? The clemency of Darius may therefore be praised, but his sacrilegious pride can by no means be excused. Commentaries on Daniel.[21]

6:15-16 *The King's Edict*

Disobeying the King's Edict. Johann

[19]*In Danielem prophetam libri duo* (1553), 77-78. [20]*Prophets,* 536. [21]CTS 24:371-72 (CO 19:17-18).

Wigand: Daniel did not rashly open the widows, as was his usual custom, only to oppose the decree of king Darius. . . . He had these reasons: (1) The second commandment of the Decalogue, in which the invocation of God is commanded, is not an *adiaphora*. (2) He preferred to seek, to honor and with ardent zeal to vindicate the glory of God in fear of the true God. For the enemies were seeking to abolish the honor of God, or at least pollute it.

. . . But the rulers and those children of the world among the Jewish captives had other reasons in view. The authority of the king, as a swollen thundering mouth, they thought must be obeyed. That is, the king's decree and all the judgments of his counselors are defended. Therefore, no one may make an attempt against it.

I respond that there is no great distinction here. The impious and unjust decree of the king must by no means be obeyed. The reason is evident: kings are under the Decalogue, not above it. God is greater than all rulers. Here are the words: *We ought to obey God rather than man* (Acts 5:29). And, *Give glory to the Lord your God* (Jer 13:16). Furthermore, the true authority of the king consists not in sin but in doing rightly. Brief Exposition of the Prophet Daniel.[22]

Disobeying an Unjust Command. Andrew Willet: Melanchthon well notes that, although Daniel did go against the king's edict and decree, yet he had committed no evil against him. So if princes command unjust and impious things, they are not hurt if these precepts be not obeyed. Neither must they think themselves despised if God is preferred before them. As the apostles' resolution was, when they were forbidden to speak in the name of Jesus, *whether it is right in the sight of God to obey you rather than God, judge* (Acts 4:19). And hereby Melanchthon justly excuses the Protestants of Germany for refusing to obey the emperor's edicts made against the profession and professors of the gospel. Sixfold Commentary upon Daniel.[23]

6:17-18 *The Lions' Den*

The Victory of Faith. Martin Luther: In the sixth chapter there is an excellent and charming story. There is a fine and godly king [Darius] who loves Daniel. The other chief advisors demand that Daniel pay for this, so they play a little courtly trick on him, finally throwing him into the lions' den. The exiled and miserable Jews were once again deeply grieved. However, God proves himself to be just and consoling, turning the game against Daniel's enemies so that they themselves must swallow what they had devised for Daniel, as Psalm 7 (vv. 14, 16) says, "they go about pregnant with mischief, giving birth to lies, and their mischief falls on their own head, their calamity on their own skull." Thus, Daniel's life is nothing other than a refined, pure mirror, in which we see the battle and victory of faith, which through the grace of God conquers all devils and people, and the great fruit and practice of this faith, which through patience and suffering are demonstrated before both God and the world. Preface to the Prophet Daniel.[24]

Darius Not a Believer. John Calvin: Darius declares the God of Israel to be the living One. But if there is a living God, he excludes all those imaginary deities whom people fancy for themselves by their own ingenuity. For it is necessary that deity should be one, and this principle is acknowledged by even the profane. However people may be deluded by their dreams, yet they all confess the impossibility of having more gods than one. They distort, indeed, God's character, but they cannot deny his unity. When Darius uttered

[22]*Explicatio Brevis* (1571), 255. [23]*Sixfold Commentary* (1610), 181. [24]WADB 11,2:10.

this praise of the God of Israel, he confesses all other deities to be mere fictions, but he shows how, as I have said, the profane hold the first principle but afterwards allow it to escape entirely from their thoughts. This passage does not prove, as some allege, the real conversion of King Darius and his sincere adoption of true piety, for he always worshiped his own idols but thought it sufficient if he raised the God of Israel to the highest rank. But, as we know, God cannot admit a companion, for he is jealous of his own glory (Is 42:8). It was too cold, then, for Darius simply to acknowledge the God whom Daniel worshiped to be superior to all others, because where God reigns, all idols must of necessity be reduced to nothing; as also it is said in Psalm 99: "Let God reign, and let the gods of all nations fall before him." Darius then proceeded so far as to devote himself to the true and only God but was compelled to pay the greatest respect to Israel's God. Meanwhile he always remained sunk in his own superstitions to which he had been accustomed. Commentaries on Daniel.[25]

6:19-24 *Daniel Saved by Faith*

God Protects Daniel. John Calvin: Thus we see that Daniel openly assigns to angels the duty of rendering assistance, while the whole power remains in the hands of God himself. He says, therefore, that he was freed by the hand and assistance of an angel but shows how the angel was the agent and not the author of his safety. God, therefore, says he, sent his angel. We have often seen how indistinctly the Chaldeans spoke when mentioning the deity; they called their deities holy, but Daniel here ascribes the entire glory to God alone. He does not bring forward a multitude of deities according to the prevalent opinion among the profane. He puts prominently forward the unity of God; and then he adds the presence of angels as assisting God's servants, showing how they perform whatever is enjoined on them. Thus the whole praise of their salvation remains with the one God, since angels do not assist whomsoever they please and are not moved by their own will but solely in obedience to God's commands.

We must now notice what follows: *God had shut the lions' mouths.* For by these words the prophet shows how lions and the most cruel beasts are in the hands of God and are restrained by his secret curb, so that they can neither rage nor commit any injury unless by God's permission. We may thus learn that savage beasts are only so far injurious to us as God may permit them to humble our pride. Meanwhile, we may perceive that no beast is so cruel as to injure us by either his claws or his teeth unless God give him the reins. And this instruction is worthy of especial notice, since we tremble at the least danger, even at the noise of a falling leaf. As we are necessarily exposed to many dangers on all sides and surrounded by various forms of death, hence we should be harassed by wretched anxiety unless this principle supported us; not only is our life under God's protection, but nothing can injure us while he directs everything by his will and pleasure. And this principle ought to be extended to the devils themselves, and to impious and wicked people, for we know the devil to be always anxious to destroy us, like a roaring lion, for he prowls about seeking whom he may devour, as Peter says (1 Pet 5:8). For we see how all the impious plot for our destruction continually, and how madly they are inflamed against us. But God, who can close the lion's mouth, will also both restrain the devil and all the wicked from hurting anyone without his permission. Commentaries on Daniel.[26]

Daniel's Protection. Heinrich Bullinger: Daniel truly relates the manner of his salvation: "My God," I say to you, king,

[25]CTS 24:377 (CO 19:21-22). [26]CTS 24:379-80 (CO 19:23-24).

who asks, "Will your God, whom you serve continually, be able to deliver you from the lions?" I say, "My God, he delivered me." Thus Daniel always gives all glory to God alone. For he is the Lord of the universe, the governor and preserver, who delivers from danger and rescues from all evils. In this manner he delivered me, says Daniel, he sent his angel and closed the mouth of the lion, so that he could not injure me. . . . We believe that God is omnipotent and that we are under his protection safe from all enemies and evils. He is able always to deliver us from all evil, if he wills. Daniel the Most Wise Prophet of God.[27]

Daniel Delivered by God. John Mayer: *Your God, whom you serve continually will deliver you.* This the king speaks to comfort Daniel, and he might believe, that it should be so, because he had doubtless heard of the deliverance of his three fellows out of the fiery furnace. Then a stone being rolled to the door of the lions' den, it was sealed with the king's seal, says Jerome, lest the princes, if they should find that the lions spared Daniel, should otherwise seek his destruction, pretending it to be done by the lions. It was also sealed with the princes' seals, lest the king should take him out again or seek some means of his preservation, but in all God's providence wrought that his almighty power might more clearly appear in his deliverance, and there was no fraud, for the comfort and confirmation of others being in greatest danger by the malice of their enemies. For dangers by lions, Aristotle, Pliny and Pererius say that if a cloth is cast on the eyes of a lion to cover them, he will not hurt a person; if the lion is full; if a person has been kind to him; or if a person lies prostrate before him in the manner of a supplicant. But Daniel was not safe by any such means, but God sending his angels to shut the lions' mouths, or as some think, taking hunger away from them in respect of Daniel and causing in them a satiety, or causing such a fantasy in them that they looked on Daniel not as prey but as friend.

Daniel being kept safe from the fury of the lions till the morning, and then called to by Darius, answers, *God sent his angel and shut the mouths of the lions, because innocency was found in me,* as he was not hurtful to any, especially not to his conscience by doing anything against it, so God provided that the lions were not able to hurt him. About this Augustine has a notable saying, "Subject yourself to him that is above you, and all things under you shall be subject to you." But because humanity through sin left him, under whom he ought to have been, he was subjected to them, above whom he ought to be. Commentary upon All the Prophets.[28]

Daniel's Faith and Works. Philipp Melanchthon: There are three notable statements in this text concerning faith and works. The principal one is concerning faith, when it says, *He believed in his God* (Dan 6:23). Although this statement is brief, nevertheless it teaches the reader the whole doctrine of faith; namely, God requires faith, and faith receives remarkable gifts. *He believed,* one may see that from the very beginning issuance of the impious decree, he did not abandon his faith and public profession but constantly confessed, called on the God of Israel, and by this faith sought and expected help from God, for the king and for himself, that true doctrine not be removed from the kingdom.

. . . God requires such faith and grants these benefits. According to Isaiah, he who trusts in the Lord will not be put to shame. Again, according to Matthew, whatever you shall ask in prayer, you will receive. Therefore, as by faith, Moses at the Red Sea, Isaiah in the city's siege and all saints in true danger receive help, so here Daniel received deliverance by faith. These testimonies oppose our adversar-

[27]*Daniel Sapientissimus*, 69-70. [28]*Prophets*, 536-37.

ies who shout many things about works and scorn the doctrine concerning faith.

The remaining two statements talk about the righteousness of works, which ought to be in believers before God and before people. Daniel eloquently says, *I was found righteous before God*. Then he adds, *Before you, king, I have done no harm* (Dan 6:22).

Therefore, you will observe in these three places, faith, likewise an inchoate obedience, which although it is impure, nevertheless pleases God in believers, who are justified by faith. It is proper that the righteousness of a good conscience be present in us, as Paul says, "Our rejoicing is this, the testimony of a good conscience" (2 Cor 1:12).

So here Daniel says, *I was found righteous before God*. This is rightly understood when the other sentence concerning faith is added, *He believed in his God*. By no means did Daniel want himself to be righteous on account of his own merit or virtues, but through mercy by faith. And nevertheless he knows to strive for the righteousness of a good conscience that is pleasing to God in believers. COMMENTARY ON THE PROPHET DANIEL.[29]

DANIEL BELIEVED. JOHN CALVIN: But we must here consider the meaning and force of the word *believing* (Dan 6:23). For the prophet does not simply speak of his deliverance as springing from believing Israel's God to be the true and only God, the maker of heaven and earth, but from his committing his life to him, from his reposing on his grace, from his fixed determination that his end must be happy if he worshiped him. Since, therefore, Daniel was certainly persuaded that his life was in God's hand and that his hope in him was not in vain, he boldly incurred danger and intrepidly suffered for the sincere worship of God; hence he says *he believed in God*.

We see then that the word *belief* is not taken coldly, as the papists dream, since their notion implies an unfolded or dead and shapeless faith, for they think faith nothing else but a confused apprehension of the Deity. Whenever people have any conception of God at all, the papists think this to be faith, but the Holy Spirit teaches us far otherwise. For we must consider the language of the apostle, who says that we do not properly believe in God unless we determine him to be a rewarder of all who diligently seek him (Heb 11:6). God is not sought by foolish arrogance, as if by our merits we could confer an obligation on him, but he is sought by faith, by humility and by invocation. But when we are persuaded that God is the rewarder of all who seek him, and we know how he ought to be sought, this is true faith. So Daniel did not doubt that God would deliver him, because he did not distrust that teaching of piety that he had learned from a boy, and through reliance on which he had always called on God. This, therefore, was the cause of his deliverance.

Meanwhile, it is clear that Daniel's trust in God did not spring from any previous instruction concerning the result, for he rather committed his life to God, since he was prepared for death. Therefore Daniel could not acknowledge this before he was cast into the cave and exposed to the lions, being ignorant whether God would deliver him, as we previously saw in the case of his companions, "God, if he pleases, will deliver us; but if not, we are prepared to worship him and to disobey your edict." If Daniel had been taught the issue beforehand, his constancy would not have deserved much praise, but since he was willing to meet death fearlessly for the worship of God and could deny himself and renounce the world, this is a true and serious proof of his faith and constancy. *He believed therefore in God*, not because he hoped for such a miracle but because he knew his own happiness to consist in persisting in the true worship of God. So Paul says, Christ is gain to me, both

[29]*In Danielem Prophetam* (1543), 98-100.

in life and in death (Phil 1:21). Daniel therefore rested in the help of God, but he closed his eyes to the event and was not remarkably anxious concerning his life, but since his mind was erected toward the hope of a better life, even if he had to die a hundred times, yet he never would have failed in his confidence, because our faith is extended beyond the boundaries of this frail and corruptible life, as all the pious know well enough. Commentaries on Daniel.[30]

Daniel Saved by Faith. Heinrich Bullinger: To those who believe, God promises abundant blessings from his grace; to those who do not believe he offers nothing. Therefore, they who believe receive benefits from God, because of the covenant and the mercy and grace of God. For the covenant is nothing other than the pure kindness of God. Those who do not believe receive nothing, since God promises nothing to unbelievers. Daniel the Most Wise Prophet of God.[31]

6:25-28 *The King's Decree*

King Darius Not a Believer. John Calvin: Here Daniel adds the king's edict, which he wished to be promulgated. And by this edict he bore witness that he was so moved by the deliverance of Daniel as to attribute the supreme glory to the God of Israel. Meanwhile, I do not think this a proof of the king's real piety, as some interpreters here extol King Darius without moderation, as if he had really repented and embraced the pure worship prescribed by the law of Moses. Nothing of this kind can be collected from the words of the edict—and this circumstance shows it, for his empire was never purged from its superstitions. King Darius still allowed his subjects to worship idols, and he did not refrain from polluting himself with such defilements; but he wished to place the God of Israel on the highest elevation, thus attempting to mingle fire and water! We have previously discussed this point. For the profane think they discharge their duty to the true God if they do not openly despise him but assign him some place or other; and, especially, if they prefer him to all idols, they think they have satisfied God. But this is all futile; for unless they abolish all superstitions, God by no means obtains his right, since he allows of no equals. Hence this passage by no means proves any true and serious piety in King Darius, but it implies simply his being deeply moved by the miracle and his celebrating through all the regions subject to him the name and glory of the God of Israel. Finally, as this was a special impulse on King Darius, so it did not proceed beyond a particular effect; he acknowledged God's power and goodness on all sides; but he seized on that specimen that was placed directly before his eyes. Hence he did not continue to acknowledge the God of Israel by devoting himself to true and sincere piety; but, as I have said, he wished him to be conspicuously superior to other gods, but not to be the only God. But God rejects this modified worship, and thus there is no reason for praising King Darius. Meanwhile his example will condemn all those who profess themselves to be catholic or Christian kings, or defenders of the faith, since they not only bury true piety, but, as far as they possibly can, weaken the whole worship of God, and would willingly extinguish his name from the world, and thus tyrannize over the pious and establish impious superstitions by their own cruelty. Darius will be a fit judge for them, and the edict here recited by Daniel will be sufficient for the condemnation of them all. Commentaries on Daniel.[32]

The King's Decree. Philipp Melanchthon: The evangelical statements in the king's decree must be observed. He says that the God

[30]CTS 24:384-85 (CO 19:27-28). [31]*Daniel Sapientissimus*, 70.
[32]CTS 24:388-89 (CO 19:30).

of Daniel is a deliverer and rescuer. He names the God of Daniel, that is, his words acknowledge and honor with faith what Daniel proclaimed. . . . God does not wish to be acknowledged or honored by anyone without his word or testimony. . . . Therefore, the king testifies that God is the true God, about whom Daniel preached the word.

Then he adds another distinction that God is a deliverer and rescuer. Now, this is a distinction between true religion and all others. Where there is knowledge of the law only doubt remains, and the dejected are not able to stand. God truly wishes to have mercy, to listen and to help. But the gospel cries out that God freely receives believers. Again, that he truly wishes to listen and to save because he requires such faith, that he wishes to be honored principally by this worship. . . . Wherefore, these statements in the edict that proclaim God a deliverer and rescuer are truly gospel, just as those words in the psalm, *Who heals the brokenhearted and binds up their wounds* (Ps 147:3). This faith is exercised daily in prayer. Commentary on the Prophet Daniel.[33]

Daniel Prefigured Christ. John Mayer: Touching Christ and his kingdom, which he had doubtless learned of Daniel. To conclude, the representation of Christ in this vision, as was said before in part, is in Daniel's coming alive again out of the lions' den into which he was put, as into a sepulcher, after which his accusers being put in were cruelly destroyed, and then the Lord's kingdom extolled and all people prohibited to speak ill of God, the Father of our Lord Jesus Christ. So Christ being laid into the sepulcher, and there a watch of lion-like soldiers set to keep it, and if he should rise again, to kill him, notwithstanding had his angels ready at hand to terrify the soldiers away, and then he arose again and came forth, being safe from all harm, and had all power given him, in heaven and in earth forevermore.

Thus it appears, in everything done here, that Daniel prefigured Christ, as in his name "the judge of God," for so it was before showed that Daniel signifies, and Christ, we believe shall come to judge the living and the dead. 2. As Daniel came out of the lions' den, so he out of the sepulcher. 3. As Daniel came from among the lions safe and sound, so he from among the soldiers. 4. As Daniel came forth from among the lions, his accusers were cast in and destroyed, so Christ came out of the sepulcher, death being not able to hurt him, the Jews his accusers were cast in, as it were, when by the Romans taken and slain. 5. As on this great miracle God was acknowledged and published to all parts of the earth, so on the miraculous rising again of Christ, false gods went down on the publishing of this in all places, and the true God and his Son Jesus Christ were acknowledged all over the earth. Commentary upon All the Prophets.[34]

[33]*In Danielem Prophetam* (1543), 101-2. [34]*Prophets*, 537.

7:1-8 DANIEL'S DREAM OF FOUR BEASTS

1In the first year of Belshazzar king of Babylon, Daniel saw a dream and visions of his
head as he lay in his bed. Then he wrote down the dream and told the sum of the matter.
2Daniel declared,[a] *"I saw in my vision by night, and behold, the four winds of heaven were*
stirring up the great sea. 3And four great beasts came up out of the sea, different from
one another. 4The first was like a lion and had eagles' wings. Then as I looked its wings
were plucked off, and it was lifted up from the ground and made to stand on two feet
like a man, and the mind of a man was given to it. 5And behold, another beast, a second
one, like a bear. It was raised up on one side. It had three ribs in its mouth between its
teeth; and it was told, 'Arise, devour much flesh.' 6After this I looked, and behold, an-
other, like a leopard, with four wings of a bird on its back. And the beast had four heads,
and dominion was given to it. 7After this I saw in the night visions, and behold, a fourth
beast, terrifying and dreadful and exceedingly strong. It had great iron teeth; it devoured
and broke in pieces and stamped what was left with its feet. It was different from all the
beasts that were before it, and it had ten horns. 8I considered the horns, and behold, there
came up among them another horn, a little one, before which three of the first horns were
plucked up by the roots. And behold, in this horn were eyes like the eyes of a man, and a
mouth speaking great things.

a Aramaic *answered and said*

Overview: The seventh chapter begins the second part of Daniel. The first part concerned memorable historical events in the Babylonian kingdom; the second deals with various visions given to Daniel. Put another way, in the first part Daniel was an interpreter and instructor of unbelieving kings; in the second part he instructs the household of believers, the church.

In the present chapter, Daniel has a vision of the four monarchies described in Daniel 2. Here he sees them under the figure of four beasts: lion, bear, leopard and a fourth with horns. As in the second chapter, so too here, Daniel gives most of his attention to the fourth beast, the Roman Empire. Our commentators spend most of their time identifying the fourth beast and the significance of the horns. Disagreement is especially found with the identity of the little horn. The suggestions offered are Julius Caesar, the pope, the Turk or the antichrist.

Two Divisions of Daniel's Book. Heinrich Bullinger: In the first part of the book, Daniel set forth several memorable things about the Babylonian kingdom, under which he lived from the former monarch to Darius for about seventy years. He did not describe all the things that happened during each of these years. . . . In the second part of the book, very many differences follow from the preceding. He has visions not like others but exhibited to him from God, through dreams and divine revelations. Daniel the Most Wise Prophet of God.[1]

The Second Part of Daniel. John Calvin: Here Daniel begins to offer instruction peculiar to the church. For God had formerly appointed him an interpreter and instructor to profane kings. But he now appoints him a teacher to the church, that he may exercise his office within it and instruct the children of God in the bosom of the church. We must notice this first of all, because thus far his predictions extended beyond the limits of the household of faith, but here Daniel's duty is restricted to the church. Commentaries on Daniel.[2]

Daniel's Second Part. John Mayer: In this chapter and hence forward, as Lyra observes, are five visions more. (1) Of four monstrous beasts, and of the coming of the Judge and of the whole proceeding of the last tribulation (Dan 7). (2) Setting forth the fight of the Persians and Grecians by a ram and a goat, and the principal conflict of the same tribulation (Dan 8). (3) Of an angel foretelling the seventy weeks to the death of the Messiah, in whom should be an end of the tribulation (Dan 9). (4) Of a man declaring the end of tribulation, and the last days (Dan 10). (5) Of the fight of Christ and his final victory and triumph under the type of the king of the south and of the north (Dan 11). Thus Lyra.

But Polanus says that in these visions the sufferings of the people of God under the four monarchies of the world are set forth, and especially in the time of Antiochus Epiphanes, when the worship and service of God were quite overturned. The end of such sufferings for the comfort of the faithful is set forth by certain days, by a mighty deliverance, and after that by the coming of the Messiah. And, yet, that the Messiah should be rejected and killed by the greatest part of the Jews, and for this their city should be destroyed, their temple overthrown and the Levitical service there abolished and never be restored again. In that time of common destruction the elect should be by the power of the Messiah preserved, and finally at Christ's second coming all the dead shall rise, some to everlasting life, some to everlasting condemnation. Commentary upon All the Prophets.[3]

Summary of Chapter. Martin Luther: In the seventh chapter the visions and prophecies of the future kingdoms begin, especially of the kingdom of Christ—for whose sake all of these visions take place. First, the four kingdoms that he indicated in chapter 2 (vv. 31-43) in that great image, he sees here again in another form, that is, as four animals. He mostly focuses on the fourth animal, the Roman Empire. He wants to say something more about it, because under that Roman Empire the greatest event on earth is to take place, that is, Christ will come, humanity will be redeemed, and the world will end. Preface to the Prophet Daniel.[4]

A Summary of Daniel. Philipp Melanchthon: Here Daniel begins with particular visions concerning the succession of empires, the advent of Christ and the struggle of the church that will be at the end times. This vision is shown in order to show the time of the coming Messiah lest believers should despair concerning the promises because of the delay and suffering. Commentary on the Prophet Daniel.[5]

7:1 *The Purpose of the Vision*

Daniel's Visions for the Church. John Calvin: *Then he wrote the dream and explained the meaning of the words.* By this phrase he teaches us how his seeing the vision was not for his own sake personally but for the common

[1]*Daniel Sapientissimus*, 73. [2]CTS 25:7 (CO 19:36). [3]*Prophets*, 537-38. [4]WADB 11,2:10. [5]*In Danielem Prophetam* (1543), 108.

edification of the church. Those who suppose Daniel to have leaped suddenly from his bed, lest he should forget the dream, offer a vain and frivolous comment. Daniel rather wished to bear witness to this vision as not peculiar to himself but common to God's elect people, and hence not only to be celebrated orally but also to be delivered to posterity for a perpetual remembrance. We must bear in mind these two points; first, Daniel wrote this prophecy that the knowledge of it might ever be celebrated among the faithful; and then he considered the interests of posterity and so left the vision written. Both these points are worthy of notice to induce us to pay greater attention to the vision, since it was not delivered for a single individual, but God chose Daniel as his minister and as the herald and witness of this oracle. Hence we see how it concerns us; it was not teaching for any single age, but it extends to us and ought to flourish till the end of the world. . . .

He repeats again, *He saw in his vision during the night.* Again, I say, Daniel affirms that he brought forward nothing but what God had authoritatively delivered to him. For we know that in the church all human traditions ought to be treated as worthless, since all people's wisdom is vanity and lies. As God alone deserves to be listened to by the faithful, so Daniel here asserts that he offers nothing of his own by dreaming in the ordinary way, but that the vision is sure and such as cannot deceive the pious. Commentaries on Daniel.[6]

7:2-3 Four Winds and Four Beasts

The Four Winds. John Mayer: First Daniel says that he *saw in his vision by night, and four winds strove on the sea, and four great beasts came up from the sea,* by these four winds, says Lyra, understand four angels set over the four monarchies of the world, who are said to strive, when each one stands for the monarchy, over which he is set, yet ready, when God makes his will known to either of them, to acquiesce and rest therein. As for their striving, it is not to be understood that they did thus all together at one time, but successively, the angel of the Babylonian monarchy against him of the Persian, striving to uphold it against Darius and Cyrus but giving way to the destruction thereof, when God had made known his will in this regard, and likewise he over the Persian against the Grecian, and he that was over the Grecian against the Roman. Commentary upon All the Prophets.[7]

The Four Beasts. Giovanni Diodati: [Dan 7:2. *The four*] By the sea is meant the world, and by the winds the changes of it, by which one empire is raised and another brought low, like the waves of the sea.

[Dan 7:3. *Beasts*] That is to say, empires, figured in this manner, because for the most part the purchase is made, the possession maintained and the government of them executed with violence and tyranny (see Ps 76:4; Song 4:8).

[Dan 7:4. *The first*] This lion represented the Chaldean Empire (Dan 2:37) by reason of its might, and ravenousness (see Is 5:29; Jer 4:7). [*Wings*] to show the Chaldeans' great celerity in their conquests (Is 5:26; Jer 4:13; 48:40; Ezek 17:3; Hab 1:8). [*Plucked*] Namely, all means of conquering or raising itself any more were taken away from it, and it was deprived of the ease and rest that it had a long time enjoyed like a beast, lying on the ground; and being subdued was brought to a reasonable civil and modest life: such the state of Babylon was, long after it had been taken by Cyrus.

[Dan 7:5. *Another*] Which is the Persian Empire (Dan 2:39; 8:3). [*Like to a bear*] for the Persians were a mountain nation, more uncivil than the Chaldeans; though they were great warriors and much inclined to set on empires and states. [*On one side*] he seems here to mean the beginning of the Persian Empire, from the one side of the world, namely, the east, from

[6]CTS 25:9-10 (CO 19:37-38). [7]*Prophets*, 538.

where they came to conquer the other three parts (Dan 8:4). [*They said*] Namely, God's secret providence did drive them on to those enterprises and made them easy for them (see Is 21:2).

[Dan 7:6. *Another*] Namely, Alexander the Great, his empire, who was very speedy in all his conquests, which is figured by the leopard, a very active beast (Hab 1:8), and by his wings (Dan 2:39, 8:5; 11:3). [*Four heads*] which were the four satrapies into which Alexander the Great's empire was divided after his death (Dan 8:8; 11:4; 1 Macc 1:9-10).

[Dan 7:7. *A fourth*] By Daniel 8:9 we may find that the chief meaning of this prophecy has a relation to the kingdoms of Syria and Egypt, possessed by the Seleucids and Ptolemies, which notwithstanding, does not hinder us from believing but that God's Spirit did look yet further; namely, to the Roman Empire, by the resemblance of it to the other, in persecuting the church, subversion and interdiction of God's service and violence done to consciences, whereon the revelation does fit many of these passages of Daniel to antichrist. . . .

[*Diverse*] seeing his tyranny over God's people tended to force people to apostasy and annihilate God's service, which none of the precedent empires had attempted. [*Ten horns*] these are the ten Seleucides, kings of Asia and of Syria, to Antiochus, comprehending him among the rest (Dan 7:24), for although he had successors, yet the people of God (in regard of whom these things are spoken) began after Antiochus to reassume their liberty under the Hasmoneans, until Christ. Pious Annotations.[8]

7:4 *The Lion*

The First Beast: The Lion. Martin Luther: Now then the first animal is the kingdom of Assyria and Babylon. It is a lion with two eagle's wings, because it is the noblest and most superior. As it was said earlier, it was a golden kingdom above all others. The two wings are the parts of the empire, Assyria and Babylon. It is given a human heart and stands on its feet, because no other kingdom has had such a king [as Nebuchadnezzar] who so marvelously came to acknowledge God. As well, no other kingdom has had so many great, righteous, and wise people in the royal court, as this kingdom did. Preface to the Prophet Daniel.[9]

The Lion. Philipp Melanchthon: The lion signifies the Chaldeans and Assyrians. The two wings signify the two particular nations, which ruled in succession, the Chaldeans and Assyrians. It was lifted above the earth and was changed into the figure of a man, that is, the kingdom would be very glorious and put aside barbarity, because it was called to the acknowledgment of God. Commentary on the Prophet Daniel.[10]

Daniel's First Beast, the Lion. John Calvin: We perceive then the reason why the prophet says, *The first beast offered to me was like a lion,* because greater integrity flourished under the Chaldeans than when all the empires were mixed together, and the Persians subdued both the Chaldeans and the Medes. For it is evident from all histories that they were a barbarous and fierce nation. They were indeed showy in their praise of virtue, since they spent their lives in austerity, and despised all luxuries and were exceedingly temperate in their living, but their ferocity and brutal cruelty rendered them detestable. *The first beast* then *was like a lion,* says he, *and had eagle's wings*; that is, although it was a lion, yet it had wings. This refers to its swiftness, since we know in how short a time the Assyrians increased their monarchy, for they had previously subdued the Chaldeans, just like a lion

[8]*Pious Annotations* (1651), 7:2-7. [9]WADB 11,2:10. [10]*In Danielem Prophetam* (1543), 109.

for swiftness. For a lion has force, spirit and cruelty for committing injuries. Besides, the prophet saw a winged lion, since they not only increased their empire by their own strength but also suddenly extended their wings in every direction. We see, then, how strength and power are denoted on the one hand, and the greatest speed on the other. He afterwards adds, *Their wings were dragged or torn off.* For when the Chaldeans desired to stretch beyond their bounds, the Lord restrained them within due limits and checked their continual victories. Their wings were then torn off, when God restrained them by the check of a bridle, lest they should wander as freely as they had formerly done.

The prophet then adds, *This beast was raised from the earth,* implying the cessation of the empire. For neither the Chaldeans nor the Assyrians were entirely destroyed; but their glory was completely taken away. The face of the beast no longer appeared when God transferred that monarchy to the Medes and Persians. Commentaries on Daniel.[11]

On the Lion. John Mayer: For these beasts the first was *like a lion*. . . .This was the king of Babylon, because as a lion among all the beasts of the forest is as king, so was he of all other people far and wide; and therefore under this name of lion he is also set forth (Is 5:29; Jer 4:13) and under the name of an eagle (Jer 48; Ezek 17). And he had two wings of an eagle, the one of riches, for which he was also set forth before by a golden head, and the other of military prowess, for in this both for might and skill he excelled all others, insomuch as that some say he was stronger than Hercules. And wings of an eagle are ascribed to him for his pride, in regard of these two, by which he was lifted up above all other people, as the eagle above all fowls of the air by the strength of his wings, as was touched before in Daniel 3. But his wings were plucked when after his strutting of himself in his pride, he was in mind made like a beast, for then he was for a long time not only as an eagle with his feathers plucked, not able to soar above others any more, and by this means kept lower and beneath them all, even the meanest person, but also whereas the eagle, his feathers being plucked, has still the mind of an eagle, he, on the contrary, was here inferior to other people also, as he had not the understanding of the simplest man in him.

And he was lifted up and made to stand on his feet as a man, which is not to be understood as being done by means of his wings, for they are said before this to have been plucked, but by the mercy of God shown again toward him in restoring him so debased. For then he was lifted up and stood erect as a man, and went not on all four, making feet of his hands, as he did before, but his face that so long had been toward the ground, as the face of a beast, was now lifted up again to look toward heaven, and as God there, by whose savor the case was thus altered with him, as man is differentiated from a beast, according to the saying, "when other animals look downward to the earth, he has given a sublime face to man and bidden him look upward" (cf. Eccles 3:21).

And a man's heart was given to him: which is just according to the saying before on the vision of the great and admirable tree in vision represented to Nebuchadnezzar (Dan 4:32), where after his driving from among people, and the heart of a man taken from him, he says, his understanding returned to him, and he looked up toward heaven. Lyra has also another interpretation of his being plucked of his feathers, when all his power and riches were taken away by the Persians, at what time he stood, as a man, that is, as a poor ordinary man of the meanest sort, and had the heart of a man given him, that is, whereas before he thought himself as good as God, now he knew by experience that he was no god but a

[11]CTS 25:13-14 (CO 19:41).

miserable man. But it is improper to say of one killed that he was lifted up and stood on his feet as a man, or that he had the heart of a man given him, when his heart's blood was shed and he perished; indeed this would be absurd, and therefore I rest in the former.

But Polanus who is for this seeks to make it probable by saying that he was made to stand on his feet as a man when his pride was abated by the Persian, he being before as a lion, and that he had the heart of a man given him because he was then as another ordinary man, and the people of that kingdom made tributary. For these beasts coming out of the sea, hereby the sea is set forth the world for the fluctuating condition of it, now flowing, now ebbing, now boisterous through winds, now calm; their rising then out of the sea is up in the world successively one after another, as God in his providence, who foreshowed this, appointed. Commentary upon All the Prophets.[12]

7:5 *The Bear and Three Ribs*

The Second Beast: The Bear. Martin Luther: The second animal, the bear, is the kingdom of Persia and Media, which destroyed the last remnant of Babylon, plucking its wings. Among its teeth are three ribs that are three great, long teeth, representing the most distinguished kings—Cyrus, Darius and Xerxes—who accomplished the most in this kingdom, devouring much flesh, that is, they conquered many great lands. Preface to the Prophet Daniel[13]

The Bear. Philipp Melanchthon: The bear signifies the Persians. The three long teeth in the mouth signify the three particular kings: Cyrus, Darius and Artaxerxes. Commentary on the Prophet Daniel.[14]

Daniel's Second Beast, The Bear. John Calvin: Here the prophet proclaims how he was instructed by a dream concerning the second beast. If we will only judge by the event, this beast doubtless represented the kingdom of the Medes and Persians, although the prophet specifies the Persians, as the Medes had long ago submitted to their yoke. *Behold,* says he, *another beast like a bear.* We know a bear to be a mean and foul animal, slothful and inert, as well as cruel. In comparing the bear with the lion, its appearance is foul and displeasing, while the lion is remarkable for beauty, although it is formidable. He compares the Persians with a bear, on account of their barbarity, since we have already pronounced that nation fierce and savage. Then, again, the Persians were not civilized like the Assyrians and Chaldeans, who dwelled in the most beautiful region in the whole world, and in a most lovely country like a most noble theater; but the Persians lay hid like wild beasts in their caves. They dwelled among their mountains and lived like the brutes. Hence the prophet compares them very appositely with a bear; nay, God showed this form to his prophet. Commentaries on Daniel.[15]

On the Bear. John Mayer: Here the kingdom of Persia is represented by a bear because a bear is baser than a lion who by subtlety gets his prey and is more cruel. He is baser, as not having so specious a form as a lion, so the Persian was poor and inhabited a barren country, and therefore lived more basely and on coarser food then the Babylonian, whose country was more fruitful. Commentary upon All the Prophets.[16]

The Three Ribs. John Calvin: The prophet then adds, *Three ribs were in the beast's mouth between its teeth; and it was thus proclaimed, Arise, eat much flesh!* Those who

[12]*Prophets,* 538-39. [13]WADB 11,2:10-12. [14]*In Danielem Prophetam* (1543), 109. [15]CTS 25:15 (CO 19:42). [16]*Prophets,* 539.

understand three definite kingdoms by the three ribs seem to refine far too minutely. I think the number indefinite, because this beast had bitten by its mouth not one rib but more; because the Persians, as we have said, drew to themselves the power of the Medes and afterwards subdued the Assyrians and Chaldeans, and Cyrus also subdued many nations, until all Asia Minor acknowledged his authority. When, therefore, the prophet speaks of three ribs, it implies the insatiable nature of this beast, since it was not content with a single body but devoured many people together. For by "many ribs," he meant much prey. This is the whole sense. Commentaries on Daniel.[17]

The Three Ribs in the Mouth of the Beast. John Mayer: By three ribs in his mouth, either three kingdoms are set forth, the Persian, Median and Babylonian, now all in the power of Cyrus, or three parts of the world, east, west and south, as some say, or rather east, south and north; as others, the east subdued by Cyrus, the south by Cambyses, in which stood Egypt and Lybia, the north by Darius Hystaspis, where the Scythians were. Commentary upon All the Prophets.[18]

God Punishes the World. John Calvin: I do not hesitate to explain the following words, *it was said to the beast,* of angels or of God himself. Some prefer to understand this of the stimulus by which Cyrus was instigated to cruelty. But since God exhibits to his prophet the image of his Providence, what I have lately suggested becomes very probable, namely, *it was said to the beast, Arise, eat much flesh;* not because God was the author of cruelty, but since he governs by his secret counsel the events that people carry on without method, his authority is here deservedly placed before our eyes; for Cyrus would not have penetrated so swiftly into different regions, and have drawn to himself so many empires and subjugated so many powerful nations, had not God wished to punish the world and had made Cyrus the instrument of slaughter. As therefore Cyrus executed God's vengeance by shedding so much human blood, the prophet declares it to have been said to him, *Arise, and eat flesh.* In one respect God was not pleased by the slaughter of so many nations by Cyrus, and by the increase of one man's power and tyranny through so much human bloodshed; but in another respect God is said to have commanded the conduct of Cyrus, since he wished to punish the world for its ingratitude, to which the most desperate obstinacy and rebellion were added. There was no remedy for these vices; hence God entrusted Cyrus with the duty of executing his judgment. Commentaries on Daniel.[19]

The Bear Eats Flesh. John Mayer: This bear is bidden eat much flesh to show that the destructions made by him in the world were by God's appointment and not at his own will, and for this end it is also said of the next, that dominion was given to it. Commentary upon All the Prophets.[20]

7:6 *The Leopard*

The Third Beast: The Leopard. Martin Luther: The third animal is the leopard with four wings and four heads. It is the kingdom of Alexander the Great of Greece. Afterwards four kingdoms came out of it, as we will hear in the next chapter. Preface to the Prophet Daniel.[21]

The Leopard. Philipp Melanchthon: The leopard signifies Alexander of Macedonia. The four wings and four heads are the four successors, for after the mighty battle the four rulers after Alexander divided the great empire:

[17]CTS 25:16 (CO 19:42-43). [18]*Prophets,* 540. [19]CTS 25:17 (CO 19:43). [20]*Prophets,* 540. [21]WADB 11,2:12.

Seleucus ruled Syria and beyond, Ptolemy Egypt, Antigonus Asia Minor, and Antipater Macedonia.

The nature of the leopard or panther corresponds to the character of the Greeks; they are spotted, fragrant and have a frightful head; they hunt their prey with their sweet odor and by concealing their heads; they fight courageously for their young and offspring, fearing no weapons; and they are made drunk with wine. COMMENTARY ON THE PROPHET DANIEL.[22]

DANIEL'S THIRD BEAST, THE LEOPARD. JOHN CALVIN: Daniel has already spoken of two empires, namely, the Chaldean and Persian. Interpreters agree in the necessity for referring this vision to the Macedonian Empire. He compares this kingdom with a leopard, or, as some translate, a panther, since Alexander obtained his great power through swiftness alone; and although it is not by any means a striking animal, yet it managed by its remarkable speed to subdue the whole east. Others bring forward many points of likeness in which the Grecian character is in accordance with the nature of the leopard. But I fear these minutiae have but little weight: it is sufficient for me that the Spirit treats here of the third empire. It was not of any importance at first and could neither terrify distant regions nor acquire subjects by its own worthiness. It then became like some swift animal, if I may say so, since the swiftness of Alexander is notorious; but he did not excel in either prudence, or gravity, or judgment, or in any other virtues. Mere rashness seized on him, and even if he had never tasted wine, his ambition would have intoxicated him. Hence Alexander's whole life was drunken; there was neither moderation nor composure in him. We see, then, how suitably this answers to the character of Alexander, although this is also extended to his successors, all of whom partook largely of the nature of their prince. Daniel says, therefore, *A beast appeared to him like a leopard.*

He also says, *It had four wings on its back, and four heads.* Some persons, as I think perversely, distinguish between the wings and the heads. They suppose the kingdom to be depicted as winged because Alexander seized on many kingdoms in a short period; but the more simple sense is this beast had four wings and four heads because Alexander had scarcely completed his victories when he died, contrary to all expectation; and after his death, every one seized a portion of the prey for himself. This, however, is certain: after the chief generals of his army had contended for many years, all histories agree in stating that the supreme power centered in four. For Seleucus obtained Asia Major, and Antigonus Asia Minor, Cassander was king of Macedon and was succeeded by Antipater, while Ptolemy the son of Lagus became the ruler of Egypt. COMMENTARIES ON DANIEL.[23]

7:7 *The Fourth Beast*

THE FOURTH BEAST. MARTIN LUTHER: Now the fourth animal with iron teeth is the truly guilty one. It is the last kingdom, that is, the Roman Empire, with it the world is to come to an end, as Daniel here says much about the Last Judgment and about the kingdom of the saints that will follow after this kingdom. PREFACE TO THE PROPHET DANIEL.[24]

DIFFICULTIES IN IDENTIFYING THE FOURTH BEAST. JOHN CALVIN: There is greater difficulty in this fourth monarchy. Those who are endued with moderate judgment confess this vision to be fulfilled in the Roman Empire, but they afterwards disagree, since what is here said of the fourth beast many transfer to the pope, when it is added a little horn sprang up; but others think the Turkish kingdom is com-

[22]*In Danielem Prophetam* (1543), 109. [23]CTS 25:17-20 (CO 19:43-44). [24]WADB 11,2:12.

prehended under the Roman. The Jews for the most part incline this way, and they are necessarily compelled to do so, since Daniel will afterwards add, I saw the throne of the Son of Man; since it is clear, from this prediction, that Christ's kingdom was erected by the overthrow of the Roman dominion, the Jews turn round, and, as I have said, join the Turkish monarchy with the Roman, since they do not find their Christ according to their imagination. And there are some of our writers who think this image ought not to be restricted to the Roman Empire but ought to include the Turkish. In my view, there is nothing probable in that opinion; I have no doubt that in this vision the prophet was shown the figure of the Roman Empire, and this will be more apparent as we go on. Commentaries on Daniel.[25]

The Fourth Beast. John Mayer: By this beast differing from all the rest, the ancients generally understand the Roman Empire, which was so diversely ruled, sometime by tribunes of the people, sometime by consuls, by dictators, by the triumviri and by emperors, and therefore it was unlike any of the kingdoms that went before it and is set forth as more terrible for the great iron teeth and horns, and the feet stamping all under foot, by subjecting them to tribute in all countries and nations. For which cause this monarchy could not by any beast be represented but only be described as a monster among beasts. Commentary upon All the Prophets.[26]

7:8 *The Horns*

The Horns. Martin Luther: He depicts that this Roman Empire will first be divided into ten kingdoms—these are the ten horns—as Syria, Egypt, Asia [Minor], Greece, [North] Africa, Spain, France, Italy, Germany, England, etc. Then a small horn will uproot three of the original ten horns. This is Mohammed or the Turk, who now has Egypt, Asia and Greece. This same little horn will fight against the saints, blaspheming Christ. This we all are experiencing before our very eyes. The Turk has had great victories against Christians and indeed denies Christ, hoisting his Mohammed over everything else. Now certainly we have nothing more to wait for except the Last Day, for the Turk will not uproot more than three of the horns. Preface to the Prophet Daniel.[27]

The Horns of the Fourth Beast. John Calvin: *I was attentive,* therefore, says he, *to the horns, and behold one small one arose among them.* Here interpreters begin to vary; some twist this to mean the pope and others the Turk, but neither opinion seems to me probable; they are both wrong, since they think the whole course of Christ's kingdom is here described, while God wished only to declare to his prophet what should happen up to the first advent of Christ. This, then, is the error of all those who wish to embrace under this vision the perpetual state of the church up to the end of the world. But the Holy Spirit's intention was completely different. We explained at the beginning why this vision appeared to the prophet—because the minds of the pious would constantly fail them in the dreadful convulsions that were at hand, when they saw the supreme dominion pass over to the Persians. And then the Macedonians broke in on them and acquired authority throughout; the whole of the east, and afterwards those robbers who made war under Alexander suddenly became kings, partly by cruelty and partly by fraud and perfidy, which created more strife than outward hostility. And when the faithful saw all those monarchies perish and the Roman Empire spring up like a new prodigy, they would lose their courage in such confused and turbulent changes. Thus this vision was presented to the prophet that all the children

[25]CTS 25:21 (CO 19:46). [26]*Prophets,* 540. [27]WADB 11,2:12.

of God might understand what severe trials awaited them before the advent of Christ. Daniel, then, does not proceed beyond the promised redemption and does not embrace, as I have said, the whole kingdom of Christ but is content to bring the faithful to that exhibition of grace that they hoped and longed for.

It is sufficiently clear, therefore, that this exhibition ought to be referred to the first advent of Christ. I have no doubt that *the little horn* relates to Julius Caesar and the other Caesars who succeeded him, namely, Augustus, Tiberius, Caligula, Claudius, Nero, and others. Although, as we said before, the counsel of the Holy Spirit must be attended to, which leads the faithful forward to the beginning of the reign of Christ, that is, to the preaching of the gospel, which was commenced under Claudius, Nero, and their successors. He calls it a *little horn*, because Caesar did not assume the name of king. Commentaries on Daniel.[28]

The Ten Horns. Andrew Willet: By the ten horns are rather understood ten kingdoms, then kings, as Greece, Macedonia, Asia, Syria, Egypt, Africa, Spain, Gaul, Germany and Illyricum. The little horn signifies Muhammad, called little in respect of his obscure beginning. The three horns plucked up before it are the three kingdoms of Syria, Egypt, Africa, which the Turk invaded. The mouth speaking proud things is the new law of the Turks brought in by Muhammad. Sixfold Commentary upon Daniel.[29]

Another Horn. Giovanni Diodati: [*Another*] That is, Antiochus called Epiphanes, who is one of the number of the above-mentioned ten kings; yet he is called another, because his tyranny over the people was especial (Dan 7:24).

[*Little*] as Daniel 8:9, because this Antiochus was the youngest among his brethren, and the kingdom did not by right belong to him; and besides, he was of an abject and despicable nature and carriage (Dan 11:21).

[*Three of*] that is, three kings, namely, Ptolomeus Philopater, king of Egypt, who had taken Syria; Antiochus the great father of Epiphanes; and Seleucus his brother, who were all three deprived either of their lives or kingdoms by Antiochus (Dan 7:24).

[*Were eyes*] this is spoken to show his natural sagacity and cunning (Dan 8:23, 25; 11:23, 32).

[*Mouth*] he was exceeding haughty in words (1 Macc 1:25), cruel in bloody decrees and a great blasphemer of God (Dan 7:25; 8:23, 25; 11:36, 1 Macc 1:46-47). See the comparison of this with pagan Rome (Rev 13:5). Pious Annotations.[30]

The Little Horn, the Antichrist and the Pope. John Mayer: But although I here agree with antiquity, both that the Roman Empire is set forth by this beast with ten horns of which I have also said enough on Revelation 17 showing what ten kings these horns were, and that the little horn was antichrist, who was to arise during the time of this empire, yet whereas they say that antichrist is yet to come toward the end of the world, and that he shall, when he comes, reign but three years and a half: in this I cannot subscribe, but, on the contrary, hold that antichrist is come and is not one man but a succession of men in the Roman state, ruling not by force at the first but by flattery and false persuasions, for which it is said that he had *eyes like the eyes of a man, and a mouth speaking great things:* for he sees according to the carnal reason of a man, whereby he conceives himself (because he is Saint Peter's successor, who had the government of Christ's church committed to him) to be as high priest, and lord over all churches

[28]CTS 25:26-27 (CO 19:50). [29]*Sixfold Commentary* (1610), 500. [30]*Pious Annotations* (1651), 7:8.

and churchmen speaking to this purpose most magnificently of himself, as Christ's vicar being over all powers not only spiritual but also temporal, it being in him to dispose of the kingdoms of the world as he pleases, putting down one and setting up another. And therefore this horn little at the first must be the pope of Rome, to whom these things do most aptly agree. COMMENTARY UPON ALL THE PROPHETS.[31]

[31] *Prophets*, 542.

7:9-28 THE ANCIENT OF DAYS AND CHRIST'S KINGDOM

9"As I looked,

thrones were placed,
and the Ancient of Days took his seat;
his clothing was white as snow,
and the hair of his head like pure wool;
his throne was fiery flames;
its wheels were burning fire.
10A stream of fire issued
and came out from before him;
a thousand thousands served him,
and ten thousand times ten thousand stood before him;
the court sat in judgment,
and the books were opened.

11"I looked then because of the sound of the great words that the horn was speaking.
And as I looked, the beast was killed, and its body destroyed and given over to be burned
with fire. 12As for the rest of the beasts, their dominion was taken away, but their lives
were prolonged for a season and a time.

13"I saw in the night visions,

and behold, with the clouds of heaven
there came one like a son of man,
and he came to the Ancient of Days
and was presented before him.

14And to him was given dominion
and glory and a kingdom,
that all peoples, nations, and languages
should serve him;
his dominion is an everlasting dominion,
which shall not pass away,
and his kingdom one
that shall not be destroyed.

15"As for me, Daniel, my spirit within me[a] was anxious, and the visions of my head
alarmed me. 16I approached one of those who stood there and asked him the truth concern-
ing all this. So he told me and made known to me the interpretation of the things. 17'These
four great beasts are four kings who shall arise out of the earth. 18But the saints of the Most
High shall receive the kingdom and possess the kingdom forever, forever and ever.'
19"Then I desired to know the truth about the fourth beast, which was different from
all the rest, exceedingly terrifying, with its teeth of iron and claws of bronze, and which
devoured and broke in pieces and stamped what was left with its feet, 20and about the ten
horns that were on its head, and the other horn that came up and before which three of
them fell, the horn that had eyes and a mouth that spoke great things, and that seemed
greater than its companions. 21As I looked, this horn made war with the saints and pre-
vailed over them, 22until the Ancient of Days came, and judgment was given for the saints
of the Most High, and the time came when the saints possessed the kingdom.
23"Thus he said: 'As for the fourth beast,

there shall be a fourth kingdom on earth,
which shall be different from all the kingdoms,
and it shall devour the whole earth,
and trample it down, and break it to pieces.
24As for the ten horns,
out of this kingdom ten kings shall arise,
and another shall arise after them;
he shall be different from the former ones,
and shall put down three kings.
25He shall speak words against the Most High,
and shall wear out the saints of the Most High,
and shall think to change the times and the law;
and they shall be given into his hand
for a time, times, and half a time.
26But the court shall sit in judgment,
and his dominion shall be taken away,
to be consumed and destroyed to the end.
27And the kingdom and the dominion
and the greatness of the kingdoms under the whole heaven
shall be given to the people of the saints of the Most High;
their kingdom shall be an everlasting kingdom,

and all dominions shall serve and obey them.'[b]

[28]*"Here is the end of the matter. As for me, Daniel, my thoughts greatly alarmed me, and my color changed, but I kept the matter in my heart."*

a Aramaic *within its sheath* **b** Or *his kingdom shall be an everlasting kingdom, and all dominions shall serve and obey him*

Overview: Daniel next sees the Ancient of Days and the Son of Man. Our commentators are divided on the identity of the Ancient of Days. Some understand here God the Father; others see this as a reference to Christ, particularly his divine nature. A third opinion is that this is a reference to the everlasting Trinity: Father, Son and Holy Spirit. If it is God the Father, then some exegesis is required to account for Christ's statements in John 5 that all judgment has been given to him by the Father. All are agreed that Son of Man is a clear reference to Christ. He is said to be "like" a Son of Man because he had not yet assumed flesh. Therefore Daniel saw him in figure and not in substance. Daniel ends with a description of the kingdom of the saints and Christ's eternal reign. Our commentators reflect on the significance of this vision of the future kingdom of Christ and how we are to cherish it and not seek to go beyond what God has revealed. As Daniel says, "Here is the end of the matter" (Dan 7:28).

7:9-12 *Ancient of Days*

The Ancient of Days. John Calvin: Daniel now relates how he saw another figure, namely, God sitting on his throne to exercise judgment. We shall see it afterwards concerning Christ, but Daniel now teaches only the appearance of God in his character of a judge. This was the reason why many persons extend this prophecy to the second advent of Christ—an interpretation by no means correct, as I shall show more copiously in the proper place. But first it is worthwhile to consider here why he says the Ancient of Days, meaning the eternal Deity himself, ascended the throne of judgment. This scene seems unnecessary, because it is the peculiar office of God to govern the world; and as we know this cannot be done without upright judgment, it follows that God has been a perpetual judge from the creation of the world. Now, even a moderate acquaintance with the Scriptures shows how well this passage suits us by appealing to our senses, for unless God's power is made conspicuous, we think it either abolished or interrupted. Hence those forms of expression that occur elsewhere, as, "How long are you silent, O Lord, and how long will you cease from us?" (Ps 13:1; Ps 9:7, and elsewhere), and God ascends his throne—for we should not acknowledge him as a judge unless he really and experimentally proved himself such. This then is the reason why Daniel says God himself was seated in judgment. Commentaries on Daniel.[1]

Christ, the Ancient of Days. Johannes Oecolampadius: Christ is introduced as the Ancient of Days, who is called the lamb that was slain from the beginning of the world, and who in the beginning was with God, so that you would become acquainted with the prophets who acknowledge Christ as God and man. Commentary on Daniel.[2]

Who Is the Ancient of Days? Andrew Willet: Some understand here the person of the Father because mention is made (Dan 7:13) of the Son of Man, which approached the Ancient of Days (Polanus). So also the

[1]CTS 25:31 (CO 19:53). [2]*In Danielem prophetam libri duo* (1553), 93-94.

Glossa Ordinaria takes it. But Christ is there called the Son of Man in respect of human nature. As he is God, he is the Ancient of Days from all eternity, as God the Father is, as he is called the *everlasting father* (Is 9:6).

Some by the Ancient of Days understand Christ the mediator; Christ is brought in as the Ancient of Days, who is the lamb that was slain from the beginning of the world (Oecolampadius). But Christ as the mediator, God and man, is described afterward (Dan 7:13) where he is called the Son of Man and approaches the Ancient of Days. The Son of Man, then, and the Ancient of Days are not all one.

Wherefore by the Ancient of Days, the everlasting God is signified (Junius), the Father, Son and Holy Spirit, who were from all eternity. For concerning the person of the Father, our Savior says, *My Father judges no one but has committed all judgment to the Son* (Jn 5:22). So, the everlasting God shall judge (Hugo), not God the Father only by his Son (as Osiander). But although the person of the Son only shall appear, yet there shall not be wanting both the Father and the Holy Ghost (Vatablus). Sixfold Commentary upon Daniel.[3]

The Ancient of Days and the Son of Man. Heinrich Bullinger: The judge who is seated on his throne is the Ancient of Days, God the Father. Without doubt the future divine and most just judgment of Christ is shown under this person. For the Father does not judge in any other way, but he gives all authority to judge also to the Son of Man: he who judged with the most just judgment judges as he receives from the Father. And the Lord Jesus in the Gospel of John says, "The Father judges no one but has given all judgment to the Son that all may honor the Son as they honor the Father. Whoever does not honor the Son does not honor the Father who sent him" (Jn 5:22-23). And next he says, "As the Father has life in himself, so he has granted that the Son has life in himself and has given him authority to execute judgment also because he is the Son of Man" (Jn 5:26-27). And this is without doubt about whom Daniel speaks.

Therefore the persons of the Father and the Son are most excellently distinguished one from the other and are not confounded. The one is the Father and the other truly the Son, both having equal authority because they are coequal, coessential and coeternal. Indeed, elsewhere the Lord says, "I and the Father are one" (Jn 10:30). We just heard that the Son is to be honored as the Father; that the Son has life in himself as the Father. Therefore, although we heard that the Son received something and the Father gave something to the Son, it is not to be held that they are unequal and that the Son has not this authority from eternity, which he receives in time from the Father. What is more clear than what the Lord himself says: "And now glorify me, Father, with your own self with the glory that I had with you before the world was" (Jn 17:5). Therefore, we assign to the divine economy what we hear the Son receives and the Father gives, as they are no less coequal and coeternal and possessing the same authority. Therefore, when we hear the most just judgment of the Father represented here, we understand by true faith that this is the judgment of Christ. Daniel the Most Wise Prophet of God.[4]

7:13-14 *The Son of Man*

The Ancient of Days Is the Son of God. John Mayer: Here by the Ancient of Days Lyra understands Christ in his divinity, and by the Son of Man brought to him Christ in his humanity, but Polanus by the first God the Father and God the Son incarnate by the second.

[3] *Sixfold Commentary* (1610), 221. The *Glossa Ordinaria* is a medieval commentary on the Bible with marginal and interlinear glosses from the Fathers. Francis Vatablus (1485–1547) was a noted Hebrew professor at the University of Paris. [4] *Daniel Sapientissimus*, 81.

I rather prefer Lyra, because God the Father has never taken to him any similitude, but the Son as a "prelude" of his incarnation, and Ezekiel 1, where one sitting on a throne above the cherubim appeared like the Son of Man, it was undoubtedly God the Son; and here is a representation of a judge, which office is by the Father deputed to the Son. There is something said like this in Revelation 20:12 where the proceedings at the day of judgment are set forth, and as there, so here the opening of the books are spoken of, but here nothing else is meant, but that it should be justly proceeded against the kings before spoken of, as when a judge now goes according to plain evidence in condemning malefactors. Commentary upon All the Prophets.[5]

Son of Man. Johann Wigand: At the final judgment, the Son of Man will appear; that is Christ, who establishes the limits of all the kingdoms of this world and whose kingdom alone will stand for eternity, with the Father and the Holy Spirit.

. . . The *Ancient of Days* seems to be a periphrasis for God the Father. To be sure this is not said exclusively because the Son and the Holy Spirit are coeternal with the Father. No space of time is to be conceived by the mind when the Son was not with the Father. Rightly condemned was Arius, who said there was a time when the Son of God was not.

And was presented before him. Here the glorification of Christ after the resurrection is described. Below Daniel says, Christ will be slain. Here mention is made of the final judgment. Brief Exposition of the Prophet Daniel.[6]

Christ the Son of Man. John Calvin: *I was,* then, says he, *attentive in visions of the night, and beheld as it were the Son of Man.* I have already said this passage cannot be otherwise taken than concerning Christ. We must now see why he uses the word "like" the Son of Man; that is, why he uses the letter *ke*, the mark for likeness. This might be twisted in favor of the folly of the Manicheaens, who thought Christ's body to be only imaginary. For, as they wrest the words of Paul and pervert their sense, that Christ was in likeness as a man (Phil 2:7), so also they may abuse the prophet's testimony, when Christ is not said to be a man but only like one. With respect to Paul's words, he is not speaking of the essence of his human nature but only of his state, for he is speaking of Christ being made man, of his condition being humble and abject and even servile. But in the passage before us the reason is different. For the prophet says, *He appeared* to him as the *Son of Man,* as Christ had not yet taken on him our flesh. And we must remark that saying of Paul's: "When the fullness of time was come, God sent his Son, made of a woman" (Gal 4:4). Christ then began to be a man when he appeared on earth as mediator, for he had not assumed the seed of Abraham before he was joined with us in brotherly union. This is the reason why the prophet does not pronounce Christ to have been man at this period but only like man, for otherwise he had not been that Messiah formerly promised under the law as the son of Abraham and David. For if from the beginning he had put on human flesh, he would not have been born of these progenitors. It follows, then, that Christ was not a man from the beginning but only appeared so in a figure. As also Irenaeus says, This was a "prelude," he uses that word. Tertullian also says, "Then the Son of God put on a specimen of humanity." This was a symbol, therefore, of Christ's future flesh, although that flesh did not yet exist. We now see how suitably this figure agrees with the thing signified, wherein Christ was set forth as the Son of Man, although he was then the eternal Word of God. . . .

[5]*Prophets*, 543. [6]*Explicatio Brevis* (1571), 266-67.

But as there are many fanatics who wrest what has been said of the person of the Mediator, as if Christ were not the true God but had a beginning from the Father at some definite period of time, we must observe how the prophet's expression is neither about the human nor the divine nature of Christ properly speaking, but a Mediator is here set before us who is God manifest in flesh. For if we hold this principle that Christ is described to us, not as either the word of God or the seed of Abraham but as Mediator, that is, eternal God who was willing to become man, to become subject to God the Father, to be made like us and to be our advocate, then no difficulty will remain. Thus he appeared to Daniel like the Son of Man, who became afterwards truly and really so. Commentaries on Daniel.[7]

Like the Son of Man. Andrew Willet: He is said to be as the Son of Man because Daniel saw only a figure of the Son of Man. For at this time, when Daniel saw this, he was not yet the Son of Man but was to be born and become man in his time (Bullinger). Because Christ had not yet put on our flesh, indeed after Christ was incarnate, when he was seen figuratively in vision, he is said to be as the Son of Man; Revelation 14:14, *I saw upon the cloud one sitting as the Son of Man.* This was said because he was not seen in his substance but in figure only. Sixfold Commentary upon Daniel.[8]

7:15-28 *Christ's Kingdom*

The Kingdom of the Saints. John Mayer: *I beheld and the same horn made war with the saints and prevailed against them until the Ancient of Days came and judgment given to the saints, and the time came that the saints possessed the kingdoms* (Dan 7:21-22). The same is said in Revelation 7. This proves the same to be set forth here, that is that the saints here spoken of are Christians, and the little horn the same antichrist, and as was before said. The kingdom of the saints spoken of before was not taken by the beasts or kings, but the saints took the kingdom, which endures forever, against those that would have all this understood of things done of old, and not in the time of the gospel. Yet Polanus being overcome by the evidence of truth, seeing the words can be translated no otherwise, but of setting forth the saints taking of the kingdom, acknowledges this to be meant of the kingdom, which they enjoy in common with Christ. However, he applies the words before going to Antiochus and the Jews, against whom he made war and prevailed until the appointed time. And by this word of the *appointed time* he seeks to evade that which is brought against his interpretation by saying that the four beasts held the kingdom of the saints until this appointed time, but then it was above ordered that the saints should come to the kingdom. How solid this is I refer to the judgment of others; to me it seems plain that the saints' taking of the kingdom here spoken of follows not so long a time after Antiochus Epiphanes, as the day of judgment, when the saints come to that everlasting kingdom, but soon after the war, wherein the beast overcame them, but now in the end the beast being destroyed, they come to enter, as it were, on that kingdom, because into a more joyful and peaceable condition in this world, being shortly after to be possessed of it actually forever. And the setting of this forth here immediately after that suffering implies that no such long time of persecution, as followed under the Roman monarchy, could come between, but that it was there stirred up by another beast or the little horn here spoken of springing up, which was the papacy. Commentary upon All the Prophets.[9]

[7]CTS 25:41-43 (CO 19:60-61). [8]*Sixfold Commentary* (1610), 226. [9]*Prophets*, 546.

The Kingdom of the Saints and Christ's Reign. John Calvin: Let us now return to the passage. Daniel first of all says, *A kingdom and power and extensive dominion, shall be given to the people of the holy ones.* This was partially fulfilled when the gospel emerged from persecution: then the name of Christ was everywhere celebrated and held in honor and esteem, while previously it had been the subject of the greatest envy and hatred. For nothing had been more hated and detested for many years than the name of Christ. God, therefore, then gave the kingdom to his people when he was acknowledged as the Redeemer of the world throughout its many changes, after having been formerly despised and utterly rejected. I may here remark again and impress on the memory what I have frequently touched on, namely, the custom of the prophets, in treating of Christ's kingdom, to extend their meaning further than its first beginnings; and they do this while they dwell on its commencement. Thus Daniel or the angel does not predict here occurrences connected with the advent of Christ as Judge of the world, but with the first preaching and promulgation of the gospel and the celebration of the name of Christ. But this does not prevent him from drawing a magnificent picture of Christ's reign and embracing its final completion. It is sufficient for us to perceive how God begins to give the kingdom to his elect people, when, by the power of his Spirit, the doctrine of the holy gospel was everywhere received in the world. Commentaries on Daniel.[10]

The Kingdom of Christ. Andrew Willet: *The high saints or the saints of the Most High shall take the kingdom* (Dan 7:18). The church of God then consists of the saints and the elect, which are ordained to everlasting salvation. So our Savior calls them his flock for whom his Father had prepared a kingdom (Lk 12:32). And again he says, *I pray not for the world but for those whom you have given me* (Jn 17:9). They then which are of the world are not of the church of Christ: hypocrites, heretics, unbelievers, carnal livers; these may well be in the church, but they are not of it. Saint John says, *They went out from us, but they were not of us. For if they had been of us, they would have continued with us* (1 Jn 2:19). Sixfold Commentary upon Daniel.[11]

The Word of God. John Mayer: *To this point the end of the matter.* This is added for a conclusion of this matter to prevent all curious inquiring after such things, as God has not been pleased to reveal: for we must be wise only according to that which is written, and not pry into other secrets of the Lord.

As for me Daniel, my thoughts were troubled in me, my countenance was changed, and I kept the matter in my heart, that is, knowing here that most sad things should befall the church of God under these monarchies, I was accordingly affected with grief, and this appeared in the paleness of my face. Daniel is here propounded as a pattern to us, that we may not be unaffected with the sufferings of God's people, against which it is declaimed (Amos 6:6). Moreover, as he, so we must keep in our hearts the words of God, as we desire, that our hearing of them may not be vain, so likewise Mary did, and who so is wise will ponder these things. Commentary upon All the Prophets.[12]

Why Does God Reveal Such Things to Us? Philipp Melanchthon: Let us examine the reasons why God reveals these things. The human mind desires knowledge of the future with such perverse curiosity. But in fact God makes known great things from the beginning: the advent of his Son, the future judgment, the resurrection of the dead, the eternal punishment of the wicked, the eternal glory of

[10]CTS 25:74 (CO 19:82-83). [11]*Sixfold Commentary* (1610), 235-36. [12]*Prophets*, 547.

believers and the exact succession or order of kingdoms before the final judgment. God did not reveal these things in vain but that his will would be carefully considered. And, indeed, this doctrine taught Daniel and others about eternal life and the future judgment. . . . We know with certainty that this doctrine, which Daniel professed, is divine, and we will not allow it to be taken away from us. COMMENTARY ON THE PROPHET DANIEL.[13]

[13]*In Danielem Prophetam* (1543), 115-16.

8:1-14 DANIEL'S VISION OF A RAM AND A GOAT

*1In the third year of the reign of King Belshazzar a vision appeared to me, Daniel,
after that which appeared to me at the first. 2And I saw in the vision; and when I saw, I
was in Susa the capital,[a] which is in the province of Elam. And I saw in the vision, and I
was at the Ulai canal. 3I raised my eyes and saw, and behold, a ram standing on the bank
of the canal. It had two horns, and both horns were high, but one was higher than the
other, and the higher one came up last. 4I saw the ram charging westward and northward
and southward. No beast could stand before him, and there was no one who could rescue
from his power. He did as he pleased and became great.*

*5As I was considering, behold, a male goat came from the west across the face of the
whole earth, without touching the ground. And the goat had a conspicuous horn between
his eyes. 6He came to the ram with the two horns, which I had seen standing on the bank of
the canal, and he ran at him in his powerful wrath. 7I saw him come close to the ram, and
he was enraged against him and struck the ram and broke his two horns. And the ram had
no power to stand before him, but he cast him down to the ground and trampled on him.
And there was no one who could rescue the ram from his power. 8Then the goat became
exceedingly great, but when he was strong, the great horn was broken, and instead of it
there came up four conspicuous horns toward the four winds of heaven.*

*9Out of one of them came a little horn, which grew exceedingly great toward the south,
toward the east, and toward the glorious land. 10It grew great, even to the host of heaven.
And some of the host and some[b] of the stars it threw down to the ground and trampled
on them. 11It became great, even as great as the Prince of the host. And the regular
burnt offering was taken away from him, and the place of his sanctuary was overthrown.
12And a host will be given over to it together with the regular burnt offering because of
transgression,[c] and it will throw truth to the ground, and it will act and prosper. 13Then I
heard a holy one speaking, and another holy one said to the one who spoke, "For how long
is the vision concerning the regular burnt offering, the transgression that makes desolate,*

and the giving over of the sanctuary and host to be trampled underfoot?" [14]*And he said to me,*[d] *"For 2,300 evenings and mornings. Then the sanctuary shall be restored to its rightful state."*

a Or *the fortified city* b Or *host, that is, some* c Or *in an act of rebellion* d Hebrew; Septuagint, Theodotion, Vulgate *to him*

Overview: The first point addressed by our commentators concerns the change in language from Aramaic to Hebrew. The difference in language indicates a difference in audience. Our commentators also discuss the similarities and differences between the vision of this chapter and the last. This chapter offers an abbreviated form of the previous vision, focusing especially on Antiochus Epiphanes. The questions raised with this vision begin immediately. Where was Daniel when he saw this vision? Was he in Babylon or Persia? Was he really in Susa, as he says? Some try to give a definite answer; others acknowledge the mystery here involved and leave the question open. Daniel proceeds with his vision about Alexander the Great and Antiochus Ephiphanes. Our commentators dwell on the final two verses of the vision and particularly the identity of the holy one and the angels. Some, following the Septuagint, think it better to retain the Hebrew word, Palmoni, rather than trying to translate it. They are agreed that this Palmoni or holy one is Christ. The other, an angel, asks about the judgment for Daniel's benefit.

Summary of the Chapter. John Mayer: In this chapter the prophet speaks no more in the Chaldean tongue, as in the seventh, but in the Hebrew, because as Polanus conjectures, the Lord sets forth these things in respect to his church in Judea. For their comfort these things were written, and not for pagans and infidels. Yet it seemed good to God by his predictions to show to the Chaldeans something whereby they might be convinced that he only is the true God, from whom nothing to come is hidden; their gods, who could not do this, were false gods and vain idols. Therefore he had the first vision of Daniel 7 written in the Chaldean tongue, by which they might have a taste of his omniscience; God also showed that all things to come to the end of the world were open and manifest to him. The principal occurrences of all times and ages to the day of judgment are revealed, and another strong argument to prove is that the fourth kingdom spoken of in the prophecy was the Roman; however, touching the little horn something like antichrist's persecution is shown to have been done by a king arising out of the Grecian kingdom, against the old church of God. Because the old church was as material for the Jews then to know, as for us Christians the proceedings of antichrist, God vouchsafed to show to Daniel another vision here representing the tragic acts that should then be done by Antiochus Epiphanes. For between the kingdom there spoken of, out of which sprang the little horn, and this here spoken of, there is this plain difference made: a fourth beast, not one springing out of the third, had ten horns; this springs out of the goat and consists but of four horns, and out of one of these springs the little horn that afterwards grew so great, whereas the little horn there is said to have come up among the ten horns. Commentary upon All the Prophets.[1]

8:1 *The Purpose of the Vision*

The Relationship Between This Vision and the Former. Andrew Willet: In the former there was a description of four kingdoms; here the Chaldean and Babylonian is omitted because it was now at hand

[1]*Prophets*, 547*.

to be abolished (Calvin), which may be the cause why from the second chapter Daniel had written in the Chaldean tongue, because those things concerned the Chaldean state, which were revealed to Daniel. Now he uses the Hebrew tongue because these things that follow in this prophecy, especially concerning the people of God, as of their great affliction under Antiochus, in this chapter and Daniel 11, and of the coming of the Messiah in Daniel 9. Sixfold Commentary upon Daniel.[2]

The Purpose of this Vision. John Calvin: Here Daniel relates another vision, differing from the former as a part from the whole. For God wished to show him first what various changes should happen before Christ's advent. The second redemption was the beginning of a new life, since God then not only restored afresh his own church, but as it were created a new people; and hence the departure from Babylon and the return to their country are called the second birth of the church. But as God at that time afforded only a taste of true and solid redemption, whenever the prophets treat of that deliverance, they extended their thoughts and their prophecies as far as the coming of Christ. God therefore, with great propriety, shows the four monarchies to his prophet, lest the faithful should grow weary in beholding the world so often convulsed and all but changing its figure and nature. Thus they would be subject to the most distressing cares, become a laughingstock to their enemies and ever remain contemptible and mean, without the power to help themselves under these constant innovations. The faithful, then, were forewarned concerning these four monarchies, lest they should suppose themselves rejected by God and deprived altogether of his care.

But now God wished to show only one part to his prophet. As the destruction of the Babylonian empire was at hand and the second kingdom was approaching, this dominion also should speedily come to its close, and then God's people should be reduced to the utmost extremity. And the chief object of this vision is to prepare the faithful to bear patiently the horrible tyranny of Antiochus, of which the prophet treats in this chapter. Now, therefore, we understand the meaning of this prophet, where God speaks of only two monarchies, for the kingdom of the Chaldeans was soon to be abolished: he treats first of the Persian kingdom and next adds that of Macedon but omits all others and descends directly to Antiochus, king of Syria. He then declares the prevalence of the most wretched confusion in the church; for the sanctuary should be deprived of its dignity and the elect people everywhere killed, without sparing even innocent blood. We shall see also why the faithful were informed beforehand of these grievous and oppressive calamities, to induce them to look up to God when oppressed by such extreme darkness. And at this day this prophecy is useful to us, lest our courage should fail us in the extreme calamity of the church, because a perpetual representation of the church is depicted for us under that calamitous and mournful state. Although God often spares our infirmities, yet the church is never free from many distresses, and unless we are prepared to undergo all contests, we shall never stand firm in the faith. This is the scope and explanation of the prophecy. Commentaries on Daniel.[3]

The Encouragement of This Vision. Johann Wigand: The next prophecy concerns the end of the second monarchy and the constitution and progress of the third. The end of this revelation is noteworthy as the church of God is warned of its trials and afflictions under the third monarchy, which certainly happened under Antiochus Epiphanes. God wanted to forewarn future generations lest they themselves suffer under the wicked king,

[2]*Sixfold Commentary* (1610), 242. [3]CTS 25:80-81 (CO 19:87-88).

being carried away from true doctrine and the worship of God; most especially lest believers suppose that so horrible and atrocious profanation of the temple and extirpation of true religion would render void the divine promises setting forth the Messiah. This prophecy shows, however, that the reinstatement of divine worship would follow. For Judas Maccabeus restored and cleansed the temple, showing the kindness of God. Brief Exposition of the Prophet Daniel.[4]

8:2 *Daniel's Location*

Where Did Daniel See the Vision? John Calvin: Some think Daniel to be then dwelling in Persia, but this view is by no means probable; for who could persuade the holy prophet of God, who had been led captive with the rest and was attached to the king of Babylon, to depart as if he had been entirely his own master and to go into Persia, when the Persians were then open enemies? This is not at all likely; and I wonder what can induce people to adopt this comment, so contrary to all reason. For we need not dispute about a matter by no means obscure if we weigh the prophet's words, as he removes all doubt by saying *he was in Susa when he saw*, that is, when he was caught up by the prophetic spirit beyond himself and above the world. The prophet does not say he dwelled in Susa, or in the neighborhood, but he was there in the vision only. The next verse, too, sufficiently shows him to have then been in Chaldea in the third year, he says, of the reign of King Belshazzar. By naming the king, he clearly expresses that he then dwelled under his power and dominion. It is clearly to be gathered from these words, without the slightest doubt, that the prophet then dwelled in Chaldea. Commentaries on Daniel.[5]

Daniel Carried by the Spirit. John Mayer: But how could Daniel, who was a captive in Babylon at this time, it being in the reign of Belshazzar, be in Susa? Polanus says that he was there only in spirit about the proving of which he uses diverse arguments, but because Daniel speaks of no such manner of being there but says plainly, I was in the palace of Susa, it is rather to be held that he was there indeed, being carried miraculously there by the Spirit of God, as Ezekiel had been by the lock of his head to the temple at Jerusalem from the land of the Chaldeans, and as the spirit took up Elijah sometime and carried him to remote places, so that Ahab, who sought to destroy him, could nowhere find him. For all arguments brought to prove that Daniel was not really now in Persia (because so he should have made himself obnoxious to the king of Babylon at his return, and he would have done this against his duty, it being the known will of God, that the Jews should dwell where they were, till the seventy years expired, and be subject to the king of Babylon and pray for the peace of that kingdom) fall to the ground, since if by the Spirit he were carried there to see these visions, and back again, he did nothing against his fidelity to the Babylonian king or that had been by the Lord forbidden the Jews in general, no more than Ezekiel, who before had been likewise carried to Jerusalem, or Jeremiah, who being the subject of the king of Judah, when according to the will of God he went to Babylon to hide a girdle by the river Euphrates, for from general rules exception of particulars is ever to be understood, all are to do so, unless God specially orders it touching some particular persons otherwise. And an argument to prove him not to have been in Chaldea now may be drawn from his change of the language in which he writes, not in the Chaldean tongue as he had done before from Daniel 2:4 to the end of Daniel 7. Commentary upon All the Prophets.[6]

[4]*Explicatio Brevis* (1571), 275. [5]CTS 25:83 (CO 19:89). [6]*Prophets*, 548.

When I Saw. Johann Wigand: It is indeed uncertain whether in spirit only or also in body he stood in Susa. It seems though that he was there only in ecstasy. For there is nothing similar to his sudden removal from one place to another. For the queen declared to Belshazzar that Daniel lived in his kingdom and was relatively near, who was able to explain mysteries and riddles. Others think that he was in Persia conducting royal business. That such a vision was shown to Daniel as if he were in Persia is not without mystery. Brief Exposition of the Prophet Daniel.[7]

I Was in Susa. Giovanni Diodati: [*I was*] Some hold that he was there in vision, as Ezekiel 8:3 and Ezekiel 40:2. Others, really and corporally, which seems to be confirmed by Daniel 10:4 and that the province of Susa was then under the Babylonian Empire, this notwithstanding, the histories make no mention. Pious Annotations.[8]

8:3-12 *Alexander the Great*

The Ram with the Two Horns. Martin Luther: In the eighth chapter Daniel has a strange vision not of the entire world, as before, but only of his people, the Jews. He explains what will happen to them before the Roman Empire and before the Christ comes, that is, under the third empire, Alexander the Great's, so that they will again be comforted and not despair in the sorrow that will come over them, as if Christ wants to abandon them again and not come. Preface to the Prophet Daniel.[9]

Alexander the Great. Giovanni Diodati: [Dan 8:5. *A he-goat*] A figure of the Grecian kingdom under Alexander the Great (Dan 8:21; see Dan 2:39; 7:6). [*From the west*] namely, from Greece and Macedon, west from Asia, where the prophet was and the Persians reigned. [*The whole*] so those great monarchies through ambition called themselves universal, though they possessed but a small part of the world (Dan 2:39), yet the most esteemed and best known. [*Touched not*] whereby is signified Alexander's extreme celerity in his conquests, as if he had flown rather than gone (see Dan 7:6). [*A notable*] Ital. *Writhen:* which is a sign of strength. [*Horn*] that is, Alexander's person in his kingdom, which is signified by the *goat.*

[Dan 8:6. *And he came*] A description of Alexander's acts against Persia, by which he overthrew the empire and made himself lord of Asia.

[Dan 8:8. *The great*] That is, Alexander died very soon, in the flower of his age and the midst of all his victories. [*Four*] these are the four satrapies or kingdoms of the Grecians, which were seized on by Alexander's captains, out of the shipwreck of his empire: Babylon towards the east, Asia towards the north, Macedon towards the west and Egypt towards the south. Which in process of time came to two: the Seleucides towards the north in Asia and the Lagides towards the south in Egypt (Dan 11:5-6). Pious Annotations.[10]

A Little Horn. Giovanni Diodati: [Dan 8:9. *A little horn*] that is, Antiochus Epiphanes. . . .

[Dan 8:12. *And a host was given*] namely, the faithful shall be in great danger of apostasy from the true religion; and Antiochus shall give them many occasions to do it and shall seek to induce them thereto: and the Lord shall put them to this trial (Dan 11:32, 35). [*Cast down*] all use, preaching and profession of God's truth and doctrine of salvation shall be forbidden and suppressed by Antiochus, who will seek to destroy even the very books of the law (1 Macc 1:5). Pious Annotations.[11]

[7]*Explicatio Brevis* 276. [8]*Pious Annotations* (1651), 8:2. [9]WADB 11,2:12. [10]*Pious Annotations* (1651), 8:5-8. [11]*Pious Annotations* (1651), 8:9, 12.

God Warns Us of Affliction. John Calvin: Now God shows his prophet what peculiarly concerned the welfare of his church, for it was of very great importance to warn the Jews of the calamities that were about to oppress them. There is nothing that more torments the minds of peole than their becoming bewildered in false imaginations and thinking the world the sport of chance, while they never ponder over the providence of God or reflect on his judgments. Hence, with this design, God wished to teach the prophet and all the pious the nature of their future afflictions, since they would thus understand how events never happened by chance, but all these scourges proceeded from God; for the same God both determines and executes his decrees, as he also predicts future events. For if nothing had been predicted, the pious would have glided gently downwards to despair in consequence of their heavy afflictions. Commentaries on Daniel.[12]

8:13-14 *The Holy One*

Palmoni Is Christ. Andrew Willet: Some retain the Hebrew word *Palmoni*, as the Septuagint, but it was not a proper name of this great angel, to whom the other angel spoke; it was a title rather or epithet given him, that *admirable or excellent angel*. . . . But this angel being spoken to as the superior, and the other angel who asked the question being set forth by the title of holy one, it is not likely that this great angel, the revealer of secrets, should be expressed by such a mean term. Therefore this *Palmoni* is understood of Christ, who is the revealer of secrets. Sixfold Commentary upon Daniel.[13]

The Angel's Questions. Johannes Oecolampadius: Who does not desire to be instructed concerning these things, about which angels longed for and asked to be taught? By these questions, the prophet, and we with him, are admonished, lest we are ashamed to learn and to be taught. If the angel himself, who beholds the face of the Father and who dwells in the midst of light, makes inquiry, then why not us, who dwell in darkness and sojourn in a strange land apart from the Lord? The angel did not ask for himself but for the sake of Daniel. He responded not to the angel but to Daniel. Thus it says in the next verse, "And he said to me." It does not say, "And he said to the other." Moreover, you know that angels are commended to us in the Scriptures. Commentary on Daniel.[14]

The Inquisitive Angel. John Mayer: But why is the angel so inquisitive of the time that this great judgment should last? Answer: First to show that the angels are affected with sorrow, and do condole together with the church of God suffering and desire a speedy end of our miseries. Second, that they are solicitous about the glory of God, who if he does not soon stretch out his almighty hand to deliver his church conflicting with misery under the hands of persecutors, they will be ready to open their blasphemous mouths and say, either he is not able to save his people, or he regards them not, and therefore it is no advantage to people to be his faithful servants. Third, the angel thus interposes himself to ask out of a desire that he had to have something answered for the comfort of Daniel and such godly ones, as he was, who could not but be greatly astonished at the hearing of those grievous judgments by a heathen king to come on God's people and sanctuary; and therefore the answer was made to Daniel, "he said to me 2300 days." And of the angels of God we should learn both to condole and to be solicitous for the church of God in misery in any place, and to stand for the comfort of one another, as it is said, weep with those that weep. Commen-

[12]CTS 25:95 (CO 19:98). [13]*Sixfold Commentary* (1610), 249. [14]*In Danielem prophetam libri duo* (1553), 102.

tary upon All the Prophets.[15]

Christ Appears As an Angel. Johannes Oecolampadius: There is no doubt that the other angel who here appears is Christ himself, who often formerly appeared to the patriarchs and prophets, and indeed in such manner that he assumed some visible form to appear before their eyes . . . as a prelude to his future assumption of a true human nature. Now the other angel Gabriel is taught by him. Christ is the teacher of the angels. Thus, he instructed Gabriel, and Gabriel instructed Daniel, and through Daniel, he instructed us. Commentary on Daniel.[16]

I Heard a Holy One. John Calvin: But while Daniel is stupefied through astonishment, God provides for his infirmity by means of an angel. Daniel himself, without doubt, inquired concerning the vision, as we shall see he did afterwards; but here God desired to meet him, as he saw the holy man so overcome by fear as scarcely to dare to make any inquiry. God, therefore, here affords no common proof of his paternal goodness and indulgence in interposing and sending his angel to make inquiries in the prophet's name. He says, then, *he heard a holy one,* meaning an angel. . . .

The sense then is, an angel comes to Christ for the sake of Daniel and of the whole church and seeks from him, as from the supreme teacher and master, the meaning of the declarations that we have just heard. We need not feel surprise at angels inquiring into eternity, as if it were unknown to them. It is the property of Deity alone to know all things, while the knowledge of angels is necessarily limited. Paul teaches us to wonder at the church being collected out of profane and strange people; this was a mystery hidden from angels themselves, before God really showed himself the father of the whole world (Eph 3:10). Hence there is no absurdity in supposing angels to inquire into mysteries, as ignorance is not necessarily deserving of blame, and as God has not raised his creatures for his own level. It is his peculiar province to know all things and to have everything under his eye. The angel desires to understand this mystery, not so much for his own sake as on account of the whole church; for we know them to be our ministers, according to the clear testimony of the apostle (Heb 1:14). As they keep watch over us so carefully, it does not surprise us to find the angel inquiring so anxiously concerning this vision and thus benefiting the whole church by the hand of Daniel. Commentaries on Daniel.[17]

[15]*Prophets,* 550. [16]*In Danielem prophetam libri duo* (1553), 102. [17]CTS 25:104-5 (CO 19:104-6).

8:15-27 THE INTERPRETATION OF THE VISION

15When I, Daniel, had seen the vision, I sought to understand it. And behold, there
stood before me one having the appearance of a man. 16And I heard a man's voice between
the banks of the Ulai, and it called, "Gabriel, make this man understand the vision." 17So
he came near where I stood. And when he came, I was frightened and fell on my face. But
he said to me, "Understand, O son of man, that the vision is for the time of the end."
18And when he had spoken to me, I fell into a deep sleep with my face to the ground.
But he touched me and made me stand up. 19He said, "Behold, I will make known to you
what shall be at the latter end of the indignation, for it refers to the appointed time of
the end. 20As for the ram that you saw with the two horns, these are the kings of Media
and Persia. 21And the goat[a] *is the king of Greece. And the great horn between his eyes*
is the first king. 22As for the horn that was broken, in place of which four others arose,
four kingdoms shall arise from his[b] *nation, but not with his power. 23And at the latter*
end of their kingdom, when the transgressors have reached their limit, a king of bold face,
one who understands riddles, shall arise. 24His power shall be great—but not by his own
power; and he shall cause fearful destruction and shall succeed in what he does, and de-
stroy mighty men and the people who are the saints. 25By his cunning he shall make deceit
prosper under his hand, and in his own mind he shall become great. Without warning he
shall destroy many. And he shall even rise up against the Prince of princes, and he shall
be broken—but by no human hand. 26The vision of the evenings and the mornings that
has been told is true, but seal up the vision, for it refers to many days from now."
27And I, Daniel, was overcome and lay sick for some days. Then I rose and went about
the king's business, but I was appalled by the vision and did not understand it.

a Or the *shaggy goat* **b** Theodotion, Septuagint, Vulgate; Hebrew *the*

Overview: Daniel seeks understanding of the vision, and before him stood one having the appearance of man. Our commentators agree that this is the Son of God, who sends the angel Gabriel, the same angel sent to the Virgin Mary, to teach Daniel. After some discussion of Gabriel, our commentators turn to the interpretation of the vision offered by him. Although they agree that the vision is about Antiochus Epiphanes, disagreement rests with whether he is a figure of the antichrist. Here some words are exchanged between our commentators. Calvin, who seems to have misunderstood Luther's comment on this text, declares him wrong and charges him with indulging his thoughts too freely. Melanchthon agrees with Luther and shows the correctness of their interpretation based on the words of Paul. Finally, our commentators discuss the significance of Daniel being overcome after this vision. A lesson is here given us that we too ought to be struck and moved by the word of God.

8:15-16a *The Appearance and Voice of a Man*

THE INTERPRETATION. MARTIN LUTHER: Daniel himself interprets the vision. The ram with the two horns is the king of Media and Persia. The goat is Alexander the great who struck Darius [III], the last king of Persia, winning his kingdom. Then Daniel says that the goat fled immediately, so that he did not even touch the earth, because Alexander went and rapidly conquered the world in twelve years, beginning when he was twenty years old and dying at the age of thirty-two. Truly no greater person (speaking in worldly terms) has or will tread the earth.

However, what quickly rises, also quickly falls. His kingdom fell apart as he died, becoming these four kingdoms: Syria, Egypt, Asia, and Greece. Now Daniel ignores two, Asia and Greece, focusing on the other two, Syria and Egypt. This is because the Jewish land is between these two. Syria to the north, and Egypt to the south. These two have an eternal dispute with one another. For this reason, because they were stuck between the door and the hinge, the Jews were plagued on both sides. Now they fell to Egypt, now Syria. Once one kingdom was superior to the other, it had to pay back its neighbor with evil, as it usually goes in wars.

In particular this was true of that libertine man, who became the king of Syria, that the histories call Antiochus the Noble, who frightfully clasped at the Jews, heaving and raging as a devil among them. He removed the worship of God from Jerusalem, profaning the temple, pillaging and taking every treasure, setting up idolatry and false images, hunting down and butchering the priests and anyone else who did not want what he wanted. He badly wanted to make out of all faiths one faith that would become the faith of the Greeks. A number of treasonous scoundrels among the Jews, who could climb no higher in society, helped him do this, as it is further described in the first chapter of 1 Maccabees (vv. 41-53). But he did not last long. PREFACE TO THE PROPHET DANIEL.[1]

THE APPEARANCE OF A MAN. JOHN CALVIN: We ought probably to interpret this passage of Christ, who is now called like a man, as formerly (Dan 7:13). For he had not yet put on our flesh, so as to be properly entitled to the name of a man; but he was here like a man, because he wished to allow the holy fathers a taste from which they might understand his future coming as mediator, when he should put on human nature as God manifest in flesh (1 Tim 3:16). Thus Daniel speaks suitably as before when he says, Christ *appeared to him under the aspect of a man.*

He does not use the particle implying fitness but says he heard the voice of a man, because he treats no longer of either a man or a figure but of a voice. It is sufficient to say at once, he was like a man, not really so, but only under the image and appearance of one. Christ therefore *appeared as a man* and is called one, since Scripture often records how angels often appeared under the form of men and are called indiscriminately either angels or men (Judg 8:3). So in this place Daniel relates the appearance of a man, or the aspect of one, improperly indeed, but without any danger of mistake; for he afterwards admonishes the faithful, how this person was not clothed with the substance of flesh but had only a human form and aspect. *I heard then a human voice in the midst of the river.* We gather from this that the same person is here intended of whom mention was lately made, because he commands the angel; whence this can be referred to Christ alone.

Gabriel, says he, *teach him.* We observe the speaker from the midst of the river here commanding Gabriel, as if superior to him. For

[1]WADB 11,2:12-14.

Gabriel as the name of an angel is sufficiently known from other passages of Scripture (Lk 1:19, 26), and its etymology, "the strength of God," is very suitable to this meaning. Without any doubt, the angel here receives his commands from Christ. Thus we see the supreme power and authority represented under the form and aspect of a man, as well as obedience portrayed in Gabriel, who discharges the duty enjoined on him. From this Christ's divinity is inferred, as he could not issue orders to angels without either having special authority or being God himself. But when the phrase "like a man" is used, we are taught his manifest superiority to humankind. And what does this imply? not angelic nature but divine. Christ by thus presenting himself under a human form shows, by a kind of foreshadowing, how he would become a man when the fullness of time arrived. Then he would really manifest himself as the head of the church and the guardian of the salvation of the pious. For he proves himself to have power over all angels when he orders Gabriel to discharge the office of the prophet's instructor. Commentaries on Daniel.[2]

The Appearance of the Son of God. Johann Wigand: *The appearance of a man* (Dan 8:15). This is understood to be the very Son of God, who appears in such form, as he would when he came for the redemption of all humankind. Although angels are accustomed to appear in the form of men, nevertheless here something appears superior to Gabriel and the rest of the angels to teach and to give commands. . . .

Gabriel (Dan 8:16). He is the same angel who was sent to Mary and whose notable sermon concerning Jesus Christ is set forth in the New Testament. "Gabriel" signifies the strength of God. Brief Exposition of the Prophet Daniel.[3]

The Voice of a Man. John Mayer: Then Daniel says that he heard the voice of a man between the banks of Ulai calling to Gabriel and bidding him to make Daniel understand the vision before going, about which he was solicitous; by way of this note that it is a study fitting the wisest of people to study what may be the meaning of heavenly visions showed by God to his servants at any time, and one who is studious about such things and seeks for resolution shall find it, as this holy prophet did, and of this I can also say the same by experience, especially in my reading through the dark passages of Ezekiel 40–41, almost without any guide but the Spirit of God, whose direction I assiduously sought.

Now for this voice of a man, it was most probably the voice of Christ called before *Palmoni* (Dan 8:13), and Gabriel an angel, this being, as Polanus notes, the only name whereby an angel is called in all the canonical Scriptures, whereas other names are by some named, as Raphael, etc. They are but human inventions; Gabriel is a fit name for any angel of God, because signifying the strength or virtue of God. Whereas Michael is afterwards also spoken of, he is none other but Christ the archangel, that is, the prince of angels, so Polanus.

. . . Whereby we see what the majesty of an angel is, and how unable humankind is to bear his presence, coming to speak to him, and how much less then are we able to bear the presence of God, that we may believe and repent at people's speaking, whom God sends, and praise him for condescending to our weakness so far, as to teach us by one another, as we are able to bear. Commentary upon All the Prophets.[4]

The Voice. Giovanni Diodati: [*A man's voice*] It should seem we must here understand it to be the Son of God, employing created an-

[2]CTS 25:111-13 (CO 19:109-11). [3]*Explicatio Brevis* (1571), 282. [4]*Prophets*, 551.

gels in that service of instructing the prophet. [*Between*] namely, between the two banks of that river, or in some island encompassed by two arms of it (see Dan 12:5, 7; Rev 10:1, 2). [*Gabriel*] The name of an angel, which signifies strong man of God (see Dan 9:21; Lk 1:26). Pious Annotations.[5]

8:16b-23 *Gabriel*

The Name Gabriel. Andrew Willet: Some do take this to be an excellent name, common to all the angels. It signifies the strength or power of God. But, it is evident from Luke 1, where this angel Gabriel was sent to the Virgin Mary, that it was the proper name of an angel. But Gregory well notes that angels are not called by names in respect of themselves, as though they could not be discerned but by their several names in that celestial city where they enjoy the vision of God. But when they come to us to minister, they do take their names of their ministry and office, as here this angel is called Gabriel, the strength of God, because he was employed in the defense of the church against the enemies here mentioned. But this further must be considered that this angel is not so called from the essential power of God but of that power that was given him to execute the Lord's commandment. And this is the only name given to angels in Scripture, for the name Michael, which signifies one as God, is ascribed to Christ, who is equal to God. Sixfold Commentary upon Daniel.[6]

Gabriel's Interpretation. Philipp Melanchthon: That this prophecy particularly addresses the history of Antiochus Epiphanes, the angel Gabriel testifies, the interpreter in the text, who, speaking with the Son of God, receives the interpretation from him. Furthermore, this locus admonishes us concerning the presence of Christ, insofar as one may see that the Son of God was always present with the patriarchs, and truly now also with the church is present, hears and governs those who call on him, as it is said in the Gospel, *Behold, I am with you*, etc. Again, *where two or three are gathered in my name, I am there in the midst of them. . . .*

I briefly add concerning the interpreter of the prophecy, whom here he calls *Palmoni*, that is, somebody wonderful, as Christ elsewhere is called "wonderful counselor" (Is 9:6). Commentary on the Prophet Daniel.[7]

The Angel's Office. John Calvin: *Behold*, therefore, says he, *I will explain to you*. He here acquires confidence for himself from his office, as he had accepted the commands divinely laid on him. And we should remark this also, since our faith will never rest or become firm unless the authority on which it is founded is fixed. As then the angel declares himself to be executing an office divinely enjoined on him, ought we to put confidence in people who conduct themselves with rashness, and, though they assume authority in God's name, yet have no certain and lawful calling? We may learn, then, how neither angels nor people ought to be held in such honor as to induce us to receive whatever they bring forward, unless the Almighty has appointed them to be his ministers and interpreters.

He then says, *I will announce to you what shall happen even at the end of the wrath*. Without doubt, the angel asserts by this phrase the suddenness of God's wrath. We are aware how instantaneously on the return of the people their enemies attacked them in Judea and never ceased to inflict on them numberless troubles. Wherefore, as soon as the Jews had returned from exile, God began to exercise them in various ways, and not without sufficient reason. Every one privately studied his own interests, but without any regard for the

[5]*Pious Annotations* (1651), 8:16. [6]*Sixfold Commentary* (1610), 252. [7]*In Danielem Prophetam* (1543), 136-37.

temple and any desire for the worship of God, and thus they were given up to avarice and caprice. Commentaries on Daniel.[8]

Can Angels Grant Understanding? Andrew Willet: The angels of themselves have no power to infuse understanding into the mind of people but he only who has created the heart of humankind can give to it understanding. And the angels themselves cannot understand the secrets and mysteries of God unless it is given unto them, as here the angel, called a holy one, inquired of Palmoni, which is Christ, the meaning of this vision. Yet when it pleases God to use the ministry of angels, they may help to make a way for our better understanding, as he who opens the window, may be said to give light unto the house, yet it is the sun properly that gives light. So the Son of righteousness illumines our hearts; the angels may help to prepare the way (Polanus). But in this place the angel does not by any secret infusion open Daniel's understanding, but by a manifest and clear interpretation of the vision. And so the Lord uses the ministry of people preaching of the gospel to open the hearts of the hearers. Sixfold Commentary upon Daniel.[9]

8:24-26 *Antiochus and the Antichrist*

Antiochus a Figure of the Antichrist. Martin Luther: Now here Daniel says of this Antiochus that after Alexander another little horn will come out of one of the four horns. This is Antiochus the Noble from the horn of Syria, who was powerful against the south, the east, and the great land, that is, the land of the Jews. Through great betrayal and trickery Antiochus took away land and many cities from the king of Egypt, as will soon be described further in chapter 11. He threw many stars to earth, that is many saintly people among the Jews were murdered. He ravaged and defiled the worship of the God of heaven in the temple, placing idols there instead.

To oppose this devil God raised up Judas Maccabeus with his brothers, who fought and did brave and faithful acts. In five years they killed nearly two hundred thousand men (2 Macc) and purified the land and the temple, restoring everything to its rightful place. As it stands here in the text (Dan 8:14), the temple will be purified after 2,300 days, which would be six years and a quarter. Antiochus raged against the Jews just as long, dying in the seventh year. The numbers line up well, as the the first book of 1 Maccabees proves (1 Macc 1:20-24; 6:16). Therefore, the angel here says that the king Antiochus will do great harm and will be a brazen and impudent king. He led a libertine and shameful life, steeped in every perversion, as the histories tell us. Still he will not, he says (Dan 8:25), be shattered by human hands. When he wanted to go to Persia to collect tribute monies, he commanded his general Lysias to slaughter and exterminate the poor Jews. However, he was not able to collect tributes, and after hearing that Judas Maccabeus had defeated and humiliated Lysias and his army, Antiochus out of great anger and impatience became very ill, because things had not gone according to plan. He died out of deep suffering and sorrow in a foreign land.

Well, this is what will happen to tyrants. This Antiochus is here set up as an example of all wicked kings and princes, especially those who rebel against God and his word. For this reason all previous teachers have also identified and interpreted this Antiochus as an image of the Antichrist, and rightly so. Such a depraved, filthy, and raving-mad tyrant must be chosen to be an image of the last horror, as many words in this chapter (8) and chapter 12 intimate and secretly reveal. Preface to the Prophet Daniel.[10]

Luther Wrong. John Calvin: Luther, in-

[8]CTS 25:117-18 (CO 19:113-14). [9]*Sixfold Commentary* (1610), 252. [10]WADB 11,2:16-18.

dulging his thoughts too freely, refers this passage to the masks of antichrist (Dan 8:22-23), but we shall trace this point afterwards. . . .

Some think this prophet refers to antichrist; thus they pass by Antiochus altogether and describe to us the appearance of antichrist, as if the angel had shown to Daniel what should happen after the second renovation of the church. The first restoration took place when liberty was restored to the people and they returned from exile to their native land, and the second occurred at the advent of Christ. These interpreters suppose this passage to unfold that devastation of the church that should take place after the coming of Christ and the promulgation of the gospel. But as we have previously seen, this is not a suitable meaning, and I am surprised that people versed in the Scriptures should so pour forth clouds on clear light. For, as we said yesterday, nothing can be clearer, or more perspicuous, or even more familiar, than this prophecy. And what is the tendency of ascribing so violently to antichrist what even mere children clearly see to be spoken of Antiochus, except to deprive Scripture of all its authority? Others speak more modestly and more considerately when they suppose the angel to treat of Antiochus for the purpose of depicting in his person the figure of antichrist. But I do not think this reasoning sufficiently sound. I desire the sacred oracles to be treated so reverently, that no one may introduce any variety according to the will of humans but simply hold what is positively certain. It would please me better to see anyone wishing to adapt this prophecy to the present use of the church and to apply to antichrist by analogy what is said of Antiochus. We know that whatever happened to the church of old belongs also to us, because we have fallen on the fullness of times.

No doubt the Holy Spirit wished to teach us how to bear our cross by making use of this example, but as I have already said, it seems to me far too frivolous to search for allegories. We should be content with true simplicity and transfer to ourselves whatever occurred to the ancient people. Commentaries on Daniel.[11]

Calvin Wrong. Philipp Melanchthon: Although the vision concerning Antiochus and the Jewish people is particularly addressed, nevertheless the prophecy also indicates the similar calamity coming on the church at the end of the world, after Christ has suffered and the gospel has gone out among the nations. That Daniel at the same time depicts the image of the impious king, waging war in the church with Christ, Paul testifies, referring to the words about Antiochus and expressly applying them to the antichrist (2 Thess 2). With this adjustment, let us hold to the testimony of Paul, let us follow his authority and lay aside the scoffing of others who do not want these words applied to antichrist. Commentary on the Prophet Daniel.[12]

The Antichrist. Johannes Oecolampadius: As we advised before, we do not take the antichrist for one person, but if any mortal appropriately fits this name it would certainly apply to Muhammad or the popes, among others, who have done very shameful things to the faithful. On this point, Origen so interprets the antichrist in *Contra Celsum* and other places. Luther rightly pours forth a torrent of words against the kingdom of the papacy, which one is not able to deny. For me, antichrist is whoever comes from us and sitting in the place of God, blasphemes the name of God and persecutes the church of Christ, whether he is a Roman or Alexandrian bishop. Moreover, one may compare the antichrist with Antiochus, as it is here put forth. Those who are led astray because of their sins are rightly

[11]CTS 25:119, 128-29 (CO 19:114, 121-22). [12]*In Danielem Prophetam* (1543), 138.

punished as they obey the antichrist. Commentary on Daniel.[13]

Death of Antiochus. John Mayer: *He shall be broken without hands.* Having so far spoken of the wicked practices and intolerable pride of Antiochus, now he shows what his end should be, namely, not by being cut off by a violent death in war but by God's just judgment seizing on him, as he was well worthy. How this was fulfilled, see 2 Maccabees 9. He had intolerable pangs in his body through a fall out of his chariot, when he hastened in a great rage towards Jerusalem, whereon his inward parts putrefied and worms bred, and an intolerable stench came from him, and so he died in extreme misery, making vows to God if he would spare him, but God's wrath would not now be pacified again toward him. Wherefore let none of however great power they be bear themselves in this way, but still walk humbly before God, because the power that is irresistible by persons is still subject to God, as this wretched tyrant before his death was made to acknowledge. But because he did it not sooner, his acknowledgement was vain and useless for him. Therefore, let us learn to confess our own weakness and wickedness before it is too late, that is, extremity of sickness forcing us to this, because so we may doubt whether we shall be accepted or no. Let us humble ourselves when we can, for the judgment of death is now begun to be executed, and so it is too late for us to repent, as when the great day of judgment of all the world comes. Commentary upon All the Prophets.[14]

8:27 *Daniel Overcome*

Daniel Weakened. John Calvin: Again, Daniel shows himself to have been so touched with the secret instinct of God that he knew for certain this vision to have been divinely presented to him. For God wished so to affect his servant, that he might embrace with greater reverence what he both heard and saw. I have already referred to our want of attention in listening to God's word as it deserves, unless some kind of fear precedes it that may rouse our minds by some means from their torpor; but this prophecy had a special intention. In an ordinary case, God did not humble his servant; but by the disease that is here mentioned, he wishes to show how this prediction related to some event of serious magnitude. Daniel, therefore, states *himself to have been astonished, as if suffering under some defect and afflicted by disease.* This disease did not happen to the prophet naturally, but it fell on him in consequence of his being suddenly terrified. And he afterwards shows this by saying no one understood the prediction. Here, then, he admonishes all the pious neither to hear nor to read this narrative with carelessness, but to summon up their utmost attention and to perceive that God here shows them things of the greatest importance, which vitally concern their salvation. This forms a reason why Daniel ought to suffer dejection and to be afflicted by disease. He next says *he returned to the king's business,* meaning his ordinary occupation. We infer from this expression the grievous error of those who think him to have been in Persia at this period, because he could not return to his duties unless he were present in the king's palace. Commentaries on Daniel.[15]

Daniel Stricken By His Visions. John Mayer: Lastly, Daniel shows how this vision affected him, for certain days he was sick and weak, so stricken was he at the miseries foreseen to come to the church, but none else knew of these things then, but he concealed them as he was commanded, when he was recovered from his sickness arising and going about the king's business and making no show in his countenance of any trouble or distraction of

[13]*In Danielem prophetam libri duo* (1553), 108-9. [13]*Prophets,* 552*. [14]CTS 25:132-33 (CO 19:124). [15]*Prophets,* 552-53.

mind for anything that he had seen. From this Polanus argues again that Daniel was all this while in Babylon, and not at Susa before spoken of, but only seemed to himself to be there. But this cannot thus be proved, for the same divine power that carried him out could suddenly bring him back again, as weak as he was, and then he, as if nothing else had befallen him in all the days that he was absent, went silently on about his business again. COMMENTARY UPON ALL THE PROPHETS.[16]

HEARING GOD'S WORD. ANDREW WILLET: Daniel was much moved at the hearing of this vision; so should the servants of God be thoroughly stricken with admiration at the mysteries of religion. Their inward selves should be moved at the hearing of God's Word. They then who are dull and heavy and have no sense or feeling when God's Word is proclaimed show that they have but carnal and cold affections and have need to be often roused up with that saying, *He who has ears to hear, let him hear.* SIXFOLD COMMENTARY UPON DANIEL.[17]

[16]*Sixfold Commentary* (1610), 261.

9:1-23 DANIEL'S PRAYER

1 In the first year of Darius the son of Ahasuerus, by descent a Mede, who was made
king over the realm of the Chaldeans—2 in the first year of his reign, I, Daniel, perceived
in the books the number of years that, according to the word of the LORD to Jeremiah the
prophet, must pass before the end of the desolations of Jerusalem, namely, seventy years.
3 Then I turned my face to the Lord God, seeking him by prayer and pleas for mercy
with fasting and sackcloth and ashes. 4 I prayed to the LORD my God and made confes-
sion, saying, "O Lord, the great and awesome God, who keeps covenant and steadfast love
with those who love him and keep his commandments, 5 we have sinned and done wrong
and acted wickedly and rebelled, turning aside from your commandments and rules. 6 We
have not listened to your servants the prophets, who spoke in your name to our kings,
our princes, and our fathers, and to all the people of the land. 7 To you, O Lord, belongs
righteousness, but to us open shame, as at this day, to the men of Judah, to the inhabitants
of Jerusalem, and to all Israel, those who are near and those who are far away, in all the
lands to which you have driven them, because of the treachery that they have committed
against you. 8 To us, O LORD, belongs open shame, to our kings, to our princes, and to
our fathers, because we have sinned against you. 9 To the Lord our God belong mercy and
forgiveness, for we have rebelled against him 10 and have not obeyed the voice of the LORD
our God by walking in his laws, which he set before us by his servants the prophets. 11 All
Israel has transgressed your law and turned aside, refusing to obey your voice. And the
curse and oath that are written in the Law of Moses the servant of God have been poured
out upon us, because we have sinned against him. 12 He has confirmed his words, which he

spoke against us and against our rulers who ruled us,[a] *by bringing upon us a great calamity. For under the whole heaven there has not been done anything like what has been done against Jerusalem.*
[13]As it is written in the Law of Moses, all this calamity has come upon us; yet we have not entreated the favor of the Lord *our God, turning from our iniquities and gaining insight by your truth.*
[14]Therefore the Lord *has kept ready the calamity and has brought it upon us, for the* Lord *our God is righteous in all the works that he has done, and we have not obeyed his voice.*
[15]And now, O Lord our God, who brought your people out of the land of Egypt with a mighty hand, and have made a name for yourself, as at this day, we have sinned, we have done wickedly.

[16]"O Lord, according to all your righteous acts, let your anger and your wrath turn away from your city Jerusalem, your holy hill, because for our sins, and for the iniquities of our fathers, Jerusalem and your people have become a byword among all who are around us.
[17]Now therefore, O our God, listen to the prayer of your servant and to his pleas for mercy, and for your own sake, O Lord,[b] *make your face to shine upon your sanctuary, which is desolate.*
[18]O my God, incline your ear and hear. Open your eyes and see our desolations, and the city that is called by your name. For we do not present our pleas before you because of our righteousness, but because of your great mercy.
[19]O Lord, hear; O Lord, forgive. O Lord, pay attention and act. Delay not, for your own sake, O my God, because your city and your people are called by your name."

[20]While I was speaking and praying, confessing my sin and the sin of my people Israel, and presenting my plea before the Lord *my God for the holy hill of my God,*
[21]while I was speaking in prayer, the man Gabriel, whom I had seen in the vision at the first, came to me in swift flight at the time of the evening sacrifice.
[22]He made me understand, speaking with me and saying, "O Daniel, I have now come out to give you insight and understanding.
[23]At the beginning of your pleas for mercy a word went out, and I have come to tell it to you, for you are greatly loved. Therefore consider the word and understand the vision."

a Or *our judges who judged us* **b** Hebrew *for the Lord's sake*

Overview: For our Lutheran commentators, this chapter is the most remarkable in the book. It serves as a compendium of the most important articles of faith; it offers clear testimony concerning the advent and death of Christ; and it teaches the chief article, justification by faith, with great clarity. For the other commentators, this chapter gives us an example of the importance of prayer and penance.

Our commentators begin with some consideration of the relationship between Jeremiah and Daniel. They then turn to Daniel's beautiful prayer and confession of faith. Daniel confesses his sins and the people's sins. Some commentators explain why Daniel embraced outward ceremonies like fasting and sackcloth; others focus more on his acknowledgment of sin. He then prays for his people in captivity and for the city of Jerusalem that they might return to their homeland and worship God in Jerusalem.

Our commentators focus mostly on the issue of righteousness and the various uses of the term throughout Daniel's prayer. Melanchthon makes a textual observation that shows Daniel's explicit appeal to Christ. Moreover, our authors emphasize at length the clear agreement between Daniel and Paul on the righteousness of faith.

The Importance of This Chapter. Philipp Melanchthon: Although every chapter contains an abundance of doctrine, nevertheless this chapter by far exceeds the others. Daniel hands down the clear testimony concerning the advent of Christ, the death of Christ, the righteousness of the New Testament and the destruction of the Jewish state. He includes the doctrine of penance in a prayer, he rightly assesses the value of his own righteousness, and he shows the righteousness of faith. Therefore, this chapter contains the most useful doctrine to confirm believers in many articles. Commentary on the Prophet Daniel.[1]

A Special Chapter in Daniel. Johann Wigand: This chapter is one of the most special in all of Daniel. It contains as it were a compendium of the most important articles of faith: God, sin, the forgiveness of sins, penance, faith, prayer, the Messiah, the end of the Jewish people, the antichrist and the destruction of the world. For that reason, we must diligently read and ponder it. To this point in the book, Daniel has described the monarchies and memorable events in his history. Now as if to analyze these things that follow the monarchy in which he lived, which is to say of the Medes and Persians, he recites the remarkable revelation concerning the restoration of the Israelite people, the renewal of Jerusalem and the coming Messiah. Daniel understood that God loved and preserved the Israelite people that he bestowed on them and adorned them with kindness and miracles, for this very reason—so that he might exhibit to them the Messiah, who would conquer the devil, redeem the human race from sin and save them from eternal condemnation. Therefore, these are such great divine revelations because they confirm the chief doctrine of the church of God that by faith alone in Christ we are justified before God, not by our works. Brief Exposition of the Prophet Daniel.[2]

Summary of the Chapter. John Calvin: In this chapter Daniel will explain to us two things. First, how very ardently he was accustomed to pray when the time of redemption, specified by Jeremiah, drew nigh; and next, he will relate the answer he received from God to his earnest entreaties. These are the two divisions of this chapter. First, Daniel informs us how he prayed when he understood from books the number of the years. From this we gather that God does not here promise his children earthly blessings but eternal life, and while they grow torpid and ease aside all care and spiritual concern, he urges them the more earnestly to prayer. For what benefit do God's promises confer on us unless we embrace them by faith? But prayer is the chief exercise of faith. This observation of Daniel's is worthy of notice. He was stimulated to prayer because he knew from books the number of the years. Commentaries on Daniel.[3]

Summary of Daniel. John Mayer: In this chapter Daniel shows how that in the first year of Darius the Mede he (understanding by Jeremiah 25 that at the end of seventy years God would bring back again the captivity of his people from Babylon) set himself by prayer and fasting most earnestly to seek God, now that this time was accomplished for the fulfilling of this his gracious promise, and in this his devotion he continued confessing sins, and the justice of God's proceedings against his people therefore, and entreating for mercy, until the Lord sent the angel Gabriel to him. Commentary upon All the Prophets.[4]

Daniel an Example for Us. John Calvin: The faithful do not so acquiesce in the prom-

[1]*In Danielem Prophetam* (1543), 153. [2]*Explicatio Brevis* (1571), 292-93. [3]CTS 25:135 (CO 19:125). [4]*Prophets*, 553.

ises of God as to grow torpid and become idle and slothful through the certainty of their persuasion that God will perform his promises, but they are rather stimulated to prayer. For the true proof of faith is the assurance when we pray that God will really perform what he has promised us. Daniel is here set before us as an example of this. For when he understood the time of deliverance to be at hand, this knowledge became a stimulus to him to pray more earnestly than he was accustomed to do. It is clear then, as we have already seen, that the prophet was diligent and anxious in this particular. He did not deviate from his usual habit when he saw the greatest risk of being put to death, for while the king's edict prohibited everyone from praying to God, he still directed his face towards Jerusalem. This was the holy prophet's daily habit. But we shall perceive the extraordinary nature of his present prayer when he says he prayed in dust-arid ashes. From this it appears how God's promise stirred him up to supplication, and hence we gather what I have lately touched on—that faith is no careless speculation, satisfied with simply assenting to God. For the stupid seem to assent by outward hearing, while true faith is something far more serious. When we really embrace the grace of God that he offers us, he meets us and precedes us with his goodness, and thus we in time respond to his offers and bear witness to our expectation of his promises. Nothing, therefore, can be better for us than to ask for what he has promised. Thus in the prayers of the saints these feelings are united, as they plead God's promises wherein they entreat him. And we cannot possibly exercise true confidence in prayer, except by resting firmly on God's word. An example of this kind is here presented to us in Daniel's case. Commentaries on Daniel.[5]

9:1-2 *Jeremiah*

Daniel Reads Jeremiah. Johann Wigand: *I perceived in the books* (Dan 9:2). The emphasis is on the words "I perceived." Although anyone among the people could have read Jeremiah, nevertheless they did not listen carefully to the time designated by him, having become greatly disheartened in exile. . . . But Daniel, on the contrary, seeing the ruination of things, the threatening disaster from foreign nations, recovered his spirit and hope, rolled open the books, prayed, groaned and inquired concerning the promises of God, read and reread what Jeremiah had foretold. Brief Exposition of the Prophet Daniel.[6]

Daniel and Jeremiah. John Calvin: Although Daniel was an interpreter of dreams, he was not so elated with confidence or pride as to despise the teaching delivered by other prophets. Jeremiah was then at Jerusalem, when Daniel was dragged into exile, where he discharged the office of teacher for a long period afterwards, so that Babylon became a kind of pulpit. And Ezekiel names him the third among the most excellent servants of God (Ezek 14:14), because Daniel's piety, integrity and holiness of life were even then celebrated. As to Jeremiah, we know him to have been either just deceased in Egypt, or perhaps to be still living, when this vision was offered to Daniel, who had perused his prophecies previously to this occasion. We observe also the great modesty of this holy man, because he exercised himself in reading the writings of Jeremiah and was not ashamed to own how he profited by them. For he knew this prophet to have been appointed to instruct himself as well as the rest of the faithful. Thus he willingly submitted to the instruction of Jeremiah and ranked himself among his disciples. And if he had not deigned to read those prophecies, he would have been unworthy to partake of the promised deliverance. As he was a member of the church, he ought to have been a disciple of

[5]CTS 25:136 (CO 19:125-26). [6]*Explicatio Brevis* (1571), 295.

Jeremiah, so in like manner, Jeremiah would not have objected to profit in his turn, if any prophecy of Daniel's had been presented to him. This spirit of modesty ought to flourish among the servants of God, even if they excel in the gift of prophecy, inducing them to learn from each other, while no one should raise himself above the common level. While we are teachers, we ought at the same time to continue as learners. Commentaries on Daniel.[7]

9:3-15 *Daniel's Prayer and Confession*

Prayer to the True God. Johann Wigand: *To the Lord God* (Dan 9:3). The emphasis is "to the true God," who reveals himself in the Word, who is one Lord, who is here signified by the word *Adonai*. And there are three persons, who are expressed by the plural number *Elohim*. Moreover, by uniting these two names, he testifies that he calls on the true God and separates his prayer from the pagan idolatry. Brief Exposition of the Prophet Daniel.[8]

Daniel's Prayer. Martin Luther: The first part of the ninth chapter is a very beautiful prayer in which Daniel pleads for his people, who were exiled in Babylon, and for the city of Jerusalem and the temple. He prays that the Jews would be able to return home and reestablish the worship of God there. The prayer is granted, and it is revealed to him how many years until the Christ will come and inaugurate his eternal kingdom. This is an incredible and great revelation of Christ, indicating the time so certainly and precisely. Preface to the Prophet Daniel.[9]

God's Covenantal Faithfulness. John Calvin: Daniel announces that *God keeps his covenant toward all who love him* (Dan 9:4). We must next notice how he adds the word *pity* to "covenant." He does not put these two words as differing from each other, *berith* and *chesed*, but unites them together, and the sentence ought to be understood by a common figure of speech, implying that God made a gratuitous covenant that flows from the fountain of his pity. What, therefore, is this agreement or covenant and pity of God? The covenant flows from God's mercy; it does not spring from either the worthiness or the merits of people; it has its cause, and stability, and effect and completion solely in the grace of God. We must notice this, because those who are not well versed in the Scriptures may ask why Daniel distinguishes mercy from covenant, as if there existed a mutual stipulation when God enters into covenant with people, and thus God's covenant would depend simply on human obedience. This question is solved when we understand the form of expression here used, as this kind of phrase is frequent in the Scriptures. For whenever God's covenant is mentioned, his clemency, or goodness or inclination to love is also added. Daniel therefore confesses, in the first place, the gratuitous nature of the covenant of God with Israel, asserting it to have no other cause or origin than the gratuitous goodness of God. He next testifies to God's faithfulness, for he never violates his agreement or departs from it, as in many other places God's truth and faithfulness are united with his clemency (Ps 36:6 and elsewhere). It is necessary for us to rely on God's mere goodness, as our salvation rests entirely with him, and thus we render to him the glory due to his pity, and thus it becomes needful for us, in the second place, to obtain a clear apprehension of God's clemency. The language of the prophet expresses both these points, when he shows how God's covenant both depends on and flows from his grace, and when he adds the Almighty's faithfulness in keeping his agreement. Commentaries on Daniel.[10]

[7]CTS 25:138-39 (CO 19:128). [8]*Explicatio Brevis* (1571), 297. [9]WADB 11,2:18. [10]CTS 25:146-47 (CO 19:133-34).

Daniel's Prayer and Ceremonies. John Calvin: Daniel is not here treating of his daily prayers. We may easily collect from the whole of his life how Daniel had exercised himself in prayer before Jeremiah had spoken of the seventy years. Because he knew the time of redemption to be at hand, he was then stimulated to more than his usual entreaties. He expresses this by saying *in fasting and sackcloth and ashes* For the saints were not accustomed to throw ashes over their heads every day, nor yet to separate themselves for prayer, by either fasting or putting on sackcloth. This action was rare, used only when God gave some sign of his wrath or when he held out some scarce and singular benefit. Daniel's present prayer was not after his usual habit, but when he put on sackcloth and sprinkled himself with ashes and endured fasting, he prostrated himself suppliantly before God. He also pleaded for pardon, as we shall afterwards see, and begged the performance of what the Almighty had surely promised.

From this we should learn two lessons. First, we must perseveringly exercise our faith by prayers; next, when God promises us anything remarkable and valuable, we ought then to be the more stirred up and to feel this expectation as a sharper stimulus. With reference to the fasting and sackcloth and ashes, we may shortly remark how the holy fathers under the law were in the habit of adding extraordinary ceremonies to their prayers, especially when they wished to confess their sins to God, and to cast themselves before him as thoroughly guilty and convicted and as placing their whole hope in their supplication for mercy. And in the present day the faithful are justified in adding certain external rites to their prayers; although no necessity either can or ought to be laid down beforehand in this case. We know also the Orientals to be more devoted to ceremonies than we are ourselves. And this difference must be noticed between the ancient people and the new church, since Christ by his advent abolished many ceremonies. For the fathers under the law were, in this sense, like children, as Paul says (Gal 4:3). The discipline that God had formerly instituted involved the use of more ceremonies than were afterwards practiced. As there is this important difference between our position and theirs, whoever desires to copy them in all their actions would rather become the ape than the imitator of antiquity. Meanwhile, we must notice that the reality remains for us, although external rites are abolished. Two kinds of prayer, therefore, exist; one that we ought to practice daily, in the morning, evening, and if possible, every moment; for we see how constancy in prayer is commended to us in Scripture (Lk 18:1; Rom 12:12; 1 Thess 5:17). The second kind is used when God denounces his wrath against us, or we have need of his special aid or seek anything unusual from him. This was Daniel's method of praying when he put on sackcloth and sprinkled himself with ashes. Commentaries on Daniel.[11]

Daniel's Prayer. Heinrich Bullinger: The prayer and confession of the prophet follows, whose argument is this: He frankly confesses his sins and the people's sins, which he neither abbreviates nor diminishes but rather exaggerates. He proclaims the righteousness of God, who himself punishes with a most just judgment. Then he entreats, seeking the forgiveness of his sins and the people's sins, the liberation and return of the people and the restitution of the temple and worship of God and the city. We too are able to ask similar things from God, as often as they beset us and difficulties oppress us. In this same prayer, Daniel lays out true penitence, which is conversion to God from Satan and sin, acknowledgement of sin, and confession, with grief over shameful sins, and by true faith receiving the remission of sins, and devoting oneself to a changed life,

[11]CTS 25:136-37 (CO 19:126-27).

from wickedness to holiness. And unless someone is gifted with true and firm faith in God, he will not rightly pray. For this reason, Daniel from the beginning of his prayer calls on God that he think of God as he prays and rouses himself in prayer, teaching who and how great this God is, who clearly is able to help. Daniel the Most Wise Prophet of God.[12]

Daniel and Confession. Philipp Melanchthon: Daniel confesses the sins of the people and gives praise to the God of justice because he justly punished the people. Then he begs for the forgiveness of sins and the return of the people. Therefore, this is true contrition to acknowledge the wrath of God against our sins, to become frightened because of the wrath of God, to suffer grief because we have offended God, to bestow on him praise because he justly punishes us and to be subject to punishment.

Here he recites this confession, "To you, O Lord, belongs righteousness, but to us open shame." This is the voice of true contrition. Just as Psalm 32 teaches, "I said I will confess my transgressions to the Lord, etc." (Ps 32:5). And Psalm 51, "Against you only have I sinned and done what is evil in your sight, so that you may be justified in your words and blameless in your judgment" (Ps 51:4). . . .

It is necessary to diligently inculcate the church with this doctrine of contrition so that they truly acknowledge sins, truly understand the punishments and calamities inflicted on us because of our sins. Just as Jeremiah says, "Your sins have kept good things from you" (Jer 5:25). And in this place, "Righteous is the Lord our God in all the works he does" (Dan 9:14). . . .

Nevertheless, it is not enough to acknowledge sins and to consider punishments, but consolation must be added. Therefore, Daniel not only put forward the doctrine of contrition but adds the other part. He teaches by his own example to pray and to hope for kindness, because of the mercy and promises. As it says elsewhere, Repent and believe the gospel. Faith added to contrition looks to the promises. So Daniel here not only says, "To you, O Lord, belongs righteousness," but also adds, "To you mercy and atonement." You promised to show compassion and to forgive. And he repeats several times this sentence, distinctly excluding merit, "We ask not by our own righteousness but because of your great mercy." Commentary on the Prophet Daniel.[13]

Confession of Daniel. Andrew Willet: Confession of sins is either public, either by the whole congregation or of one and more before the congregation; or private, either of one's sins by himself or in the name of many. And each of these confessions is either ordinary or extraordinary. This confession of Daniel was of the latter sort, wherein he confesses not his own sins only but also the sins of his people. And if Daniel, so holy a man, yet confesses his sins in his prayer, how much more ought we sinful people always in our prayers to make our confession, as the prophet David says, *Then I acknowledged my sin to you, etc., and you forgave the punishment of my sin* (Ps 32:5). Sixfold Commentary upon Daniel.[14]

Daniel's Confession. John Calvin: The greatest part of this prayer is an entreaty that God would pardon his people. Whenever we ask for pardon, the testimony of repentance ought to precede our request. For God announces that he will be propitious and easily entreated when people seriously and heartily repent (Is 58:9). Thus confession of guilt is one method of obtaining pardon, and for this reason Daniel fills up the greater part of his prayer with the confession of his sinfulness. He reminds us of this, not for the sake of boasting but to instruct us by his own example

[12]*Daniel Sapientissimus*, 94. [13]*In Danielem Prophetam* (1543), 156-58. [14]*Sixfold Commentary* (1610), 361.

to pray as we ought. He says, therefore, *he prayed and made confession.* The addition of "my God" to the word *Jehovah* is by no means superfluous. *I prayed,* he says, *to my God.* He here shows that he did not utter prayers with trembling, as people too often do, for unbelievers often flee to God, but without any confidence. They dispute with themselves whether their prayers will produce any fruit; Daniel, therefore, shows us two things openly and distinctly, since he prayed with faith and repentance. By the word *confession* he implies his repentance, and by saying *he prayed to God,* he expresses faith and the absence of all rashness in throwing away his prayers, as unbelievers do when they pray to God confusedly and are all the while distracted by a variety of intruding thoughts. *I prayed,* says he, *to my God.* No one can use this language without a firm reliance on the promises of God, and assuming that he will prove himself ready to be entreated. COMMENTARIES ON DANIEL.[15]

9:16-19 *Righteousness*

FOR THE SAKE OF CHRIST. PHILIPP MELANCHTHON: And he says by name, "Hear, O God, the prayer of your servant, consider your deserted temple, for the sake of the Lord" (Dan 9:17), that is, hear, consider, because of the Lord. Now among the Hebrews this particle is inserted, so that Daniel speaking to God as a second person, *Hear, O God, consider,* etc., afterwards adds a third person in the end, *for the sake of the Lord.* For that reason, the Jewish interpretation is *for the sake of Abraham.* But this interpretation is contrary to the text and is to be repudiated.

Daniel understood not Abraham to be the Lord of the people, but rather the promised Savior, as it is said in the psalm, "The Lord said to my Lord, sit at my right hand, etc." (Ps 110:1). There is no doubt but that Daniel here understood Christ, saying *for the sake of the Lord,* that is, *for the sake of Christ.* There are similar sermons on contrition and faith extant everywhere in the prophets. Jeremiah says, "Though our iniquities testify against us, O Lord, act for your name's sake, we have sinned against you, our Savior in times of trouble, do not abandon us, etc." (Jer 14:7-8). COMMENTARY ON THE PROPHET DANIEL.[16]

DANIEL AND PAUL AGREE. PHILIPP MELANCHTHON: Here readers are admonished that they observe this prayer by Daniel, for the purpose of confirming the teaching that is passed down by Paul concerning the righteousness of faith. For here Daniel puts forward the certain and clear testimony of Paul's teaching. Now some clever people try to change the teaching of Paul to fit human opinion on the righteousness of works and cry out wildly that this is to be accepted by us. They deny those statements that all people are under sin, our works do not merit reconciliation, the natural person is full of vice and not able to satisfy the law; likewise they deny that freely by mercy people are declared righteous for the sake of Christ, not for the sake of works.

. . . Let us then consider that when Paul speaks about righteousness before God, it is necessary that his teaching agree with the prophets and patriarchs. And it is clear that in the succession of the prophets they teach the same thing. They testify that all people are under sin, and they impugn human righteousness. And they in turn put forward the gratuitous mercy revealed in the promises by God for sake of the promised Savior. They decree that this mercy is to be received by faith and in such they affirm our forgiveness.

There is one unanimous voice among all the prophets. For that reason Peter says, "To him give all the prophets witness, that through his name all who believe in him shall receive remission of sins" (Acts 10:43). And this is the

[15]CTS 25:142-43 (CO 19:131). [16]*In Danielem Prophetam* (1543), 158-59.

liberation promised through the Messiah to be delivered from sin, restored to perfect righteousness and eternal life. . . . That Paul agrees here with Daniel is clear. Daniel says, "To you, O Lord, belongs righteousness, but to us open shame" (Dan 9:7). He acknowledges the whole church to have sin. And he expressly says, "We pray not because of our righteousness, etc." (Dan 9:18). . . . Therefore just as Paul removes merit and asserts that all are under sin, indeed impressing the need for certain grace, so too here Daniel teaches, saying, "not because of our righteousness, etc." Again, as Paul says, sins are remitted by grace, so too here he cries out, "we flee to your great mercy" (Dan 9:18) and specifically names the mediator, saying, "for the sake of the Lord" (Dan 9:17). As often as mention is made of mercy, its correlative, faith, is to be understood, by which we receive mercy. Therefore Daniel agrees with Paul entirely. Commentary on the Prophet Daniel.[17]

God's Righteousness. John Calvin: [Daniel] subjoins, O Lord, may your anger be averted according to all your righteousness, and your indignation from your city Jerusalem, the mountain of your holiness (Dan 9:16). We observe how Daniel here excludes whatever merit there might be in the people. In reality they did not possess any, but I speak according to that foolish imagination that people can scarcely put off. They always take credit to themselves, although they are convicted of their sins a hundred times over, and still desire to conciliate God's favor by pleading some merit before God. But here Daniel excludes all such considerations when he pleads before God his own justice and uses the strong expression "according to all your righteousness." Those who take this word *righteousness* to mean "judgment" are in error and inexperienced in interpreting the Scriptures; for they suppose God's justice to be opposed to his pity. But we are familiar with God's righteousness as made manifest, especially in the benefits he confers on us. It is just as if Daniel had said that the single hope of the people consisted in God's having regard to himself alone and by no means to their conduct. Hence he takes the righteousness of God for his liberality, gratuitous favor, consistent fidelity and protection, which he promised his servants: O God, therefore, he says, according to all your promised mercies; that is, you do not fail those who trust in you, you promise nothing rashly, and you are not accustomed to desert those who flee to you; oh! by your very justice, succor us in our distress. Commentaries on Daniel.[18]

Daniel's Use of Righteousness. Johann Wigand: *Righteousness* (Dan 9:7). Here Daniel speaks concerning the righteousness of the law. There is a twofold righteousness of God, as he himself makes clear: the strict righteousness of God expressed in the law and the propitious righteousness handed down in the gospel. . . . *O Lord, according to your righteous acts* (Dan 9:16). We ask for your mercy. Here righteousness does not signify that strict righteousness of the law but of the gospel, by which God, according to pure and immeasurable mercy, wishes to receive sinners by grace for the sake of the Messiah. Brief Exposition of the Prophet Daniel.[19]

God's Mercy and Forgiveness. John Calvin: *To God,* says he, *belong mercies and forgiveness.* No doubt Daniel took this phrase from Moses, especially from that remarkable and memorable passage where God pronounces himself a severe avenger, yet full of mercy, inclined to clemency and pardon and exercising much forbearance (Ex 34:6). As, therefore, Daniel held the impossibility of God putting away his affectionate feelings of pity, he takes this as the main point of his teaching, and it

[17]*In Danielem Prophetam* (1543), 159-62. [18]CTS 25:176-77 (CO 19:154). [19]*Explicatio Brevis* (1571), 304, 306.

becomes the chief foundation for his hopes and his petition for pardon. He argues thus, *To God belong loving kindnesses;* therefore, as he can never deny himself, he will always be merciful. This attribute is inseparable from his eternal essence; and however we have rebelled against him, yet he will never either cast away or disdain our prayers.

We may conclude from this passage that no prayers are lawful or rightly composed unless they consist of these two members. First, all who approach God ought to cast themselves down before him and to acknowledge themselves deserving of a thousand deaths; next, to enable them to emerge from the abyss of despair and to raise themselves to the hope of pardon, they should call on God without fear or doubt, and with firm and stable confidence. This reliance on God can have no other support than the nature of God himself, and to this he has borne ample testimony. Commentaries on Daniel.[20]

Mercy and Pardon. Giovanni Diodati: [*To the Lord*] Namely, the glory of saving us in this extreme height of our sins belongs to you only: seeing it cannot be, but out of the infiniteness of your mercy and pardon, without our conferring anything, but only the feeling of our sin and misery, which may move your compassion. Pious Annotations.[21]

9:20-23 *Gabriel's Answer*

Daniel's Prayer Answered. John Calvin: Here Daniel begins to show us that his prayers were by no means useless, nor yet without their fruit, as Gabriel was sent to elevate his mind with confidence and to lighten his grief by consolation. He next sets him forth as a minister of the grace of God to the whole church, to inspire the faithful with the hope of a speedy return to their country and to encourage them to bear their afflictions until God should open a way for their return. Next, as to ourselves, we need not wonder at God's refusing at times an answer to our prayers, because those who seem to pray far better than the rest scarcely possess a hundredth part of the zeal and fervor required. On comparing our method of prayer with this vehemence of the prophet, surely we are in truth very far behind him; and it is by no means surprising, if, while the difference is so great, the success should be so dissimilar. And yet we may be assured that our prayers will never be in vain, if we follow the holy prophet at even a long interval. If the limited amount of our faith hinders our prayers from emulating the prophet's zeal, yet God will nevertheless listen to them, so long as they are founded in faith and penitence. Commentaries on Daniel.[22]

[20]CTS 25:159 (CO 19:142). [21]*Pious Annotations* (1651), 9:16. [22]CTS 25:187-88 (CO 19:161-62).

9:24-27 The Seventy Weeks

24"Seventy weeks[a] are decreed about your people and your holy city, to finish the trans-
gression, to put an end to sin, and to atone for iniquity, to bring in everlasting righteous-
ness, to seal both vision and prophet, and to anoint a most holy place.[b] 25Know therefore
and understand that from the going out of the word to restore and build Jerusalem to the
coming of an anointed one, a prince, there shall be seven weeks. Then for sixty-two weeks
it shall be built again with squares and moat, but in a troubled time. 26And after the
sixty-two weeks, an anointed one shall be cut off and shall have nothing. And the people
of the prince who is to come shall destroy the city and the sanctuary. Its[c] end shall come
with a flood, and to the end there shall be war. Desolations are decreed. 27And he shall
make a strong covenant with many for one week,[d] and for half of the week he shall put an
end to sacrifice and offering. And on the wing of abominations shall come one who makes
desolate, until the decreed end is poured out on the desolator."

a Or *sevens;* also twice in verse 25 and once in verse 26 **b** Or *thing,* or *one* **c** Or *His* **d** Or *seven;* twice in this verse

Overview: The final section of this chapter has captured the attention of many. Here the precise time is given by Daniel when the Messiah would come. There is no clearer designation given in all the prophets. The seventy weeks are taken by our commentators as weeks of years and not of days; as such one week is understood to represent seven years, and the total of seventy weeks represents 490 years. Daniel used weeks of years because of Jeremiah's prophecy of the seventy years. Therefore, the two prophecies are analogous, though pointing to different things.

In this prophecy, we have the advent of Christ indicated with great clarity. Daniel also enumerates the benefits of Christ: the destruction of sin, the establishment of an everlasting righteousness and the gift of eternal life. Our commentators spend as much time, if not more, discussing these benefits of Christ than the seventy weeks. In these benefits, they all see the great truths of the Reformation expressed by Daniel, especially the imputation of Christ's righteousness to those who acknowledge their utter sinfulness and by faith trust in Christ alone.

Our commentators turn next to a consideration of the law and its demands. Christ came not to abolish the law but to fulfill it. For this reason, Christ suffers death on the cross for our sins. All of this is indicated in the text: the Messiah, the Prince, who is Christ, shall be cut off. Moreover, the sanctuary and the city are destroyed. For our commentators, the sequence of events here described (the advent of the Messiah, the benefits of the Messiah, his death and the destruction of the sanctuary and city) all clearly show that Jesus was the promised Messiah and no other is to be expected, as the destruction of the city by the Romans makes clear.

9:24 *The Seventy Weeks, Sealing Up Sins, Eternal Righteousness*

The Time of the Messiah. Johann Wigand: This is a special gem or doctrine that is set forth in Daniel. This prophecy is the divine revelation in which the precise time is designated when the Messiah would come, who will bring blessing to all humankind. . . . So clear a designation of time is not to be found in any other prophet. Brief Exposition of the Prophet Daniel.[1]

The Prophecy of the Seventy Weeks. Philipp Melanchthon: The prophecy that follows that was handed down by Daniel concerning the seventy weeks, which is a clear testimony against the Jews about the time of Christ's advent and the end of the Jewish state. Daniel briefly mentions many things that would happen in this prophecy. When he spoke about Christ's advent, he at once also taught about the benefits that would be brought about. The promises are interpreted clearly regarding the future when sin would be destroyed, an everlasting righteousness would be established and a new and eternal life begun. He adds also that Christ would die but nevertheless many people would be given his benefits, and afterward there would be an end to the Jewish state. This is the greatest of prophecies in which such clear testimonies are put forward concerning many articles against the Jews.

First, this locus refutes the error that the law must be retained and the political kingdom of the Messiah established. If righteousness will be everlasting, again, if the Messiah will be put to death, it follows that the Mosaic law must not be retained and there will be no worldly kingdom. Second, this prophecy passes down testimony concerning the suffering of Christ. Commentary on the Prophet Daniel.[2]

The Seventy Weeks. Martin Luther: These seventy weeks, as the angel proclaims, are considered by all teachers to be weeks of years, not weeks of days. In other words, a week consists of seven years instead of seven days. Reason confirms this. Seventy weeks do not even make two years, which is no extraordinary time for such a magnificent revelation. So now, these seventy weeks make 490 years, which is how long one should wait for the Christ. After that time he will inaugurate his kingdom. Now it must be determined where and when these seventy weeks begin. The angel announces them as beginning in that year when a command goes out that Jerusalem is to be rebuilt. For he says "from that time on, when the word goes out that Jerusalem is to be rebuilt," etc (9:25). Some have greatly smeared and distorted this.

So that we correctly calculate this, we should begin the seventy years in the second year of king Darius, called "the long handed." In the same year the word of the lord came to the prophets Haggai and Zechariah that Zerubbabel would rebuild the temple, as we find in the first chapter of both prophets (Hag 1:1-15; Zech 1:1-17). Darius gave this same command, which was sent out as recorded in Ezra 6 (vv. 6-15), agreeing with the calculation of the years. From this instruction or word, that went out from Haggai, to Christ's baptism, when he assumed his office and his kingdom or the new covenant began (here the angel describes him as a prince), is actually 483 years or sixty-nine weeks. The angel here says, "until the time of Christ the Prince there will be seven weeks and then sixty-two weeks"—that is, sixty-nine weeks.

Then the calculation of the years looks like this: from the second year of Darius to Alexander the Great are 145 years, as Metasthenes writes, from Alexander to Christ's birth 311 years, as the histories demonstrate, and from Christ's birth to his baptism thirty years, as in Luke 3 (v. 23). All together this is 486 years

[1]*Explicatio Brevis* (1571), 329. [2]*In Danielem Prophetam* (1543), 164-65.

or sixty-nine weeks. Three years remain which one must strike from the calculation. It often happens that in such calculations and histories a half year is called a whole year. We cannot find and determine all days and hours so precisely, when we write history it is enough for us that we come pretty close, especially since we have a text specifically concerned with the essentials. Preface to the Prophet Daniel.[3]

Three Parts of Seventy Weeks. Martin Luther: Now, the angel divides these seventy weeks into three parts. "In the first seven weeks, that is forty-nine years," he says, "the wall and streets will be rebuilt during a time of distress." It was indeed a sour time to them, because the surrounding lands strongly opposed them (Neh 2:10; 4; 6). This agrees with what the Jews said to Christ in John 2 (v. 20): "This temple was built in forty-six years, and you will build it in three days?" "Then after sixty-two weeks," he says, "the Christ will be killed." Here he indicates what will happen after these sixty-nine weeks are over and the Christ has now begun his ministry: the Christ will be crucified (which happened in the fourth year after the sixty-nine weeks, and after the beginning of his ministry) and the city of Jerusalem will finally be destroyed, and Judaism will come to an end (which happened afterwards through the Romans).

The one last week, that is, seven years, is the time following the sixty-nine weeks, when, as it was said, the Christ will be killed. And that took place in this way, he says (Dan 9:27), he will make the covenant with many for one week. The preaching of Christ went out mightily in those seven years, both through Christ himself into the fourth year and afterwards through the apostles, proclaiming the promised mercy. And in the middle of the week, that is, in the fourth year after Christ's baptism, he was killed. Then the sacrificial system was cast aside, that is, through Christ's death, which is the true sacrifice, the Jewish sacrificial system and worship of God came to an end. Soon after, as he here says (Dan 9:27), an idol was placed in the temple by the Romans under Emperor Caius Caligula as a sign that the temple and Judaism were to be ended. Preface to the Prophet Daniel.[4]

The Seventy Weeks. John Calvin: This passage has been variously treated and so distracted and almost torn to pieces by the various opinions of interpreters that it might be considered nearly useless on account of its obscurity. But, in the assurance that no prediction is really in vain, we may hope to understand this prophecy, provided only we are attentive and teachable according to the angel's admonition and the prophet's example. I do not usually refer to conflicting opinions, because I take no pleasure in refuting them, and the simple method that I adopt pleases me best, namely, to expound what I think delivered by the Spirit of God. But I cannot escape the necessity of confuting various views of the present passage. . . .

Our prophet alludes to the seventy years of Jeremiah, and I am surprised that the advocates of our side have not considered this, as no one suggests any reason why Daniel reckons years by weeks. Yet we know this figure to be purposely used, because he wished to compare seventy weeks of years with the seventy years. And whoever will take the trouble to consider this likeness or analogy will find the Jews slain with their own sword. For the prophet here compares God's grace with his judgment; as if he had said, the people have been punished by an exile of seventy years, but now their time of grace has arrived; nay, the day of their redemption has dawned, and it shone forth with continual splendor, shaded, indeed, with a few clouds, for 490 years until the advent of Christ. The prophet's language must be interpreted as follows: Sorrowful darkness has

[3]WADB 11,2:18-22. [4]WADB 11,2:24-26.

brooded over you for seventy years, but God will now follow up this period by one of favor of sevenfold duration, because by lightening your cares and moderating your sorrows, he will not cease to prove himself propitious to you even to the advent of Christ. This event was notoriously the principal hope of the saints who looked forward to the appearance of the Redeemer. . . .

We began yesterday to show how foolishly the rabbis corrupt by their comments this prophecy of which we are now treating; for they suppose the angel to be treating of the continual wrath of God, which the Jewish people had partially experienced, and which was still to be of longer duration and greater severity, according to their supposition. We have explained how openly this is opposed to the words of Daniel, who here promises the return of God's favor to his people and then shows the object and intention of the Holy Spirit. By this consolation he wished to lighten the sorrow of the holy man whom we have already seen to be extremely anxious about the state of the church that he then perceived to be so deplorable. The phrase on which we have already commented confirms the same point, for the angel promises, at the arrival of the predicted period, *an end to sin and wickedness and iniquity, because iniquity should then be expiated.* He next promises *the approach of eternal righteousness;* and lastly adds, *the sealing of the vision and prophecy, together with the spiritual anointing of the Holy of Holies.* Everyone admits this to be a promise of a blessing more excellent than anything under the law. No other interpretation can possibly be received than that which refers it to the advent of Christ and the entire restoration of the church of God. Commentaries on Daniel.[5]

Seventy Weeks of Daniel. Giovanni Diodati: [Dan 9:24. *Seventy weeks*] Namely, you have prayed to God concerning the seventy years of the people's captivity, which the Lord has appointed. And I will tell you, moreover, that after the accomplishment of those years, there is seventy times seven years (which are weeks of years), that is to say, 490 years, appointed for the lasting of the people and of the city of Jerusalem, after it is relieved from its present desolation: in which time the Messiah shall come, fulfill the prophecies, expiate and satisfy for the sins of the world by his death and establish the true righteousness of the gospel, which shall remain forever; through which all believers shall be absolved and justified and by his Spirit be regenerate to a new and godly life, and he himself shall be consecrated and made an everlasting King, sitting at the right hand of God his Father, having obtained the fullness of God's Spirit, as head of his church. And after all this the city and the nation shall be destroyed by the Romans. . . .

[Dan 9:27. *And he*] Namely, Christ having come, and conversant in the world, shall in one of those weeks by the gospel renew the covenant of grace (with the Jews who shall believe) that he had made with their forefathers and shall ratify it by new sacraments. [*Of the week*] Namely, of that week that remains after the sixty-nine, to make up the number of seventy: for indeed the revolts and troubles of the Jews lasted three years and a half, or four, after the threescore and nine weeks. [*Shall cause*] Namely, through the desolation of the temple by the Romans, the Jewish service and sacrifices shall be abolished. Pious Annotations.[6]

Daniel's Seventy Weeks. William Pemble: When Daniel's seventy weeks begin is uncertain. Some will have them begin in the first year of Cyrus; some in the second of Darius Nothus; others in the twentieth of Artaxerxes Mnemon. A person may follow his judgment, for neither the one nor the other is

[5]CTS 25:195-96, 200, 203 (CO 19:167, 170, 172). [6]*Pious Annotations* (1651), 9:24-27.

defined in the text (Dan 9:25) but is absolutely put, *from the outgoing of the Word*, which we know went forth in three kings' reigns.

But for the end and period of them it must necessarily be at the death of Christ and not, as some will have it, at the destruction of Jerusalem by the Romans. It is plain (Dan 9:24). But to grant this proposition true, though uncertain, that Daniel's seventy weeks begin at the first year of Cyrus, does it not then follow that from the first year of Cyrus are precisely 490 years. For numbers are either taken properly when they note that which naturally they signify. Improperly, or figuratively, when they signify more or less, in regard of the circumstance of matter and the speaker's intention. . . .

Let us consider the drift and scope of the angel's speech. Daniel understands by books that the seventy years of captivity were now even at an end. Because of this he prays that God would be merciful to the people and the holy city. An angel is sent to him and talks to him, not of the seventy years of captivity to be ended under Cyrus but of seventy times seven years of most glorious deliverance from the slavery of hell and the devil to be purchased by Christ. As if the angel had thus said, "You, Daniel, think of seventy years, at the end of which your people are to have a deliverance from carnal servitude under Babylon and a restoration of an earthly Jerusalem. But I give you to understand of a far more glorious liberty and freedom from Satan's slavery to be purchased by Christ for your people after seventy times seven years. Do not you think of seventy years, which are now even gone and past, but of seventy times seven years, which when they are come to end, your people and city for whom you pray shall obtain this great blessing."

Wherefore this is spoken in allusion to the seventy years of captivity to show that God's mercy should exceed his judgments, seventy times, which from that time should endure seventy times seven years, till the coming of Christ, and afterwards forever. It is therefore a prophetical prediction and not a historical relation, and the circumscription of time is used only for memory sake; that after these many years, they should be sure to obtain such a deliverance, as greater than which they could desire nothing more. . . .

That the seventy weeks are not to be understood precisely, but by a synecdoche, is thus proved. Seventy weeks are determined on your people, says Gabriel (Dan 9:24). That these are whole and full is proved by their partition. For there are seven weeks from the going forth of the commandment (Dan 9:25) and sixty-three weeks when the street and wall shall be built; and again, after threescore and two weeks, Christ shall be slain. But not presently after those sixty-nine weeks but in the middle of the last week (Dan 9:27).

. . . Christ died in the midst of the last week. This is manifest, for Christ then died when sacrifice and oblation ceased. This is proved by the ninth and tenth chapters in the Epistle to the Hebrews [Heb 9–10]. But sacrifice and oblation ceased in the midst of the last week. This Daniel expressly says (Dan 9:27). THE PERIOD OF THE PERSIAN MONARCHY.[7]

THE DIVISION OF WEEKS. JOHN MAYER: The angel speaks here, (1) Generally of that which should be done in the seventy weeks altogether, *For your people and the holy city to finish transgression.* (2) He distinguishes these weeks into seven weeks and sixty-two weeks (Dan 9:25-26) and one week again into two, in the first part of which *the sacrifice should cease*, and then for the *overspreading of abominations he shall make it desolate* [Dan 9:27]. Touching the general, that by seventy weeks are not simply understood so many weeks, but so many weeks of years is plain, because otherwise after their return out of captivity they should have had their city destroyed again in one year and eighteen weeks, which was before it was built

[7]*Persian Monarchy* (1659), 353-56.

again, indeed which is as strange, both city and temple must have been built in seven weeks, and therefore the rabbis themselves, seeing into this, acknowledge weeks of years to be here meant, as I have in the place before cited showed. In saying seventy weeks he alludes to the seventy years that had passed during which they suffered by a tedious captivity, but now he shows that they, being returned into their own land, should dwell there again seven times as long as they had lived in exile, in which time an expiation for sin should be made, and everlasting righteousness by the Messiah or Christ brought in, and his whole time is ten jubilees, wherein this reckoning of weeks of years first begun, only before it there was a week of years, the last of which was holy, in which they might neither sow nor reap but let the land rest, and for the rest of old on the seventh year, and the year after seven times seven, now seventy weeks, consisting of ten times such a number are appointed to show the rest to come to all the truly faithful by the Messiah.

And as Polanus notes, here are three benefits coming by Christ to the faithful reckoned up: (1) to keep from defection; (2) to seal transgressions; and (3) to expiate sin, in which words he renders it instead of these, *to finish transgression, to make an end of sin and to make reconciliation for iniquity*. By keeping from defection he understands the keeping of the remnant of the faithful from falling from God's grace through unbelief in Christ, when so many of that nation should by *sealing up transgressions*, being forgiving, their sins being hidden and covered, the expiation by Christ offering himself for their sins, as the epistle to the Hebrews will well bear this reading and exposition.

. . . But before we come to the opening of this further, I will return again to Daniel 9:24. And first, by the keeping from defection the obsignation of sin and the expiation thereof, Polanus rightly says that one part of the benefit coming by Christ is meant; namely, the taking away of evil, and by the bringing in of *everlasting righteousness*, the other part which stands in the collation of good. The evil taken away is (1) of sin, when through sanctification attained by the spirit sin is mortified and it reigns no more in our mortal bodies. (2) Of guilt, the handwriting that is against us, being cancelled. (3) Of punishments out of God's justice due for our sins either in this or in the world to come, for from all these the true believer is delivered through him our most blessed Savior and Redeemer. Commentary upon All the Prophets.[8]

The Weeks of Daniel. Joseph Mede: The weeks of Daniel are a divine chronology of the time during which the legal service of the sanctuary should continue when it is restored after the Babylonian captivity. During which time the city of Jerusalem should also be reinhabited, its walls rebuilt, and some sixty-two weeks after that Messiah, the Redeemer, should be anointed. Indeed, he will be cut off and rejected of his own. For which, when the whole seventy weeks (the time allotted) should expire, their sanctuary and city should again be razed and their commonwealth utterly dissolved.

Seventy weeks are determined or allotted (Dan 9:24): That is, the holy city shall again be restored, and seventy weeks of years are allotted and limited for its continuance and your people with it. And for this end, that during its standing, the Messiah, according to vision and prophecy, may come to expiate sin and be anointed in his kingdom.

. . . Here I distinguish the beginning of the times of the holy city from the beginning of Jerusalem. For the holy city is so called of the temple as the principal part. Therefore the time of its restitution is to be reckoned from the time the temple was built. But by Jerusalem is understood (as appears in the next verse) the external buildings and walls of the

[8]*Prophets*, 553-55.

city, which were not restored until some time after the temple and sanctuary were finished. Daniel's Weeks.[9]

Christ Will Seal Up Sins. John Calvin: A remarkable passage now follows concerning the office of Christ. The angel foretells what they were to expect from Christ. First of all, he announces remission of sins; for he points this out by the form of expression, *to prohibit* or close up *wickedness, to seal up sinfulness and to expiate iniquity* (Dan 9:24). It does not surprise us to find the angel using many phrases in a matter of such importance. Such repetition in the language seems to us superfluous, but the knowledge of salvation is comprehended under this head. We are thus informed how God is reconciled to us by gratuitous pardon, and this is the reason why the angel insists on this subject by so many words. . . .

What, then, is the meaning of the phrase "Christ at his advent will seal up sins and expiate iniquities"? Here, as I have said, a difference is shown between the condition of the old and the new church. The fathers indeed had hopes of remission of their sins, but their condition was inferior to ours in two respects. Their teaching was not so plain as ours, nor were their promises so full and steadfast. We excel them also in another respect. God bears witness to us that he is our Father, and so we flee to him with the utmost freedom and fearlessness; and, in addition to this, Christ has already reconciled us to the Father by his blood (Rom 8:15; Gal 4:6). Thus we are superior to them, not only in our instruction but in effect and completeness, since at this day God not only promises us the pardon of our sins but also testifies and affirms their entire blotting out and becoming abolished through the sacrifice of Christ his Son. This difference is openly denoted by the angel when he says, *Sins should be closed up and sealed, and iniquities also expiated* when Christ came. Hence we stated previously how something better was promised than the fathers experienced before the manifestation of Christ. Commentaries on Daniel.[10]

Reconciling Iniquity. Andrew Willett: The Vulgar Latin reads, *to take away sin*. So also Lyra, Hugo, Pintus, with others, and here also Pererius shows three ways a thing may be taken away: by washing and wiping, by scraping, as a blot in writing, and by dissipating or dissolving, as when a cloud or mist is dispersed. And so in all these phrases sin is said to be taken away. David says in Psalm 51, *wash away my sin*. Saint Paul says that Christ has erased the handwriting of our sin (Col 2). And in Isaiah (Is 44:22), the Lord says, *I have put away your transgression as a cloud*. This sense is true, but it is not well grounded, for the word *caphar* signifies to expiate, reconcile, not to take away.

Some by this expiation and reconciliation understand the taking away of the guilt of sin, by which we are made guilty of eternal damnation (Polanus). But that seems to be signified before in the *sealing of sins*, that they should be had in remembrance of our condemnation. By this, then, is signified that Christ has made reconciliation for sin, that is, he satisfies in his death on the cross for our faults and punishment (Bullinger).

Thus by these three words here used that are translated wickedness, sins and iniquity, all manner of sins whatsoever are implied (sin only against the Holy Spirit excepted), which may thus be distinguished *wickedness* against God, *sin* in ourselves and *iniquity* against our neighbor (Hugo). And here this benefit taking away sins is set forth in three degrees: in restraining the act, in sealing them up in respect of the guilt unto condemnation and in making expiation for the fault and essence itself. Sixfold Commentary upon Daniel.[11]

[9]*Daniel's Weeks*, 1-3. [10]CTS 25:215-16 (CO 19:180-81). [11]*Sixfold Commentary* (1610), 287.

Eternal Righteousness. John Calvin: *To bring in eternal righteousness.* This righteousness depends on the expiation. For how could God reckon the faithful just, or impute righteousness to them, as Paul informs us, unless by covering and burying their sins or purging them in the blood of Christ (Rom 4:11)? Is not God himself appeased by the sacrifice of his Son? These phrases, then, must be united, *Iniquity shall be expiated, and eternal righteousness brought manifestly forward.* No righteousness will ever be found in mortals, unless they obtain it from Christ; and if we use great accuracy of expression, righteousness cannot exist in us otherwise than through that gratuitous pardon that we obtain through the sacrifice of Christ. Meanwhile, Scripture purposely unites together remission of sins and righteousness, as also Paul says, Christ died for our sins and rose again for our justification (Rom 4:25). His death procured satisfaction for us, so that we should not always remain guilty or be subject to the condemnation of eternal death, and then by his resurrection he procured righteousness for us and acquired eternal life.

The reason why the prophet here treats justice as perpetual or "of the ages" is this: the fathers under the law were compelled to please God by daily sacrifices. There would have been no necessity for repeating sacrifices, as the apostle admonishes us, if there had been any inherent virtue in a single sacrifice to appease the Almighty (Heb 10:1). But since all the rites of the law tended to the same purpose of foreshadowing Christ as the one and perpetual victim for reconciling people to God, daily sacrifices must necessarily be offered; as we formerly said, these satisfactions were plainly insufficient for procuring righteousness. Therefore Christ alone brought in eternal righteousness—his death alone sufficed for expiating all transgressions. For Christ suffered not only to satisfy for our sins, but he sets before us his own death in which we should acquiesce. Hence this eternal justice depends on the enduring effect of the death of Christ, since the blood of Christ flowed as it were before God, and while we are daily purged and cleansed from our pollution, God is also daily appeased for us. We observe, then, how righteousness was not completely revealed under the law but is now set before us under the gospel. Commentaries on Daniel.[12]

Christ's Righteousness. Johannes Oecolampadius: Who will be given to the Jews to blot out sins, bring about righteousness and fulfill prophecy? Who will be anointed by the Holy Spirit, who is the true tabernacle of God, other than Christ? About him Isaiah says, "He was wounded for our transgressions, he was bruised for our iniquities. On him was the chastisement that brought us peace, and we were healed by his stripes" (Is 53:5). John testifies, "Behold, the Lamb of God, who takes away the sins of the world" (Jn 1:29). And in Romans, "Christ died for our sins, and he rose for our justification" (Rom 4:25). And in Hebrews, "Now he has appeared once for all at the end of the ages to put away sin by the sacrifice of himself" (Heb 9:26). And indeed Christ procured for us such good things, that is, the destruction of sin, grace, the gift of righteousness, because he himself is made our righteousness. Of such goods we are made partakers by regeneration, imparted by the Spirit of righteousness. Commentary on Daniel.[13]

Righteousness Through Christ. Heinrich Bullinger: We obtain righteousness through Christ or we are justified through Christ. It is not enough to be made clean before God without also being just, or being clothed in righteousness before him. There is no person alive on earth who is righteous before God. We are all sinners, and we are without the glory of God. However, we are justified

[12]CTS 25:216-17 (CO 19:181-82). [13]*In Danielem prophetam libri duo* (1553), 120.

freely, as the apostle says, by faith in Christ, without works of the law (Gal 2:16). Therefore Daniel, speaking about this righteousness says, "an everlasting righteousness will be brought about." Daniel the Most Wise Prophet of God.[14]

Everlasting Righteousness and Our Justification. John Mayer: The good collated is everlasting righteousness, which is not only that of sanctification, because it is but in part, but the righteousness by which the believer stands righteous, and so shall stand forever. This is a perfect righteousness in every way, which is by the law required. In none is this righteousness to be found but in Christ alone, who came not to dissolve the law but to fulfill it. Yet this righteousness is made ours by faith through imputation, whereby we come to be accepted before God for perfectly righteous, as if we had in everything all the days of our lives fulfilled all righteousness.

Question: If it is so, that Christ in fulfilling the law in all things brought in everlasting righteousness, as has been said, what need was there that he should die for our justification and salvation? Answer: It was necessary for us that Christ should suffer death for us sinners, that we might be delivered from everlasting death, and that by fulfilling all righteousness he should make a compensation for our unrighteousness. For the precepts of the law cannot be satisfied but by doing them, and the condemnation of the law for transgressions cannot be satisfied but by dying for them and bearing the punishment due them. Therefore, Christ, by bearing the punishment due to us and by his obedience, covered and abolished our disobedience. Thus likewise Justin Martyr taught of old, saying, As Adam subjected all people to death by sinning and made all our nature obnoxious to sin, so Christ revoked and abolished all this by leading a life free from all sin and suffering death for our sins. Indeed in suffering he fulfilled all righteousness, which was begun, and he continued in such righteousness all his life. In his death his obedience was most perfected, and the greatest love of all was shown.

If it is said, when God gave Adam a commandment to be kept at the first and annexed a penalty in case he should break it, we cannot conceive that any other thing was meant, but either he should keep the commandment or die the death. Therefore Christ having kept it in everything, which was since given in charge, it should seem that there was no need to the bringing in of righteousness, that he should suffer death also. Solution: It is true, if Adam had obeyed that commandment and never broken it, he could not have been required to bear the punishment of death also. But he transgressed, and we in him, and therefore both this punishment must be born, and Christ, who came as a second Adam, must obey and persevere in obedience also to the end, that through him standing in the stead of him and his sinful posterity, perfect righteousness might again be brought in, and we delivered from Adam's unrighteousness in both parts forever.

If it is said, because Christ's perfect obedience is ours, we need not live in obedience to God's laws, but as we lust. I answer as follows. He obeyed not only to make a compensation for our disobedience but also to give us example, as he says, *Learn of me, etc.*, and therefore disobedience and looseness of life in us are inconsistent with faith in him. Indeed, how can he be judged to believe in Christ that follows him not as far as he is able, but rather goes from him and follows his enemies, the devil, the world and the flesh? Commentary upon All the Prophets.[15]

Christ's Perfect Righteousness. Andrew Willet: It must of necessity follow, if that Christ has obtained and purchased for

[14]*Daniel Sapientissimus*, 100. [15]*Prophets*, 555-56.

us a perfect and absolute redemption, that he has discharged our whole debt, not only in satisfying for the punishment of the law but in imputing also to us his innocence and obedience as may appear by these reasons.

1. Christ is of greater power to communicate to us his innocence than Adam was to derive unto us the guilt of his sin and disobedience. Then as by Adam sin was propagated and death came in by sin (Rom 5:12), so it is necessary that we should receive from Christ not only exemption from death by his death but be clothed also with his righteousness.

2. We cannot stand in judgment before God unless we are endued with perfect justice. Now perfect justice is that whereby the commandments of God are exactly fulfilled, which was performed not only by that one act of Christ's death but by the perfect innocence and holiness of his whole life. Therefore, the whole obedience of Christ must be imputed and communicated unto us.

3. Christ discharged our whole debt. Now we are debtors not only in respect of the punishment of the law, which by our disobedience we have deserved. But the law exacts also of us perfect obedience, and integrity from sin. In both these respects then we have need of Christ.

4. The apostle says directly *that Christ is the end of the law for righteousness to everyone who believes* (Rom 10:4). That is, by faith the righteousness of Christ in fulfilling the law is imputed to us in as full and ample manner as if we had fulfilled the law ourselves.

5. If Christ has not fulfilled the law for us, it would follow that the law remains still to be fulfilled by us, which is impossible. SIXFOLD COMMENTARY UPON DANIEL.[16]

9:25 *Messiah the Prince*

THE NAMING OF CHRIST. JOSEPH MEDE: *Unto Messiah the prince* (Dan 9:25), that is, to *Christos Basileus* (Lk 23:2, Mk 15:32), or *Christos Kyrios*, as the angel styles him (Lk 2:11). There is no exposition, no interpretation of any passage in this prophecy could seem so harsh, but I would be content to admit it, rather than yield that by MESSIAH the PRINCE here named should be meant any other than Christ our Lord and Redeemer. For I am persuaded that the church of Israel in the gospel (and from them the apostles took it) had no other place of Scripture from which they did or could ascribe the name of Christ and Messiah unto him except this one from Daniel. For there is no other prophecy in all the Old Testament besides this where that name is directly given him, but only by way of type. DANIEL'S WEEKS.[17]

MESSIAH SHALL BE CUT OFF. JOHN CALVIN: The angel here asserts, *Christ should die*, and at the same time he specifies the kind of death by saying *nothing shall remain to him*. This short clause may be taken in various senses, yet I do not hesitate to represent the angel's meaning to be this: Christ should so die as to be entirely reduced to nothing. Some expound it thus: the city or the people shall be as nothing to him; meaning, he shall be divorced from the people, and their adoption shall cease, since we know the Jews to have so fallen away from true piety by their perfidy as to be entirely alienated from God and to have lost the name of a church. But that is forced. Others think it means it shall be neither hostile nor favorable; and others, nothing shall remain to him in the sense of being destitute of all help; but all these comments appear to me too frigid. The genuine sense, I have no doubt, is as follows: the death of Christ should be without any attractiveness or loveliness, as Isaiah says (Is 53:2). In truth, the angel informs us of the ignominious character of Christ's death, as if he should vanish from the sight of people through want of comeliness. *Nothing*, therefore, *shall*

[16]*Sixfold Commentary* (1610), 288. [17]*Daniel's Weeks*, 11.

remain to him, says he; and the obvious reason is, because people would think him utterly abolished. Commentaries on Daniel.[18]

9:26-27 *Abomination of Desolations*

The Temple and the Abomination of Desolation. John Mayer: Jerusalem was then so full of abominable sins, as Josephus says, that if the Romans had not come to destroy them and their city, it might well have been expected that God should have rained down fire and brimstone to consume them, as he did on Sodom.

. . . Of these words the meaning is that for the Jews abominable sins universally corrupting all the land, the city and temple should be ruined. It shall so continue after the desolation, to which it should be brought forever, desolation being thus, as it were, added to desolation. And therefore if any think of the rebuilding of Jerusalem again after the Jews' conversion, they are by this manifestly concluded against us, holding contrary to the truth. For although the Lord says, your habitation shall be left desolate, until you say, Blessed be he that comes in the name of the Lord, . . . it cannot hence be inferred that the Jerusalem and temple of wood and stone shall be built there again, but a glorious church in that land spiritually understood.

And whereas many rabbis of the Jews blindfold their eyes from seeing into the true meaning of this place by diverting them to some other interpretations, none of them yet can deny that the time here set is long ago past, ever since the destruction of Jerusalem by the Romans. By consequence the Messiah cannot be yet to come, as they expect, but came then, and was approved by God's angels, and an almighty power showing itself in him. So that nothing but a spiritual judgment on their souls, whereby they seeing see and perceive not, hinders them from seeing to believe to this day. And when this judgment shall be taken off, they shall see and look up to him whom they have pierced, and mourn. Until then, however, by the greatest evidence of reason out of their own prophets, they cannot be made to do.

And therefore pray we to the Lord to hasten the taking off of the veil of blindness and give them a sight of him, who in all their sacrifices was continually pointed at, that beholding at length his glory and unparalleled love, they may melt into tears for their so long continued obstinacy, and be saved. Commentary upon All the Prophets.[19]

Who Is the One Who Makes Desolate? Joseph Mede: But who is this desolator, or maker of desolations, who should command over this wing of abominations and bring these Gentiles against the holy city? The words in the original stand indifferent to be applied either to the Roman general or messiah. But I could not render them so indifferently. For if I render them, *And in half a week a desolator shall cause the sacrifice and offering to cease, and that* (being) *over a wing of abominations,* or, *Over a wing of abominations* (shall he be) *who makes desolate.* This desolater would then seem to be some other than the Messiah, that is, the Roman general. But render them as I do, *And making desolation, or being a desolater, he shall cause the sacrifice and offering to cease, and [commanding] over a wing of abominations, be a desolator.* Either way they will have reference to Messiah the Prince, who is the person meant in the words immediately before: *He shall confirm a covenant with many one week.* And this I most incline to, so that the person spoken of may be the same throughout. A reason also appears for the addition that this desolater should be over an army of abominations. For if a foreign general were only meant, what need was there of this addition? What other army could such a one lead but Gentiles? But that Messiah himself should command

[18]CTS 25:221 (CO 19:185). [19]*Prophets,* 558-59.

over an army of idolaters, this needed a special intimation.

And surely the Roman army, though an army of abominations, was in this service the army of Messiah. So the parable aiming at this prophecy tells us (Matthew 22:7). When the king heard how spitefully they entreated his messengers who came to tell them, the wedding to which they had been bidden was ready: "*He was wroth* (says the text) *and sent forth his armies and destroyed those murderers, and burned up their city.*" DANIEL'S WEEKS.[20]

[20]*Daniel's Weeks,* 44-45.

10:1-21 DANIEL'S TERRIFYING VISION OF A MAN

*1In the third year of Cyrus king of Persia a word was revealed to Daniel, who was
named Belteshazzar. And the word was true, and it was a great conflict.[a] And he under-
stood the word and had understanding of the vision.*

*2In those days I, Daniel, was mourning for three weeks. 3I ate no delicacies, no meat or
wine entered my mouth, nor did I anoint myself at all, for the full three weeks. 4On the
twenty-fourth day of the first month, as I was standing on the bank of the great river (that
is, the Tigris) 5I lifted up my eyes and looked, and behold, a man clothed in linen, with
a belt of fine gold from Uphaz around his waist. 6His body was like beryl, his face like
the appearance of lightning, his eyes like flaming torches, his arms and legs like the gleam
of burnished bronze, and the sound of his words like the sound of a multitude. 7And I,
Daniel, alone saw the vision, for the men who were with me did not see the vision, but a
great trembling fell upon them, and they fled to hide themselves. 8So I was left alone and
saw this great vision, and no strength was left in me. My radiant appearance was fear-
fully changed,[b] and I retained no strength. 9Then I heard the sound of his words, and as I
heard the sound of his words, I fell on my face in deep sleep with my face to the ground.*

*10And behold, a hand touched me and set me trembling on my hands and knees. 11And
he said to me, "O Daniel, man greatly loved, understand the words that I speak to you,
and stand upright, for now I have been sent to you." And when he had spoken this word
to me, I stood up trembling. 12Then he said to me, "Fear not, Daniel, for from the first day
that you set your heart to understand and humbled yourself before your God, your words
have been heard, and I have come because of your words. 13The prince of the kingdom of
Persia withstood me twenty-one days, but Michael, one of the chief princes, came to help
me, for I was left there with the kings of Persia, 14and came to make you understand what
is to happen to your people in the latter days. For the vision is for days yet to come."*

*15When he had spoken to me according to these words, I turned my face toward the
ground and was mute. 16And behold, one in the likeness of the children of man touched*

my lips. Then I opened my mouth and spoke. I said to him who stood before me, "O my lord, by reason of the vision pains have come upon me, and I retain no strength. 17*How can my lord's servant talk with my lord? For now no strength remains in me, and no breath is left in me."*

18*Again one having the appearance of a man touched me and strengthened me.* 19*And he said, "O man greatly loved, fear not, peace be with you; be strong and of good courage." And as he spoke to me, I was strengthened and said, "Let my lord speak, for you have strengthened me."* 20*Then he said, "Do you know why I have come to you? But now I will return to fight against the prince of Persia; and when I go out, behold, the prince of Greece will come.* 21*But I will tell you what is inscribed in the book of truth: there is none who contends by my side against these except Michael, your prince."*

a Or *and it was about a great conflict* **b** Hebrew *My splendor was changed to ruin*

OVERVIEW: Next follows a vision so terrifying that Daniel loses his strength and breath. This vision is related to what follows in the rest of the book. Our commentators begin by emphasizing the truth of prophecy and then turn their attention to Daniel's mourning and fasting. Some comments are here given on the proper use of fasting for Christians.

Daniel alone sees this vision. His companions, seized with fear, fled. There is no agreement on the identity of the man clothed in linen. Some see this man as an angel; others as Palmoni (Dan 8:13), who is Christ, the Son of God. By far the more pressing question for our commentators is the identity of Michael. Although some commentators are more reserved in their judgment on this question, most acknowledge Michael to be the Son of God. The minority opinion understands Michael as an angel. Even less clarity is to be found with the identity of the one in the likeness of man. Some see Christ; others suggest that it could be either an angel, the Son of God or Michael. Finally, comment is made regarding good and bad angels.

SUMMARY OF THE CHAPTER. JOHN CALVIN: The tenth chapter now follows, which Daniel introduces as a preface to the eleventh and twelfth. He relates the manner in which he was affected when the last vision was presented to him. This he briefly explains as referring to events about to occur until the advent of Christ; and then he extends it to the final day of the resurrection. God had previously predicted to his prophet the future condition of the church from its return from Babylon to the advent of Christ, but in the eleventh chapter he more distinctly and clearly points with the finger to every event, as we shall perceive in proceeding with our comments. In this chapter Daniel assures us that the prophecies that he is about to discuss are worthy of more than ordinary attention; when the angel appeared, he was immediately affected with sorrow and grief; then he was one moment astonished and the next cast down by the secret instinct of the Spirit; he lay like a dead man, till he was restored again and again by the angel of God. COMMENTARIES ON DANIEL.[1]

10:1 *Daniel's Name and True Prophecy*

DANIEL WHO IS BELTESHAZZAR. JOHN CALVIN: Interpreters, again, seek for a reason why he mentions his own name as Belteshazzar; some think it celebrates some honor to which he was raised; others treat it as commending the superiority of his abilities, as the name implies—descended from heaven; while oth-

[1]CTS 25:231 (CO 19:191).

ers bring forward various conjectures. I have no hesitation in stating Daniel's wish to erect some illustrious monument of his vocation among the Medes, Persians and Chaldeans. There, most probably, he was usually called Belteshazzar, and the name Daniel was almost buried in oblivion, and so he wished to testify to his being no stranger to the people of God, although he suffered a foreign name to be imposed on him, for we have already seen the impossibility of his avoiding it. I therefore think the prophet had no other intention than to render this prophecy notorious throughout all those regions in which he was well known under the name of Belteshazzar. Besides this, he wished to testify to his countrymen that he was not entirely cut off from the church through being called Belteshazzar by the Chaldeans; for he was always the same, and while banished from his country, was endued with the Spirit of prophecy, as we have previously seen. As the name of Daniel was almost unknown in Chaldea, he wished to make known the existence of both his names. Commentaries on Daniel.[2]

True and False Prophecy. Andrew Willet: *A thing was revealed to Daniel* (Dan 10:1). To the end that this might appear to be a true vision, Daniel is named both by his original name and that which was given him in Chaldea, namely, Belteshazzar, to whom the Lord had showed many visions before. So before we receive any prophecy, we must acknowledge them to be prophets, which are the ministers, such as the Lord uses to reveal himself to. Therefore Hananiah, who prophesied that the Lord would break the yoke of the king of Babylon (Jer 28), was not to be heard because the Lord used not to speak by him. Such were the revelations which in time past Montanus and Priscilla pretended, and the Enthusiasts and Anabaptists in these days, which are not to be credited because they are known not to be prophets. Sixfold Commentary upon Daniel.[3]

The True Word of Prophecy. Johann Wigand: The Hebrew may be understood as "the word was true" or "the truth of the word." This relates to our understanding. For he strongly asserts that this was not some illusion, not an uncertain dream, but the prophetic truth revealed from heaven. . . . God sometimes reveals his word mediately through angels or people and sometimes immediately. Now when we are faced with hardship and suffering, let us flee to the revealed word and not seek private visions. Indeed all things are revealed that will be before the end times. Therefore, let us draw consolation from the solid word of God, and let us entrust all other things to the mercy and omnipotence of God.

God does not mock us with confusing words like the old Delphic oracles . . . but reveals what is certain, true and effective, which believers rightly understand. Brief Exposition of the Prophet Daniel.[4]

Daniel Understood the Vision. John Calvin: *He understood the vision*; by this assertion he confirms the prophecy that he is about to explain, and thus assures us of his not uttering anything either perplexed or obscure. He also induces all the pious to hope for the exercise of the same understanding as he had himself attained; as if he had said, I know what God wished; he has explained to me by his angel various events that I will now set forth in their own order; let everyone peruse these prophecies attentively and reverently, and may God grant him the same gift of understanding and lead him to certain knowledge. The information conveyed by the prophet belongs to all

[2]CTS 25:232 (CO 19:192). [3]*Sixfold Commentary* (1610), 439. Montanus and Priscilla were both regarded as the heresiarchs of the second-century movement identified as Montanism. A feature of this movement, alluded to here by Willet, was emphasis on the continuing prophetic work of the Holy Spirit through such figures as the prophet Montanus and the prophetess Priscilla. [4]*Explicatio Brevis* (1571), 366-67.

the pious, to deter them from sluggishness and despair. Commentaries on Daniel.[5]

10:2-3 *Mourning and Fasting*

Daniel's Mourning. Philipp Melanchthon: The revelation that is described in the above chapter happened in the first year of Cyrus, by whom an edict for the restitution of Jerusalem was issued at some point after this revelation. Some of the Jews began to return and to build. Then all were full of happiness, joy and good hope. The godly gave thanks to God because the old residence, temple and worship of the church had been restored; they celebrated the prophecy of Jeremiah; they praised God, who through the voice of Jeremiah miraculously protected a remnant of the people. For the younger people, it was delightful to see the home of their ancestors, to have the temple and divine worship restored, to enjoy freedom and a pious devotion. They acknowledged that their exile had been profitable for the propagation of doctrine. They considered Cyrus and many others to be converts to true piety, and they rejoiced to have the king's support, who in rule and virtue excelled all other kings. Those joys mollified the exile for the old Daniel, who had been away from his homeland for eighty-six years.

. . . Such joys were three years later followed by great sadness. Cyrus divided his kingdom; he prohibited by a new edict the building of the temple. At some point after this, Cyrus himself was killed. In the royal court a reversal of all things occurred: the godly, who had been highly regarded during the reign of Cyrus, were excluded, treated with hatred and oppressed. The superstitions of the Gentiles were restored. Heathen rulers, inimical to true doctrine, were called to the court. This is why Daniel was in such mourning. No one is able to express this sufficiently: he grieved over the demise of his friend, the king; he grieved over the abuse to be afflicted on the name of God. . . . Therefore the new vision shown now to Daniel not only confirmed him and the other believers in this present danger but also showed to their posterity the particular changing of rulers and their calamities, which threatened the Jews. Commentary on the Prophet Daniel.[6]

Daniel's Age and Mourning. John Mayer: Here follows the third vision of Daniel in the third year of Cyrus, king of Persia, when he was very old. For he was carried captive into Babylon in the third year of Jehoiakim, king of Judah, from which to the end of his reign was eight years, from which point, to that captivity in the eleventh year of Zedekiah, makes nineteen. To this add the seventy years of the Babylonian captivity, and we shall come to eighty-nine. One year of Darius and two of Cyrus make ninety-two. To this add his age when he was carried captive (happily but seven or eight) all together make one hundred or thereabouts. Yet at this great age Daniel, living in great honor and estimation and without doubt abounding with all comforts of this life, for the high place wherein he was set by Darius (Dan 6), gave his mind more to understand the mystical things of God. Since more had been revealed before to him and to the end that he might attain to an understanding of this, he sequestered himself from the delights of this life, pleasant wines and delicate fare, and continued mourning three full weeks.

From this note that he who is enlightened in the knowledge of the mystical things of God rests not satisfied in that which he has attained to but earnestly desires to be filled yet with more such knowledge. So sweet does he find this, which already he has, as David himself, to whom the word of God was sweeter than the honeycomb. This stands against all those that care not for such knowledge, or if they do, have

[5]CTS 25:233-34 (CO 19:193). [6]*In Danielem Prophetam* (1543), 211-14.

no such earnest desire to it. Any modicum here suffices them. Truly this shows that they are altogether without divine understanding to this time. Indeed, as soon as this enters the mind, there is a desire bred by all means to know more and more.

Again, to get spiritual knowledge, the flesh must not be pampered, but abstinence used. And because it is not to be doubted that Daniel joined to his abstinence assiduous prayer, for so he did in Daniel 9, it must at all times, when we address ourselves to increase it, be sought by praying likewise. Commentary upon All the Prophets.[7]

Daniel Mourns. Giovanni Diodati: [*I eat no*] Namely, I abstained from all meats in which one might rejoice, either in respect of the quality of the food, or of the company that was at them or any delight I took in them. I fasted with bread and water, which is called in Scripture living with the bread of affliction and the water of sorrow. [*Anoint*] for in times of rejoicing people did anoint their faces with sweet-smelling oils when they went to the table. On the contrary, in time of mourning, they did abstain from it (Eccles 9:8; Mt 6:17). Pious Annotations.[8]

Daniel's Fasting. John Calvin: But he now states he had not tasted delicate bread, that is, made of fine flour, and had not tasted either wine or flesh, during the time in which the building of the temple had been impeded. We must diligently notice this, for many celebrate fasting as if it were a principal part of the worship of God. They think it an act of obedience peculiarly pleasing to God. But this is a gross error, since fasting by itself ought to be treated as a matter unimportant and indifferent. It deserves no praise unless with reference to its object. Now the objects of fasting are various; the principal one is this, to enable the faithful suppliantly to deprecate God's wrath with the solemn testimony of their repentance and to stimulate each other to more fervor in their prayers. Ordinary daily prayers do not require fasting; but when any great necessity presses on us, that exercise is added by way of help, to increase the alertness and fervor of our minds in the pouring forth of prayer. For this reason the Scriptures often connect fasting with sorrow, and Daniel here follows the usual practice. We perceive then the reason of his rejecting all delicacies in meat and drink, through his desire to withdraw himself entirely from all hindrances and to become more intent on his prayers.

I now touch but briefly on fasting, because I cannot stop on casual passages like these. We should notice, however, how foolishly and absurdly fasting is observed in these days among the papists, who think they have discharged that duty by eating but once in the day and abstaining from flesh. The rule of fasting among the papists is, to avoid flesh and not to partake of either supper or dinner. But real fasting requires something far different from this, namely, perfect abstinence from all delicacies. For Daniel extends this fasting even to bread. He says he did not taste wine, meaning he abstained from all wine. Then, as to the word *flesh*, he does not mean only that of oxen, or calves, or lambs, or fowls or birds in general, but all food except bread is included under the term *flesh*. For Daniel did not trifle childishly with God, as the papists do at this day, who feed without any religious scruple on the best and most exquisite provisions, so long as they avoid flesh. This appears more clearly from the statement that he did not eat pleasant bread, that is, made of fine flour or the very best of the wheat. He was content with plain bread to satisfy his necessities. This abundantly proves the superstition of those who distinguish between flesh and eggs and fish.

Now, fasting consists in this—the imposition of a bridle on people's lusts, eating

[7]*Prophets*, 559. [8]*Pious Annotations* (1651), 10:3.

only sparingly and lightly what is absolutely necessary, and being content with black bread and water. We now understand how fasting in this and similar passages is not taken for that temperance that God recommends to us throughout the whole course of our lives. The faithful ought to be habitually temperate, and by frugality to observe a continual fast; they ought not to indulge in immoderate food and drink and in luxurious habits, lest they should debilitate the mind and weaken the body by such indulgences. As a mark of mourning and an exercise of humility, the faithful may impose on themselves the law of fasting beyond their ordinary habits of sobriety when they feel any sign of God's wrath and desire to stimulate themselves to fervor in prayer, according to our former statements, and to confess themselves in the face of the whole world guilty before the tribunal of God. Such was Daniel's intention in not permitting himself to taste pleasant bread, or to drink wine or to eat flesh. Commentaries on Daniel.[9]

Daniel Fasts. Andrew Willet: *I ate no pleasant food.* Daniel, intent to humble himself by fasting, did not only abstain from flesh but from wine also, indeed from fine bread and from other delicates, as in anointing himself with oil. Whereby their nice superstition or superstitious niceness is reproved, who though they forebear the eating of flesh in their fastings, yet will fill their bellies with other delicate meats, with dainty fish and curious confections. But here Daniel contents himself with coarse bread and water (Calvin). Neither did he thus fast, as thereby thinking to merit anything at God's hand, but only that he might be the more humbled thereby and to make his prayers more fervent and effectual (Osiander). Sixfold Commentary upon Daniel.[10]

10:4-12 *Daniel's Vision*

Daniel Alone Saw. Johann Wigand: This vision was offered only to Daniel. For at the beginning, when his friends beheld the splendor of the angel, they were seized with fear and fled. Daniel would not have been able to bear the glorious presence of the angel had he not been divinely roused and strengthened. The same experience came on Paul at his conversion. Brief Exposition of the Prophet Daniel.[11]

The Manner of Daniel's Vision. John Calvin: Daniel now begins to relate the manner in which the vision was offered to him. He says when he stood on the bank of the river a man appeared to him, different from the common order of people. He calls him a man but shows him to be endued or adorned with attributes that inspire full confidence in his celestial glory. We have elsewhere stated how angels are called men, whenever God wished them to put on this outward form. The name of men is therefore used metaphorically whenever they assumed that form by God's command, and now Daniel speaks after the accustomed manner. Meanwhile, some absurdly imagine angels to have been really men, since they assumed this appearance and were clothed in a human body. We ought not to believe them to be really men, because they appeared under a human form. Christ, indeed, was really man, in consequence of his springing from the seed of Abraham, David and Adam. But as regards angels, God clothes them for a single day or a short period in bodies, for a distinct purpose and a special use. Wherefore I assert the gross error of those who suppose angels to become men, as often as they are corporeally visible in a human form. Still they may be called men, because Scripture accommodates itself to our senses, as we know sufficiently well. Daniel therefore says he saw a man, and afterwards distinguishes him from the human race and

[9]CTS 25:237-38 (CO 19:195-96). [10]*Sixfold Commentary* (1610), 390. [11]*Explicatio Brevis* (1571), 370.

shows fixed and conspicuous marks inscribed on him, which discover him to be an angel sent down from heaven, and not a mere earthly mortal. COMMENTARIES ON DANIEL.[12]

DANIEL SEES CHRIST. JOHN MAYER: *I saw a man whose loins were girt with fine gold of Uphaz, in linen, and his face as lightning, his eyes as lamps, etc.* This man, according to Lyra, was an angel, but Polanus will have him the same that appeared before to him (Dan 8:13), who is called *Palmoni, the numberer of secrets,* which he proves from Daniel 12:7, where an angel inquires of this man how long it should be to the end of these wonders, and he confirmed by oath that it should be a time and times and half a time, which implies that this man was so great in understanding that the angels had light and understanding from him, as a fountain of knowledge; we read also of the like appearance, where no one doubts but that it was Christ. He had a linen garment to set forth his priestly office because the priests wear linen garments; a *girdle of fine gold of Uphaz,* to set forth by the girdle his readiness, as a servant to do his Father's will, because good servants are said to stand with their loins girded and their lamps burning; by the fine gold of which it was made, his purity, stability, when tried in the fire, and virtue medicinal, that was in him to heal the diseased. His body like beryl, that is, of a sky color, showed him to be heavenly; his face like lightning for celerity, showing how soon he should shine from one part of the heaven to the other, all over the world; *his eyes like lamps,* to show his clear seeing of all things even in the darkest and most hidden places. Lastly, *his arms and his feet like burnished brass,* his strength being hereby set forth to stamp on and break in pieces all people who oppose him, as he that has brazen arms and feet can easily break in pieces a potter's vessels of earth. COMMENTARY UPON ALL THE PROPHETS.[13]

ALLEGORY AND PROPHECY. JOHN CALVIN: Without doubt, the prophet beheld something different from a human form, for the purpose of his clearly ascertaining the vision not to be a man but an angel in the form of man. I leave the allegory here, although it proceeds throughout the whole verse. I am aware of the plausible nature of allegories, but when we reverently weigh the teachings of the Holy Spirit, those speculations that at first sight pleased us exceedingly vanish from our view. I am not captivated by these enticements myself, and I wish all my hearers to be persuaded of this—nothing can be better than a sober treatment of Scripture. We ought never to fetch from a distance subtle explanations, for the true sense will, as I have previously expressed it, flow naturally from a passage when it is weighed with maturer deliberation. COMMENTARIES ON DANIEL.[14]

AN ANGEL OR CHRIST? ANDREW WILLET: *There was a man clothed in linen* (Dan 10:5). Not that he was a man indeed, but he appeared in human shape. Some think that this was the angel Gabriel (Theodoret, Carthusianus, Lyra), who was, they think, the special protector of the Jews in captivity, as Michael was of those which were returned (Gregory the Great). Cardinal Hugo, Calvin, Bullinger and Osiander are of the opinion that it was an angel. And Pererius's reason is because in the visions showed to Daniel the angel Gabriel is expressed by name, that was sent to declare the meaning of the vision to the prophet. But it does not follow that therefore this was the angel Gabriel who appeared in this glorious manner. It was the angel Gabriel who afterward speaks with Daniel; but it was Christ who in this glorious manner manifested himself.

. . . Therefore this is our answer: It was the person of Christ, the Son of God, which was seen by Daniel in that great majesty. And he is

[12]CTS 25:240-41 (CO 19:198). [13]*Prophets,* 559-60. [14]CTS 25:242-43 (CO 19:199).

that Michael afterward spoken of. But it was the angel Gabriel who had the communication with Daniel. For the prophet himself distinguishes the person of the angel from him who appeared in that glory. Sixfold Commentary upon Daniel.[15]

The Angel Sent to Daniel. Johann Wigand: *I came* (Dan 10:12). This is the highest dignity. Your prayers were efficacious and have been considered by God. He sent me, an angel, to you.

The prince (Dan 10:13). This is the second part of the narration or the basis of the consolation. I, the heavenly angel, in the palace of the Persian prince, I withstood the impious advisors who were guided by an evil spirit, having the assistance of Michael, the prince of the Israelite people, that is, the very Son of God. From this account, the type fits with Revelation 12:7, where Michael and his angels fight against the dragon. Brief Exposition of the Prophet Daniel.[16]

10:13-14 *The Identity of Michael*

The Angel Michael. Philipp Melanchthon: The prince, Michael, whom here and below is called the prince of the people of God, was present with the good angel. I understand him to be the very Son of God, the Logos, as he is named by John. Above he writes about that prince in the midst of the vision in Daniel 8 where the angel seeks the interpretation of the vision from his Lord. . . . It is certain that the Son of God is always present with his church and defends it against the fury of the devil. John says, "All things were made by him." He speaks not only about the condition of things but also about the glorious liberation of the church. He protected the people in the Red Sea and in the wilderness. He defended Joseph, Gideon, Samuel, David, Elijah, Elisha, and other faithful leaders of his people. Jacob said, "The angel, who redeemed me from all evil, bless these boys" (Gen 48:16). These words refer to the Son of God, who truly delivers from all evil, especially from sin, from the wrath of God, from eternal death and from the treachery of the devil. Not without reason he specifically says "from all evil." This glory is not able to be attributed to the ministry of angels, who, although they protect the bodies of believers, nevertheless are not able to deliver from sin or eternal death. Commentary on the Prophet Daniel.[17]

Does Michael Represent Christ? John Calvin: He adds next, *Behold! Michael, one of the chief leaders or princes, came to strengthen me*. Some think the word *Michael* represents Christ, and I do not object to this opinion. Clearly enough, if all angels keep watch over the faithful and elect, still Christ holds the first rank among them, because he is their head and uses their ministry and assistance to defend all his people. But as this is not generally admitted, I leave it in doubt for the present and shall say more on the subject in the twelfth chapter. From this passage we may clearly deduce the following conclusion: angels contend for the church of God both generally and for single members, just as their help may be needed. This we know to be a part of the occupation of angels, who protect the faithful according to Psalm 34:8. They fix their camp in a circuit round them. God, therefore, plants his angels against all the endeavors of Satan, and all the fury of the impious who desire to destroy us and are ever plotting for our complete ruin. If God were not to protect us in this way, we should be utterly undone. We

[15]*Sixfold Commentary* (1610), 375-76. Theodoret of Cyrus (c. 393–c. 460) was an important theologian of the fifth-century Antiochene school. Dionysius the Carthusian (1402–1471) was a Flemish theologian and mystic. Gregory the Great (c. 540–604) was a reforming pope, theologian and exegete. Cardinal Hugo of Florence (c. 1200–1263) was a Dominican theologian and biblical scholar. [16]*Explicatio Brevis* (1571), 372. [17]*In Danielem Prophetam* (1543), 214-16.

are aware of Satan's horrible hatred to us, and of the mighty fury with which he assails us; we know how skillfully and variously he contrives his artifices; we know him as the prince of this world, dragging and hurrying the greater part of humankind along with him, while they impiously pour forth their threats against us. What prevents Satan from daily absorbing a hundred times over the whole church both collectively and individually? It clearly becomes necessary for God to oppose his fury, and this he does by angels. While they are contending for us and for our safety, we do not perceive this hidden malice, because they conceal it from us. COMMENTARIES ON DANIEL.[18]

THE ANGEL MICHAEL AND THE SON OF GOD. JOHANN WIGAND: *Behold Michael* (Dan 10:13). Whether you understand this to be a superior angel or the very Son of God, both are acceptable. With that in mind, let us interpret it as the Son of God since the text goes on to say, *the Prince of the Israelite people*, that is, of the true church. Moreover, Paul teaches the true Son of God to be the prince and overseer of his people. And Jacob says in Genesis 48:16, *The angel who has kept me from all evil, bless the boys, and among them let my name be called on*, etc. Now to rescue from all evil is not consistent with a creature but rather the Creator. Similarly to bless is the work of God. Thereafter his name is most excellent. Now the name Michael signifies "Who is like God?" BRIEF EXPOSITION OF THE PROPHET DANIEL.[19]

THE IDENTITY OF MICHAEL THE ANGEL. GIOVANNI DIODATI: [*The prince*] That is, Cambyses, the son of Cyrus, who governed the kingdom, while his father was employed in foreign wars. Now Cambyses was an enemy to the Jews and hindered the restoration of Jerusalem; and this angel remained in Persia to repress him the space of three weeks, which was the time of Daniel's fasting (Dan 10:2) whereby the execution of his commission against Daniel was stayed. Others understand this of some evil angel, prince of the world; particularly assisting to these evil counsels that were against the church.

[*Michael*] Jude calls him archangel (Jude 9), that is, an angel of eminent degree who commanded others (Dan 10:21). He is termed head of the church and defender of the same (Dan 12:1), and head of the angels (Rev 12:7). Therefore many think that it is the Son of God himself, as indeed Michael signifies "Who is like to God?" And so the meaning would be that the Son of God had joined his divine power to the work of this created angel for the defense of his church.

[*One of the*] if Michael is the Son of God, by these chief princes may be understood the persons of the most Holy Trinity. If a created angel, the archangels (see 1 Thess 4:16). So angels are called principalities and powers (Rom 8:38; Eph 3:10; Col 1:16). PIOUS ANNOTATIONS.[20]

THE ANGEL MICHAEL. ANDREW WILLET: This Michael was none other than Christ, the Son of God, the prince and chief of the angels. The reasons are these: (1) the word *Michael* signifies *who is as God*. Therefore it cannot be inferred that he is not God, for the essence of the Son is not compared with the essence of the Father, but the comparison is of their persons. And so Christ is called the image of the invisible God (Col 1:15), the engraved image of his person (Heb 1:3). (2) He is called the chief of the angels, who are called princes in comparison with all other earthly princes. The word here used signifies as well *the first* as *one*. As the word of the same sense is taken in Daniel 1:21, *he was unto the first year of Cyrus*. Christ then was not one but the first or chief of the princes, that is, the angels. (3) This Michael is called the prince of the

[18]CTS 25:253 (CO 19:206-07). [19]*Explicatio Brevis* (1571), 372. [20]*Pious Annotations*, 10:13.

people of God (Dan 10:21), who is Christ, and the great prince (Dan 12:1). (4) He is said to help the angels; then he was greater than the angels, for there is no power greater than the angelic power, but the divine only. Polanus and Melanchthon consent that Michael is not here a created angel but Christ Jesus, the Son of God, the prince of the angels. Calvin leaves it as a thing indifferent. Sixfold Commentary upon Daniel.[21]

The Identity of Michael. John Mayer: It is as great a question who Michael, whom he calls their prince, was, whom he says helped him, for if by Michael the Son of God is understood, as ours hold, and by the man before spoken of, Christ, how can he speak of him as of a third person? To these, I find nothing said by anyone in way of resolution. And therefore it seems necessary to me to understand by the man before spoken of, not the Son of God, but an angel of God representing God, as an angel many times does and speaks accordingly, one superior to another of an inferior rank, according to instruction given from God, and so it may be conceived to have been done (Dan 12:7), and then the prince of Persia must needs be another angel by God set over Persia, as the guardian of that kingdom, or rather one of the devil's angels swaying by his suggestions the king of Persia to oppose the building of the temple in enmity against the people of God, who most earnestly desired the going forward of that work. For that God sets any good angel over a heathen kingdom to be a guardian to it, to intermeddle so much, as to argue before God for a wicked king being permitted to hinder a good work, I cannot believe, although there are some who stand for this, saying it is not unbecoming of a good angel so to do, provided that when God reveals his will, he cease to stand any further for it. Of the devil's angels, see Revelation 12:7, where it is said *the Dragon and his angels fought, and Michael and his angels.*

It is true, the Son of God, Christ Jesus is shown to John in the like manner as this man here, but it is not therefore necessary to conclude that he was the same. . . . And if we take that glorious man for an angel of God showing himself to Daniel, and the prince of Persia for an angel of the devil, and Michael called the prince of the Jews, for a principal angel of God placed as guardian over Judea, and the Jews in chief, all things will very well agree. The angel of the Dragon or devil might by opposing through God's permission retard a good angel's coming to Daniel to comfort him, and he might in a kind of duel be held by him in Persia during the time here spoken of, and then by Michael a principal angel coming in to his help, prevail to come away and assure Daniel of the constant purpose of God to stand for his temple and people. And touching Michael, it is not said any otherwise, but *Michael one of the chief princes came to help me,* not the prince over them, as Christ is, but one among them, implying that there were more such princes of God. . . .

And from that which is here said, also, we may argue that Michael was not the Son of God, but a principal angel, because he says that he helped him in fighting, hereby implying that he was but his fellow and confederate, as it were, as one prince that comes in time of war to help another. But what is it that he says, *I will tell you what is written in the Scripture of truth:* by the Scripture of truth is meant the decree of God, which is spoken of as written indelibly, to show the certainty that neither Daniel nor any of his faithful people might be discouraged for the troubles in present or in future, as being assured that nothing that may seem cross to the good promised to them came or could come to pass without God, but as he had decreed for the exercise of their faith and patience and the chastisement of them for their sins. Commentary upon All the Prophets.[22]

[21]*Sixfold Commentary* (1610), 384. [22]*Prophets*, 561-62.

A Prophecy About Christ and the Church. John Calvin: He next adds, *at the end of the days* By this expression the angel commends God's grace toward the prophet, as he was its special minister. His mission was not only to announce to him the occurrences of three or four years, or of any brief period, but he had to extend his predictions over many years, even to the extremity of the days. I willingly refer this period to the renovation of the church that happened at the advent of Christ. The Scriptures in using the phrase "the last days or times" always point to the manifestation of Christ, by which the face of the world was renewed. It is exactly similar to the angel saying he would make Daniel fully acquainted with all future events, until the final redemption of the people, when Christ was exhibited for the salvation of his church. Hence the angel embraces the 490 years of which he had spoken. For Christ's advent determined the fullness of times, and the subjoined reason suits the passage exceedingly well.

... For when the angel testifies, *the vision is yet for days*, it means, although God permits his people to be miserably afflicted, yet by this new proof he shows that he had not entirely cast them off. Some vision remained; that is, by the light of prophecy he will always manifest his care for his chosen, and they may even anticipate a happy issue out of all their sorrows. We now understand the angel's meaning when he says *the vision is yet for days*. Prophecies, indeed, ceased soon afterwards, and God no longer sent other prophets to his people, yet their teaching always remained permanent like a finger post, for in it was completed the whole series of times up to the advent of Christ. His children were never destitute of all necessary consolation; for although there were no prophets surviving who could instruct the people in God's commands by the living voice, yet Daniel's teaching flourished for nearly five hundred years after his death. It also performed its part in supporting the courage of the pious and showing them the firmness of God's covenant not withstanding all opposition. Although the church was agitated in a variety of ways, yet God is consistent in all his promises, until the complete redemption of his church by the advent of his only-begotten Son. Commentaries on Daniel.[23]

10:15-21 *Christ and Angels*

One in the Likeness of Man. Johannes Oecolampadius: You have again God, by the word of the gospel, strengthen those who tremble and grow weak because of knowledge of the law and judgment. The gospel, on the other hand, is faith in Jesus, the Son of God, who is made like the sons of men, obtaining the remission of sins and appeasing the Father for us. Therefore, he says, that great angel, who is Christ, in some way made himself known to Daniel in the likeness of man and gently touched his lip. Daniel showed his faith by speaking with him, expressing his weakness that had fallen on him from the greatness of the vision. Again, the prophet acknowledged his poverty and confessed that as a servant he is not able to speak with the Lord. Commentary on Daniel.[24]

The Instrument of God. Johann Wigand: *And behold one in the likeness* (Dan 10:16). This you may understand as either an angel, the Son of God or Michael. As mentioned above, all are acceptable. To touch the lip and to bestow strength of heart and mind is a benefit of God, even though angels are able to be instruments of God, through whom God works what he wishes. Just as the laying on of hands by the apostles healed the sick and raised the dead. Brief Exposition of the Prophet Daniel.[25]

[23]CTS 25:255-56 (CO 19:208-9). [24]*In Danielem prophetam libri duo* (1553), 139. [25]*Explicatio Brevis* (1571), 373.

Good and Bad Angels. Martin Luther: The tenth chapter is a preface to the eleventh. Still in this chapter Daniel writes an extraordinary account of angels, as is recorded nowhere else in Scripture, namely, that the good angels fight with the evil angels, defending humanity. Also he calls the evil angels princes, saying, "the prince of Greece" (Dan 10:20). From this we may understand why in the courts of kings and princes it is so wild and out of control, and why they prevent good, serving up instead war and sorrow. It is because these devils are there, scampering and scratching, or preventing anything from going as it ought to. For example, the Jews were supposed to be freed from Babylon through the kings of Persia, this never would have happened, even if the kings would have liked to have helped. Therefore, this angel here says that he has to do it; he must fight against the prince of Persia. Still he worries that once he leaves, the prince of Greece will come. As if we were to say, "whenever we fend off sorrow, the devil always raises up some new tragedy; if you were freed from the Babylonians, then you would be plagued by the Greeks." Enough of this now, it would take up too much space and time to speak further about this. Preface to the Prophet Daniel.[26]

The Prince of Persia. John Mayer: Here it is questioned who is meant by the prince of Persia, and resolved by the ancients, an angel set over that kingdom, but whether good or bad, they agree not; some say that it was a bad angel, holding that every kingdom has two angels set over it, one good and another evil, the good to move them that inhabit it to good and to stand for the good, and the evil to instigate it to evil. Therefore say they an evil angel is here meant, who stirred up the Persian king against the Jews, to hinder the putting into execution of Cyrus's decree for the building of the temple, as I have shown, that it was done on Ezra, both in the time of Cyrus and Cambyses his son. Others, that it was a good angel, who would not have the Persians to want such a people to serve them, as Pharaoh in times past would not, but to hold them still in the country, that were there, and to give to such as were gone into Judea so great discouragement that they might rather be willing to return again than to continue there still. Commentary upon All the Prophets.[27]

Daniel Honors the Angel. John Calvin: *And how shall the servant of this my Lord be able to speak with that my Lord?* The demonstrative, *zeh*, seems to be used by way of amplifying, according to the phrase common enough in our day, with such a one. Daniel does not simply point out the angel's presence but wishes to express his rare and singular excellence. Dispute would be both superfluous and out of place should any one assert the unlawfulness of ascribing such authority to the angel. For, according to my previous remark, the prophet uses the common language of the times. He never intended to detract in any way from the monarchy of God. He knew the existence of only one God, and Christ to be the only prince of the church; meanwhile, he freely permitted himself to follow the common and popular form of speech. And truly we are too apt either to avoid or neglect religious ceremony in the use of words. Although we maintain that the prophet followed the customary forms of expression, he detracted nothing from God by transferring it to the angel, as the papists do when they manufacture innumerable patron saints and despoil Christ of his just honor. Daniel would not sanction this but treated the angel with honor, as he would any remarkable and illustrious mortal, according to my previous assertion. He knew him to be an angel, but in his discourse with him he did not give way

[26]WADB 11,2:30. [27]*Prophets*, 560-61.

to any empty scruples. As he saw him under the form of a man, he conversed with him as such; and with reference to the certainty of the prophecy, he was clearly persuaded of the angel's mission as a heavenly instructor. COMMENTARIES ON DANIEL.[28]

[28]CTS 25:260 (CO 19:211-12).

11:1-45 THE KINGS OF THE SOUTH AND THE NORTH

1And as for me, in the first year of Darius the Mede, I stood up to confirm and strengthen him.

2And now I will show you the truth. Behold, three more kings shall arise in Persia, and a fourth shall be far richer than all of them. And when he has become strong through his riches, he shall stir up all against the kingdom of Greece. 3Then a mighty king shall arise, who shall rule with great dominion and do as he wills. 4And as soon as he has arisen, his kingdom shall be broken and divided toward the four winds of heaven, but not to his posterity, nor according to the authority with which he ruled, for his kingdom shall be plucked up and go to others besides these.

5Then the king of the south shall be strong, but one of his princes shall be stronger than he and shall rule, and his authority shall be a great authority. 6After some years they shall make an alliance, and the daughter of the king of the south shall come to the king of the north to make an agreement. But she shall not retain the strength of her arm, and he and his arm shall not endure, but she shall be given up, and her attendants, he who fathered her, and he who supported[a] her in those times.

7And from a branch from her roots one shall arise in his place. He shall come against the army and enter the fortress of the king of the north, and he shall deal with them and shall prevail. 8He shall also carry off to Egypt their gods with their metal images and their precious vessels of silver and gold, and for some years he shall refrain from attacking the king of the north. 9Then the latter shall come into the realm of the king of the south but shall return to his own land.

10His sons shall wage war and assemble a multitude of great forces, which shall keep coming and overflow and pass through, and again shall carry the war as far as his fortress. 11Then the king of the south, moved with rage, shall come out and fight against the king of the north. And he shall raise a great multitude, but it shall be given into his hand. 12And when the multitude is taken away, his heart shall be exalted, and he shall cast down tens of thousands, but he shall not prevail. 13For the king of the north shall again raise a multitude, greater than the first. And after some years[b] he shall come on with a great army and abundant supplies.

14In those times many shall rise against the king of the south, and the violent among your own people shall lift themselves up in order to fulfill the vision, but they shall fail.

15 Then the king of the north shall come and throw up siegeworks and take a well-fortified
city. And the forces of the south shall not stand, or even his best troops, for there shall be
no strength to stand. 16 But he who comes against him shall do as he wills, and none shall
stand before him. And he shall stand in the glorious land, with destruction in his hand.
17 He shall set his face to come with the strength of his whole kingdom, and he shall bring
terms of an agreement and perform them. He shall give him the daughter of women to
destroy the kingdom,[c] but it shall not stand or be to his advantage. 18 Afterward he shall
turn his face to the coastlands and shall capture many of them, but a commander shall
put an end to his insolence. Indeed,[d] he shall turn his insolence back upon him. 19 Then
he shall turn his face back toward the fortresses of his own land, but he shall stumble and
fall, and shall not be found.

20 Then shall arise in his place one who shall send an exactor of tribute for the glory of
the kingdom. But within a few days he shall be broken, neither in anger nor in battle. 21 In
his place shall arise a contemptible person to whom royal majesty has not been given. He
shall come in without warning and obtain the kingdom by flatteries. 22 Armies shall be ut-
terly swept away before him and broken, even the prince of the covenant. 23 And from the
time that an alliance is made with him he shall act deceitfully, and he shall become strong
with a small people. 24 Without warning he shall come into the richest parts[e] of the prov-
ince, and he shall do what neither his fathers nor his fathers' fathers have done, scattering
among them plunder, spoil, and goods. He shall devise plans against strongholds, but only
for a time. 25 And he shall stir up his power and his heart against the king of the south
with a great army. And the king of the south shall wage war with an exceedingly great and
mighty army, but he shall not stand, for plots shall be devised against him. 26 Even those
who eat his food shall break him. His army shall be swept away, and many shall fall down
slain. 27 And as for the two kings, their hearts shall be bent on doing evil. They shall speak
lies at the same table, but to no avail, for the end is yet to be at the time appointed. 28 And
he shall return to his land with great wealth, but his heart shall be set against the holy cov-
enant. And he shall work his will and return to his own land.

29 At the time appointed he shall return and come into the south, but it shall not be
this time as it was before. 30 For ships of Kittim shall come against him, and he shall be
afraid and withdraw, and shall turn back and be enraged and take action against the holy
covenant. He shall turn back and pay attention to those who forsake the holy covenant.
31 Forces from him shall appear and profane the temple and fortress, and shall take away
the regular burnt offering. And they shall set up the abomination that makes desolate.
32 He shall seduce with flattery those who violate the covenant, but the people who know
their God shall stand firm and take action. 33 And the wise among the people shall make
many understand, though for some days they shall stumble by sword and flame, by cap-
tivity and plunder. 34 When they stumble, they shall receive a little help. And many shall
join themselves to them with flattery, 35 and some of the wise shall stumble, so that they
may be refined, purified, and made white, until the time of the end, for it still awaits the
appointed time.

36 And the king shall do as he wills. He shall exalt himself and magnify himself above
every god, and shall speak astonishing things against the God of gods. He shall prosper
till the indignation is accomplished; for what is decreed shall be done. 37 He shall pay
no attention to the gods of his fathers, or to the one beloved by women. He shall not

pay attention to any other god, for he shall magnify himself above all. [38]*He shall honor*
the god of fortresses instead of these. A god whom his fathers did not know he shall
honor with gold and silver, with precious stones and costly gifts. [39]*He shall deal with*
the strongest fortresses with the help of a foreign god. Those who acknowledge him he
shall load with honor. He shall make them rulers over many and shall divide the land
for a price.[f]

[40]*At the time of the end, the king of the south shall attack*[g] *him, but the king of the north*
shall rush upon him like a whirlwind, with chariots and horsemen, and with many ships.
And he shall come into countries and shall overflow and pass through. [41]*He shall come*
into the glorious land. And tens of thousands shall fall, but these shall be delivered out of
his hand: Edom and Moab and the main part of the Ammonites. [42]*He shall stretch out his*
hand against the countries, and the land of Egypt shall not escape. [43]*He shall become ruler*
of the treasures of gold and of silver, and all the precious things of Egypt, and the Libyans
and the Cushites shall follow in his train. [44]*But news from the east and the north shall*
alarm him, and he shall go out with great fury to destroy and devote many to destruction.
[45]*And he shall pitch his palatial tents between the sea and the glorious holy mountain. Yet*
he shall come to his end, with none to help him.

a Or *obtained* **b** Hebrew *at the end of the times* **c** Hebrew *her, or it* **d** The meaning of the Hebrew is uncertain **e** Or *among the richest men* **f** Or *land as payment* **g** Hebrew *thrust at*

OVERVIEW: Our commentators understand this chapter to detail the historical events of the Persian kingdom, the monarchy of Alexander the Great and the two kingdoms of Syria and Egypt. Moreover, we see in this chapter God's use of his prophets to comfort his people who suffer oppression and torment under godless rulers. The pollution of the temple and of the worship of God by Antiochus Epiphanes is foretold. Amid such persecution, the faithful, preserved by God, are made more constant and resolute in their faith. Our commentators spend a good deal of time discussing Antiochus and sorting out his chronology and actions. Many see a relationship between Antiochus and antichrist. Some attention is given to the identity of the king (Dan 11:36-39). Possibilities include Antiochus, antichrist, the Romans or even the pope. Daniel ends the chapter with the hope of promised deliverance. Indeed, as one commentator puts it, this final section of deliverance became an inestimable treasury and comfort to the faithful.

ARGUMENT OF THE CHAPTER. JOHANN WIGAND: This is a clear narration of future things during the second and third monarchy and what will happen by their conduct. By such things the omnipotence of God is seen. . . . The end of this revelation, that the church of God might understand, is about the happenings and changes of future things. There they might learn that among the fury and political upheaval of the world, the church is miraculously and powerfully preserved by God; to be sure, not without difficulty, that is, tribulation and affliction. For the church of God in this world dwells hospitably amid godless people, among whom they are not able not to be oppressed and tormented, and yet they are divinely preserved.

There are five parts to the chapter: (1) the destruction of the Persian monarchy; (2) the third monarchy and principally Alexander the Great; (3) the posterity of Alexander, who held the third monarchy; (4) how the Syrian and Egyptian kings especially clashed; (5) the affliction of the Jewish church, especially under

Antiochus Epiphanes. To be sure, consolation for the preservation of God's people is mixed in with these prophecies. Brief Exposition of the Prophet Daniel.[1]

Summary of the Chapter. Philipp Melanchthon: Now begins the prophecy about the kingdoms; God at the same time encourages Daniel and forewarns his descendants concerning the impending calamities. These words are a very clear testimony showing that the doctrine of the prophets is handed down from God. And because this prophecy promises deliverance, it indicates that those people who cling to the prophetic doctrine are under the protection of God. Therefore believers are strengthened, so that they do not rebel against God or abandon the profession of this doctrine. Commentary on the Prophet Daniel.[2]

Summary of Daniel 11. John Calvin: This chapter seems like a historical narrative under the form of an enigmatic description of events then future. The angel relates and places before his eyes occurrences yet to come to pass. We gather from this very clearly how God spoke through his prophets; and thus Daniel, in his prophetic character alone, is a clear proof to us of God's peculiar favor toward the Israelites. Here the angel discusses not the general state of the world but first the Persian kingdom, then the monarchy of Alexander and afterwards the two kingdoms of Syria and Egypt. From this we cleverly perceive how the whole discourse was directed to the faithful. God did not regard the welfare of other nations but wished to benefit his church, and principally to sustain the faithful under their approaching troubles. It was to assure them of God's never becoming forgetful of his covenant, and of his so moderating the convulsions then taking place throughout the world, as to be ever protecting his people by his assistance. Commentaries on Daniel.[3]

The Relationship Between Daniel 10 and Daniel 11. Andrew Willet: Is the vision in the eleventh chapter different from the previous vision in the tenth chapter? Jerome, who takes the first words of verse one to be uttered by Daniel, that he prayed for the prosperity of Darius, thinks that this vision is different from the former, for that happened in the third year of Cyrus (Dan 10:1) and this in the first of Darius. And so his opinion is that when Daniel prayed for Darius in his first year, then these things were revealed to him by the angel. And so there is in the text a sudden change of the person: for in the second verse the angel speaks, *behold, now I will show you,* whereas the former words were uttered by Daniel. . . .

But the better opinion is that this vision continues from the last chapter, which Lyra proves, because this chapter begins with a Hebrew conjunction, which shows a coherence with the former. And it may further be thus confirmed in the former chapter (Dan 5:14). The angel says, *I am come to show you what shall come to the people in the latter days.* These things are not there declared to the prophet. The things then that should befall the people of God, which the angel came to declare to the people, are those things that are expressed in this chapter.

Some do make this first verse a part of the former chapter and will have this to be the sense, as Michael helped me, so I again helped Michael (Bullinger). But it shall appear that the angel says not here that he helped or strengthened Michael but Darius rather. Sixfold Commentary upon Daniel.[4]

11:1-2a *The Angel and the Truth*

The Angel Fought for Whom? John Calvin: Interpreters explain this verse in various

[1]*Explicatio Brevis* (1571), 399. [2]*In Danielem Prophetam* (1543), 236. [3]CTS 25:268-69 (CO 19:217). [4]*Sixfold Commentary* (1610), 396-97.

ways (Dan 11:1). Some think the angel fought for the Persian king, and follow up their opinion, because he did not for the first time begin now to defend that monarchy in favor of the chosen people but had done so from the very beginning. Others refer this to Michael, as the angel declares that he introduced the assistance of Michael. But that is forced and cold. I do not hesitate to state the argument to be from the greater to the less, and we have an instance of this in a tragedy of Ovid's. I have been able to preserve you; do you ask whether I can destroy you? Thus the angel says, I have erected the Persian monarchy; I have not the slightest doubt of my present power to restrain these kings, lest they should pour forth their fury on the people. The full meaning is this, the king of the Persians is nothing and can do nothing except through me. I was God's servant in transferring the monarchy of the Medes and Chaldeans to the Persians, as well as that of the Babylonians to the Medes. God, says he, entrusted me with that office, and so I placed Darius on the throne. You now see how completely I have him in my power, and how I can prevent him from injuring my people should he be so inclined. When the angel boasts of *his standing forward to help Darius*, he claims nothing to himself but speaks as it were in the person of God. For angels have no power distinct from God's when he uses their agency and assistance. There is no reason for any inquiry whether the angel ought to use this boastful language and claim anything for himself. For he does not claim anything as really his own, but he shows himself to have been an agent in the change of dynasty when Babylon was subdued by the Medes and the empire transferred to Darius. Commentaries on Daniel.[5]

I Will Show You the Truth. Andrew Willet: The truth is only revealed in Scripture; the truth of God is first manifested unto the world in Christ, as he says, *I am the way, the truth and the life* (Jn 14:6). And this truth is revealed in Scripture, as our blessed Savior says, *Your Word is the truth* (Jn 17:17). The Scriptures of truth are committed to the church, which is called the pillar of truth (1 Tim 3:15), not because it bears up the truth, but it rather is born up by the truth. But both because the truth of God is only revealed to the church as here the angel delivers the truth of this prophecy to Daniel. And the truth is set forth and professed in the world by the church, as a light set on a pillar or a beacon raised on a mountain. Sixfold Commentary upon Daniel.[6]

Prophecy and History. John Mayer: *And the king of the south shall be strong, and one of his princes, and he shall be strong above him, and he shall have dominion,* and it *shall be a great dominion.* Having spoken of the division of Alexander's kingdom into four, here leaving two, he declares only things to come concerning the other two, with whom the Jews had to do. And it is to be noted that the angel in his predictions of things to be done many years after is so punctual, as that a historian writing things done cannot more exactly set them forth, that the fourth king from Cyrus should be so rich, that he should go against the Grecians, that from among them a more mighty king should arise, that this kingdom should be divided into four, but not of his children but strangers, and that of the four two should be most remarkable, and lastly, particular passages between these two and those in a long process of time one after another. For what does this show but that there is an omniscient and omnipotent God who rules over all the world and decrees long before how all the weighty affairs of kingdoms shall be transacted from time to time, that we may believe in him and serve him, and fear him only, and if we do so, be comforted in

[5]CTS 25:266-67 (CO 19:216-17). [6]*Sixfold Commentary* (1610), 438.

our greatest adversities, for they come not to us at the will of people but of God, who is our God and Father. Commentary upon All the Prophets.[7]

11:2b-20 *Four Kings*

The Four Kings. Martin Luther: In the eleventh chapter Daniel prophesies to his people, the Jews, almost the same prophesy as in chapter eight—about Alexander the Great, the two kingdoms, Syria and Egypt, but most of all about Antiochus (called the Noble), who will plague the Jews. However, he depicts these same things in such a way that his words also describe the Antichrist by the person of Antiochus. So really he is describing these end times of ours just before the Last Day. For all teachers agree that these prophecies about Antiochus point to the Antichrist. His words demonstrate and compel us to understand that he does not only mean Antiochus the Noble, but instead groups together Antiochus the Noble and the Antichrist, willingly obscuring his clear and understandable words.

Three kings, he says (Dan 11:2), will arise in Persia. He does not mean that Persia will only have so few kings, as the Jews think, because they have had at least ten kings. These four are chosen to arise in Persia, because they are more extraordinary than all the others. After Cyrus came Cambyses, Darius, and Xerxes—these are the four most elite kings of Persia. Of the four Xerxes was the richest. He fought against the Greeks with an innumerable army. But infamously he lost; he himself barely escaped. After that comes Alexander with his four successors, not from his family or blood. Now come the two kingdoms, Syria and Egypt, and how they quarrel and hack at one another. . . . After Alexander the kingdom of Egypt became very powerful, as Daniel (11:5) says here, as well as the kingdom of Syria, so that neither could conquer or enslave the other as they so often had tried and would have liked to have done. Preface to the Prophet Daniel.[8]

Who are the Four Kings? William Pemble: The former verse shows this was in the first year of Darius the Mede. Therefore, where it is said, "There shall stand up [yet] three kings," the sense is that from or after Darius the Mede there shall be three kings in Persia; namely, Cyrus, Cambyses, Darius Hystaspis. The fourth is plainly Xerxes, as appears by that of his great riches and his huge and mighty preparations made to invade Greece. Now since it is as clear as day that the fourth was Xerxes, the other three can be no other than Cyrus, Cambyses and Darius Hystaspis.

The only objection that can be made is of a magician named Smerdis, who took on him to be the son of Cyrus and usurped the throne after Cambyses, against whom he conspired. But the answer is that the Holy Spirit does not hold him worth the naming, and he bears no place in holy Scripture among the kings of Persia. The reason for this is either that his time was short (for before he saw seven months the nobles conspired against him and suppressed him), or that he, who was a conspirator, is rather to be called a tyrant than a king. It is out of question the Holy Spirit does pass this magician or Smerdis over. Some do take the odd months that this Smerdis usurped and add them to the time of Cambyses, and so give him somewhat a longer time of reign than I have done. So small a difference is not worth discussing. The Period of the Persian Monarchy.[9]

War Between the Kingdoms. Martin Luther: The first war arose between Antiochus II Theos and Ptolemy II Philadelphus. However, because they warred against one another for so long, they made a truce. Ptolemy II

[7] *Prophets*, 563-64. [8] WADB 11,2:30-34. [9] *Persian Monarchy* (1659), 349.

Philadelphus was an especially fine king. He enjoyed peace and every kind of art, employed numerous learned people, and had a beautiful library collected from all over the world. He even had done many good things for the Jews, magnificently adorning the temple and upholding the worship of God in Jerusalem. I even regard him as one of the righteous kings. He gave his only daughter, named Berenice, to Antiochus II Theos, so that the peace might hold even more firmly. He died soon after. However, Berenice, as the daughter of a powerful king and now as a powerful queen herself and woman of the court, strived to make her son the heir of the kingdom of Syria. But she failed. Laodice, the former queen of Antiochus II Theos, along with her two sons, Seleucus II Callinicus and Antiochus Hierax, were set against Berenice and her son as enemies, wanting themselves to inherit the kingdom instead. Laodice poisoned her husband Antiochus II Theos. After that she instructed her two sons to hound Berenice, their stepmother. They hunted her down, finally killing her and her child, along with the entire courtly retinue. This is what Daniel (11:6) here means when he says, "She will not retain the strength of her arm, as well her seed will not survive, instead she will be handed over to death with her child, her attendants, even with her lord the king, by whom she had become so mighty."

Ptolemy III Euergetes, Berenice's brother, punished and avenged such wickedness. He warred against the two brothers, Seleucus and Antiochus, hunted them down, ransacked their kingdom, and then returned home again. Soon after this, these two brothers finally perished painfully and wretchedly (as the just fruit of matricide). Daniel (11:7) here speaks of this, saying, "the king of the South will move with his army against the king of the North and will be victorious." PREFACE TO THE PROPHET DANIEL.[10]

11:21-35 *Persecution of God's People*

CORRUPTION OF GOD'S WORSHIP. JOHN CALVIN: We stated in the last lecture the seriousness of the test by which God proved the faithfulness of his people, in allowing Antiochus such unbounded liberty to pollute the temple and to abolish, for a time, all the sacrifices and services. He next set up in the midst of the temple that abomination that cast down the spirits of the pious, for that prodigy could not be witnessed without the most profound astonishment. No one could suppose it possible that God would expose his own sanctuary to such dishonor, as it was the only one that he had chosen in the whole world. It now follows, *And he shall deceive the transgressors of the covenant with blandishment, but a people knowing their God will retain it firmly and practice it.* Here Daniel more clearly expresses what he had previously said of the corruption and overthrow of God's worship, as Antiochus should enticingly win over to himself a perfidious portion of those who were nominally, at least, God's people . . .

He says then, *these should be deceived by the blandishments of Antiochus.* He doubtless offered to the priests and to others what he thought they would value most; one he set over the temple, another he deceived with vain and fallacious promises for a time, by distributing a variety of gifts among them. In this way he corrupted them all by his flatteries. To these the prophet opposes the sincere worshipers of God, and the Hebrew copula ought to be understood here as implying this contrast. He had already spoken of many as deceived by vain promises and had called them transgressors of the covenant; he now adds, *But the people who know God shall strengthen themselves and shall do it.* The angel means that the perfidy of those of whom he had spoken should not prevail with the pious to lead them into the same alliance of wickedness and to hurl them headlong into the same snares. Although such

[10]WADB 11,2:34-38.

was the perfidy of these revolters, yet *all who know God*, says he, *shall strengthen themselves*.

This passage is specially worthy of notice, as experience teaches how very few stand their ground when many fall away. The example of one often draws with it a hundred into the same rule; but the constancy of a hundred is scarcely sufficient to retain one in his position. In this case we behold the depth of our natural depravity. For we are not only moved but shaken by the very slightest breezes, and even when God sets before us a firm resting place, still we do not cease our vacillation. When an apostle sets before us the examples of the saints, he says, a cloud of witnesses is ever gazing on us, with the view of retaining us in the fear of God and in the pure confession of our faith (Heb 12:1). But that cloud vanishes too soon from our view. Meanwhile, if any trifler whom we know to be a person of no weight, and whom we have ourselves condemned—if such a one should decline even so little from the right way, we think such an example sufficient to excuse us. Wherefore I had good reason for stating how this passage lays open to us our perverse and malignant disposition. We can scarcely be attracted toward God by a multiplicity of appliances, but we are easily dragged toward the devil to our own destruction. Hence we ought diligently to meditate on this passage and continually to reflect on the prophet's language. Commentaries on Daniel.[11]

The Abomination and Idolatry. Giovanni Diodati: [*The abomination*] according to some it is the idol of the Olympic Jupiter (2 Macc 6:2), according to others an idolatrous altar erected above God's (1 Macc 1:54, 59) for which things the people refusing to consent to idolatry were destroyed and the temple and God's service made desolate.

[Dan 11:32. *By flatteries*] namely, by gifts, promises and allurements he shall draw the Jews of his side to prostitute themselves to idolatry: to draw others to it by their example. [*The people*] namely, the true believers; among whom, God's true people shall be preserved, shall show themselves constant and perseverant in his pure service. [*Do exploits*] namely, shall overcome all their great combats and temptations.

[Dan 11:33. *That understand*] namely, those whom God shall have enlightened by his Word and Spirit shall instruct and strengthen their brethren by their doctrine and example. Others understand this of a certain religious society, which was newly set up in those days, called the Asideans: that is to say, pious and holy, very understanding and zealous in the law of God (see 1 Macc 2:42; 7:13; 2 Macc 14:6).

[Dan 11:34. *They shall be*] namely, by Matthias and other Asmoneans or Maccabees (1 Macc 2:1; 2 Macc 8:1. *Many*] namely, among the Jews, who having (before) suffered themselves to be drawn to idolatry, when they see some enlargement by the means of the Maccabees, shall unite themselves to their brethren: yet without any inward piety, zeal or constancy.

[Dan 11:35. *Shall fall*] namely, many of them shall suffer martyrdom, that the trial of their faith and the purification of their hearts and works may be in this world, by the fire of afflictions, to their everlasting salvation (see Dan 12:10). [*To the time*] namely, which is appointed by God's decree, to have an end of these persecutions. Pious Annotations.[12]

True Knowledge of God. John Calvin: So here, *the people who shall know their God* means his true people—those whom he acknowledges as his elect. The angel here makes a distinction between the pious children of Abraham and the pious worshipers of God. It is worthy of careful observation that the angel assigns their knowledge of God as the cause

[11]CTS 25:322-24 (CO 19:254-56). [12]*Pious Annotations* (1651), 11:31-35.

and foundation of their constancy. How then, we may ask, does it come to pass that some few are left, when the apostates thus prostitute themselves? Because their knowledge of God shall prevail, and enable them to overcome these attacks, and bravely to repel them and to become superior to any temptations. We see, then, the source which our own fortitude is derived—the knowledge of God. This acknowledgment is no vain and cold imagination but springs from that faith that spreads its living root in our hearts. Hence it follows, we do not really acknowledge God unless we boldly contend when we are put to the test and remain firm and stable, although Satan endeavors, by various machinations, to weaken our faithfulness. And unless we persist in that firmness that is here described, it is quite clear that God has never been truly and really acknowledged by us. . . .

This instruction must now be applied to our own times. We observe in these days how many fall off from the church. Persecution sifts all those who profess to belong to Christ, and thus many are winnowed like chaff, and but a small portion remain steadfast. Their backsliding ought not to overthrow our faithfulness when they so carelessly forsake all piety, either through being enticed by the allurements of Satan or deceived by the conduct of the ungodly. Let us bear in mind the assertion of the angel, and thus the true knowledge of God will reign supreme in our hearts, and we shall still proceed in the course we have pursued. And to show how consistently the faithful progress in the teaching of the law and the gospel, he says, *they shall strengthen themselves and shall do it.* Here the word "to do" is taken in the sense of to "execute" — "exploiter," as we say in France; meaning, they shall summon their courage to discharge their duty; for the word "to do" or "to execute" is referred to the vocation of the pious; they should not be sluggish or slothful in the discharge of their duty, says the prophet, but should gather courage for these contests. And whence? from the acknowledgment of God. We observe, too, that faith is no idle feeling or cold imagination, lying suffocated in our minds, but an energizing principle. For we may say that from faith springs strength, and from strength execution, and thus we avoid all slothfulness in our calling. Commentaries on Daniel.[13]

The Purpose of Persecution. Andrew Willet: There are two ends of persecution. The one is that trial may be made of the constancy and faithfulness of the servants of God. The other to purge out that dross that is in them and to wash them white. Whereby we see that the most faithful servants of God have their blemishes, errors and imperfections, and therefore had need to be purged. Sixfold Commentary upon Daniel.[14]

God Preserves a Remnant. John Calvin: Lastly, the angel signifies how small a seed God should preserve in his church as the teachers and rulers of others, though but few in number; as Isaiah says, God shall consume his people, but that consumption should leave some remnant, and then it shall flow forth (Is 10:22). The sentiment of this passage is the same; even if many should degenerate and depart from the faith, and this spirit should extend to the whole people, yet some few should stand firm perhaps ten in a thousand—and these should be God's ministers in gathering together a new church; and thus the land that was formerly sterile should profit by this irrigation and produce new seed. *Those,* therefore, *who shall be wise among the people shall teach many.* While the angel is here predicting the future, we ought to take to ourselves this admonition: the more each of us becomes proficient in the faith, the more he ought to exert his utmost endeavors to teach his rude and

[13]CTS 25:325-26 (CO 19:256-57). [14]*Sixfold Commentary* (1610), 439.

ignorant neighbors according to this exhortation of the angel. God does not stretch forth his hand to us to lead each of us to follow his own course but to assist others and to advance their spiritual progress. We read therefore here a condemnation of the slothfulness of those on whom God has bestowed much knowledge and faith, when they fail to use the trust committed to them for the edification of their brethren. This prediction of the angel ought to influence each of us, as a law and rule, to seek the profit of his brethren according to the measure of his intelligence. . . .

In conclusion, then, the angel demonstrates how God never approves of any teachers as true and legitimate unless they deliver their message as if ready to defend it and prepared to seal it with their blood whenever it shall be necessary. We must read the two clauses together, *Those who teach many the worship of God shall fall by the sword and the flame*; meaning, they would rather fall or perish a hundred times by the sword and the flame than desist from their office of teaching. Besides, the angel here mentions the various kinds of death, for the sake of exhortation; for, had he mentioned only *the sword*, he would not have fully expressed the usefulness of this instruction. Whatever teachers God sets over his church, they are not fully proved in the discharge of their duty by overcoming a single form of temptation, but they must contend with foes on the right hand and on the left and must not allow the variety of their perils to weaken either their constancy or their fortitude. If the sword threatens them on one side, and fire on the other, if they must suffer the spoiling of their goods and banishment from home, nevertheless these teachers must persevere in their course. We observe, then, the multiplicity of conflicts here enumerated by the angel, to teach us the strength of the grace of the Spirit in supporting the teachers and rulers of the church and in preventing them from yielding to any temptations while contending even with the sword, and fire, and exile and the spoiling of their goods. Commentaries on Daniel.[15]

11:36-39 *Antiochus Epiphanes*

Saints Must Be Purged and Cleansed. John Calvin: The angel points out from the result how persecutions that seem to issue in the destruction of the church are yet profitable and salutary to the children of God, as this is the method of their being *purified, and cleansed and whitened* (Dan 11:36). But we must always remember how some defiling dregs, which require clearing out, remain in the elect, nay, even among the holy martyrs. The angel does not here treat of hypocrites or of ordinary believers but of whatever is most conspicuous and most perfect in the church, and yet asserts their need of purification. None, therefore, he concludes, possess such sanctity and purity as to prevent the remnant of some pollution that requires to be removed. Hence it becomes necessary for them to pass through the furnace and to be purified like gold and silver. This is extended to all God's martyrs.

This reminds us of the great folly of the papists, in imagining the merits of saints to be transferred to us, as if they had more than they required for themselves. Indulgences, as they call them, depend on this error, according to the following reasoning: had Peter lived to the ordinary period of human life, he would have proved faithful to the end and then would have merited the crown of the heavenly kingdom; but when he went beyond this and poured out his blood in martyrdom, some merits were superabundant; these ought not to be lost, and hence the blood of Peter and Paul profit us at this day for the remission of sins. This is the papal theology, and these miserable sophists are not ashamed of these gross blasphemies, while they vomit forth such foul sacrilege. But the angel's teaching is far different: the mar-

[15]CTS 25:328-30 (CO 19:258-60).

tyrs themselves are benefited by meeting death for their adherence to the truth, because God *purges and cleanses* and refines *and whitens them*. The angel would not have said this except some admixture of dross still defiled the purity of the saints. But this doctrine ought to be more than enough to animate us to undergo all dangers when we see ourselves stained and polluted with hidden dross; besides this, we ought certainly to determine that death would be profitable in this sense, as God will then purge us from those vices by which we are both infected and defiled. Whence the value of the repetition here; the angel does not simply say *to purge* them but adds *to cleanse and whiten them*. Whatever holiness may shine forth in the best of people, yet many stains and much defilement he concealed within them; and thus in consequence of their many failings, persecution was always useful to them. Commentaries on Daniel.[16]

The Early Years of Antiochus Epiphanes. Martin Luther: Now after the death of Philopator, Antiochus [III] the Great armed himself even more fiercely against Philopator's son, called Ptolemy [V] Epiphanes who was still a mere child around four or five years old. As it usually happens, whenever a lord must have a regent his subjects rebel against him, and so it was with Antiochus and other kings, like Philip of Greece, who all wanted to divvy up the land of the child Epiphanes. Also during this time there was great discord throughout the land. The Jews, too, defected from him to Antiochus. So, Daniel (11:13-16) here says that King Antiochus will return and that many will rise against the child Epiphanes, so that the forces of the south, that is, the troops of Epiphanes in Phoenicia and Judea, even at Jerusalem, were not able to stand. Instead Antiochus conquered all of these lands, coming even to that great land in Jerusalem. There the Jews helped him hunt down all of the troops of Epiphanes. For this, Antiochus greatly honored the Jews, granting them many gifts and great freedom.

But still he wanted to go even farther, to conquer Egypt. So Ptolomy Epiphanes appealed to the Romans, so that Antiochus had to stop abruptly and make peace with Ptolomy Epiphanes, giving him his daughter, Cleopatra. But Antiochus did not do this with good intentions, rather, as Daniel (11:17) says here, he wanted to ruin Epiphanes. Antiochus thought that through his daughter he could snatch the kingdom away from the boy. The queen and the Egyptians, however, thwarted this plan. After this Antiochus warred against the islanders in Asia (like Daniel [11:18-19] says), capturing many of them. But the Romans arrayed themselves against him, forcing him back, stripping him of this glorious cloak, in fact almost all of Asia Minor. He returned home, traveling to Persia, where he wanted to steal gold from a temple in Elymais (1 Macc 6:1-3). But the peasants resisted fiercely, striking him down with his entire army, straight to death. He remained in a foreign land, never to be found again.

Now before this, since the Romans defeated Antiochus, he had sent his son Antiochus, called the Noble who was the lowest and least esteemed of his sons, to Rome as a hostage or pledge. When he died, his son Seleucus Philopator became king, but he was a stupid man, as Daniel says here, better suited to be a thug or hangman than a king. Because he aimed for nothing noble or honest he soon died. So Antiochus the Noble secretly ran away from Rome. Although he was so despised and the kingdom was deliberately not given to him, (as Daniel [11:21] says) still he came slithering, pretending that he meant well, so that through trickery he became king. This is the last king that Daniel writes about, the "noble" and "righteous" child, who handled everything with deceits and pranks, lying and deceiving,

[16]CTS 25:336-37 (CO 19:263-64).

not as a king, but rather as a libertine rouge. His pranks were boorishly crude, and as we will see, he did not even seek any appearance of honor. Because of this wicked and depraved brat this vision (Dan 8:2-14) took place, as a comfort to the Jews whom he plagued with every kind of trouble. Preface to the Prophet Daniel.[17]

The Later Years of Antiochus Epiphanes. Martin Luther: Now just as Antiochus had deceitfully overtaken the kingdom, so he expanded it through the same craftiness. Since the king of Egypt, his sister's son named Ptolemy [VI] Philometor, was still too young, Antiochus acted as though he wanted to be a faithful regent to his nephew, occupying the cities of Syria, Phoenicia, and Judea. When the governors of Egypt demanded them back, Antiochus flatly refused to do so. Then the conflict began. Daniel (11:21-22) here says of this, that he will break over the Egyptians like a tide (that is, he will overwhelm Philometor's forces and troops), because Antiochus seized the victory.

But this prank was not enough for him, instead he planned to seize all of Egypt. So he made a treaty with Philometor's commanders, again acting as if he were doing it all for his nephew's best interest, as a "faithful" regent. With such lies (as Daniel [11:23-24] says here) he came into Egypt with only a few troops. The Egyptians opened wide every gate for this beloved uncle. Antiochus snatched the crown, placing it on his own head, making himself the king of Egypt, robbing, pillaging, and ravaging the entire land of Egypt. Just as the text says here [Dan 11:24], he did this with trickery, something that not one of his ancestors had been able to do even with force. Then he returned home.

In the meanwhile King Philometer was now grown and ready to take the kingdom, wanting to take back what was his by force. Thus, the two kings arrayed themselves against one another. But soon that "noble" child, Antiochus, saw that Philometor was too strong for him. So, he relied on his usual "virtue." With money he instigated a mutiny, so that Philometor's own people would kill him. Although many were slaughtered, still he did not conquer the land. So, he once again made peace with his nephew, eating and talking with him over a meal, saying "I would gladly visit Egypt one more time." But now no one would trust him any more. And as Daniel (11:27) says here, both kings sought the demise of the other, under the facade of peace. With numerous possessions Antiochus turned to go home again. On the way, through deceit and trickery, he entered Jerusalem, villainously ransacking the temple and the city, as 1 Maccabees (1:20-28) states and also as Daniel (11:28) says here, "His heart will be set against the holy covenant."

A little over two years later, since his lying and childish tricks would no longer help him, Antiochus dedicated himself to conquering Egypt with force, now marching to his nephew not as a regent, but as an enemy. However, Daniel (11:29) says, "he will not succeed as he did before." The Romans—who, through the will of King Philometor's father, were appointed as his regents and protectors—sent a senator, Marcus Popilius, with troops to Antiochus, commanding him to leave Egypt. However, he again wanted to make use of his old "virtue," trying to dismiss the Romans with kind words, claiming that he wanted to go take council with his friends. But with the staff in his hand Marcus Popilius made a circle in the sand around Antiochus, since he stood by the sea, and proclaimed: "This is what the Senate of Rome says: You will not leave this circle until you speak your answer, whether you will have war or peace." Disgraced, Antiochus had to retreat and return home again.

He returned again through Jerusalem,

[17]WADB 11,2:38-44.

wreaking havoc on the house of God, God's worship and God's people, since he could not direct his anger or avenge his disgrace against anyone else than against God and his kingdom. Many wicked brats among the Jews helped him and served him, until God raised up Judas Maccabeus and his brothers against him, just as it is shown above in chapter 8 and as Daniel (11:30-35) explains here in the text. PREFACE TO THE PROPHET DANIEL.[18]

ANTIOCHUS, ANTICHRIST AND THE POPE. JOHN MAYER: And now it is time to make application of all that has been said of this Antiochus to antichrist, the pope of Rome. That antichrist is here set forth is the tenet of Jerome and of all antiquity, indeed some expound it altogether of antichrist, or at the least as fulfilled in him, being but in part fulfilled in Antiochus. For these words, says Lyra, *he shall not regard the God of his fathers, or any God* (Dan 11:37), cannot apply to Antiochus, since that he was an idolater as well as his fathers, and now, when he put down all other rites about other gods, yet he was a worshiper of Jupiter. But by that which has been already said we may see that it is not inaptly applied to Antiochus, because that however it be said, *he shall not regard any god*, yet it is added for further explication, *he shall honor a god with gold and precious stones*, whereby we are given to understand that by any god is not meant any god at all, but any god used to be worshiped and honored by his ancestors or countrymen. Wherefore it is to be held that the things here prophesied were all fulfilled in Antiochus, but in speaking thus of him the Spirit of God had a further aim, in him and the abominations committed by him, to set forth the antichrist, and that not one yet to come, being one particular person, who should reign three years and a half, 1260 days, as has been generally held of old, but the pope of Rome being, as it were, one continued antichrist in each pope succeeding his predecessor for so many years, as the days before spoken of. And this may well be made undeniably to appear, if we begin with Antiochus and from there proceed throughout all that is prophesied of him; and lay the pope's beginning and proceedings hereunto in his horrible pride and ambition, and trampling underfoot the laws and ordinances of God under his feet and setting up his own on pain of death to be obeyed and followed by all people. . . .

Bellarmine from that which is said [Dan 11:36-37] begins arguments to prove that the pope was not prefigured by Antiochus and therefore is not antichrist, for he is well known to be a worshiper of God the Father, God the Son and God the Holy Spirit, here called the God of Gods, and the God of his fathers. Answer: He does indeed in show, but in truth he denies him and exalts himself above him, because he takes on him above the holy Word of God, that being thus preferred that comes from him. COMMENTARY UPON ALL THE PROPHETS.[19]

NOT ABOUT ANTIOCHUS OR ANTICHRIST. JOHN CALVIN: This passage is very obscure (Dan 11:36-39) and has consequently been explained in very opposite ways by interpreters. And whatever is obscure is usually doubtful, and there would be little utility and no termination if I were to narrate the opinions of them all. I shall therefore follow another method, and omitting all superfluous labor, I shall simply inquire about the angel's meaning. I must, however, refer briefly to opinions received by the consent of the majority, because they occupy the minds of many and thus close the door to the correct interpretation. The Jews, for instance, are not agreed among themselves, and their difference of opinion only serves to produce and perpetuate darkness rather than to diffuse the clearness of light. Some explain it of Antiochus, and oth-

[18]WADB 11,2:44-48. [19]*Prophets*, 573, 577.

ers of the Romans, but in a manner different from that which I shall afterwards state. The Christian expositors present much variety, but the greater number incline toward antichrist as fulfilling the prophecy. Others, again, use greater moderation by supposing antichrist to be here obliquely hinted at, while they do not exclude Antiochus as the type and image of antichrist. This last opinion has great probability, but I do not approve of it and can easily refute it. Antiochus did not long survive the pollution of the temple, and then the following events by no means suit the occurrences of this time. Nor can his sons be fairly substituted in his place, and hence we must pass on to some other king, distinct from Antiochus and his heirs. As I have already stated, some of the rabbis explain this of the Romans, but without judgment, for they first apply the passage to Vespasian, and Titus his son, and then extend it to the present times, which is utterly without reason, as they chatter foolishly, according to their usual custom. Those who explain it of antichrist have some color of reason for their view, but there is no soundness in their conclusion, and we shall perceive this better in the progress of our exposition. We must now discover what king the angel here designates. First of all, I apply it entirely to the Roman Empire, but I do not consider it to begin at the reign of the Caesars, for this would be unsuitable and out of date, as we shall see. . . .

We lay this down at once. The angel did not prophesy of Antiochus or any single monarch but of a new empire, meaning the Roman. We have the reason at hand why the angel passes directly from Antiochus to the Romans. God desired to support the spirits of the pious, lest they should be overwhelmed by the number and weight of the massacres that awaited them and the whole church even to the advent of Christ. It was not sufficient to predict the occurrences under the tyranny of Antiochus; for after his time, the Jewish religion was more and more injured, not only by foreign enemies but by their own priesthood. Nothing remained unpolluted, since their avarice and ambition had arrived at such a pitch that they trod underfoot the whole glory of God and the law itself. The faithful required to be fortified against such numerous temptations until Christ came, and then God renewed the condition of his church. The time, therefore, that intervened between the Maccabees and the manifestation of Christ ought not to be omitted. The reason is now clear enough why the angel passes at once from Antiochus to the Romans. . . .

Let us remember, then, that the angel is not now speaking of Antiochus, nor does he make a leap forward to antichrist, as some think, but he means a perpetual series. Thus the faithful would be prepared for all assaults that might be made on their faith, if this rampart had not been interposed. Commentaries on Daniel.[20]

Antiochus a Warning and an Example. John Mayer: Lastly, in this whole prophecy touching Antiochus men like him are pointed at, and their destiny is read; if any man by flattery and deceitful means comes to power, or having attained power is insatiable through the ambitiousness of his mind, or abuses his power against the servants of God, the worship or house of God, to cruelty or rapine, or to the altering of good laws grounded on the law of God, or to be lifted up in pride, let him think that he is in Antiochus threatened with a miserable end. His rise out of the dust to sit with princes, his good success in all his undertakings, and the increase of his wealth and dominion, if he is such a one, are no arguments of God's favor toward him but a lifting of him up, as it were, for a time on high, that he might take the greater fall; the fatting of him up, that his body being filled with ill humors may break out into diseases most tormenting and incurable, and the using of him but as a rod in

[20]CTS 25:338-40, 344 (CO 19:265-66, 269).

his indignation to chastise his people provoking him to anger, being afterwards to be cast into the fire. The time shall certainly come when the good success of such shall be turned into evil, and joy for overcoming into sorrow for being overcome, and his greater forces being shamefully beaten and put to flight before lesser. He who is wise will consider this and not argue from his success in an unwarranted way time after time, that his cause is good, and it shall never happen otherwise to him, but measure the goodness of his cause by the true rule of the Word, which only can justify their actions, and not either their good intentions or success in their undertakings. COMMENTARY UPON ALL THE PROPHETS.[21]

PRIDE AND HUMILITY. JOHN CALVIN: *And he shall not pay attention to other gods, because he shall magnify himself against them all* (Dan 11:37). The cause is here assigned why this king should be a gross despiser of all deities, and fierce and barbarous against all mortals, *because he should magnify himself above them all.* That pride so blinded the Romans as to cause them to forget both piety and humanity; and so this intolerable self-confidence of theirs was the reason why they paid no honor to any deity and trampled all mortals under foot. Humility is certainly the beginning of all true piety; and this seed of religion is implanted in the heart of people, causing them whether they will or not to acknowledge some deity. But the Romans were so puffed up by self-consequence as to exalt themselves above every object of adoration and to treat all religions with contemptuous scorn; and in thus despising all celestial beings, they necessarily looked down on all humankind, which was literally and notoriously the fact. COMMENTARIES ON DANIEL.[22]

11:40-45 *Deliverance*

HOPE OF PROMISED DELIVERANCE. JOHN CALVIN: *They shall come,* then, *into the desirable land, and many regions shall fall* (Dan 11:41), meaning no hope should remain for the Jews after the arrival of the Romans, as victory was already prepared to their hand. The angel's setting before the faithful this material for despair was not likely to induce confidence and comfort, but, as they were aware of these divine predictions, they knew also that the remedy was prepared by the same God who had admonished them by means of the angel. It was in his power to save his church from a hundred deaths. This prophecy became an inestimable treasury, inspiring the faithful with the hope of the promised deliverance. The angel will afterwards add the promise intended to support and strengthen and revive their drooping spirits. But he here announces that God's aid should not immediately appear, because he would give the Romans full permission to exercise a cruel sway, tyranny and robbery throughout the whole of Asia and the east. COMMENTARIES ON DANIEL.[23]

[21] *Prophets*, 582. [22] CTS 25:350-51 (CO 19:274). [23] CTS 25:261-62 (CO 19:281).

12:1-13 The End Times

1“At that time shall arise Michael, the great prince who has charge of your people. And there shall be a time of trouble, such as never has been since there was a nation till that time. But at that time your people shall be delivered, everyone whose name shall be found written in the book. 2And many of those who sleep in the dust of the earth shall awake, some to everlasting life, and some to shame and everlasting contempt. 3And those who are wise shall shine like the brightness of the sky above;[a] *and those who turn many to righteousness, like the stars forever and ever. 4But you, Daniel, shut up the words and seal the book, until the time of the end. Many shall run to and fro, and knowledge shall increase.”*

5Then I, Daniel, looked, and behold, two others stood, one on this bank of the stream and one on that bank of the stream. 6And someone said to the man clothed in linen, who was above the waters of the stream,[b] *“How long shall it be till the end of these wonders?” 7And I heard the man clothed in linen, who was above the waters of the stream; he raised his right hand and his left hand toward heaven and swore by him who lives forever that it would be for a time, times, and half a time, and that when the shattering of the power of the holy people comes to an end all these things would be finished. 8I heard, but I did not understand. Then I said, “O my lord, what shall be the outcome of these things?” 9He said, “Go your way, Daniel, for the words are shut up and sealed until the time of the end. 10Many shall purify themselves and make themselves white and be refined, but the wicked shall act wickedly. And none of the wicked shall understand, but those who are wise shall understand. 11And from the time that the regular burnt offering is taken away and the abomination that makes desolate is set up, there shall be 1,290 days. 12Blessed is he who waits and arrives at the 1,335 days. 13But go your way till the end. And you shall rest and shall stand in your allotted place at the end of the days.”*

a Hebrew *the expanse;* compare Genesis 1:6-8 **b** Or *who was upstream;* also verse 7

Overview: This final chapter announces the return of Michael, the deliverance of the saints and the resurrection of the dead. Some will be raised to everlasting life and some to everlasting contempt. Our commentators return to the question of Michael's identity. All are agreed that Michael is here the true Son of God, Jesus Christ, by the description of his person (equal to God), his office (he is the great prince) and his benefit (he protects his people from Satan and his ministers). The consolations of this chapter are especially emphasized. Our commentators note God's promised preservation and protection of his people, the gathering of his people by the pure doctrine of the gospel and their salvation and final resurrection.

A number of issues are discussed with Daniel's final vision. Two angels appear and inquire of the man clothed in linen. The man clothed in linen is the Son of God, who is set forth as both God and man. Moreover, agreement is seen between Daniel and John's Revelation. Because of the obscurity of what was here revealed, Daniel heard without understanding and seeks clarification from the Lord, asking as the angel before him had. Exactly what Daniel did not understand is debated by our commentators. A final comment is made about the desolation of the temple and its final destruction. Our authors bring their commentaries to a close by reflecting on the final words to Daniel that he stand firm in his allotted place, which is in Christ. Luther closes our commentary by commending the book of Daniel to all Christians, who will here find encouragement, joy and strength.

Summary of the Chapter. John Mayer: After the prophecy touching Antiochus Epiphanes, and his rage against the people of God and miserable end, to which God in his just judgment brought him therefore, here follows an amplification of the same for the arming of the servants of God with patience to bear their sufferings under him and to comfort them by declaring Michael their prince, his victory over the devil and his limbs and firstborn Antiochus and their deliverance, he being destroyed, and joyful resurrection to follow to everlasting glory. Commentary upon All the Prophets.[1]

12:1 *End Times and the Return of Michael*

The End Times. Johann Wigand: This chapter concerns the end time of this world and the judgment of the Son of God over all the living and the dead. . . . Consolation is added to lift up and strengthen the church of Christ, lest it is disheartened by those fierce tempests and confused by the end times, during which Antiochus will disturb consciences and believers will again be persecuted to death, and, in addition to this, many places will be ravaged by the mad Turks, and their empire will be harsher and sadder. The godlessness, rebellion, extravagance, greed and other evils of people will increase. For Christ says that those living at the end of the world will be like those in the days of Noah and Lot (Lk 17:27-30). Brief Exposition of the Prophet Daniel.[2]

In That Time. Andrew Willet: 1. Some refer this time to the last time of the world after that great antichrist shall have raged against the church of Christ, which shall continue three years and a half (Lyra, with other writers of that side). But we hold that to be a dream that any such singular antichrist shall come in the end of the world.

2. Bullinger understands it of the coming of Christ to judgment when there shall be such great tribulation as never was in the world before. This may seem like an argument because afterward mention is made of the resurrection (Dan 12:2). But that is added as a consolation. They who were not temporally delivered in those troublesome times yet should be sure to rise to life everlasting.

3. Some do expound this prophecy of the persecution in the last times under the Turk (Melanchthon) and the Roman antichrist (Osiander).

4. Calvin refers it to the time of Christ's coming in the flesh.

5. Junius in his commentary interprets it of all the time of the gospel, the beginning of which is in his first coming, and the end of his second.

6. But it is most properly referred to that time when Antiochus left half his army with Lysias while he went to Elymais in Persia, for about the same time did Judas Maccabeus, by the assistance of the great prince of the church, Michael, which is Christ Jesus, recover Jeru-

[1]*Prophets*, 582-83. [2]*Explicatio Brevis* (1571), 425, 443.

salem and purge the temple, which had been defiled (2 Macc 10). SIXFOLD COMMENTARY UPON DANIEL.[3]

THE RETURN OF MICHAEL, THE SON OF GOD. JOHANNES OECOLAMPADIUS: *And in that time Michael shall arise* (Dan 12:1). The Lord himself will judge on behalf of the people of God in that most perilous time. Although the Lord on that day will be surrounded with the service of angels, nevertheless the Lord himself will be the one who delivers his own people, and for this reason the Lord is Michael, the great Prince, who shall arise to do battle for the children of his people. I know that others belonging to the synagogue refer to the angel prince differently, but the way I think is supported by Saint John, who in Revelation 19 says the one who does battle for his people is seated on a white horse, who is righteous, faithful and true, judges the orphans, whose clothes are dipped in blood (as is alluded to in the words of Isaiah 63) and his troops are on white horses. Finally, from his mouth comes forth a sword sharp on both sides, by which he strikes down the nations and rules with a rod of iron. Written on his thigh and robe is King of kings and Lord of lords, and moreover his name is Word of God. . . . John harmonizes well what is said here in Daniel about the great prince with his King of kings. According to the meaning of the name Michael in Hebrew, "Who is like God," we are lead beautifully to Christ. Again that John understood this fact in Revelation when he writes about the great battle in heaven between Michael and his angels with the dragon is further significant. For there the devil was cast down from heaven to earth, and, as it says in the passage from Revelation 19, into a lake of fire. COMMENTARY ON DANIEL.[4]

MICHAEL, THE SON OF GOD. GIOVANNI DIODATI: [Dan 12:1. *At that time*] namely, after the destruction of all the foresaid monarchies (see Dan 2:44). [*Michael*] namely, the Son of God, shall appear in the flesh and by God his Father be established everlasting King of his church (Dan 10:13, 21; Josh 5:14-15). [*Which stands*] namely, who is their protector against all their enemies (Ps 54:4). [*A time*] this seems to have a relation to the extreme calamities that the Jews suffered under the Romans, after Christ's ascent into heaven (Mt 24:21). [*Your people*] namely, God shall deliver his elect out of the general reprobation, and extermination of the Jewish nation (see Mt 24:22; Rom 9:27, 29). [*In the book*] namely, of eternal life (Ps 69:28; Lk 10:20; Phil 4:3; Rev 3:5; 13:8).

[Dan 12:2. *Many of them*] The angel goes on to the accomplishment of Christ's kingdom and the eternal salvation of the church, at the last resurrection, which will be joined with the final destruction of its enemies. [*That sleep*] a Scripture term, to show the immortality of the soul and repose of believers after the death of the body, with the certainty of the resurrection. [*To shame*] See Isaiah 66:24; Romans 9:21.

[Dan 12:3. *That be wise*] Namely, the true believers, who in this life are enlightened by the Holy Spirit in faith, shall enjoy the light of glory in the kingdom of heaven. He alludes to the understanding people, of which he had spoken in the time of Antiochus (Dan 11:33, 35). [*That turn many*] namely, the faithful ministers of the gospel, which being received by a lively faith is the only means to be justified before God (Rom 1:16-17) and to be sanctified in newness of life (1 Tim 4:16; Jas 5:19-20). [*As the stars*] See 1 Corinthians 15:41.

[Dan 12:4. *Shut up*] The use and clear understanding of these prophecies is not for this present time (Dan 12:9) but for the times of their fulfillment, which is appointed by God. [*Shall run to and fro*] namely, shall endeavor to seek out these prophecies to be instructed,

[3]*Sixfold Commentary* (1610), 467. [4]*In Danielem prophetam libri duo* (1553), 161.

comforted and strengthened. [*Knowledge*] that is to say, God by his Spirit, and the events shall give full knowledge of these things, which are as yet but obscurely foretold (see Is 29:18; Jer 23:20). PIOUS ANNOTATIONS.[5]

THE RETURN OF MICHAEL AND OUR CONSOLATION. JOHANN WIGAND: *And in that time* (Dan 12:1). Consolation, and this is especially for all present circumstances, cares, protection and liberation by Michael, the great prince, that is, the very Son of God about whom mention has already been made in Daniel 10. Christ explains and makes clear these things: Behold, he says, I am with you to the end of the age (Mt 28:20). Again, I will not leave you as orphans (Jn 14:18). What could be said more sweetly than that Jesus Christ, the Son of God and Son of Man, our Savior, does not wish to abandon us, wishes to attach himself to us in a friendly manner and wishes to protect us against all danger and adversity? If God is for us, says Paul, who can be against us (Rom 8:31)? . . . This Michael is the one who is omnipotent, who conquers the world and its ruler, who crushes the head of the serpent, who holds power over this world and the one to come. We are kept safe by the Lord who is near us and protects us, and although we die, we will live and reign with him. BRIEF EXPOSITION OF THE PROPHET DANIEL.[6]

MICHAEL THE GREAT PRINCE. JOHANN WIGAND: *The great prince* (Dan 12:1). In Isaiah 9 Jesus Christ is called the Prince of peace, who here is called the great prince. He is the prince because all are subject under his feet (Ps 8:6). There are two reasons why he is rightly called prince. First, by reason of creation, because all things are created through him. Why, therefore, is he not rightly named the prince of all things? Second, by reason of merit, because he conquers the world and subjects it, along with its ruler, the devil, to himself. And so he is rightly called prince. In Revelation 1, he is said to be the prince of the kings of the earth.

He is "great"—indeed more accurately he is called the greatest and most righteous prince—because God is omnipotent, the author and governor of the heavens and earth, who made and makes all things, and whatever else he wishes. BRIEF EXPOSITION OF THE PROPHET DANIEL.[7]

MICHAEL. ANDREW WILLET: Here are three things concerning Christ:

1. His person; he is called Michael, that is, as God, one equal to God, a distinct person from the Father but of the same essence, power, eternity, who is the brightness of his glory and the engraved form of his person (Heb 1:3).

2. His office is described; he is the great prince: the government is on his shoulder (Is 9:6); the Lord of lords and the King of kings (Rev 17:14); the mighty protector and defender of his church.

3. The benefit that we have is this—this Michael stands for his people to defend them from the rage of Satan and of his ministers. Our blessed Savior says, I give to them eternal life, and they shall never perish, neither shall any pluck them out of my hand (Jn 10:28). SIXFOLD COMMENTARY UPON DANIEL.[8]

A TIME OF ANGUISH. JOHANN WIGAND: *A time of trouble* (Dan 12:1). Various tribulations. Truly this is a most splendid name to be called the people of God, the church of Christ, the children of God and heirs of eternal life. . . . Here God himself foretells for us through the angel far off and serious afflictions, disturbances, hardships and suffering, which will not be brought to an end until the coming of Christ in judgment, although a certain liberation and alleviation of such things is repeatedly granted by the mercy of this Michael, lest

[5]*Pious Annotations* (1651), 12:1-4. [6]*Explicatio Brevis* (1571), 443-44. [7]*Explicatio Brevis* (1571), 445. [8]*Sixfold Commentary* (1610), 483.

the seed of the saints be entirely extinguished on earth, and in order that some propagation of heavenly doctrine continue. Thus, the very Son of God, made man for us, sings forth: You will be hated by all people because of my name (Mt 10:22); I send you forth as sheep in the midst of wolves (Mt 10:16); If they persecuted me, they will persecute you (Jn 15:20); Whoever wishes to follow me must take up his cross (Mt 16:24). And Paul cries out, All who wish to lead a godly life in Christ Jesus will suffer persecution (2 Tim 3:12). Brief Exposition of the Prophet Daniel.[9]

God's Preservation of His Church. John Calvin: The angel no longer relates future occurrences specially but proclaims God to be in general the guardian of his church, so as to preserve it wonderfully amid many difficulties and dreadful commotions, as well as in the profound darkness of disaster and death. This is the meaning of this sentence. This verse consists of two parts: the first relates to that most wretched period that should be full of various and almost numberless calamities; and the second assures us of God's never-failing protection and preservation of his church by his own innate power. In this second part the promise is restricted to the elect, and thus a third clause may be distinguished, but it is only an addition to the second just mentioned. At the close of the verse, the angel presents us with a definition of the church, as many professed to be God's people who were not really so. He says, *Michael, the prince of the people, should stand up* (Dan 12:1). Then he states the reason, *The calamities of that period should be such as were never witnessed from the beginning of the world.* As he addresses Daniel, he says, *sons of your people*; for he was one of the sons of Abraham, and the nation from which Daniel sprang was in that sense his. From this it follows that the calamities of which he will by and by treat belong to the true church, and not to the profane nations. The singular aid of Michael would not have been needed unless the church had been oppressed with the most disastrous distresses. We perceive, then, the angel's meaning to be according to my explanation. The church should be subject to most numerous and grievous calamities until the advent of Christ, but yet it should feel God's propitious disposition, ensuring its own safety under his aid and protection.

By Michael many agree in understanding Christ as the head of the church. But if it seems better to understand Michael as the archangel, this sense will prove suitable, for under Christ as the head, angels are the guardians of the church. Whichever is the true meaning, God was the preserver of his church by the hand of his only-begotten Son, and because the angels are under the government of Christ, he might entrust this duty to Michael. Commentaries on Daniel.[10]

12:2-4 *Salvation and Resurrection*

The End of the World and Consolations for the Faithful. Philipp Melanchthon: There are four consolations handed down in this place that ought always to be kept in mind by all believers.

The first is that the church will not be completely destroyed but shall endure amid trials. For that reason he says, "The wise shall make many understand" (Dan 11:33). Here and in other testimonies is to be understood concerning the perpetual preservation of the church. Similarly Christ says, "I am with you always unto the end of the age" (Mt 28:20). And in Isaiah, " 'This is my covenant with them,' says the Lord. 'My Spirit that is on you, and my words that I have put in your mouth shall not depart out of your mouth or out of the mouth of your offspring,' says the Lord, 'from this time forth and forevermore' " (Is 59:21). This is a brilliant description of the church . . . in

[9]*Explicatio Brevis* (1571), 447. [10]CTS 25:367-68 (CO 19:286).

which the voice of the gospel is heard and the Holy Spirit directs hearts.

The second consolation that is found here concerns the future members of the church, who, wherever they are found, are surrounded by the pure doctrine of the gospel. For, as he here says, there will be a scattering of the people. Under the Turkish kingdom, under other kings and popes hostile to the pure doctrine of the gospel, here and there believers will be scattered. These people hold to this consolation that the church is not bound to a political state, but all people, wherever they might be, who call on God by faith, truly acknowledge Christ and flee from idolatry are members of the church of God. By thought, will and confession they are joined with other members. They demonstrate this: "My sheep hear my voice" (Jn 10:27). Again, "If you abide in me, and my word abides in you, ask whatever you wish and it shall be for you" (Jn 15:7). Again, "Wherever two or three are gathered in my name, I am in the midst of them" (Mt 18:20). These Scriptures have been passed down so that the believers scattered everywhere would have consolation, thinking neither that the church is political nor bound to one state but rather to the voice of the gospel and the true invocation of God.

The third consolation is that when the church endures persecution it is protected by the Son of God. Here in this text it is said, "At that time shall arise Michael, the great prince, who protects the children of your people." By this word all believers are confirmed, whom Christ himself impresses on them, saying, "I am with you to the end of the age." Amid such scattering, amid such hardship, believers are thought to be deserted by God. . . . Although the godless think these people to be neglected by God, nevertheless it is certain that they are brought relief and defended by the Son of God. . . . As he says, "I will not leave you as orphans" (Jn 14:18).

The fourth consolation is (which here also the angel relates) that hardship will not continue forever. Let us often speak about this hope that believers are promised a glorious deliverance and eternal joy. The godless are warned with an eternal punishment. Here Daniel says, "Many will be raised from the dust of the earth, some to eternal glory, some to neverending torment." Commentary on the Prophet Daniel.[11]

Final Day of Resurrection. John Calvin: The angel seems here to mark a transition from the commencement of the preaching of the gospel to the final day of the resurrection, without sufficient occasion for it. For why does he pass over the intermediate time during which many events might be the subject of prophecy? He unites these two subjects very fitly and properly, connecting the salvation of the church with the final resurrection and with the second coming of Christ. Wherever we may look around us, we never meet with any source of salvation on earth. The angel announces the salvation of all the elect. They are most miserably oppressed on all sides, and wherever they turn their eyes, they perceive nothing but confusion. Hence the hope of the promised salvation could not be conceived by people before the elect raise their minds to the second coming of Christ. It is just as if the angel had said, God will be the constant preserver of his church, even to the end; but the manner in which he will preserve it must not be taken in a carnal sense, as the church will be like a dead body until it shall rise again. . . .

Meanwhile it is necessary to add this second point; as long as we fix our eyes only on this present state of things and dwell on what the world offers us, we shall always be like the dead. And why so? Our life ought to be hid with Christ in God. Our salvation is secure, but we still hope for it, as Paul says in another passage (Rom 8:23-24). What is hoped

[11] *In Danielem Prophetam* (1543), 367-72.

for is not seen, says he. This shows us how completely seasonable is the transition from this doctrine respecting God's elect to the last advent of Christ. Commentary of Daniel.[12]

Turn Many to Righteousness. John Mayer: *And they that be wise shall shine as the brightness of the firmament, and they that turn many to righteousness as the stars.* Here it is showed in what a glorious estate the elect shall be in the life to come, how greatly so ever they be abased in this life, and in saying *they that turn many,* he alludes to Daniel 11:33, *they that understand shall instruct many,* for who are the wise who turn others but those who understand and instruct many? And who are they, but such as Mattathias and Judas Maccabeus and his brethren; who taught the law of God both in doctrine and life, abhorring themselves from doing contrary, indeed being leaders to others in suffering for the truth, as Daniel 11:33 where after that he had spoken of the intelligent instructing many, he says, yet they were slain by the sword and flame. Wherefore here is showed in what a high degree of glory the faithful ministers of the Word shall be that stand to their own doctrine, which they received from God, to the death for the encouragement of us all against the malignity and contempt of the wicked world, that neither for fear of dangers nor hope of reward we may ever go from this our duty but persist in it to our lives' end. And this is a ground of that tenet touching the degrees of heavenly glory. But when the wise and such as turn others are spoken of, the faithful of any calling are not excluded from having a part in this glory, but only more eminency of glory is promised to instructors and converters, for *turning many to righteousness,* it is *justifying many or making many just,* which is done when by the teaching and examples of faithful pastors many are converted, for in the instant one is converted he is justified, and the preacher being the instrument of this is said to justify, as Saint Paul tells Timothy, that by continuing in doctrine, exhortation and prayer, he shall both save himself and those who hear him, for properly God only justifies by forgiving sins, a person only instrumentally when by his preaching a sinner is converted, and by virtue of the office committed to him, he is absolved from his sins. Commentary upon All the Prophets.[13]

Ministers of Justification. John Calvin: *And those who shall justify many* shall be *like stars,* says he (Dan 12:3). He repeats the same thing in other words, and now speaks of *stars,* having formerly used the phrase *the brightness of the firmament,* in the same sense; and instead of "those who are endued with understanding," he says *those who shall have justified.* Without doubt, the angel here especially denotes the teachers of the truth, but in my opinion he embraces also all the pious worshipers of God. Not one of God's children ought to confine their attention privately to themselves, but as far as possible, everyone ought to interest himself in the welfare of his brethren. God has deposited the teaching of his salvation with us, not for the purpose of our privately keeping it to ourselves but of our pointing out the way of salvation to all humankind. This, therefore, is the common duty of the children of God—to promote the salvation of their brethren. By this word *justifying,* the angel means not that it is in the power of one person to justify another, but the property of God is here transferred to his ministers. Meanwhile, we are as clearly justified by any teaching that brings faith within our reach, as we are justified by the faith that springs from the teaching. Why is our justification ever ascribed to faith? Because our faith directs us to Christ in whom is the complete perfection of justification, and thus our justification may be ascribed equally to the faith taught and the doctrine that teaches it. And those who bring

[12]CTS 25:373-74 (CO 19:290). [13]*Prophets,* 584-85.

before us this teaching are the ministers of our justification. The assertion of the angel, in other words, is this: the children of God, who being devoted entirely to God and ruled by the spirit of prudence, point out the way of life to others, shall not only be saved themselves but shall possess surpassing glory far beyond anything that exists in this world. This is the complete explanation. Commentaries on Daniel.[14]

The Gospel Turns Many to Righteousness. Andrew Willet: This philosophy cannot convert people to righteousness. For as the stars do somewhat brighten the night, but they cannot expel darkness, so philosophy may give some light to the understanding, but it cannot utterly chase away ignorance or give true knowledge. It is the light of the gospel that chases away darkness, as the apostle says: "The night is past, the day is come" (Rom 13:12). And Christ only has the words of the eternal life (Jn 6:68). Sixfold Commentary upon Daniel.[15]

12:5 *Daniel's Vision*

Angels Appearing as Men. John Calvin: When he says *he beheld* (Dan 12:5), he commends to our notice the certainty of the vision. Unless he had been attentive and had applied his mind seriously to these mysteries, his narrative would have failed to produce confidence. But as his mind was completely calm, and he was desirous of receiving the instruction conveyed by God through his angel, not the slightest doubt can be thrown on what he so faithfully delivers to us. He speaks of angels as if they were men, for the reason previously assigned. He does not imply their being really men but uses that expression in consequence of their outward appearance, for as they had a human face, they were called men. I do not assert their bodies to be merely imaginary, nor will I say Daniel saw only special forms and human shapes, for God might have clothed his angels in real bodies for the time, and yet they would not on that account become men. For Christ took on him our flesh and was truly man, while he was God manifest in flesh (1 Tim 3:16). But this is not true of angels, who received only a temporary body while performing the duties of their office. Commentaries on Daniel.[16]

Two Angels and the Son of God. John Mayer: To this point has been the consolation of the faithful against all their sufferings by that cruel tyrant Antiochus Epiphanes in respect of the happy issue of their grievous sufferings. Now because an appointed time and the time of the end had been spoken of, but this end was yet unknown, two angels are brought in inquiring of the man clothed in linen, spoken of in Daniel 10:3, how long it should be to the end of these wonders. He answered by swearing for further confirmation, lifting up his right hand and his left to heaven, *that it should be for a time, times and a part; when he shall have accomplished to scatter the power of the holy people, all these things shall be fulfilled.* The angels appear and are heard to enquire of the Son of God, to show their solicitude for the good of the faithful and their deliverance out of danger, as being ministering spirits sent out for their good. And whereas commonly in swearing by him that lives forever the right hand only is lifted up, he now lifts up both his right hand and his left, because two angels stood one on the one side of the river and the other on the other, as having respect to them both together from the place where he stood, which was on the waters, arguing his power over peoples set forth often by waters; see the like, Revelation 10:5-6. Commentary upon All the Prophets.[17]

[14]CTS 25:376-77 (CO 19:292). [15]*Sixfold Commentary* (1610), 484. [16]CTS 25:381 (CO 19:295). [17]*Prophets*, 585-86.

12:6-7 *The Man Clothed in Linen*

The Man Clothed in Linen. John Calvin: We know there is but one teacher of people and angels—the Son of God, who is eternal wisdom and truth. This passage may be referred to Christ, but as I cannot make any positive assertion, I am content with the simple statement already made. Commentaries on Daniel.[18]

The High Priest in Linen. Andrew Willet: Here first the person of the Son of God is set forth, being both God and man. This appearing in human form was a prelude and foreshowing of his incarnation and assuming of our flesh. For his dignity, he is the Word of his Father, from him all the elect, both angels and people, receive their illumination and knowledge, *for in him are hid all the treasures of wisdom and knowledge* (Col 2:3). For his office, he is our high priest, which is signified by his linen garments. For his authority, he has rule and power over all nations and therefore he stands on the waters, which signify the people. His mercy also and love appear, being ready to declare to the angels the thing that they desired. Sixfold Commentary upon Daniel.[19]

Daniel and John Agree. Johannes Oecolampadius: *And I heard a man clothed in linen.* This verse is also in John's Revelation. In the tenth chapter of Revelation, he says, "The angel whom I saw standing on the sea and on the land raised his hand to heaven, and the things that are therein, and the earth, and the things that are therein, and the sea, and the things that are therein, because there is time no longer. But in the days of the voice of the seventh Angel, when he shall begin to sound the trumpet, the mystery of God shall be completed, just as he has declared to his servants the prophets" (Rev 10:5-7). Whoever does not here see that John calls on Daniel as a witness understands nothing. There is nothing opposed in what is said. While Daniel says "standing on the sea," John says "on the land and sea." Daniel says "raised his right and left hand toward heaven." John simply says "he raised his hand to heaven." For here the greater power of Christ is shown because he fills all things and is the Lord of heaven, earth and sea. Indeed, raising the hand to heaven does not indicate a vow of obedience, as is most often understood, but it is evidence of power. John confirms this by an oath, swearing by means of the living God who created the heavens, earth, sea, and all that is in it. Thus you see that he swears by himself, whose hands extend beyond the heavens and whose feet are above the earth and sea, and he reveals himself to be Lord of them. For these reasons, there is no difference in the oath. Commentary on Daniel.[20]

12:8-9 *Hearing Without Understanding*

Daniel Heard Without Understanding. John Calvin: Now Daniel begins to ask questions in accordance with the angel's example. He had first heard one angel inquiring of the other; he next summons up courage, and becomes desirous of information and asks what should be the end or issue? He says, *he heard without understanding* (Dan 12:8). By the word *hearing*, he bears witness to the absence of ignorance, slothfulness or contempt. Many depart without any perception of a subject, although it may be very well explained, because they were not attentive to it. But here the prophet asserts that he heard; implying it would be no fault of his diligence if he did not understand, because he was desirous of learning and had exerted all his powers, as we formerly intimated, and yet he confesses *he did not understand*. Daniel does not mean to profess utter stupidity but restricts his igno-

[18]CTS 25:382 (CO 19:296). [19]*Sixfold Commentary* (1610), 484. [20]*In Danielem prophetam libri duo* (1553), 164.

rance to the subject of this interrogation. Of what then was Daniel ignorant? Of the final issue. He could not attain to the meaning of these predictions, which were so extremely obscure, and this was needful to their full and thorough comprehension. It is quite clear that God never utters his word without expecting fruit; as it is said in Isaiah, I have not spoken unintelligibly, nor have I said to the seed of Jacob, seek me in vain (Is 45:19). God was unwilling to leave his prophet in this perplexity of hearing without understanding, but we are aware of distinct degrees of proficiency in the school of God. Again, sufficient revelation was notoriously conferred on the prophets for the discharge of their office, and yet none of them ever perfectly understood the predictions they delivered. We know, too, what Peter says, They ministered more for our times than for their own (1 Pet 1:12). They were by no means useless to their own age, but when our age is compared with theirs, certainly the instruction and discipline of the prophets is more useful to us and produces richer and riper fruit in our age than in theirs. We are not surprised, then, at Daniel confessing *he did not understand*, so long as we restrict the words to this single instance. Commentaries on Daniel.[21]

Daniel's Lack of Understanding. John Mayer: *Then I heard but understood not, and I said, (O my Lord) what shall be the end of these things?* Hereby Daniel means that he heard him say, a *time, and times and part*. But what he meant by this he knew not, intimating a desire that he had to be further informed about this. Whence note that even prophets did not understand some things that were showed them without a further light given to them by him who knows all secrets. Therefore we much less, which ingenuity made Daniel to acknowledge, but pride, on the contrary, makes people now in their own opinion ignorant of nothing. But Paul says, as Daniel confesses, *we know but in part*, and says, *if anyone thinks that he knows anything he knows nothing yet as he ought to know*, that is, if he thinks so highly of himself that he knows anything, and that nothing is so obscure but he understands it, he is void of all true understanding. The first point to be made is that we, with Daniel, ought to know and acknowledge our own ignorance in humility. We must seek that God would enlighten us, who *gives wisdom to all who ask and upbraids no one*.

Then he answered me, Go your way, Daniel, for the words are closed up and sealed to the time of the end. That is, "inquire no further into this matter; let it suffice for you to have had so much revealed to you. As I have already showed you, and without troubling your mind any further, with what has been revealed, go to your grave in peace, for no more of these mysteries shall be understood until the things prophesied of begin to be accomplished. Until that time they shall remain closed and sealed up, as was said before." Wherein an item is given to us to rest satisfied with that knowledge that God has been pleased to reveal to us in his Word, and not to be inquisitive into such things, as he has shut up yet from our understanding, as his great secrets, according to that of Moses, "The secret things of the Lord belong to the Lord, but the revealed to us and to our children" (Deut 29:29). Commentary upon All the Prophets.[22]

Daniel Understood Not. Andrew Willet: Some think that Daniel here inquired of the end of the world, as the apostles asked of Christ. And as Christ answered his apostles that the day and hour of his coming was not known, indeed, not even to the angels, the like answer is made to Daniel here (Bullinger and Oecolampadius). But as has been often shown before, this prophecy concerns not the end of

[21]CTS 25:385 (CO 19:298). [22]*Prophets*, 586-87.

the world. Daniel only desired to know what should befall his own people. Sixfold Commentary upon Daniel.[23]

12:10 *Purification*

The Faithful Need Constant Purification. John Calvin: Again, the angel mentions the persecutions that were at hand for the purpose of arming the faithful for the approaching conflicts (Dan 12:10). We know from other sources how tender and weak our minds naturally are, for as soon as any cause for fear arises, before it comes to blows, we fall down lifeless through terror. As, therefore, our natural imbecility is so great, we necessarily require many stimulants to patience, and to urge us to contend with earnestness, and never to yield to any temptations. This is the reason why the angel announces the necessity for such multiplied purifications, *to cleanse them,* as wheat from chaff; *to whiten them,* as cloth by the fuller; and *to melt them,* as metal to be separated from dross.

First of all, as I have previously explained, he admonishes Daniel and all the pious of the future state of the church, to lead them to prepare and gird themselves for battle and to gather up their unconquered fortitude, since the condition of life set before them is that of forcing their way through the midst of troubles. This is one point. Again, the angel shows the practical utility of this kind of life, which might otherwise seem too bitter. We naturally refuse the cross because we feel it contrary to our disposition, while God shows the pious that nothing can be more profitable to them than a variety of afflictions. This is a second point. But afflictions by themselves might possibly consume us, and hence we are cast into a furnace. Now, then, could we expect these sufferings to promote our salvation, except God changed their nature in some wonderful way, as their natural tendency is to bring about our destruction? But while we are *melted down, and whitened, and cleansed,* we perceive how God consults for our welfare by pressing us with his cross and causing us to submit to adversity.

Now, third, the angel shows the insufficiency of one single act of cleansing, and our need of many more. This is the object of this numerous heaping together of words, *they shall be cleansed, and whitened, and melted down,* or poured forth. He might have embraced the whole idea in a single word; but, as through our whole lives God never ceases to test us in various ways, the angel heaps together these three words to show the faithful their need of continual cleansing as long as they are clothed in flesh; just as garments that are in daily use have need of continual washing. However snowy a mantle may be, it becomes soiled immediately when used for even a single day, requiring constant ablution to restore it to its original purity. Thus we are brought in contact with the defilements of sin; and as long as we are pilgrims in this world, we necessarily become subject to constant pollution. And as the faithful also are infected with the contagion of numerous iniquities, they require daily purification in different ways. We ought, then, diligently to notice these three distinct processes. Commentaries on Daniel.[24]

12:11-12 *Abomination of Desolation*

Abomination That Makes Desolate. Andrew Willet: Jerome and Theodoret understand here the discontinuing of the true service of God by antichrist at his coming. He shall bring in a horrible desolation and abolish the true service of God. He shall forbid the service and worship of God. But neither does this prophecy concern the end of the world nor yet shall there be any such singular antichrist.

Pererius and Pintus, with other Romanists, understand this of the abrogating of the

[23]*Sixfold Commentary* (1610), 479. [24]CTS 25:387-88 (CO 19:299-300).

sacrifice of the Mass, and in the stead of it antichrist shall command himself to be worshiped. So also Cardinal Hugo says antichrist shall cause himself to be worshiped. But the idolatrous sacrifice of the Mass is rather the abomination of desolation itself, whereby the true service of Christ and the right use of the Eucharist according to Christ's institution is abolished. Neither shall this abomination be antichrist himself, but he shall set up this abomination. . . .

Bullinger thinks it is the abominable laying waste of the nation and city of the Jews as the destruction of Jerusalem by the Romans. But this prophecy was rather fulfilled in the time of Antiochus as afterward shall be showed.

Calvin understands the sacrifices of the Jews, which were abominable, after the sacrifice of Christ's death performed on the cross. . . .

Osiander thinks this abominable desolation to be the idolatrous service brought into the church by the Roman antichrist. But then can not the time here described by days agree, for more than so many days or months has the true service of God been corrupted by them and so many years, as here are named days, God forbid that antichrist's corrupt religion should continue.

Wherefore this abomination that shall be set up was no other than the profanation of the temple by Antiochus, when he caused that abominable idol of Jupiter Olympus to be brought into the temple and the daily sacrifice to cease (1 Macc 1:57; 2 Macc 6:2). SIXFOLD COMMENTARY UPON DANIEL.[25]

DESTRUCTION OF THE TEMPLE. JOHN CALVIN: In consequence of the obscurity of this passage (Dan 12:11-12) it has been twisted in a variety of ways. At the end of the ninth chapter I have shown the impossibility of its referring to the profanation of the temple that occurred under the tyranny of Antiochus; on this occasion the angel bears witness to such a complete destruction of the temple, as to leave no room for the hope of its repair and restoration. Then the circumstances of the time convince us of this. For he then said, Christ shall confirm the covenant with many for one week and shall cause the sacrifices and oblation to cease. *Afterwards, the abomination that stupifies shall be added,* and desolation or stupor, and then death will distill, says he, on the astonished or stupefied one. The angel, therefore, there treats of the perpetual devastation of the temple. So in this passage, without doubt, he treats of the period after the destruction of the temple; there could be no hope of restoration, as the law with all its ceremonies would then arrive at its termination. With this view Christ quotes this passage in Matthew 24, while he admonishes his hearers diligently to attend to it. Let him who reads, understand, says he. We have stated this prophecy to be obscure, and hence it requires no ordinary degree of the closest attention. First of all, we must hold this point; the time now treated by the angel begins at the last destruction of the temple. That devastation happened as soon as the gospel began to be promulgated. God then deserted his temple, because it was only founded for a time and was but a shadow, until the Jews so completely violated the whole covenant that no sanctity remained in either the temple, the nation or the land itself. Some restrict this to those standards that Tiberius erected on the very highest pinnacle of the temple, and others to the statue of Caligula, but I have already stated my view of these opinions as too forced. I have no hesitation in referring this language of the angel to that profanation of the temple that happened after the manifestation of Christ, when sacrifices ceased and the shadows of the law were abolished. COMMENTARIES ON DANIEL.[26]

[25]*Sixfold Commentary* (1610), 480. [26]CTS 25:389-90 (CO 19:301-2).

12:13 *Stand Firm*

Our Allotted Place in Christ. Johann Wigand: *And stand in your allotted place* (Dan 12:13). That is, the place of the justified and the blessed. Christ explains this in Matthew 25, where he says that there are two groups that will be brought before his tribunal, one of the goats who will be damned, and the other the sheep who will be saved. Daniel will stand in his place, which is to say, among the sheep of Christ's flock who will be saved. This is the greatest consolation to know that we will be in our place among the justified. About these things it is not necessary for us to search in hidden places but rather to observe what is revealed and certain. It is not according to the accusing and terrifying law but according to the sweetly consoling gospel. For Christ redeemed us from the curse of the law; he called us through his word of grace; he regenerated us in baptism; he sealed this by the testament of his body and blood; he gave us the pledge of the Holy Spirit, giving a witness to our spirit that we are children of God. All these things we have by the gratuitous mercy of God and by the merit of Christ, who bore our sins. Brief Exposition of the Prophet Daniel.[27]

Stand Firm. Heinrich Bullinger: He adds a splendid promise for the consolation of those who persevere: "And you shall rest without doubt in body and soul." And indeed the soul of Daniel, separated from his body by death, is brought to his ancestors, in the bosom of Abraham, in which he has peace and rest. . . .

In addition it is noted, *And you shall stand in your allotted place at the end of the days* (Dan 12:13). You shall stand, he says, without doubt in complete integrity in both body and soul. You will stand, I say, resuscitated from where you fell in death. Then, you shall stand in your allotted place. . . . You will claim and take up your portion or inheritance. These words are most plainly and best expressed by Saint Paul, who says, "We must all appear before the tribunal of Christ so that everyone might report those things that were done in the body, whether it be good or bad" (2 Cor 5:10). Indeed this is the lot or inheritance of the saints—immortality or eternal life, which befalls the saints, glorified in soul as well as body. Most elegantly this holy and divine book is concluded with this statement in which the final payment, as it were, is shown to all believers, and eternal life is promised to all those who persevere. Our merciful Father deigns to grant this to us by the merit of his beloved Son, Jesus, our Lord, to whom be praise and glory and thanksgiving for all his benefits, forever and ever. Amen. Daniel the Most Wise Prophet of God.[28]

All Christians Must Read Daniel. Martin Luther: We command all good Christians to read this book of Daniel. During these miserable last times, he is so comforting and helpful to them. But he is of absolutely no benefit to the godless, just as he says at the end (Dan 12:10), "The godless remain godless, understanding nothing." Such prophecies of Daniel and other prophets were not only written so we could know about old stories and future afflictions, as if to satisfy our curiosity with fresh news, rather this book was written so that the saints would be comforted and made joyful, that their faith and hope would be strengthened through patience. Here they see and hear that their sorrows have an end, they are free from sin, death, the Devil, and all evil (under which they presently groan), and they will come to Christ in heaven, in his blessed and eternal kingdom. This is just like when Christ comforts his apostles in Luke 21[:28] with dreadful news: "When you see these things, look up, lift up your heads, because your redemption is near," etc.

This is why we see here that Daniel always

[27]*Explicatio Brevis* (1571), 462. [28]*Daniel Sapientissimus*, 139-40.

ends every passage and vision, however frightful they are, with joy, namely, with Christ's kingdom and future coming. For the sake of this future coming, the last and most important thing, all such passages and visions were created, interpreted and written. So whoever wants to benefit from reading Scripture, should not get caught up or trapped in the events or stories, going no further than them, but rather should feed and comfort his heart in the promised and certain coming of our Redeemer Jesus Christ, who is the blessed and joyous redemption from this valley of death and misery. May our beloved Lord and Savior guide us to this, and may he with the Father and the Holy Spirit be praised forever. Amen. Preface to the Prophet Daniel[29]

[29]WADB 11,2:128-130.

Map of the Reformation

Timeline of the Reformation

	German Territories	France	Spain	Italy	Switzerland	Netherlands	British Isles
1337-1453		Hundred Years' War					Hundred Years' War
1378-1415		Western Schism (Avignon Papacy)		Western Schism			
1384							d. J. Wycliffe
1414-1418							
1415				Council of Constance; d. J. Huss			
1450	Invention of printing press						
1452				b. Leonardo da Vinci (d. 1519)			
1453				Fall of Constantinople			
1455-1485							War of Roses; Rise of House of Tudor
1456	Gutenberg Bible						
1460							
1466		b. Jacques Lafèvres d'Étaples (d. 1536)					
1467						b. Desiderius Erasmus (d. 1536)	b. John Colet (d. 1519)
1475				b. Michelangelo (d. 1564)			
1478	b. Wolfgang Capito (d. 1541)		Ferdinand and Isabella				b. Thomas More (d. 1535)
1480	b. Balthasar Hubmaier (d. 1528); b. Andreas Bodenstein von Karlstadt (d. 1541)						
1481-1530			Spanish Inquisition				
1482					b. Johannes Oecolampadius (d. 1531)		
1483	b. Martin Luther (d. 1546)						
1484					b. Huldrych Zwingli (d. 1531)		
1485	b. Johannes Bugenhagen (d. 1554)						b. Hugh Latimer (d. 1555)

	German Territories	France	Spain	Italy	Switzerland	Netherlands	British Isles
1486	r. Frederick the Wise, Elector (d. 1525); b. Johann Eck (d. 1543)						
1488							b. Miles Coverdale (d. 1568)
1489	b. Thomas Müntzer (d. 1525); b. Kaspar von Schwenckfeld (d. 1561)						b. Thomas Cranmer (d. 1556)
1491	b. Martin Bucer (d. 1551)		b. Ignatius Loyola (d. 1556)				
1492			Defeat of Moors in Grenada; Columbus discovers America; Explusion of Jews from Spain				
1494							b. William Tyndale (d. 1536)
1496	b. Andreas Osiander (d. 1552)					b. Menno Simons (d. 1561)	
1497	b. Philipp Melanchthon (d. 1560); b. Wolfgang Musculus (d. 1563)						
1498				d. Girolamo Savonarola	b. Conrad Grebel (d. 1526)		
1499	b. Johannes Brenz (d. 1570)			b. Peter Martyr Vermigli (d. 1562)			
1500			r. Charles V (-1558)				
1501	b. Erasmus Sarcerius (d. 1559)						
1502	Founding of University of Wittenberg				b. Heinrich Bullinger (d. 1575)		
1504							
1505	Luther joins Augustinian Order						
1506				Resotration of St. Peter's begins			
1507				Sale of indulgences approved to fund building			
1509		b. John Calvin (d. 1564)					r. Henry VIII (-1547)

	German Territories	France	Spain	Italy	Switzerland	Netherlands	British Isles
1510	Luther moves to Rome						b. Nicholas Ridley (d. 1555)
1511	Luther moves to Wittenberg						
1512				Sistene Chapel completed			
1512-1517				Fifth Lateran Council; rejection of Conciliarism			
1513	Luther lectures on Psalms			r. Pope Leo X (-1521)			b. John Knox (d. 1572)
1515	Luther lectures on Romans	r. Francis I (-1547); b. Peter Ramus (d. 1572)					
1516		Est. French National Church (via Concordat of Bologna); b. Theodore Beza (d. 1605)		Concordat of Bologna		publication of Erasmus's Greek New Testament	
1517	Tetzel sells indulgences in Saxony; Luther's Ninety-Five Theses						
1518	Heidelberg Disputation; Luther examined by Eck at Diet of Augsburg			Diet of Augsburg			
1519	Leipzig Disputation		Cortés conquers Aztecs; Portuguese sailor Magellan circumnavigates the globe		Zwingli appointed pastor of Grossmünster in Zurich; b. Rudolf Gwalther (d. 1576)		
1520	Publication of Luther's Three Treatises; Burning of Papal Bull in Wittenberg		Coronation of Charles V	Papal Bull v. Luther: Exurge Domine			
1521	Luther excommunicated; Diet/Edict of Worms - Luther condemned; Luther in hiding; Melanchthon's *Loci Communes*	French-Spanish War (-1526)	French-Spanish War; Loyola converts	Papal excommunication of Luther			Henry VIII publishes Affirmation of the Seven Sacraments against Luther; awarded title "Defender of the Faith" by Pope
1521-1522	Disorder in Wittenberg; Luther translates New Testament						

	German Territories	France	Spain	Italy	Switzerland	Netherlands	British Isles
1521-1525		First and Second Hamburg Valois War					
1522	Luther returns to Wittenberg; Luther's NT published; criticizes Zwickau prophets; b. Martin Chemnitz (d. 1586)		Publication of Complutensian Polyglot Bible under Cisneros		Sausage Affair & reform begins in Zurich under Zwingli		
1523	Knight's Revolt	Bucer begins ministry in Strasbourg	Loyola has religious experiences, which cause the writing of Spiritual Exercises	r. Pope Clement VII (-1534)	Iconoclasm in Zurich		
1524-1526	Peasants' War						
1524	Luther criticizes peasants					Erasmus's disputation On Free Will	
1525	Luther marries; execution of Thomas Müntzer				Abolition of mass in Zurich; disputation on baptism; first believers' baptism performed in Zurich		
1526					Zurich council mandates mandatory capital punishment of Anabaptists	Publication of Tyndale's English translation of NT	
1527				Sack of Rome	First Anabaptists beheaded in Zurich; drafting of Schleitheim Confession		
1528	Execution of Hubmaier						
1529	Diet of Speyer; evangelical "protest"; publication of Luther's catechisms; Marburg Colloquy; siege of Vienna by Turkish forces	Abolition of mass in Strasbourg					Thomas More appointed chancellor to Henry VIII
1530	Diet of Augsburg; Confession of Augsburg		Charles V crowned Holy Roman Emperor				

	German Territories	France	Spain	Italy	Switzerland	Netherlands	British Isles
1531	Formation of Schmalkaldic League				d. H. Zwingli; succeeded by H. Bullinger		
1532		Publication of Calvin's commentary on Seneca; conversion of Calvin					
1533		Nicholas Cop addresses University of Paris; Cop and Calvin implicated as "Lutheran" sympathizers					Thomas Cranmer appointed as Archbishop of Canterbury; Henry VIII divorces
1534	First edition of Luther's Bible published	Affair of the Placards; Calvin flees		Jesuits founded			Act of Supremacy; English church breaks with Rome
1535	Sack of Anabaptists at Münster						d. Thomas More; d. John Fisher
1536	Wittenberg Concord; b. Kaspar Olevianus (d. 1587)				First edition of Calvin's Institutes published; Calvin arrives in Geneva (-1538)	Publication of Tyndale's translation of NT; d. W. Tyndale	d. A. Boleyn; Henry VIII dissolves monasteries (-1541)
1537					Calvin presents ecclesiastical ordinances to Genevan Council		
1538					Calvin exiled from Geneva; arrives in Strasbourg (-1541)		
1539		Calvin publishes second edition of Institutes in Strasbourg					Statute of Six Articles; publication of Coverdale's Wheat Bible
1540				Papal approval of Jesuit order			d. Thomas Cromwell
1541	Colloquy of Regensberg	French translation of Calvin's Institutes published			d. A. Karlstadt; Calvin returns to Geneva (-1564)		
1542				Institution of Roman Inquisition			War between England and Scotland; James V of Scotland defeated; Ireland declared sovereign kingdom

	German Territories	France	Spain	Italy	Switzerland	Netherlands	British Isles
1543	Copernicus publishes De Revolutionibus						
1545-1547	First session of Council of Trent; Schmalkaldic Wars; d. Martin Luther			Council of Trent			
1547	Defeat of Protestants at Mühlberg	d. Francis I; r. Henri II (-1559)					d. Henry VIII; r. Edward VI (-1553)
1548	Augsburg Interim (-1552)						
1549					Consensus Tigurinus between Calvin and Bullinger		First Book of Common Prayer published
1551-1552	Second session of Council of Trent			Council of Trent			Cranmer's Forty-Two Articles
1553							Book of Common Prayer revised; d. Edward VI; r. Mary I (1558)
1554							Richard Hooker (d. 1600)
1555	Diet of Augsburg; Peace of Augsburg; establishes legal territorial existence of Lutheranism and Catholicism	First mission of French; pastors trained in Geneva					b. Robert Rollock (d. 1599); d. Hugh Latimer; d. Nicholas Ridley
1556			Charles V resigns			b. Sibbrand Lubbert (d. 1625)	d. Thomas Cranmer
1557					Michael Servetus executed in Geneva		Alliance with Spain in war against France
1558			d. Charles V				b. William Perkins (d. 1602); d. Mary I; r. Elizabeth I (-1603)
1559		d. Henry II; r. Francis II (-1560); first national synod of French reformed churches (1559) in Paris		First index of prohibited books issued	Final edition of Calvin's Institutes; founding of Genevan Academy	b. Jacobus Arminius (d. 1609)	Elizabethan Settlement
1560	d. P. Melanchthon	d. Francis II; r. Charles IX (1574); Edict of Toleration created peace with Huguenots					Kirk of Scotland established

	German Territories	France	Spain	Italy	Switzerland	Netherlands	British Isles
1561-1563	Third session of Council of Trent			Council of Trent			
1561						Belgic Confession	
1562		Massacre of Huguenots begins French Wars of Religion (-1598)					
1563	Heidelberg Catechism						
1564				b. Galileo (d. 1642)	d. J. Calvin		b. William Shakespeare (d. 1616)
1566				Roman Catechism			
1567						Spanish occupation	Abdication of Scottish throne by Mary Stuart; r. James VI (-1603)
1568						Dutch movement for liberation (-1645)	
1570				Papal Bull Regnans in Excelsis excommunicates Elizabeth I			Elizabeth I excommunicated
1571	b. Johannes Kepler (d. 1630)		Spain defeats Ottoman navy at Battle of Lepanto				
1572		Massacre of Huguenots on St. Bartholomew's Day		r. Pope Gregory XIII (-1583)		William of Orange invades	
1574		d. Charles IX; r. Henri III (d. 1589)					
1576		Declaration of Toleration; formation of Catholic League		b. Giovanni Diodati (d. 1649)		Sack of Antwerp; Pacification of Ghent	
1577	Lutheran Formula of Concord						England alies with Netherlands against Spain
1578			Truce with Ottomans				Sir Francis Drake circumnavigates the globe
1579			Expeditions to Ireland			Division of Dutch provinces	
1580	Lutheran Book of Concord						

	German Territories	France	Spain	Italy	Switzerland	Netherlands	British Isles
1581			d. Teresa of Avila				Anti-Catholic statutes passed
1582				Gregorian Reform of calendar			
1583							b. David Dickson (d. 1663)
1584		Treaty of Joinville with Spain	Treaty of Joinville; inducted into Catholic League; defeats Dutch at Antwerp			Fall of Antwerp; d. William of Orange	
1585		Henri of Navarre excommunicated		r. Pope Sixtus V (-1590)			
1586							Sir Francis Drake's expedition to West Indies; Sir Walter Raleigh in Roanoke
1587		Henri of Navarre defeats royal army					d. Mary Stuart of Scotland
1588		Henri of Navarre drives Henri III from Paris; assassination of Catholic League Leaders	Armada destroyed				English Mary defeats Spanish Armada
1589		d. Henri III; r. Henri (of Navarre) IV (-1610)	Victory over England at Lisbon				Defeated by Spain in Lisbon
1590		Henri IV's siege of Paris					Alliance with Henri IV
1593		Henri IV converts to Catholicism					
1594		Henri grants toleration to Huguenots					
1595		Henri IV declares war on Spain; received into Catholic Church		Pope Sixtus accepts Henri IV into Church			Alliance with France
1596		b. René Descartes (d. 1650)					
1598		Edict of Nantes; toleration of Huguenots; peace with Spain	Treaty of Vervins; peace with France				
1603							d. Elizabeth I; r. James I (James VI of Scotland) (-1625)

	German Territories	France	Spain	Italy	Switzerland	Netherlands	British Isles
1605						b. Rembrandt (d. 1669)	Guy Fawkes and gunpowder plot
1606							Jamestown Settlement
1607							b. John Milton (d. 1674)
1608							
1610		d. Henri IV; r. Louis XIII (-1643)					
1611							Publication of Authorized English Translation of Bible (AV/KJV)
1616							b. John Owen (d. 1683)
1617							b. Ralph Cudworth (d. 1689)
1618-1648	Thirty Years' War						
1618/19						Synod of Dort	
1620							English Puritans land in Massachusetts
1640				Diodati's Italian translation of Bible published			
1642-1649							English civil wars; d. Charles I; r. Oliver Cromwell (1649-1660)
1643		d. Louis XIII; r. Louis XIV (-1715)					
1648		Treaty of Westphalia ends Thirty Years' War					
1660							English Restoration; d. Oliver Cromwell; r. Charles II (-1685)
1688							Glorious Revolution; r. William and Mary (-1702)

Biographical Sketches of Reformation-Era Figures

Johannes Aepinus (1499–1553). German preacher and theologian. Aepinus studied under Martin Luther,* Philipp Melanchthon* and Johannes Bugenhagen* in Wittenberg. Because of his Lutheran beliefs, Aepinus lost his first teaching position in Brandenburg. He fled north to Stralsund and became a preacher and superintendent at Saint Peter's Church in Hamburg. In 1534, he made a diplomatic visit to England but could not convince Henry VIII to embrace the Augsburg Confession. His works include sermons and theological writings. Aepinus became best known as leader of the Infernalists, who believed that Christ underwent torment in hell after his crucifixion.

Johann Agricola (c. 1494–1566). German pastor and theologian. Agricola studied under Martin Luther* and attended the Leipzig Disputation with him in 1519; he also participated in the burning of the papal bull held in 1520, both events painting him as a loyal Luther follower. Eventually Agricola strayed from Luther's distinction between law and gospel. He saw the gospel as the reason for recognition of sin, rather than the law. Luther responded by writing anonymous pamphlets debating the subject of antinomianism. Despite his aberrant view, Agricola refused to leave the Lutheran Church. To assuage relations, in 1540 Agricola moved to Berlin and published a recantation of his views. Doing so abated the public debate, but Luther and Agricola were never personally reconciled, even though Agricola continued to revere his former teacher. In all, Agricola served as a catechist, the head of a grammar school, a preacher, a lecturer on the faculties of the University of Leipzig and Wittenberg, and a court chaplain.

Jacobus Arminius (1559–1609). Dutch pastor and theologian. Arminius was a vocal critic of high Calvinist scholasticism, whose views were repudiated by the synod of Dort (1618–1619). Arminius was a student of Theodore Beza* at the academy of Geneva. He served as a pastor in Amsterdam and later joined the faculty of theology at the university in Leiden, where his lectures on predestination were popular and controversial. Predestination, as Arminius understood it, was the decree of God determined on the basis of divine foreknowledge of faith or rejection by humans who are the recipients of prevenient, but resistible, grace.

Richard Baxter (1615–1691). English Puritan minister. Baxter was a leading Puritan pastor, evangelist and theologian, known throughout England for his landmark ministry in Kidderminster and a prodigious literary output, producing 135 books in just over forty years. Baxter came to faith through reading William Perkins,* Richard Sibbes and other early Puritan writers and was the first cleric to decline the terms of ministry in the national English church imposed by the 1662 Act of Uniformity; Baxter wrote on behalf of the more than 1700 who shared ejection from the national church. He hoped for restoration to national church ministry, or toleration, that would allow lawful preaching and pastoring. Baxter sought unity in theological, ecclesiastical, sociopolitical and personal terms and is regarded as a forerunner of Noncomformist ecumenicity, though he was defeated in his efforts at the 1661 Savoy Conference to take seriously Puritan objections to the revision of the 1604 Prayer Book. Baxter's views on church ministry were considerably hybrid: he was a paedobaptist, Nonconformist minister who approved of synodical Episcopal government and fixed liturgy. He is most known for his classic writings on the Christian life, such as *The Saints' Everlasting Rest and A Christian Directory,* and pastoral ministry, such as *The Reformed Pastor.* He also produced *Catholick Theology,* a large volume squaring current Reformed, Lutheran, Arminian and Roman Catholic systems with each other.

Theodore Beza (1516–1605). French pastor and professor. Beza was compatriot and successor to John Calvin* as leader of the French Reformed ecclesial communities. He was a noteworthy New Testament scholar whose *Codex Bezae* formed the basis of the New Testament section of the English Geneva Bible (1560). A leader in the academy and the church, Beza served as rector at the Lausanne and Geneva academies. He enjoyed an international reputation through his correspondence with key European leaders. Beza developed and extended Calvin's doctrinal thought, reconfiguring the doctrine of election (e.g., supralapsarian predestination) and the relational basis of eucharistic presence.

Georg Blaurock (1492–1529). Swiss Anabaptist. Blaurock (a nickname meaning "blue coat," because of his preference for this garment) was one of the first leaders of Switzerland's radical reform movement. In the first public disputations on baptism in Zurich, he argued for believers' baptism and was the first person to receive adult believers' baptism there, having been baptized by Conrad Grebel* in 1525. Blaurock was arrested several times for performing mass adult baptisms and engaging in social disobedience by disrupting worship services. He was eventually expelled from Zurich but continued preaching and baptizing in various Swiss cantons until his execution.

Thieleman Jans van Braght (1625–1664). Dutch Mennonite preacher. After demonstrating great ability with languages this cloth merchant was made preacher in his hometown of Dordrecht in 1648. He served in this office for the next sixteen years, until his death. This celebrated preacher had a reputation for engaging in debate wherever an opportunity presented itself, particularly concerning infant baptism. The publication of his book of martyrs, *Het Bloedigh Tooneel of Martelaersspiegel (1660; Martyrs' Mirror),* proved to be his lasting contribution to the Mennonite tradition. *Martyrs' Mirror* is heavily indebted to the earlier martyr book Offer des Heeren (1562), to which Braght added many early church martyrs who rejected infant baptism, as well as over 800 contemporary martyrs.

Johannes Brenz (1499–1570). German Lutheran reformer and clergyperson. Brenz was converted to the reformation cause after hearing Martin Luther* speak; later, Brenz became a student of Johannes Oecolampadius.* His central achievement lay in his talent for organization. As city preacher in Schwäbisch-Hall and afterward in Württemberg and Tübingen, he oversaw the introduction of reform measures and doctrines and new governing structures for ecclesial and educational communities. Brenz also helped establish Lutheran orthodoxy through treatises, commentaries and catechisms. He defended Luther's position on eucharistic presence against Huldrych Zwingli* and opposed the death penalty for religious dissenters.

Guillaume Briçonnet (1470–1534). French abbot and bishop. Briçonnet created a short-lived circle of reformist-minded humanists in his diocese under the sponsorship of Marguerite d'Angoulême. His desire for ecclesial reform developed throughout his prestigious career (including positions as royal chaplain to the queen, abbot at Saint-Germain-des-Prés and bishop of Meux), influenced by Jacques Lefèvre d'Étaples.* Briçonnet encouraged reform through ministerial visitation, Scripture and preaching in the vernacular and active study of the Bible. When this triggered the ire of the theology faculty at the Sorbonne in Paris, Briçonnet quelled the activity and departed, envisioning an ecclesial reform that proceeded hierarchically.

Martin Bucer (1491–1551). German Reformed theologian and ecclesiastical leader. A Dominican friar, Bucer was influenced by Desiderius Erasmus* during his doctoral studies at the University of Heidelberg, where he began corresponding with Martin Luther.* After advocating reform in Alsace, Bucer was excommunicated and fled to Strausbourg, where he became a leader in the city's Reformed ecclesial and educational communities. Bucer sought concord between Lutherans and Zwinglians and Protestants and Catholics. He emigrated to England, becoming a professor at Cambridge. Bucer's greatest theological concern was the centrality of Christ's sacrificial death, which achieved justification and sanctification and orients Christian community.

Johannes Bugenhagen (1485–1558). German Lutheran pastor and professor. Bugenhagen, a priest and lecturer at a Premonstratensian monastery, became a city preacher in Wittenberg during the reform efforts of Martin Luther* and Philipp Melanchthon.* Initially influenced by his reading of Desiderius Erasmus,* Bugenhagen grew in evangelical orientation through Luther's works; later, he studied under Melanchthon at the University of Wittenberg, eventually serving as rector and faculty member there. Bugenhagen was a versatile commentator, exegete and lecturer on Scripture. Through these roles and his development of lectionary and devotional material, Bugenhagen facilitated rapid establishment of church order throughout many German provinces.

Heinrich Bullinger (1504–1575). Swiss Reformed pastor and theologian. Bullinger succeeded Huldrych Zwingli* as minister and leader in Zurich. A primary author of the First and Second Helvetic Confessions (1536; 1566), Bullinger was drawn toward reform through the works of Martin Luther* and Philipp Melanchthon.* After Zwingli died, Bullinger was vital in maintaining adherence to the cause of reform; he oversaw the expansion of the Zurich synodal system while preaching, teaching and writing extensively. One of Bullinger's lasting legacies was the development of a federal view of the divine covenant with humanity, making baptism and the Eucharist covenantal signs.

John Bunyan (1628–1688). English Nonconformist preacher and writer. Bunyan was an English Puritan Independent, or Congregationalist, a noted preacher and beloved writer, whose *Pilgrim's Progress* is one of the best-selling English language titles in history. Born to a working-class family, Bunyan was largely unschooled, gaining literacy (and entering the faith) through reading the Bible and such early Puritan devotional works as *The Plain Man's Pathway to Heaven* and *The Practice of Piety*. Following a short stint in Cromwell's parliamentary army, in which Bunyan narrowly escaped death in combat, he turned to a preaching minister, succeeding John Gifford as pastor at the Congregational church in Bedford. A noted preacher, Bunyan drew large crowds in itinerant appearances and it was in the sermonic form that Bunyan developed his theological outlook, which was an Augustinian-inflected Calvinism. Bunyan's opposition to the Book of Common Prayer and refusal of official ecclesiastical licensure lead to multiple imprisonments, where he wrote much of his famous allegorical spiritual literary works, including *Pilgrim's Progress, The Holy City, Prison Meditations* and *Holy War.*

Georg Calixtus (1586–1656). German Lutheran theologian. Calixtus studied at the University of Helmstedt where he developed regard for Philipp Melanchthon.* Between his time as a student and later as a professor at Helmstedt, Calixtus traveled through Europe seeking a way to unite and reconcile Lutherans, Calvinists and Catholics. He attempted to fuse these denominations through use of the Scriptures, the Apostles' Creed, and the first five centuries, interpreted by the Vincentian canon. Calixtus's position was stamped "syncretism" and yielded further debate even after his death.

John Calvin (1509–1564). French Reformed pastor and theologian. In his *Institutes of the Christian Religion,* Calvin provided a theological dogmatics for the Reformed churches. Calvin's gradual conversion to the cause of reform occurred through his study with chief humanist scholars in Paris, but he spent most of his career in Geneva (excepting a three-year exile in Strausbourg with Martin Bucer*). In Geneva, Calvin reorganized the structure and governance of the church and established an academy that became an international center for theological education. He was a tireless writer, producing his *Institutes,* theological treatises and Scripture commentaries.

Wolfgang Capito (1478?–1541). German humanist, reformer and theologian. Capito, a Hebrew scholar, produced a Hebrew grammar and published several Latin commentaries on books of the Hebrew Scriptures. He corresponded with Desiderius Erasmus* and fellow humanists. Capito translated Martin Luther's* early works into Latin for the printer Johann Froben. On meeting Luther, Capito was converted to Luther's vision, left Mainz and settled in Strasbourg, where he lectured on Luther's theology to the city clergy. With Martin Bucer,* Capito reformed liturgy, ecclesial life and teachings, education, welfare and government. Capito worked for the theological unification of the Swiss cantons with Strasbourg.

Martin Chemnitz (1522–1586). German Lutheran theologian. A leading figure in establishing Lutheran orthodoxy, Chemnitz studied theology and patristics at the University of Wittenburg, later becoming a defender of Philipp Melanchthon's* interpretation of the doctrine of justification. Chemnitz drafted a compendium of doctrine and reorganized the structure of the church in Wolfenbüttel; later, he led efforts to reconcile divisions within Lutheranism, culminating in the Formula of Concord (1577). One of his chief theological accomplishments was a modification of the christological doctrine of the *communicatio idiomatium,* which provided a platform for understanding the sacramental presence of Christ's humanity in the Eucharist.

John Colet (1467–1519). English Catholic priest, preacher and educator. Colet, appointed dean of Saint Paul's Cathedral by Henry VII, was a friend of Desiderius Erasmus*, on whose classical ideals Colet reconstructed the curriculum of Saint Paul's school. Colet was convinced that the foundation of moral reform lay in the education of children. Though an ardent advocate of reform, Colet, like Erasmus, remained loyal to the Catholic Church throughout his life. Colet's agenda of reform was oriented around spiritual and ethical themes, demonstrated in his commentaries on select books of the New Testament and the writings of Pseudo-Dionysius the Areopagite.

Miles Coverdale (1488–1568). English reformer and bishop. Coverdale is known for his translations of the Bible into English, completing William Tyndale's* efforts and later producing the Great Bible commissioned by

Henry VIII (1539). A former friar, Coverdale was among the Cambridge scholars who met at the White Horse Tavern to discuss Martin Luther's* ideas. During Coverdale's three terms of exile in Europe, he undertook various translations, including the Geneva Bible (1560). He was appointed bishop of Exeter by Thomas Cranmer* and served as chaplain to Edward VI. Coverdale contributed to Cranmer's first edition of the Book of Common Prayer (1549).

Thomas Cranmer (1489–1556). English archbishop and theologian. Cranmer supervised church reform and produced the first two editions of the Book of Common Prayer (1549; 1552). As a doctoral student at Cambridge, he was involved in the discussions at the White Horse Tavern. Cranmer contributed to a religious defense of Henry VIII's divorce; Henry then appointed him Archbishop of Canterbury. Cranmer cautiously steered the course of reform, accelerating under Edward VI. After supporting the attempted coup to prevent Mary's assuming the throne, Cranmer was convicted of treason and burned at the stake. Cranmer's legacy is the splendid English of his liturgy and prayer books.

Caspar Cruciger (1504–1548). German Lutheran theologian. Recognized for his alignment with the theological views of Philipp Melanchthon,* Cruciger was a scholar respected among both Protestants and Catholics. In 1521, Cruciger came Wittenberg to study Hebrew and remained there most of his life. He became a valuable partner for Martin Luther* in translating the Old Testament and served as teacher, delegate to major theological colloquies and rector. Cruciger was an agent of reform in his birthplace of Leipzig, where at the age of fifteen he had observed the disputation between Luther and Johann Eck.*

Hans Denck (c. 1500–1527). German Anabaptist and radical reformer. Denck, a crucial early figure of the German Anabaptist movement, combined medieval German mysticism with the radical sacramental theology of Andreas von Bodenstein Karlstadt* and Thomas Müntzer.* Denck argued that the exterior forms of Scripture and sacrament are symbolic witnesses secondary to the internally revealed truth of the Sprit in the human soul. This view led to his expulsion from Nuremberg in 1525; he spent the next two years in various centers of reform in the German territories. At the time of his death, violent persecution against Anabaptists was on the rise throughout northern Europe.

David Dickson (1583?–1663). Scottish clergyperson, preacher, professor and theologian. Dickson defended the Presbyterian form of ecclesial reformation in Scotland and was recognized for his iteration of Calvinist federal theology and expository biblical commentaries. Dickson served for over twenty years as professor of philosophy at the University of Glasgow before being appointed professor of divinity. He opposed the imposition of Episcopalian measures on the church in Scotland and was active in political and ecclesial venues to protest and prohibit such influences. Dickson was removed from his academic post following his refusal of the oath of supremacy during the Restoration era.

Giovanni Diodati (1576–1649). Italian reformer and translator. Diodati was from an Italian banking family who fled for religious reasons to Geneva. There he trained under Theodore Beza*; on completion of his doctoral degree, Diodati became professor of Hebrew at the academy. He was an ecclesiastical representative of the church in Geneva (for whom he was a delegate at the Synod of Dordrect in 1618) and a toiler for reform in Venice. Diodati's chief contribution to the Italian reform movement was a translation of the Bible into Italian (1640–1641), which remains the standard translation in Italian Protestantism.

Johann Eck (Johann Maier of Eck) (1486–1543). German Catholic theologian. Though Eck was not an antagonist of Martin Luther* until the dispute over indulgences, Luther's Ninety-five Theses (1517) sealed the two as adversaries. After their debate at the Leipzig Disputation (1519), Eck participated in the writing of the papal bull that led to Luther's excommunication. Much of Eck's work was written to oppose Protestantism or to defend Catholic doctrine and the papacy; *The Enchiridion* was a manual written to counter Protestant doctrine. He participated in the assemblies at Regensburg and Augsburg and led the Catholics in their rejection of the Augsburg Confession.

Desiderius Erasmus (1466–1536). Dutch humanist and educationist. Erasmus, a celebrated humanist scholar, was recognized for translations of ancient texts, reform of education according to classical studies, moral and spiritual writings and the first printed edition of the Greek New Testament. A former Augustinian who never left the Catholic Church, Erasmus addressed deficiencies he saw in the church and society, challenging numerous prevailing doctrines but advocating reform. He envisioned a simple, spiritual Christian life shaped by the teaching of Jesus and ancient wisdom. He was often accused of collusion with Martin Luther* on account of some resonance of their ideas but hotly debated Luther on human will.

Sebastian Franck (1499–1542). German theologian and radical reformer. Franck became a Lutheran in 1525, but by 1529 he began to develop ideas that distanced him from Protestants and Catholics. Expelled from Strasbourg and later Ulm due to his controversial writings, Franck spent the end of his life in Basel. Franck emphasized God's word as a divine internal spark that cannot be adequately expressed in outward forms. Thus he criticized religious institutions and dogmas. His work consists mostly of commentaries, compilations and translations. In his sweeping historical *Chronica* (1531), Franck supported numerous heretics condemned by the Catholic Church and criticized political and church authorities.

Johann Gerhard (1582–1637). German Lutheran theologian, professor and superintendent. Gerhard is considered one of the most eminent Lutheran theologians, after Martin Luther* and Martin Chemnitz.* After studying patristics and Hebrew at Wittenberg, Jena and Marburg, Gerhard was appointed superintendent at the age of twenty-four. In 1616 he was appointed to a post at the Universtiy of Jena, where he reintroduced Aristotelian metaphysics to theology and gained widespread fame. His most important work was the nine-volume *Loci Theologici* (1610–1625). He also expanded Chemnitz's harmony of the Gospels *(Harmonia Evagelistarum)*, which was finally published by Polykarp Leyser* in 1593. Gerhard was well-known for an irenic spirit and an ability to communicate clearly.

Conrad Grebel (c. 1498–1526). Swiss radical reformer. Grebel, considered the father of the Anabaptist movement, was one of the first defenders and performers of believers' baptism, for which he was eventually imprisoned in Zurich. One of Huldrych Zwingli's* early compatriots, Grebel advocated rapid, radical reform, clashing publicly with the civil authorities and Zwingli. Grebel's views, particularly on baptism, were influenced by Andreas Bodenstein von Karlstadt* and Thomas Müntzer.* Grebel advocated elimination of magisterial involvement in governing the church; instead, he envisioned the church as lay Christians determining their own affairs with strict adherence to the biblical text, and unified in volitional baptism.

William Greenhill (1591–1671). English noncomformist clergyman. Greenhill attended and worked at Magdalen College. He ministered in the diocese of Norwich but soon left for London, where he preached at Stepney. Greenhill was a member of the Westminster Assembly of Divines and was appointed the parliament chaplain by the children of Charles I. Oliver Cromwell included him among the preachers who helped draw up the Savoy Declaration.

Greenhill was evicted from his post following the Restoration, after which he pastored independently. Among Greenhill's most significant contributions to church history was his Exposition of the Prophet of Ezekiel.

Rudolf Gwalther (1519–1586). Swiss preacher and reformer. Gwalther was a consummate servant of the Reformed church in Zurich, its chief religious officer and preacher, a responsibility fulfilled previously by Huldrych Zwingli* and Heinrich Bullinger.* Gwalther provided sermons and commentaries and translated the works of Zwingli into Latin. He worked for many years alongside Bullinger in structuring and governing the ecclesial communities in Zurich; as well, Gwalther strove to strengthen the connections to the Reformed churches on the Continent and England: he was a participant in the Colloquy of Regensburg (1541) and an opponent of the Formula of Concord (1577).

Balthasar Hubmaier (1480/5–1528). German Anabaptist reformer. Hubmaier, a former priest who studied under Johann Eck,* is identified with his leadership in the peasants' uprising at Waldshut. Hubmaier served as the cathedral preacher in Regensberg, where he became involved in a series of anti-Semitic attacks. He was drawn to reform through the early works of Martin Luther*; his contact with Huldrych Zwingli* made Hubmaier a defender of more radical reform, including believers' baptism and a memorialist account of the Eucharist. His involvement in the Peasants' War led to his extradition and execution by the Austrians.

Hans Hut (1490–1527). German Anabaptist. Hut was an early leader of a mystical, apocalyptic strand of Anabaptist radical reform. His theological views were shaped by Andreas Bodenstein von Karlstadt,* Thomas Müntzer* and Hans Denck,* by whom Hut had been baptized. Hut rejected society and the established church and heralded the imminent end of days, which he perceived in the Peasants' War. Eventually arrested for practicing believers' baptism and participating in the Peasants' War, Hut was tortured and died accidentally in a fire in the Augsburg prison. The next day, the authorities sentenced his corpse to death and burned him.

Andreas Bodenstein von Karlstadt (Carlstadt) (1486–1541). German reformer and theologian. Karlstadt, an early associate of Martin Luther* and Philipp Melanchthon* at the University of Wittenberg, participated alongside Luther in the dispute at Leipzig with Johann Eck.* He also influenced the configuration of the Old Testament canon in Protestantism. During Luther's captivity in Wartburg, Karlstadt oversaw reform in Wittenberg. His acceleration of the pace of reform brought conflict with Luther, so Karlstadt left Wittenberg, eventually settling at the University of Basel as professor of Old Testament (after a sojourn in Zurich with Huldrych Zwingli*). During his time in Switzerland, Karlstadt opposed infant baptism and repudiated Luther's doctrine of Christ's real presence in the Eucharist.

John Knox (1513–1572). Scottish preacher and reformer. Knox, a fiery preacher to monarchs and zealous defender of high Calvinism, was a leading figure of reform in Scotland. Following imprisonment in the French galleys, Knox went to England, where he became a royal chaplain to Edward VI. At the accession of Mary, Knox fled to Geneva, studying under John Calvin* and serving as a pastor. Knox returned to Scotland after Mary's death and became a chief architect of the reform of the Scottish church (Presbyterian), serving as one of the authors of the book of discipline and writing many pamphlets and sermons.

François Lambert (Lambert of Avignon) (1487–1530). French reformer and theologian. In 1522, after becoming drawn to the writings of Martin Luther* and meeting Huldrych Zwingli,* Lambert left the Franciscan order. He spent time in Wittenberg, Strasbourg, and

Hesse, where Lambert took a leading role at the Homberg Synod (1526) and in creating a biblically based plan for church reform. He served as professor of theology at Marburg University from 1527 to his death. After the Marburg Colloquy (1529), Lambert accepted Zwingli's symbolic view of the Eucharist. Lambert produced nineteen books, mostly biblical commentaries that favored spiritual interpretations; his unfinished work of comprehensive theology was published posthumously.

Hugh Latimer (c. 1485–1555). English bishop, preacher and reformer. Latimer was celebrated for his sermons critiquing the idolatrous nature of Catholic practices and the social injustices visited on the underclass by the aristocracy and the individualism of Protestant government. After his support for Henry's petition of divorce he served as a court preacher under Henry VIII and Edward VI. Latimer became a proponent of reform following his education at Cambridge University and received license as an unbounded preacher. Following Edward's death, Latimer was tried for heresy, perishing at the stake with Nicholas Ridley* and Thomas Cranmer.*

Jacques Lefèvre d'Étaples (Faber Stapulensis) (1460?–1536). French humanist, publisher and translator. Lefèvre d'Étaples studied classical literature and philosophy, as well as patristic and medieval mysticism. He advocated the principle of *ad fontes*, issuing a full-scale annotation on the corpus of Aristotle, publishing the writings of key Christian mystics, and contributing to efforts at biblical translation and commentary. Although he never broke with the Catholic Church, his views prefigured those of Martin Luther,* for which he was condemned by the University of Sorbonne in Paris. He then found refuge in the court of Marguerite d'Angoulême, where he met John Calvin* and Martin Bucer.*

Sibrandus Lubbertis (c. 1555–1625). Dutch Calvinist reformer and theologian. Lubbertis, a key figure in the establishment of orthodox Calvinism in the Frisian province, studied theology at Wittenburg and Geneva (under Theodore Beza*) before his appointment as professor of theology at the University of Franeker. Throughout his career, Lubbertis advocated for high Calvinist theology, defending it in disputes with representatives of Socinianism, Arminianism and Roman Catholicism. Lubbertis criticized the Catholic theologian Robert Bellarmine and fellow Dutch reformer Jacobus Arminius*; the views of the latter he opposed as a prominent participant in the Synod of Dort (1618–1619).

Martin Luther (1483–1546). German priest, professor, reformer and theologian. While a professor in Wittenberg, Luther reinterpreted the doctrine of justification. Convinced that righteousness comes only from God's grace, he disputed the sale of indulgences with the Ninety-five Theses. Luther's positions brought conflict with Rome; his denial of papal authority lead to excommunication. He also challenged the Mass, transubstantiation and communion under one kind. Though Luther was condemned by the Diet of Worms, the Elector of Saxony provided him safe haven. Luther returned to Wittenberg with public order collapsing under Andreas Bodenstein von Karlstadt*; Luther steered a more cautious path of reform. His rendering of the Bible and liturgy in the vernacular, as well as his hymns and sermons, proved extensively influential.

Georg Major (1502–1574). German Lutheran theologian. Major was on the theological faculty of the University of Wittenberg, succeeding as dean Johannes Bugenhagen* and Philipp Melanchthon.* One of the chief editors on the Wittenberg edition of Luther's works, Major, however, is most identified with the controversy bearing his name, in which he stated that good works are necessary to salvation. Major qualified his statement, which was in reference to the totality of the Christian life. The Formula of Concord rejected the statement, ending the controversy. As a theologian,

Major further refined Lutheran views of the inspiration of Scripture and the doctrine of the Trinity.

Thomas Manton (1620–1677). English Nonconformist minister. Manton, educated at Oxford, was a nonconformist minister, serving for a time as lecturer at Westminster Abbey and rector of St. Paul's, Covent Garden, and was a strong advocate of Presbyterianism. He was known as a rigorous evangelical Calvinist who preached long expository sermons. At different times in his ecclesial career he worked side-by-side with Richard Baxter* and John Owen.* In his later life, Manton's nonconformist position led to his ejection as a clergyman from the Church of England (1662) and eventual imprisonment (1670). Although a voluminous writer, Manton was best known for his preaching. At his funeral in 1677, he was dubbed "the king of preachers."

John Mayer (1583–1664). Anglican priest and biblical exegete. Mayer dedicated much of his life to biblical exegesis, writing a seven-volume commentary on the entire Bible (1627–1653). Styled after Philipp Melanchthon's* *locus* method, Mayer's work avoided running commentary, focusing instead on textual and theological problems. He was a parish priest for fifty-five years. In the office of priest Mayer also wrote a popular catechism, *The English Catechisme, or a Commentarie on the Short Catechisme* (1621), which went through twelve editions in his lifetime.

Joseph Mede (1586–1638). Anglican biblical scholar, Hebraist and Greek lecturer. A man of encyclopedic knowledge, Mede was interested in numerous fields, varying from philology and history to mathematics and physics, although millennial thought and apocalyptic prophesy were clearly his chief interests. Mede's most important work was *Clavis Apocalyptica* (1627, later translated into English as *The Key of the Revelation*). This work examined the structure of Revelation as the key to its interpretation. Mede saw the visions as a connected and chronological sequence hinging around Revelation 17:18. He is remembered as an important figure in the history of millenarian theology. He was respected as a mild-mannered and generous scholar who avoided controversy and debate, but who had many original thoughts.

Philipp Melanchthon (1497–1560). German educator, reformer and theologian. Melanchthon is known as the partner and successor to Martin Luther* in reform in Germany and for his pioneering *Loci Communes*, which served as a theological textbook. Melanchthon participated with Luther in the Leipzig disputation, helped implement reform in Wittenberg and was a chief architect of the Augsburg Confession. Later, Melanchthon and Martin Bucer* worked for union between the reformed and Catholic churches. On account of Melanchthon's more ecumenical disposition and his modification from Luther on several doctrines, he was held in suspicion by some.

Thomas Müntzer (c. 1489–1525). German radical reformer. As a preacher in the town of Zwickau, Müntzer was influenced by German mysticism and, growing convinced that Martin Luther* had not carried through reform properly, sought to restore the pure apostolic church of the New Testament. Müntzer's radical ideas led to expulsions from various cities; he developed a highly apocalyptic theology, in which he heralded the last days that would establish the pure community out of suffering, prompting Müntzer's proactive role in the peasants' rebellion, which he perceived as a crucial apocalyptic event. Six thousand of Müntzer's followers were annihilated by magisterial troops; Müntzer was executed.

Wolfgang Musculus (1497–1563). Pastor, reformer and theologian from Lorraine. Musculus produced translations, biblical commentaries and an influential theological text, *Loci Communes Sacrae Theologiae* (*Commonplaces of Sacred Theology*), outlining a Zwinglian theology. Musculus began to study theology while at a Benedictine monastery; he departed in 1527 and became secretary to Martin Bucer* in Strasbourg. He was later installed as a pastor in Augsburg, eventually performing the first evangelical liturgy in the city's cathedral. Though Musculus was active in the pursuit of the reform agenda, he was also concerned for ecumenism, participating in the Wittenberg Concord (1536) and discussions between Lutherans and Catholics.

Johannes Oecolampadius (Johannes Huszgen) (1482–1531). Swiss-German humanist, reformer and theologian. Oecolampadius (an assumed name meaning "house light") assisted with Desiderius Erasmus's* Greek New Testament, lectured on biblical languages and exegesis and completed an influential Greek grammar. After joining the evangelical cause through patristics and the work of Martin Luther,* Oecolampadius went to Basel, where he lectured on biblical exegesis and participated in ecclesial reform. On account of Oecolampadius's effort, the city council passed legislation restricting preaching to the gospel and releasing the city from compulsory Mass. Oecolampadius was a chief ally of Huldrych Zwingli,* whom he supported at the Marburg Colloquy (1529).

Kaspar Olevianus (1536–1587). German Calvinist reformer and theologian. Olevianus is celebrated for composing the Heidelberg Catechism and producing a critical edition of Calvin's *Institutes* in German. Olevianus studied theology with including John Calvin,* Theodore Beza,* Heinrich Bullinger* and Peter Martyr Vermigli.* As an advocate of Reformed doctrine, Olevianus oversaw the shift from Lutheranism to Calvinism throughout Heidelberg, organizing the city's churches after Calvin's Geneva. The Calvinist ecclesial vision of Olevianus entangled him in a dispute with another Heidelberg reformer over the rights of ecclesiastical discipline, which Olevianus felt belonged to the council of clergy and elders rather than civil magistrates.

John Owen (1616–1683). English Puritan theologian. Owen is one of the most widely admired Puritan theologians, recognized for his theological acuity and arduous, yet irenic, defense of the Reformed faith in such works as *The Death of Death in the Death of Christ*, *Of Communion with God the Father, Son and Holy Spirit* and *The Glorious Mystery of the Person of Christ*. Owen trained at Oxford University, where he was later appointed dean of Christ Church and vice chancellor of the university, following his service as chaplain to Oliver Cromwell. He was also a member of the British Parliament and participated in the Savoy Conference (which reviewed the Book of Common Prayer in the attempt to mediate between Presbyterian and Anglican clergy on the issues of ordination and order of service). Although Owen began his career as a Presbyterian minister, he eventually departed to the party of Independents. Owen's authorial achievement was wide-ranging, with a corpus containing multi-volumes of sermons, biblical commentaries (including seven volumes on the book of Hebrews), theological treatises and controversial monographs (including disputations with Arminians, Anglicans, Catholics and Socinians). At the center of Owen's theological vision was a high and integrative view of Scripture, Christ and the Spirit.

William Perkins (1558–1602). English Puritan preacher and theologian. Perkins was a highly regarded Puritan Presbyterian preacher and biblical commentator in the Elizabethan era. He studied at Cambridge University and later became a fellow of Christ's Church college as preacher and professor, Perkins was acclaimed for his sermons and lectures. Even more, Perkins gained an esteemed reputation for his ardent exposition of Calvinist reformed doctrine in the style of Petrus Ramus,* becoming one of the first English reformed theologians to achieve international recognition. Perkins influenced the federal Calvinist shape of Puritan theology and the vision of logical, practical expository preaching.

Petrus Ramus (1515–1572). French humanist philosopher and reformer. Ramus was an influential professor of philosophy and logic at the French royal college in Paris; he converted to Protestantism and left France for Germany, where he came under the influence of Calvinist thought. Ramus was a trenchant critic of Aristotle and noted for his method of classification based on a deductive movement from universals to particulars, the latter becoming branching divisions that provided a visual chart of the parts to the whole. His system profoundly influenced Puritan theology and preaching. After returning to Paris, Ramus died in the Saint Bartholomew's Day Massacre.

Nicholas Ridley (1502?–1555). English bishop and reformer. Ridley was a student and fellow at Cambridge University who was appointed chaplain to Archbishop Thomas Cranmer* and is thought to be partially responsible for Cranmer's shift to a symbolic view of the Eucharist. Cranmer promoted Ridley twice: as bishop of Rochester, where he openly advocated Reformed theological views, and, later, as bishop of London. Ridley assisted Cranmer in the revisions of the Book of Common Prayer. Ridley's support of Lady Jane Grey against the claims of Mary to the throne led to his arrest; he was tried for heresy and burned at the stake with Hugh Latimer.*

Robert Rollock (1555?–1599). Scottish clergyperson, educator and theologian. Rollock was deeply influenced by Petrus Ramus's* system of logic, which he implemented as a tutor and (later) principal of Edinburgh University and in his expositions of the Bible. Rollock, as a divinity professor and theologian, was instrumental in diffusing a federalist Calvinism in the Scottish church; he lectured on theology using the texts of Theodore Beza* and articulated a highly covenantal interpretation of the biblical narratives. He was a prolific writer of sermons, expositions, commentaries, lectures and occasional treatises.

Erasmus Sarcerius (1501–1559). German Lutheran ecclesial leader, educator and pastor. Sarcerius served as educational superintendent, court preacher and pastor in Nassau and, later, in Leipzig. The hallmark of Sarcerius's reputation was his ethical emphasis as exercised through ecclesial oversight and family structure; he also drafted disciplinary codes for regional churches in Germany. Sarcerius served with Philipp Melanchthon* as Protestant delegates at the Council of Trent (1552), though both withdrew prior to the dismissal of the session; he eventually became an opponent of Melanchthon, contesting the latter's understanding of the Eucharist at a colloquy in Worms in 1557.

Menno Simons (c. 1496–1561). Dutch Anabaptist leader. Simons led a separatist Anabaptist group in the Netherlands who would later be called Mennonites, known for renunciation of the world and nonviolence. A former priest, Simons rejected Catholicism through the influence of Anabaptist disciples of Melchior Hoffmann and based on careful study of Scripture, in which he found no support for transubstantiation or infant baptism. Following the sack of Anabaptists at Münster, Simons committed to a nonviolent way of life. Simons proclaimed a message of radical discipleship of obedience and inner purity, marked by voluntary adult baptism and communal discipline.

Daniel Toussain (1541–1602). Swiss Reformed pastor and professor. Toussain became pastor at Orléans after attending college in Basel. After the third War of Religion, Toussain was exiled, eventually returning to Montbéliard, his birthplace. In 1571, he faced opposition there from the strict Lutheran rulers and was eventually exiled due to his influence over the clergy. He returned to Orléans but fled following the Saint Bartholomew's Day Massacre (1572), eventually becoming pastor in Basel. He relocated to Heidelberg in 1583 as pastor to the new regent, becoming professor of theology at the university, and he remained there until his death.

William Tyndale (Hychyns) (1494–1536). English reformer, theologian and translator. Tyndale was educated at Oxford University, where he was influenced by the writings of humanist thinkers. Believing that piety is fostered through personal encounter with the Bible, he asked to translate the Bible into English; denied dispensation, Tyndale left for the Continent to complete the task. His New Testament was the equivalent of a modern-day best seller in England but was banned and ordered burned. Tyndale's theology was oriented around justification, the authority of Scripture and Christian obedience; Tyndale emphasized the ethical as a concomitant reality of justification. He was martyred in Brussels before completing his English translation of the Old Testament, which Miles Coverdale* finished.

Juan de Valdés (1500/10–1541). Spanish theologian and writer. Although Valdés adopted an evangelical doctrine, had Erasmian affiliations and published works that were listed on the Index of Prohibited Books, Valdés rebuked reformers for creating disunity and never left the Catholic Church. His writings included translations of the Hebrew Psalter and various biblical books, a work on the Spanish language and several commentaries. Valdés fled to Rome in 1531 to escape the Spanish Inquisition and worked in the court of Clement VII in Bologna until the pope's death in 1534. Valdés subsequently returned to Naples, where he led the reform- and revival-minded Valdesian circle.

Peter Martyr Vermigli (1499–1562). Italian humanist, reformer and theologian. Vermigli was one of the most influential theologians of the era, held in common regard with such figures as Martin Luther* and John Calvin.* In Italy, Vermigli was a distinguished theologian, preacher and advocate for moral reform; however, during the reinstitution of the Roman Inquisition Vermigli was fled to Protestant regions in northern Europe. He was eventually appointed professor of divinity at Oxford University, where Vermigli delivered acclaimed disputations on the Eucharist. Though Vermigli's works are now being rediscovered, he was widely noted for his deeply integrated biblical commentaries and theological treatises.

Johann Wigand (1523–1587). German Lutheran theologian. Wigand is most noted as one of the compilers of the *Magdeburg Centuries*, a German ecclesiastical history of the first thirteen centuries of the church. He was a student of Philipp Melanchthon* at the University of Wittenburg and became a significant figure in the controversies dividing Lutheranism. Strongly opposed to Roman Catholicism, Wigand lobbied against innovations in Lutheran theology that appeared sympathetic
to Catholic thought. In the later debates, Wigand's support for Gnesio-Lutheranism established his role in the development of confessional Lutheranism. Wigand was appointed bishop of Pomerania after serving academic posts at the universities in Jena and Königsburg.

Andrew Willet (1562–1621). Anglican priest, professor, and biblical expositor. Willet was a gifted biblical expositor and powerful preacher. He walked away from a promising university career in 1588 when he was ordained a priest in the Church of England. For the next 33 years he served as a parish priest. Willet's commentaries summarized the present state of discussion while also offering practical applications for preachers—they have been cited as some of the most technical commentaries of the early seventeenth century. His most important publication was *Synopsis Papismi, or a General View of Papistrie (1594)*, in which he responded to many of Robert Bellarmine's critiques. After years of royal favor, Willet was imprisoned in 1618 for a month after presenting to King James I his opposition to the "Spanish Match" of Prince

Charles to the *Infanta* Maria. Willet died after being thrown from his horse while returning home from a trip to London. While serving as a parish priest for thirty-three years, he wrote forty-two works, most of which were either commentaries on books of the Bible or controversial works against Catholics.

Huldrych Zwingli (1484–1531). Swiss humanist, preacher, reformer and theologian. Zwingli, a parish priest, was influenced by the writings of Desiderius Erasmus* and taught himself Greek. While a preacher to the city cathedral in Zurich, Zwingli enacted reform through sermons, public disputations and conciliation with the town council, abolishing the Mass and images in the church. Zwingli broke with the lectionary preaching tradition, instead preaching serial expository biblical sermons. He later was embroiled in controversy with Anabaptists over infant baptism and with Martin Luther* at the Marburg Colloquy (1529) over Zwingli's symbolic view of the Eucharist. Zwingli, serving as chaplain to Zurich's military, was killed in battle.

Bibliography

Sources and Translations Used in This Volume

Baxter, Richard. *The Practical Works of Richard Baxter.* 4 vols. Reprint ed. Ligonier, Penn.: Soli Deo Gloria Publications, 1990.

Braght, Tieleman J. van. *A Martyrology of the Churches of Christ, Commonly Called Baptists, During the Era of the Reformation.* Edited by Edward Bean Underhill. 2 vols. London: Hanserd Knollys Society, 1850.

Bullinger, Heinrich. *Daniel Sapientissimus Dei Propheta.* Zurich: C. Froschouerus, 1576.

Bullinger, Heinrich. *The Decades of Bullinger.* 4 vols. Cambridge: Cambridge University Press, 1849–1852.

Bunyan, John. *Solomon's Temple Spiritualized.* In *Complete Works of John Bunyan.* Philadelphia: Bradley, Garretson, 1872.

Calvin, John. *Commentaries on the Book of the Prophet Daniel.* Translated by Thomas Myers. 2 vols. Edinburgh: Calvin Translation Society, 1847; reprint, Grand Rapids: Eerdmans, 1948.

Calvin, John. *Commentaries on the First Twenty Chapters of the Book of the Prophet Ezekiel.* Translated by Thomas Myers. 2 vols. Edinburgh: Calvin Translation Society, 1847; reprint, Grand Rapids: Eerdmans, 1948.

Calvin, John. *Institutes of the Christian Religion.* Edited by John T. McNeill. Translated by Ford Lewis Battles. 2 vols. Philadelphia: Westminster Press, 1960.

The Catholic Encyclopedia. Edited by Charles G. Herbermann et al. 16 vols. New York: The Encyclopedia Press, 1907–1914.

Chemnitz, Martin. *The Harmony of the Four Evangelists.* Edited by Polycarp Leyser and Johann Gerhard. Translated by Richard J. Dinda. Malone, Tex.: The Center for the Study of Lutheran Orthodoxy, 2009.

Chemnitz, Martin. *Ministry, Word and Sacraments: An Enchiridion.* Translated by Luther Poellot. St. Louis, Mo.: Concordia Publishing House, 1981.

Denck, Hans. "Reflection on the Book of the Prophet Micah (1532)." In *Selected Writings of Hans Denck,* ed. E. J. Furcha, 35-181. Lewiston, N.Y.: Edwin Mellen, 1989.

———. "The Law of God (1526)." In *Selected Writings of Hans Denck,* ed. E. J. Furcha, 215-244. Lewiston, N.Y.: Edwin Mellen, 1989.

Dictionary of National Biography. Edited by Leslie Stephen and Sidney Lee. 63 vols. London: Smith, Elder, 1885–1900.

Diodati, Giovanni. *Pious Annotations upon the Holy Bible*. London: Nicolas Fussell, 1651.
Geneva Study Bible. 1599.
Gerhard, Johann. *Theological Commonplaces: On the Nature of Theology and Scripture*. Translated by Richard J. Dinda. St. Louis, Mo.: Concordia Publishing House, 2006.
Gerhard, Johann. *Theological Commonplaces: On the Nature of God and on the Trinity*. Translated by Richard Dinda. St. Louis, Mo.: Concordia Publishing House, 2007.
Gerhard, Johann. *Postilla: An Explanation of the Sunday and Most Important Festival Gospels of the Whole Year*. Translated by Elmer Hohle. 2 vols. Malone, Tex.: The Center for the Study of Lutheran Orthodoxy, 2001.
Greenhill, William. *An Exposition of Ezekiel*. Carlisle, Penn.: Banner of Truth Trust, 1994.
Luther, Martin. *Luther's Works* [American edition]. 55 vols. St. Louis, Mo.: Concordia Publishing House; Philadelphia: Fortress Press, 1955–1986.
———. *D. Martin Luthers Werke, Kritische Gesamtausgabe*. 72 vols. Weimar: Verlag Hermann Böhlaus Nachfolger, 1883–.
———. *D. Martin Luthers Wereke, Kritische Gesamtausgabe: Deutsche Bibel*. 12 vols. Weimar: Hermann Böhlaus Nachfolger, 1906–1961.
———. *The Precious and Sacred Writings of Martin Luther*. Ed. John Nicholas Lenker. 31 vols. Minneapolis: Lutherans in All Lands, 1903–1938.
———. *The Complete Sermons of Martin Luther*. Ed. John Nicholas Lenker. Grand Rapids: Baker Books, 2000.
Manton, Thomas. *The Complete Works of Thomas Manton*. 22 vols. Worthington, Penn.: Maranatha Publications, 1970.
Mayer, John. *A Commentary upon All the Prophets Both Great and Small*. London: Abraham Miller and Ellen Cotes, 1652.
Meade, Matthew. *The Vision of the Wheels, Seen by the Prophet Ezekiel, Opened and Applied: Partly at the Merchant's Lecture in Broad Street, and Partly at Stepney, on January 31, 1688–89*. Edinburgh: Thomas Turnbull, 1799.
Meade, Matthew. *The Sermons of Matthew Meade*. Reprint ed. Ligonier, Penn.: Soli Deo Gloria Publications, 1991.
Mede, Joseph. *Daniel's Weeks: An Interpretation of part of the Prophecy of Daniel*. London: John Clark, 1643.
Melanchthon, Philipp. *In Danielem Prophetam Commentarius*. Leipzig: Nicolaus Wolrab, 1543.
Oecolampadius, Johannes. *Commentarius in Ezechielem Prophetam*. Geneva: Crispiniana, 1553.
Oecolampadius, Johannes. *Commentariorum In Danielem Prophetam Libri Duo*. Geneva: Ioannis Crispini, 1553.
Owen, John. *The Works of John Owen*. 16 vols. London: Banner of Truth Trust, 1965–1968.
Oxford Dictionary of National Biography. 60 vols. Oxford: Oxford University Press, 2004.
Oxford Encyclopedia of the Reformation. 4 vols. Oxford: Oxford University Press, 1996.
Pemble, William. *The Period of the Persian Monarchy*. Oxford: John Adams, Edw. and John Forrest, 1659.
Racovian Catechism. London: Longman, Hurst, Rees, Orme & Brown, 1818.
Raupius, Jakob. *Commentarius Synopticus In Prophetam Ezechielem*. Arnstadt: Christiani a Saher, 1655.
Selected Writings of Hans Denck, 1500–1527. Translated by E. J. Furcha. Lewiston, N.Y.: Edwin Mellen Press, 1989.

Simons, Menno. *A Foundation and Plain Instruction of the Saving Doctrine of Our Lord Jesus.* Translated by Daniel Rupp. Lancaster, Penn.: Elias Barr, 1863.

The Book of Concord: The Confessions of the Evangelical Lutheran Church. Edited by Theodore G. Tappert. Philadelphia: Fortress Press, 1959.

Wigand, John. *Danielis Prophetae Explicatio Brevis.* Jena: Guntherus Huttichius, 1571.

Willet, Andrew. *A Sixfold Commentary upon the Most Divine Prophecy of Daniel.* Cambridge: Leonard Greene, 1610.

Author Index

Subject Index

Scripture Index